Analysis of panels and limited dependent variable models

This important collection brings together leading econometricians to discuss recent advances in the areas of the econometrics of panel data, limited dependent variable models, and limited dependent variable models with panel data.

The chapters in this collection can be grouped into two broad categories. The chapters by Amemiya; Arellano, Bover, and Labeaga; Geweke and Keane; Lee; and El-Gamal and Grether primarily deal with different aspects of limited dependent variable models and sample selectivity. The second group of chapters, by Nerlove; Ahn and Schmidt; Kiviet; Davies and Lahiri; Baillie and Baltagi; Hsiao, Pesaran, and Tahmiscioglu; and Pesaran and Zhao, consider issues that arise in estimation of dynamic (possibly) heterogeneous panel data models.

Overall, the contributors focus on the issues of simplifying complex real world phenomena into easily generalizable inferences from individual outcomes. As the contributions of G.S. Maddala in the fields of limited dependent variables and panel data have been particularly influential, it is a fitting tribute that this volume is dedicated to him.

Analysis of panels and limited dependent variable models

In honour of G. S. Maddala

Edited by
CHENG HSIAO, KAJAL LAHIRI,
LUNG-FEI LEE, AND
M. HASHEM PESARAN

CAMBRIDGE
UNIVERSITY PRESS

CAMBRIDGE UNIVERSITY PRESS
Cambridge, New York, Melbourne, Madrid, Cape Town, Singapore,
São Paulo, Delhi, Dubai, Tokyo

Cambridge University Press
The Edinburgh Building, Cambridge CB2 8RU, UK

Published in the United States of America by Cambridge University Press, New York

www.cambridge.org
Information on this title: www.cambridge.org/9780521131001

First published 1999
Reprinted 2000, 2001
This digitally printed version 2010

A catalogue record for this publication is available from the British Library

ISBN 978-0-521-63169-3 Hardback
ISBN 978-0-521-13100-1 Paperback

Contents

Contributors

Seung Chan Ahn *Arizona State University, Tempe*
Takeshi Amemiya *Stanford University*
Manuel Arellano *CEMFI, Madrid*
Richard T. Baillie *Michigan State University*
Badi H. Baltagi *Texas A&M University*
Olympia Bover *Bank of Spain, Madrid*
Anthony Davies *West Virginia University*
Mahmoud A. El-Gamal *Rice University*
John Geweke *University of Minnesota and Federal Reserve Bank of Minneapolis*
David M. Grether *California Institute of Technology*
Cheng Hsiao *University of Southern California*
Michael Keane *University of Minnesota and Federal Reserve Bank of Minneapolis*
Jan F. Kiviet *University of Amsterdam*
José M. Labeaga *Universitat Pompeu Fabra, Barcelona*
Kajal Lahiri *State University of New York at Albany*
Lung-Fei Lee *Hong Kong University of Science and Technology*
Marc Nerlove *University of Maryland*
M. Hashem Pesaran *University of Cambridge and University of Southern California*
Peter Schmidt *Michigan State University*
A. Kamil Tahmiscioglu *University of Wisconsin at Milwaukee*
Zhongyun Zhao *Merck-Medco Managed Care LLC*

G.S. Maddala, 1933–1999

On June 4, 1999 G.S. Maddala (universally known as "G.S.") passed away in Columbus, Ohio just a few months before this *Festschrift* could come out. We had hoped very much to dedicate this volume to him in person, but this was not to be. At the time of his death, G.S. held the University Eminent Scholar Professorship in the Department of Economics at Ohio State University. He is survived by his wife Kameswari, "Kay", and several members of his immediate family: his daughter, Tara, and his son, Vivek, both of San Francisco; and two sisters who live in India.

The curriculum vita that is appended at the end of this volume traces G.S.'s long and productive career, and his research contributions. In an interview conducted a month before his death (*Econometric Theory,* Vol 15, 1999, pp. 753–776), G.S. discussed the influences that shaped his academic life and work, and the salient features of his philosophy. The readers will be happy to know that his colleagues at the Ohio State University have launched a University endowed G.S. Maddala Memorial Lecture Series, and an Award to an outstanding econometrics graduate student. Also, the proceedings of the 2nd Workshop on Applied Bayesian Methods in Econometrics and Forecasting recently held at the Indian Statistical Institute, Bangalore have been dedicated in honour and memory of him. G.S.'s family have donated his personal collections of books and journals to the economics department of Andhra University (India), which has dedicated a part of their library to his memory.

With a deep sense of loss we also note the death of Zvi Grilisches, the Paul M. Warburg Professor of Economics at Harvard University, on November 4, 1999. Zvi was G.S.'s mentor at the University of Chicago in the early 60s, and very kindly wrote an affectionate "Foreword" to this volume.

We are delighted to see that the *Festschift* is being reprinted within a year of its first publication, reflecting the significant interest in G.S.'s work and legacy that exists in the conomics profession today.

Foreword

GS [G.S. Maddala] came to Chicago with a very strong statistical background (a BA in Mathematics from Andhra University and an MA in Statistics from Bombay University) and immediately impressed everyone who came into contact with him. When he showed up in my econometrics class it was clear that here was somebody from whom I could learn. A teacher is lucky when that happens. His first published paper (*Econometrica*, 1962) on the quarterly consumption function came out of this class. It was joint work with Robert Lucas, Neil Wallace, and myself. Not bad company.

At Chicago, we tried to convert GS to empirical work. He did a first-rate dissertation on "Productivity and Technological Change in the Bituminous Coal Industry" (*Journal of Political Economy*, 1965) and a pioneering study of international diffusion of new steel making techniques (*Economic Journal*, 1967). But whether it was the profession's cool reception to empirical work in general or the pull of his first love, almost all of his subsequent work has been in econometric methodology, where he has been both an innovator and a great expositor and synthesizer. He has worked in almost all areas of econometrics: distributed lags, generalized least squares, panel data, simultaneous equations, errors in variables, tests of significance, switching and market disequilibrium models, qualitative and limited dependent variable models, selection and self-selection biases, exact small sample distributions of estimators, outliers and bootstrap methods, Bayesian econometrics, and more. A veritable textbook of econometrics, which he proceeded to write most successfully in several versions. Nor was it all just pure methodology. Substantive issues were also examined: estimates of liquid asset demands, functional forms for income distributions and production functions, returns to education and discrimination in loan markets, the meaning of rationality in expectations, and issues in the estimation of rational expectations models. All of his papers are serious papers where an effort is made to grapple with substantive and important questions.

Through his textbooks and the book on limited and dependent qualitative variables and his many students, he became the preeminent teacher of econometrics in this country and an authority on almost every question that he touched. His influence has been widely felt. He is one of the "fathers" of modern panel data analysis (together with Yair Mundlak and Marc Nerlove) and he was one of the early proponents of Bayesian techniques in econometrics. And he is probably the most widely cited econometrician today. At least, he is cited more times (325 and 348) in the years that I examined the Social Sciences Citation Index (1994 and 1996) than each of the six econometricians who won the Clark Medal during the last 30 years or so. True, his citations are heavily concentrated (146 to the Limited Dependent Variables book, 43 to the Introduction to Econometrics, and 47 to the Variance Components Pooling of Cross-Section and Time-Series Data paper), but even if one were to exclude the book citations, he is still being cited at about the same rate as the median Clark medalist. Quite an achievement and a testimony to his influence.

GS has an unassuming and quiet way. But he also has something that is close to perfect pitch in econometrics: when he sees work that is "off," that strikes somehow the wrong note, it bothers him, and his irritation often produces pearls of papers. While much of his work is constructive, much is also critical of many current fads in econometrics. In this he reminds me of a story told about Morris Cohen, the City College philosopher who was accused of being too critical and not constructive enough. Cohen replied: "I am a plumber, I unstop toilets." That is also a very important contribution. A contribution which may not have been appreciated enough. For many years GS toiled on the periphery of the academic circus. The recognition of his contributions reflected by this volume is, therefore, both overdue and most welcome. It could not have happened to a nicer guy.

Zvi Griliches
Harvard University

Introduction

The chapters in this volume bring together important recent advances in the areas of (i) econometrics of panel data, (ii) limited dependent variable models, and (iii) limited dependent variable models with panel data. Panel data offers researchers many more possibilities than pure cross-sectional or time series data. Like cross-sectional data, panel data describes each of a number of individuals. Like time series data, it describes changes through time. By blending characteristics of both cross-sectional and time series data, panel data can be used, for example, to (i) expand sample size, (ii) allow the specification of more complicated behavioral hypotheses, (iii) capture cross-sectional variation and dynamic behavior, (iv) lessen the problem of multicollinearity, (v) provide possibilities for reducing omitted variable and estimation biases, (vi) improve accuracy of parameter estimates, (vii) obtain more accurate prediction of individual outcomes. However, the analysis of panel data also raises a number of new issues. For instance, in the case of short dynamic panel data models with large cross-section units, it is known that dealing with the initial values and incidental parameters problem can be complex. In other applications, such as non-linear panel data models with fixed effects, a general solution to the problem may not exist. A notable example is estimation of probit models with fixed effects. Also panel data based on economic surveys are very often qualitative in nature, and have limited variations due to self-selection, and truncation.

This collection focuses on the issues of simplifying complex real-world phenomena into easily generalizable inference from individual outcomes. Since Maddala's contributions in the fields of limited dependent variables and panel data have been particularly influential, it is a fitting tribute to his legacy that we dedicate this volume to him.

Professor G.S. Maddala is one of the leading figures in the econometrics profession and has made highly influential contributions covering almost every area of econometrics. He has been an unerring source of wise counsel to a generation of students, colleagues, and journal editors who have come in contact with him. Moreover, Maddala writes econometrics in plain English. He likes to convey the basic ideas in simple words. His main econometrics textbook, in various editions, has been an important source for the training of students. His Econometric Society monograph on *Limited Dependent and Qualitative Choice Variables* is among the most cited technical books on econometrics. Professor Maddala has also provided invaluable service to practicing econometricians through a large number of timely surveys covering a wide range of topics, including the analysis of sample selectivity bias as it pertains to health care markets, the econometrics of panel data models, limited dependent variable models using panel data, the analysis of expectations using survey data, a perspective on the use of limited dependent and qualitative variable models in accounting research, specification tests in limited dependent variable models, structural change and unit roots, and bootstrapping time series models. These surveys not only summarize the state of the art at the time but have been sources of inspiration. A complete list of these surveys and other publications of Professor Maddala is provided at the end of this volume.

The chapters in this collection can be grouped into two broad categories. The chapters by Amemiya; Arellano, Bover and Labeaga; Geweke and Keane; Lee; and El-Gamal and Grether primarily deal with different aspects of limited dependent variable models and sample selectivity. The second group of papers by Nerlove; Ahn and Schmidt; Kiviet; Davies and Lahiri; Baillie and Baltagi; Hsiao, Pesaran, and Tahmiscioglu; and Pesaran and Zhao consider issues that arise in estimation of dynamic (possibly) heterogeneous panel data models.

The two chapters by Amemiya, and Arellano, Bover and Labeaga consider how to take account of selectivity or censoring issues using panel data. Data censoring can create much difficulty in estimation and inference because of the unobservability of the true state. Surprisingly, panel data can sometimes make an inherently intractable problem easier to solve. The chapter by Amemiya provides a unified treatment of a duration model in which left censoring arises because (i) spells in the middle of continuation at the time of the first observation are either completely observed or partially observed; (ii) spells which start after the time of the first observation are either observed or not observed; or (iii) for a single individual we either observe a single spell or a sequence of spells in different states. Amemiya derives the maximum likelihood estimator when these models are fully specified. He also shows that, in certain situations, a less efficient but more robust method, which does not require the full knowledge of the model specification, may be possible and desirable.

The chapter by Arellano, Bover and Labeaga considers an autoregressive method with random effects for a latent variable which is only partly observed due to a selection mechanism. They show that the intractability of a dynamic model subject to censoring using a single time series can be successfully overcome by noting that the sub-samples of the panel data that only included individuals without censored past observations are exogenously selected. They suggest an easy to implement asymptotic least squares method to estimate features of the distribution of the censored endogeneous variable conditional on its past. They also apply these methods to analyze the dynamics of female labor supply and wages using PSID data.

Geweke and Keane consider the binary choice model where the distribution of the underlying disturbances is assumed to be a mixture of normal densities, which is an important generalization of the standard normal probit model widely used in the literature. The mixture normal specification, by allowing mixing on both the mean and the variance parameters, and by increasing the number of the distributions in the mixtures provides a highly flexible formulation, thus enabling the researcher to explore the possible effects of a wide range of departures from the standard normal probit model. The chapter implements a Bayesian approach showing how Gibbs sampling techniques can be used to carry out the necessary computations. Geweke and Keane contrast their approach to the semiparametric methods developed in the literature for the estimation of the parameters of the probit model, and discuss the pros and cons of their procedure as compared with that of the semiparametric methods. The finite sample performance of the estimation procedure is studied by means of a number of Monte Carlo experiments. A substantive empirical application is also provided where women's labor force participation is investigated using a subset of data from the Panel Study of Income Dynamics.

The chapter by Lung-Fei Lee considers the estimation of limited dependent variable models under rational expectations in the time series context. Serial correlation in disturbances and dynamic structures with lagged dependent variables are considered and incorporated in the estimation. He shows that the simulated maximum likelihood method is feasible for the estimation of such models. A general simulation method with broad applicability is suggested. It is proved that a unique rational expectations solution exists even when the equations characterizing the rational expectations solution are simulated. For a long time series, the potential numerical underflow issue in the simulation of rational expectations solution and likelihood function can be solved with a recursive weighting simulation scheme. Variance reduction in the simulation is possible for models with renewal property. Lung-Fei Lee conducts a number of Monte Carlo experiments to study the finite sample performance of the proposed estimation method.

The chapter by El-Gamal and Grether provides a Monte Carlo study on finite sample performance of their EC (estimation-classification) estimator and algorithm for panel data probit models. The situation under investigation is that each observed individual in a panel may belong to one of a fixed but possibly unknown number of types. The study has found that the EC-estimator can be better than the familiar fixed effects estimator. A diagnostic statistic called the average normalized entropy is also found to be a very useful indicator of possible misclassifications.

The second group of papers deal with panel data models. The chapter by Nerlove re-examines the estimation of dynamic panel data models and studies the sensitivity of the coefficient estimates of both the "state" variable and the other explanatory variables to the econometric method employed. He examines this sensitivity in the context of recent empirical studies of growth rate convergence using panel data from the Penn World Tables. Models with country-specific intercepts and models with country-specific trends are estimated. Even though the primary purpose of the chapter is to assess the performance of alternative estimators, all the results reported support the conventional interpretation of the coefficient of the lagged dependent variable in terms of growth convergence conditional on savings and population growth rates. He shows that the use of the fixed-effects estimator favors the results toward finding a relatively rapid convergence. However, when the maximum likelihood estimation technique is employed, unconditional on the initial observations, very slow convergence is obtained. Biases in the estimates of the coefficient of the "state" variable for all of the usual methods of panel data analysis tend to induce biases in the estimates of the coefficients of other variables as well. Consequently, Nerlove argues that the conclusions of many of the recent studies of the determinants of growth employing dynamic panel data models may largely reflect the econometric methods employed.

In their chapter Ahn and Schmidt consider efficient use of moment conditions in panel data models. In panel data models with strictly exogenous time-varying regressors, the number of moment conditions rapidly increases with the number of time series observations. In terms of asymptotic efficiency, it would always be desirable to use as many moment conditions as possible. However, in finite samples, the biases in generalized method of moments (GMM) estimates tend to increase with the number of moment conditions used. Ahn and Schmidt derive conditions to identify redundant moment conditions. They also propose a modified generalized instrumental variable (MGIV) estimator that is asymptotically equivalent to the GMM estimator when the errors are conditionally homoskedastic. When the errors are conditionally heteroskedastic, the MGIV estimator is less efficient than the full GMM estimator asymptotically. However, their

Monte Carlo results suggest that, in finite samples, the MGIV estimator with heteroskedasticity adjusted asymptotic standard errors performs better than the full GMM estimator.

The chapter by Kiviet provides asymptotic expansions of least squares and instrumental variables estimators for dynamic panel data models. The dynamic panel data model includes lagged dependent variables and a weakly exogenous regressor. Analytic results are obtained by deriving the expectation of higher-order expansions of estimation errors. Those analytical results have strong implications on small sample properties of various estimators of these models.

The chapter by Davies and Lahiri is concerned with the analysis of expectations from the surveys of professional forecasters carried out by American Statistical Association – National Bureau of Economic Research (ASA–NBER). They provide a generalization of the panel data model used by Keane and Runkle (1990), which allows for a more complex correlation structure across the forecast errors over different individuals, target dates, and at different horizons. Within this framework they examine a number of issues raised by Keane and Runkle, notably the problem associated with the use of revised July figures (that could not have been available to the respondents), the proper accounting of aggregate shocks, and the appropriate choice of the forecast horizon. Based on their test results they conclude that on the whole the hypothesis that the ASA-NBER panel have been rational in predicting the inflation rate over the period 1968(4)–1991(4) is rejected. According to their analysis more than 70 percent of the forecasters failed to meet the rationality criteria in the sense of Muth (1961).

The chapter by Baillie and Baltagi considers prediction problems for the regression model with one-way error component disturbances. The expression for the asymptotic mean squared errors of prediction from various predictors are derived. Theoretical and simulation results indicate that it is important to allow for parameter uncertainty in forming prediction confidence intervals.

The chapter by Hsiao, Pesaran, and Tahmiscioglu implements a Bayesian approach to estimate dynamic panel data models when the coefficients are assumed to be randomly distributed across cross-sectional units using Markov Chain Monte Carlo (MCMC) methods. They establish the asymptotic equivalence of the Bayes estimator and the mean group estimator of Pesaran and Smith (1995), and show that the Bayes estimator is asymptotically normal for large N (the number of units) and large T (the number of time periods) so long as $\cdot N/T \to 0$ as both N and $T \to \infty$. The performance of the Bayes estimator for the short-run coefficients is compared against alternative estimators using both simulated and real data. The Monte Carlo results show that the Bayes estimator has better sampling properties than other estimators for both small and moderate T samples. The analysis of the real data yields new results on Tobin's q model.

The problem of estimation for the long-run coefficients in dynamic heterogeneous panels is taken up in the chapter by Pesaran and Zhao. This chapter investigates the finite T bias of the estimators of the mean long-run coefficients of a heterogeneous dynamic panel. Three approaches of bias corrections are applied to derive individual long-run coefficients before taking their averages. The first approach applies to the Kiviet–Phillips bias correction to individual short-run coefficients before deriving their long-run coefficients. This is referred to as "naive" bias corrected (NBC) procedure. The second approach makes the bias correction directly to the individual long-run coefficients. Two variants are considered, DBC_1 and DBC_2. Both are unbiased to order $O(T^{-1})$ but the DBC_1 estimator contains some higher-order bias corrections. The third approach uses the average of the replica of the long-run coefficients derived from bootstrap generated short-run coefficients as the individual long-run coefficients (*BSBC*). Monte Carlo studies are conducted to evaluate the effectiveness of these bias-correction procedures in reducing the small sample bias. It is found that the NBC procedure fails in all cases. The *BSBC* performs poorly in cases where the true coefficient of the lagged dependent variable is relatively large. The DBC_2 performs reasonably well, although only the DBC_1 outperforms the bootstrap method. When the coefficient of the lagged dependent variable is around 0.8 or above, none of the above-mentioned estimators seems to work.

References

Keane, M.P. and D.E. Runkle (1990), "Testing the Rationality of Price Forecasts: New Evidence from Panel Data," *American Economic Review*, 80: 714–735.

Muth, J.F. (1961), "Rational Expectations and the Theory of Price Movements," *Econometrica*, 29: 315–355.

Pesaran, M.H. and R.P. Smith (1995), "Estimating Long-Run Relationships from Dynamic Heterogeneous Panels," *Journal of Econometrics*, 68: 79–113.

1 A note on left censoring

TAKESHI AMEMIYA

1 Introduction

Left censoring occurs in a duration model when a statistician observes only those spells which either are in the middle of continuation at the time of the first observation or start during the observation period. It is assumed that the statistician has no record of those spells which had ended by the time of the first observation. A special treatment of the problem is necessary because ignoring left censoring will overestimate the mean duration as longer spells tend to be observed more frequently than shorter spells. This is called selectivity bias.

Different cases of left censoring arise depending on the following considerations: (1) Spells in the middle of continuation at the time of the first observation are either completely or partially observed. Suppose such a spell started at s, continued on to 0 (the time of the first observation), and ended at t. The statistician may observe only s (by asking how long the spell had lasted), only t, or both. (2) Spells which start after the time of the first observation are either observed or not observed. (3) For a single individual we either observe a single spell or a sequence of spells in different states.

In each possible case we will consider how the selectivity bias is eliminated. If the model is fully specified, this is accomplished by the method of maximum likelihood estimation, which is fully efficient. However, in certain situations, a less efficient but more robust method, which does not require the full knowledge of the model specification, may be possible and desirable.

Although we treat the case of a homogeneous population, the adjustment for a heterogeneous population is simple as it will be indicated in appropriate places.

The problem of left censoring is dealt with only scantily in the general

The first version of this chapter appeared as CEPR Publication No. 235 on March 1991. The author is indebted to Aaron Edlin and Tony Lancaster for helpful comments.

statistical literature. For example, standard textbooks on duration analysis such as Kalbfleisch and Prentice (1980) or Cox and Oakes (1984) devote less than a page to the problem. Miller (1981) mentions only a different kind of left censoring from what we discuss here. One can find more discussion in the econometric literature (for example, see Lancaster (1979), Flinn and Heckman (1982), Ridder (1984), and Amemiya (1985)). Here we try to give a more complete, unified treatment of the subject.

2 A single state model

The duration data are generated according to the following scheme: a duration starts in an interval $[a, b]$, which encloses 0, and the starting time X is distributed according to density $h(x)$. Duration T is distributed according to density $f(t)$ and distribution function $F(t)$. We assume that X and T are independent. The statistician observes only those spells which end or are censored after 0. We will consider three types of left censoring and for each type will derive the likelihood function assuming a homogeneous population. The result can be easily modified for the case of a heterogeneous population, as we will indicate below.

Type 1 left censor

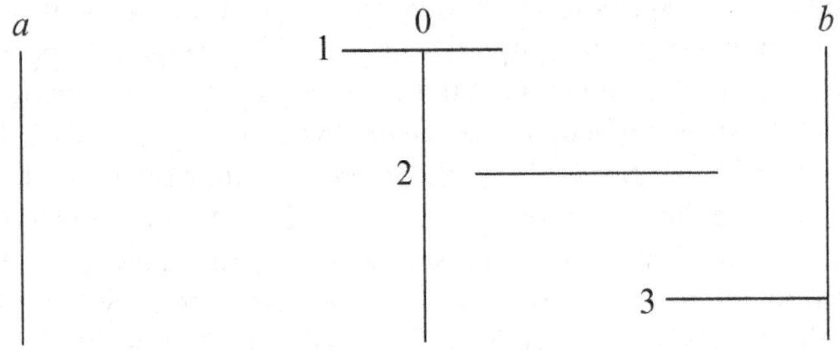

Here the spell that was going on at time 0 is completely observed. Three kinds of spells are depicted in the above figure; we will write the likelihood function as a product of three parts corresponding to the three kinds. Each part is to be divided by the probability of observing a spell. Define

$$A_1 = \{x,t \mid t > -x,\ 0 > x > a\} \text{ and } A_2 = \{x,t \mid x > 0\}.$$

Then

$$P_1 \equiv P(A_1) = \int_a^0 h(x)[1 - F(-x)]dx \tag{1}$$

$$P_2 \equiv P(A_2) = \int_0^b h(x)dx. \tag{2}$$

The probability of observing a spell, denoted by P, is $P_1 + P_2$. Finally, the likelihood function can be written as

$$L_1 = \prod_1 h(x_i)f(t_i) \prod_2 h(x_i)f(t_i) \prod_3 h(x_i)[1 - F(b - x_i)] \prod_{all} P^{-1}. \tag{3}$$

Note that the first and second kinds of spells are treated symmetrically. In the next section we will show that dividing the first part by P_1 and the second and third part by P_2 leads to a consistent but less-efficient estimator.

Type 2 left censor

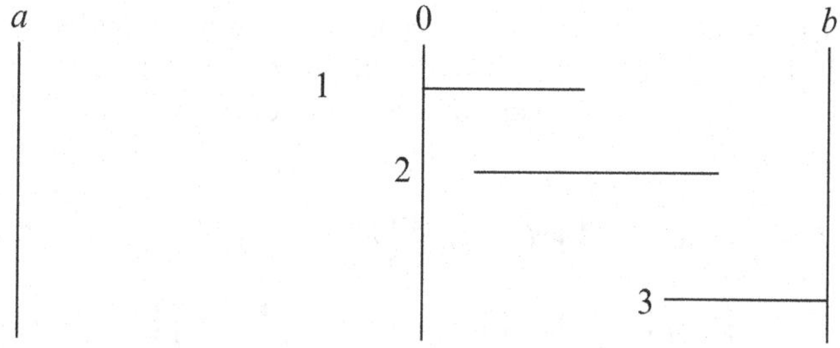

Here the spell that was going on at time 0 is observed only after 0. The likelihood function differs from (3) only in its first part and is given by

$$L_2 = \prod_1 \int_a^0 h(x)f(t_i - x)dx \prod_2 h(x_i)f(t_i) \prod_3 h(x_i)[1 - F(b - x_i)] \prod_{all} P^{-1}. \tag{4}$$

Type 3 left censor

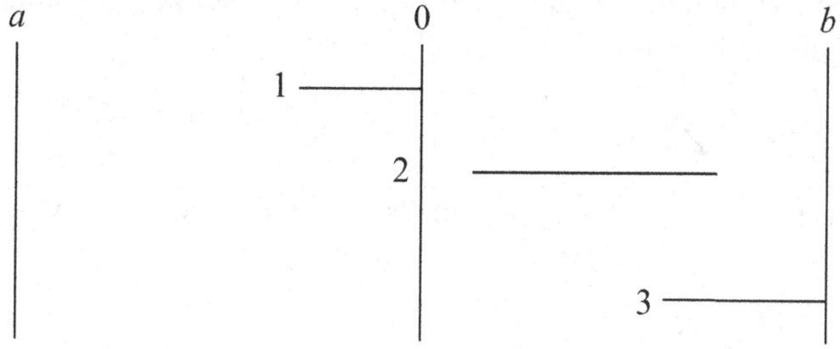

Here the spell that was going on at time 0 is observed only up to 0. Again, the likelihood function differs from (3) and (4) only in its first part.

$$L_3 = \prod_1 h(x_i)[1 - F(t_i)] \prod_2 h(x_i) f(t_i) \prod_3 h(x_i)[1 - F(b - x_i)] \prod_{all} P^{-1}. \quad (5)$$

So far we have assumed a homogeneous population. The necessary adjustment for a heterogeneous population is straightforward. Merely add subscript i to h, f, F, a, and b, and hence also to P. Otherwise, the likelihood function (3), (4), or (5) is unchanged.

3 Why divide by P

Now we answer the question posed after equation (3): Why is it less efficient to divide the first part by P_1 and the second and third part by P_2? We will consider Type 1 left censor; the other types can be similarly analyzed. For simplicity we will assume that there is no right censoring. Therefore, there are only two kinds of spells and the spell which reaches b is observed until its end. In this case the correct likelihood function is (3) except the third part. We will first give a heuristic and then a rigorous argument.

Rewrite (3) as

$$\begin{aligned} L_1 &= \prod_1 h(x_i) f(t_i) \prod_2 h(x_i) f(t_i) \prod_{all} P^{-1} \\ &= \prod_1 h(x_i)[f(t_i)] P_1^{-1} \prod_2 h(x_i) f(t_i) P_2^{-1} \prod_1 P_1/P \prod_2 P_2/P \equiv L_{11} L_{12}, \quad (6) \end{aligned}$$

where L_{11} consists of the first two products. From the above it is clear that dividing the two parts separately by P_1 and P_2 means ignoring L_{12}. It means ignoring information that a particular spell is either the first kind or the second kind. The estimator that maximizes L_{11} is a conditional maximum likelihood estimator; therefore, it is consistent but less efficient.

To advance a rigorous argument, we must introduce a parameter vector θ to estimate. Although we will treat θ as a scalar in the subsequent analysis, an extension to the vector case is obvious. Suppose f depends on θ but h does not. Taking the natural logarithm of the first line of (6) and ignoring h because it does not depend on θ, we have

$$\log L_1 = \sum_{i=1}^{n} \log f(t_i) - n \log P \quad (7)$$

where n is the number of observed spells. Differentiating (7) with respect to θ and noting P_2 does not depend on θ, we have

$$\frac{\partial \log L_1}{\partial \theta} = \sum_{i=1}^{n} \frac{1}{f} \frac{\partial f}{\partial \theta} - \frac{n}{P} \frac{\partial P_1}{\partial \theta}. \quad (8)$$

Although it is not necessary to do so because a maximum likelihood estimator is generally consistent, we can directly check it by noting

$$E\frac{1}{N}\frac{\partial \log L_1}{\partial \theta}=\int_A \frac{1}{f}\frac{\partial f}{\partial \theta} hfdtdx-\frac{\partial P_1}{\partial \theta}=\frac{\partial}{\partial \theta}\int_A hfdtdx-\frac{\partial P_1}{\partial \theta}=0 \tag{9}$$

where $A=A_1\cup A_2$ and N is the total number of spells both observed and unobserved.

Differentiating (8) again with respect to θ

$$\frac{\partial^2 \log L_1}{\partial \theta^2}=-\sum_{i=1}^{n}\frac{1}{f^2}\left[\frac{\partial f}{\partial \theta}\right]^2+\sum_{i=1}^{n}\frac{1}{f}\frac{\partial^2 f}{\partial \theta^2}+\frac{n}{P^2}\left[\frac{\partial P_1}{\partial \theta}\right]^2-\frac{n}{P}\frac{\partial^2 P_1}{\partial \theta^2}. \tag{10}$$

Therefore

$$-E\frac{1}{N}\frac{\partial^2 \log L_1}{\partial \theta^2}=\int_A \frac{1}{f}\left[\frac{\partial f}{\partial \theta}\right]^2 hdtdx-\frac{1}{P}\left[\frac{\partial P_1}{\partial \theta}\right]^2. \tag{11}$$

As usual, the asymptotic variance of $\sqrt{N}(\hat{\theta}-\theta)$ is given by the inverse of (11).

Next, taking the log of L_{11} and ignoring the terms that do not depend on θ

$$\log L_{11}=\sum_{i=1}^{n}\log f(t_i)-n_1\log P_1-n_2\log P_2. \tag{12}$$

Therefore

$$\frac{\partial \log L_{11}}{\partial \theta}=\sum_{i=1}^{n}\frac{1}{f}\frac{\partial f}{\partial \theta}-\frac{n_1}{P_1}\frac{\partial P_1}{\partial \theta}. \tag{13}$$

As in (9), we can show

$$E\frac{1}{N}\frac{\partial \log L_{11}}{\partial \theta}=0 \tag{14}$$

which implies the consistency of the estimator that maximizes L_1. As in the case of L, the asymptotic variance is the inverse of

$$-E\frac{1}{N}\frac{\partial^2 \log L_{11}}{\partial \theta^2}=\int_A \frac{1}{f}\left[\frac{\partial f}{\partial \theta}\right]^2 hdtdx-\frac{1}{P_1}\left[\frac{\partial P_1}{\partial \theta}\right]^2. \tag{15}$$

Since L_{11} is a conditional likelihood function, this result is correct, but one can also directly show the equality of (15) to $N^{-1}V(\partial \log L_{11}/\partial \theta)$.

By comparing (15) with (11), one can readily see the inefficiency of the estimator that maximizes L_{11} relative to the true maximum likelihood estimator.

4 A simple example

In this section we will evaluate the variances of the above two maximum likelihood estimators in a very simple duration model. We will also calculate the degree of inconsistency of an estimator which does not correct for selective bias. We assume that spells start either at -1 or at 0 with equal probabilities. From either starting point, a spell lasts for 1.5 with probability p and 0.5 with probability $1-p$. We observe only those spells which end after 0. Supposing we observe m_1 spells which started at -1 and lasted for 1.5, n_1 spells which started at 0 and lasted for 1.5 and n_2 spells which started at 0 and lasted for 0.5, how should we estimate p?

Ignoring selectivity

This estimator maximizes the product of unadjusted probabilities

$$S=p^{m_1+n_1}(1-p)^{n_2}. \tag{16}$$

Therefore, $\tilde{p}=(m_1+n_1)/(m_1+n_1+n_2)$ and plim $\tilde{p}=p-(p^2-p)/(1+p)$. The parameter p is overestimated because the short spells that started at -1 were not observed.

Maximizing conditional LF

The conditional likelihood function (aside from a constant term), the conditional maximum likelihood estimator, and its asymptotic distribution are given by

$$L_1=p^{n_1}(1-p)^{n_2} \tag{17}$$

$$\hat{p}_1=\frac{n_1}{n_1+n_2} \tag{18}$$

$$\sqrt{N}(\hat{p}_1-p)\rightarrow N\{0,2p(1-p)\} \tag{19}$$

where N is the total number of spells including those which are not observed. Note that since (18) defines the estimator explicitly, (18) can be verified directly by a central limit theorem. However, the asymptotic variance may also be obtained as the inverse of the information matrix as we did in the previous section. The same remark applies to the next estimator.

Maximizing full LF

The full likelihood function (aside from a constant term), the maximum likelihood estimator, and its asymptotic distribution are given by

$$L = p^{m_1+n_1}(1-p)^{n_2}(1+p)^{-(m_1+n_1+n_2)} \tag{20}$$

$$\hat{p} = \frac{m_1+n_1}{m_1+n_1+2n_2} \tag{21}$$

$$\sqrt{N}(\hat{p}-p) \rightarrow N\{0, p(1-p)(1+p)\}. \tag{22}$$

From (19) and (22), we see the extent of the inefficiency of the conditional maximum likelihood estimator.

5 Observe only spells continuing at 0

In this section we consider the model in which duration data are generated by the same scheme as in section 2 but we observe only those spells which are continuing at time 0. Since we can concentrate on the starting time in the interval $[a, 0]$, we will assume that the support of density $h(x)$ is $[a, 0]$. We assume a homogeneous population, but the adjustment for the case of a heterogeneous population is simple as in section 2. As before, we consider three types of censoring. For each type the likelihood function is the first part of the likelihood function of section 2 divided this time not by P but by P_1. Thus

$$L_1 = \Pi h(x_i) f(t_i) P_1^{-1} \tag{23}$$

$$L_2 = \Pi \int_a^0 h(x) f(t_i - x) dx \, P_1^{-1} \tag{24}$$

$$L_3 = \Pi h(x_i)[1 - F(t_i)] P_1^{-1}. \tag{25}$$

When we take $h(x)$ as uniform density and take the limit of a going to $-\infty$, we obtain the three formulae (11.2.75), (11.2.76), and (11.2.71), respectively, given in Amemiya (1985, p. 448).

6 Method which does not require starting-time distribution

Next, we will consider Type 1 left censor as adapted in the model of section 5 above, for which the full likelihood function is (23), and discuss a consistent estimator which does not require the knowledge of $h(x)$. It is the estimator that maximizes the product of conditional densities of t given x. This estimator was used by Lancaster (1979), and its properties were studied by Ridder (1984). Such an estimator is useful because it is often difficult for a researcher to specify $h(x)$ correctly. The aforementioned formulae in Amemiya do not depend on $h(x)$ but this was accomplished by an arbitrary assumption of its uniformity. Although we treat the case of a homogeneous population, the adjustment for a heterogeneous population is simple as in section 2. This estimator maximizes

$$L^* = \prod_{i=1}^{n} \frac{f(t_i)}{1 - F(-x_i)}. \tag{26}$$

Clearly, it is a conditional maximum likelihood estimator. Taking the logarithm

$$\log L^* = \sum_{i=1}^{n} \log f(t_i) - \sum_{i=1}^{n} \log[1 - F(-x_i)]. \tag{27}$$

Differentiating (27) with respect to θ

$$\frac{\partial \log L^*}{\partial \theta} = \sum_{i=1}^{n} \frac{1}{f}\frac{\partial f}{\partial \theta} + \sum_{i=1}^{n} \frac{1}{1-F}\frac{\partial F}{\partial \theta}. \tag{28}$$

Consistency follows from noting

$$\begin{aligned} E\frac{1}{N}\frac{\partial \log L^*}{\partial \theta} &= \int_{A_1} \frac{1}{f}\frac{\partial f}{\partial \theta} hfdtdx + \int_{A_1} \frac{1}{1-F}\frac{\partial f}{\partial \theta} hfdtdx \\ &= \frac{\partial}{\partial \theta}\int_a^0 h(x)[1 - F(-x)]dx + \frac{\partial}{\partial \theta}\int_a^0 h(x)F(-x)dx \\ &= \frac{\partial}{\partial \theta}\int_a^0 h(x)dx \\ &= 0. \end{aligned} \tag{29}$$

Differentiating (28) again with respect to θ

$$\begin{aligned} \frac{\partial^2 \log L^*}{\partial \theta^2} = &-\sum_{i=1}^{n} \frac{1}{f^2}\left[\frac{\partial f}{\partial \theta}\right]^2 + \sum_{i=1}^{n} \frac{1}{f}\frac{\partial^2 f}{\partial \theta^2} + \sum_{i=1}^{n} \frac{1}{(1-F)^2}\left[\frac{\partial F}{\partial \theta}\right]^2 \\ &+ \sum_{i-1}^{n} \frac{1}{1-F}\frac{\partial^2 F}{\partial \theta^2}. \end{aligned} \tag{30}$$

Using

$$E\frac{1}{f^2}\left[\frac{\partial f}{\partial \theta}\right]^2 = \int_{A_1} \frac{1}{f}\left[\frac{\partial f}{\partial \theta}\right]^2 hdtdx \tag{31}$$

$$E\frac{1}{f}\frac{\partial^2 f}{\partial \theta^2} = \frac{\partial^2}{\partial \theta^2}\int_a^0 h(x)[1 - F(-x)]dx \tag{32}$$

$$E\frac{1}{(1-F)^2}\left[\frac{\partial F}{\partial \theta}\right]^2 = \int_a^0 \frac{1}{1-F}\left[\frac{\partial F}{\partial \theta}\right]^2 hdtdx \tag{33}$$

$$E\frac{1}{1-F}\frac{\partial^2 F}{\partial \theta^2} = \frac{\partial^2}{\partial \theta^2}\int_a^0 h(x)[F(-x)]dx \tag{34}$$

we have

$$-E\frac{1}{N}\frac{\partial^2 \log L^*}{\partial \theta^2} = \int_{A_1} \frac{1}{f}\left[\frac{\partial f}{\partial \theta}\right]^2 hdtdx - \int_a^0 \frac{1}{1-F}\left[\frac{\partial F}{\partial \theta}\right]^2 hdtdx. \tag{35}$$

The information matrix of the full maximum likelihood estimator that maximizes (23) is analogous to (15) except that the integration in the right-hand side is over the set A_1. Thus

$$-E\frac{1}{N}\frac{\partial^2 \log L_1}{\partial \theta^2} = \int_{A_1} \frac{1}{f}\left[\frac{\partial f}{\partial \theta}\right]^2 hdtdx - \frac{1}{P_1}\left[\frac{\partial P_1}{\partial \theta}\right]^2. \tag{36}$$

That (36) is greater than (35) follows from the Cauchy–Schwartz inequality

$$E_x U^2\, E_x V^2 \geq (E_x UV)^2 \tag{37}$$

where $E_x(Z) = \int_a^0 zh(x)dx$, $U = \frac{1}{\sqrt{1-F}}\frac{\partial F}{\partial \theta}$, and $V = \sqrt{1-F}$.

Unfortunately, a simple consistent estimator which does not require the knowledge of $h(x)$ has not been found for Type 2 or Type 3 left censor in the model of section 5. In the model of section 2, there exists an even simpler consistent estimator of θ which does not require the knowledge of h, provided h does not depend on θ. It works for any of the three types and simply amounts to maximizing the second and third product each divided by P_2: namely

$$\text{Maximize} \prod_2 h(x_i)f(t_i)P_2^{-1} \prod_3 h(x_i)[1-F(b-x_i)]P_2^{-1}.$$

In the case of Type 1 left censor, this method can be combined with the method proposed earlier to obtain a more efficient estimator: namely, that which maximizes

$$L^* = \prod_1 h(x_i)f(t_i)[1-F(-x_i)]^{-1} \prod_2 h(x_i)f(t_i)P_2^{-1} \prod_3 h(x_i)$$
$$[1-F(b-x_i)]P_2^{-1}. \tag{38}$$

If $h(x)$ does not depend on θ as before, $h(x_i)$ and P_2 can be eliminated from the right-hand side of (38). The estimator is consistent and its asymptotic variance can be obtained by the same method described above.

There is an alternative method, which, although not consistent, may work reasonably well for Type 2 left censor in the model of section 5. In this method, the term after the product symbol in the right-hand side of (24) is specified to be an appropriate function of t and a new set of parameters. This method can be easily adjusted for heterogeneous population and has been used in empirical applications (see, for example, Gritz (1993)).

7 Semiparametric estimation of $h(x)$ and θ

Goto (1993 and 1996) considered the semiparametric maximum likelihood estimation of density $h(x)$ and the parameter θ that appears inside f in the model (23). He proved that when the maximizing value of $h(x)$ is inserted back into (23), one obtains the conditional likelihood function (26). Thus, we can interpret the conditional maximum likelihood estimator that maximizes (26) as the semiparametric maximum likelihood estimator of the model (23).

We will give a sketch of the proof. We are to maximize

$$L=\prod_{i=1}^{n}\frac{h(x_i)f(t_i)}{\int_a^0 h(x)[1-F(-x)]dx} \tag{39}$$

with respect to function $h(\cdot)$. We can take $h(\cdot)$ to be a step function taking the value of h_i over the interval of length d around the observed x_i and zero elsewhere, where $d=(\Sigma h_k)^{-1}$. Then, since

$$\int_a^0 h(x)[1-F(-x)]dx \cong \sum_k dh_k[1-F(-x_k)] \tag{40}$$

we can write (39) as

$$L=\prod_{i=1}^{n}\frac{h_i f(t_i)}{\sum_{k=1}^{n} h_k(\sum_j h_j)^{-1}[1-F(-x_k)]} \tag{41}$$

Therefore, we should maximize

$$\prod_{i=1}^{n}\frac{h_i f(t_i)}{\sum_k h_k[1-F(-x_k)]} \text{ subject to } \sum_k h_k = 1. \tag{42}$$

Differentiating the logarithm of the above with respect to each h_i and setting the derivative equal to zero, we obtain

$$\frac{1}{h_i} - \frac{na_i}{\sum h_k a_k} = 0 \tag{43}$$

where we have defined $a_i = 1 - F(-x_i)$. These can be rewritten as

$$h_i = \left(\frac{a_1}{a_i}\right) h_1,\ i = 1, 2, \ldots, n. \tag{44}$$

Summing both sides of the above over i and noting $\sum_k h_k = 1$, we obtain

$$h_i = \frac{1}{a_i \sum_k (a_k)^{-1}}. \tag{45}$$

Finally, putting (45) back into the maximand in (42) yields

$$\frac{1}{n^n} \prod_{i=1}^{n} \frac{f(t_i)}{1 - F(-x_i)} \tag{46}$$

which is the same as (26) except for a factor which does not depend on θ.

8 Separate estimation of $h(x)$

The density $h(x)$ may also be estimated using a sample either independent of that used to estimate θ or an augmented sample including that used to estimate θ. Nickell (1979) used the method but did not analyze its effect on the asymptotic distribution of the maximum likelihood estimator of θ.

We consider the estimator of θ that maximizes

$$\hat{L}_1 = \Pi f(t_i) \hat{P}_1^{-1} \tag{47}$$

where $\hat{P}_1 = \int_a^0 \hat{h}(x)[1 - F(-x)]dx$. As $\hat{h}(x)$, we can, for example, use the following simple method: divide the interval $[a, 0]$ into small intervals of length d and for each interval estimate $h(x)$ by the relative frequency of the workers who became unemployed in the augmented sample. If the size of the independent or augmented sample is K, we must have $d \to 0$ and $dK \to \infty$. In this case we have (see Bickel and Doksum (1977, p. 385))

$$|\hat{h}(x) - h(x)| = O\left(\frac{1}{\sqrt{dK}}\right) \tag{48}$$

provided that $h(x)$ is continuous in $[a, 0]$.

If we denote this estimator by $\hat{\theta}$, its asymptotic distribution can be obtained from

$$\sqrt{N}(\hat{\theta}-\theta)=-\left(\frac{1}{\sqrt{N}}\frac{\partial \log \hat{L}_1}{\partial \theta}\right)\left(\frac{1}{N}\frac{\partial^2 \log \hat{L}_1}{\partial \theta^2}\right)^{-1}. \tag{49}$$

The second-derivative term above divided by N will converge to the same limit as if h were not estimated, provided that $d \to 0$ and $dK \to \infty$. So, here, we will only consider the first derivative part. We have

$$\frac{1}{\sqrt{N}}\frac{\partial \log \hat{L}_1}{\partial \theta} \cong \frac{1}{\sqrt{N}}\sum_{i=1}^{N}\left(D\frac{1}{f}\frac{\partial f}{\partial \theta}-\frac{\partial P_1}{\partial \theta}\right)-\frac{1}{P_1}\frac{\partial P_1}{\partial \theta}\frac{1}{\sqrt{N}}\sum_{1}^{N}(D-P_1)$$
$$+\int_a^0 \sqrt{N}\,[\hat{h}(x)-h(x)]\Psi(x)dx, \tag{50}$$

where $\Psi(x)=\partial F(-x)/\partial\theta + P_1^{-1}(\partial P_1/\partial\theta)[1-F(-x)]$ and $D_i=1$ if $T_i > -X_i > 0$ and 0 otherwise. From (48) and (50) it is clear that only when K goes to infinity at the rate faster than N, estimating h has no effect on the asymptotic distribution.

It is better to estimate P_1 by $\hat{P}_1=\int_a^0 [1-F(-x)]d\hat{H}(x)$, where $\hat{H}$ is the empirical distribution function. Thus, $\hat{P}_1=\frac{1}{K}\sum_{i=1}^{K}[1-F(-x_i)]$. In this case, we can show

$$\frac{1}{\sqrt{N}}\frac{\partial \log \hat{L}_1}{\partial \theta} \cong \frac{1}{\sqrt{N}}\sum_{i=1}^{N}\left(D\frac{1}{f}\frac{\partial f}{\partial \theta}-\frac{\partial P_1}{\partial \theta}\right)+\sqrt{N}\int_a^0 \frac{\partial F}{\partial \theta}d[\hat{H}(x)-H(x)] \tag{51}$$

but since

$$\sqrt{K}\int_a^0 \frac{\partial F}{\partial \theta}d[\hat{H}(x)-H(x)] \to N[0, V(\partial F/\partial\theta)], \tag{52}$$

the asymptotic variance of this estimator adds $cV(\partial F/\partial\theta)$ to that of the maximum likelihood estimator with the known $h(x)$, where $cK=N$ for some constant c (see Prakasa Rao (1987, p. 391)).

9 Two-states model

In this section we consider a model in which an individual starts a spell in either state 1 or state 2 at time a, with probability p and $1-p$ respectively. The transition from state 1 to 2 occurs with density function $f_1(t)$ and distribution function $F_1(t)$. The transition from 2 to 1 is done according to $f_2(t)$

and $F_2(t)$. The statistician starts observing spells at time 0. As in section 2, the spells that are continuing at time 0 will be completely or partially observed, leading to the three types of censoring. The subsequent spells of an individual, after the spell that is continuing at 0 terminates, will be observed up to time b. However, unlike in section 2, possible selectivity bias need not be taken into account for these subsequent spells, because the starting time of a subsequent spell is determined by the end of the preceding spell. For this reason this model has more similarity to the model of section 5. Although we treat the case of a homogeneous population, the adjustment for a heterogeneous population is simple as in section 2.

We need to distinguish the following two cases: (1) the statistician observes spells in both states at time 0; (2) the statistician observes only spells in one of the states at time 0. We will assume that the subsequent spells of both states will be observed, but this is not a crucial assumption.

Observe both states

The likelihood functions corresponding to the three types of censoring can be written as follows:

$$L_1 = \prod_1 h_1(x_i) f_1(t_i) \prod_2 h_2(x_i) f_2(t_i) \tag{53}$$

$$L_2 = \prod_1 \int_a^0 h_1(x) f_1(t_i - x) dx \prod_2 \int_a^0 h_2(x) f_2(t_i - x) dx \tag{54}$$

$$L_3 = \prod_1 h_1(x_i)[1 - F_1(t_i)] \prod_2 h_2(x_i)[1 - F_2(t_i)] \tag{55}$$

where the numbers at the bottom of the product sign refer to the two states rather than two kinds of spells as in section 2.

A feature of this model which makes it more complex than the single-state model is that $h(x)$ is a very complicated function of p, f_1, and f_2. Thus, if θ is the vector of parameters that characterize f_1 and f_2, we can no longer assume that $h(x)$ does not depend on θ. This fact makes the full maximum likelihood estimator generally very complicated and increases the advisability of a simple consistent estimator which does not require $h(x)$. We will briefly indicate how $h_1(x)$ can be determined. It can be calculated by summing the densities of all the possible event histories prior to x. First of all, $x = a$ with probability p. Therefore, strictly speaking, we should allow for the possibility that hs that appear in the right-hand side of (53) and (55) are probabilities and the integral in (54) is a Stieltjes integral. The second possibility is that an individual starts in state 2 at time a and moves once to state 1 at time x, for which the density is

$$(1-p)f_2(x-a) \tag{56}$$

The third possibility is that an individual starts in state 1 at time a, moves to state 2, comes back to state 1 at time x, for which the density is

$$p\int_a^x f_1(y-a)f_2(x-y)dy. \tag{57}$$

Summing all these densities *ad infinitum*, $h_1(x)$ is evaluated. $h_2(x)$ can be analogously derived.

To verify the correctness of our likelihood functions, it is useful to check the consistency of the maximum likelihood estimator. We will do this for (53). We have

$$\frac{\partial \log L_1}{\partial \theta} = \sum_1 \frac{1}{h_1}\frac{\partial h_1}{\partial \theta} + \sum_1 \frac{1}{f_1}\frac{\partial f_1}{\partial \theta} + \sum_2 \frac{1}{h_2}\frac{\partial h_2}{\partial \theta} + \sum_2 \frac{1}{f_2}\frac{\partial f_2}{\partial \theta} \tag{58}$$

$$E\frac{1}{N}\frac{\partial \log L_1}{\partial \theta} = \frac{\partial P_1}{\partial \theta} + \frac{\partial P_2}{\partial \theta} = 0 \tag{59}$$

where P_1 is the probability an individual is in state 1 at time 0 and is given by

$$P_1 = \int_a^0 h_1(x)[1-F_1(-x)]dx \tag{60}$$

Clearly, $P_2 = 1 - P_1$.

Observe one state

Without loss of generality, we assume we observe only spells in state 1 at time 0. The likelihood functions corresponding to the three types of censoring can be written as follows

$$\underline{L}_1 = \prod h_1(x_i)f_1(t_i)P_1^{-1} \tag{61}$$

$$\underline{L}_2 = \prod \int_a^0 h_1(x)f_1(t_i-x)dxP_1^{-1} \tag{62}$$

$$\underline{L}_3 = \prod h_1(x_i)[1-F_1(t_i)]P_1^{-1}. \tag{63}$$

These likelihood functions are not any simpler than those in the previous case.

Method which does not require starting-time distribution

As in section 6, this method works only for type 1 left censor. This estimator maximizes the following conditional likelihood functions: L_1^* for the case of observing both states and $\underline{L}_1^*$ for the case of observing only state 1.

$$L_1^* = \prod_1 \frac{f_1(t_i)}{1 - F_1(-x_i)} \prod_2 \frac{f_2(t_i)}{1 - F_2(-x_i)} \tag{64}$$

$$\underline{L}_1^* = \prod \frac{f_1(t_i)}{1 - F_1(-x_i)}. \tag{65}$$

The consistency of these estimators can be shown by tracing the argument in section 6.

It is instructive to recognize the term after the product symbol in (61) and (65) as successive conditional likelihood functions of the term after the first product symbol in (53). The term after the first product symbol in (53) can be written as the product of three terms as follows

$$hf = \frac{f}{1 - F} \frac{h(1 - F)}{P} P \tag{66}$$

where we have omitted the subscript 1 from all the letters. The product of the first two terms in the right-hand side of (66) gives the term in (61) and the first term alone in the right-hand side of (66) gives the term in (65).

References

Amemiya, T. (1985), *Advanced Econometrics*, Cambridge, Mass.: Harvard University Press.

Bickel, P. and K. Doksum (1977), *Mathematical Statistics*, Oakland: Holden-Day.

Cox, D.R. and D. Oakes (1984), *Analysis of Survival Data*, London: Chapman and Hall.

Flinn, C.J. and J.J. Heckman (1982), "Models for the Analysis of Labor Force Dynamics," *Advances in Econometrics*, 1: 35–95.

Goto, F. (1993), "Consistency and Efficiency of Semiparametric Estimators in Left Censored Duration Models," Unpublished Ph.D. Thesis. Stanford University.

(1996), "Achieving Semiparametric Efficiency Bounds in Left Censored Duration Models," *Econometrica*, 64: 439–442.

Gritz, R.M. (1993), "The Impact of Training on the Frequency and Duration of Employment," *Journal of Econometrics*, 57: 21–51.

Kalbfleisch, J.D. and R.L. Prentice (1980), *The Statistical Analysis of Failure Time Data*, New York: John Wiley & Sons.

Lancaster, T. (1979), "Econometric Methods for the Duration of Unemployment," *Econometrica*, 47: 939–956.

Miller, R.G. (1981), *Survival Analysis*, New York: John Wiley & Sons.

Nickell, S. (1979), "Estimating the Probability of Leaving Unemployment," *Econometrica*, 47: 1249–1266.
Prakasa Rao, B.L.S. (1987), *Asymptotic Theory of Statistical Inference*, New York: John Wiley & Sons.
Ridder, G. (1984), "The Distribution of Single-Spell Duration Data," in G.R. Neumann and N.C. Wertergaard-Nielsen (eds.), *Studies in Labor Market Dynamics*, Springer Verlag.

2 Autoregressive models with sample selectivity for panel data

MANUEL ARELLANO, OLYMPIA BOVER, AND
JOSÉ M. LABEAGA

1 Introduction

Recent studies have developed econometric procedures for the analysis of the time series properties of panel data sets consisting of large numbers of short individual time series (e.g., Anderson and Hsiao (1981), Chamberlain (1984), Holtz-Eakin, Newey, and Rosen (1988), and Arellano and Bond (1991)). The analysis is typically based on empirical autoregressive equations including time and individual effects, and possibly observed time-varying exogenous variables. Individual effects are removed by differencing and lagged variables are used as instruments in order to retrieve consistent estimators of the autoregressive coefficients of the levels equation. Alternatively, one could choose moving average processes and components of variance to model the autocovariance matrix of the data in first differences, using methods of moments estimation and testing as well (as done, for example, by Abowd and Card (1989)). In either case, the motivation for this type of analysis with micro data is often to establish a mapping between the observed dynamic interactions and those implied by a theoretical model, or at least to test particular time series implications of such model.

The purpose of this chapter is to formulate procedures for the analysis of the time series behavior of panel data subject to censoring. We apply these methods to analyze the dynamics of female labor supply and wages using PSID data. We follow the standard latent variable approach to models with selectivity and assume a linear autoregressive model for a latent variable which is only partly observed due to a selection mechanism.

These models arise as a natural limited-dependent-variable extension of similar linear models, and may be a representation of the reduced form

An earlier version of this chapter was presented at the Mannheim Meeting on Labour Markets, 19–22 March 1992, and at the European Meeting of the Econometric Society, Brussels, August 1992. We are grateful to two anonymous referees for helpful comments on this work. All remaining errors are our own.

of interesting structural models. In this regard, it is important to distinguish an interest in the dynamics of the censored variable given the selection rule, from a concern with the dynamics of the selection process. For example, in terms of our application, we are interested in the time series behavior of female labor supply and wages conditional on participation and individual effects. If the focus were on the dynamics of participation, it would be important to model dependence on past states as well as unobserved heterogeneity (see Heckman (1981) for a menu of alternative models). In effect, the models we consider are strictly speaking models of selectivity in the sense that qualitative choice models are not covered, since at least some values of the latent variables (not just their sign) must be observed.

The chapter is organized as follows. Section 2 presents the model and compares our assumptions with those typically made for linear models. Section 3 discusses methods of parameter estimation and testing. The basic method of estimation can be regarded as an application of the asymptotic least squares procedures of Gourieroux, Monfort, and Trognon (1985). Section 4 contains the application to female labor supply and wages using two samples from the Michigan database. Finally, section 5 presents some concluding remarks.

2 The model

We begin by considering a first-order autoregression for a scalar latent variable y_{it}^* including an individual effect η_i. The index i denotes cross-sectional observations and t refers to time periods. Specifically, we have

$$y_{it}^* = \alpha y_{i(t-1)}^* + \eta_i + v_{it} \quad |\alpha| < 1 \tag{1}$$

with

$$E(v_{it} | y_{i1}^*, \ldots, y_{i(t-1)}^*) = 0.$$

The variable y_{it}^* is observed subject to endogenous selection. We use the notation y_{it} for the observed variable, and the sample consists of N independently distributed individual time series of length T. Throughout, T is small and N is large. This framework will include truncated and Type I and Type II Tobit censored autoregressive models (using the terminology of Amemiya (1985), see below).

Even in the absence of selection, equation (1) presents the problem that the permanent effect η_i is unobserved. However, the equation error in first differences satisfies

$$\mathrm{E}(\Delta y_{it}^* - \alpha \Delta y_{i(t-1)}^* | y_{i1}^*, \ldots, y_{i(t-2)}^*) = 0 \tag{2}$$

which implies moment restrictions on the joint distribution of $(y_{i1}^*, \ldots, y_{iT}^*)$, but marginal with respect to η_i. In particular we have the following $(T-2)(T-1)/2$ orthogonality conditions

$$E[y_{i(t-j)}^*(\Delta y_{it}^* - \alpha \Delta y_{i(t-1)}^*)] = 0 \quad (j=2,\ldots,(t-1);\ t=3,\ldots,T) \tag{3}$$

which are the basis for instrumental variables inferences in the linear model without selectivity.

For later use, we notice that the orthogonality conditions (3) can also be written in terms of the coefficients of the best linear predictors of y_{it}^* and $y_{i(t-1)}^*$ given $(y_{i1}^*, \ldots, y_{i(t-2)}^*)$. Letting

$$\pi_{t-1} = [E(x_{i(t-2)}x'_{i(t-2)})]^{-1}\, E(x_{i(t-2)}y_{i(t-1)}^*) \tag{4}$$

$$p_t = [E(x_{i(t-2)}x'_{i(t-2)})]^{-1}\, E(x_{i(t-2)}y_{it}^*) \tag{5}$$

where $x_{i(t-2)} = (y_{i1}^*, \ldots, y_{i(t-2)}^*)'$, the orthogonality conditions in (3) can be written as

$$(p_t - \pi_{t-1}) = \alpha(\pi_{t-1} - q_{t-2}) \quad (t=3,\ldots,T) \tag{6}$$

where q_{t-2} is a $(t-2)\times 1$ vector which has one in the last position and zero elsewhere. Clearly, the coefficients p_t are related to the π_t and the relation is given by

$$p_t = (I_{t-2} \vdots \pi_{t-1})\pi_t. \tag{7}$$

This approach is attractive because it places no restrictions on the distribution of the effects given the observed conditioning variables. However, it cannot be directly used in our case since we only observe sample moments conditional on selection. That is, we do not observe sample counterparts of the population regression coefficients π_t.

In fact, the selection model is unidentified in the absence of additional prior restrictions on the distribution of the latent variable. If T were sufficiently large, we could choose to place restrictions on the conditional distribution of y_{it}^* while treating the realizations of η_i as parameters to be estimated. Honoré (1992) presents a static Type I Tobit model with fixed effects together with a consistent and asymptotically normal estimator for that model with fixed T and large N. Honoré's estimator places no restrictions on the distribution of η_i given the exogenous variables. In return, he requires the distribution of the errors given the exogenous variables and the effects to be fully stationary, hence ruling out time series heteroskedasticity. In a similar vein. Honoré (1993) gives moment conditions that do not depend on η_i for a Type I Tobit model with a lagged dependent variable, strictly exogenous variables and stationary and serially uncorrelated errors.

Here we achieve identification by placing restrictions on the conditional distribution of the latent variables y_{it}^* given $y_{i1}^*, \dots, y_{i(t-1)}^*$ but not η_i. Firstly, we specify the mean of $y_{it}^* | y_{i1}^*, \dots, y_{i(t-1)}^*$ as an unrestricted (non-Markovian) linear regression. That is, we assume that this mean coincides with the corresponding linear projection (which, for example, would be the case if the y_{it}^* were jointly normally distributed). This amounts to specifying the mean of the effects given $y_{i1}^*, \dots, y_{i(T-1)}^*$ and so we assume some knowledge of the conditional distribution of η_i. In doing this we follow the work of Chamberlain (1984). Secondly, additional features of the distribution of $y_{it}^* | y_{i1}^*, \dots, y_{i(t-1)}^*$ will be specified to overcome the selection problem, using methods existing in the literature. A benefit of this approach is that we can consider Type I and Type II censored models within the same framework. Another advantage is that non-stationary errors (like errors with time series heteroskedasticity) are not ruled out.

In general we have

$$E(y_{it}^* | y_{i1}^*, \dots, y_{i(t-1)}^*) = \alpha y_{i(t-1)}^* + E(\eta_i | y_{i1}^*, \dots, y_{i(t-1)}^*) \tag{8}$$

and we assume

$$E(y_{it}^* | y_{i1}^*, \dots, y_{i(t-1)}^*) = \pi_{t1} y_{i1}^* + \dots + \pi_{t(t-1)} y_{i(t-1)}^* = \pi'_t x_{i(t-1)} \quad (t = 2, \dots, T) \tag{9}$$

which implies that

$$E(\eta_i | y_{i1}^*, \dots, y_{i(T-1)}^*) = \lambda_1 y_{i1}^* + \dots + \lambda_{T-1} y_{i(T-1)}^*. \tag{10}$$

Notice that given (8) and (9), all the conditional expectations $E(\eta_i | x_{it})$ are linear and their coefficients are functions of $\lambda_1, \dots, \lambda_{T-1}$ and α. Using the law of iterated expectations we have

$$\begin{aligned} E(\eta_i | x_{it}) &= E(\lambda_1 y_{i1}^* + \dots + \lambda_{T-1} y_{i(T-1)}^* | x_{it}) \\ &= \sum_{k=1}^{t} \lambda_k y_{ik}^* + \sum_{j=1}^{T-t-1} \lambda_{t+j} E(y_{i(t+j)}^* | x_{it}) \end{aligned}$$

and for $j \geq 2$

$$E(y_{i(t+j)}^* | x_{it}) = \pi'_{t+j} \prod_{s=1}^{j-1} (I_{t+j-s-1} \vdots \pi_{t+j-s})' x_{it}.$$

The coefficients π_t are non-linear functions of α and the λs, with the latter being nuisance parameters. For example, with $T = 3$, α is uniquely determined given the πs. In this case we have

$$E(y_{i2}^* | y_{i1}^*) = \pi_{21} y_{i1}^*$$

$$E(y_{i3}^* | y_{i1}^*, y_{i2}^*) = \pi_{31} y_{i1}^* + \pi_{32} y_{i2}^*$$

and

$$\pi_{21} = (\alpha + \lambda_1)/(1 - \lambda_2), \quad \pi_{31} = \lambda_1, \quad \pi_{32} = \alpha + \lambda_2.$$

Solving for α we obtain

$$\alpha = \frac{(\pi_{31} + \pi_{21}\pi_{32}) - \pi_{21}}{\pi_{21} - 1} = \frac{p_{31} - \pi_{21}}{\pi_{21} - 1} = \frac{E(y_{i1}^* \Delta y_{i3}^*)}{E(y_{i1}^* \Delta y_{i2}^*)}.$$

The expression on the right-hand side is the population counterpart of the Anderson and Hsiao (1981) instrumental variables estimator used in linear models. With $T > 3$ there are $(1/2)(T-2)(T-1) - 1$ overidentifying restrictions given the π_ts. Notice that with $T = 3$ a second-order autoregression with individual effects would not be identified. Here we assume that although T is small, it is sufficiently large to avoid problems of lag truncation.

When $\alpha > 0$, the dependence of y_{it}^* on both $y_{i(t-1)}^*$ and η_i generates positive autocorrelation on y_{it}^*. Having assumed that the reduced-form autoregression (9) is a linear one, the structure of the model apportions the overall serial correlation in y_{it}^* between the autoregressive and the permanent components.

In the censored sample selection model, the observed variable y_{it} is given by

$$y_{it} = d_{it} y_{it}^* \tag{11}$$

where d_{it} is a binary selection indicator. In the Type I model d_{it} takes the form

$$d_{it} = 1(y_{it}^* > 0) \tag{12}$$

where $1(A)$ denotes an indicator function in the event A, while in the Type II model we have

$$d_{it} = 1(\gamma_t' w_{it} + \varepsilon_{it} > 0) \tag{13}$$

where ε_{it} is an unobserved error term and w_{it} is a vector of variables which includes $x_{i(t-1)}$, but may also contain other variables known on *a priori* grounds to be independent of $y_{it}^* \mid x_{i(t-1)}$. In this sense, predictors of the individual effects η_i would be excluded. Finally, in the truncated model, y_{it} consists of observations from the distribution of y_{it}^* conditional on $y_{it}^* > 0$.

Although most of the discussion on estimation methods will be conducted in terms of the first-order scalar autoregression presented above, the analysis is intended to cover the following pth-order vector autoregression

$$y_{it}^* = \delta_t + \sum_{j=1}^{p} A_j y_{i(t-j)}^* + \eta_i + v_{it}$$
$$E(v_{it} \mid y_{i1}^*, \ldots, y_{i(t-1)}^*) = 0 \tag{14}$$

where y^*_{it} is a $g \times 1$ vector of (at least partly) latent variables, η_i is a $g \times 1$ vector of individual effects and δ_t is a vector of time effects treated as parameters to be estimated (in the empirical section we consider a bivariate model with $p=2$ and time effects). The first-order scalar autoregression without time effects is notationally much simpler to work with and yet does not miss any essential aspect of the more general vector problem. Another remark is that our framework is consistent with, but does not require the stronger assumption $E(v_{it}|y^*_{i1},\ldots,y^*_{i(t-1)},\eta_i)=0$.

3 Estimation and hypothesis testing

3.1 Estimating the reduced form

We begin by considering the estimation of the set of $(T-1)$ equations

$$E(y^*_{it}|y^*_{i1},\ldots,y^*_{i(t-1)}) = \pi'_t x_{i(t-1)} \quad (t=2,\ldots,T) \tag{15}$$

in the case where the selection mechanism is censored Type I, so that $d_{it}=1(y^*_{it}>0)$. Let $h_{i(t-1)}$ be the indicator function of the event $(y^*_{i1}>0,\ldots,y^*_{i(t-1)}>0)$. The coefficient vector π_t will be estimated using the sub-sample with $h_{i(t-1)}=1$, so that each estimated π_t will be based on a different sub-sample. Notice that these sub-samples are exogenously selected for the purpose of estimating π_t. The choice of estimator will depend on the assumptions we make about the distribution of $y^*_{it}|x_{i(t-1)}$. We give the details for a fully parametric normal model, but the same ideas can be applied to any asymptotically normal semiparametric method (like the trimmed least squares estimator due to Powell (1986), which is a popular semiparametric alternative that we employ in the empirical application, and is described in appendix B). Our analysis can also accommodate exogenous variables with some straightforward modifications, which are discussed in appendix C.

Assuming that

$$y^*_{it}|x_{i(t-1)} \sim N(\pi'_t x_{i(t-1)},\sigma^2_t) \tag{16}$$

we can choose $\hat{\theta}_t=(\hat{\pi}'_t,\hat{\sigma}_t)'$ to maximize

$$L_t = \sum_{i=1}^{N} h_{i(t-1)}\left[d_{it}\ln\frac{1}{\sigma_t}\phi\left(\frac{y_{it}-\pi'_t x_{i(t-1)}}{\sigma_t}\right)+ (1-d_{it})\ln\Phi\left(\frac{-\pi'_t x_{i(t-1)}}{\sigma_t}\right)\right] = \sum_{i=1}^{N}\ell_{it}(\pi_t,\sigma_t) \quad (t=2,\ldots,T) \tag{17}$$

where $\phi(.)$ and $\Phi(.)$ are, respectively, the *pdf* and the *cdf* for a standard normal variable.

The resulting stacked vector of estimates $\hat{\pi} = (\hat{\pi}_2' \dots \hat{\pi}_T')'$ can be regarded as maximizing the criterion function

$$L(\theta) = \sum_{t=2}^{T} L_t(\theta_t). \tag{18}$$

Thus, $\hat{\pi}$ is not a full maximum likelihood estimator, since $L(\theta)$ does not take into account the correlation between variables corresponding to different time periods.

Subject to standard regularity conditions, a first-order expansion of $\partial L(\hat{\theta})/\partial\theta$ about the true values of θ gives

$$\left(-\frac{1}{N}\operatorname{diag}\left\{\frac{\partial^2 L_t}{\partial\theta_t \partial\theta_t'}\right\}\right)\sqrt{N}(\hat{\theta}-\theta) = \frac{1}{\sqrt{N}}\sum_{i=1}^{N}\begin{pmatrix}\partial\ell_{i2}/\partial\theta_2\\ \vdots \\ \partial\ell_{iT}/\partial\theta_T\end{pmatrix} + o_p(1) \tag{19}$$

from which a joint limiting normal distribution for $\sqrt{N}(\hat{\theta}-\theta)$ can be obtained. A consistent estimator of the asymptotic covariance matrix of $\sqrt{N}(\hat{\theta}-\theta)$ is given by

$$\hat{V}_\theta = \hat{H}_\theta^{-1}\hat{\Psi}_\theta\hat{H}_\theta^{-1} \tag{20}$$

where

$$\hat{H}_\theta = \operatorname{diag}\{N^{-1}\partial^2\hat{L}_t/\partial\theta_t\partial\theta_t'\}$$

and

$$\hat{\Psi}_\theta = N^{-1}\sum_{i=1}^{N}\left\{\frac{\partial\hat{\ell}_{it}}{\partial\theta_t}\cdot\frac{\partial\hat{\ell}_{is}}{\partial\theta_s'}\right\}$$

where $\hat{\ell}_{it} = \ell_{it}(\hat{\pi}_t, \hat{\sigma}_t)$ and $\hat{L}_t = \Sigma_{i=1}^N \hat{\ell}_{it}$.

The previous method for the Type I Tobit model illustrates the particularities involved in the estimation of the system of equations (15). In the case of the Type II Tobit model, the parametric method most frequently used in practice is Heckman's two-step estimator (see Heckman (1979)) which can be applied to (15), equation by equation on the basis of subsamples with $h_{i(t-1)} = 1$, where now

$$h_{i(t-1)} = 1(d_{i1} = 1, \dots, d_{i(t-1)} = 1).$$

In such a case let us redefine $\hat{\theta}_t = (\hat{\pi}_t, \hat{\phi}_t)'$ to minimize

$$S_t = \sum_{i=1}^{N} h_{it}[y_{it} - \pi_t' x_{i(t-1)} - \phi_t \lambda(\hat{\gamma}_t' w_{it})]^2 = \sum_{i=1}^{N} s_{it}(\theta_t, \hat{\gamma}_t) \tag{21}$$

where $\lambda(.) = \phi(.)/\Phi(.)$, and $\hat{\gamma}_t$ are probit estimates of γ_t in (13) using the subsample with $h_{i(t-1)} = 1$. That is, $\hat{\gamma}_t$ maximizes

$$L_{pt} = \sum_{i=1}^{N} h_{i(t-1)}[d_{it} \ln \Phi_{it} + (1 - d_{it}) \ln(1 - \Phi_{it})]$$

$$= \sum_{i=1}^{N} \ell_{pit}(\gamma_t) \tag{22}$$

with $\Phi_{it} = \Phi(\gamma_t' w_{it})$. Using similar arguments as above we can obtain

$$H_t \sqrt{N}(\hat{\theta}_t - \theta_t) = B_t \frac{1}{\sqrt{N}} \sum_{i=1}^{N} m_{it} + o_p(1) \quad (t = 2, \ldots, T) \tag{23}$$

where

$$m_{it} = \begin{pmatrix} \partial s_{it} / \partial \theta_t \\ \partial \ell_{pit} / \partial \gamma_t \end{pmatrix}$$

$$B_t = \left[I \vdots - \left(\frac{\partial^2 S_t}{\partial \theta_t \partial \gamma_t'} \right) \left(\frac{\partial^2 L_{pt}}{\partial \gamma_t \partial \gamma_t'} \right)^{-1} \right]$$

and

$$H_t = \frac{1}{N} \frac{\partial^2 S_t}{\partial \theta_t \partial \theta_t'}.$$

From such expressions one can obtain a joint limiting normal distribution for $\sqrt{N}(\hat{\theta} - \theta)$. A consistent estimator of the (t,s) block of the asymptotic covariance matrix of $\sqrt{N}(\hat{\theta} - \theta)$ is given by

$$\widehat{\text{Cov}}(\hat{\theta}_t, \hat{\theta}_s) = \hat{H}_t^{-1} \hat{B}_t \left(\frac{1}{N} \sum_{i=1}^{N} \hat{m}_{it} \hat{m}_{is}' \right) \hat{B}_s' \hat{H}_s^{-1} \tag{24}$$

where the symbols are as before but replacing true parameters by their estimated values.

There are also available asymptotically normal semiparametric two-step alternatives to Heckman's estimator, like the series estimator of Newey (1988) and the weighted kernel estimator of Powell (1987), both of which can also be applied to our context (see also Newey, Powell, and Walker (1990)).

3.2 *Asymptotic least squares estimation*

We turn to consider the estimation of the autoregressive coefficient α. Given consistent and asymptotically normal estimates of π_t, it would be possible to obtain joint minimum distance (MD) estimates of α and the λs (see Chamberlain (1982)). However, the π_t are highly non-linear functions of these parameters and, moreover, the λs are not parameters of direct interest. For these reasons, it is more convenient to exploit the instrumental variable restrictions in the form of the relationship between α and the π_t given in (6). Stacking the equations we have

$$f(\alpha,\pi)=(p-\pi^1)-\alpha(\pi^1-q)=0 \tag{25}$$

where $p=(p_3'\ldots p_T')', \pi^1=(\pi_2'\ldots\pi_{T-1}')'$ and $q=(q_1'\ldots q_{T-2}')'$. The vector p consists of functions of $\pi=(\pi_2'\ldots\pi_T')'$ of the form given in (7).

Given $T>3$ and some consistent and asymptotically normal estimator $\hat{\pi}$ together with a consistent estimator of its asymptotic covariance matrix $\hat{V}_\pi$, say, an asymptotic least squares (ALS) estimator of α is given by

$$\hat{\alpha}=\arg\min_\alpha f(\alpha,\hat{\pi})'A_N f(\alpha,\hat{\pi})=\frac{(\hat{\pi}^1-q)'A_N(\hat{p}-\hat{\pi}^1)}{(\hat{\pi}^1-q)'A_N(\hat{\pi}^1-q)} \tag{26}$$

where $\hat{p}=p(\hat{\pi})$ and A_N is a weighting matrix (see Gourieroux, Monfort, and Trognon (1985), and Gourieroux and Monfort (1995, chapter 9, section 1)). The optimal choice of A_N for given $\hat{\pi}$ is $\hat{V}_r^{-1}$, which corresponds to the inverse of a consistent estimate of the asymptotic covariance matrix of $f(\alpha,\hat{\pi})$

$$V_r=QV_\pi Q' \tag{27}$$

where Q is a $(1/2)(T-1)(T-2)\times(1/2)(T-1)T$ matrix given by

$$Q=\frac{\partial f(\alpha,\pi)}{\partial\pi'}=(\mathrm{I}\otimes\pi^0)'\frac{\partial \mathrm{vec}C}{\partial\pi'}+C\frac{\partial\pi^0}{\partial\pi'}-(1+\alpha)\frac{\partial\pi^1}{\partial\pi'}$$

and

$$C=\mathrm{diag}[(1:\pi_2),\ldots,(I_{T-2}:\pi_{T-1})]$$

$$\pi^0=(\pi_3'\ldots\pi_T')'.$$

The estimated variance $\hat{V}_r$ can be obtained replacing V_π by $\hat{V}_\pi$ in (27) and evaluating Q at $\hat{\pi}$ and a preliminary consistent estimate of α. The optimal ALS estimator of α based on $f(\alpha,\hat{\pi})$ is asymptotically equivalent to the optimal MD estimator of α based on $\hat{\pi}-\pi(\alpha,\lambda_1,\ldots,\lambda_{T-1})$ and solved jointly with the λs (see Alonso-Borrego and Arellano (1999)).

A consistent estimate of the asymptotic variance of $\sqrt{N}(\hat{\alpha}-\alpha)$ for arbitrary A_N is given by

$$\widehat{\mathrm{avar}}(\hat{\alpha})=\frac{(\hat{\pi}^1-q)'A_N\hat{V}_rA_N(\hat{\pi}^1-q)}{[(\hat{\pi}^1-q)'A_N(\hat{\pi}^1-q)]^2}. \tag{28}$$

3.3 *Estimates based on orthogonal deviations*

As an alternative to the moment conditions for the errors in first differences given in (3), we can use similar moments for errors in forward orthogonal deviations (see Arellano and Bover (1995)). Contrary to the first-differenced errors, the errors in orthogonal deviations are free from serial correlation if the original errors are not autocorrelated. Namely, we have

$$E[x_{i(t-1)}(\tilde{y}^*_{it} - \alpha \tilde{y}^*_{i(t-1)})] = 0 \quad (t = 2, \ldots, T-1) \tag{29}$$

where

$$\tilde{y}^*_{it} = c_t[y^*_{it} - \frac{1}{(T-t)}(y^*_{i(t+1)} + \ldots + y^*_{iT})]$$

$$\tilde{y}^*_{i(t-1)} = c_t[y^*_{it-1} - \frac{1}{(T-t)}(y^*_{it} + \ldots + y^*_{i(T-1)})]$$

and $c_t^2 = (T-t)/(T-t+1)$. As shown by Arellano and Bover (1995), in linear models the two sets of moments produce the same optimal GMM estimates, but this will not be the case here in general. Contrary to the linear case, in our context there are no natural one-step estimators that are optimal under certain assumptions. Thus we may expect preliminary consistent estimates based on first differences (and the two-step estimates based on them) to show a different behavior from those based on orthogonal deviations.

The moment conditions (29) translate into the following restrictions among linear projection coefficients and the parameter α

$$g_t(\alpha, \pi) = \left[\pi_{t|t-1} - \frac{1}{(T-t)}(\pi_{t+1|t-1} + \ldots + \pi_{T|t-1})\right] - \alpha\left[q_{t-1} - \frac{1}{(T-t)}(\pi_{t|t-1} + \ldots + \pi_{T-1|t-1})\right] = 0 \tag{30}$$

where

$$\pi_{t+j|t} = [E(x_{it}x'_{it})]^{-1}E(x_{it}y^*_{i(t+j)})$$

so that in the previous notation $\pi_t = \pi_{t|t-1}$ and $p_t = \pi_{t|t-2}$. As before, the coefficients $\pi_{t+j|t}$ are linked by the law of iterated projections and can all be expressed as functions of $(\pi_2 \ldots \pi_T)$.[1] Stacking the g_t functions the analysis can proceed as in the first-difference case developed above.

3.4 *Testing the overidentifying restrictions*

When $T > 3$, there are $(1/2)(T-1)(T-2)-1$ overidentifying restrictions implied by the model which can be tested. The testing of these constraints

[1] Specifically, we have

$$\pi_{t|t-j} = (I_{t-j} \vdots \pi_{t-j+1|t-j} \vdots \ldots \vdots \pi_{t-1|t-j})\pi_{t|t-1}.$$

is facilitated by the fact that the minimized optimal ALS criterion multiplied by the sample size has a limiting chi-squared distribution with degrees of freedom equal to the number of overidentifying restrictions (a proof of this result can be found in Gourieroux and Monfort (1989, vol. II, p. 175, and 1995, vol. II, p. 154) and a similar method is proposed by Szroeter (1983)). Thus, the test statistic is given by

$$S = Nf(\hat{\alpha},\hat{\pi})'\hat{V}_r^{-1}f(\hat{\alpha},\hat{\pi}). \tag{31}$$

This test statistic can be regarded as an extension to sample selection models of the Sargan specification tests of overidentifying restrictions for linear panel data GMM estimators considered by Arellano and Bond (1991) (cf. Sargan (1958) and (1988)). On the same lines, it is also possible to consider extensions of Sargan difference tests in order to discriminate between nested hypotheses.

3.5 *Consistent OLS estimation using predicted differences*

Calculation of the optimal ALS estimator of α requires a preliminary consistent estimator in order to obtain $\hat{V}_r$. The following estimator can be computed in one step (given the $\hat{\pi}_t$) and has a straightforward interpretation.

Let us define

$$\Delta\hat{y}^*_{it|t-1} = x'_{i(t-1)}(\hat{\pi}_t - q_{t-1}) \tag{32a}$$

$$\Delta\hat{y}^*_{it|t-2} = x'_{i(t-2)}(\hat{p}_t - \hat{\pi}_{t-1}). \tag{32b}$$

Then we consider the OLS regression of $\Delta\hat{y}^*_{i|t-2}$ on $\Delta\hat{y}^*_{i(t-1)|t-2}$ for all periods and individuals with $h_{i(T-2)} = 1$

$$\tilde{\alpha} = \frac{\Sigma_{i=1}^N h_{i(T-2)}\,\Sigma_{t=3}^T \Delta\hat{y}^*_{i(t-1)|t-2}\Delta\hat{y}^*_{it|t-2}}{\Sigma_{i=1}^N h_{i(T-2)}\,\Sigma_{t=3}^T (\Delta\hat{y}^*_{i(t-1)|t-2})^2}. \tag{33}$$

Simple algebra reveals that

$$\tilde{\alpha} = \frac{\Sigma_{t=3}^T(\hat{\pi}_{t-1} - q_{t-2})'M_{t-2}(\hat{p}_t - \hat{\pi}_{t-1})}{\Sigma_{t=3}^T(\hat{\pi}_{t-1} - q_{t-2})'M_{t-2}(\hat{\pi}_{t-1} - q_{t-2})} \tag{34}$$

where $M_{t-2} = \Sigma_{i=1}^N\, h_{i(T-2)}x_{i(t-2)}x'_{i(t-2)}$. Therefore, $\tilde{\alpha}$ is a non-optimal ALS estimator of the form given in (26) with weighting matrix given by

$$A_N = \text{diag}(M_1, \ldots, M_{T-2})$$

and estimated asymptotic covariance matrix of the form given by (28). Clearly, an alternative consistent OLS estimator can be calculated along the same lines using predicted orthogonal deviations as opposed to first differences.

4 An application to female labor supply and wages

We estimate separate autoregressive equations for annual hours of work and log wages (average hourly earnings) for two different samples of the Panel Study of Income Dynamics (PSID), covering the periods 1970–1976 and 1978–1984. In both cases the observations correspond to prime-age, white, married women from the random PSID sub-sample that were continuously married to the same husband, and who were 30–65 years old in 1968 (for the first sample) or 1976 (for the second). After selecting the samples with the criteria above, and removing some inconsistencies and non-respondents, we had 660 women available in the first sample, and 804 in the second.

The starting point for each dataset is the following second-order bivariate autoregression.

$$h^*_{it} = a^h_t + b^h_1 h^*_{i(t-1)} + b^h_2 h^*_{i(t-2)} + c^h_1 \ln w^*_{i(t-1)} + c^h_2 \ln w^*_{i(t-2)} + \eta^h_i + v^h_{it} \tag{35a}$$

$$\ln w^*_{it} = a^w_t + b^w_1 h^*_{i(t-1)} + b^w_2 h^*_{i(t-2)} + c^w_1 \ln w^*_{i(t-1)} + c^w_2 \ln w^*_{i(t-2)} + \eta^w_i + v^w_{it} \quad (t = 3,\ldots,7) \tag{35b}$$

where h^*_{it} is the supply of hours of work for individual i in period t and $\ln w^*_{it}$ is the natural log of the wage of individual i in period t. The variables η^h_i and η^w_i are individual effects, and a^h_t and a^w_t are time effects.

Inferences will be based on the following conditional moment restrictions

$$\begin{aligned}
&E(\Delta v^h_{i4} \mid h^*_{i1}, h^*_{i2}, \ln w^*_{i1}, \ln w^*_{i2}) = 0 \\
&E(\Delta v^h_{i5} \mid h^*_{i1}, h^*_{i2}, h^*_{i3}, \ln w^*_{i1}, \ln w^*_{i2}, \ln w^*_{i3}) = 0 \\
&E(\Delta v^h_{i6} \mid h^*_{i1}, \ldots, h^*_{i4}, \ln w^*_{i1}, \ldots, \ln w^*_{i4}) = 0 \\
&E(\Delta v^h_{i7} \mid h^*_{i1}, \ldots, h^*_{i5}, \ln w^*_{i1}, \ldots, \ln w^*_{i5}) = 0
\end{aligned} \tag{36}$$

and similarly for first-differenced log wage errors (actually, we shall use errors in orthogonal deviations for which similar conditions hold). Both h^*_{it} and w^*_{it} are subject to censoring with a common selection mechanism. The unconditional non-participation rates for all individuals and time periods are around 50 per cent in the first sample and 40 per cent in the second. However, conditional non-participation rates for the sequence of subsamples on which inferences will be based are much lower as can be seen

Table 2.1. Conditional participation frequencies

Sub-sample	Size	No. of non-participants	Percentage
		First sample, 1970–1976, N = 660 (Period 1 = 1970)	
$h_1>0, h_2>0$	$N_1=303$	$no(h_3=0 \mid h_1>0, h_2>0)=30$	9.9
$h_1>0,\ldots,h_3>0$	$N_2=273$	$no(h_4=0 \mid h_1>0,\ldots,h_3>0)=13$	4.8
$h_1>0,\ldots,h_4>0$	$N_3=260$	$no(h_5=0 \mid h_1>0,\ldots,h_4>0)=16$	6.2
$h_1>0,\ldots,h_5>0$	$N_4=244$	$no(h_6=0 \mid h_1>0,\ldots,h_5>0)=18$	7.4
$h_1>0,\ldots,h_6>0$	$N_5=226$	$no(h_7=0 \mid h_1>0,\ldots,h_6>0)=16$	7.1
		Second sample, 1978–1984, N = 804 (Period 1 = 1978)	
$h_1>0, h_2>0$	$N_1=438$	$no(h_3=0 \mid h_1>0, h_2>0)=25$	5.7
$h_1>0,\ldots,h_3>0$	$N_2=413$	$no(h_4=0 \mid h_1>0,\ldots,h_3>0)=27$	6.5
$h_1>0,\ldots,h_4>0$	$N_3=386$	$no(h_5=0 \mid h_1>0,\ldots,h_4>0)=25$	6.5
$h_1>0,\ldots,h_5>0$	$N_4=361$	$no(h_6=0 \mid h_1>0,\ldots,h_5>0)=23$	6.4
$h_1>0,\ldots,h_6>0$	$N_5=338$	$no(h_7=0 \mid h_1>0,\ldots,h_6>0)=19$	5.6

from table 2.1. The frequency of non-participants is under 10 percent for the four sub-samples corresponding to the period 1970–6, and even lower for those of the more recent period. This suggests that LDV estimates of the linear projection coefficients π_t will have a small bias whatever the truth of the linear conditional expectation assumption and of the specification of the selection mechanism. Some additional descriptive information on the two datasets is provided in table A1 in the appendix.

Tables 2.2 and 2.3 contain results for the hours and wage equations, respectively. To the basic autoregressive equations we have added two children variables which are treated as predetermined variables in the estimation (a dummy for a child less than six years old and another for a child between six and nine). All the results we present include these children dummies, but their exclusion does not alter the observed dynamics of hours and wages in our data.

All the results reported in both tables are optimal ALS estimates based on moment conditions in orthogonal deviations. The preliminary consistent estimates are OLS using predicted differences in orthogonal deviations. The differences among the columns are in the way the reduced-form coefficients are estimated, or in the number of moment conditions used. Columns labelled OLS present optimal ALS estimates based on OLS estimates of the reduced-form coefficients for the sequentially censored sub-samples. Thus,

Table 2.2. *Hours equations (Optimal ALS estimates using orthogonal deviations)*

	OLS reduced-form projections	LS with selectivity correction	Measurement error correction
Panel A: Sample 1970–1976			
h_{t-1}	0.167	0.188	0.310
	(3.38)	(3.10)	(3.74)
h_{t-2}	0.126	0.120	0.145
	(2.95)	(2.32)	(2.30)
$\ln w_{t-1}$	20.37	83.01	287.59
	(0.48)	(1.41)	(4.88)
$\ln w_{t-2}$	94.76	123.84	85.40
	(2.81)	(3.18)	(2.29)
D_{1t}	−312.46	−310.26	−362.02
	(−3.99)	(−3.73)	(−3.51)
D_{2t}	−43.16	−41.95	−98.45
	(−0.87)	(−0.76)	(−1.30)
S	82.68(58)	63.47(58)	56.00(42)
Panel B: Sample 1978–1984			
h_{t-1}	0.466	0.379	0.337
	(11.2)	(6.46)	(5.29)
h_{t-2}	−0.051	−0.072	0.002
	(−1.47)	(−2.08)	(0.52)
$\ln w_{t-1}$	253.56	232.72	−13.01
	(4.91)	(4.20)	(−0.22)
$\ln w_{t-2}$	−20.44	−28.52	−104.67
	(−0.58)	(−0.77)	(−3.07)
D_{1t}	−250.07	−209.30	−152.67
	(−3.85)	(−2.84)	(−1.43)
D_{2t}	−16.62	7.97	−246.94
	(−0.29)	(0.14)	(−4.38)
S	54.61(58)	56.09(58)	37.73(42)

Notes:
(i) Time dummies are included in all equations.
(ii) Figures in parentheses are t-ratios.
(iii) D_{1t}=1 if at least one child less than six years old is present.
D_{2t}=1 if at least one child older than five and younger than ten years old is present.
(iv) S is the chi-squared test statistic of overidentifying restrictions.
(v) Estimates in cols. (1) and (2) use variables dated $t-2$ and less as instruments, while the estimates in col. (2) use only variables dated at most $t-3$.
(vi) Estimates in cols. (2) and (3) use Heckman's estimates of the reduced form.

Table 2.3. *Wage equations (Optimal ALS estimates using orthogonal deviations)*

	OLS reduced-form projections	LS with selectivity correction	Measurement error correction
Panel A: Sample 1970–1976			
h_{t-1}	0.00027	0.00020	0.00022
	(7.15)	(3.87)	(4.48)
h_{t-2}	0.00006	0.00006	−0.00025
	(1.78)	(1.60)	(−5.90)
$\ln w_{t-1}$	0.140	0.210	0.576
	(2.92)	(3.72)	(23.0)
$\ln w_{t-2}$	0.078	0.079	−0.281
	(2.72)	(1.84)	(−10.7)
D_{1t}	−0.015	−0.014	−0.071
	(−0.41)	(−0.34)	(−1.13)
D_{2t}	0.149	0.118	0.009
	(4.48)	(3.15)	(0.17)
S	76.98(58)	80.37(58)	56.02(42)
Panel B: Sample 1978–1984			
h_{t-1}	0.00040	0.00043	0.00036
	(11.9)	(10.3)	(8.30)
h_{t-2}	0.00012	0.00012	0.00012
	(5.56)	(4.79)	(3.82)
$\ln w_{t-1}$	−0.167	−0.089	−0.172
	(−3.99)	(−1.81)	(−4.45)
$\ln w_{t-2}$	−0.106	−0.092	−0.132
	(−5.54)	(−4.07)	(−6.19)
D_{1t}	0.020	0.005	0.269
	(0.46)	(0.11)	(5.08)
D_{2t}	−0.038	−0.051	0.053
	(−1.00)	(−1.33)	(1.35)
S	48.57(58)	44.77(58)	32.52(42)

Notes:
See table 2.2.

these estimates do not correct for selectivity, but given the low conditional non-participation rates in the samples we would not expect them to differ substantially from those with selectivity corrections. The estimates shown in the remaining two columns are based on Heckman's estimates of the reduced-form coefficients. Those in the second columns of tables 2.2 and 2.3 use the same moments as the ones in the first columns, and as expected the differences between the two sets of estimates are small. Finally, the estimates in the third columns are also based on Heckman's estimates of the reduced form, but only use instrumental variables dated t–3 or less. The motivation for these estimates arises from a concern with measurement errors in observed wages, which would invalidate the moment conditions given in (36). However, if the measurement error is not serially correlated, by back-dating the conditioning variables one period, the mean independence of the first-differenced errors is restored. Tables A2 and A3 in the appendix show some additional ALS estimates of the hours and wage equations based on Powell's (1986) symmetrically censored LS estimates of the reduced form, and also Tobit estimates with and without allowance for measurement errors in wages.

Starting with the results for the hours equations, there are some significant differences between the estimates with and without measurement error corrections which, nevertheless, are not signaled by the test statistics of overidentifying restrictions. There appears to be an increase of the effect of past hours of work on current hours in the second period, which is consistent with the notion of a trend towards a steadier involvement with the labor market for those who participate. The estimated effects of lagged wages on hours of work are not robust, and lack a clear pattern. In the first sample the effect is stronger when allowing for measurement error in wages, but this situation is reversed in the second sample. Lastly, the empirical coefficients of the children dummies have the expected sign, but their magnitude becomes consistently smaller when moving from the first panel to the second.

Turning to the wage equations, the estimates in this case exhibit larger differences between the two periods. Firstly, there is a positive effect of lagged wages (net of individual effects) in the first period, which disappears altogether – or becomes even negative – in the second period. Secondly, there is a positive effect of lagged hours on wages whose size doubles from the first period to the second. The change in the effect of lagged wages suggests higher occupational mobility, while the change in the effect of lagged hours points to higher returns to experience. Finally, in no case have the children dummies a significant effect on wages.

Table 2.4 presents alternative estimates without individual effects for comparison. The reported estimates are pooled OLS for each of the two

Table 2.4. *Levels equations without individual effects. OLS estimates for the sample of participants in previous periods*

	Hours equations		Wage equations	
Panel A: Sample 1970–1976 (1,306 observations)				
h_{t-1}	0.663	0.659	0.00029	0.00029
	(13.9)	(13.9)	(7.74)	(7.76)
h_{t-2}	0.127	0.131	−0.00011	−0.00010
	(2.75)	(2.87)	(−2.89)	(−2.63)
$\ln w_{t-1}$	205.46	205.69	0.514	0.484
	(4.62)	(4.45)	(10.3)	(9.66)
$\ln w_{t-2}$	−42.59	−34.50	0.239	0.206
	(−0.92)	(−0.70)	(4.56)	(3.94)
D_{1t}	—	−191.39	—	−0.104
		(−1.79)		(−1.41)
D_{2t}	—	−61.66	—	−0.011
		(−1.09)		(−0.24)
Education	—	−14.15	—	0.040
		(−1.13)		(3.44)
Age	—	−5.35	—	−0.0035
		(−2.89)		(−2.52)
Panel B: Sample 1978–1984 (1,936 observations)				
h_{t-1}	0.542	0.539	0.0002	0.0002
	(16.0)	(16.2)	(5.25)	(5.92)
h_{t-2}	0.218	0.215	−0.00007	−0.000002
	(6.59)	(6.62)	(−0.22)	(−0.08)
$\ln w_{t-1}$	4.20	−0.073	0.349	0.325
	(0.12)	(−0.002)	(8.52)	(8.24)
$\ln w_{t-2}$	39.99	33.36	0.360	0.329
	(1.00)	(1.07)	(8.67)	(8.03)
D_{1t}	—	−268.89	—	−0.363
		(−4.19)		(−5.27)
D_{2t}	—	−19.28	—	0.032
		(−0.28)		(0.51)
Education	—	9.37	—	0.066
		(1.02)		(6.74)
Age	—	−3.96	—	0.0004
		(−2.60)		(0.29)

Notes:
(i) Time dummies are included in all equations.
(ii) Figures in parentheses are *t*-ratios robust to heteroskedasticity.
(iii) $D_{1t}=1$ if at least one child less than six years old is present.
$D_{2t}=1$ if at least one child older than five and younger than ten years old is present.

samples of participants in previous periods (table A4 presents Tobit estimates for the same models and data). As expected, the wage equations without permanent effects show a stronger autoregressive pattern for lagged wages. It is, however, noticeable that there is a change in the pattern of serial dependence in wages between the two panels, which is broadly consistent with the results found for the models with individual effects. Notice that these equations include education and age variables, whose effects are captured by individual and year effects in the equations in orthogonal deviations.

We now turn to interpret the previous empirical autoregressions in terms of a life-cycle labor supply framework. Let us consider the following labour supply equation

$$h^*_{it} = \mu_{it} + \beta \ln w^*_{it} + \beta \ln \lambda_{it} \tag{37}$$

where μ_{it} reflects variation in preferences due to individual and time-specific factors, λ_{it} is the marginal utility of wealth, and the parameter β divided by h^*_{it} represents the intertemporal substitution elasticity. Browning, Deaton, and Irish (1985, pp. 521–52) obtain the profit function from which this equation can be derived.[2] They also show (see also Heckman and MaCurdy (1980), and MaCurdy (1981)) that the first difference of $\ln\lambda_{it}$ can be approximated by a time effect plus a serially uncorrelated innovation ξ_{it}. The innovation ξ_{it} will be correlated with current wages but uncorrelated to all lagged variables in the individual's information set.

We assume that μ_{it} can be represented as the sum of time and individual effects, the effects of children, and a disturbance term v_{it}. Given the observed autoregressive behavior of hours of work and the fact that in model (37) this behavior can only be rationalized through serial correlation in v_{it}, we specify

$$v_{it} = \rho v_{i(t-1)} + \varepsilon_{it}.$$

Excluding children dummies for simplicity of presentation, the labor supply equation in first differences can be written in the form

$$\Delta h^*_{it} = \Delta\delta_t + \rho\Delta h^*_{i(t-1)} + \beta\Delta\ln w^*_{it} - \rho\beta\Delta\ln w^*_{it(t-1)} + (\xi_{it} - \rho\xi_{i(t-1)} + \Delta\varepsilon_{it}). \tag{38}$$

Let us denote a simplified model for the change in log wages excluding second-order lags as

$$\Delta\ln w^*_{it} = \Delta a^w_t + c\Delta\ln w^*_{i(t-1)} + b\Delta h^*_{i(t-1)} + \Delta v^w_{it}. \tag{39}$$

[2] Equation (37) assumes that labor supply and goods are additive within periods. The introduction of an extra term of the form $w^{*-1/2}_{it}$ to relax this assumption (as suggested by Browning, Deaton, and Irish (1985)) would make impossible the direct mapping with our VAR. The estimates of the effect of this additional variable reported by Browning *et al.* for cohorts male labor supply never turned out to be significantly different from zero.

Now combining equations (38) and (39), the life-cycle labor supply model implies that the process for hours follows

$$\Delta h^*_{it} = \Delta a^h_t + m\Delta h^*_{i(t-1)} + \gamma \Delta \ln w^*_{i(t-1)} + \Delta v^h_{it} \tag{40}$$

where

$$\begin{aligned} m &= \rho + \beta b \\ \gamma &= \beta(c - \rho) \\ a^h_t &= \delta_t + \beta a^w_t \\ \Delta v^h_{it} &= \xi_{it} - \rho \xi_{i(t-1)} + \Delta \varepsilon_{it} + \beta \Delta v^w_{it}. \end{aligned} \tag{41}$$

Therefore, under the previous interpretation the coefficient on lagged wages in the autoregressive hours equation can be regarded as an estimate of $\beta(c-\rho)$, where β divided by h^*_{it} gives the intertemporal labor supply elasticity. However, given the lack of robustness of the estimated effects of lagged wages on hours of work, we may expect the implied estimates of β to be very imprecise (indeed if $c-\rho=0$ the parameter β would be unidentified). This result is similar to the finding of Abowd and Card (1989) for male labor supply using moving average representations, and suggests that the dynamics of hours and wages in these data sets contain little information on intertemporal labor supply responses.

5 Concluding remarks

The methods developed in this chapter are based on the observation that the sub-samples which only include individuals without censored past observations (those with $h_{i(t-1)} = 1$) are exogenously selected for the purpose of estimating features of the distribution of y^*_{it} conditional on its past. In the application to female labor supply and wages presented in section 3, it turns out that most of the selectivity due to censoring is accounted for by the permanent effects, and our methods make precise the sense in which this is so. For other applications, however, these procedures may retain very few or no observations with $h_{i(t-1)} = 1$ for the larger values of t. In practice, such a problem could be addressed by considering distributions that are conditional on the more recent observations only. In effect, if the linearity of the conditional expectation of y^*_{it} given $(y^*_{i1}, \ldots, y^*_{i(t-1)})$ holds, we might expect this to hold for any time sequence since the initial observation is often arbitrary. In such cases, we could rely on the linearity of the conditional expectation of y^*_{it} given $y^*_{i(t-1)}, \ldots, y^*_{i(t-s)}$ for any t and s in devising asymptotic least squares estimates of the parameters of interest. This may create a trade off between the number of moment restrictions being used and the actual sample size, which remains to be explored. Future work will also have to address ways of relaxing some of the distributional assumptions, and consider ways of introducing stationarity restrictions.

Appendix A Descriptive statistics and additional parameter estimates

Table A1. *Descriptive statistics*

	Full sample		Sample of participants in previous periods	
	Mean	St. Dev.	Mean	St. Dev.
Panel A: Sample 1970–1976				
Participation	0.506	0.500	0.928	0.257
Hours	672.7	839.4	1379.6	732.9
Wages	1.847	2.899	3.837	3.060
Partic. (1972)	0.483	0.500	0.901	0.299
Hours (1972)	650.4	852.5	1319.6	808.6
Wages (1972)	1.571	2.422	3.102	2.413
Partic. (1976)	0.515	0.500	0.929	0.257
Hours (1976)	682.0	827.7	1426.0	687.9
Wages (1976)	2.379	3.771	4.570	3.282
D_1	0.096	0.295	0.038	0.192
D_2	0.115	0.319	0.084	0.278
Sample size	4,620(=660×7)		1,306	
Panel B: Sample 1978–1984				
Participation	0.615	0.487	0.939	0.238
Hours	849.9	871.2	1433.2	719.5
Wages	3.637	5.094	6.367	5.961
Partic. (1980)	0.651	0.477	0.943	0.232
Hours (1980)	883.2	870.8	1397.1	726.9
Wages (1980)	3.422	4.185	5.135	4.491
Partic. (1984)	0.610	0.488	0.950	0.219
Hours (1984)	857.3	888.4	1486.3	722.3
Wages (1984)	4.561	7.214	8.040	8.990
D_1	0.082	0.274	0.069	0.253
D_2	0.078	0.269	0.084	0.278
Sample size	5,628(=804×7)		1,936	

Notes:
(i) Wages are average hourly earnings.
(ii) D_1=1 if at least one child less than six years old is present.
(iii) D_2=1 if at least one child older than five and younger than ten years old is present.
(iv) The "samples of participants in previous periods" includes participants and non-participants conditional on participation in the previous years available in the data. They effectively combine the sequentially censored sub-samples described in table 2.1.

Table A2. *Hours equations (Optimal ALS estimates using orthogonal deviations)*

	Tobit reduced-form projections	SCLS reduced-form projections	Measurement error correction
Panel A: Sample 1970–1976			
h_{t-1}	0.423	0.179	0.248
	(6.34)	(3.89)	(2.85)
h_{t-2}	−0.001	0.155	0.167
	(−0.26)	(3.74)	(2.99)
$\ln w_{t-1}$	−101.19	9.82	−94.44
	(−1.35)	(0.28)	(−1.13)
$\ln w_{t-2}$	−45.35	83.53	−87.84
	(−1.04)	(2.48)	(−1.69)
D_{1t}	−302.53	−312.268	−236.47
	(−4.61)	(−4.56)	(−2.74)
D_{2t}	−14.46	−60.09	−229.18
	(−0.20)	(−1.18)	(−2.44)
S	93.22(58)	91.24(58)	74.02(42)
Panel B: Sample 1978–1984			
h_{t-1}	0.219	0.478	0.394
	(3.78)	(11.1)	(6.49)
h_{t-2}	−0.071	−0.055	0.043
	(−2.31)	(−1.71)	(0.83)
$\ln w_{t-1}$	141.34	207.13	−255.38
	(3.02)	(4.14)	(−4.76)
$\ln w_{t-2}$	−119.07	−32.50	−166.13
	(−4.41)	(−0.98)	(−6.15)
D_{1t}	−294.65	−309.36	−247.40
	(−3.70)	(−4.84)	(−2.32)
D_{2t}	25.32	−29.51	−138.49
	(0.42)	(−0.54)	(−1.64)
S	48.83(58)	74.64(59)	45.98(42)

Notes:
(i) Time dummies are included in all equations.
(ii) Figures in parentheses are t-ratios.
(iii) $D_{1t}=1$ if at least one child less than six years old is present.
$D_{2t}=1$ if at least one child older than five and younger than ten years old is present.
(iv) S is the chi-squared test statistic of overidentifying restrictions.
(v) Estimates in cols. (1) and (2) use variables dated $t-2$ and less as instruments, while the estimates in col. (3) use only variables dated at most $t-3$.
(vi) Estimates in cols. (1) and (3) use Tobit estimates of the reduced form.
(vii) Estimates in col. (2) use Powell's (1986) symmetrically censored least squares (SCLS) estimates of the reduced form.

Table A3. *Wage equations (Optimal ALS estimates using orthogonal deviations)*

	Tobit reduced-form projections	SCLS reduced-form projections	Measurement error correction
Panel A: Sample 1970–1976			
h_{t-1}	0.0004	−0.00002	0.0004
	(8.07)	(−0.44)	(7.65)
h_{t-2}	0.0001	−0.0002	0.00015
	(2.70)	(−1.20)	(3.17)
$\ln w_{t-1}$	0.237	0.282	0.301
	(3.89)	(2.17)	(5.79)
$\ln w_{t-2}$	0.051	0.119	0.022
	(1.54)	(1.85)	(0.71)
D_{1t}	−0.063	1.218	−0.410
	(−0.48)	(7.45)	(−3.16)
D_{2t}	0.143	0.525	0.139
	(2.31)	(9.75)	(2.63)
S	53.67(58)	59.05(58)	48.20(42)
Panel B: Sample 1978–1984			
h_{t-1}	0.00033	0.00029	0.00034
	(5.93)	(8.67)	(5.46)
h_{t-2}	0.00009	0.00007	0.00011
	(2.87)	(3.47)	(2.16)
$\ln w_{t-1}$	0.067	−0.217	−0.197
	(1.75)	(−5.07)	(−3.77)
$\ln w_{t-2}$	0.025	−0.098	−0.161
	(1.10)	(−4.17)	(−5.43)
D_{1t}	−0.352	−0.410	−0.464
	(−4.42)	(−13.1)	(−4.94)
D_{2t}	0.122	−0.107	−0.032
	(1.60)	(−3.14)	(−0.32)
S	53.35(58)	60.11(58)	52.83(42)

Notes:
See Table A2.

Table A4. *Levels equations without individual effects. Tobit estimates for the sample of participants in previous periods*

	Hours equations		Wage equations	
Panel A: Sample 1970–1976 (1,306 observations)				
h_{t-1}	0.717	0.714	0.00034	0.00034
	(13.4)	(13.4)	(7.73)	(7.75)
h_{t-2}	0.101	0.105	−0.00014	−0.00013
	(1.97)	(2.08)	(−3.14)	(−2.92)
$\ln w_{t-1}$	245.70	247.36	0.560	0.529
	(4.77)	(4.62)	(10.1)	(9.47)
$\ln w_{t-2}$	−63.23	−54.93	0.225	0.194
	(−1.23)	(−1.02)	(3.97)	(3.45)
D_{1t}	—	−240.01	—	−0.139
		(−2.03)		(−1.69)
D_{2t}	—	−58.30	—	−0.012
		(−0.98)		(−0.23)
Education	—	−16.00	—	0.038
		(−1.20)		(3.05)
Age	—	−5.96	—	−0.0039
		(−2.99)		(−2.30)
Panel B: Sample 1978–1984 (1,936 observations)				
h_{t-1}	0.569	0.566	0.0002	0.0002
	(15.8)	(15.9)	(5.45)	(6.09)
h_{t-2}	0.217	0.213	−0.00001	−0.000008
	(6.18)	(6.18)	(−0.32)	(−0.20)
$\ln w_{t-1}$	12.09	7.24	0.362	0.336
	(0.32)	(0.19)	(8.19)	(7.91)
$\ln w_{t-2}$	28.32	30.57	0.364	0.333
	(0.83)	(0.90)	(8.22)	(7.64)
D_{1t}	—	−302.06	—	0.032
		(−4.30)		(0.50)
D_{2t}	—	−14.82	—	0.0002
		(−0.21)		(0.12)
Education	—	11.17	—	0.068
		(1.15)		(6.53)
Age	—	−4.21	—	0.004
		(−2.63)		(0.10)

Notes:
(i) Time dummies are included in all equations.
(ii) Figures in parentheses are t-ratios.
(iii) $D_{1t}=1$ if at least one child less than six years old is present.
$D_{2t}=1$ if at least one child older than five and younger than ten years old is present.

Appendix B Type I Tobit with symmetric trimming

Assuming that $y^*_{it}|x_{i(t-1)}$ has a symmetric distribution with heteroskedasticity of unknown form, we can estimate consistently the π_t using Powell's (1986) symmetrically censored least squares method (SCLS). The SCLS estimator $\tilde{\pi}_t$ solves the iteration

$$\tilde{\pi}_t^{r+1} = \left(\sum_{i=1}^{N} h_{i(t-1)} \varphi_{it}(\tilde{\pi}_t^r) x_{i(t-1)} x'_{i(t-1)} \right)^{-1}$$

$$\sum_{i=1}^{N} h_{i(t-1)} \varphi_{it}(\tilde{\pi}_t^r) x_{i(t-1)} \min \{y_{it}, 2x'_{i(t-1)} \tilde{\pi}_t^r\} \tag{B.1}$$

where $\varphi_{it}(\tilde{\pi}_t^r) = 1(x'_{i(t-1)} \tilde{\pi}_t^r > 0)$ for $r \geq 1$ and $\varphi_{it}(\tilde{\pi}_t^0) = 1$ (that is, the initial value is the OLS estimator).

In this case, since the SCLS estimation criterion is not differentiable we cannot use the argument of section 3 for normal Tobit or Heckman's estimator in order to obtain the asymptotic covariance matrix of $\tilde{\pi} = (\tilde{\pi}'_2 \ldots \tilde{\pi}'_T)'$. However, Powell (1986) following the approach of Huber (1967) obtains an asymptotic relation (see equation (A.15) of his paper) which combined for our $(T-1)$ equations can be written as

$$(\text{diag}\{C_t\}) \sqrt{N}(\tilde{\pi} - \pi) = \frac{1}{\sqrt{N}} \sum_{i=1}^{N} \begin{pmatrix} \psi_{i2}(\pi_2) \\ \vdots \\ \psi_{iT}(\pi_T) \end{pmatrix} + o_p(1) \tag{B.2}$$

where

$$C_t = \frac{1}{N} \sum_{i=1}^{N} E[h_{i(t-1)} 1(0 < y_{it} < 2x'_{i(t-1)} \pi_t) x_{i(t-1)} x'_{i(t-1)}]$$

and

$$\psi_{it}(\pi_t) = 1(x'_{i(t-1)} \pi_t > 0) v_{it} x_{i(t-1)}$$

$$v_{it} = \min\{y_{it}, 2x'_{i(t-1)} \pi_t\} - x'_{i(t-1)} \pi_t.$$

From this expression a joint limiting normal distribution for $\sqrt{N}(\tilde{\pi} - \pi)$ can be obtained. A consistent estimator of the asymptotic covariance matrix of $\sqrt{N}(\tilde{\pi} - \pi)$ is given by

$$\tilde{V}_\pi = (\text{diag}\{\tilde{C}_t^{-1}\}) \tilde{\Psi}_\pi (\text{diag}\{\tilde{C}_t^{-1}\}) \tag{B.3}$$

where $\tilde{C}_t$ is a "natural" estimator of C_t and $\tilde{\Psi}_\pi$ has the following block structure

$$\tilde{\Psi}_\pi = \frac{1}{N} \sum_{i=1}^{N} \{\psi_{it}(\tilde{\pi}_t) \psi'_{is}(\tilde{\pi}_s)\}.$$

Appendix C Models with exogenous variables

The analysis for autoregressive models can accommodate exogenous variables in a straightforward manner. Suppose that model (1) is extended to include a strictly exogenous variable z_{it}

$$y^*_{it} = \alpha y^*_{i(t-1)} + \beta z_{it} + \eta_i + v_{it} \tag{C.1}$$

such that

$$E(v_{it} | y^*_{i1}, \ldots, y^*_{i(t-1)}, z_{i1}, \ldots, z_{iT}) = 0. \tag{C.2}$$

This assumption implies that

$$E(x_{it(t-2)} \Delta v_{it}) = 0 \quad (t = 3, \ldots, T) \tag{C.3}$$

or

$$(p_t - \pi_{t-1}) = \alpha(\pi_{t-1} - q_{t-2}) + \beta h_t \quad (t = 3, \ldots, T) \tag{C.4}$$

where $x_{i(t-2)}$ has been redefined as

$$x_{i(t-2)} = (y^*_{i1}, \ldots, y^*_{i(t-2)}, z_{i1}, \ldots, z_{iT})' \tag{C.5}$$

and p_t, π_{t-1}, and q_{t-2} are also redefined accordingly, h_t is a selection vector of known constants such that

$$h_t = [E(x_{i(t-2)} x'_{i(t-2)})]^{-1} E(x_{i(t-2)} \Delta z_{it}). \tag{C.6}$$

The discussion in the main text will apply provided we can assume

$$E(y^*_{it} | x_{i(t-1)}) = \pi'_i x_{i(t-1)} \tag{C.7}$$

together with sufficient distributional assumptions about the distribution of $y^*_{it} | x_{i(t-1)}$ in order to identify its mean in the presence of selectivity.

References

Abowd, J.M. and D. Card (1989), "On the Covariance Structure of Earnings and Hours Changes," *Econometrica*, 57: 411–445.

Alonso-Borrego, C. and M. Arellano (1999), "Symmetrically Normalized Instrumental-Variable Estimation Using Panel Data," *Journal of Business and Economic Statistics* (forthcoming).

Amemiya, T. (1985), *Advanced Econometrics*, Oxford: Blackwell.

Anderson, T.W. and C. Hsiao (1981), "Estimation of Dynamic Models with Error Components," *Journal of the American Statistical Association*, 76: 598–606.

Arellano, M. and S.R. Bond (1991), "Some Tests of Specification for Panel Data: Monte Carlo Evidence and an Application to Employment Equations," *Review of Economic Studies*, 58: 277–297.

Arellano, M. and O. Bover (1995), "Another Look at the Instrumental Variable Estimation of Error-Components Models," *Journal of Econometrics*, 68: 29–51.

Browning, M., A. Deaton, and M. Irish (1985), "A Profitable Approach to Labor Supply and Commodity Demands over the Life-Cycle," *Econometrica*, 53: 503–543.

Chamberlain, G. (1982), "Multivariate Regression Models for Panel Data," *Journal of Econometrics*, 18: 5–46.

(1984), "Panel Data," in Z. Griliches and M.D. Intrilligator (eds.), *Handbook of Econometrics*, vol. II, Elsevier Science.

Gourieroux, C. and A. Monfort (1989), *Statistique et Modèles Econométriques*, vol. II, Paris: Économica.

(1995), *Statistics and Econometric Models*, vols. I and II. Cambridge University Press.

Gourieroux, C., A. Monfort, and A. Trognon (1985), "Moindres Carrés Asymptotiques," *Annales de l'Inséé*, 58: 91–122.

Heckman, J.J. (1979), "Sample Selection Bias as a Specification Error," *Econometrica*, 47: 153–161.

(1981), "Statistical Models for Discrete Panel Data," in C.F. Manski and D. McFadden (eds.), *Structural Analysis of Discrete Data with Econometric Applications*, Cambridge, Mass.: MIT Press.

Heckman, J.J. and T.E. MaCurdy (1980), "A Life-Cycle Model of Female Labour Supply," *Review of Economic Studies*, 47: 47–74.

Holtz-Eakin, D., W. Newey, and H. Rosen (1988), "Estimating Vector Autoregressions with Panel Data", *Econometrica*, 56: 1371–1395.

Honoré, B. (1992), "Trimmed LAD and Least Squares Estimation of Truncated and Censored Regression Models with Fixed Effects," *Econometrica*, 60: 533–565.

(1993), "Orthogonality Conditions for Tobit Models with Fixed Effects and Lagged Dependent Variables," *Journal of Econometrics*, 59: 35–61.

Huber, P.J. (1967), "The Behaviour of Maximum Likelihood Estimates Under Nonstandard Conditions," *Proceedings of the Fifth Berkeley Symposium on Mathematical Statistics and Probability*, 1: 221–233.

MaCurdy, T.E. (1981), "An Empirical Model of Labor Supply in a Life-Cycle Setting," *Journal of Political Economy*, 89: 1059–1085.

Newey, W.K. (1988), "Two Step Series Estimation of Sample Selection Models," unpublished discussion paper, Princeton University.

Newey, W.K., J.L. Powell, and J.R. Walker (1990), "Semiparametric Estimation of Selection Models: Some Empirical Results," *The American Economic Review Papers and Proceedings*, 80: 324–328.

Powell, J.L. (1986), "Symmetrically Trimmed Least Squares Estimation for Tobit Models," *Econometrica*, 54: 1435–1460.

(1987), "Semiparametric Estimation of Bivariate Latent-Variable Models," Social Systems Research Institute, University of Wisconsin-Madison, Working Paper No. 8704.

Sargan, J.D. (1958), "The Estimation of Economic Relationships Using Instrumental Variables," *Econometrica*, 26: 393–415.

(1988), "Testing for Misspecification after Estimating Using Instrumental Variables," in E. Maasoumi (ed.), *Contributions to Econometrics: John Denis Sargan*, vol. I, Cambridge University Press.

Szroeter, J. (1983), "Generalized Wald Methods for Testing Nonlinear Implicit and Overidentifying Restrictions," *Econometrica*, 51: 335–353.

3 Mixture of normals probit models

JOHN GEWEKE AND MICHAEL KEANE

1 Introduction

In econometric specifications of dichotomous choice models, the probit and logit specifications are commonly used. Other specifications have been suggested (Maddala (1983, pp. 27–32), Aldrich and Nelson (1984)), but in econometric applications, the probit and logit specifications have been used almost exclusively. The probit model is easy to use, and the logit specification is even more tractable. Because the probit specification can be made free of the problem of independence of irrelevant alternatives (Hausman and McFadden (1984)) when moving from dichotomous to polytomous choice, whereas the logit specification cannot, the probit model has become a mainstay in econometrics, and it is likely to remain one.

It is widely appreciated that any misspecification of functional form in a dichotomous choice model will lead to inconsistent estimates of conditional choice probabilities. In particular, if a probit specification is maintained when a different specification is true, misleading inferences about conditional choice probabilities and the effects of changes in covariates on these probabilities may result. In this chapter, we consider strict generalizations of the probit specification that remain within the class of linear dichotomous choice models:

$$\mathrm{P}(d_t = 1) = \mathrm{P}(\beta' \mathbf{x}_t + \varepsilon_t > 0)$$

where d_t is the choice indicator, $\mathbf{x}_t$ is a vector of covariates, and ε_t is an i.i.d. disturbance. Our approach is fully parametric and Bayesian. This approach permits us to obtain explicit evaluations of $\mathrm{P}(d_t = 1 \mid \mathbf{x}_t = \mathbf{x}^*)$ for any $\mathbf{x}^*$,

John Geweke wishes to acknowledge financial support from National Science Foundation grant SBR-9514865, Michael Keane from NSF grant SBR-9511186. We thank Robin Carter, Daniel Houser, and seminar participants at the University of Western Ontario for comments on an earlier draft, but blame only each other for remaining errors. We thank John Landon-Lane and Lance Schibilla for research assistance. The views expressed herein are those of the authors and not necessarily those of the Federal Reserve Bank of Minneapolis or the Federal Reserve System.

which are ultimately the focus of any application, and makes it possible to compare alternative generalizations with each other as well as with the conventional probit model. These evaluations and comparisons can, in principle, be accomplished with all Bayesian approaches to dichotomous choice (see, for example, Zellner and Rossi (1984), Albert and Chib (1993), Koop and Poirier (1993)). However, recent developments in numerical methods have greatly simplified the computation of posterior moments and Bayes factors. The class of specifications taken up here is the mixture of normals distribution, in which

$$p(_{\varepsilon}) = (2\pi)^{-1/2}\sum_{j=1}^{m} p_j h_j^{1/2} \exp[-0.5h_j(\varepsilon - \alpha_j)^2].$$

The generation of the shock may be described by first drawing from one of m specified normal distributions, with probabilities $p_1, \ldots, p_m$, and then drawing the shock ε from that distribution.

There is a large literature in econometric theory that has taken a semiparametric approach to this problem by dealing with consistent estimation of β and making regularity assumptions about the distribution of the shock rather than specifying it. The development of this approach includes Cosslett (1983), Manski (1985), Gallant and Nychka (1987), Powell, Stock, and Stoker (1989), Horowitz (1992), Ichimura (1993), and Klein and Spady (1993). Lewbel (1997) extends this approach to include consistent estimation of moments of ε. This approach and the one taken here are complementary. Both break free of the normality assumption of the probit model. On the one hand, the semiparametric approach introduces a series of approximations that yields consistent estimates of covariate coefficients given weak assumptions (for example, differentiability of the density function) about the shock distribution, whereas we make no claim that the mixture of normals family will similarly accommodate all such distributions. On the other hand, our method leads directly to exact inference for $P(d_t = 1 | \mathbf{x}_t = \mathbf{x}^*)$, which the semiparametric approach does not do even asymptotically.

The organization of the chapter is simple. The next section describes the mixture of normals probit model, beginning by extending the treatment of the probit model by Albert and Chib (1993) and moving through to the development of a Markov Chain Monte Carlo posterior simulator and the evaluation of the marginal likelihood. Experiments with artificial data provide some evidence on the ability of different models within the class to cope with alternative shock distributions. These are reported in section 3. A substantive example pertaining to women's labor force participation, which uses a subset of the Panel Study of Income Dynamics (PSID) with 1,555 observations, and an informative prior is presented in section 4. In this example, the conventional probit model is overwhelmingly rejected in favor of the mixture of normals probit model; However, subsequent work with this same data set (Geweke and Keane (1999)) has shown that with a more diffuse prior distribution for the coefficients, the conventional probit and mixture of normals models have similar marginal likelihoods, so Bayes factors do not strongly favor either model. Some fairly obvious extensions of this work are mentioned in the concluding section.

2 Bayesian inference for probit models

In the probit model, the observables are $\underset{k\times T}{\mathbf{X}'} = [\mathbf{x}_1, \ldots, \mathbf{x}_T]$ and $\mathbf{d}' = (d_1, \ldots, d_T)$, $d_t = 0$ or 1. The relationships of interest are

$$\tilde{y}_t = \beta'\mathbf{x}_t + \varepsilon_t,\ d_t = \chi_{[0,\infty)}(\tilde{y}_t)\ (t = 1, \ldots, T) \tag{1}$$

where the indicator function $\chi_S(z) = 1$ if $z \in S$ and $\chi_S(z) = 0$ if $z \notin S$. Let $\tilde{\mathbf{y}}' = (\tilde{y}_1, \ldots, \tilde{y}_T)$.

2.1 Conventional probit model

In the conventional probit model

$$\varepsilon_t|\mathbf{X} \overset{IID}{\sim} \mathrm{N}(0,1) \tag{2}$$

and it is convenient to complete this model with the prior distribution $\beta \sim \mathrm{N}(\underline{\beta}, \underline{\mathbf{H}}_\beta^{-1})$, where $\underline{\beta} \in \mathrm{R}^k$ and $\underline{\mathbf{H}}_\beta$ is a $k \times k$ positive definite precision matrix

$$\mathrm{p}(\beta) = (2\pi)^{-k/2}|\underline{\mathbf{H}}_\beta|^{1/2} \exp[-0.5(\beta - \underline{\beta})'\underline{\mathbf{H}}_\beta(\beta - \underline{\beta})] \tag{3}$$

Albert Chib (1993) develop a Gibbs sampling algorithm for Bayesian inference in this model. From (1) and (2)

$$\begin{aligned} \mathrm{p}(\mathbf{d},\tilde{\mathbf{y}} \mid \beta,\mathbf{X}) &= \mathrm{p}(\tilde{\mathbf{y}} \mid \beta,\mathbf{X})\mathrm{p}(\mathbf{d} \mid \tilde{\mathbf{y}}) \\ &= (2\pi)^{-T/2} \exp[-0.5(\tilde{\mathbf{y}} - \mathbf{X}\beta)(\tilde{\mathbf{y}} - \mathbf{X}\beta)]\Pi_{t=1}^{T}[d_t\chi_{[0,\infty]}(\tilde{y}_t) + \\ &\quad (1 - d_t)\chi_{(-\infty,0)}(\tilde{y}_t)] \qquad (4) \\ &= \Pi_{t=1}^{T}(2\pi)^{-1/2} \exp[-0.5(\tilde{\mathbf{y}} - \beta'\mathbf{x}_t)^2][d_t\chi_{[0,\infty)}(\tilde{y}_t) + \\ &\quad (1 - d_t)\chi_{(-\infty,0)}(\tilde{y}_t)] \qquad (5) \end{aligned}$$

The joint posterior density β and $\tilde{\mathbf{y}}$ is $\mathrm{p}(\beta,\tilde{\mathbf{y}} \mid \mathbf{d},\mathbf{X}) \propto \mathrm{p}(\mathbf{d},\tilde{\mathbf{y}} \mid \beta,\mathbf{X})\mathrm{p}(\beta)$. When we take the product of the joint density (4) and the prior density (3) and examine the kernel of this expression in β

$$\beta|(\tilde{\mathbf{y}},\mathbf{X}) \sim \mathrm{N}(\bar{\beta},\bar{\mathbf{H}}_\beta^{-1}),\ \bar{\mathbf{H}}_\beta = \underline{\mathbf{H}}_\beta + \mathbf{X}'\mathbf{X},\ \bar{\beta} = \bar{\mathbf{H}}_\beta^{-1}(\underline{\mathbf{H}}_\beta\underline{\beta} + \mathbf{X}'\tilde{\mathbf{y}}). \tag{6}$$

Taking $\mathrm{p}(\mathbf{d},\tilde{\mathbf{y}} \mid \beta,X)$ in the form (5)[2], we have the T conditionally independent distributions

$$\tilde{y}_t|(\mathbf{d},\beta,\mathbf{X}) = \tilde{y}_t|(d_t,\beta,\mathbf{x}_t) \sim \mathrm{N}(\beta'\mathbf{x}_t,1)$$
$$\text{subject to } \tilde{y}_t \geq 0 \text{ if } d_t = 1 \text{ and } \tilde{y}_t < 0 \text{ if } d_t = 0. \quad (7)$$

Beginning from an arbitrary point $\beta^{(0)} \in \mathrm{R}^k$, we construct the sequence $\{\beta^{(r)},\tilde{\mathbf{y}}^{(r)}\}$ by drawing sequentially from the T distributions in (7) and the distribution (6). (In all results reported subsequently for this model, $\beta^{(0)} \sim \mathrm{N}(\underline{\beta},\underline{\mathbf{H}}^{-1})$.) Given any point $(\beta^*,\tilde{\mathbf{y}}^*)$ in the support of $\mathrm{p}(\beta,\tilde{\mathbf{y}}\,|\,\mathbf{d},\mathbf{X})$ and any subset A of the support with positive Lebesgue measure, the probability of moving from $(\beta^*,\tilde{\mathbf{y}}^*)$ into A in one iteration of this algorithm is strictly positive. Therefore, the process $\{\beta^{(r)},\tilde{\mathbf{y}}^{(r)}\}$ is ergodic (Tierney (1994), Geweke (1997a, section 3.3)), which implies that if $\mathrm{E}[\mathrm{g}(\beta)|\mathbf{d},\mathbf{X}]$ exists, then $R^{-1}\sum_{m=1}^{M}\mathrm{g}(\beta^{(m)}) \xrightarrow{a.s.} \mathrm{E}[\mathrm{g}(\beta)|\mathbf{d},\mathbf{X}]$.

2.2 *Mixture of normals probit model*

In the mixture of normals probit model

$$\varepsilon_t = \sum_{j=1}^{m} e_{tj}(\alpha_j + h_j^{-1/2}\eta_t),\ \alpha' = (\alpha_1,\ldots,\alpha_m) \in \mathrm{R}^m,\ \mathbf{h}' = (h_1,\ldots,h_m) \in \mathrm{R}_+^m \quad (8)$$

$$\eta_t|\mathbf{X} \overset{IID}{\sim} \mathrm{N}(0,1). \quad (9)$$

The random vectors $\mathbf{e}_t' = (e_{t1},\ldots,e_{tm})$ are i.i.d., each with a multinomial distribution with parameters $p_J = \mathrm{P}(e_{tj} = 1)(j = 1,\ldots,m)$

$$\mathbf{e}_t \overset{IID}{\sim} \mathrm{MN}(p_1,\ldots,p_m),\ \mathbf{p}' = (p_1,\ldots,p_m) \in S_m \quad (10)$$

where S_m is the unit simplex in R^m.

Without further restrictions, the model is clearly unidentified in the sense that more than one set of values of the parameters in (1) and (8–10) imply the same $\mathrm{p}(\mathbf{d}|\mathbf{X})$. Three specific identified versions of the model are of interest, each consisting of a set of further restrictions on (1) and (8–10).

In the *full mixture of normals model*

(i) rank $(\mathbf{X}) = k$ and $\mathbf{a}'\mathbf{X}' \neq (1,\ldots,1)$ for any $k \times 1$ vector $\mathbf{a}$;
(ii) $p_j > 0\,\forall j$;
(iii) the support of $\beta'\mathbf{x}_t$ is a set of positive Lebesgue measure;
(iv) either
  (a) $\alpha_{j-1} < \alpha_j\ (j = 2,\ldots,m)$ or
  (b) $h_{j-1} < h_j\ (j = 2,\ldots,m)$; and
(v) $h_j^* =$ for some j^*.

In the *scale mixture of normals model*, $\alpha_j = 0\ (j = 1,\ldots,m)$, $\mathbf{X}$ may (and generally does) include an intercept, and (iv(b)) obtains. In the *mean mixture of normals model*, $h_j = 1\ (j = 1,\ldots,m)$ and (iv(a)) obtains. The orderings in (iv) are labeling restrictions that prevent interchanging the components of the mixture; obviously, other labeling restrictions are possible.

For Bayesian inference, it is convenient to complete the model with independent prior distributions for β, α, $\mathbf{h}$, and $\mathbf{p}$. The prior distribution for β is (3). Except in the scale mixture of normals model, $a \sim N(\underline{\alpha}, \underline{\mathbf{H}}_{\alpha}^{-1})$, where $\underline{\alpha} \in R^m$ and $\underline{\mathbf{H}}_{\alpha}$ is an $m \times m$ positive definite matrix

$$p(\alpha) = (2\pi)^{-m/2} |\underline{\mathbf{H}}_{\alpha}|^{1/2} \exp[-0.5(\alpha - \underline{\alpha})' \underline{\mathbf{H}}_{a} (\alpha - \underline{\alpha})] \quad (11)$$

subject to (iv(a)) in the mean mixture of normals model and in the full mixture of normals model if (iv(b)) is not invoked.

Except in the mean mixture of normals model, $\underline{s}_j^2 h_j \sim \chi^2(\underline{\nu}_j)$ $(j \neq j^*)$, where $\underline{s}_j^2 > 0$ and $\underline{\nu}_j > 0$. If(iv(b)) is not imposed, then the prior density of $\mathbf{h}$ is

$$p(\mathbf{h}) = \prod_{j=1, j \neq j^*}^{m} [2^{\underline{\nu}_j/2} \Gamma(\underline{\nu}_j/2)]^{-1} (\underline{s}_j^2)^{\underline{\nu}_j/2} h_j^{(\underline{\nu}_j - 2)/2} \exp(-0.5 \underline{s}_j^2 h_j). \quad (12)$$

If (iv(b)) is imposed, then the support is truncated accordingly, and the normalization constant must be adjusted.

Finally, $p(\mathbf{p}) \sim \text{Beta}(\mathbf{r})$, $\mathbf{r} \in R_+^m$

$$p(\mathbf{p}) = [\Gamma(\textstyle\sum_{j=1}^{m} r_j) / \prod_{j=1}^{m} \Gamma(r_j)] \prod_{j=1}^{m} p_j^{(r_j - 1)}. \quad (13)$$

Since the likelihood function

$$p(\mathbf{d} | \beta, \alpha, \mathbf{h}, \mathbf{p}, \mathbf{X}) = \prod_{t=1}^{T} \langle d_t \textstyle\sum_{j=1}^{m} p_j \Phi[h_j^{1/2}(\alpha_j + \beta' \mathbf{x}_t)] + (1 - d_t)\{1 - \textstyle\sum_{j=1}^{m} p_j \Phi[h_j^{1/2}(\alpha_j + \beta' \mathbf{x}_t)]\} \rangle \quad (14)$$

is bounded between zero and one

$$p(\mathbf{d} | \beta, \alpha, \mathbf{h}, \mathbf{p}, \mathbf{X}) p(\beta) p(\alpha) p(\mathbf{h}) p(\mathbf{p}) \quad (15)$$

is finitely integrable over its support, and, consequently, the posterior distribution $p(\beta, \alpha, \mathbf{h}, \mathbf{p} | \mathbf{X})$, proportional to (15), exists. Since β, α, $\mathbf{h}$, and $\mathbf{p}$ have prior moments of all orders, they also have posterior moments of all orders. And since for any specified $\mathbf{x}_{T+s} (s > 0)$, $p(d_{T+s} = 1 | \beta, \alpha, \mathbf{h}, \mathbf{p}, \mathbf{x}_{T+s})$ is bounded between zero and one, $p(d_{T+s} = 1 | \mathbf{x}_{T+s}, \mathbf{X})$ has posterior moments of all orders.

2.3 *A posterior simulator*

In the mixture of normals probit model

$$p(d, \tilde{\mathbf{y}}, \mathbf{e} | \beta, \alpha, \mathbf{h}, \mathbf{p}, \mathbf{X}) = p(\mathbf{e} | \mathbf{p}) p(\tilde{\mathbf{y}} \mid \mathbf{e}, \beta, \alpha, \mathbf{h}, \mathbf{X}) p(\mathbf{d} | \tilde{\mathbf{y}}).$$

When we define $L_t = (j{:}e_{tj} = 1)$ and $T_j = \sum_{t=1}^{T} e_{tj}$

$$p(\mathbf{e} | \mathbf{p}) = \prod_{t=1}^{T} \prod_{j=1}^{m} p_j^{e_{tj}} = \prod_{j=1}^{m} p_j^{T_j} \quad (16)$$

$$p(\tilde{\mathbf{y}} \mid \mathbf{e}, \beta, \alpha, \mathbf{h}, \mathbf{X}) = (2\pi)^{-T/2} \prod_{j=1}^{m} h_j^{T_j/2} \exp[-0.5 \textstyle\sum_{t=1}^{T} h_{Lt}^{1/2} (\tilde{y}_t - \alpha' \mathbf{e}_t - \beta' \mathbf{x}_t)^2] \quad (17)$$

$$p(\mathbf{d} | \tilde{\mathbf{y}}) = \prod_{t=1}^{T} [d_t \chi_{(0,\infty)}(\tilde{y}_t) + (1 - d_t) \chi_{(-\infty,0)}(\tilde{y}_t)] \quad (18)$$

The product of (16), (17), and (18) and the prior density kernels (3), (11), (12), and (13) is a kernel of the posterior distribution of the latent variables $\mathbf{e}$ (equivalently, $\{L_t\}_{t=1}^{T}$) and $\tilde{\mathbf{y}}$ and the parameter vectors β, α, $\mathbf{h}$, and $\mathbf{p}$. Posterior distributions for individual groups of latent variables and parameters, conditional on all the other latent variables and parameters and the data, are easily derived from these expressions as follows.

The kernel in $\tilde{\mathbf{y}}$ is the product of (17) and (18), from which the $\tilde{y}_t$ are conditionally independent with

$$\tilde{y}_t \sim \mathrm{N}(\beta'\mathbf{x}_t + \alpha'\mathbf{e}_t, h_{L_t}^{-1}) \text{ subject to } \tilde{y}_t \geq 0 \text{ if } d_t = 1 \text{ and } \tilde{y}_t < 0 \text{ if } d_t = 0.$$

The kernel in $\{L_t\}_{t=1}^{T}$ is the product of (16) and (17), which shows that the L_t are conditionally independent with

$$\mathrm{P}(L_t = j) \propto p_j \exp[-0.5 h_j^{1/2}(\tilde{y}_t - \alpha_j - \beta'\mathbf{x}_t)^2].$$

The kernel in β is the product of (3) and (17), from which

$$\beta \sim \mathrm{N}(\bar{\beta}, \bar{\mathbf{H}}_\beta^{-1}),\ \bar{\mathbf{H}}_\beta = \underline{\mathbf{H}}_\beta + \textstyle\sum_{t=1}^{T} h_{L_t}\mathbf{x}_t\mathbf{x}_t',\ \bar{\beta} = \bar{\mathbf{H}}_\beta^{-1}\big(\underline{\mathbf{H}}_\beta\underline{\beta} + \textstyle\sum_{t=1}^{T} h_{L_t}\mathbf{x}_t\tilde{y}_t\big).$$

The kernel in α is the product of (11) and (17), which yields

$$\alpha \sim \mathrm{N}(\bar{\alpha}, \bar{\mathbf{H}}_\alpha^{-1}),\ \bar{\mathbf{H}}_\alpha = \underline{\mathbf{H}}_\alpha + \textstyle\sum_{t=1}^{T} \mathbf{e}_t\mathbf{e}_t',\ \bar{\alpha} = \bar{\mathbf{H}}_\alpha^{-1}[\underline{\mathbf{H}}_\alpha\underline{\alpha} + \textstyle\sum_{t=1}^{T} \mathbf{e}_t(\tilde{y}_t - \beta'\mathbf{x}_t)]$$

subject to $\alpha_1 < \ldots < \alpha_m$ if this labeling restriction has been invoked. (The algorithm of Geweke (1991) provides for efficient imposition of the inequality constraints.)

The kernel in $\mathbf{h}$ is the product of (12) and (17), which indicates

$$\bar{s}_j^2 h_j \sim \chi^2(\bar{\nu}_j),\ \bar{s}_j^2 = \underline{s}_j^2 + \textstyle\sum e_{tj}(\tilde{y}_t - \alpha_j - \beta'\mathbf{x}_t)^2,\ \bar{\nu}_j = \underline{\nu}_j + T_j$$

for $j \neq j^*$ and subject to $h_1 < \ldots < h_m$ if the labeling restriction on $\mathbf{h}$ has been invoked. Whether or not this restriction applies, it is straightforward to draw the h_j sequentially.

Finally, the posterior kernel in $\mathbf{p}$ is the product of (13) and (16)

$$\mathbf{p} \sim \mathrm{Beta}(r_1 + T_1, \ldots, r_m + T_m).$$

It is straightforward to verify that the lower semicontinuity and boundedness conditions of Roberts and Smith (1994) for ergodicity of the Gibbs samplers are satisfied by the posterior distribution. Therefore, any starting value $(\beta^{(0)}, \alpha^{(0)}, \mathbf{h}^{(0)}, \mathbf{p}^{(0)})$ may be used. As a practical matter, however, we have found that unless the dimension k of β is small, convergence is slow if the initial values are drawn from the respective prior distributions (3), (11), (12), and (13). In the case of a labeling restriction on $\mathbf{h}$, the difficulty is that since $\beta^{(0)}$ is quite unrepresentative of the posterior distribution with very high probability, initial values of $h_j^{(r)}$ tend to be quite small for $j<j^*$, or, if $h_1=1$, initial values of $\beta_j^{(r)}$ become quite small, and many thousands of iterations are required before convergence to the posterior distribution. (A similar problem arises with a labeling restriction on α.) This difficulty is avoided by drawing $\beta^{(0)}$ from (3), sampling in the conventional probit model for a few hundred iterations, and then beginning a full set of draws in the mixture of normals probit model.

2.4 Comparison of models

To this point, the number of mixtures m has been taken as given. In fact, it will be of some interest to compare the plausibility of alternative values of m, and, in particular, to compare mixture of normals models ($m>1$) with the conventional probit model. It may also be of interest to compare alternative specifications of prior distributions. We can do this formally by means of Bayes factors using the extensions of the method of Gelfand and Dey (1994) outlined in Geweke (1997b).

Generically, for a model j with data density $\mathrm{p}_j(\mathbf{y}\,|\,\theta_j)$, completed with a prior density $\mathrm{p}_j(\theta_j)$, $\theta_j \in \Theta_j$, the marginal likelihood may be defined

$$M_j = \int_{\Theta_j} \mathrm{p}_j(\mathbf{y}\,|\,\theta_j)\mathrm{p}_j(\theta_j)d\theta_j. \tag{19}$$

(It is important that the data and prior densities be properly normalized, that is, that $\int_Y \mathrm{p}(\mathbf{y}\,|\,\theta_j)d\mathbf{y} = 1\,\forall\,\Theta_j \in \Theta_j$ and $\int_{\Theta_j}\mathrm{p}(\theta_j)d\theta_j = 1$.) The Bayes factor in favor of model j versus model k is M_j/M_k. Gelfand and Dey (1994) point out that if $\mathrm{f}_j(\theta_j)$ is any function with the property $\int_{\Theta_j}\mathrm{f}_j(\theta_j)d\theta_j = 1$, then the posterior expectation of $\mathrm{f}_j(\theta_j)/\mathrm{p}_j(\mathbf{y}\,|\,\theta_j)\mathrm{p}_j(\theta_j)$ in model j is M_j^{-1}

$$\int_{\Theta_j} \frac{\mathrm{f}_j(\theta_j)}{\mathrm{p}_j(\mathbf{y}\,|\,\theta_j)\mathrm{p}_j(\theta_j)}\mathrm{p}(\theta_j\,|\,\mathbf{y})d\theta_j = \int_{\Theta_j} \frac{\mathrm{f}_j(\theta_j)}{\mathrm{p}_j(\mathbf{y}\,|\,\theta_j)\mathrm{p}_j(\theta_j)} \cdot \frac{\mathrm{p}_j(\mathbf{y}\,|\,\theta_j)\mathrm{p}_j(\theta_j)}{\int_{\Theta_j}\mathrm{p}_j(\mathbf{y}\,|\,\theta_j)\mathrm{p}_j(\theta_j)}d\theta_j$$

$$= \frac{1}{\int_{\Theta_j}\mathrm{p}_j(\mathbf{y}\,|\,\theta_j)\mathrm{p}_j(\theta_j)}.$$

Thus, if $\{\theta_j^{(r)}\}$ is the output of an ergodic posterior simulator

$$R^{-1}\sum_{r=1}^{R}\mathrm{f}_j(\theta_j^{(r)})/\mathrm{p}(\mathbf{y}\,|\,\theta_j^{(r)})\mathrm{p}(\theta_j^{(r)}) \xrightarrow{a.s.} M_j^{-1}.$$

Gelfand and Dey (1994) also observe that for convergence to occur at a practical rate, it is quite helpful if $\mathrm{f}_j(\theta_j)/\mathrm{p}_j(\mathbf{y}\,|\,\theta_j)\mathrm{p}_j(\theta_j)$ is bounded above. If $\mathrm{f}_j(\theta_j)$ has "thick tails" relative to $\mathrm{p}_j(\mathbf{y}\,|\,\theta_j)\mathrm{p}_j(\theta_j)$, then this will not be the case. For the case of continuous θ_j, Geweke (1997b) avoids this problem by taking $\mathrm{f}_j(\theta_j)$ to be the density of a multivariate normal distribution centered at $\hat{\theta}_j = R^{-1}\Sigma_{r=1}^{R}\theta_j^{(r)}$ with variance $R^{-1}\Sigma_{r=1}^{R}(\theta_j^{(r)} - \hat{\theta}_j)(\theta_j^{(r)} - \hat{\theta}_j)'$, truncated to a highest density region of the multivariate normal distribution.

In the mixture of normals probit model, this procedure is not practical if applied to the augmented parameter vector ($\beta,\alpha,\mathbf{h},\mathbf{p},\tilde{\mathbf{y}},\mathbf{e}$) used in the posterior simulator, because the length of this vector is more than twice the sample size. But since the probability function (15) for **d** is available in essentially closed form, with $\tilde{\mathbf{y}}$ and **e** marginalized analytically, the procedure can be applied by using the parameter vector ($\beta,\alpha,\mathbf{h},\mathbf{p}$) and the product of (15) with the prior densities (3), (12), (13), and (14). (In accounting for the labeling restrictions, the normalization factor for the prior density can be found by independence Monte Carlo; accuracy on the order of 10^{-3} in the logarithm of the normalizing constant can typically be achieved in a few seconds. This means that this source of approximation error will contribute only about 0.1 percent to the evaluation of the marginal likelihood (19).) To increase the accuracy of the approximation, it is helpful to reparameterize the h_j by $\log(h_j^{1/2})$ and **p** by $\log(p_j/p_m)$ (j = 1,…,m – 1). Since the truncated normal density $f_j(\theta_j)$ may still not be contained in the support of the parameter space because of labeling restrictions, the normalizing constant for this distribution must be systematically adjusted by Monte Carlo as well.

3 Some results with artificial data

Before proceeding to substantive applications, we conducted some experiments with artificial data. The main purpose of these experiments was to check software and gain some appreciation of how large a sample might be required to produce posterior moments that differ in an interesting way from prior moments, how much computing time would be required, and – by implication – what might be the practical scope for application of the methods described in section 2. As a byproduct, the experiments provide some indication of the ability of these methods to detect departures from the conventional probit model specification and of the mixture of normals probit models to approximate other distributions of the disturbance. The latter questions are of no interest to purely subjective Bayesians, but are probably of considerable concern to non-Bayesians.

We used five data generating processes (DGPs), shown in table 3.1. In each process, there is a single explanatory variable with mean zero and standard deviation five, and a coefficient of one. The first three processes are special cases of the mixture of normals probit specification. The first is a conventional probit model. The second and third are mixtures of two normals, the third having a bimodal distribution of the shock ε_t. In the

Table 3.1. *Artificial data generating processes*

All data sets: $x_t \overset{IID}{\sim} N(0, 25)$

Data sets 1–4: $\tilde{y}_t = \beta x_t + \varepsilon_t,\ \beta = 1$

(x_t, ε_t) i.i.d.

$$d_t = \begin{cases} 1 \text{ if } \tilde{y}_t > 0 \\ 0 \text{ if } \tilde{y}_t \leq 0 \end{cases}$$

Data set 1: Normal (conventional probit specification)

$\varepsilon_t \sim N(0, 1)$

Data set 2: Scale mixture of two normals

$$\varepsilon_t \sim \begin{cases} N(0, 1)\ (p_1 = 0.5) \\ N(0, 25)\ (p_2 = 0.5) \end{cases}$$

Data set 3: Full mixture of two normals

$$\varepsilon_t \sim \begin{cases} N(1.5, 1.0)\ (p_1 = 0.667) \\ N(-3.0, 4.0)\ (p_2 = 0.333) \end{cases}$$

Data set 4: Cauchy distribution

$\varepsilon_t \sim \text{Cauchy}(0, 1)$

Data set 5: Logit distribution

$P(y_t = 1 | x_t) = \exp(x_t)/[1 + \exp(x_t)]$

fourth DGP, the shock is Cauchy, and in the fifth, it is logit. The sample size is 2,000 in every process.

We used three model specifications, shown in table 3.2. In each specification the prior distribution of the slope and intercept coefficients is independent standard normal. In the specifications with two or more mixtures, the prior correlation of the intercept coefficients is 0.8, which indicates that the coefficients are believed to be close together relative to their distance from zero. The first model is the conventional probit model. The second model has two mixtures: a labeling restriction on the precision and a setting of the larger precision to unity. The parameters of the prior distribution are chosen so that the upper 5 per cent of the distribution for h_1 is truncated by the labeling restriction $h_1 < 1$ and so that the 0.05 quantile is $h_1 = 0.01$. Thus, this prior distribution allows considerable scope for a leptokurtic distribution. The third model has three mixtures, again using a labeling restriction on the precisions, with $h_2 = 1$. The smaller precision has the same prior distribution as in the preceding model. For the larger prior precision, the lower 5 per cent of the distribution is truncated by the labeling restriction $h_3 > 1$, and the 0.95 quantile is $h_3 = 10$.

We carried out computations on a Sun Ultra 200 Sparcstation using

Table 3.2. *Model specifications (Artificial data)*

All models:

$$\tilde{y}_t = \beta x_t + \varepsilon_t$$
$$\varepsilon_t | (x_1, \ldots, x_T) \text{ i.i.d.}$$
$$d_t = \begin{cases} 1 \text{ if } \tilde{y}_t > 0 \\ 0 \text{ if } \tilde{y}_t \leq 0 \end{cases}$$
$$\beta \sim N(0, 1)$$

Conventional probit model:

$$\varepsilon_t | (x_1, \ldots, x_T) \sim N(\alpha, 1)$$
$$\alpha \sim N(0, 1)$$

Two full mixtures:

$$P[\varepsilon_t | (x_1, \ldots, x_T) \sim N(\alpha_j, h_j^{-1})] = p_j$$
$$\begin{pmatrix} \alpha_1 \\ \alpha_2 \end{pmatrix} \sim N\left(\begin{pmatrix} 0 \\ 0 \end{pmatrix}, \begin{bmatrix} 1.0 & 0.8 \\ 0.8 & 1.0 \end{bmatrix}\right)$$
$$3.832 h_1 \sim \chi^2(0.996),\ h_2 = 1,\ h_1 < h_2$$
$$(p_1, p_2) \sim \text{Beta } (5, 5)$$

Three full mixtures:

$$P[\varepsilon_t | (x_1, \ldots, x_T) \sim N(\alpha_j, h_j^{-1})] = p_j$$
$$\begin{pmatrix} \alpha_1 \\ \alpha_2 \\ \alpha_3 \end{pmatrix} \sim N\left(\begin{pmatrix} 0 \\ 0 \\ 0 \end{pmatrix}, \begin{bmatrix} 1.0 & 0.8 & 0.8 \\ 0.8 & 1.0 & 0.8 \\ 0.8 & 0.8 & 1.0 \end{bmatrix}\right)$$
$$3.832 h_1 \sim \chi^2(0.996),\ h_2 = 1,\ 1.076 h_3 \sim \chi^2(4.85);\ h_1 < 1 < h_3$$
$$(p_1, p_2, p_3) \sim \text{Beta } (3.5, 3.5, 1)$$

software written in Fortran 77. In each computation 10,000 iterations of the Gibbs sampler were employed, and the last 8,000 were used in the approximation of posterior moments. Computation time was 14 minutes for the conventional probit model, 28 minutes for the mixture of two normals, and 39 minutes for the mixture of three normals. Since the draws exhibit positive serial correlation, there is less information in 8,000 iterations than there would be in 8,000 hypothetical i.i.d. drawings from the posterior distribution. The ratio of the number of such i.i.d. draws to the number required in any given posterior simulator is the relative numerical efficiency of that posterior simulator. In the conventional probit model relative numerical efficiency for the Gibbs sampler was between 0.1 and 0.2 for most moments. In the mixture of two normals, it was between 0.01 and 0.06. In the mixture of three normals, it was between 0.005 and 0.05.

Table 3.3. *Marginal likelihoods*[1]

Data set	Conventional probit	Two full mixtures	Three full mixtures
1 (Normal)	− 261.7 (0.08)	− 263.5 (0.16)	− 269.5 (0.35)
2 (Scale mixture)	− 771.1 (0.02)	− 743.1 (0.08)	− 744.4 (0.15)
3 (Full mixture)	− 621.5 (0.03)	− 601.6 (0.07)	− 602.8 (0.43)
4 (Cauchy)	− 772.9 (0.02)	− 695.0 (0.19)	− 695.0 (0.14)
5 (Logit)	− 246.5 (0.07)	− 248.2 (0.14)	− 248.4 (0.18)

Note:
[1] Numerical standard errors of numerical approximations are shown in parentheses.

Discrimination between models using Bayes factors is of considerable interest. Table 3.3 shows marginal likelihoods for all data sets and models. Consider first the data generated from the conventional probit model (set 1). The Bayes factor in favor of the conventional probit model is 16 over the two-mixture model and 2,440 over the three-mixture model. The intuitive interpretation of this result is that while the mixture models are correctly specified, they spread prior probability over a larger space than does the conventional probit model, which leaves less probability for the DGP. This is an example of how Bayes factors penalize excessive parameterization.

For the data generated from the two-mixture specification, the Bayes factor against the incorrectly specified conventional probit model is overwhelming (about 1.45×10^{12}). The three-mixture model is correctly specified, but, again, the penalty for excessive parameterization is exhibited in a Bayes factor of 3.7 in favor of the two-mixture model. Results for the full-mixture data (set 3) are similar. For the case in which the distribution of the disturbance is Cauchy, the Bayes factor between the two-mixture models is one, but the Bayes factor against the conventional probit specification is huge: 6.78×10^{33}. Neither the two- nor the three-mixture model provides an improvement on the conventional probit model in the case of the logistic distribution, with the Bayes factor in favor of the conventional probit model being 5.5 against the two-mixture model and 6.7 against the three-mixture model. In view of the well-documented great similarity of the probit and logit specifications (Maddala (1983)), these findings for the logit data are not surprising.

The predictive distributions, $P(d=1|x)$, are the main focus of interest in any application of these models. Figures 3.1 through 3.5 show some aspects of these distributions for the five data sets, respectively. Each

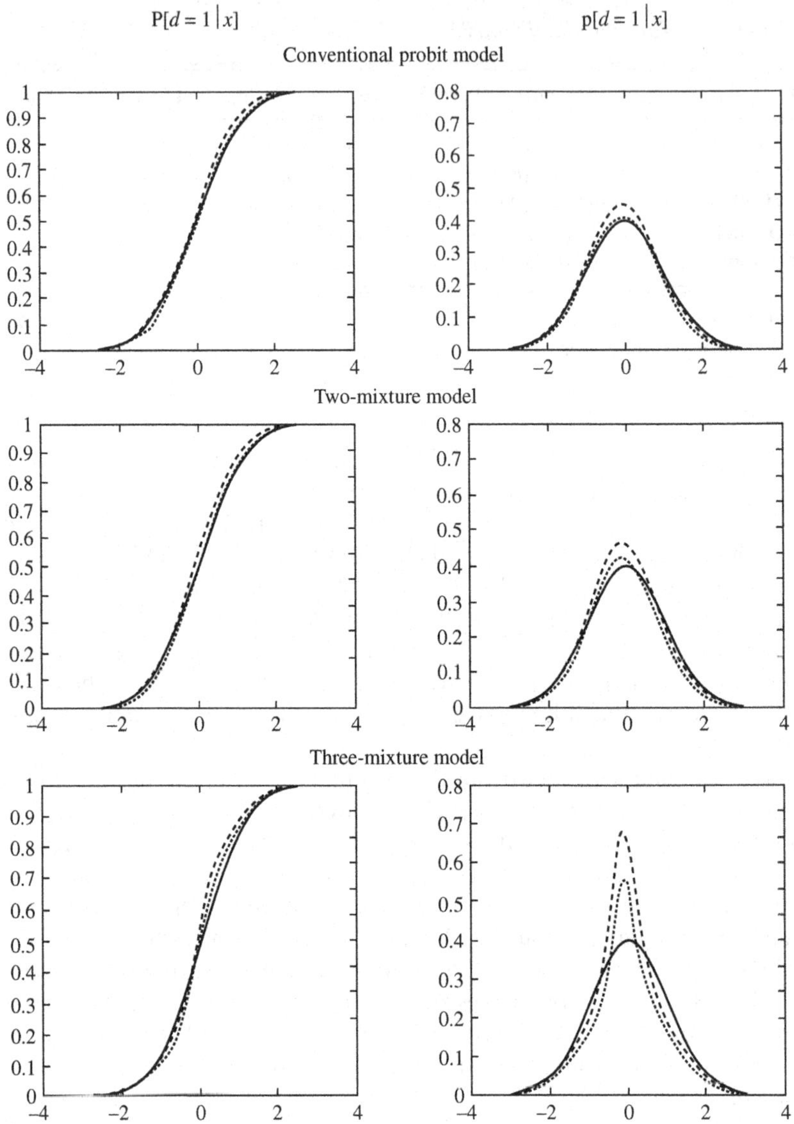

Figure 3.1 Population values and posterior quartile values: Normal DGP

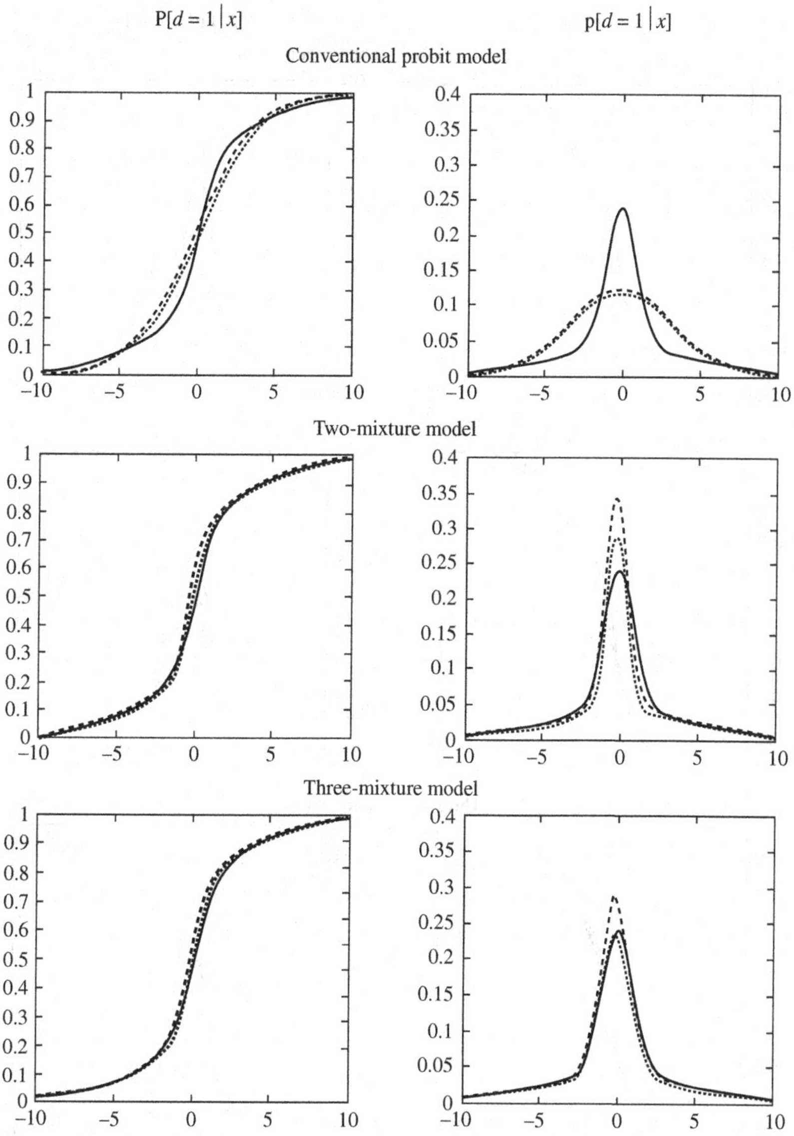

Figure 3.2 Population values and posterior quartile values: Scale mixture DGP

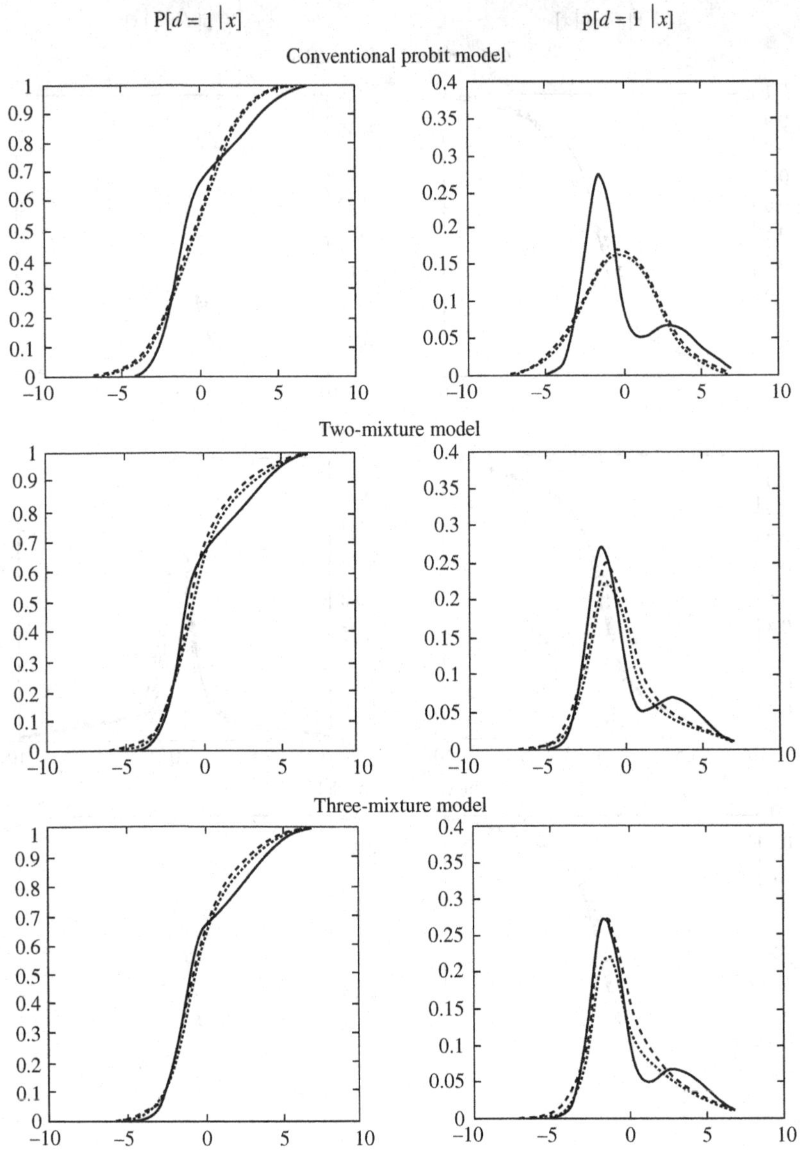

Figure 3.3 Population values and posterior quartile values: Full mixture DGP

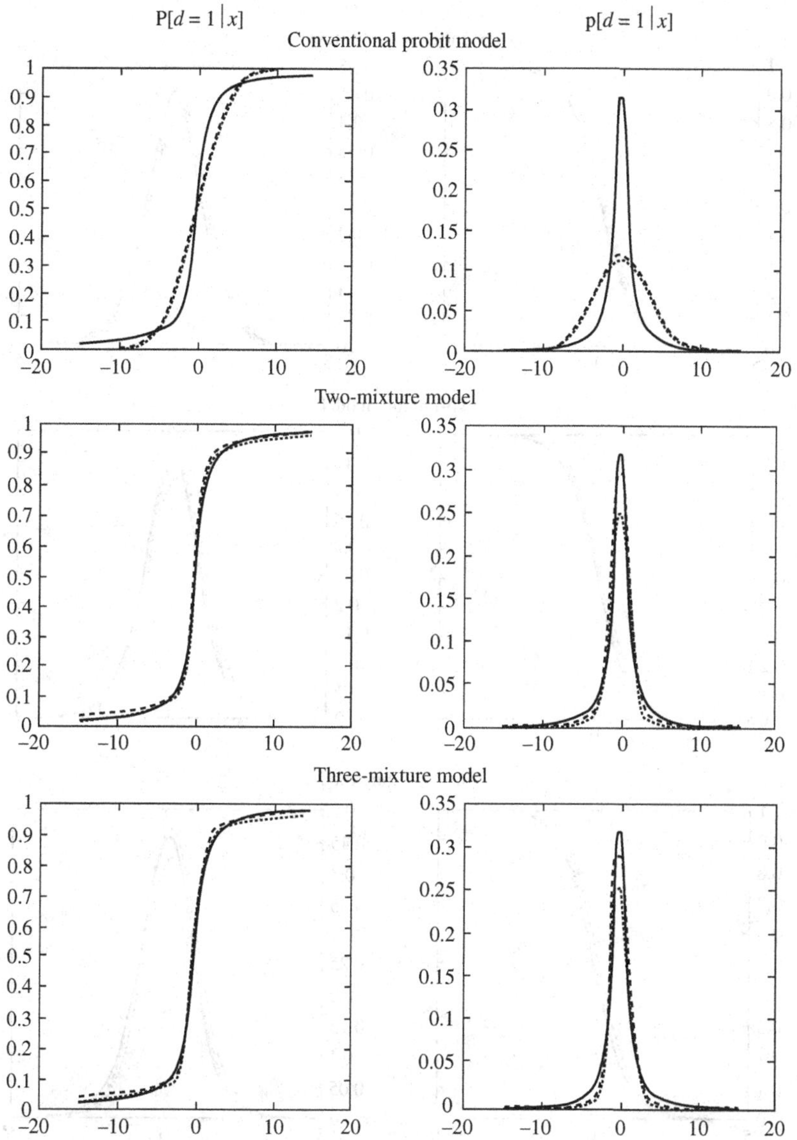

Figure 3.4 Population values and posterior quartile values: Cauchy DGP

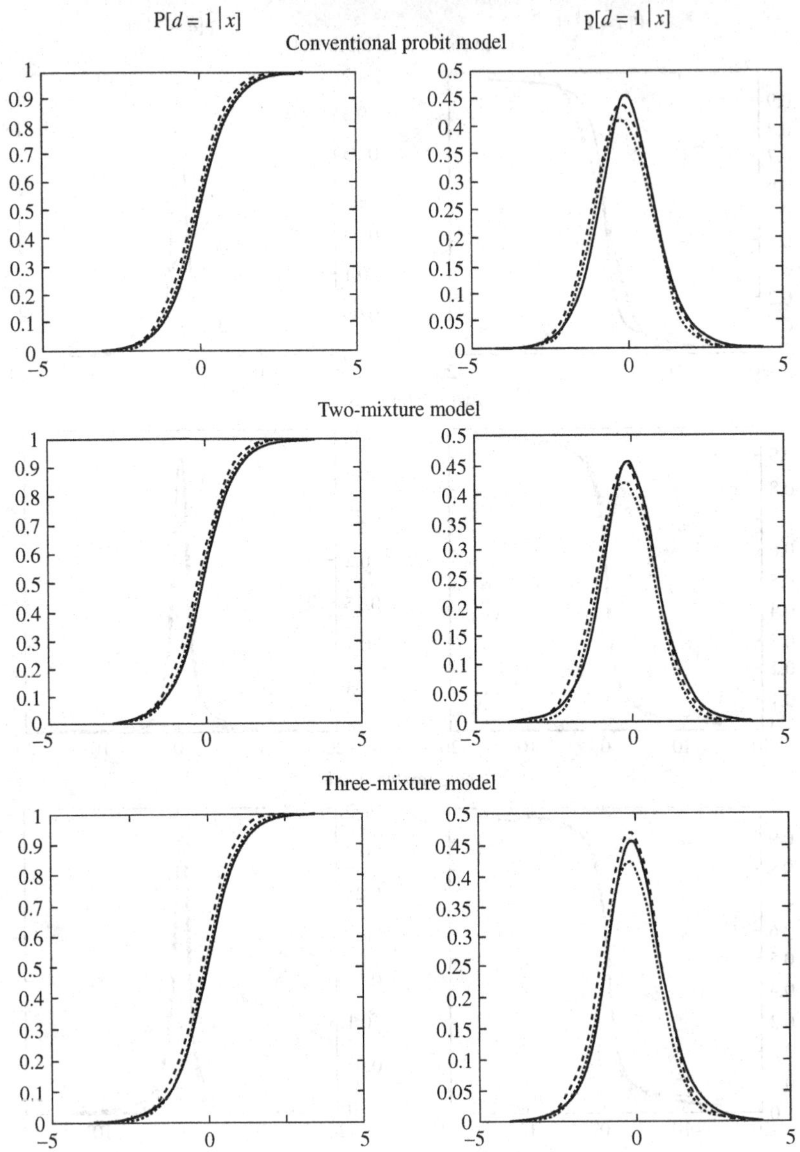

Figure 3.5 Population values and posterior quartile values: Logistic DGP

figure corresponds to one of the artificial DGPs shown in table 3.1, and each contains six panels. Each panel shows a relevant range of x values on the horizontal axis. The three panels on the left indicate the value of $P(d=1|x)$ in the DGP with a solid line and the 0.25 and 0.75 posterior quantiles for this population value with dotted and dashed lines, respectively. The three panels on the right indicate the derivative of $P(d=1|x)$ with respect to x in the DGP with a solid line, and 0.25 and 0.75 posterior quantiles for this population value with dotted and dashed lines. The upper pair of panels shows results for the conventional probit model, the middle pair for the two full-mixture model, and the third pair for the three full-mixture model.

Results for the conventional probit DGP are shown in figure 3.1. For a well-specified model and large sample sizes, we expect that the population value of $P(d=1|x)$ and its first derivative would be bracketed by the posterior 0.25 and 0.75 quantiles about half the time. On the one hand, the conventional probit DGP is a special case of all three model probability density functions (pdfs), but the posterior interquartile values match the population $P(d=1|x)$ better for the conventional probit specification than for either of the mixture models. On the other hand, there are not many values of x for which there is a serious discrepancy between posterior and DGP in the sense that the true value lies more than an interquartile range's width from the boundary of the interquartile range itself. The obvious deterioration in the visual match between distributions evident in figure 3.1, in moving from the conventional probit to the more complicated mixture of normals models, is reflected in the marginal likelihoods in the first row of table 3.3.

In the case of the scale mixture of normals DGP (figure 3.2), the conventional probit model correctly specifies a symmetric distribution of the disturbance but cannot capture the thick tails of the population density. The most obvious feature of figure 3.2 is the distance of the posterior interquartile values from the population values of $P(d=1|x)$ for the conventional probit model and the corresponding closeness for the mixture models. This is reflected in the marginal likelihood values in the second row of table 3.3. Interquartile ranges are larger for the two-mixture model than for the conventional probit model and slightly larger yet for the three-mixture model. But the fit of the conventional probit model is so bad that its probability is very low relative to the other two (as indicated in the second row of table 3.3). The three-mixture model looks a little closer to the DGP than does the two-mixture model in the interquartile range metric, but the interquartile range is sufficiently larger and it receives a little lower marginal likelihood.

The full mixture of normals DGP implies a bimodal pdf for the shock. None of the models captures the bimodality, as indicated in figure 3.3, but the mixture models come much closer than does the conventional probit model. As was the case for the scale mixture of normals DGP, interquartile ranges increase with model complexity. The conventional model has difficulty with the tails, complicated by the asymmetry of the distribution. Although the population distribution of ε_t has mean zero, its median is positive. The distribution in the conventional probit specification is symmetric, and this causes overprediction rather than underprediction of $P(d=1|x)$ for small values of x. The mixture models exhibit difficulties that are similar qualitatively but of considerably less importance quantitatively. This behavior is due to the prior distribution of α, in which the standard deviation of $\alpha_1 - \alpha_2$ is 0.63, whereas the population value of $\alpha_1 - \alpha_2$ is over seven times this value. The prior is centered at a symmetric distribution, and so under- and overprediction similar to the conventional probit model results.

Results using the Cauchy DGP are shown in figure 3.4. The difficulty of the conventional probit model in coping with the very thick tails of the Cauchy distribution is obvious. By contrast, both mixture models provide good approximations to the true predictives $P(d=1|x)$ over a very wide range.

Finally, figure 3.5 compares posterior quartiles with DGP values in the case of a logistic DGP. The three models approximate the population value in similar ways, and interquartile ranges are about the same for all three. None of the models matches the thick tails of the logistic, but the discrepancy is not large in comparison with interquartile ranges. The visual similarity of the three models, evident in figure 3.5, is reflected in the closeness of the marginal likelihoods shown in the fifth row of table 3.3.

4 An example: labor force participation of women

To provide a substantive application of the mixture of normals probit model, we use an otherwise standard regression for women's labor force participation, employing data from the PSID. The data pertain to those women observed in 1988, observed since the time they became a household head or spouse, for whom an uninterrupted history of annual hours worked is available, whose parents' educational attainment is available, and for whom spouse income and number of children are known. The sample size is 1,555. From the data, we construct 17 covariates, shown in table 3.4. If a woman reports positive hours of work for 1988, she is a labor force participant; 80 per cent of the women in the sample are labor force participants.

For the purposes of this illustration, independent Gaussian priors were constructed for each of the 17 covariate coefficients. In each case, the prior distribution has mean zero. The standard deviation is chosen by considering a large but reasonable effect of a change in the corresponding covariate on the probability of labor force participation, given that the probability of labor force participation is about one-half. This construction of the informative prior distribution for β is shown in table 3.5, which provides the

Table 3.4. *Covariate definitions (PSID labor force participation)*

1	Black	1 if black; else 0
2	Age (single)	Age if not married; else 0
3	Age (married)	Age if married; else 0
4	Education	Years of schooling
5	Married	1 if married; else 0
6	Kids	1 if children present; else 0
7	#Kids	Number of children present
8	Spouse$	Spouse's income in current (1988) dollars; 0 if no spouse
9	Spouse$0	1 if spouse present with no income; else 0
10	Family$	Household unearned income
11	F-HS	1 if father graduated from high school but not college; else 0
12	F-Coll	1 if father graduated from college; else 0
13	M-HS	1 if mother graduated from high school but not college; else 0
14	M-Coll	1 if mother graduated from college; else 0
15	AFDC$	Monthly AFDC income if woman does not work in current (1988) dollars
16	Food$	Monthly food stamp eligibility if woman does not work in current (1988) dollars
17	WorkExp	Cumulative number of hours worked since becoming a household head

prior standard deviation for each coefficient along with the reasoning about effects on probability of labor force participation that led to the choice.

The prior distribution for the mean vector α of the normal mixture is the same as that used for the artificial data. The full specification of the normal mixture models is based on combinations of four prior distributions for precisions, indicated at the bottom of Table 3.5. Priors A and D were introduced in the experiments with artificial data. Prior B constrains the precision to be less than one, but places much smaller probability on very low precisions than does prior A. Prior C constrains the precision to be greater than one, but places smaller probability on high precisions than does prior D.

We report results for 13 models, shown in table 3.6. Besides the conventional probit models, there are two groups of mixture of normals probit models. The first group uses full mixtures of normals, and the second group uses scale mixtures of normals, thereby imposing symmetry of the shock distribution. The idea is to vary the number of mixtures by using combinations of the prior distributions for precisions shown in table 3.5 and labeling restrictions on precisions to identify the mixtures. In the case of mixtures of two and three normals, some alternative prior distributions are used to gauge the effect of alternative prior distributions for the mixtures on marginal likelihood.

Formal model comparison is straightforward based on the marginal

Table 3.5. *Model specifications (PSID labor force participation)*

Description	Prior standard deviation	Derivation of prior standard deviation
Covariate priors (Gaussian, mean zero)		
1 Black	0.125	$\Delta p = 0.05$ at $p = 0.5$
2 Age (single)	0.00417	$\Delta p = 0.05$ for 55 vs. 25 at $p = 0.5$
3 Age (married)	0.03333	$\Delta p = 0.40$ for 55 vs. 25 at $p = 0.5$
4 Education	0.00417	$\Delta p = 0.10$ for 10 vs. 16 at $p = 0.5$
5 Married	0.125	$\Delta p = 0.05$ at $p = 0.5$
6 Kids	0.250	$\Delta p = 0.10$ at $p = 0.5$
7 #Kids	0.125	$\Delta p = 0.05$ at $p = 0.5$
8 Spouse$	3.57×10^{-6}	$\Delta p = 0.05$ per \$35,000 at $p = 0.5$
9 Spouse$0	0.125	$\Delta p = 0.05$ at $p = 0.5$
10 Family$	3.57×10^{-6}	$\Delta p = 0.05$ per \$35,000 at $p = 0.5$
11 F-HS	0.05	$\Delta p = 0.02$ at $p = 0.5$
12 F-Coll	0.05	$\Delta p = 0.02$ at $p = 0.5$
13 M-HS	0.10	$\Delta p = 0.04$ at $p = 0.5$
14 M-Coll	0.10	$\Delta p = 0.04$ at $p = 0.5$
15 AFDC$	6.25×10^{-4}	$\Delta p = 0.25$ per \$1,000 at $p = 0.5$
16 Food$	6.25×10^{-4}	$\Delta p = 0.25$ per \$1,000 at $p = 0.5$
17 WorkExp	6.25×10^{-5}	$\Delta p = 0.05$ per year (2,000 hours)

Normal mixture means

All means 0, all variances 4, all covariances 3.2

Values of $\underline{s}^2$ and $\underline{\nu}$	*Derivation of* $\underline{s}^2$ and $\underline{\nu}$
Normal mixture precisions: $\underline{s}^2 h \sim \chi^2(\underline{\nu})$	
(A) $\underline{s}^2 = 3.832$, $\underline{\nu} = 0.996$	$P(h \leq 0.01) = P(h > 1) = 0.05$
(B) $\underline{s}^2 = 21.16$, $\underline{\nu} = 12.1$	$P(h \leq 0.25) = P(h > 1) = 0.05$
(C) $\underline{s}^2 = 31.36$, $\underline{\nu} = 45.9$	$P(h \leq 1) = P(h > 2) = 0.05$
(D) $\underline{s}^2 = 1.076$, $\underline{\nu} = 4.85$	$P(h \leq 1) = P(h > 10) = 0.05$

likelihoods shown in table 3.6. The most striking feature of the results is the poor performance of the conventional probit model relative to the mixture of normals probit models. Relative to the conventional probit model, the Bayes factor in favor of the mixture of normals model with the smallest marginal likelihood (the full mixture of two normals employing $h_A \leq 1$) is 200,000. Relative to this latter model, the Bayes factor in favor of the mixture of normals model with the largest marginal likelihood (the scale mixture of four normals) is 445. A second regular feature of the results is that for both the full-mixture and the scale-mixture groups, marginal likelihood increases as the number of mixtures is increased from two to three

Table 3.6. *Summary of prior specifications and marginal likelihoods (PSID labor force participation)*

			Log marginal likelihood	
Model	Beta prior for **p**	Precisions mixed	Approximation	Numerical standard error
Conventional probit	—	—	−566.61	0.012
Full mixture, 2 normals	5.0, 5.0	$h_A \leq 1$	−554.4	0.19
Full mixture, 2 normals	5.0, 5.0	$h_B \leq 1$	−554.2	0.15
Full mixture, 3 normals	3.5, 3.5, 1.0	$h_A \leq 1 \leq h_D$	−550.6	0.34
Full mixture, 3 normals	3.5, 3.5, 1.0	$h_B \leq 1 \leq h_C$	−553.0	0.34
Full mixture, 4 normals	1.5, 2.0, 1.5, 1.0	$h_A \leq h_B \leq 1 \leq h_D$	−549.1	0.19
Full mixture, 5 normals	1.5, 2.0, 3.5, 0.5, 0.5	$h_A \leq h_B \leq 1 \leq h_C \leq h_D$	−551.4	0.22
Scale mixture, 2 normals	5.0, 5.0	$h_A \leq 1$	−553.9	0.33
Scale mixture, 2 normals	5.0, 5.0	$h_B \leq 1$	−553.7	0.12
Scale mixture, 3 normals	3.5, 3.5, 1.0	$h_A \leq 1 \leq h_D$	−551.9	0.39
Scale mixture, 3 normals	3.5, 3.5, 1.0	$h_B \leq 1 \leq h_C$	−552.3	0.12
Scale mixture, 4 normals	1.5, 2.0, 1.5, 1.0	$h_A \leq h_B \leq 1 \leq h_D$	−548.3	0.15
Scale mixture, 5 normals	1.5, 2.0, 3.5, 0.5, 0.5	$h_A \leq h_B \leq 1 \leq h_C \leq h_D$	−548.5	0.19

or four and then decreases slightly for the mixture of five normals. The mixtures of four and five normals provide an extremely rich family for a univariate distribution, with anywhere from 6 (scale mixture of four normals) to 13 (full mixture of five normals) parameters. Nevertheless, these models more than carry their own weight in the sense that this increased uncertainty about the form of the distribution is more than compensated for by the better explanation of the data. A final regular feature of the results is evidence in favor of scale-mixture models as opposed to full-mixture models. However, this evidence is not strong. In some cases, the difference is on the order of numerical approximation error, and in one case, the full-mixture model is preferred.

Posterior moments of the covariate coefficients in the conventional probit model, and in the scale mixture of four normals model, are shown in table 3.7. The coefficients in the two models have different meanings, since the distributions of the shocks in the models are not the same. Nevertheless, the posterior means and standard deviations are quite similar. Seven of the seventeen covariates are important in the sense that their posterior means are on the order of the large but reasonable effects used to choose the prior standard deviations (see table 3.5). These posterior means are also several posterior standard deviations from zero in each case. Probability of labor force participation declines with age for both single and married women. As expected, the effect is greater for married than single women, which corresponds to a change in probability of about 12 percent over 30 years for married women and 35 percent over 30 years for single women if labor force participation probabilities are around 50 percent. Labor force participation probability declines by about 20 percent with the first child and by about 6 percent for each child thereafter (again, beginning from participation probabilities of around 50 percent). Spouse income, Aid to Families with Dependent Children (AFDC), food stamp benefits, and cumulative work experience all have strong effects on the probability of labor force participation. Further details on these effects are presented below.

From the sampled values for the parameters of the distributions, it is straightforward to construct the posterior distribution of the probability density of the shock term ε_t. These densities are shown in figures 3.6 and 3.7 for the scale mixture of four normals (the model with the highest marginal likelihood of those considered) and, for comparison, the full mixture of four normals (in which the Bayes factor relative to the scale mixture is a respectable 0.45). In each figure, the posterior median and interquartile ranges are shown for each ordinate. The leptokurtosis in the scale mixture of four normals is immediately evident in figure 3.6. When the ratio of the third to the first quartile is considered, this figure suggests that the posterior uncertainty in the seven parameters of this distribution is most

Table 3.7. *Covariate coefficient posterior moments (PSID labor force participation)*

		Normal prior	Posterior			
			Conventional probit		Scale mixture of four normals	
	Intercept	$(0, 4^2)$	1.213	(0.183)	1.019	(0.222)
1	Black	$(0, 0.125^2)$	0.0158	(0.0781)	0.037	(0.0708)
2	Age (single)	$(0, 0.00417^2)$	−0.0104	(0.0038)	−0.0099	(0.0038)
3	Age (married)	$(0, 0.03333^2)$	−0.0288	(0.0066)	−0.0274	(0.0066)
4	Education	$(0, 0.00417^2)$	0.0023	(0.0042)	0.0021	(0.0041)
5	Married	$(0, 0.125^2)$	0.189	(0.117)	0.206	(0.117)
6	Kids	$(0, 0.250^2)$	−0.361	(0.135)	−0.383	(0.144)
7	#Kids	$(0, 0.125^2)$	−0.151	(0.045)	−0.129	(0.056)
8	Spouse$	$(0, (3.57 \times 10^{-6})^2)$	-7.29×10^{-6}	(2.29×10^{-6})	-6.89×10^{-6}	(2.27×10^{-6})
9	Spouse$0	$(0, 0.125^2)$	−0.00650	(0.117)	0.00186	(0.116)
10	Family$	$(0, (3.57 \times 10^{-6})^2)$	-1.07×10^{-6}	(2.92×10^{-6})	-0.77×10^{-6}	(2.83×10^{-6})
11	F-HS	$(0, 0.05^2)$	0.0300	(0.0445)	0.0238	(0.0429)
12	F-Coll	$(0, 0.05^2)$	−0.0074	(0.0474)	−0.0180	(0.0473)
13	M-HS	$(0, 0.10^2)$	−0.0223	(0.0675)	−0.0265	(0.0628)
14	M-Coll	$(0, 0.10^2)$	−0.0113	(0.0863)	−0.0102	(0.0855)
15	AFDC$	$(0, (6.25 \times 10^{-4})^2)$	-5.88×10^{-4}	(3.06×10^{-4})	-5.07×10^{-4}	(2.82×10^{-4})
16	Food$	$(0, (6.25 \times 10^{-4})^2)$	-12.18×10^{-4}	(4.39×10^{-4})	-10.77×10^{-4}	(4.26×10^{-4})
17	WorkExp	$(0, (6.25 \times 10^{-5})^2)$	11.80×10^{-5}	(0.83×10^{-5})	12.36×10^{-5}	(2.24×10^{-5})

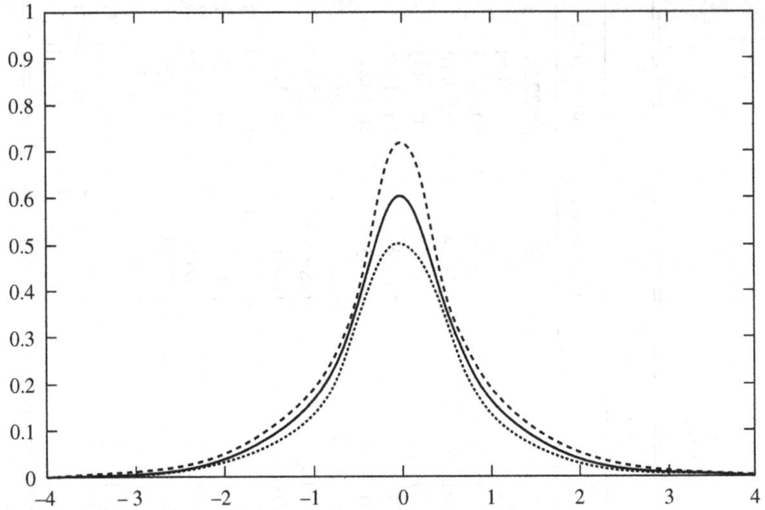

Figure 3.6 Disturbance pdf scale mixture of four normals

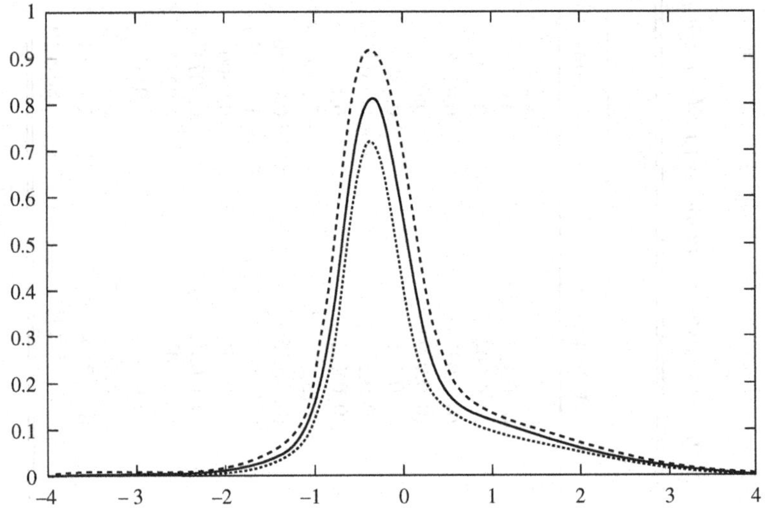

Figure 3.7 Disturbance pdf full mixture of four normals

manifest near the origin and in the tails of the probability density. The full mixture of four normals density, which depends on ten parameters, is shown in figure 3.7. This distribution is strongly negatively skewed, a mode that is near zero but distinctly negative, and a thick positive tail.

Some predictive distributions of interest are shown in table 3.8. Two examples are studied. In each example results are shown for the conventional probit model and for the mixture of normals probit model with the highest marginal likelihood. In the first example, the probability of labor force participation for a 30-year-old woman with two children and no spouse present is examined, as AFDC and food stamp benefit levels (given no labor force participation) are changed from no benefits to the sample average for a woman in this situation in 1988 to the sample maximum. In the conventional probit model, the increase of benefits from zero to the maximum increases the probability of labor force non-participation from 0.042 to 0.174, while in the scale mixture of four normals model, the increase is only from 0.049 to 0.131. Notice that the posterior standard deviation of the labor force participation probabilities is lower in the scale-mixture model than in the conventional probit model in every case: uncertainty about the individual parameters in this model, taken in isolation, does not imply greater uncertainty about the predictive probabilities than in the case of the conventional probit model where there is no uncertainty about the shape of the shock distribution.

In the second example shown in table 3.8, cumulative labor market experience and spouse's income are varied for a married woman aged 30 with two children so as to vary the probability of labor force participation between roughly 0.01 and 0.99. Differences in the posterior means of participation probabilities can be appreciable, reaching 0.078 (about one posterior standard deviation) for a woman with no labor market experience and a spouse earning $75,000 per year. Ratios for participation or non-participation approach two when these probabilities are small. When probabilities of both participation and non-participation are substantial, the posterior standard deviations in the conventional probit model tend to be smaller, whereas when one is small and one is large, there is less uncertainty in the scale mixture of normals model.

A graphical presentation of the second example is given in figures 3.8 and 3.9. Each figure shows posterior 0.25 and 0.75 quantities from the conventional probit model (dotted lines) and the scale mixture of four normals model (dashed lines). Figure 3.8 contrasts the predicted probability of labor market participation as hours of experience are varied. The difference is greatest at around 7,000 hours (3.5 years) of experience, where the mixture models imply a substantially higher probability of participation. The 0.25 quantile of the mixture posterior is about the same as the 0.75 quantile of

Table 3.8. *Effects of some covariates on labor force participation probability*

	Posterior moments of probability			
	Conventional probit		Scale mixture of four normals	
AFDC and food stamp benefits				
Base case: Unmarried, not black, 2 kids, age 30, 12 years education, 6.25 years work experience				
AFDC = \$0, Food stamps = \$0	0.958	(0.015)	0.951	(0.012)
AFDC = \$289, Food stamps = \$197	0.908	(0.019)	0.921	(0.014)
AFDC = \$633, Food stamps = \$344	0.826	(0.047)	0.869	(0.036)
AFDC and Food stamps 0 vs. max	−0.131	(0.052)	−0.083	(0.039)
Some combinations of work experience and spouse's income				
Base case: Married, not black, 2 kids, age 30, 12 years education				
Experience 10 years; income \$25,000	0.992	(0.004)	0.983	(0.006)
Experience 8 years; income \$25,000	0.974	(0.009)	0.969	(0.008)
Experience 6 years; income \$25,000	0.932	(0.019)	0.939	(0.014)
Experience 4 years; income \$25,000	0.846	(0.033)	0.877	(0.027)
Experience 2 years; income \$25,000	0.710	(0.049)	0.744	(0.058)
Experience 0 years; income \$25,000	0.534	(0.061)	0.497	(0.089)
Experience 0 years; income \$50,000	0.463	(0.063)	0.399	(0.089)
Experience 0 years; income \$75,000	0.393	(0.070)	0.315	(0.090)
Experience 0 years; income \$100,000	0.326	(0.079)	0.249	(0.090)
Experience 0 years; income \$150,000	0.215	(0.089)	0.159	(0.083)
Experience 0 years; income \$200,000	0.136	(0.088)	0.106	(0.074)
Experience 0 years; income \$500,000	0.011	(0.042)	0.018	(0.039)

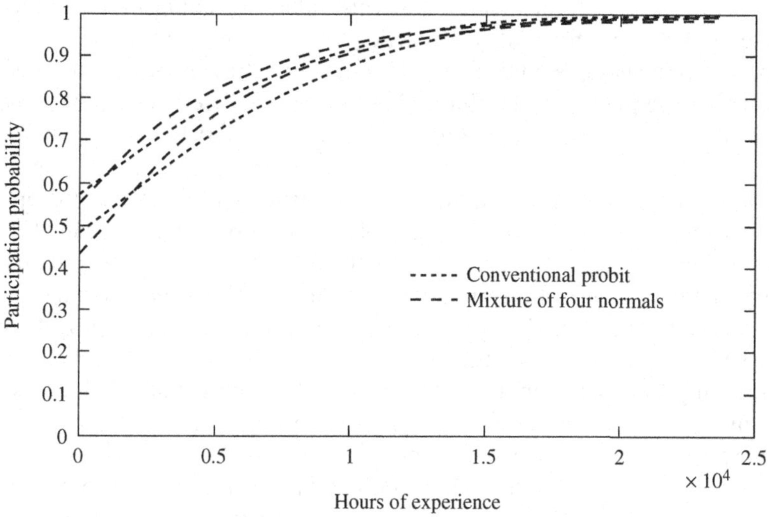

Figure 3.8 Labor force participation probability as a function of experience

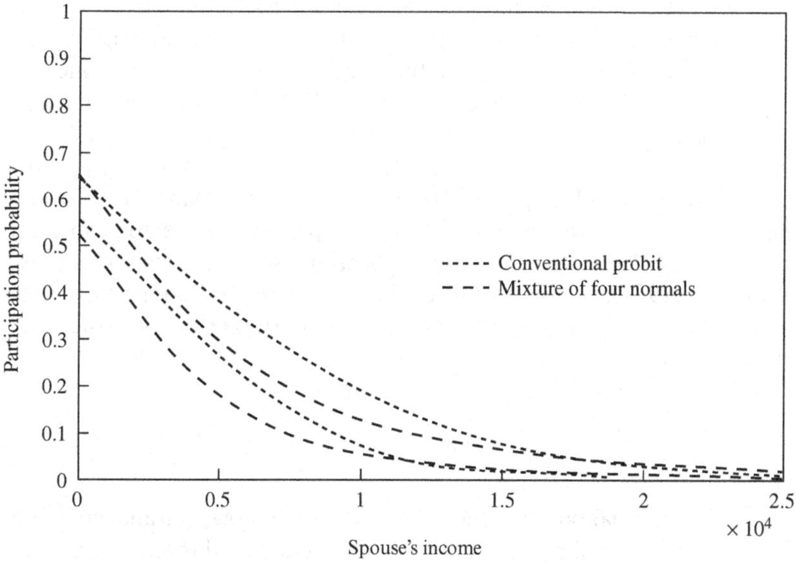

Figure 3.9 Labor force participation probability as a function of spouse's income

the conventional probit posterior at this value. As hours of experience increase, however, probability of participation in the conventional probit model approaches one much faster than in the mixture model. Both effects are the consequence of the thin tails of the normal relative to the scale mixture of four normals. Qualitatively similar characteristics are seen in the comparison for labor market participation probability as a function of spouse income in figure 3.9. As income rises, participation probability drops. Over a long range, the participation probability drops faster in the mixture model, but eventually it is overtaken by the probability in the conventional probit model because of the thinner tails of the shock density in that model.

At least in this example, the mixture of normals probit model provides a marked improvement over the conventional probit model. The data are sufficiently informative about the nature of the distribution of the shock that the most preferred model has four mixtures with six free parameters in the distribution, and the most flexible model – five mixtures with 13 free parameters – is still in the running, with posterior probability about 4.5 percent that of the most preferred model. Moreover, distributions of predictive probabilities of the kind usually studied with this model differ substantially between the conventional probit and mixture models. The mixture models imply a weaker effect of welfare benefit levels and a stronger effect of spouse income on labor force participation than does the conventional probit model. The prior distribution for the coefficient vector was the one displayed in Table 3.5 in all of these models. Subsequent work with this data set (Geweke (1998)) showed that a more diffuse prior distribution for the coefficient vector increases the marginal likelihood in all models. In particular, with a more diffuse prior distribution, posterior means for the coefficient on age, work experience, and food stamp benefits increase in absolute value in all of the models. Another application using this data set (Geweke and Keane (1999)) showed that given the more diffuse prior distribution for the coefficients, the marginal likelihoods for all the models is about the same, and therefore, Bayes factors favor neither the conventional model nor the mixture of normals models strongly over the other.

5 Conclusion

In the conventional probit model, there are no unknown parameters in the distribution of the shock term. We have generalized this specification by adopting mixtures of normals distributions in which the probability density of the shock term is governed by many unknown parameters. We found in a set of experiments with artificial data that our models are very successful at recognizing departures from normality when they are present (that is, Bayes factors strongly favored the mixture models when errors were in fact normal mixtures or Cauchy). Conversely, when errors are in fact normal (or very close to normal), our models recognized that as well. We were pleasantly surprised that samples with about 2,000 observations would be so informative for the distribution of the shock in a linear latent variable model.

Against this background, it is reasonable to contemplate several extensions of this work. This generalization of the mixture of normals model to the multivariate case is straightforward as is its incorporation into Markov Chain Monte Carlo methods for the multinomial probit model that we have described elsewhere (Geweke, Keane, and Runkle (1994, 1997)). In view of the irregular likelihood surface in the dimensions of the variance matrix in this model (Keane (1992)), whether full or scale mixture of models will succeed as generalizations of the multinomial probit model seems to us very much an open question. An alternative extension is to mix distributions other than the normal or to mix the normal and/or several other families. The Student's t family is an obvious candidate, itself a continuous scale mixture of normal distributions to which methods similar to those used here can be applied (Geweke (1993)). Since the research reported in this chapter was completed, these extensions have been developed and are discussed in Geweke and Keane (1999). Finally, we note that the assumption of linearity in the covariates $\mathbf{x}_t$ is as much a convenient assumption in most applications as is normality in the conventional probit model. Relaxing this assumption in favor of the obvious expansion families (for example, Taylor or Laurent series) is straightforward and lends itself well to incorporation of subjective priors in the way we have done here. Clearly, there are interactions between relaxing both linearity and normality; in the limit, one cannot do both. We plan to explore these issues in future work.

References

Albert, J.H. and S. Chib (1993), "Bayesian Analysis of Binary and Polychotomous Response Data," *Journal of the American Statistical Association*, 88: 669–679.

Aldrich, J. and F. Nelson (1984), *Linear Probability, Logit, and Probit Models*, Beverly Hills: Sage Publications.

Cosslett, S.R. (1983), "Distribution-Free Maximum Likelihood Estimator of the Binary Choice Model," *Econometrica*, 51, 765–782.

Gallant, A.R. and D.W. Nychka (1987), "Semi-Nonparametric Maximum Likelihood Estimation," *Econometrica*, 55: 363–390.

Gelfand, A.E. and D.K. Dey (1994), "Bayesian Model Choice: Asymptotics and Exact Calculations," *Journal of the Royal Statistical Society Series B*, 56: 501–514.

Geweke, J. (1991), "Efficient Simulation from the Multivariate Normal and Student-t Distributions Subject to Linear Constraints," in E.M. Keramidas (ed.), *Competing Science and Statistics: Proceedings of the Twenty-Third Symposium on the Interface*, Fairfax: Interface Foundation of North America, Inc., pp. 571–578.

(1993), "Bayesian Treatment of the Independent Student-t Linear Model," *Journal of Applied Econometrics*, 8: S19–S40.

(1997a), "Posterior Simulators in Econometrics," in D. Kreps and K.F. Wallis (eds.), *Advances in Economics and Econometrics: Theory and Applications*, vol. III, Cambridge: Cambridge University Press, pp. 128–165.

(1997b), "Simulation-Based Bayesian Inference for Economic Time Series," in R.S. Mariano, T. Schuermann, and M. Weeks (eds.), *Simulation-Based Inference in Econometrics: Methods and Applications*, Cambridge: Cambridge University Press.

(1998), "Using Simulation Methods for Bayesian Econometric Models: Inference, Development, and Communication," (with discussion and rejoinder), *Econometric Reviews*, forthcoming.

Geweke, J. and M. Keane (1999), "Computationally Intensive Methods for Integration in Econometrics," in J.J. Heckman and E.E. Leamer (eds.), *Handbook of Econometrics*, vol. 5, Amsterdam: North-Holland, forthcoming.

Geweke, J., M. Keane, and D. Runkle (1994), "Alternative Computational Approaches to Inference in the Multinomial Probit Model," *Review of Economics and Statistics*, 76: 609–632.

(1997), "Statistical Inference in the Multinomial Multiperiod Probit Model," *Journal of Econometrics*, 80: 125–166.

Hausman, J. and D. McFadden (1984), "Specification Tests for the Multinomial Logit Model," *Econometrica*, 52: 1219–1240.

Horowitz, J.L. (1992), "A Smoothed Maximum Score Estimator for the Binary Response Model," *Econometrica*, 60: 505–531.

Ichimura, H. (1993), "Semiparametric Least Squares (SLS) and Weighted SLS Estimation of Single-Index Models," *Journal of Econometrics*, 58: 71–120.

Keane, M.P. (1992), "A Note on Identification in the Multinomial Probit Model," *Journal of Business and Economic Statistics*, 10: 193–200.

Klein, R.W. and R.H. Spady (1993), "An Efficient Semiparametric Estimator for Binary Response Models," *Econometrica*, 61: 387–421.

Koop, G. and D.J. Poirier (1993), "Bayesian Analysis of Logit Models Using Natural Conjugate Priors," *Journal of Econometrics*, 56: 323–340.

Lewbel, A. (1997), "Semiparametric Estimation of Location and Other Discrete Choice Moments," *Econometric Theory*, 13: 32–51.

Maddala, G.S. (1983), *Limited Dependent and Qualitative Variables in Econometrics*, Cambridge: Cambridge University Press.

Manski, C.F. (1985), "Semiparametric Analysis of Discrete Response: Asymptotic Properties of the Maximum Score Estimator," *Journal of Econometrics*, 27: 313–333.

Powell, J.L., J.H. Stock, and T.M. Stoker (1989), "Semiparametric Estimation of Index Coefficients," *Econometrica*, 57: 1403–1430.

Roberts, G.O. and A.F.M. Smith (1994), "Simple Conditions for the Convergence of the Gibbs Sampler and Metropolis-Hastings Algorithms," *Stochastic Processes and Their Applications*, 49: 207–216.

Tierney, L. (1994), "Markov Chains for Exploring Posterior Distributions" (with discussion and rejoinder), *Annals of Statistics*, 22: 1701–1762.

Zellner, A. and P.E. Rossi (1984), "Bayesian Analysis of Dichotomous Quantal Response Models," *Journal of Econometrics*, 25, 365–393.

4 Estimation of dynamic limited-dependent rational expectations models

LUNG-FEI LEE

1 Introduction

The problem of rational expectations (RE) in limited dependent variable (LDV) models was first considered in Chanda and Maddala (1983). Maddala (1993) provided more detailed discussions on expectation formation under different assumptions used by agents as well as different estimation methods. The specification and estimation of such models have further been investigated in Maddala (1990, 1993), Pesaran (1990), Donald and Maddala (1992), Lee (1994), Pesaran and Ruge-Murcia (1996, 1998), and Pesaran and Samiei (1995). Under some general conditions, the RE solution exists and is unique (Pesaran and Samiei (1992a), Donald and Maddala (1992), Lee (1994), and Pesaran and Ruge-Murcia (1996)). The usefulness of such models in empirical studies can be found in Shonkwiler and Maddala (1985) and Holt and Johnson (1989) for agricultural commodities markets with price supports and Pesaran and Samiei (1992a, 1992b) and Edin and Vredin (1993) for models with exchange rate determination under a target zone.

For the estimation of limited-dependent rational expectations (LDRE) models, Pesaran and Samiei (1992a) have suggested the maximum likelihood (ML) method. Estimated models have, so far, assumed serially independent disturbances. Even though dynamics can easily be introduced through the inclusion of observed lagged dependent variables without complication (Pesaran and Samiei (1992b)), neither dynamic structures involving lagged latent dependent variables nor serially correlated disturbances are allowed. As these models are used for time series data, it is of interest to consider the model estimates with serial correlation or latent dynamic structures in addition to the inclusion of observed lagged dependent variables. In this article, we investigate and propose methods for the

Financial support from the RGC of Hong Kong under grant no. HKUST595/96H for my research is gratefully acknowledged. I would like to thank Professors Cheng Hsiao, Kajal Lahiri, G.S. Maddala, and M. Hashem Pesaran for valuable comments.

estimation of dynamic LDV models under RE. With serial correlation, likelihood functions will involve multiple integrals with large dimensions depending on sample size and the number of censored observations over time. Equations characterizing RE solutions will involve similar multivariate probabilities as RE involves conditional probabilities conditional on past information sets. Simulation estimation may be feasible with simulation estimation methodologies.

Various simulation estimation methods and simulation procedures for drawing random variables have been proposed in statistics and econometrics literature. The simulated maximum likelihood method (SML) with a simulated likelihood (SL) has been proposed in Lerman and Manski (1981). Methods of simulated moments and simulated scores have been introduced in McFadden (1989) and Hajivassiliou and McFadden (1990). Simulated pseudo-maximum likelihood methods are proposed in Gourieroux and Montfort (1993). The performance of simulation methods depends on simulators for relevant functions involving integrals. Various simulators have been proposed for multinomial probabilities of discrete choice models. The Geweke–Hajivassiliou–Keane (GHK) simulator provides an adequate approximation (see the evidence in Hajivassiliou, McFadden, and Ruud (1996)). Hendry and Richard (1992) suggested simulation techniques for evaluating likelihood functions of dynamic latent variables models based on sequential factorizations of joint densities of observable and latent variables.

This article considers simulation estimation of dynamic LDRE models. For the estimation of LDV models, the ML method is desirable (Tobin (1958)). Other methods based moments are rather inefficient (Amemiya (1973), Heckman (1976), and Warner (1976)). The SL estimation of LDV models without RE has been investigated in Lee (1996). The simulation procedure is based on a recursive formulation of the GHK simulator of Geweke (1991), Borsch-Supan and Hajivassiliou (1990), and Keane (1994), and sequential factorizations of joint densities for dynamic latent variables models in Hendry and Richard (1992). Monte Carlo results in Lee (1996) provide evidence of good performance of the SML approach. Models with RE introduce additional complications as the RE solution at each period is an explanatory variable in a regression equation. The RE solution needs to be derived from its characterization equation at each period before a SL can be formulated. With serial correlation, the characterization equation is analytically intractable but needs to be simulated. We consider a procedure that incorporates the simulation of RE solutions. It is important that a simulated rational expectations (SRE) solution will exist and is unique under simulation.

We address some important issues related to the simulation of conditional expectations and the likelihood function. In the time series context, as a SL involves products of conditional densities and probabilities, its computation may suffer from machine imprecision and numerical underflow. In Lee (1996), a transformation of the SL function into a formulation involving the summation of terms over time overcomes the computational difficulty. In the LDRE model, the simulation of conditional expectations raises an additional but related computational issue. To overcome this additional difficulty, a recursive weighing scheme is proposed. Likelihood simulation is a by-product of the recursive weighing algorithm. Autoregressive dynamic models may possess a renewal property that allows variance-reduction techniques to be applied to likelihood simulation and RE solution simulation. We formulate our simulation procedure via the recursive weighing algorithm to incorporate such variance-reduction techniques. Monte Carlo experiments are provided to investigate these issues and our proposed simulation approaches.

The chapter is organized as follows. In section 2, we discuss dynamic structure and serial correlation problems in LDV models under RE. Section 3 investigates the existence and uniqueness of RE solutions under simulation. Section 4 provides a SL algorithm that is applicable to general dynamic LDRE models. We discuss the potential numerical underflow issue in simulation and suggest a recursive weighting scheme and a likelihood transformation to overcome the numerical difficulty. Variance reduction techniques in RE solutions and likelihood simulations are introduced in section 5 for models with a renewal property. Monte Carlo results are provided in section 6. Final conclusions are drawn in section 7.

2 Serial correlation and dynamics in LDV models under RE

2.1 *One-limit and two-limit LDRE models*

LDVs were introduced in econometrics in Tobin (1958) and Amemiya (1973). The problem of RE in LDV models was first considered in Chanda and Maddala (1983). Consider the one-limit model with expectations. Let

$$y_t^* = \gamma y_t^e + x_t \beta + u_t \tag{1}$$

be the underlying latent equation before censoring. The x_t is a vector consisting of strictly exogenous variables and predetermined observed variables. The observed dependent variable (for example, market price for a price support model) is

$$y_t = \max\{y_t^*, p_{tl}\} \tag{2}$$

where p_{tl} is the lower bound (support price). Let $\mathcal{T}_{t-1}$ be the information set available at time $t-1$ when the expectation y_t^e of y_t is formed. The agent's expectation is rational in that the expected y_t given past information is an unbiased predictor of the actual y_t, i.e.

$$y_t^e = E(y_t | \mathcal{T}_{t-1}) \tag{3}$$

The bound p_{tl} is fully credible and is in the agent's information set $\mathcal{T}_{t-1}$. To be specific, $\mathcal{T}_{t-1}$ is assumed to be generated by observed y_{t-1} and by all its past lagged values (also by all corresponding strictly exogenous variables and bounds). The agent at time $t-1$ does not know whether y_t is above or below p_{tl}. In the general time series setting, the disturbance u_t can be serially correlated. In addition to y_t^e, some components of x_t may not be perfectly predictable and, in that case, the agent is assumed to form the expectation x_t^e of x_t at $t-1$. Thus $x_t = x_t^e + v_t$ where v_t are i.i.d. and are independent of all *u*s.

Let $w_t = u_t + v_t\beta$ and let $F_t(w_t)$ and $f_t(w_t)$ denote, respectively, the conditional distribution and conditional density w_t conditional on $\mathcal{T}_{t-1}$, i.e., conditional on $\bar{y}_{t-1}$ and past events of censoring at t, where $\bar{y}_t = (y_t, y_{t-1}, \ldots, y_1)$ (and exogenous variables x, x^e and bounds which are suppressed in all expressions on expectations, densities, and probabilities through the text for simplicity). Denote $C_{tl}(q) = p_{tl} - \gamma q - x_t^e\beta$. For the one-limit model in (1)–(2), the RE y_t^e can be characterized as a solution to the following equation (Lee (1994))

$$\begin{aligned} y_t^e = p_{tl}F_t(C_{tl}(y_t^e)) + \{\gamma y_t^e + x_t^e\beta + \\ E(w_t | \bar{y}_{t-1}, w_t > C_{tl}(y_t^e))\}[1 - F_t(C_{tl}(y_t^e))]. \end{aligned} \tag{4}$$

In Lee (1994), under regularity conditions that the absolute first conditional moment $E(|w_t||\bar{y}_{t-1})$ of w_t exists and the conditional distribution $F_t(w_t)$ of w_t is absolutely continuous with an everywhere positive density $f_t(w_t)$, it was shown that the RE solution of (4) exists and is unique for $\gamma < 1$. For $\gamma = 1$, it is unique if the solution exists. For $\gamma > 1$, there are either multiple solutions or no solution. The proof of this result is general in that serially correlated disturbances are allowed and are applicable to any univariate or multivariate distribution. In Pesaran and Samiei (1992a) and Donald and Maddala (1992), they considered only serially uncorrelated cases with normal distribution for $F_t(w_t)$. With serial correlation in u_t, the implied conditional distribution $F_t(w_t)$ will be quite complicated and nonnormal even when $\bar{u}_t = (u_t, u_{t-1}, \ldots, u_1)$ is jointly normal. This is so because the observed $\bar{y}_t$ involves continuous and discrete components. Serial correlation introduces complication in the computation of $F_t(w_t)$ and in the numerical methods for solving y_t^e from (4). The value of y_t^e is essentially needed in any estimation method for the model.

LDV models with two limits also have interesting empirical applications (Pesaran and Samiei (1992a)). For the two-limit model under RE, the existence and uniqueness of RE are even more elementary. A two-limit model is for the case where the dependent variable is bounded from above and below, say, respectively, by p_{tu} and p_{tl}, where $p_{tu} > p_{tl}$. The observed dependent variable y_t at t is

$$y_t = \min\{p_{tu}, \max\{y_t^*, p_{tl}\}\} \tag{5}$$

where y_t^* is in (1). For the two-limit model, in addition to $C_{tl}(q)$, define a function corresponding to the upper bound $C_{tu}(q) = p_{tu} - \gamma q - x_t^e\beta$. The RE solution y_t^e of the two-limit model is characterized by the following equation (Lee (1994, proposition 2)):

$$\begin{aligned} y_t^e = {} & p_{tl}F_t(C_{tl}(y_t^e)) + p_{tu}[1 - F_t(C_{tu}(y_t^e))] + \\ & \{\gamma y_t^e + x_t^e\beta + E(w_t | \bar{y}_{t-1}, C_{tl}(y_t^e) < w_t < C_{tu}(y_t^e))\}[F_t(C_{tu}(y_t^e)) - \\ & F_t(C_{tl}(y_t^e))]. \end{aligned} \tag{6}$$

For the two-limit model, the RE solution y_t^e from (6) exists for any value of γ. The solution is unique if $\gamma \leq 1$ (Lee (1994, proposition 3)).

These models can be generalized to incorporate the dynamic structure, for example

$$y_t^* = \gamma y_t^e + \sum_{j=1}^{\infty} y_{t-j}^* \alpha_j + \sum_{k=1}^{\infty} y_{t-k}\delta_k + x_t\beta + u_t. \tag{7}$$

Under a stationarity assumption, the reduced form y_t^* will be a linear function of y_t^e with additional lagged values of y_{t-s}^e and y_{t-s} for $s \geq 1$ as explanatory variables. The dynamic generalization does not invalidate the existence and uniqueness of the RE solutions in (4) and (6) with proper modifications of the explanatory variables. Subsequent analysis and proposed estimation methods can also be applied to such dynamic models.

2.2 *Likelihood functions*

With serial correlation, the likelihood functions of the LDRE models will involve multi-dimensional integrals with a dimension depending on the number of observed *y*s at their bounds. Given sample observations of size T, suppose observed dependent variables of y at $t_1, t_2, \ldots, t_m$ are the bound (i.e., censored), and the remaining observed dependent variables are not censored. Let I_t be an indicator of censoring or non-censoring at t. Denote $\bar{I}_t = (I_t, \ldots, I_1)$. Let the joint density of observed and censored latent dependent variables for this model be $f(\bar{y}_T, \bar{I}_T, y_{t1}^*, \ldots, y_{tm}^*)$, where unknown parameters are suppressed for simplicity. The likelihood function for the one-limit model is (Lee and Maddala (1985)):

$$L_1(\bar{y}_T, \bar{I}_T) = \int_{-\infty}^{p_{t_m l}} \cdots \int_{-\infty}^{p_{t_1 l}} f(\bar{y}_T, \bar{I}_T, y_{t1}^*, \ldots, y_{tm}^*) d\bar{y}_T^* \tag{8}$$

where $\bar{y}_t^*$ denotes the vector of all censored y^*s preceding up to period t.

For the two-limit model, given a sample of size T, suppose that observed dependent variables attain lower bounds at $t_1, \ldots, t_m$ and upper bounds $s_1, \ldots, s_k$, then the likelihood function will be

$$L_2(\bar{y}_T, \bar{I}_T) = \int_{p_{s_k u}}^{\infty} \cdots \int_{p_{s_1 u}}^{\infty} \int_{-\infty}^{p_{t_m l}} \cdots \int_{-\infty}^{p_{t_1 l}} f(\bar{y}_T, \bar{I}_T, y^*_{s1}, \ldots, y^*_{sk}, y^*_{t1}, \ldots, y^*_{tm}) d\bar{y}^*_T. \quad (9)$$

2.3 Serial correlation and inconsistent estimation

In a Tobit regression model (without dynamics), it is known that the Tobit ML estimate, which ignores serial correlation in disturbance, is still consistent (Robinson (1982)). This is so because the first two moments of the marginal distribution have been correctly used in estimating equations. For the LDRE model, there are more problematic issues when serial correlation in disturbance is ignored. When serial correlation in a LDRE model is ignored, an econometrician will solve the RE y_t^e as $E(y_t)$, while the agent's RE is $E(y_t | \bar{y}_{t-1})$. The econometrician would use the specification

$$y_t^* = \gamma E(y_t) + x_t \beta + u_t^* \quad (10)$$

instead of the correct specification $y_t^* = \gamma E(y_t | \bar{y}_{t-1}) + x_t \beta + u_t$ in (1) for the estimation. By comparing (10) with (1), $u_t^* = u_t + \gamma[E(y_t | \bar{y}_{t-1}) - E(y_t)]$. The error u_t^* is composed of the original disturbance u_t and the additional error $E(y_t | \bar{y}_{t-1}) - E(y_t)$ due to the misspecification of the RE solution. If the econometrician did not realize the existence of the serial correlation in the disturbance, u_t^* would be regarded as the structural disturbance u_t in the model. In such a circumstance, if u_t were normally distributed, the distribution of u_t^* would be assumed to be normal. However, such a distributional assumption would be a misspecification even if u_t were truly normally distributed. This is so because the additional error due to misspecification of the RE solution need not be normally distributed. Indeed, the exact distribution will be rather too complicated to be determined. With misspecification in distribution, the likelihood estimator, by ignoring serial correlation, might be inconsistent.

3 RE solution and simulation

The existence of an RE solution is fundamental in RE models. For the one-limit model, the RE solution needs to be solved from (4) and that of the two-limit model from (6). As the conditional probabilities and conditional expectations involved at each t are multi-dimensional, they are analytically intractable. In this section, we suggest simulation methods which can circumvent these problems. With proper simulators for the equations (4) and (6), the RE solutions can then be derived.

Consider the one-limit model. The $F_t(w_t)$ is the conditional distribution function of w_t conditional on $\bar{y}_{t-1}$. It follows that $F_t(a) = \int_{-\infty}^{a} f(w_t|\bar{y}_{t-1})dw_t$. The formulation of the conditional distribution function looks simple but is not, because the conditional density $f(w_t|\bar{y}_{t-1})$ can be quite complicated due to censoring. For the one-limit model, let $I_{1t} = 1$ if $y_t^* \leq p_{tl}$ and 0 otherwise. It follows that

$$F_t(a) = \int_{-\infty}^{a}\int_{-\infty}^{\infty}\cdots\int_{-\infty}^{\infty} f(w_t, \bar{y}_{t-1}, \bar{I}_{t-1}, \bar{y}^*_{t-1})d\bar{y}^*_{t-1}dw_t \Big/ \int_{-\infty}^{\infty}\cdots\int_{-\infty}^{\infty} f(\bar{y}_{t-1}, \bar{I}_{t-1}, \bar{y}^*_{t-1})d\bar{y}^*_{t-1} \tag{11}$$

$$= \frac{\int_{-\infty}^{\infty}\cdots\int_{-\infty}^{\infty}[\int_{-\infty}^{a} f(w_t|\bar{y}_{t-1}, \bar{I}_{t-1}, \bar{y}^*_{t-1})dw_t] f(\bar{y}_{t-1}, \bar{I}_{t-1}, \bar{y}^*_{t-1})d\bar{y}^*_{t-1}}{\int_{-\infty}^{\infty}\cdots\int_{-\infty}^{\infty} f(\bar{y}_{t-1}, \bar{I}_{t-1}, \bar{y}^*_{t-1})d\bar{y}^*_{t-1}}$$

where $\bar{I}_t = (I_t, \ldots, I_1)$. With general latent dynamic or serial correlation structures, at each t, the dimension of the integral in the denominator can be as large as the number of censored periods preceding the period t. The dimension of the integral in the numerator is one larger. Effective simulation methods are needed to estimate these probabilities. The $F_t(w)$ can be simulated by simulating both the numerator and denominator. The mixed continuous and discrete density $f(\bar{y}_t, \bar{I}_t, \bar{y}_t^*)$ can be factored into a product of univariate conditional densities and probabilities. To be specific, suppose that censoring occurs at $t_1 < t_2 < \ldots < t_m$ in a sample of size T. The mixed joint density can be factorized into

$$f(\bar{y}_T, \bar{I}_T, \bar{y}_T^*) = \prod_{s \notin \{t_1, t_2, \ldots, t_m\}} f(y_s|\bar{y}_{s-1}, \bar{I}_{s-1}, \bar{y}^*_{s-1}).$$

$$\prod_{s \in \{t_1, t_2, \ldots, t_m\}} P(I_{1s} = 1|\bar{y}_{s-1}, \bar{I}_{s-1}, \bar{y}^*_{s-1})$$

$$\prod_{s \in \{t_1, t_2, \ldots, t_m\}} f(y_s^*|I_{1s} = 1, \bar{y}_{s-1}, \bar{I}_{s-1}, \bar{y}^*_{s-1}). \tag{12}$$

This decomposition suggests a simulation procedure.The product of densities

$$\prod_{s \in \{t_1, t_2, \ldots, t_m\}} f(y_s^*|I_{1s} = 1, \bar{y}_{s-1}, \bar{I}_{s-1}, \bar{y}^*_{s-1}) \tag{13}$$

can be used for drawing random variables. Each of the density components in (13) is a univariate truncated conditional density. Random variables

$y^*_{t_1},\ldots,y^*_{t_m}$ can be recursively drawn from these univariate truncated densities. With a finite number of independent simulation runs (paths), R, and simulated sample paths $y^{*(r)}_{t_1},\ldots,y^{*(r)}_{t_m}$, the denominator in (11) can be simulated by the unbiased simulator

$$\frac{1}{R}\sum_{r=1}^{R}\prod_{s=1}^{t-1} f(y_s|\bar{y}_{s-1},\bar{I}_{s-1},\bar{y}^{*(r)}_{s-1})^{1-I_{1s}}P(I_{1s}=1|\bar{y}_{s-1},\bar{I}_{s-1},\bar{y}^{*(r)}_{s-1})^{I_{1s}} \tag{14}$$

and the numerator in (11) can be simulated by

$$\frac{1}{R}\sum_{r=1}^{R}\int_{-\infty}^{a} f(w_t|\bar{y}_{t-1},\bar{I}_{t-1},\bar{y}^{*(r)}_{t-1})dw_t$$

$$\prod_{s=1}^{t-1} f(y_s|\bar{y}_{s-1},\bar{I}_{s-1},\bar{y}^{*(r)}_{s-1})^{1-I_{1s}}P(I_{1s}=1|\bar{y}_{s-1},\bar{I}_{s-1},\bar{y}^{*(r)}_{s-1})^{I_{1s}} \tag{15}$$

Therefore, $F_t(a)$ in (11) can be simulated by

$$\hat{F}_{t,R}(a)=\sum_{r=1}^{R}\left[\int_{-\infty}^{a} f(w_t|\bar{y}_{t-1},\bar{I}_{t-1},\bar{y}^{*(r)}_{t-1})dw_t\right]\omega_{1,t-1}(\bar{y}^{*(r)}_{t-2}) \tag{16}$$

where

$$\omega_{1,t-1}(\bar{y}^{*(r)}_{t-2})=\frac{\prod_{s=1}^{t-1} f(y_s|\bar{y}_{s-1},\bar{I}_{s-1},\bar{y}^{*(r)}_{s-1})^{1-I_{1s}}P(I_{1s}=1|\bar{y}_{s-1},\bar{I}_{s-1},\bar{y}^{*(r)}_{s-1})^{I_{1s}}}{\sum_{r=1}^{R}\prod_{s=1}^{t-1} f(y_s|\bar{y}_{s-1},\bar{I}_{s-1},\bar{y}^{*(r)}_{s-1})^{1-I_{1s}}P(I_{1s}=1|\bar{y}_{s-1},\bar{I}_{s-1},\bar{y}^{*(r)}_{s-1})^{I_{1s}}} \tag{17}$$

can be regarded as a weight for the rth simulation path. The term related to a conditional expectation in (4) can similarly be simulated. Since

$$E(w_t|\bar{y}_{t-1},w_t>a)[1-F_t(a)]$$

$$=\int_{a}^{\infty} w_t f(w_t|\bar{y}_{t-1},\bar{I}_{t-1})dw_t$$

$$=\int_{-\infty}^{\infty}\left[\int_{a}^{\infty} w_t f(w_t|\bar{y}_{t-1},\bar{I}_{t-1},\bar{y}^*_{t-1})dw_t\right] f(\bar{y}_{t-1},\bar{I}_{t-1},\bar{y}^*_{t-1})d\bar{y}^*_{t-1}\Big/\int_{-\infty}^{\infty}$$

$$f(\bar{y}_{t-1},\bar{I}_{t-1},\bar{y}^*_{t-1})d\bar{y}^*_{t-1},$$

this term can be simulated by

$$\hat{B}^{(1)}_{t,R}(a)=\sum_{r=1}^{R}\left[\int_{a}^{\infty} w_t f(w_t|\bar{y}_{t-1},\bar{I}_{t-1},\bar{y}^*_{t-1})dw_t\right]\omega_{1,t-1}(\bar{y}^{*(r)}_{t-2}). \tag{18}$$

With simulators in (16) and (18), the RE characterization equation in (4) can be simulated as

$$\hat{y}^e_{t,R} = p_{tl}\hat{F}_{t,R}(C_{tl}(\hat{y}^e_{t,R})) + (\gamma\hat{y}^e_{t,R} + x^e_t\beta)[1 - \hat{F}_{t,R}(C_{tl}(\hat{y}^e_{t,R}))] + \hat{B}^{(1)}_{t,R}(C_{tl}(\hat{y}^e_{t,R})). \tag{19}$$

The solution $\hat{y}^e_{t,R}$ of (19) is a simulator for y^e_t. As R tends to infinity, $\hat{y}^e_{t,R}$ will converge in probability to y^e_t.

For the two-limit model, the simulation should be modified to take into account the upper bound censoring in addition to the lower bound censoring. For this model, $I_t = (I_{1t}, I_{2t}, I_{3t})$ where each of the three components of I_t is a dichotomous indicator such that $I_{1t} = 1$ if $y^*_t \leq p_{tl}$, $I_{2t} = 1$ if $y^*_t \geq p_{tu}$, and $I_{3t} = 1$ if $p_{tl} < y^*_t < p_{tu}$. The $F_t(a)$ in (11) can be simulated by

$$\hat{F}_{t,R}(a) = \sum_{r=1}^{R}\left[\int_{-\infty}^{a} f(w_t|\bar{y}_{t-1}, \bar{I}_{t-1}, \bar{y}^{*(r)}_{t-1})dw_t\right]\omega_{2,t-1}(\bar{y}^{*(r)}_{t-2}) \tag{20}$$

where

$$\omega_{2,t-1}(\bar{y}^{*(r)}_{t-2}) = \tag{21}$$

$$\frac{\prod_{s=1}^{t-1} P(I_{1s}=1|\bar{y}_{s-1}, \bar{I}_{s-1}, \bar{y}^{*(r)}_{s-1})^{I_{1s}} P(I_{2s}=1|\bar{y}_{s-1}, \bar{I}_{s-1}, \bar{y}^{*(r)}_{s-1})^{I_{2s}} f(y_s|\bar{y}_{s-1}, \bar{I}_{s-1}, \bar{y}^{*(r)}_{s-1})^{I_{3s}}}{\sum_{r=1}^{R}\prod_{s=1}^{t-1} P(I_{1s}=1|\bar{y}_{s-1}, \bar{I}_{s-1}, \bar{y}^{*(r)}_{s-1})^{I_{1s}} P(I_{2s}=1|\bar{y}_{s-1}, \bar{I}_{s-1}, \bar{y}^{*(r)}_{s-1})^{I_{2s}} f(y_s|\bar{y}_{s-1}, \bar{I}_{s-1}, \bar{y}^{*(r)}_{s-1})^{I_{3s}}}$$

is the rth weight. The random draw $y^{*(r)}_t$ in $\bar{y}^{*(r)}_t$ is from $f(y^*_t|I_{1t} = 1, \bar{y}_{t-1}, \bar{I}_{t-1}, \bar{y}^*_{t-1})$ when $I_{1t} = 1$, and from $f(y^*_t|I_{2t} = 1, \bar{y}_{t-1}, \bar{I}_{t-1}, \bar{y}^*_{t-1})$ if $I_{2t} = 1$. The $E(w_t|\bar{y}_{t-1}, a_1 < w_t < a_2)\}[F_t(a_2) - F_t(a_1)]$ in (6) can be simulated by

$$\hat{B}^{(2)}_{t,R}(a_1, a_2) = \sum_{r=1}^{R}\left[\int_{a_1}^{a_2} w_t f(w_t|\bar{y}_{t-1}, \bar{I}_{t-1}, \bar{y}^{*(r)}_{t-1})dw_t\right]\omega_{2,t-1}(\bar{y}^{*(r)}_{t-2}). \tag{22}$$

With simulators in (21) and (22), the RE characterization equation in (6) can be simulated as

$$\begin{aligned}\hat{y}^e_{t,R} = {} & p_{tl}\hat{F}_{t,R}(C_{tl}(\hat{y}^e_{t,R})) + p_{tu}[1 - \hat{F}_{t,R}(C_{tu}(\hat{y}^e_{t,R}))] + \\ & (\gamma\hat{y}^e_{t,R} + x^e_t\beta)[\hat{F}_{t,R}(C_{tu}(\hat{y}^e_{t,R})) - \hat{F}_{t,R}(C_{tl}(\hat{y}^e_{t,R}))] + \\ & \hat{B}^{(2)}_{t,R}(C_{tl}(\hat{y}^e_{t,R}), C_{tu}(\hat{y}^e_{t,R})).\end{aligned} \tag{23}$$

With simulation, the existence and uniqueness of the SRE solution $\hat{y}^e_{t,R}$ is essential for estimation. With the above simulation approach, without regard for the number of simulation draws, the simulated characterization equation for each of the models possesses a similar monotonicity property as the corresponding original characterization equation. For the one-limit model, the SRE solution exists and is unique when $\gamma < 1$. As for the two-limit model, the SRE solution exists and is unique when $\gamma \leq 1$. The proofs can be found in the appendix. The success of finding an SRE numerically is also crucial in any estimation method as it is an explanatory variable needed to formulate the dynamic equation and hence any estimating function. Numerical methods of root finding can be effective if a root is bracketed in an interval (Press *et al.* (1992)). The characterizations of the SRE solution in (19) and (23) have the desirable bracketing property for root finding.

4 Likelihood simulation and recursion

Our proposed likelihood simulation method happens to be a by-product of the RE simulation. For the one-limit model, with a sample $(\bar{y}_T, \bar{I}_T)$ of size T, the mixed continuous and discrete joint density of the sample is $f(\bar{y}_T, \bar{I}_T) = \int f(\bar{y}_T, \bar{I}_T, \bar{y}_T^*) d\bar{y}_T^*$, which can be simulated as

$$\hat{L}_{1,R}(\theta) = \frac{1}{R}\sum_{r=1}^{R}\prod_{s=1}^{T} f(y_s \mid \bar{y}_{s-1}, \bar{I}_{s-1}, \bar{y}_{s-1}^{*(r)})^{1-I_{1s}} P(I_{1s} = 1 \mid \bar{y}_{s-1}, \bar{I}_{s-1}, \bar{y}_{s-1}^{*(r)})^{I_{1s}} \tag{24}$$

from (14). For the two-limit model, the likelihood function can be simulated as

$$\hat{L}_{2,R}(\theta) = \frac{1}{R}\sum_{r=1}^{R}\prod_{s=1}^{T} P(I_{1s} = 1 \mid \bar{y}_{s-1}, \bar{I}_{s-1}, \bar{y}_{s-1}^{*(r)})^{I_{1s}} P(I_{2s} = 1 \mid \bar{y}_{s-1}, \bar{I}_{s-1}, \bar{y}_{s-1}^{*(r)})^{I_{2s}} f(y_s \mid \bar{y}_{s-1}, \bar{I}_{s-1}, \bar{y}_{s-1}^{*(r)})^{I_{3s}} \tag{25}$$

This SL approach can be justified as an importance-sampling approach for likelihood simulation. The product of truncated densities for random draws provides practical and desirable approximations to the ideal importance-sampling density (Lee (1996)). The SL functions in (24) and (25) are general in that they can be applied to dynamic LDRE models with any order of lagged dependent variables or serial correlation. As its derivation does not depend on any specific parametric distribution, it is applicable to models with normal or non-normal disturbances.

While this simulation approach is general, there are some issues that should be addressed. The first issue is the possibility of numerical underflow in the computation of the SLs in (24) or (25) with long time series data. There are concerns about the computation of the SL as numerical underflow can occur. The SL is an average of products of conditional densities and probabilities. As values of conditional densities and probabilities can be numerically small, when T becomes larger, the value of products will become smaller. With large T, it is quite likely that values of products will be smaller than the numerical precision of computing. This same issue raises concern about the ML estimation of random effect probit panel data models in Borjas and Sueyoshi (1994). For the random effect probit panel model, the difficulty occurs because a single integral of the random component is present in the Gaussian quadrature evaluation of the likelihood function. In Lee (1996), a stable formulation of SL based on a transformation is suggested. For the LDRE model, this numerical issue is also relevant for the simulation of the RE solution. The simulators for conditional probabilities and expectations in (16), (18), (20), and (22) depend on the computation of weights in (17) and (21). In the following paragraph, we suggest a recursive scheme for the computation of weights in (17) and (21). The stable SL formulation can be regarded as a by-product of the recursive weighting scheme.

Consider the simulation of weights in (17) of the one-limit model. Define $\omega_{10}(\bar{y}_{-1}^{*(r)}) = 1/R$ for $r = 1,\ldots,R$, to start the recursion. From its definition in (17), the weight at t can be rewritten as

$$\omega_{1t}(\bar{y}_{t-1}^{*(r)}) = \frac{f(y_t|\bar{y}_{t-1},\bar{I}_{t-1},\bar{y}_{t-1}^{*(r)})^{1-I_{1t}}P(I_{1t}=1|\bar{y}_{t-1},\bar{I}_{t-1},\bar{y}_{t-1}^{*(r)})^{I_{1t}}\omega_{1,t-1}(\bar{y}_{t-2}^{*(r)})}{\sum_{r=1}^{R} f(y_t|\bar{y}_{t-1},\bar{I}_{t-1},\bar{y}_{t-1}^{*(r)})^{1-I_{1t}}P(I_{1t}=1|\bar{y}_{t-1},\bar{I}_{t-1},\bar{y}_{t-1}^{*(r)})^{I_{1t}}\omega_{1,t-1}(\bar{y}_{t-2}^{*(r)})}. \tag{26}$$

The computation of weights can be recursively based on (26). Since the sum of all the weights for $r = 1,\ldots,R$, is a unity, individual weights should not be all very small. Possibly numerical underflow has been effectively eliminated by the normalization of weights in the recursive weighting scheme. Similarly, the computation of weights in (21) of the two-limit model can be recursive as

$$\omega_{2,t}(\bar{y}_{t-1}^{*(r)}) = \frac{P(I_{1t}=1|\bar{y}_{t-1},\bar{I}_{t-1},\bar{y}_{t-1}^{*(r)})^{I_{1t}}P(I_{2t}=1|\bar{y}_{t-1},\bar{I}_{t-1},\bar{y}_{t-1}^{*(r)})^{I_{2t}}f(y_t|\bar{y}_{t-1},\bar{I}_{t-1},\bar{y}_{t-1}^{*(r)})^{I_{3t}}\omega_{2,t-1}(\bar{y}_{t-2}^{*(r)})}{\sum_{r=1}^{R} P(I_{1t}=1|\bar{y}_{t-1},\bar{I}_{t-1},\bar{y}_{t-1}^{*(r)})^{I_{1t}}P(I_{2t}=1|\bar{y}_{t-1},\bar{I}_{t-1},\bar{y}_{t-1}^{*(r)})^{I_{2t}}f(y_t|\bar{y}_{t-1},\bar{I}_{t-1},\bar{y}_{t-1}^{*(r)})^{I_{3t}}\omega_{2,t-1}(\bar{y}_{t-2}^{*(r)})} \tag{27}$$

For likelihood simulation of the one-limit model, define a sequence of functions c_{1t} for $t = 1,\ldots,T$ as follows

$$c_{1t}(\bar{y}_t,\bar{I}_t) = \sum_{r=1}^{R}[f(y_t|\bar{y}_{t-1},\bar{I}_{t-1},\bar{y}_{t-1}^{*(r)})]^{1-I_{1t}} [P(I_{1t}=1|\bar{y}_{t-1},\bar{I}_{t-1},\bar{y}_{t-1}^{*(r)})]^{I_{1t}}\omega_{1,t-1}(\bar{y}_{t-2}^{*(r)}). \tag{28}$$

By successive substitution of (26) into (28), one can check that

$$\prod_{t=1}^{T} c_{1t}(\bar{y}_t,\bar{I}_t) = \frac{1}{R}\sum_{r=1}^{R}\prod_{t=1}^{T}[f(y_t|\bar{y}_{t-1},\bar{I}_{t-1},\bar{y}_{t-1}^{*(r)})]^{1-I_{1t}}$$
$$[P(I_{1t}=1|\bar{y}_{t-1},\bar{I}_{t-1},\bar{y}_{t-1}^{*(r)})]^{I_{1t}}.$$

The log SL function in (24) can be rewritten as

$$\log\hat{L}_{1,R}(\theta) = \prod_{t=1}^{T}\log\{c_{1t}(\bar{y}_t,\bar{I}_t)\}$$
$$= \sum_{t=1}^{T}\log\left\{\sum_{r=1}^{R}[f(y_t|\bar{y}_{t-1},\bar{I}_{t-1},\bar{y}_{t-1}^{*(r)})]^{1-I_{1t}}\right.$$
$$\left.[P(I_{1t}=1|\bar{y}_{t-1},\bar{I}_{t-1},\bar{y}_{t-1}^{*(r)})]^{I_{1t}}\omega_{1,t-1}(\bar{y}_{t-2}^{*(r)})\right\}. \quad (29)$$

The weights could not be very small for all r, and $c_{1t}(\bar{y}_t,\bar{I}_t)$, which involves an average of weighted simulated conditional densities or probabilities, would not suffer from numerical underflow in its evaluation. For the two-limit model, the log SL in (25) can be reformulated as

$$\log\hat{L}_{2,R}(\theta) = \sum_{t=1}^{T}\log\left\{\sum_{r=1}^{R}P(I_{1t}=1|\bar{y}_{t-1},\bar{I}_{t-1},\bar{y}_{t-1}^{*(r)})^{I_{1t}}\right.$$
$$P(I_{2t}=1|\bar{y}_{t-1},\bar{I}_{t-1},\bar{y}_{t-1}^{*(r)})^{I_{2t}}.f(y_t|\bar{y}_{t-1},\bar{I}_{t-1},\bar{y}_{t-1}^{*(r)})^{I_{3t}}$$
$$\left.\omega_{2,t-1}(\bar{y}_{t-2}^{*(r)})\right\}. \quad (30)$$

5 Renewal and variance reduction

The suggested simulation procedures for simulating the RE solution and likelihoods are general and can be applied to models with general serial correlations or dynamics. Simulation estimation of certain simple but important dynamic models with a renewal property can be improved. When the renewal property is taken into account, it may be possible to simulate likelihood functions with reduced variance (Lee (1996)). For LDRE models, reduced variance techniques can also be applied to the simulation of the RE solution.

The concept of renewal can be formally defined for our models. It concerns properties of a stochastic process with reference to observed samples. Consider a one-limit model with sample observations censored at $t_1,\ldots,t_m$ with $t_1<t_2<\ldots<t_m$. Denote $\bar{y}_{[t,s]}^{*}$ a subvector of $\bar{y}_t^{*}$ which contains all censored latent variables from time s to t where $s<t$. To be specific, suppose

that $t_1 < \ldots < t_{l-1} < s \leq t_l < \ldots < t_k \leq t$, then $\bar{y}^*_{[t,s]} = (y^*_{t_k}, \ldots, y^*_{t_l})$. The one-limit model is said to have the renewal property at t if, for all j such that $j > t$

$$f(y_j | I_j = 0, \bar{y}_{j-1}, \bar{I}_{j-1}, \bar{y}^*_{j-1}) = f(y_j | I_j = 0, \bar{y}_{j-1}, \bar{I}_{j-1}, \bar{y}^*_{[j-1,t]}),$$
$$P(I_j = 1 | \bar{y}_{j-1}, \bar{I}_{j-1}, \bar{y}^*_{j-1}) = P(I_j = 1 | \bar{y}_{j-1}, \bar{I}_{j-1}, \bar{y}^*_{[j-1,t]}),$$
$$f(y^*_j | I_j = 1, \bar{y}_{j-1}, \bar{I}_{j-1}, \bar{y}^*_{j-1}) = f(y^*_j | I_j = 1, \bar{y}_{j-1}, \bar{I}_{j-1}, \bar{y}^*_{[j-1,t]}),$$

and, if $I_t = 1$

$$f(y^*_t | I_t = 1, \bar{y}_{t-1}, \bar{I}_{t-1}, \bar{y}^*_{t-1}) = f(\bar{y}^*_t | I_t = 1, \bar{y}_{t-1}, \bar{I}_{t-1}). \tag{31}$$

The first three conditions in (31) mean that censored latent lagged variables on the past of t provide no additional information for relevant future conditional densities and probabilities of t. The last condition of (31) is relevant only when the sample is censored at t and a simulation of y^*_t is needed. The concept of renewal can similarly be defined for the two-limit model. Models with an autoregressive dynamic structure or autoregressive disturbances have the renewal property. For an LDRE model with autoregressive process of order one (AR(1)), the process is renewed at t if sample observation of y is not censored either at $t-1$ or t. If y_t and y_{t-1} are both censored, the last condition in (31) will apparently not be satisfied. For an AR(2) process, renewal occurs at t if y_{t-1} is not censored. For an AR(3) process, it requires that both y_{t-1} and y_{t-2} are not censored. Models with neither latent lagged dependent variables nor serial correlation have the renewal property at each period.

An implication of the renewal property for our models is that likelihood functions that involve higher dimensional integrals can be decomposed into products of functions involving lower dimensional integrals. The mixed joint density of dependent variables in (12) of the one-limited model can be rewritten as

$$\begin{aligned} f(\bar{y}_T, \bar{I}_T, \bar{y}^*_T) = \prod_{t=1}^{T} & f(y_t | \bar{y}_{t-1}, \bar{I}_{t-1}, \bar{y}^*_{t-1})^{1-I_{1t}} \\ & P(I_{1t} = 1 | \bar{y}_{t-1}, \bar{I}_{t-1}, \bar{y}^*_{t-1})^{I_{1t}} \\ & \prod_{s \in \{t_1, t_2, \ldots, t_m\}} f(y^*_s | I_{1-s} = 1, \bar{y}_{s-1}, \bar{I}_{s-1}, \bar{y}^*_{s-1}). \end{aligned} \tag{32}$$

Suppose that renewal occurs at t, then

$$\begin{aligned} f(\bar{y}_T, \bar{I}_T, \bar{y}^*_T) = \prod_{j=t+1}^{T} & f(y_j | \bar{y}_{j-1}, \bar{I}_{j-1}, \bar{y}^*_{[j-1,t]})^{1-I_{1j}} \\ & P(I_{1j} = 1 | \bar{y}_{j-1}, \bar{I}_{j-1}, \bar{y}^*_{[j-1,t]})^{I_{1j}} \end{aligned}$$

$$\prod_{j\in\{t_1,t_2,\ldots,t_m\},j\geq t} f(y_s^*|I_{1j}=1,\bar{y}_{j-1},\bar{I}_{j-1},\bar{y}^*_{[j-1,t]})$$

$$\prod_{s=1}^{t} f(y_s|\bar{y}_{s-1},\bar{I}_{s-1},\bar{y}^*_{s-1})^{1-I_{1s}}P(I_{1s}=1|\bar{y}_{s-1},\bar{I}_{s-1},\bar{y}^*_{s-1})^{I_{1s}}$$

$$\prod_{s\in\{t_1,t_2,\ldots,t_m\},s<t} f(y_s^*|I_{1s}=1,\bar{y}_{s-1},\bar{I}_{s-1},\bar{y}^*_{s-1}), \tag{33}$$

can be partitioned into two different components without overlapping successive latent variables. Suppose that $t_1<\ldots<t_k<t\leq t_{k+1}<\ldots<t_m$, the likelihood in (8) becomes

$$L_1(\bar{y}_T,\bar{I}_T)=\int_{-\infty}^{p_{t_m l}}\cdots\int_{-\infty}^{p_{t_{k+1} l}}\prod_{j=t+1}^{T} f(y_j|\bar{y}_{j-1},\bar{I}_{j-1},\bar{y}^*_{[j-1,t]})^{1-I_{1j}}$$

$$P(I_{1j}=1|\bar{y}_{j-1},\bar{I}_{j-1},\bar{y}^*_{[j-1,t]})^{1-I_{1j}}$$

$$\prod_{j\in\{t_1,t_2,\ldots,t_m\},j\geq t} f(y_j^*|I_{1j}=1,\bar{y}_{j-1},\bar{I}_{j-1},\bar{y}^*_{[j-1,t]})d\bar{y}^*_{[T,t]}$$

$$\int_{-\infty}^{p_{t_k l}}\cdots\int_{-\infty}^{p_{t_1 l}}\prod_{s=1}^{t} f(y_s|\bar{y}_{s-1},\bar{I}_{s-1},\bar{y}^*_{s-1})^{1-I_{1s}}$$

$$P(I_{1s}=1|\bar{y}_{s-1},\bar{I}_{s-1},\bar{y}^*_{s-1})^{I_{1s}}$$

$$\prod_{s\in\{t_1,t_2,\ldots,t_m\},s<t} f(y_s^*|I_{1s}=1,\bar{y}_{s-1},\bar{I}_{s-1},\bar{y}^*_{s-1})d\bar{y}_t. \tag{34}$$

A large dimensional integral has been effectively divided into two integrals with smaller dimensions. With renewal at several periods, further divisions of integrals are possible. Given such a division of integrations, the simulation can be done separately for each integral of a smaller dimension. Variance reduction can be achieved by the following reason. Suppose that random variables $z_1,\ldots,z_m$ are mutually independent with means $E(z_j)=\mu_j$, $j=1,\ldots,m$. Let $(z_{1,r},\ldots,z_{m,r})$, $r=1,\ldots,R$, be vectors of realizations of the zs. The estimator based on a product of sample means $\prod_{j=1}^{m}(\frac{1}{R}\sum_{r=1}^{R}z_{j,r})$ has smaller variance than the simple sample average estimator $\frac{1}{R}\sum_{r=1}^{R}(\prod_{j=1}^{m}z_{j,r})$ for the estimation of $\prod_{j=1}^{m}\mu_j$ (Lee (1996)).

With renewal, variance reduction techniques can be easily implemented for the RE solution and the likelihood simulation via a modification of the recursive weighting scheme in (26) or (27). Whenever the process is renewed at a period, say t, set $\omega_{1t}(\bar{y}^{*(r)}_{t-1})=1/R$ for all $r=1,\ldots,R$, instead of the formulation in (26) for the one-limit model, and set $\omega_{2t}(\bar{y}^{*(r)}_{t-1}) = 1/R$ instead of (27) for the two-limit model. Such a modification will renew the simulation of paths for censored variables by ignoring the history of past simulated paths of t. This is desirable as past simulated paths have no effective implication for simulators of future components. With this modification, the corresponding SLs in (29) and (30) capture the variance reduction formulation. To see this, consider (26) and (28) at $t+1$ for the one-limit model. As $\omega_{1t}(\bar{y}^{*(r)}_{t-1}) = 1/R$ after modification, the renewal property of (32) implies that

$$c_{1,t+1}(\bar{y}_{t+1}, \bar{I}_{t+1}) = \sum_{r=1}^{R} f(y_{t+1} | \bar{y}_t, \bar{I}_t, \bar{y}^{*(r)}_{[t,t]})^{(1-I_{1,t+1})} P(I_{1,t+1} = 1 | \bar{y}_t, \bar{I}_t, \bar{y}^{*(r)}_{[t,t]})^{I_{1,t+1}}$$

and

$$\omega_{1,t+1}(\bar{y}^{*(r)}_t) = \frac{f(y_{t+1} | \bar{y}_t, \bar{I}_t, \bar{y}^{*(r)}_{[t,t]})^{(1-I_{1,t+1})} P(I_{1,t+1} = 1 | \bar{y}_t, \bar{I}_t, \bar{y}^{*(r)}_{[t,t]})^{I_{1,t+1}}}{\sum_{r=1}^{R} f(y_{t+1} | \bar{y}_t, \bar{I}_t, \bar{y}^{*(r)}_{[t,t]})^{(1-I_{1,t+1})} P(I_{1,t+1} = 1 | \bar{y}_t, \bar{I}_t, \bar{y}^{*(r)}_{[t,t]})^{I_{1,t+1}}}.$$

The $\bar{y}^{*(r)}_{[t,t]}$ is either an empty element when $I_t = 0$ or it is a random value drawn from the density $f(y^*_t | I_{1t} = 1, \bar{y}_{t-1}, \bar{I}_{t-1}, \bar{y}^*_{t-1}) = f(y^*_t | I_{1t} = 1, \bar{y}_{t-1}, \bar{I}_{t-1})$. These quantities at the period $t+1$ behave as quantities at the first period and y^*_t behaves as an initial value for simulation. In a model with AR(1) process, as the process is renewed at a non-censored period or at a period when its sample observation in the preceding last period is not censored, the largest dimension of integrals that need to be simulated corresponds to the largest number of successively censored periods in a sample.

6 Monte Carlo experiments and results

To investigate computational aspects and finite sample properties of proposed estimators, Monte Carlo experiments are performed. Several different models with various bounds are considered. The models considered include one- and two-limit models with fixed and varying censoring bounds. We compare estimators under various censoring circumstances and study the effects by ignoring serial correlation in estimation.

The underlying regression equation for all our experiments is specified as

$$y^*_t = \beta_1 + \beta_2 x_t + \gamma y^e_t + u_t, \quad u_t = \rho u_{t-1} + \varepsilon_t \tag{35}$$

where ε_t are i.i.d. $N(0, \sigma)$. The regressor is generated from the process $x_t = 0.6x_{t-1} + v_t$ where v_t are i.i.d. $N(0,2)$ and are independent of all εs. The xs are therefore serially correlated with a first-order autocorrelation coefficient 0.6

and its variance is about 3.1. The parameter values of the x_t process is assumed to be known in the estimation for simplicity. For a two-limit LDRE model with fixed bounds, the lower and upper bounds are $p_{tl} = -2.0$ and $p_{tu} = 2.0$ for all t. For the one-limit LDRE model, the lower bound is $p_{tl} = -2.0$ and there is no upper bound. To study more possible effects of bounds on SML estimates of parameters in models, the bounds in some cases are enlarged or become stochastic. The regressor x_t is, in most cases, assumed to be not perfectly predictable and its expected value x_t^e is known to be $0.6x_{t-1}$ at t. We will also consider cases with a perfectly predictable x_t.[1]

In all experiments, the true unknown parameters are set to $\beta_1 = 0$, $\beta_2 = 1$, $\gamma = 0.5$, $\rho = 0.5$, and $\sigma = 1$. These designs imply an R^2 about 0.9 for the corresponding regression equation of y_t on x_t from (35) in an RE model with a perfectly predictable x_t but without censoring. For data generation, the RE y_t^e at each t is needed before a sample observation y_t can be generated from (35) with a censoring mechanism. Simple observations are generated in a recursive fashion. Starting with initial values of $y_0^* = 0$, $y_0 = 0$, $x_0 = 0$ and $u_0 = 0$, a SRE y_t^e is solved from the simulated RE characterization equation. y_1^* and y_1 are then generated from (35). Recursively, given $\bar{y}_{t-1}$, a SRE y_t^e is solved and y_t^* *and* y_t are generated. As the SRE expectation has been shown to lie between the bounds, we use the straightforward bisection method for root finding from the numerical recipes (Press *et al.* (1992)). This may not necessarily be the quickest method but it is one that cannot fail. The SREs are used as the true RE in our sample. To minimize the implicit measurement error problem, the number of simulation runs is set to 500. This number of simulation runs is unnecessarily large for our purpose. As we have experimented with simulation runs of 100 and 600, SRE solutions in the majority of cases are identical up to five or six digits. While 100 simulation runs might be sufficient, we desire to use 500 runs instead. With carefully computed weights, the SRE can be derived for each period in all sample data simulations without problems.

For estimation, since the existence and uniqueness of the RE solution for both one-limit and two-limit models are necessary in an optimization algorithm, the restriction that $\gamma \leq 1$ is imposed. This is achieved by reparameterizing γ such that $\gamma = 1 - e^{-\theta}$ with θ being an unrestricted unknown parameter on $(-\infty, \infty)$. Similarly, restrictions are imposed on ρ with values on $(-1,1)$ and the non-negativity constraint is also imposed

[1] The imperfect predictability of regressors is important for parameter identification. In a linear expectation model with a perfectly predictable x_t and with neither serial correlation nor censoring, as $y_t^e = (\beta_1 + \beta_2 x_t)/(1-\gamma)$, x_t and y_t^e in (35) will be perfectly linearly correlated and the identification of regression coefficients is impossible. With serial correlation and censoring, non-linearity in expectation may help identification. The possibility of utilizing the non-linearity of the RE solution for the LDRE (without serial correlation) to identify otherwise unidentified parameters has been considered in Pesaran and Samiei (1995).

on σ in estimation. The optimization subroutine used is the DFP from the GQOPT package.[2] Lengths of each time series are chosen to be either $T=50$ or $T=100$. To investigate the potential sensitivity of SML estimate with respect to the number of simulation runs, simulated runs with $R=30$ and larger $R=100$ are tried. For each case, results on the SML estimate are based on 400 replications. Summary statistics of SML estimates on the empirical mean (Mean) and empirical standard deviation (SD) are reported for each parameter. Estimates of standard errors of SML estimates based on numerical second-order derivatives are directly available from the GQOPT package. These estimates are reported under the column "Est.SD1." As an alternative, standard errors of estimates based on analytical second-order derivatives of simulated likelihoods are reported under "Est.SD2." Analytical derivatives of first and second orders from our simulated likelihoods are complex but can be derived with assistance from the symbolic mathematics package Mathematica. In addition, we also report the maximized logarithmic SL value (F). In some cases, optimization sub-routines might not converge, thus the number of successful convergent cases (con#) is reported.

Table 4.1 reports SML estimates of the model (35) with fixed censoring bands $(-2,2)$. For this design, about 42 percent of samples are, on average, censored – a half for each bound. All the initial estimates except σ start from zero. The initial starting value of σ is unity. The estimates in the first two rows of table 4.1 are SML estimates where the initial values of the SL are correctly specified. The numerical optimization sub-routine is stable. All iterations converge successfully without failure. The results show that the SML estimates are similar and not sensitive to the number of simulation runs R for both samples of size $T=50$ and $T=100$. The average maximized log simulated likelihood values Fs are almost exactly the same with respect to R. There are some upward biases in the estimates of β_2 and ρ and some downward biases for the estimates of γ. As the sample length increases from $T=50$ to $T=100$, the biases of β_2 and γ decrease. For both sample sizes, these biases are small. The SD decreases on average according to the $\sqrt{T}$ rate as the sample length increases. The SML estimates provide reasonably accurate estimates of the parameters of the model. The Est.SD1s based on numerical second-order derivatives of the simulated log likelihood function from the GQOPT option have substantially underestimated corresponding (empirical) SDs of this model. Statistical inference based on them such as the significance test will not be reliable. Estimated standard errors of the SML estimates based on analytical second-order derivatives, Est.SD2s, provide

[2] GQOPT is a general purpose numerical optimization package written by Professor Richard E. Quandt and the late Professor Stephen M. Goldfeld at Princeton University. The version used is the version 6.08. The sub-routines are written in Fortran.

Table 4.1. *SML estimation of LDRE model: non-perfectly predictable regressors, fixed bounds* $(-2, 2)$

True parameters: $\beta_1 = 0$, $\beta_2 = 1$, $\gamma = 0.5$, $\rho = 0.5$, and $\sigma = 1$

	Mean	SD	Est.SD1	Est.SD2	Mean	SD	Est.SD1	Est.SD2
	$T=50$,	$R=30$			$T=50$,	$R=100$		
β_1	−0.0232	(0.3090)	[0.1271]	[0.3888]	−0.0182	(0.2949)	[0.1603]	[0.3652]
β_2	1.0712	(0.1671)	[0.0857]	[0.1412]	1.0735	(0.1721)	[0.0883]	[0.1390]
γ	0.4804	(0.1625)	[0.0809]	[0.1597]	0.4834	(0.1651)	[0.0722]	[0.1554]
ρ	0.5236	(0.1318)	[0.0526]	[0.1194]	0.5203	(0.1290)	[0.0499]	[0.1154]
σ	0.9957	(0.1504)	[0.0949]	[0.1456]	0.9969	(0.1493)	[0.1016]	[0.1450]
	$F=-49.66$,	con#	400		$F=-49.66$,	con#	400	
	$T=100$,	$R=30$			$T=100$,	$R=100$		
β_1	−0.0065	(0.2051)	[0.1100]	[0.2524]	−0.0032	(0.2069)	[0.1030]	[0.2479]
β_2	1.0564	(0.1179)	[0.0537]	[0.0884]	1.0583	(0.1202)	[0.0588]	[0.0887]
γ	0.4914	(0.1162)	[0.0556]	[0.1010]	0.4943	(0.1178)	[0.0572]	[0.0992]
ρ	0.5291	(0.0867)	[0.0352]	[0.0789]	0.5291	(0.0900)	[0.0364]	[0.0769]
σ	1.0194	(0.1111)	[0.0667]	[0.0971]	1.0217	(0.1107)	[0.0692]	[0.0976]
	$F=-102.41$,	con#	400		$F=-102.32$,	con#	400	
	Initial value misspecification							
	$T=50$,	$R=30$			$T=50$,	$R=100$		
β_1	−0.0032	(0.2999)	[0.1354]	[0.3200]	−0.0017	(0.2962)	[0.1335]	[0.2923]
β_2	1.0664	(0.1594)	[0.0773]	[0.0957]	1.0645	(0.1646)	[0.0839]	[0.0887]
γ	0.4842	(0.1691)	[0.0771]	[0.0512]	0.4838	(0.1716)	[0.0719]	[0.0504]
ρ	0.5190	(0.1305)	[0.0527]	[0.0670]	0.5189	(0.1325)	[0.0487]	[0.0645]
σ	0.9987	(0.1459)	[0.0922]	[0.0625]	1.0008	(0.1495)	[0.0930]	[0.0601]
	$F=-49.93$,	con#	398		$F=-49.96$,	con#	398	
	SRE based on 100 random draws							
	$T=50$,	$R=30$			$T=100$,	$R=100$		
β_1	0.0025	(0.2945)	[0.1257]	[0.3180]	0.0081	(0.2043)	[0.1308]	[0.2529]
β_2	1.0648	(0.1649)	[0.0795]	[0.0890]	1.0540	(0.1114)	[0.0559]	[0.0890]
γ	0.5055	(0.1552)	[0.0703]	[0.0466]	0.4971	(0.1061)	[0.0580]	[0.0977]
ρ	0.5057	(0.1377)	[0.0486]	[0.0599]	0.5326	(0.0828)	[0.0343]	[0.0789]
σ	0.9909	(0.1531)	[0.0930]	[0.0640]	1.0130	(0.1019)	[0.0630]	[0.0970]
	$F=-49.62$,	con#	399		$F=-102.57$,	con#	400	

Table 4.1. (*cont.*)

True parameters: $\beta_1 = 0$, $\beta_2 = 1$, $\gamma = 0.5$, $\rho = 0.5$, and $\sigma = 1$

	Mean	SD	Est.SD1	Est.SD2	Mean	SD	Est.SD1	Est.SD2
	Ignoring correlation							
	$T=50$				$T=100$			
β_1	−0.0280	(0.2869)	—	—	−0.0132	(0.2013)	—	—
β_2	1.0702	(0.2124)	—	—	1.0369	(0.1399)	—	—
γ	0.4771	(0.2216)	—	—	0.4905	(0.1663)	—	—
σ_u	1.2601	(0.2424)	—	—	1.2952	(0.1841)	—	—
	$F=-57.55$,	con#	399		$F=-119.48$,	con#	400	

Notes:
Mean: empirical mean; SD: empirical standard deviation; Est.SD1 and Est.SD2: estimates of SD of SML estimates based on, respectively, numerical and analytical second-order derivatives of SL; T: length of a time series; R: number of simulation runs; F: maximized log SL value; con#: number of successful convergent cases.

much better approximations for this model for both T equal to 50 or 100. Figures 4.1 and 4.2 report q-q plots of quantiles of the SML estimates against standard normal quantiles, respectively, for $T=50$ and $T=100$. These plots are derived from the statistical package S-plus. One can conclude from these q-q plots that distributions of the SML estimates are approximately normal.

To investigate the potential problem of misspecified initial values in estimation, we collect a sample after the stochastic process has been operated for 50 periods. As the SL assumes the initial values to be zeros, there is a misspecified initial value problem. The SMLs with misspecified initial values are reported under the block entitled "Initial value misspecification." The Fs show slightly worse model fitting than the previous ones without initial value problems. There are two cases of non-convergence. But the SML estimates with or without initial value problems are very similar. These results show that misspecification of initial values does not seem to be an issue for parameter estimation even for $T=50$. However, both the Est.SD1s and Est.SD2s are not adequate.

As mentioned in previous paragraphs, samples are generated with SRE solutions derived from the simulated RE characterization equations with 500 simulation runs. Such samples are not ideal. An ideal sample should be the one with the RE solutions from analytical characterization equations. To show that our SML estimates may or may not suffer from simulation errors in the samples, different samples with simulated characterization equations based on 100 simulation runs are generated. The SML estimates for these

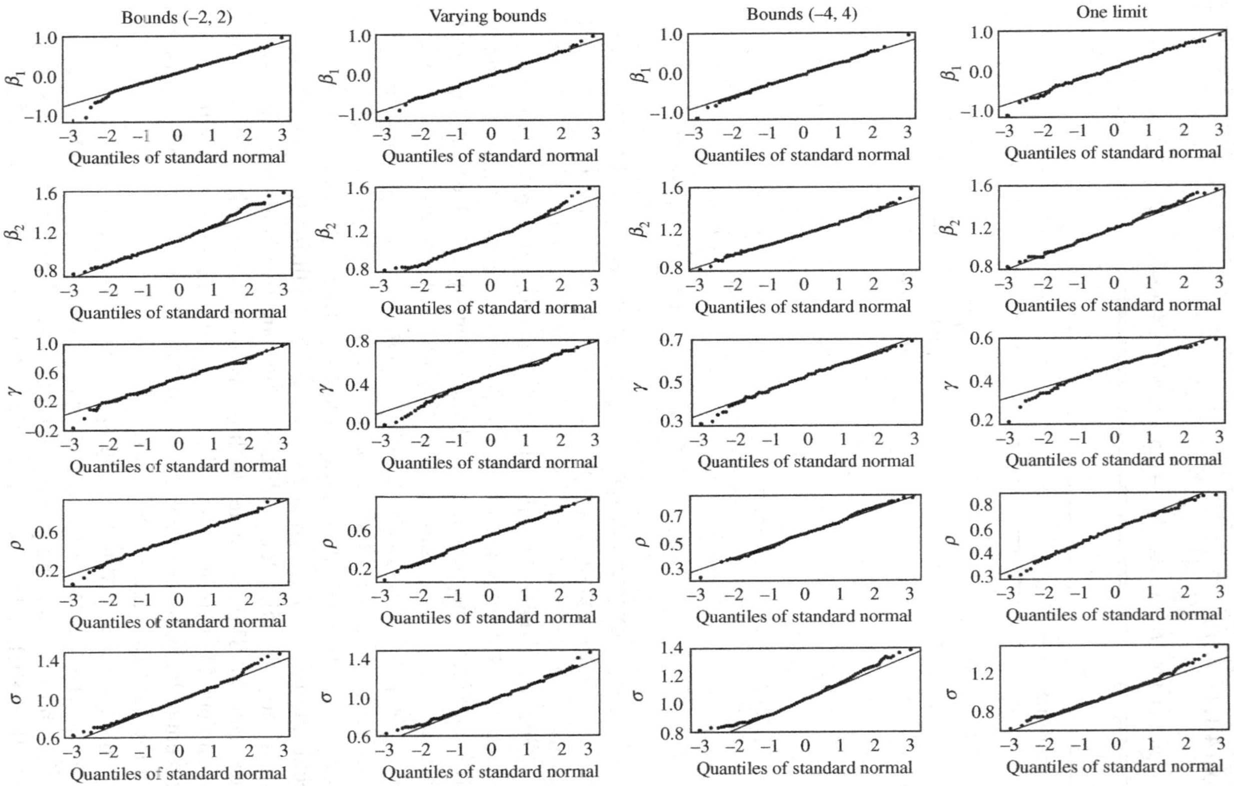

Figure 4.1 Normal probability plots of SMLEs for $T = 50$

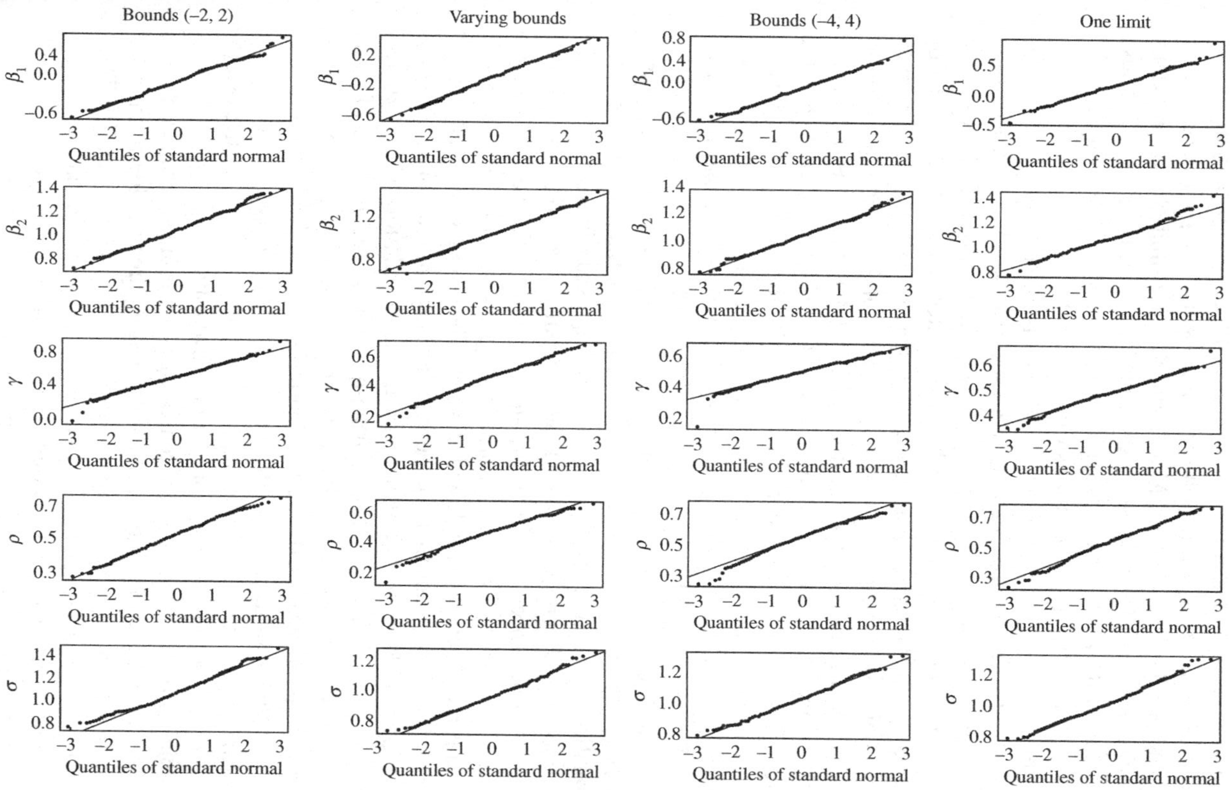

Figure 4.2 Normal probability plots of SMLEs for $T = 100$

samples are reported under the columns "SRE based on 100 random draws." Except for some small changes on the estimates of γ and ρ for the case of $T = 50$ and $R = 30$, results on the Means and SDs are similar to the previous corresponding ones. Est.SD2s show some sensitivity with respect to T. Those for samples with $T = 50$ do not provide better approximations than Est.SD1. They provide better approximations when $T = 100$.

When serial correlation is ignored, the likelihood function will be misspecified and the corresponding ML estimator may be inconsistent. To investigate this potential issue, we report on the last row block under the entity "Ignoring correlation" likelihood estimates of the LDRE model by assuming $\rho = 0$. The econometrician will likely regard the variance estimate of equation (10) as an estimate σ_u^2 – the variance of u_t. Assuming stationarity in the data generating process, the corresponding true σ_u is $(1 - \rho^2)^{-1/2}$, which is approximately equal to 1.1547. The results indicate that the misspecification of the serial correlation provides substantial upward biases in the estimation of σ_u. The upward bias can persist or become worse for longer time series with $T = 100$. Except for more downward bias in the estimate of ρ when $T = 50$, the Means of estimates of βs and γ are similar to those that take serial correlation into account. The SDs for all the parameters except the intercept are, however, much larger than those with serial correlation. The fitted average F values are significantly smaller than the corresponding F values of the SL with serial correlation. To illustrate numerical differences in SRE solutions that take serial correlation into account compared with those ignoring it, figure 4.3 reports such solutions from the first generated sample with $T = 100$. The values with the label "$E(y|y_{-1})$" are SRE solutions that take serial correlation into account and those with the label "$E(y)$" are those that ignore serial correlation. The differences of $E(y|y_{-1}) - E(y)$ are summarized in a q-q plot in the second panel of figure 4.3. As these errors, due to the RE solutions, are not too far from a normal distribution, the likelihood function that has ignored serial correlation does not suffer much from a misspecification of distributional assumption. This may explain the similarity of estimates of βs and γ. As the variance of $E(y|y_{-1}) - E(y)$ is not zero, it contributes to the overestimation of σ_u^2.

Table 4.2 reports results where censoring bounds are stochastic. Sample data are generated with the specification that p_{tu} are i.i.d. log normal distributed with mean 2 and a unity variance and $p_{tl} = -p_{tu}$ for all t. These bounds are assumed to be known to the agent in their formulation of rational expectations. Because the bounds are changing, corresponding bands are sometimes narrower and sometimes wider. On the average, about 45 percent of the samples are censored, which implies 3 percent more censoring than the samples for table 4.1. The SML estimates of parameters in this model are similar to those with fixed bounds except SDs of estimates of γ,

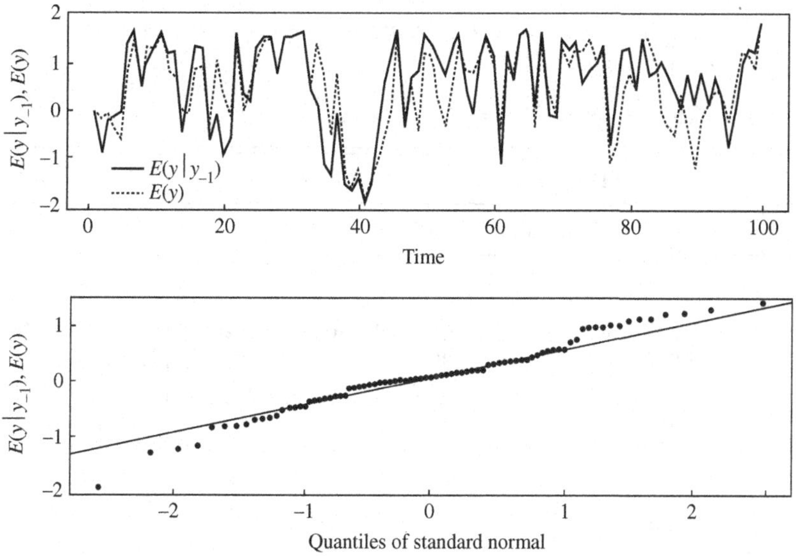

Figure 4.3 RE solutions, the first sample, $T = 100$

which are now larger. When serial correlation is ignored for estimation in this case, such a misspecification has more severe consequences. In addition to upward biases of estimates of σ_u, there are much larger upward biases in estimates of γ. All the variances of SML estimates, by ignoring serial correlation, are larger than those incorporating serial correlation in SLs.

Table 4.3 reports estimates where the censoring bounds are fixed over time with $p_{tl} = -4$ and $p_{tu} = 4$. The band width is wider by a factor of two. The total percentage of samples being censored is reduced to 14.5 percent on average. As with previous cases, the SML estimates are insensitive to the number of simulation runs R. With a wider fixed band, all the SDs of parameter estimates, except the intercept term, are smaller than those of table 4.1. The wider band has the strongest effect in the reduction of variance in the SML estimates of γ. The SDs in table 4.3 are reduced by more than half those in table 4.1. There are some downward biases in the SML estimates of γ and upward biases for ρ. The magnitude of the bias of ρ is larger than that in table 4.1 with a narrower fixed band. Overall, in terms of mean squared errors, the ones of ρ in table 4.3 are smaller than those in table 4.1.[3]

[3] Intuitively, one might expect that this would be the case as more information could be retained with less censoring. However, with rational expectation, this is not obvious as different degrees of censoring have different effects on the RE solution. The RE solution is an explanatory variable which changes according to different degrees of censoring.

Table 4.2. *SML estimation of LDRE model: non-perfectly predictable regressors, varying bounds*

True parameters: $\beta_1=0$, $\beta_2=1$, $\gamma=0.5$, $\rho=0.5$, and $\sigma=1$

	Mean	SD	Est.SD1	Est.SD2	Mean	SD	Est.SD1	Est.SD2
	Varying upper and lower bounds							
$T=50$	$R=30$				$R=100$			
β_1	−0.0188	(0.2981)	[0.1114]	[0.3555]	−0.0035	(0.2857)	[0.1164]	[0.3657]
β_2	1.0772	(0.1746)	[0.0878]	[0.1359]	1.0791	(0.1699)	[0.0881]	[0.1353]
γ	0.4815	(0.1276)	[0.0574]	[0.1208]	0.4867	(0.1284)	[0.0604]	[0.1224]
ρ	0.5144	(0.1327)	[0.0451]	[0.1178]	0.5187	(0.1291)	[0.0508]	[0.1166]
σ	0.9919	(0.1460)	[0.0865]	[0.1385]	0.9915	(0.1462)	[0.0925]	[0.1411]
	$F=-47.83$,	con#	400		$F=-47.83$,	con#	399	
$T=100$	$R=30$				$R=100$			
β_1	−0.0094	(0.1946)	[0.1016]	[0.2373]	−0.0131	(0.1933)	[0.1153]	[0.2244]
β_2	1.0554	(0.1211)	[0.0556]	[0.0883]	1.0566	(0.1220)	[0.0667]	[0.0854]
γ	0.4863	(0.0890)	[0.0461]	[0.0778]	0.4884	(0.0881)	[0.0538]	[0.0765]
ρ	0.5309	(0.0974)	[0.0340]	[0.0736]	0.5335	(0.0966)	[0.0401]	[0.0700]
σ	1.0134	(0.1020)	[0.0606]	[0.0909]	1.0122	(0.1034)	[0.0667]	[0.0886]
	$F=-98.11$,	con#	400		$F=-98.03$,	con#	400	
	Ignoring correlation							
	$T=50$				$T=100$			
β_1	−0.0071	(0.3327)	—	—	−0.0202	(0.2227)	—	—
β_2	1.1487	(0.2149)	—	—	1.1178	(0.1562)	—	—
γ	0.6898	(0.3564)	—	—	0.7141	(0.2333)	—	—
σ_u	1.2577	(0.2225)	—	—	1.3002	(0.1665)	—	—
	$F=-56.03$,	con#	400		$F=-116.04$,	con#	400	

Note:
See table 4.1.

With wider fixed censoring bounds, the optimization sub-routine is slightly more unstable as 1.5 percent to 5 percent repetitions do not converge. By ignoring serial correlation in disturbances, the ML estimates are less efficient and the estimates of σ_u are biased upward. The magnitude of the upward bias of σ_u is larger than that in table 4.1 when serial correlation is ignored. In table 4.3, we also investigate the possible effects of ignoring censoring in the estimation of the model. A likelihood function is formulated

Table 4.3. *SML estimation of LDRE model: non-perfectly predictable regressors, wider bounds (−4, 4)*

True parameters: $\beta_1=0$, $\beta_2=1$, $\gamma=0.5$, $\rho=0.5$, and $\sigma=1$

	Mean	SD	Est.SD1	Est.SD2	Mean	SD	Est.SD1	Est.SD2
	Wider bounds (−4, 4)							
$T=50$	$R=30$				$R=100$			
β_1	−0.0080	(0.2768)	[0.1276]	[0.4831]	−0.0259	(0.2909)	[0.1205]	[0.4784]
β_2	1.0561	(0.1348)	[0.0798]	[0.1156]	1.0602	(0.1338)	[0.0801]	[0.1162]
γ	0.4842	(0.0703)	[0.0358]	[0.0656]	0.4841	(0.0693)	[0.0328]	[0.0649]
ρ	0.5665	(0.1003)	[0.0295]	[0.1049]	0.5681	(0.0969)	[0.0328]	[0.1049]
σ	1.0228	(0.1323)	[0.0803]	[0.1266]	1.0326	(0.1324)	[0.0779]	[0.1294]
	$F=-63.89$, con# 392				$F=-63.91$, con# 394			
$T=100$	$R=30$				$R=100$			
β_1	−0.0022	(0.2105)	[0.1151]	[0.3390]	−0.0030	(0.2040)	[0.1047]	[0.3380]
β_2	1.0484	(0.0976)	[0.0521]	[0.0786]	1.0448	(0.0961)	[0.0504]	[0.0770]
γ	0.4841	(0.0541)	[0.0221]	[0.0447]	0.4807	(0.0531)	[0.0233]	[0.0446]
ρ	0.5663	(0.0805)	[0.0217]	[0.0713]	0.5721	(0.0787)	[0.0215]	[0.0720]
σ	1.0375	(0.0962)	[0.0514]	[0.0867]	1.0402	(0.1025)	[0.0540]	[0.0867]
	$F=-129.94$, con# 380				$F=-129.99$, con# 383			
	Ignoring correlation							
	$T=50$				$T=100$			
β_1	−0.0380	(0.2686)	—	—	−0.0103	(0.1797)	—	—
β_2	1.0595	(0.1802)	—	—	1.0291	(0.1126)	—	—
γ	0.4693	(0.1121)	—	—	0.4804	(0.0818)	—	—
σ_u	1.3752	(0.2487)	—	—	1.4076	(0.1771)	—	—
	$F=-77.52$, con# 397				$F=-159.68$, con# 392			
	Ignoring censoring							
	$T=50$				$T=100$			
β_1	−0.0099	(0.2066)	—	—	−0.0026	(0.1411)	—	—
β_2	0.8593	(0.1070)	—	—	0.8567	(0.0721)	—	—
γ	0.4428	(0.0617)	—	—	0.4450	(0.0428)	—	—
ρ	0.6347	(0.1052)	—	—	0.6479	(0.0689)	—	—
σ	0.9615	(0.1051)	—	—	0.9775	(0.0742)	—	—
	$F=-68.69$, con# 393				$F=-139.34$, con# 396			

Notes:
See table 4.1.

as if there is no censoring in the observations of y. This likelihood function is misspecified in that censored observations of y are treated as uncensored observations and the RE solution y_t^e is computed as $(\beta_1 + \beta_2 x_t^e)/(1-\gamma)$. By ignoring censoring, the effects of misspecification are serious. The ML estimates of all parameters except the intercept are all biased. The estimates of γ are biased downward and upward biases of ρ are severe. The estimates of β_2 and σ are also biased downward. The downward bias of β_2 is severe.

Table 4.4 reports estimates for the one-limit LDRE model where the lower bound is fixed at $p_{tl} = -2$ and there is no upper bound. The percentage of samples being censored is about 20.5 percent on average. The estimates in table 4.4 in many aspects are quite similar to the results in table 4.3 with wider fixed bounds. The SML estimates have some downward biases for γ and upward biases for ρ. The magnitude of these biases are similar to those in table 4.3. The SDs of the SML estimates are smaller than those of the two-limit model in table 4.1.

Table 4.5 reports results for cases where x_t is perfectly predictable. Parameters of the RE model (35) could not be identifiable if there were neither zero correlation nor censoring as the RE solution y_t^e would be a linear function of x_t. As RE solutions with serial correlation disturbances and censoring are complex non-linear functions of x_t, non-linearity might provide weak identification of unknown parameters. The results in table 4.5 indicate that the identification of the parameters β_2, γ, and ρ are fragile. There are very severe downward biases in γ and upward biases in β_2 and ρ. The SDs of these estimates become much larger than those of table 4.1. The SD of β_2 and γ are indeed more than double. Stochastic varying bounds help the situation a little bit as the magnitude of biases in β_2 and γ are reduced. But the remaining biases are still severe and SDs are relatively much larger.

Because both the numerical and analytical second-order derivatives approaches for SD estimations can substantially underestimate empirical SDs, especially for short time series, statistical inferences based on Wald type statistics may be unreliable. An alternative inference approach is the simulated likelihood ratio test. To investigate the performance of the likelihood ratio approach based on the simulated likelihood for our models, we focus on testing the hypothesis that $\rho = 0$. Table 4.6 reports SML estimates with the correct restriction $\rho = 0$ imposed and those without this restriction imposed.[4] There are some downward biases in the estimates of γ for both approaches with or without imposing the restriction. These biases decrease

[4] The initial values for the unconstrained estimation are from the constrained MLE. The DFP subroutine converges in a few iterations, which render the Est.SD1 too large to be reliable. The reported Est.SD1s are from estimates with initial zero values as in the previous cases. The latter takes more time for convergence. The SMLEs with constrained MLEs as initial estimates provide a slightly better fit in terms of fitted F values. But the SMLEs are similar.

Table 4.4. *SML estimation of LDRE model: non-perfectly predictable regressors, one-limit bounds* $(-2, \infty)$

True parameters: $\beta_1=0$, $\beta_2=1$, $\gamma=0.5$, $\rho=0.5$, and $\sigma=1$

	Mean	SD	Est.SD1	Est.SD2	Mean	SD	Est.SD1	Est.SD2
	Lower bound only $(-2, \infty)$							
$T=50$	$R=30$				$R=100$			
β_1	−0.0056	(0.2979)	[0.1215]	[0.5103]	0.0044	(0.2918)	[0.1300]	[0.4910]
β_2	1.0521	(0.1340)	[0.0635]	[0.1174]	1.0540	(0.1374)	[0.0707]	[0.1167]
γ	0.4814	(0.0700)	[0.0302]	[0.0668]	0.4775	(0.0731)	[0.0339]	[0.0680]
ρ	0.5623	(0.1147)	[0.0291]	[0.1151]	0.5650	(0.1114)	[0.0328]	[0.1111]
σ	1.0167	(0.1376)	[0.0712]	[0.1307]	1.0150	(0.1405)	[0.0749]	[0.1289]
	$F=-60.54$, con# 397				$F=-60.48$, con# 395			
$T=100$	$R=30$				$R=100$			
β_1	0.0154	(0.2088)	[0.0834]	[0.3243]	0.0177	(0.2240)	[0.0986]	[0.3271]
β_2	1.0442	(0.0991)	[0.0438]	[0.0783]	1.0430	(0.1018)	[0.0462]	[0.0786]
γ	0.4795	(0.0497)	[0.0203]	[0.0449]	0.4786	(0.0493)	[0.0197]	[0.0451]
ρ	0.5612	(0.0860)	[0.0234]	[0.0728]	0.5615	(0.0856)	[0.0208]	[0.0730]
σ	1.0346	(0.0984)	[0.0542]	[0.0871]	1.0348	(0.1030)	[0.0534]	[0.0877]
	$F=-123.06$, con# 392				$F=-123.04$, con# 392			
	Ignoring correlation							
	$T=50$				$T=100$			
β_1	−0.0500	(0.2741)	—	—	−0.0325	(0.1946)	—	—
β_2	1.0529	(0.1845)	—	—	1.0280	(0.1245)	—	—
γ	0.4718	(0.1193)	—	—	0.4879	(0.0825)	—	—
σ_u	1.3549	(0.2624)	—	—	1.4040	(0.1841)	—	—
	$F=-73.17$, con# 398				$F=-150.15$, con# 400			

Notes:
See table 4.1.

as the sample length T increases. The SDs of SML estimates with restrictions imposed have slightly larger SDs than those without restrictions imposed. This indicates that sample lengths of T equal to 50, 100, or 200 might not be large enough for asymptotic efficiency results to hold. Again, Est.SD2 can provide reasonably good approximations to the estimation of SDs only for a large T. Table 4.7 reports empirical levels of significance and power of likelihood ratio tests. The nominal levels of significance at

Table 4.5. *SML estimation of LDRE model: perfectly predictable regressors*

True parameters: $\beta_1 = 0$, $\beta_2 = 1$, $\gamma = 0.5$, $\rho = 0.5$, and $\sigma = 1$

	Mean	SD	Est.SD1	Mean	SD	Est.SD1
	Fixed upper and lower bounds (−2, 2)					
$T=100$	$R=30$			$R=100$		
β_1	−0.0120	(0.2692)	[0.2012]	−0.0150	(0.2596)	[0.2011]
β_2	1.4209	(0.3160)	[0.1435]	1.4042	(0.3341)	[0.1315]
γ	0.1729	(0.2634)	[0.1363]	0.1850	(0.2762)	[0.1314]
ρ	0.5840	(0.1001)	[0.0726]	0.5784	(0.0979)	[0.0729]
σ	1.0365	(0.1264)	[0.0855]	1.0324	(0.1276)	[0.0836]
	$F=-91.96$,	con#	395	$F=-91.80$,	con#	397
	Varying upper and lower bounds					
$T=100$	$R=30$			$R=100$		
β_1	−0.0059	(0.2475)	[0.1765]	−0.0059	(0.2456)	[0.1884]
β_2	1.2789	(0.2817)	[0.1436]	1.2568	(0.2754)	[0.1615]
γ	0.3105	(0.1964)	[0.1045]	0.3211	(0.1955)	[0.1073]
ρ	0.5607	(0.1152)	[0.0744]	0.5619	(0.1099)	[0.0753]
σ	1.0346	(0.1287)	[0.0850]	1.0284	(0.1299)	[0.0843]
	$F=-88.97$,	con#	399	$F=-88.88$,	con#	398

Notes:
See table 4.1.

conventional levels based on a $\chi^2(1)$ distribution under-report the empirical levels of significance. With the sample size $T=100$, at 2.5 percent and 5 percent levels of significance, the empirical levels of significance are double. With smaller sample size $T=50$, the empirical levels of the significance can be more than double. At the 5 percent level of significance, the actual empirical level is 14 percent. Its accuracy slightly improves for longer time series $T=200$ but the overrejection is still substantial.[5] With the distorted empirical sizes, the interpretation of power will be more conservative. Even so, the results show that the likelihood test statistic has good power.

[5] The overrejection phenomenon tends to occur for SML or simulated pseudo-maximum likelihood estimators when models are complicated. Standard formulas on estimated standard errors of parameter estimates tend to underestimate the empirical standard errors (see, e.g. Laroque and Salanie (1993)). There does not seem to have a systematic procedure which can take into account simulation errors with a finite number of random draws.

Table 4.6. *SML estimation of LDRE model: non-perfectly predictable regressors; zero correlated disturbances*

True parameters: $\beta_1=0$, $\beta_2=1$, $\gamma=0.5$, $\rho=0.0$, and $\sigma=1$ Fixed bounds $(-2, 2)$

	Mean	SD	Est.SD1	Est.SD2	Mean	SD	Est.SD1	Est.SD2
	Imposing restriction $\rho=0$							
	$T=50$				$T=100$			
β_1	−0.0074	(0.1363)	[0.0638]	—	−0.0095	(0.0881)	[0.0298]	—
β_2	1.0493	(0.1580)	[0.0970]	—	1.0226	(0.1146)	[0.0639]	—
γ	0.4705	(0.1677)	[0.0765]	—	0.4904	(0.1192)	[0.0449]	—
σ	1.0103	(0.1536)	[0.0802]	—	1.0066	(0.1159)	[0.0561]	—
	$F=-51.30$,	con#	399		$F=-104.11$,	con#	400	
	$T=200$							
β_1	0.0004	(0.0588)	[0.0203]	—				
β_2	1.0101	(0.0777)	[0.0422]	—				
γ	0.4919	(0.0853)	[0.0263]	—				
σ	1.0011	(0.0746)	[0.0309]	—				
	$F=-209.99$,	con#	400					
	Unconstrained estimation							
	$T=50$,	$R=30$			$T=50$,	$R=100$		
β_1	−0.0032	(0.1204)	[0.0719]	[0.1777]	−0.0021	(0.1199)	[0.0635]	[0.1699]
β_2	1.0204	(0.1511)	[0.0978]	[0.0926]	1.0223	(0.1520)	[0.1037]	[0.0848]
γ	0.4833	(0.1648)	[0.0699]	[0.0460]	0.4815	(0.1647)	[0.0851]	[0.0467]
ρ	−0.0470	(0.1390)	[0.0535]	[0.0525]	−0.0460	(0.1386)	[0.0614]	[0.0507]
σ	0.9649	(0.1380)	[0.0821]	[0.0557]	0.9659	(0.1382)	[0.0888]	[0.0538]
	$F=-50.41$,	con#	399		$F=-50.42$,	con#	399	
	$T=100$,	$R=30$			$T=100$,	$R=100$		
β_1	−0.0003	(0.0772)	[0.0494]	[0.1329]	−0.0004	(0.0768)	[0.0404]	[0.1334]
β_2	1.0078	(0.1070)	[0.0782]	[0.0896]	1.0084	(0.1066)	[0.0691]	[0.0904]
γ	0.4952	(0.1121)	[0.0539]	[0.0980]	0.4983	(0.1127)	[0.0430]	[0.0986]
ρ	−0.0218	(0.0876)	[0.0442]	[0.0823]	−0.0215	(0.0887)	[0.0415]	[0.0817]
σ	0.9823	(0.0993)	[0.0630]	[0.0893]	0.9835	(0.0997)	[0.0566]	[0.0893]
	$F=-103.31$,	con#	400		$F=-103.30$,	con#	400	
	$T=200$,	$R=30$			$T=200$,	$R=100$		
β_1	0.0053	(0.0521)	[0.0335]	[0.0911]	0.0052	(0.0522)	[0.0451]	[0.0910]
β_2	1.0071	(0.0732)	[0.0479]	[0.0608]	1.0065	(0.0734)	[0.0501]	[0.0607]
γ	0.4939	(0.0801)	[0.0320]	[0.0661]	0.4940	(0.0801)	[0.0374]	[0.0658]
ρ	−0.0096	(0.0637)	[0.0264]	[0.0565]	−0.0096	(0.0635)	[0.0369]	[0.0565]
σ	0.9937	(0.0702)	[0.0386]	[0.0598]	0.9928	(0.0701)	[0.0394]	[0.0597]
	$F=-209.20$,	con#	400		$F=-209.20$,	con#	400	

Notes:
See table 4.1.

Table 4.7. *SL ratio tests for zero correlation model: expected regressors, fixed bounds (−2, 2)*

Other parameters: $\beta_1 = 0$, $\beta_2 = 1$, $\gamma = 0.5$, and $\sigma = 1$

	0.5%	1.0%	2.5%	5%	10%
Level of significance	$\rho = 0$				
T = 50, R = 30	0.0251	0.0426	0.0902	0.1429	0.2206
T = 50, R = 100	0.0276	0.0476	0.0877	0.1429	0.2206
T = 100, R = 30	0.0100	0.0275	0.0550	0.1050	0.2000
T = 100, R = 100	0.0100	0.0275	0.0525	0.1200	0.2000
T = 200, R = 30	0.0150	0.0250	0.0450	0.0775	0.1825
T = 200, R = 100	0.0150	0.0225	0.0425	0.0925	0.1800
Power	$\rho = 0.5$				
T = 50, R = 30	0.8246	0.8722	0.9223	0.9373	0.9649
T = 50, R = 100	0.8195	0.8697	0.9173	0.9399	0.9674
T = 100, R = 30	1.0000	1.0000	1.0000	1.0000	1.0000
T = 100, R = 100	1.0000	1.0000	1.0000	1.0000	1.0000

Notes:
T – length of a time series; R – number of simulation runs.

7 Conclusions

In this chapter, we have considered stimulation estimation of LDRE models in the context of time series regression. The existing empirical literature on the estimation of these models assumes serial independent disturbances and no dynamic structures involving lagged latent variables. We consider estimation methods that allow general serial correlation and dynamic structures in models. With serial correlation or dynamics, multiple integrals appear in conditional probabilities, expectations, and likelihood functions. As one-limit and two-limit models have interesting applications in economics, we consider estimation for both models.

An important component in an LDRE model is the RE solution of a model. For an LDRE model, a non-linear equation characterizes the RE solution. As the characterization equation involves conditional probabilities and expectation functions, simulation techniques are needed to simulate the characterization equation in addition to the likelihood simulation. We discuss simulation procedures for the computation of the SRE solution. We show that the SRE solution exists and can be unique under similar circumstances as for the existence and uniqueness of the RE solution of a model. The SRE solution is bracketed by censoring limits. Numerical methods for root finding are effective given the bracketing. With the SRE solution available, the SML method is feasible. The SL function turns out to be a by-product of the RE solution simulation. The likelihood simulation can be justified as an importance-sampling approach. The corresponding importance-sampling densities are practical and desirable approximations of ideal importance-sampling densities of likelihood functions of these models. We address variance reduction and possible numerical underflow issues in likelihood simulation. Numerical underflow can occur in the simulation of the RE solution and in likelihood simulation with long time series samples. We introduce a recursive weighing procedure which can avoid the numerical problem. Variance-reduction techniques in likelihood simulation can be applied to models with a renewal property.

Monte Carlo experiments are provided to demonstrate finite sample properties of the suggested approaches of simulation estimation. The proposed SL approach is numerically stable. The intermediate step of solving the RE from its characteristic equation does not create numerical difficulty. Identification of unknown parameters of the LDRE model depends crucially on exogenous variables being imperfectly predictable. Ignoring serial correlation in estimation provides relatively inefficient parameter estimates and possible bias and inconsistent estimates. The likelihood approach, by ignoring censoring, suffers severely from the misspecification of the likelihood function and errors of the RE solution. The SMLE estimates are reasonably accurate. Biases are small and decrease as the sample increases. Statistical inference, however, can be difficult for samples with short or moderate lengths. Due to the complexity of these models and their likelihood functions, estimated SDs of SML estimates based on numerical second-order derivatives of simulated likelihood are substantially underreported. Estimated SDs based on analytical second-order derivatives provide much better approximation for relatively long time series. Additionally, the simulated likelihood ratio test can be reliable only for large samples.

Appendix: Existence and uniqueness of SRE solution

For the one-limit model, define $\hat{H}^{(1)}_{t,R}(q) = q - p_{tl}\hat{F}_{t,R}(C_{tl}(q)) - (\gamma q + x^e_t\beta)[1 - \hat{F}_{t,R}(C_{tl}(q))] - \hat{B}^{(1)}_{t,R}(C_{tl}(q))$. With (16) and (18), it is straightforward to show that

$$d\hat{H}^{(1)}_{t,R}(q)/dq = 1 - \gamma \sum_{l=1}^{R} \left[\int_{C_{tl}(q)}^{\infty} f(w_t | \bar{y}_{t-1}, \bar{I}_{t-1}, \bar{y}^{*(r)}_{t-1}) dw_t \right] \omega_{1,t-1}(\bar{y}^{*(r)}_{t-2}).$$

When $\gamma < 1$, it follows that $d\hat{H}^{(1)}_{t,R}(q)/dq > 0$, i.e. $\hat{H}^{(1)}_{t,R}(q)$ is a strictly increasing function. Since $\hat{B}^{(1)}_{t,R}(a) > a[1 - \hat{F}_{t,R}(a)]$ for any a from (16) and (18) (the strict inequality holds under the general regularity condition that $f(w_t|\bar{y}_{t-1}, \bar{I}_{t-1}, \bar{y}^*_{t-1})$ is positive everywhere)

$$\begin{aligned}\hat{H}^{(1)}_{t,R}(p_{tl}) &= (p_{tl} - \gamma p_{tl} - x^e_t\beta)[1 - \hat{F}_{t,R}(C_{tl}(p_{tl}))] - \hat{B}^{(1)}_{t,R}(C_{tl}(p_{tl}))\\ &< (p_{tl} - \gamma p_{tl} - x^e_t\beta)[1 - \hat{F}_{t,R}(C_{tl}(p_{tl}))] -\\ &\quad (C_{tl}(p_{tl}))[1 - \hat{F}_{t,R}(C_{tl}(p_{tl}))] = 0.\end{aligned}$$

On the other hand, it is easy to check that $\lim_{q\to\infty} \hat{H}^{(1)}_{t,R}(q) = \infty$ when $\gamma < 1$. Hence $\hat{H}^{(1)}_{t,R}(q) = 0$ has a unique solution, i.e., a SRE solution of (19) exists and is unique.

For the two-limit model, define

$$\begin{aligned}\hat{H}^{(2)}_{t,R}(q) &= q - p_{tl}\hat{F}_{t,R}(C_{tl}(q)) - p_{tu}[1 - \hat{F}_{t,R}(C_{tu}(q))] -\\ &\quad (\gamma q + x^e_t\beta)[\hat{F}_{t,R}(C_{tu}(q)) - \hat{F}_{t,R}(C_{tl}(q))] - \hat{B}^{(2)}_{t,R}(C_{tl}(q), C_{tu}(q)).\end{aligned}$$

The SRE from (33) can be equivalently solved from the equation $\hat{H}^{(2)}_{t,R}(q) = 0$. At p_{tl},

$$\begin{aligned}\hat{H}^{(2)}_{t,R}(p_{tl}) &= (p_{tl} - \gamma p_{tl} - x^e_t\beta)[1 - \hat{F}_{t,R}(C_{tl}(p_{tl}))] -\\ &\quad (p_{tu} - \gamma p_{tl} - x^e_t\beta)[1 - \hat{F}_{t,R}(C_{tu}(p_{tl}))] -\\ &\quad \sum_{r=1}^{R}\left[\int_{C_{tl}(p_{tl})}^{C_{tu}(p_{tl})} w_t f(w_t|\bar{y}_{t-1}, \bar{I}_{t-1}, \bar{y}^{*(r)}_{t-1})dw_t\right]\omega_{2,t-1}(\bar{y}^{*(r)}_{t-2}).\end{aligned}$$

Since

$$\begin{aligned}C_{tl}(q)\int_{C_{tl}(q)}^{C_{tu}(q)} f(w_t|\bar{y}_{t-1}, \bar{I}_{t-1}, \bar{y}^*_{t-1})dw_t &< \int_{C_{tl}(q)}^{C_{tu}(q)} w_t f(w_t|\bar{y}_{t-1}, \bar{I}_{t-1}, \bar{y}^*_{t-1})dw_t\\ &< C_{tu}(q)\int_{C_{tl}(q)}^{C_{tu}(q)} f(w_t|\bar{y}_{t-1}, \bar{I}_{t-1}, \bar{y}^*_{t-1})dw_t,\end{aligned}$$

it follows that $\hat{H}^{(2)}_{t,R}(p_{tl}) < (p_{tl} - p_{tu})[1 - \hat{F}_{t,R}(C_{tu}(p_{tl}))] < 0$. Similarly $\hat{H}^{(2)}_{t,R}(p_{tu}) > (p_{tu} - p_{tl})\hat{F}_{t,R}(C_{tl}(p_{tu})) > 0$. As $\hat{H}^{(2)}_{2,R}(p_{tl})$ is continuous, a SRE solution exists and is lying between p_{tl} and p_{tu}. The derivative of $\hat{H}^{(2)}_{t,R}(q)$ is $\frac{d\hat{H}^{(2)}_{t,R}(q)}{dq} = 1 - \gamma\sum_{r=1}^{R}[\int_{C_{tl}(q)}^{C_{tu}(q)} f(w_t|\bar{y}_{t-1}, \bar{I}_{t-1}, \bar{y}^{*(r)}_{t-1})dw_t]\omega_{2,t-1}(\bar{y}^{*(r)}_{t-2})$, which is strictly positive when $\gamma \leq 1$. Thus, when $\gamma \leq 1$, the SRE solution is unique.

References

Amemiya, T. (1973), "Regression Analysis When the Dependent Variable is Truncated Normal," *Econometrica*, 41: 997–1016.

Borjas, G.J. and G.T. Sueyoshi (1994), "A Two-Stage Estimator for Probit Models with Structural Group Effects," *Journal of Econometrics*, 64: 165–182.

Borsch-Supan, A. and V. Hajivassiliou (1990), "Smooth Unbiased Multivariate Probability Simulators for Maximum Likelihood Estimation of Limited Dependent Variable Models," *Journal of Econometrics*, 58: 347–368.

Bratley, P., B.L. Fox, and L.E. Schrage (1987), *A Guide to Simulation*, second edition (Springer-Verlag, New York).

Chanda, A.K. and G.S. Maddala (1983), "Methods of Estimation for Models of Markets with Bounded Price Variation under Rational Expectations," *Economics Letters*, 13: 181–184.

Donald, G.S. and G.S. Maddala (1992), "A Note on the Estimation of Limited Dependent Variables Models Under Rational Expectations," *Economics Letters*, 38: 17–23.

Edin, P. and A. Vredin (1993), "Devaluation Risk in Target Zones: Evidence from the Nordic Countries," *The Economic Journal*, 103: 161–175.

Geweke, J. (1989), "Bayesian Inference in Econometric Models using Monte Carlo Integration," *Econometrica* 24: 1317–1339.

(1991) "Efficient Simulation from the Multivariate Normal and Student-t Distributions Subject to Linear Constraints," in *Computer Science and Statistics: Proceedings of the Twenty-Third Symposium on the Interface*, American Statistical Association, VA, 571–578.

Gourieroux, C. and A. Monfort (1993), "Simulation-Based Inference: A Survey with Special Reference to Panel Data Models," *Journal of Econometrics*, 59: 5–33.

Hajivassiliou, V. and D. McFadden (1990), "The Method of Simulated Scores, with Application to Models of External Debt Crises," Manuscript, Cowles Foundation Discussion Paper no. 967, Yale University.

Hajivassiliou, V., D. McFadden, and P. Ruud (1996), "Simulation of Multivariate Normal Rectangle Probabilities and Their Derivatives: Theoretical and Computational Results," *Journal of Econometrics*, 72: 85–134.

Heckman, J.J. (1976), "The Common Structure of Statistical Models of Truncation, Sample Selection and Limited Dependent Variables and a Simple Estimator for Such Models," *Annals of Economic and Social Measurement*, 5: 475–492.

Hendry, D.F. and J.F. Richard (1992), "Likelihood Evaluation for Dynamic Latent Variable Models," in H.M. Amman, D.A. Belsley, and L.F. Pau (eds.), *Computational Economics and Econometrics*, Amsterdam: Kluwer.

Holt, M.T. and S.R. Johnson (1989), "Bounded Price Variation and Rational Expectations in an Endogeneous Switching Model of the US Corn Market," *Review of Economics and Statistics*, 71: 605–613.

Keane, M.P. (1994), "A Computationally Practical Simulation Estimator for Panel Data," *Econometrica*, 62: 95–116.

Laroque, G. and B. Salanie (1993), "Simulation-Based Estimation of Models with Lagged Latent Variables," *Journal of Applied Econometrics*, 8: S119–S133.

Lee, L.F. (1994), "Rational Expectations in Limited Dependent Variable Models," *Economics Letters*, 46: 97–104.

(1996), "Estimation of Dynamic and ARCH Tobit Models," Manuscript, Department of Economics, The Hong Kong University of Science and Technology, Hong Kong.

Lee, L.F. and G.S. Maddala (1985), "The Common Structure of Tests for Selectivity Bias, Serial Correlation, Heteroskedasticity and Non-Normality in the Tobit Model," *International Economics Review*, 26: 1–20.

Lerman, S. and C. Manski (1981), "On the Use of Simulated Frequencies to Approximate Choice Probabilities," in C. Manski and D. McFadden (eds.), *Structural Analysis of Discrete Data with Econometric Applications*, Cambridge, MA: MIT Press, 305–319.

Maddala, G.S. (1990), "Estimation of Dynamic Disequilibrium Models with Rational Expectations: The Case of the Commodity Markets," in L.A. Winters and D. Sapsford (eds.), *Primary Commodity Prices: Economic Models and Policy*, Cambridge University Press.

(1993), "Estimation of Limited Dependent Variable Models under Rational Expectations," in G.S. Maddala, C.R. Rao, and H.D. Vinod (eds.), *Handbook of Statistics*, vol. XI, North Holland: Elsevier Publishers B.V. 175–194.

McFadden, D. (1989), "A Method of Simulated Moments for Estimation of Discrete Choice Models without Numerical Integration, *Econometrica*, 57: 995–1026.

Pesaran, M.H. (1990), "Comment on Maddala's Paper," in L.A. Winters and D. Sapsford (eds.), *Primary Commodity Prices: Economic Models and Policy*, Cambridge University Press.

Pesaran, M.H. and F.J. Ruge–Murcia (1996), "Limited-Dependent Rational Expectation Models with Stochastic Thresholds," *Economics Letters*, 51: 267–276.

(1998), "Limited-Dependent Expectations Models with Jumps – An Application to Exchange Rate Target Zones," *Journal of Business and Economic Statistics* (forthcoming).

Pesaran, M.H. and H. Samiei (1992a), "Estimating Limited-Dependent Rational Expectations Models with an Application to Exchange Rate Determination in a Target Zone," *Journal of Econometrics*, 53: 141–163.

(1992b), "An Analysis of the Determination of Deutsche Mark/French Franc Exchange Rate in a Discrete-Time Target Zone," *The Economic Journal*, 102: 388–401.

(1995), Limited-Dependent Rational Expectations Models with Future Expectations," *Journal of Economics Dynamics and Control*, 19: 1325–1353.

Press, W.H., S.A. Teukolsky, W.T. Vetterling, and B.P. Flannery (1992), *Numerical Recipes*, Cambridge University Press.

Robinson, P.M. (1982), "On the Asymptotic Properties of Estimators of Models Containing Limited Dependent Variables," *Econometrica*, 50: 27–41.

Shonkwiler, J.S. and G.S. Maddala (1985), "Modelling Expectations of Bounded Prices: An Application to the Market for Corn," *Review of Economics and Statistics*, 67: 634–641.

Tobin, J. (1958), "Estimation of Relationships for Limited Dependent Variables," *Econometrica*, 26: 24–36.

Warner, D. (1976), "A Monte-Carlo Study of Limited Dependent Variable Estimation," in *Studies in Nonlinear Estimation*, Cambridge, MA: Ballinger, Chapter 10.

5 A Monte Carlo study of EC estimation in panel data models with limited dependent variables and heterogeneity

MAHMOUD A. EL-GAMAL AND DAVID M. GRETHER*

1 Introduction

In El-Gamal and Grether (1995), El-Gamal and Grether (1996), we introduced an estimation-classification (EC) estimator for panel data models. Accompanying the estimator, we provided an EC algorithm which ensured the linearity of the number of required computations and the number of types in the population (k), the number of individuals in the sample (n), and the number of time series observations per individual (T). The EC estimator was shown to be consistent as T and n go to infinity. Moreover, it was shown in El-Gamal and Grether (1996) that if we have a $\sqrt{nT}$ consistent and asymptotically normal (CAN) estimator in the homogeneous case ($k=1$), then the EC estimator will consistently estimate k, and obtain (CAN) estimators of the k sets of parameters, with a block-diagonal variance–covariance matrix.[1]

The general framework of the estimator is a panel model with heterogeneity of unknown type, whereby we observe data $(y_{it}, \vec{x}_{it})$ for n individuals over T_i time periods each. It is assumed that there are k (unknown) types of individuals parameterized by $(\theta_1,\ldots,\theta_k)\in\Theta^k$ (unknown); where Θ is the parameter space indexing the individuals' likelihood function. Thus, individual i's data, is assumed to be generated by

$$(y_{it}, x_{it})_{t=1}^{Ti} \sim \prod_{j=1}^{k}\left(f\left(\{y_{it}, x_{it}\}_{t=1}^{Ti};\theta_j\right)\right)^{\delta_{ij}}$$

* Department of Economics, 1180 Observatory Drive, University of Wisconsin, Madison, WI 53706-1393, and DHSS, 228-77, Caltech, Pasadena, CA 91125. We acknowledge financial support from NSF grant #SBR-9320497 to the California Institute of Technology and The University of Wisconsin at Madison.

[1] In other words, the sufficient regularity conditions for CAN under $k=1$ together with the assumption of independence across individuals are also sufficient conditions for CAN (with block-diagonal covariance matrix) of the EC estimator in the case of $k>1$.

where $\delta_{ij} \in \{0,1\}$, with $\sum_{j=1}^{k} \delta_{ij} = 1$ define the memberships of individuals to types. Note that in the EC context, the δ_{ij}s are treated as parameters (to be estimated) as opposed to nuisance parameters (to be integrated out, e.g., using the EM algorithm as in the mixtures literature).

If, for example, each individual's data are generated by one of k regression functions, then the types would be defined by a vector of regression parameters. Note that some parameters could be constant across types, though for notational convenience we do not specifically indicate common values.

In the simplest framework considered in this chapter, each individual's data are assumed independent of each other individual, thus producing an overall log likelihood function of the data $\{(y_{it}, \vec{x}_{it})\}_{i=1;t=1}^{i=n,t=T_i}$

$$\mathfrak{L}(k;\theta_1,\ldots,\theta_k;\{\delta_{ij}\}) = \sum_{i=1}^{n} \sum_{j=1}^{k} \left(\delta_{ij} \log f\left(\{y_{it}, x_{it}\}_{t=1}^{T_i}; \theta_j \right) \right).$$

It is useful to consider the special case of a fixed effects model. In that framework, $k=n$, and the θ_js differ only on one component (the intercept term). In that special case, it is obvious that for $n \uparrow \infty$ and a fixed T, the θ_js cannot be estimated consistently. It is also clear in that framework that if $T \uparrow \infty$ for a fixed n, the θ_js can be consistently estimated. Whether T is large or small relative to n in a given sample is an issue that cannot be determined by asymptotic theory, it is simply a property of a data set.

In an influential paper, Heckman and MaCurdy (1980) provided the following argument for estimating fixed effects for $n=425$ with only $T=8$ observations per household:

> If the number of panel observations per person becomes large, and if the number of persons in the sample becomes large, maximum likelihood estimators . . . are consistent and asymptotically normally distributed. (p. 59)

> Since the number of observations per household is fixed, it is not possible to consistently estimate fixed effects . . . (p. 59)

> Whether or not this is a serious problem cannot be settled *a priori*. All samples are finite, and many cannot be imagined to become infinite . . . (p. 59)

As is explained in detail in section 2, the approach we take treats the δ_{ij}s as parameters to be estimated. Thus, given k, the individuals are classified (or clustered, as there is no training set available) to one of the k types. The other parameters (θ_js) are then estimated conditional upon the classification in an iterative procedure. For our approach to be useful it does not matter whether T is large or small relative to n, but whether T is large enough so that the assignments to types can be made with sufficient accuracy.

An alternative to treating the δ_{ij}s as parameters is to treat them as missing data, and employ the EM algorithm (Dempster *et al.* (1977), Redner and Walker (1984), Little and Rubin (1987)). In the case of $k=n$ (as in the fixed effects model), the issue of whether the δ_{ij}s are parameters, nuisance parameters, or missing data, is irrelevant. However, in the case of $k<n$ (which is preferable from the point of view of parsimony), treating the δ_{ij}s as parameters (as in the EC algorithm) implies the need for their estimation (via penalized maximum likelihood in EC), whereas treating them as missing data or nuisance parameters implies the need for integrating them out (as in EM). Little and Rubin (1983) criticize the estimation of the δ_{ij} via maximum likelihood on the basis of inconsistency for a fixed T as in $n\uparrow\infty$. Our response in El-Gamal and Grether (1995) and El-Gamal and Grether (1996) was similar in spirit to the large T argument of Heckman and MaCurdy (1980) discussed above for the special case of fixed effects. Moreover, we devise a large T approximation to the EM algorithm, by means of which we can produce a diagnostic statistic (called Average Normalized Entropy, or ANE), to determine the goodness of the large T approximation. If T is found not to be sufficiently large to trust the EC estimates, the latter become consistent initial conditions for the EM algorithm as suggested by Little and Rubin (1987), which is very useful given the slowness of convergence of that algorithm, despite the acceleration methods devised to improve its speed.[2] On a more substantive level, treating the δ_{ij}s as nuisance parameters may be inappropriate if the motivation of an empirical study (e.g., targeting marketing to specific types of consumers) requires treating them as the most interesting parameters to be estimated.

A more recent appeal to using a large T approximation to address issues of heterogeneity in panels is discussed in Pesaran *et al.* (1996) (and the references therein) in the context of dynamic panels. In this paper as in other recent research in econometrics (see, e.g., Maddala (1991), Maddala (1996)), the question of the adequacy of fixed effects in treating panel heterogeneity is revived. The so-called "pooling problem" (whether it is appropriate to assume homogeneity of all parameters other than the intercept) becomes more acute in the dynamic case with lagged dependent variables and possible persistence (e.g., unit roots) in the exogeneous variables. Pesaran *et al.* (1996) show that the estimated parameters can exhibit perverse behavior in this environment, where the bias increases with the degree of persistence in the exogeneous variables. Their recipe is to allow for heterogeneity in parameters other than the intercept (as a number of studies

[2] For the importance of finding good initial conditions for the EM algorithm, see the discussion in Tanner (1996, chapter 4).

referenced therein suggest that "slope heterogeneity" is pervasive in economic panels), and to utilize a large T approximation to justify the procedure:

> Therefore, in general, slope heterogeneity cannot be ignored and assuming it away on the grounds that one is dealing with relatively small T may not be justifiable. In such circumstances it is perhaps more prudent to admit the limitations of one's data and be more cautious about the conclusions . . . (p. 146)

The remainder of this chapter will proceed as follows. In section 2, we state the EC estimator, EC algorithm, and the large T approximation to the EM algorithm and ANE formally. In section 3, we discuss the general design of our Monte Carlo study of the unpoolable-slopes probit and poolable-slopes probit. In section 4, we show the results of our Monte Carlo analysis, and in section 5, we provide some concluding remarks.

2 The EC-EM and large *T* approximation setup

Under the outlined model of heterogeneity in the introduction, our log likelihood function is

$$\mathfrak{L}(k;\theta_1,\dots,\theta_k;\{\delta_{ij}\}) = \sum_{i=1}^{n}\sum_{j=1}^{k}\left(\delta_{ij}\log f\left(\{y_{it}, x_{it}\}_{t=1}^{T_i};\theta_j\right)\right).$$

Our EC estimator maximizes this likelihood function less a non-stochastic penalty function which grows in n and k

$$(\hat{k},\hat{\theta}_1,\dots,\hat{\theta}_{\hat{k}}) = \text{argmax}_{k',\theta_1,\dots,\theta_{k'}} \left\{\sum_{i=1}^{n}\left(\max_{h\in\{1,\dots,k'\}} \log f\left(\{y_{it}, x_{it}\}_{t=1}^{T_i};\theta_j\right)\right) - \text{penalty}(n,k')\right\}$$

When the penalty function ($-penalty(n,k')$) is log of a prior on the parameter space, this estimator is similar to minimum description length (Rissanen (1978)) and minimum message length (Wallace and Boulton (1968)). In this chapter, we shall take our prior on $(\theta_1,\dots,\theta_k)$ to be an improper flat prior, but in any given application (as in El-Gamal and Grether (1995), El-Gamal and Grether (1996)) there may be theoretical considerations which produce a more informed prior. We shall impose a hierarchical prior $1/2^k$ for $k=1,2,\dots$, and $k!/k^n$ (the reciprocal of the leading term of the sum of Stirling numbers of the second type determining the number of possible $\{\delta_{ij}\}$ configurations). This yields a penalty function $penalty(n,k') = k' \log(2) + n \log(k') - \log(k'!)$.

In El-Gamal and Grether (1996), we proved that if the estimator $\hat{\theta}_1$ is $\sqrt{nT}$-CAN when $k=1$, then our EC estimator $(\hat{\theta}_1,\dots,\hat{\theta}_k)$ is $\sqrt{nT}$-CAN when we take limits as $T\uparrow\infty$, and $n\uparrow\infty$. The implementation of the EC estimation, however, can be very difficult if we need to compare the log likelihood for all possible $k^n/k!$ possible classifications. However, the EC estimator as written above implicitly maximizes over all possible $\{\delta_{ij}\}$ configurations by employing the EC algorithm. All that is needed to implement this EC estimation using the EC algorithm is to perform a maximization over Θ^k, where Θ is the parameter space for each type. The steps used by the EC algorithm are as follows:

Algorithm EC

For any given $\phi = (k', \theta_1, \ldots, \theta_{k'})$:

For each individual i:

Calculate $lf_i(h;\phi) = \log f(\{y_{it}, x_{it}\}_{t=1}^{T}; \theta_h)$, for $h \in \{1, \ldots, k'\}$.

Choose $h \in \{1, \ldots, k'\}$ to maximize $lf_i(h;\phi)$ over $h \in \{1, \ldots, k'\}$. Call the maximal value $lf_i(\phi)$. (This corresponds to maximizing over the δ_{ij}s for individual i, conditional on the k' proposed parameter vectors.)

Sum the obtained log likelihoods $lf_i(\phi)$ over individuals $i \in \{1, \ldots, n\}$. Call the outcome $lf(\phi)$.

Start with $k' = 1$, then proceed to $k' = 2, 3, \ldots$, stopping when

$$[lf(k';\theta_1, \ldots, \theta_{k'}) - \text{penalty}(n,k')] > [lf(k'+1;\theta_1, \ldots, \theta_{k'+1}) - \text{penalty}(n,k'+1)].$$

(Where, for each k', we use a maximization sub-routine to maximize over $(\theta_1, \ldots, \theta_{k'})$).

A natural and consistent starting point for the parameter estimation can be constructed from individual level estimates. First, estimate a separate function for each individual, and then cluster the estimates into k groups taking the centroids as the initial estimates. One can attempt to guard against getting trapped in local maxima by restarting the procedure at different starting points obtained by random perturbations on the original point.[3]

The EC estimator is consistent as $T \uparrow \infty$, but when T is small, misclassifications of subjects will result in a small sample bias in the estimated $\hat{\theta}_j$s. To determine whether this bias is sufficiently significant to warrant our attention, we proposed a large-T approximation to the EM algorithm for obtaining posterior probabilities on individual classifications. The EM algorithm for this mixture model would start with guesses π_j^0 on the proportions of each type in the population, and guess $\theta^0 = (\theta_1^0, \ldots, \theta_k^0)$. Then, for the E-step of the τth iteration, the posteriors on individual classifications would be calculated using Bayes' rule:

[3] This randomized strategy was used in El-Gamal and Grether (1996), but not in the current study.

$$p^{\tau}(\{\delta_{ij}=1\})=p_{ij}^{\tau}=\frac{\pi_j^{\tau-1}f(\{y_i,\vec{x}_i\}_{t=1}^{Ti}|\theta^{\tau},\{\delta_{ij}=1\})}{\sum_{l=1}^{k}\pi_l^{\tau-1}f(\{y_i,\vec{x}_i\}_{t=1}^{Ti}|\theta^{\tau},\{\delta_{il}=1\})}$$

set

$$\pi_j^{\tau}=\frac{1}{n}\sum_{i=1}^{n}p_{ij}^{\tau}$$

and calculate

$$Q(\theta,\theta^{\tau})=\sum_{i=1}^{n}\sum_{j=1}^{k}p_{ij}^{\tau}\log\left[f(\{y_{it},\vec{x}_i\}_{t=1}^{Ti}|\theta^{\tau})\right].$$

Then, the M-step would maximize $Q(\theta,\theta^{\tau})$ to produce $\theta^{\tau+1}$, and we iterate the E and M-steps until convergence.

A large T approximation to this EM algorithm would start with θ^0 initialized at the EC estimate $(\hat{\theta}_1,\ldots,\hat{\theta}_k)$, and the M-step would be by-passed in each iteration. The iteration of the E-steps would converge to posteriors on the classifications. If those posteriors are very concentrated on the groups to which the individuals were assigned, then the expected number of possible misclassifications is small, and the resulting small sample bias is also small. The summary statistic we use to quantify the closeness of the p_{ij}s to zeros and ones (and thus their closeness to the δ_{ij}s) is called the average normalized entropy (ANE):

$$\text{ANE}(k)=-\frac{1}{n}\sum_{i=1}^{n}\sum_{j=1}^{k}p_{ij}\log_k(p_{ij})$$

which is zero when the p_{ij}s are equal to the δ_{ij}s. ANE always lies between zero and one, with small numbers reflecting crisp classifications and negligible small sample biases, and large ANEs reflecting weak classifications and significant potential biases.

3 The Monte Carlo probits experimental design

In this chapter, we implement two experimental designs to study the relative performance of EC estimation and fixed effects estimation in panel models with limited dependent variables. The data generating process in both cases is a simple probit model

$$y_{it}^{*}=\sum_{j=1}^{2}\delta_{ij}(\alpha_j+\beta_j x_{it})+\varepsilon_{it},$$

$$y_{it}=\begin{cases}1 & \text{if } y_{it}^{*}>0,\\ 0 & \text{otherwise.}\end{cases}$$

Where we shall generate $\varepsilon_{it} \sim$ i.i.d. $N(0,1)$, $x_{it} \sim$ i.i.d. $N(0,1)$, and $\Pr\{\delta_{i1}\} = \mathrm{PR}\{\delta_{i2}\} = 0.5$.

In Design I, we shall make the slopes unpoolable, with $\alpha_1 = 1$, $\alpha_2 = -1$, $\beta_1 = -1$, $\beta_2 = 1$. We shall then simulate 1,000 data sets with $n = 20$, and $T = 3,5,10,20$. For each simulated data set, we shall estimate $(\alpha_1,\beta_1,\alpha_2,\beta_2,\{\delta_{ij}\})$ using the EC algorithm. We shall also estimate $(\{\alpha_i\}_{i=1}^{20},\beta)$ for the fixed effects model, and, for comparison (α,β) for a pooled model. In Design II, we implement the same steps as in Design I, except for making the slopes poolable, by setting $\beta_1 = \beta_2 = 0.5$.

Using the 1000 simulated data sets for each design and each longitudinal sample size, we can construct and compare the distributions of resulting point estimates, and, in the case of the EC algorithm, misclassifications and ANEs. We can thus compare the efficiency gains of allowing $k \ll n$ in the poolable slopes case, as well as the gains from allowing for unpoolable slopes in Design 1.

All of the simulations were conducted on a Sun Ultra2 with two 167MHz CPUs. The simulation code was written in Gauss, using the MaxLik4.0 likelihood maximization sub-routine to estimate the pooled probits (2 parameters), the EC probits ($2 \times k$ parameters for $k = 1,2,3$), and the fixed effects probits ($n + 1$ parameters). Following the "road-map to the large T approximation" which we introduced in El-Gamal and Grether (1996), we started by estimating n probits (2 parameters each) for the n individuals, as well as one pooled probit (2 parameters) for the entire sample ($k = 1$). For $k = 2,3$, we then applied a k-means clustering algorithm to the n point estimates for the n individuals, using the algorithm of MacQueen (1967).[4] The k-centroids so produced were used as an initial condition for the EC multiprobit estimation, and produced reasonably fast convergence. For the fixed effects estimates, we used the individual $\hat{\alpha}_i$s from the n individual probits, and the $\hat{\beta}$ from the pooled probit, to initialize the search for the $(n + 1)$ parameters that maximize the fixed effects probit likelihood function. The average number of seconds used per simulation (for individual estimates, k-clustering, the $k = 1,2,3$ EC estimates and the fixed effects estimates) ranged from approximately 9 seconds for $T = 3$ to approximately 30 seconds for $T = 20$.

[4] We note that for sufficiently small sample sizes, the y_{it}s may be perfectly explained using a linear combination of the x_{it}s for some individuals. In such cases, the parameters for such individuals are identifiable only up to scale. In our Monte Carlo analysis, we applied a uniform rescaling of all individual probit estimates in such cases. We note that this is only used for finding reasonable (consistent) starting positions for the EC maximization, which identifies the parameters by pooling the data of all individuals within each type.

Table 5.1. *Misclassifications and ANE: means and STDs*

T	μ(mis)	σ(mis)	μ(ANE)	σ(ANE)
3	2.19	2.39	0.15	0.10
5	0.79	1.4	0.07	0.07
10	0.07	0.43	0.01	0.01
20	0.00	0.04	0.00	0.00

4 Monte Carlo results

For each of the two designs (unpoolable and poolable), we produce ten graphs. The first two graphs show the densities of the number of misclassifications and the ANE statistics, respectively, in the 1,000 simulations each for $T=3,5,10,20$. The next eight graphs per design are in four pairs for $T=3,5,10,20$. For each value of T, the pair of graphs show the densities of α and β estimates over the 1,000 simulations each, for the pooled estimates ($k=1$), and the EC estimates ($k=2$), as well as the fixed effects estimates. All densities are smoothed with a Gaussian kernel, and Silverman's rule of thumb bandwidth. In the remainder of this section, we shall bring to the reader's attention some of the more interesting features of the 10 plots for each design. It is our view, however, that "a picture is worth a 1000 words," and ocular examination of the smoothed densities is the best way to understand the behavior of our EC estimator relative to the fixed effects approach.

4.1 Design I: Unpoolable slopes

Figures 5.1 and 5.2 illustrate the speed with which the proportion of individuals misclassified by EC declines as T increases. Table 5.1 provides some summary statistics on the means and standard deviations of the number of misclassifications (out of 20 individuals), and the ANE statistic. It is clear that the proportion misclassified and the ANEs move together as predicted; hence reinforcing our recommendation to use the ANE as a measure of the degree of misclassification (and small sample estimation bias). We note that for Ts of modest size, the proportion misclassified is below 5 per-cent, as reflected also by the average ANE of 0.15. This suggests that T values similar to those in Heckman and MaCurdy (1980) may be sufficient for EC to perform very well, whereas we shall see in later discussion that fixed effects estimators perform rather poorly for this value of T. For T larger than 10, misclassifications are extremely rare, and the potential small sample estimation bias is negligible. This is in accordance with our results

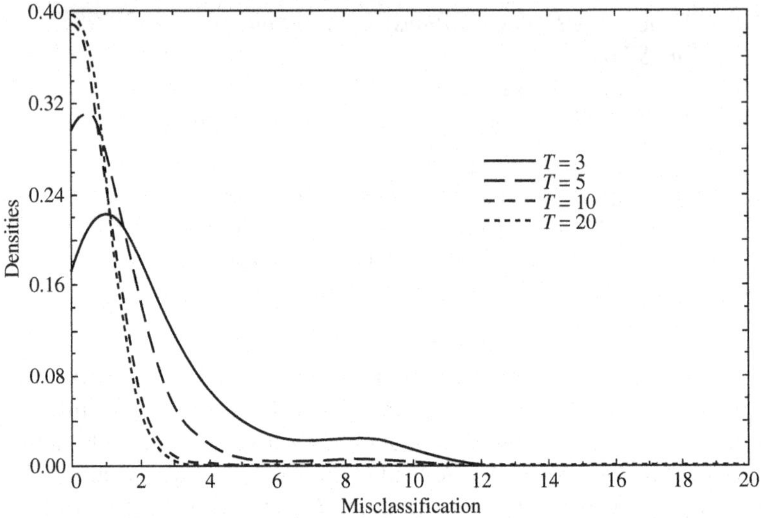

Figure 5.1 Densities of misclassification for $n = 20$, $T = 3, 5, 10, 20$

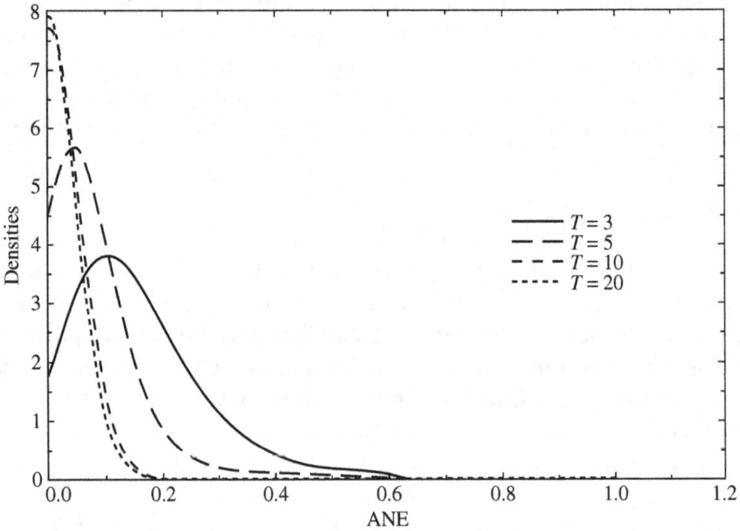

Figure 5.2 Densities of ANE for $n = 20$, $T = 3, 5, 10, 20$

Table 5.2. *Distribution of estimated k*

T	$\%\hat{k}=1$	$\%\hat{k}=2$	$\%\hat{k}>2$
3	4.8	63.1	32.1
5	0.0	81.9	18.1
10	0.0	88.7	11.3
20	0.0	92.5	7.5
50	0.0	95.0	5.0

in El-Gamal and Grether (1995), and El-Gamal and Grether (1996), where it was found with $T=14$ to 19 that the ANEs were reasonably small.

Table 5.2 shows the distribution of estimates of k (the number of types) as we vary T. It is clear in this table that the vast proportion of cases lead to correct estimation of $\hat{k}=2$, with the proportion starting above half and growing quickly as T gets larger. In tables 5.2 and 5.4 the column $\hat{k}>2$ implies that the penalized maximum likelihood for $k=3$ was larger than for $k=2$. Since we were interested mainly in the proportion of correctly estimated $\hat{k}$s we did not attempt to find the actual value of $\hat{k}$ beyond knowing that it is greater than the correct value (2).

Figures 5.3 through 5.10 illustrate the improvement in EC and fixed effects estimation. They show the rapid improvement in EC estimation, with modest biases for $T=3,5$, which are, however, much smaller than the corresponding biases in fixed effects estimates. For $T=10,20$, the EC estimators are performing extremely well, whereas the fixed effects estimates still exhibit a strong inward bias, and much larger variance, due to their inability to pool individuals with similar behavior.

4.1 Design II: Poolable slopes

Figures 5.11 and 5.12 illustrate the speed with which the proportion of individuals misclassified by EC declines as T increases. Table 5.3 provides some summary statistics on the means and standard deviations of the number of misclassifications (out of 20 individuals), and the ANE statistic. We notice from table 5.3 that the proportion of misclassifications, and the ANEs are somewhat higher in this poolable case than they were in the non-poolable case. This is mainly due to the fact that we are not imposing the conditions that $\beta_1 = \beta_2$. We note, however, that for $T=20$, the ANEs are virtually identical with those for the non-poolable case, and the proportion of misclassified individuals is very insignificant, despite the fact that we do not impose $\beta_1=\beta_2$.

Table 5.4 is the analog of Table 5.2, showing the behavior of $\hat{k}$ as T varies,

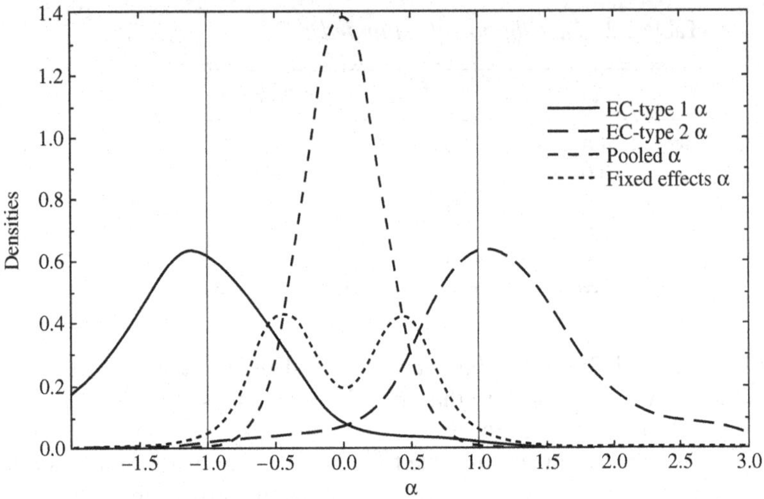

Figure 5.3 αs $T = 3$, $n = 20$, unpoolable βs

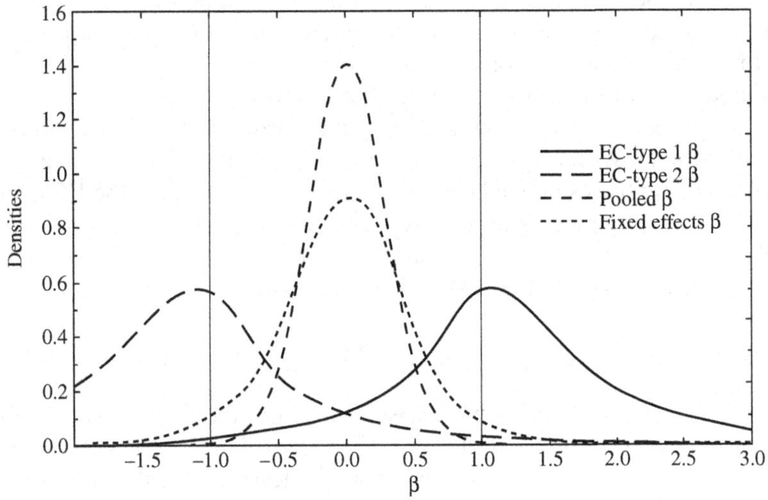

Figure 5.4 βs $T = 3$, $n = 20$, unpoolable βs

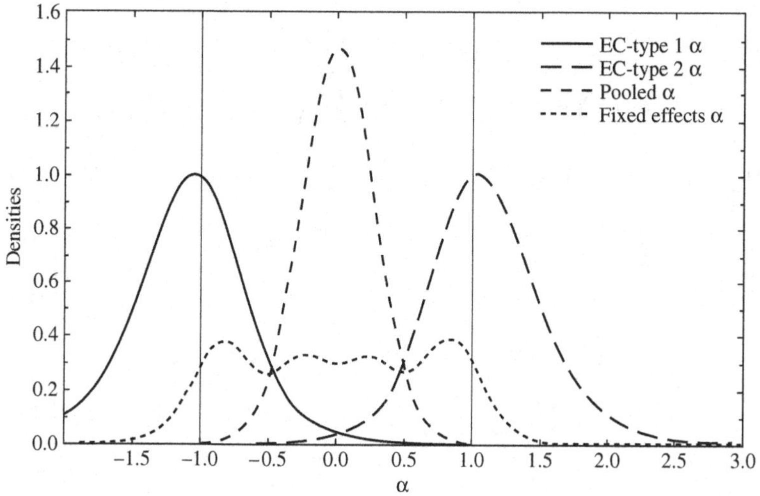

Figure 5.5 αs $T = 5$, $n = 20$, unpoolable βs

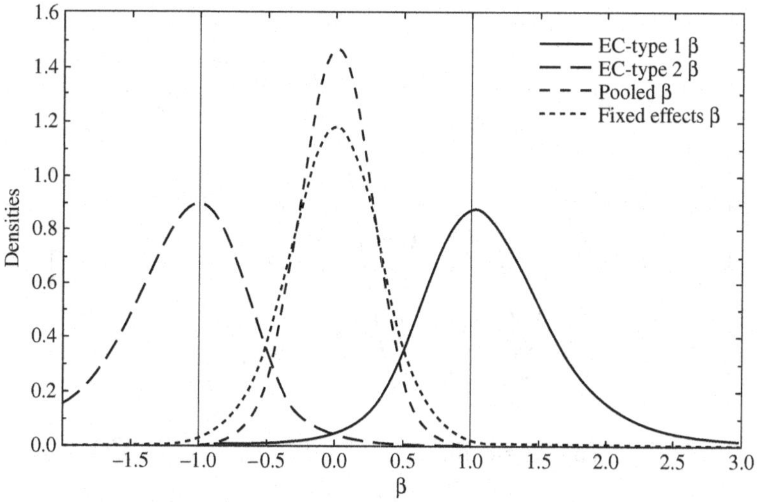

Figure 5.6 βs $T = 5$, $n = 20$, unpoolable βs

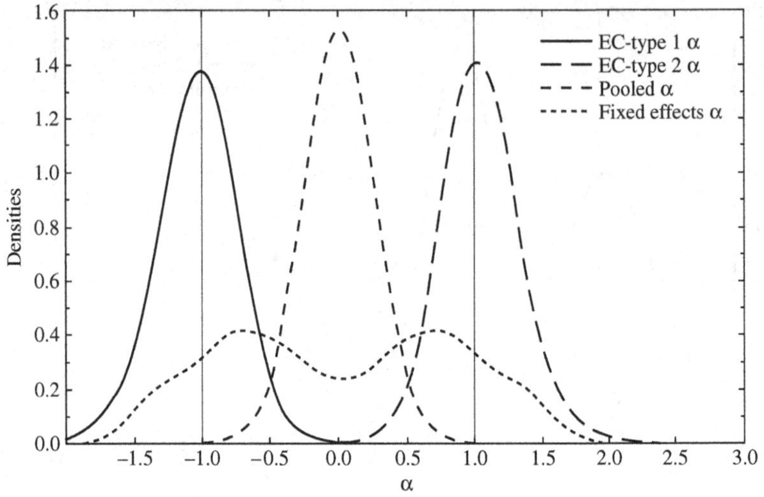

Figure 5.7 αs $T = 10, n = 20$, unpoolable βs

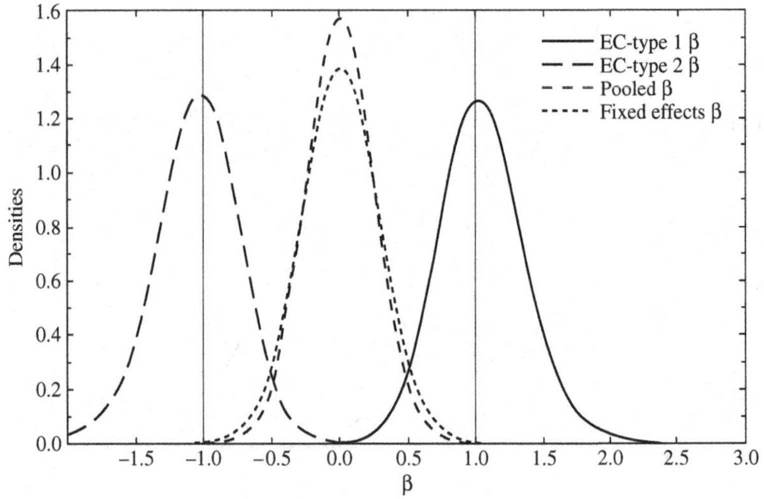

Figure 5.8 βs $T = 10, n = 20$, unpoolable βs

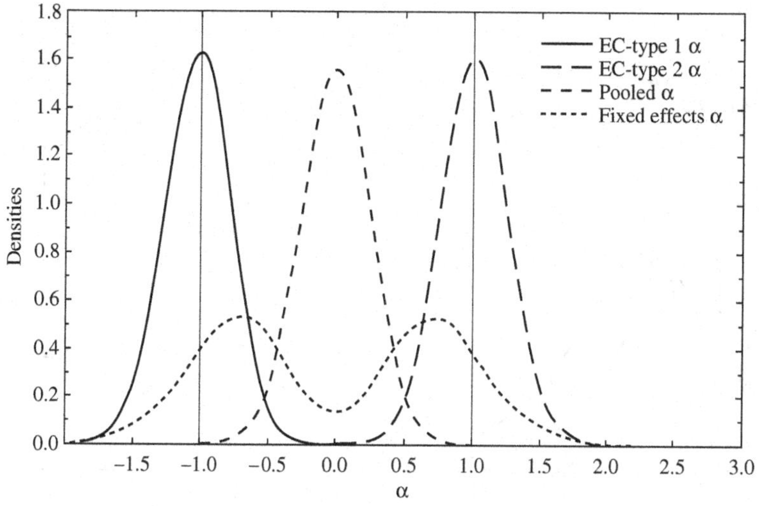

Figure 5.9 αs $T = 20$, $n = 20$, unpoolable βs

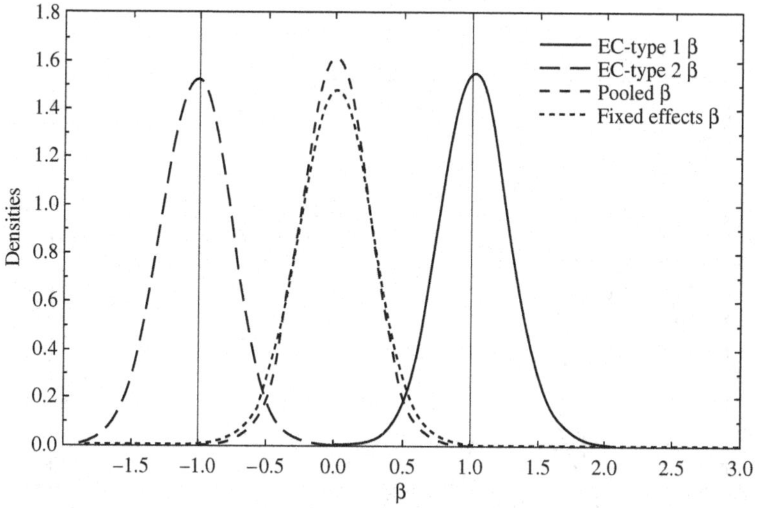

Figure 5.10 βs $T = 20$, $n = 20$, unpoolable βs

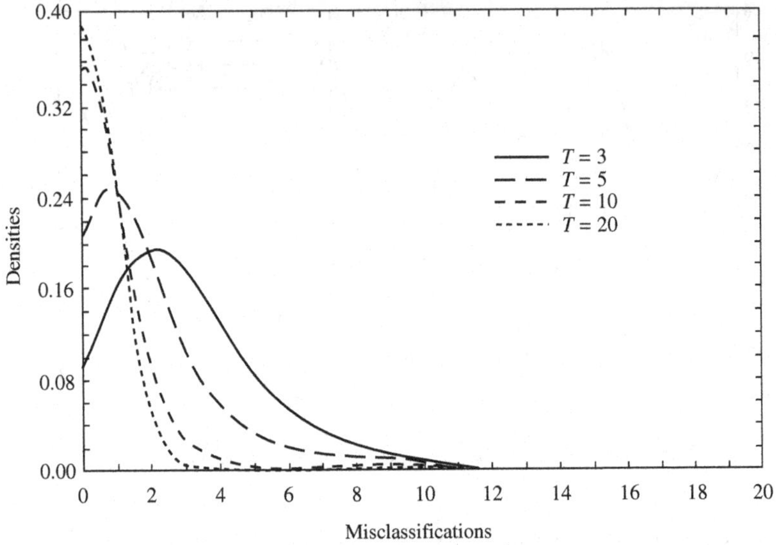

Figure 5.11 Densities of misclassification for $n = 20$, $T = 3, 5, 10, 20$, poolable slopes

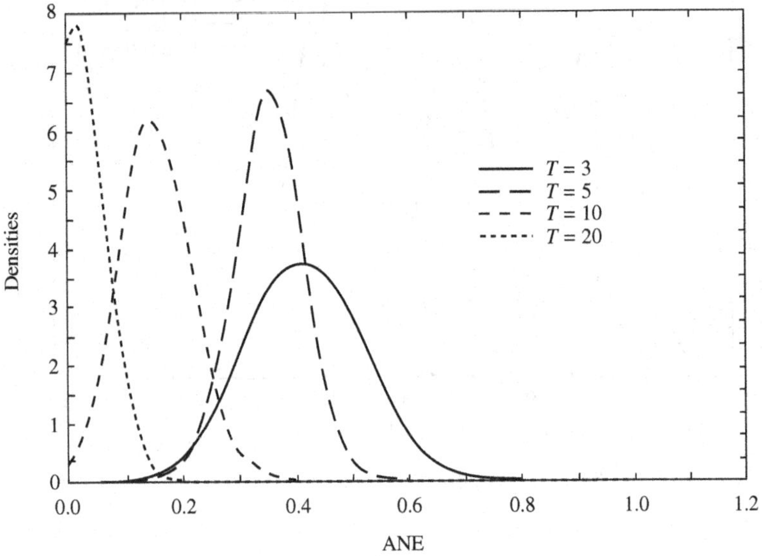

Figure 5.12 Densities of ANE for $n = 20$, $T = 3, 5, 10, 20$, poolable slopes

Table 5.3. *Misclassifications and ANE: means and STDs*

T	μ(mis)	σ(mis)	μ(ANE)	σ(ANE)
3	2.93	2.12	0.20	0.12
5	1.65	1.94	0.13	0.09
10	0.36	1.02	0.03	0.04
20	0.04	0.52	0.00	0.00

Table 5.4. *Distribution of estimated k*

T	$\%\hat{k}=1$	$\%\hat{k}=2$	$\%\hat{k}>2$
3	16.9	58.2	24.9
5	1.6	75.0	23.4
10	0.0	85.4	14.6
20	0.0	89.7	10.3

for the case of $\beta_1=\beta_2$. It can readily be seen by comparing Tables 5.2 and 5.4 that there is a tendency in the poolable case to estimate $\hat{k}=2$ correctly somewhat less often. For small values of T, both $\hat{k}=1$ and $\hat{k}>2$ occur more often in the poolable case, though not significantly so. In general, the main pattern in tables 5.2 and 5.4 is the fast convergence of almost all simulations to the correct estimation of $\hat{k}=2$ as T gets larger.

Figures 5.13 through 5.20 show that for $T=3,5$, the EC estimators still do significantly better on estimating α_1 and α_2, both in terms of bias and variance, than the fixed effects model. Despite the fact that the fixed effects model imposes the restriction that $\beta_1=\beta_2$, its performance in estimating β is not significantly better than the EC estimators, even for T as small as 3 and 5. With $T=10,20$, the EC estimators are clearly superior to the fixed effects estimators for α, and the performance in estimating β is virtually identical in terms of bias and variance. Hence, even with the handicap of not imposing $\beta_1=\beta_2$, the EC estimator recovers quickly for reasonable values of T. Needless to say, larger values of n can only improve the behavior of the EC estimate once T reaches this sufficiently large range (due to pooling more data within each group, thus reducing the estimation error).

5 Concluding remarks

The calculations exhibited in the previous section illustrate that the EC algorithm is not only feasible, but performs well in panels with values of T

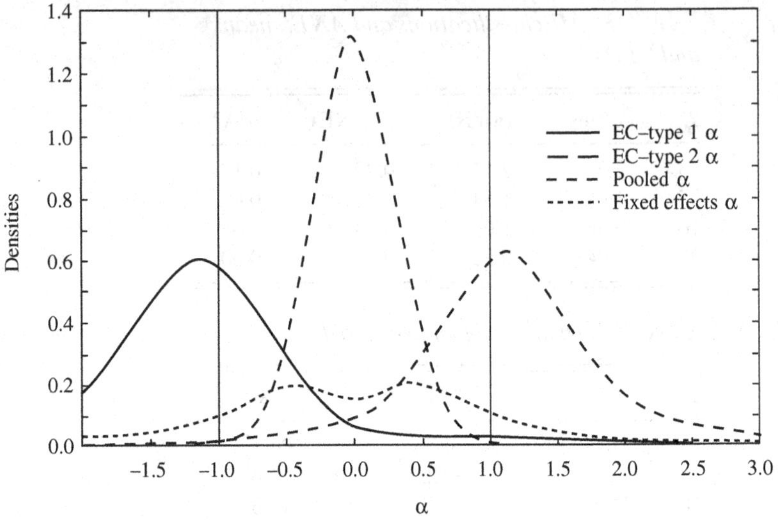

Figure 5.13 αs $T = 3, n = 20$, poolable βs

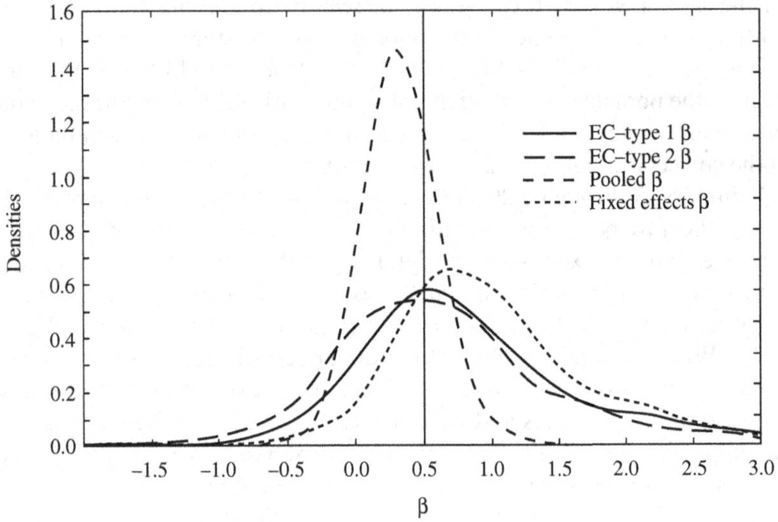

Figure 5.14 βs $T = 3, n = 20$, poolable βs

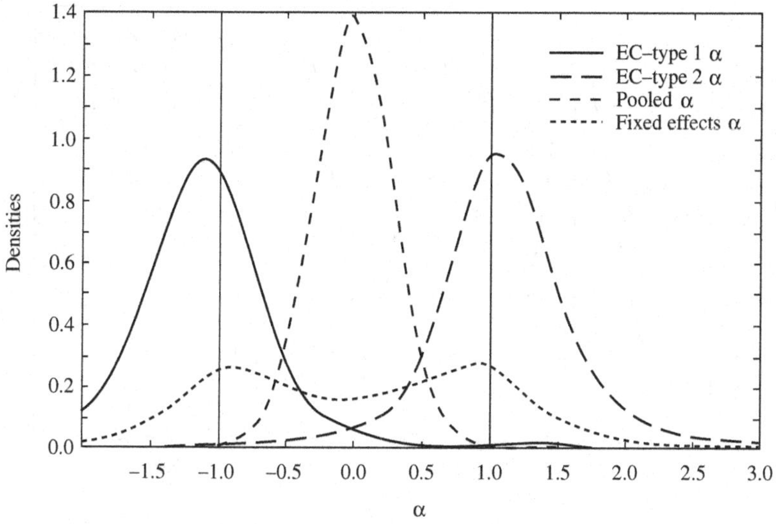

Figure 5.15 αs $T = 5, n = 20$, poolable βs

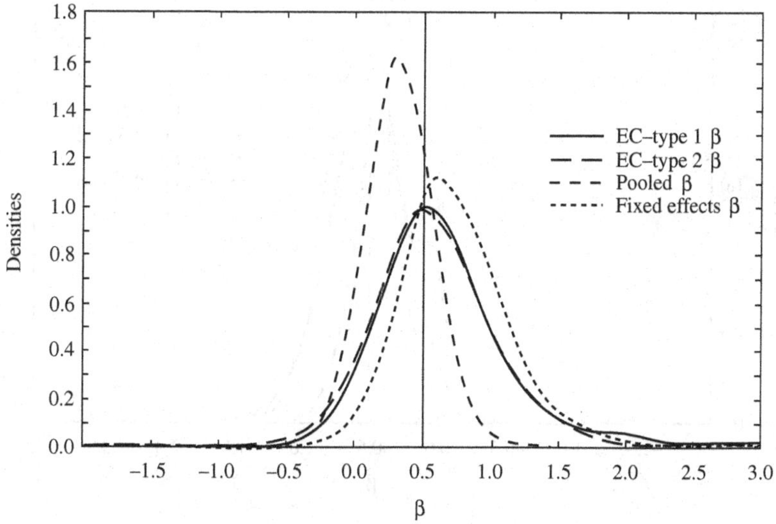

Figure 5.16 βs $T = 5, n = 20$, unpoolable βs

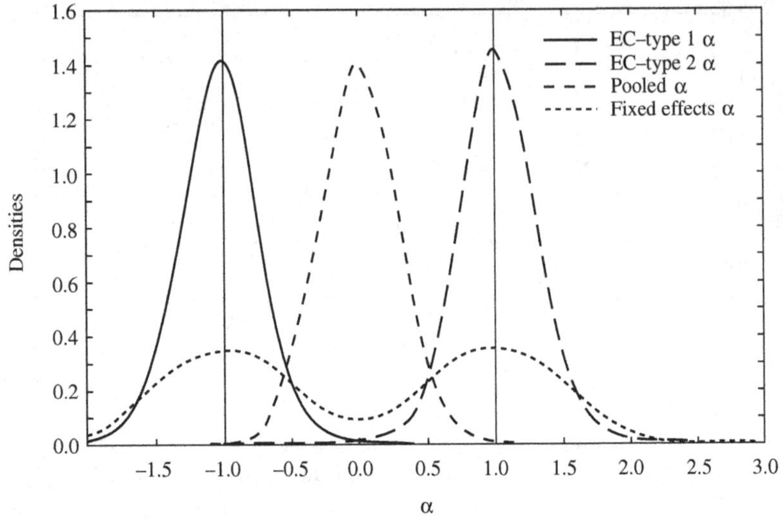

Figure 5.17 αs $T = 10, n = 20$, poolable βs

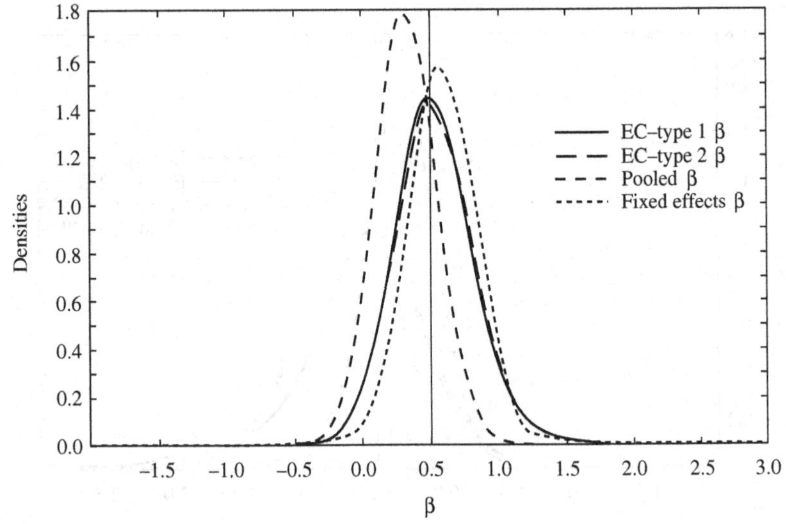

Figure 5.18 βs $T = 10, n = 20$, poolable βs

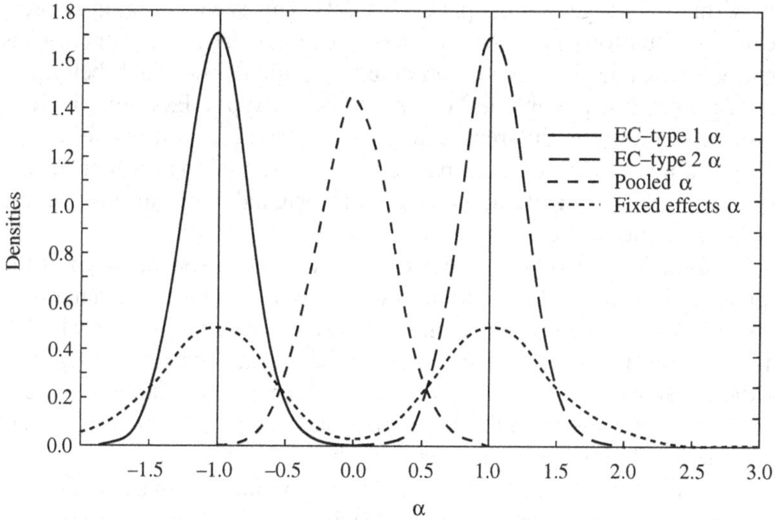

Figure 5.19 αs $T = 20$, $n = 20$, poolable βs

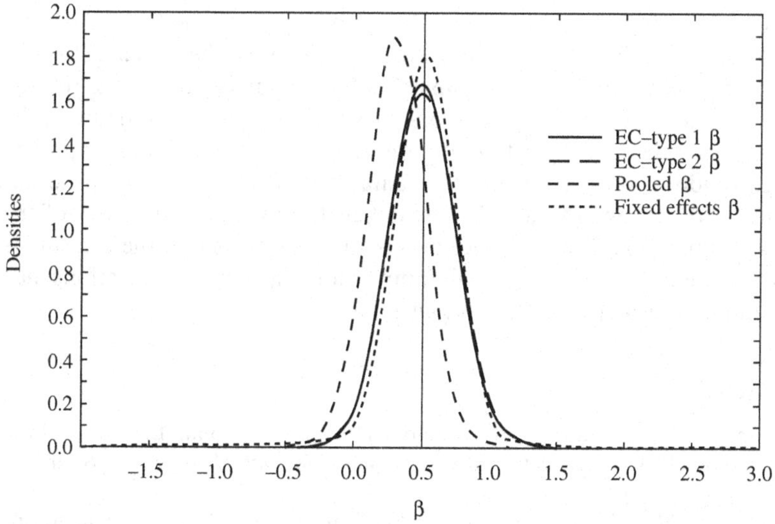

Figure 5.20 βs $T = 20$, $n = 20$, poolable βs

well within the range of most panel data sets. This is encouraging as there are many situations in which the basic idea underlying the method is directly applicable. That is, the observed individuals may each belong to one of a fixed but possibly unknown number of types. Examples include consumers adopting different shopping strategies, countries following different kinds of development paths, workers responding to intermittent spells of unemployment, and, as in our original applications, people making inference judgments.

The statistical theory of the EC estimator is based on asymptotic approximations as T goes to infinity with n going to infinity or remaining constant. As pointed out earlier in the chapter it does not matter whether T is large relative to n or not. What is crucial is that T be sufficiently large for the classification of the units to types to be made with sufficient precision. If such precise classification is possible, small sample biases arising from misclassification can be ignored safely.

Given this asymptotic approximation, the econometrician needs a means to determine if the sample sizes available are sufficiently large. We suggest that once the individuals have been classified into types, the researcher may calculate the posterior probability that each individual unit belongs to each of the active types using our large-T approximation to the EM algorithm. If these probabilities are close to zeros and ones, then the data are strongly in agreement with the assignment of individuals to types. If the classifications are not crisp, then one may wish to study the mixture of the types using the EM algorithm, or consider an entirely different approach (e.g., random effects models) to the data. We introduced a diagnostic statistic ANE designed to aid the researcher in judging the crispness of the classifications. The performance in this study suggests that the measure is indeed useful in identifying small samples for which misclassifications may result in biases in parameter estimates.

References

Dempster, A., N. Laird, and D. Rubin (1977), "Maximum Likelihood from Incomplete Data via the EM algorithm," *Journal of the Royal Statistical Society B*, 39: 1–38.

El-Gamal, M. and D. Grether (1995), "Are People Bayesian? Uncovering Behavioral Strategies," *Journal of the American Statistical Association*, 90 (432): 1137–1145.

(1996), "Unknown Heterogeneity, the EC-EM Algorithm, and Large *T* Approximation," SSRI working paper No 9622. University of Wisconsin at Madison.

Heckman, J. and T. MaCurdy (1980), "A Life Cycle Model of Female Labour Supply," *Review of Economic Studies*, 47: 47–74.

Little, R. and D. Rubin (1983), "On Jointly Estimating Parameters and Missing Data," *The American Statistician*, 37: 218–220.
(1987), *Statistical Analysis with Missing Data*, New York: Wiley.
MacQueen, J. (1967), "Some Methods of Classification and Analysis of Multivariate Observations," *Proceedings of the 5th Berkeley Symposium on Mathematical Statistics and Probability*, 1: 281–297.
Maddala, G. (1991), "To Pool or Not to Pool: That is the Question," *Journal of Quantitative Economics*, 7: 255–264.
(1996), "The Pooling Problem," in L. Matyas and P. Sevestre (eds.), *The Econometrics of Panel Data: A Handbook of the Theory with Applications*, Boston: Kluwer Academic Publishers.
Pesaran, H., R. Smith, and K. Im (1996), "Dynamic Linear Models for Heterogeneous Panels," in L. Matyas and P. Sevestre (eds.), *The Econometrics of Panel Data: A Handbook of the Theory with Applications*, Boston: Kluwer Academic Publishers, pp. 145–195.
Redner, R. and H. Walker (1984), "Mixture Densities, Maximum Likelihood and the EM Algorithm," *Siam Review*, 26(2): 195–239.
Rissanen, J. (1978), "Modeling by Shortest Data Description," *Automatica*, 14: 465–471.
Tanner, M. (1996), *Tools for Statistical Inference, Third Edition*, New York: Springer-Verlag.
Wallace, C. and D. Boulton (1968), "An Information Measure for Classification," *Computer Journal*, 11: 185–195.

6 Properties of alternative estimators of dynamic panel models: an empirical analysis of cross-country data for the study of economic growth

MARC NERLOVE

1 Introduction

One of the most important implications of the classic papers of Solow (1956) and Swan (1956) is that the lower the starting level of real per capita GDP, relative to the long run of steady state position, the faster is the growth rate. The Solow–Swan model assumes a constant-returns-to-scale production function with two inputs, capital and labor, and substitution between inputs, a constant savings rate, constant rate of growth of population, and neutral technical change, all exogenously given. Convergence of economies starting out at different levels of per capita income to the same steady state rate of growth reflects the diminishing returns to capital implied by the production function assumed: economies starting out with lower levels of real per capita

This chapter draws extensively from "Growth Rate Convergence, Fact or Artifact? An Essay in Panel Data Econometrics," prepared for the Sixth Conference on Panel Data Econometrics, Amsterdam, 28–29 June 1996. The research on which it is based was supported by the Maryland Agricultural Experiment Station, Project A-53.

My interest in the question of how the econometric approach might have influenced recent findings with respect to the convergence hypothesis was stimulated by reading Islam (1995a). Although I wound up going directly to the Penn World Tables for the data underlying the analyses presented here, I began by working with the series Islam was kind enough to supply and for which I am greatly indebted to him.

I thank Hashem Pesaran for helpful discussions, and Robert Barro, Michael Binder, William Greene, Kajal Lahiri, G.S. Maddala, and C. Spohr for useful comments. Pietro Balestra suggested the method used to obtain the likelihood function for the differenced model. Special thanks are due to Anke Meyer, with whom I discussed every aspect of this work.

I am also indebted to Jinkyo Suh and Timothy Thomas for computational counsel and their assistance in straightening out the GAUSS programs which I wrote to obtain the results reported here. Suh also checked and double checked all derivations and verified that my programs accurately reflected the formulae derived and carried out further analyses for this revision in connection with the differenced model.

This chapter is dedicated to my long-time friend and one-time colleague G.S. Maddala.

GDP relative to the long-run or steady state position have less capital per worker and therefore higher rates of return to capital. I will refer to this as the standard Barro-Baumol (BB) sense of the meaning of convergence. There is a good deal of current discussion regarding the appropriate definition of "convergence."[1] My purpose here is not to question this notion of convergence but rather to show that estimates of the coefficient of the lagged dependent variable in a dynamic panel model which has been used to study this phenomenon are extremely sensitive to the method of estimation employed. Because the steady state of the Solow–Swan model depend on the savings rate, the rate of growth of the population, and the rate of technical progress, many have argued that these factors need to be held constant in attempting to test the hypothesis of growth rate convergence. Convergence is, in this case, conditional. Convergence may also be conditional on other factors such as the accumulation of human capital or investment in infrastructure or, indeed, other unobserved factors which are trending at different rates in different countries or regions.[2]

The problem of BB-convergence in the standard neoclassical model is treated both theoretically and empirically in the recent text by Barro and Sala-i-Martin (1995) and empirically in a recent paper by Islam (1995a). Bernard and Durlauf (1996) provide a useful framework for understanding the time-series and cross-sectional tests of the BB-convergence hypothesis and its relation to alternative definitions. Quah (1996) discusses the problem of convergence in more general form and distinguishes several different varieties. He argues that "Simply because panel data techniques happen to apply to data with extensive cross-section and time series variation does not mean they are at once similarly appropriate for analyzing convergence." While I do not fault Quah's conclusion, current discussions do emphasize panel data and methods and derive strong conclusions regarding BB-convergence and the significance of other determinants of growth from such data. It is therefore appropriate to consider how these conclusions, *within the context of BB-convergence*, are affected by the econometric methods employed.

Perhaps even more important than the problem of convergence is the question of the determinants of growth. The World Bank Project on Economic Growth lists 15 published papers and 15 working papers almost

[1] Bernard and Durlauf (1995) give a nice discussion emphasizing the restrictiveness of the approach, going back to the earlier work of Barro (1991) and Baumol (1986), on which my analysis of econometric methods is based (see also Quah (1996)), and which is the most prevalent. Other recent contributions include Islam (1995b), Caselli, Esquivel, and Lefort (1996), and the fine survey by de la Fuente (1997).

[2] When population growth is endogenously determined, this implication of convergence, conditional or otherwise, of the neoclassical model of economic growth does not necessarily follow; see Nerlove and Raut (1997).

all of which involve dynamic panel data analysis or cross-section analysis with a state variable or initial condition.[3] Although the focus of these papers is not convergence but the effects of the other variables included, if the coefficient of the state variable in the statistical analysis is inconsistently estimated, in this sense "biased," then the coefficient of any variable correlated with the state variable will also be biased. Hence, quite misleading conclusions may be drawn concerning the significance, sign, and relative magnitude of other factors included in the analysis, conclusions which may significantly affect the policy implications of the analysis.

Section 2 examines recent empirical investigations of BB-convergence and the rate of convergence and argues that most are flawed by failure to allow for the inconsistencies of single cross-section or panel studies in a dynamic context.[4] In a dynamic context a single cross section is best viewed as a panel with time dimension 1. I do not attempt here a general review of the effects of the methods used in more general studies of the determinants of growth, but elsewhere I have examined the effects on the estimated coefficients of the Barro and Lee (1993) estimates of the stock of human capital.[5]

In section 3, I discuss four common methods of estimating the coefficient of the "state" variable interpreted in terms of the rate of convergence (and thus testing for convergence), and show that these four methods yield estimates which satisfy an inequality derived by Sevestre and Trognon (1996). One broad class of estimates with which I do not deal here are those based on the generalized method of moments and the so-called matrix method due to Chamberlain (1984), or derived from his work (Holtz-Eakin, Newey, and Rosen (1988) and Arellano and Bond (1991)).[6] These methods are not only somewhat difficult to implement but the resulting estimates are, by

[3] See http//www.worldbank.org/html/prdmg/grthweb.

[4] This point is also made by Caselli *et al.* (1996) in a study which came to my attention after Nerlove (1996) was written. A recent study by Lee *et al.* (1996) arrives at similar conclusions but proposes a number of alternatives different from those investigated here. In particular, I believe that their formulation of what they call the unconditional likelihood function is quite different from that proposed here because they include deterministic trends in their model and cannot therefore directly formulate the likelihood *unconditional on the initial observations* (see footnote 11).

[5] See the appendix to Nerlove (1996).

[6] For an extensive exposition of these methods and a very general formulation, see Crépon and Mairesse (1996). The method is based on a series of transformations of the basic equation (1); the resulting equation is then estimated as a cross-section regression on the original explanatory variables in all periods. Caselli *et al.* (1996) use a variant which is an application of the GMM method applied to the first differences of the series. They then use the stock or state variables as instruments. This implies that they are predetermined and therefore conditions on their values. If indeed the process, originally or in first-difference form, is stationary, the procedure does discard the information in the initial observations, which is just what unconditional ML seeks to avoid. Since conditional ML should give estimates with the same desirable properties as GMM and is very easy to compute under these circumstances, it is not clear to me why Caselli *et al.*, and others have avoided its use.

construction, insensitive to the way in which initial values of the "state" variable have presumably been generated. Below I argue that, if the process generating the data in the sample period is stationary, or can be made so by suitable transformation of the data, the initial values of the state variable convey a great deal of information about that process since they reflect how it has operated in the past. Thus conditioning on those initial conditions is clearly an undesirable feature especially when the time dimension of the panel is short.

In section 3.6, I present a new method of maximum likelihood estimation based on the density of the observations *unconditional on the initial or starting values of the dependent variable*. I argue more generally for methods of inference which look at more than just the maximum of the likelihood function, on the basis of the *likelihood principle* of Fisher (1922, 1925). This approach fully takes into account what information the initial conditions contain about how the process has operated in the past and is thus of special relevance to short time-dimension ("shallow") panels. I extend this method to the case of country-specific trends. These make the underlying processes being investigated nonstationary, but simple forms of nonstationarity can be removed by differencing the data.

Finally, in section 4, I apply all six methods to two panel data sets drawn from the Penn World Tables, for both a model with country-specific intercept effects and one with country-specific trends. The results show clearly how misleading the standard estimates can be in assessing growth rate convergence and in the estimation of the significance and magnitude of other variables included. The contrast between the conditional and the unconditional ML estimates for a small cross-section dimension and their similarity for a large cross-section dimension is illustrated, as is the importance of looking at the likelihood function itself more broadly. I also show that the usual procedures for doing feasible GLS or for obtaining starting values for ML are seriously flawed and likely to yield negative estimates of the random time persistent cross-sectional effects. The results also show that biases in the estimate of the coefficient of the lagged value of the dependent variable are transmitted to the estimates of other coefficients in the model, making inferences about the determinants of growth problematic unless appropriate econometric methods are used.

Section 5 concludes.

2 Recent empirical investigations of convergence and the rate of convergence

Let y_t = per capita output, k_t = the capital–labor ratio, s = the savings rate, δ = the depreciation rate of capital, and n = the exogenous rate of population growth and labor force. All of these variables may differ over time as indicated by their subscript t, but also, in a cross-country context, they are certain to differ from one country to another in a fashion which persists over time. An additional subscript is introduced in the sections which follow this one to indicate that fact. If the production function is Cobb–Douglas, $y_t = A_t k_t^{\alpha}$, where A_t reflects other than conventional factors of production affecting growth and where α, the elasticity of per capita output with respect to the capital–labor ratio, is often interpreted in terms of capital's share as implied by payment of capital at its marginal product. Under these circumstances it can easily be shown using a simple partial adjustment model that

$$\log y_t = \frac{\alpha(1-\gamma)}{1-\alpha}[\log s - \log(n+\delta)] + \frac{1-\gamma}{1-\alpha}\log A_t + \gamma \log \gamma_{t-1}. \quad (1)$$

The speed of convergence to equilibrium is inversely proportional to γ, with growth convergence $0<\gamma<1$. In equilibrium, per capita GDP depends only on the parameters n and s, and on the time path of A_t. In an empirical context, these differ from time to time and country to country. Clearly the extent of convergence is conditional on s, n, δ and the time path of A_t. In empirical investigations, changing n and s and sometimes a measure of changing A_t have been introduced. Below I examined models in which A_t is assumed to be constant although differing from one country to another and an alternative formulation in which A_t can be represented by a simple linear trend which plausibly also differs from country to country.

Equation (1) has been widely used to examine the hypothesis of growth convergence (Mankiw *et al.* (1992, p. 410), Barro and Sala-i-Martin (1995, chapter 12), Islam (1995a, p. 1133), Lee *et al.* (1996), Caseli, *et al.* (1996)). In empirical work, y_t is replaced by real per capita GDP; when varying s and n are taken into account, s is replaced by an average savings rate over the period t-l to t, and n is replaced by the growth rate of population over the period t-l to t. It is usual to use rates averaged over several years; following Islam (1995a), I have used quinquennial averages. The restriction on the coefficients of $\ln(s)$ and $\ln(n+\delta)$, which arises from the constant-returns-to-scale assumption, implies that $\ln(s)$ and $\ln(n+\delta)$ can be collapsed into a single variable. Testing the growth convergence hypothesis, in this context, resolves largely around the coefficient γ of the lagged level of per capita real GDP. If this is positive but much less than one, the implication is that on average countries with low initial values are growing faster than those with high initial values and is therefore evidence of convergence. Whereas, if this coefficient is close to one, perhaps even slightly larger than one, the implication is that initial values have little or no effect or even a perverse one on subsequent growth; such a finding is therefore evidence against the neoclassical theory which implies convergence. For example, if $\gamma = 0.9$, convergence to within 90 per cent of final equilibrium occurs only in 22 periods, which, given quinquennial data, implies 110 years! Similarly, 0.8 requires 53 years, 0.7, 32 years, while 0.2 requires only 7 years, and 0.1 is within 90 per cent in 5 years.[7]

The estimates of γ for the levels model presented below using cross-country quinquennial data are generally in excess of 0.7 no matter what econometric procedure is employed, but vary over a wide range depending on the method, 0.7 to 0.98. But for the differenced model, many estimates of γ are much smaller in the vicinity of 0.5.[8] It is apparent that, for all practical purposes, coefficients in excess of 0.7 represent negligible convergence, since, with unchanging s, n, and A, it would take more than a generation to achieve 90 per cent of equilibrium real per capita GDP. Most recent studies attempt to test whether $\gamma = 1$; however, this is a test for a unit root in $\log y_{it}$. Even under the best of circumstances testing for a unit root is problematic (see Diebold and Nerlove (1990)). Here the problems are compounded by the short time dimension of the typical panel. Basing a test on the size of γ rather than equality with 1 finesses a host of problems of the sort discussed extensively in Diebold and Nerlove (1990).[9]

Tests based on a single cross section (which can be viewed as a panel of time dimension 1) or on pooled cross-section time series (panel) data generally have yielded contradictory results: pooled panel data studies tend to reject the hypothesis of BB-convergence (relatively high γs), even after controlling for population growth rates, savings rates, and other variables. Dynamic fixed-effects models are, of course, not possible for a single cross section, but recent work (Islam, 1995a) using a dynamic fixed-effects panel model yields results supporting convergence. There are serious problems with tests such as those which rely on the estimated coefficients of the lagged, or initial value, of the dependent variable in dynamic panel models or in the special case of a single cross section, which arise from two sources of bias. In this chapter, I show some of these findings are probably artifacts arising from biases in the econometric methods employed. This demonstrates the sensitivity of the conclusions drawn about γ to the econometric method employed, irrespective of the validity of the relationship estimated.

7 Derivation of the model and the calculations behind this statement are given in Nerlove (1996, pp. 5–8 and appendix table 2).

8 Using a GMM estimator Caselli *et al.*, obtained an estimate of about 0.51–0.53, i.e. much more rapid convergence and close to the estimates obtained for the 94-country sample using either conditional or unconditional ML. My estimates for the 22-country sample are much higher, however.

9 Barnard and Durlauf (1995) use cointegration techniques on rather longer time series for 15 OECD countries to test alternative time series definitions of convergence and contrast the results with the standard BB-formulation.

The first source of bias are omitted variables, especially infrastructure and investments over time in infrastructure, and the natural resource base available to each country in cross-sectional or panel studies. Systematic differences across countries or regions will systematically bias the conclusions. Because such variables are likely to be correlated with savings or investment rates in conventional or in human capital, and with population growth rates it is not altogether clear what the net effect of omitting them on the coefficient of the initial value will be in a single cross section. But in a pooled model it is clear that, to the extent such differences are persistent, they will be highly correlated with the initial value and therefore omitting them will bias the coefficient of that variable upwards toward one and thus toward rejecting convergence. This source of bias has been well known since the early paper by Balestra and Nerlove (1966) and is well supported by the Monte Carlo studies reported in Nerlove (1971). In this light, it is not surprising that pooled panel data, or single cross sections, which are a special case of panels with $T=1$, even with inclusion of additional variables, often reject convergence.

Second, since there are likely to be many sources of cross-country or cross-region differences, many of which cannot be observed or directly accounted for, it is natural to try to represent these by fixed effects in a panel context. But, as is well known from the Monte Carlo investigations reported in Nerlove (1971) and demonstrated analytically by Nickell (1981), inclusion of fixed effects in a dynamic model biases the coefficient of the initial value of the dependent variable included as an explanatory variable downwards, toward zero and therefore toward support for the convergence hypothesis. This may account for Islam's (1995a) recent findings.

Alternative estimates based on more appropriate random-effects models, such as two-stage feasible generalized least squares or maximum likelihood conditional on the initial observations are also biased in small samples and inconsistent in large, or in the case of instrumental variable estimates have poor sampling properties or are difficult to implement. For example, the papers by Knight, Loayza, and Villaneuva (1993), Loayza (1994), and Islam (1995a) employ a method, among others, proposed by Chamberlain (1984), generally referred to as the Π-matrix approach.[10] The alternative of unconditional maximum likelihood suggested in Nerlove and Balestra (1996) is implemented for the first time in this paper.[11]

[10] See also Crépon and Mairesse (1996).

[11] Lee *et al* (1997) also estimate from what they maintain is an unconditional likelihood function, but inasmuch as they do not transform to stationarity (their relationship includes both a constant and a linear trend), I do not think their formulation of the likelihood function is based on the unconditional density of the dependent variable as proposed here. In fact, they estimate from a likelihood based on the *conditional* density of the dependent variable given the initial value. The relation between conditional and unconditional likelihood is discussed at length in Nerlove (1997).

Even if one has little interest in the question of convergence, or its rate, per se, the question of whether the coefficient of the state variable, lagged dependent or initial value, is biased in the sense of being inconsistent is an important one since biases in this coefficient will affect the estimates of the coefficients of other variables correlated with it and their levels of significance. To the extent such estimates are important in the formulation of policies to promote growth, the matter is indeed a serious one.[12]

In the remainder of this chapter, I investigate the sensitivity of the coefficient of the lagged dependent or state variable to the econometric method employed as well as the sensitivity of the estimates of the coefficients for other variables included. All of the results reported, except those for pooled panel data, support the growth convergence hypothesis conditional on savings and population growth rates but illustrate the rather different estimates of the rates of convergence, and of the coefficients of other explanatory variables, obtained when different estimation techniques are used. In addition, a technique for examining the shape of sections of a high-dimensional likelihood function is developed which reveals interesting and somewhat unexpected relationships among the various estimates.

3 Alternative methods for estimation[13]

A good summary of the current state of knowledge about the properties of various estimators in dynamic panel models is contained in Sevestre and Trognon (1996). Trognon (1978) was the first to show the possible inconsistency of maximum likelihood conditional on the initial individual observations. Nickell (1981) shows the inconsistency of the estimates of the fixed effects in a dynamic panel model. Kiviet (1995) derives exact results for the bias of leading estimators. In this section, following Sevestre and Trognon, I review the leading estimators and their properties for dynamic panel models. I will assume a random effects model for the disturbance for the reasons set forth in Nerlove and Balestra (1996) and because fixed effects can be viewed as a special case from the standpoint of estimation.

For simplicity, in this section I restrict attention to the simple model containing one exogenous variable x_{it} and one lagged value of the dependent

[12] For example in (1) the parameter α could be derived from the coefficient of the variable log $s - \log(n+\delta)$ as coefficient/(coefficient $+ 1 - \gamma$), so there is a double source of bias. Indeed, a number of authors accept or reject statistical formulations based on the estimated value of α which should approximate capital's share.

[13] I rely extensively in this section on the excellent discussion of Sevestre and Trognon, chapter 7 in Mátyás and Sevestre (1996, pp. 120–144). Additional alternatives, more appropriate when longer time series are available, are treated by Lee *et al.* (1997) and are not discussed or implemented here.

variable y_{it-1} as explanatory. Extension to the case in which more than one exogenous explanatory variable is included presents no serious difficulty.

$$y_{it} = \alpha + \beta x_{it} + \gamma y_{it-1} + \mu_i + \varepsilon_{it},\ i = 1,\ldots,N,\ t = 1,\ldots,T. \tag{2}$$

Taking deviations from overall means eliminates the constant α. The usual assumptions are made about the properties of the μ_i and the ε_{it}.

(i) $E(\mu_i) = E(\varepsilon_{it}) = 0$, all i and t,

(ii) $E(\mu_i \varepsilon_{it}) = 0$, all i and t,

(iii) $E(\mu_i \mu_j) = \begin{cases} \sigma_\mu^2 & i = j \\ 0 & i \neq j, \end{cases}$

(iv) $E(\varepsilon_{it} \varepsilon_{js}) = \begin{cases} \sigma_\varepsilon^2 & t = s,\ i = j \\ 0 & \textit{otherwise} \end{cases}$

Both μ_i and ε_{it} are assumed to be uncorrelated with x_{it} for all i and t. While this assumption is far from innocuous, for example, if savings rates or population growth are not independent of per capita income or unobserved factors which affect it, I adopt it here, not only because it is conventional but because one has to cut off somewhere. Clearly, however, y_{it-1} cannot be assumed to be uncorrelated with μ_i. It is clear, therefore, that OLS applied to (2) ignoring the component nature of the disturbances $\mu_{it} = \mu_i + \varepsilon_{it}$, which I call the *pooled regression*, will yield inconsistent estimates. In particular, if $\gamma > 0$, γ_{pooled} is "biased" upwards. So, just as in the case of ordinary serial correlation β_{pooled} is also "biased" and the OLS residuals understate the amount of serial correlation, which in this case is measured by the intraclass correlation coefficient ρ. This parameter measures the extent of unobserved or latent time-invariant, individual-specific, variation relative to the total unobserved variation in the sample, $\sigma_\mu^2/(\sigma_\mu^2 + \sigma_\varepsilon^2)$. It is extremely important in understanding the nature of the variation, both observed and unobserved, in the panel.

3.1 *Inconsistency of the pooled-sample OLS estimates of the dynamic error components model*

Since the panel has two dimensions, it is possible to consider asymptotic behavior as $N \to \infty$, $T \to \infty$, or both. Generally speaking it is easier to increase the cross-section dimension of a panel, so the most relevant asymptotics are as $N \to \infty$. This is called *semi-asymptotics* in the panel data literature. It is not necessary to assume $|\gamma| < 1$ as long as T is fixed, but the way in which the initial values of the dependent variable, y_{i0}, are assumed to be generated is crucial. To see why, write (2) as

$$y_{it} = \gamma^t y_{i0} + \sum_{j=0}^{t-1} \gamma^j \beta x_{it-j} + \frac{1-\gamma^t}{1-\gamma}\mu_i + v_{it}, \text{ where } v_{it} = \sum_{j=0}^{t-1} \gamma^j \varepsilon_{it-j}. \quad (3)$$

Equation (3) expresses y_{it} as the sum of four terms: the first $\gamma^t y_{i0}$, depends on the initial values; the second on lagged values of the exogenous variable; the third on the individual, time-invariant, component of residual variance; and the fourth on lagged values of the remaining component. This last term is an autoregressive process with initial values $v_{i0} = 0$ and $v_{it} = \gamma v_{it-1} + \varepsilon_{it}$. It need not be assumed to be stationary as long as T is fixed. It does not make sense in this context to assume that y_{i0} are uncorrelated with either the μ_i or the lagged values of x_{it}s. On the other hand, ε_{i0} is a random variable with mean 0 and variance σ_ε^2 independently and identically distributed for all i. Thus, the initial observation can be written as a function of lagged xs, the μ_i and ε_{i0}:

$$y_{i0} = f(x_{i0}, x_{i-1}, \ldots, \mu_i, \varepsilon_{i0}). \quad (4)$$

Clearly, if the individual effects μ_i are assumed to be fixed and the lagged xs to be given the y_{i0} are also fixed and uncorrelated with the disturbances in (3), $v_{it}, t = 1, \ldots, T$. But, if the individual effects are considered to be random, as Nerlove and Balestra (1996) have argued they should be, the initial observations are not exogenous since they are correlated with them, as they are part of the disturbance term, namely the third and fourth terms of (3).

It is common in the literature on panel data to assume that the y_{i0} are i.i.d. random variables which are characterized by their second moments and correlations with the individual effects, and not necessarily generated by the same process which generates the rest of the y_{it}s. The properties of various estimators depend on the process generating them. One possibility is to try to model and estimate this process together with the dynamic panel model (2).

3.2 *Inconsistency of the OLS estimators of the dummy variable, or fixed-effects, model*

The ordinary least squares estimates of both the coefficient of the lagged dependent variable and the exogenous variable are inconsistent in the fixed-effects model. As is well known, the fixed-effects model is equivalent to taking deviations from individual (country) means and then estimating an ordinary OLS regression

$$y_{it} - \bar{y}_i = \beta(x_{it} - \bar{x}_i) + \gamma(y_{i,t-1} - \bar{y}_{i,t-1}) + v_{it} \text{ where } v_{it} = \varepsilon_{it} - \bar{\varepsilon}_i. \quad (5)$$

Although $\sigma_{x\varepsilon}=0$,

$$\sigma^2_{y(-1)\varepsilon}=\rho N \overset{\lim}{\rightarrow} \infty \frac{1}{T}\sum_t (y_{i,t-1}-\bar{y}_{i,-1})(\varepsilon_{it}-\bar{\varepsilon}_{i,-1})$$

$$=-\frac{1}{T^2}\frac{T-1-T\gamma+\gamma^T}{(1-\gamma)^2}\sigma^2_\varepsilon \neq 0. \tag{6}$$

Thus, the OLS estimates of both β and γ in the fixed-effects model are inconsistent, although as $T \rightarrow \infty$, the inconsistency disappears. But for finite, typically small T, it remains (see Nickell (1981, p. 1424). For $T=10$ and $\gamma=0.5$, for example, the "bias" of the OLS estimate of γ, say c, is proportional to -0.16, the factor of proportionality being the OLS estimate of the variance of c from the within regression. It is always negative, implying that the bias of the OLS estimate of β, say b, is therefore upward. This conclusion holds regardless of whether one assumes the true model is fixed or random effects.

Although the inconsistency will be small when T is moderate to large, small values of T are typically the case. Nonetheless, Nerlove (1971) suggested using the fixed-effects model to estimate ρ for FGLS, in contrast to the earlier suggestion of Balestra and Nerlove (1966), hereinafter BN, of a consistent instrumental variable approach. BN also suggested but did not implement a method based on estimating ρ from the pooled and fixed-effects regressions. Rejection of instrumental variables by Nerlove (1971) was based on the instability of the results in Monte Carlo trials. Since the OLS estimates of the parameters from pooled or fixed-effects regressions are inconsistent, the estimates of ρ based on this regression will also be, hence, the FGLS estimates computed using them will not generally be consistent. In the results reported here, an estimate of ρ is derived from the estimate of residual variance from both the fixed-effects and the pooled regressions, as suggested by Balestra and Nerlove (1966), and is not consistent.

Many authors (e.g., Greene (1993, pp. 475–477), Judge *et al.* (1988, pp. 484–488, hereinafter GJ), suggest basing an estimate of ρ on the cross-section regression of the overall means and either the pooled or fixed-effects regression. This suggestion unfortunately often leads to negative estimates of ρ and unwarranted rejection of the model. These estimates are also inconsistent. The GJ suggestion is, unfortunately, utilized in most computer packages for implementing FGLS for panel data or obtaining starting values for ML, and often leads to the adoption of badly biased fixed-effects OLS when a negative estimate of ρ is obtained.

The GJ suggestion is to regress the group means of the independent variable on the group means of the dependent variables

$$\bar{y}_i = \alpha + \beta\bar{x}_i + w_i, \text{ where } w_i = \mu_i + \bar{\varepsilon}_i. \tag{7}$$

The variance of w_i is $\sigma^2_\mu + \frac{\sigma^2_\varepsilon}{T}$. The purely cross-sectional variation of the individual means gives us information on both the slope and the overall constant in the regression. This is often called the *between groups* regression. In many panel data problems purely cross-sectional variation may dominate, but this variation may not give us much information about the true value of the slope of the independent variable if the regression also contains a lagged value of the dependent variable. The residual SNN = RSSB/N from this regression estimates $\sigma^2_\mu + \frac{\sigma^2_\varepsilon}{T}$. But it will not be a very good estimate if the regression is estimated by OLS, since (7) will tend to fit too well if cross-section variation dominates the data.[14] σ^2_μ is then estimated as $\sigma^2_w - \frac{\sigma^2_\varepsilon}{T}$, where an estimate of σ^2_μ can be obtained from the fixed-effects regression. If T is large, the estimated value of σ^2_μ is not likely to be negative no matter how well the between groups regression fits. But if T is small, and particularly if the regression contains a lagged value of the dependent variable on the right-hand side, the chances of obtaining a negative, and therefore unacceptable, estimates of ρ are high irrespective of the validity of the model.[15]

[14] For example, when a lagged value of the dependent variable is included as one of the explanatory variables, its mean may be very close to the mean of the unlagged variable; then the fit of (7) may be nearly perfect. The estimated residual variance may be close to zero in this case. In general, if there is a lot of associated cross-sectional variation, the residual of this relationship may be very small. If combined with the estimate of σ^2_ε obtained from the within regression, the implied estimate of σ^2_μ may well turn out to be negative (see Greene (1993, pp. 474–476)). But this does not imply that the model is misspecified. Balestra and Nerlove (1966, p. 607) suggest estimating σ^2_μ from the fixed-effects model as the "variance" of the implied constant terms: $\sigma^2_\mu = \frac{1}{N}\sum_i(\bar{y}_i - \bar{y} - \hat{\beta} - \bar{x}))^2$, where $\hat{\beta}$ is the OLS estimate of β in that regression. This suggestion is the one implemented in Nerlove (1971). Alternatively, if a regression with dummy variables for each individual, overall constant suppressed, has been estimated, it suffices to compute the variance, sum of squared deviations from the mean value divided by N, to estimate σ^2_μ.

[15] In footnote 21, I compare three different estimates of ρ based on the above OLS regressions: (1) the original suggestion of Balestra and Nerlove (1966); (2) an estimate based only on the fixed-effects regression (Nerlove (1971)); and the suggestion of Judge *et al.* (1988) and Greene (1993), which is the basis for most computer packages doing panel econometrics. The first, and earliest, suggestion generally yields results closer to the maximum likelihood estimates than the others. The second yields estimates which are generally considerably higher. The last yields results which are far too low and often found to be negative, although not in the results reported here. I have presented estimates of ρ obtained by all three methods and compared them with estimates of ρ obtained from conditional and from unconditional maximum likelihood below in the table in footnote 22.

3.3 *Generalized least squares and feasible GLS*

The means or between regression and the fixed-effects regression both contain information about the parameters of the model: the means regression reflects purely cross-sectional variation; whereas the fixed-effects regression reflects the individual variation over time. GLS combines these two types of information with weights which depend on the characteristic roots of $Euu' = \sigma^2 \Omega$. The individual means themselves are weighted by the reciprocal of the square root of $\xi = 1 - \rho + T\rho$, while the deviations from these means are weighted by the reciprocal of the square root of $\eta = 1 - \rho$. A representative transformed observation is

$$y^*_{it} = \xi^{-1/2}\bar{y}_{i.} + \eta^{-1/2}(y_{it} - \bar{y}_i), \; i = 1, \ldots, N, \; t = 1, \ldots, T.$$

Thus y^*_{it} is a *weighted* combination (weighted by the reciprocals of the square roots of the characteristic roots of Ω) of individual means of the original observations $\bar{y}_{i\cdot}$ and the deviations from individual means $(y_{it} - \bar{y}_{i.})$. The other variables are similarly transformed to x^*_{it} and y^*_{it-1}. GLS amounts to running the OLS regression:

$$y^*_{it} = \alpha^* + \beta x^*_{it} + \gamma y^*_{it-1} + v_{it}. \tag{8}$$

v_{it} is the transformed disturbance. Note that the constant has a different interpretation.

Let $\theta^2 = \eta/\xi = (\xi^{-1/2}/\eta^{-1/2})^2$ be the relative weight of the between variation to the within variation. Note that this weight tends to 0 from above as $T \rightarrow \infty$, i.e., the within information dominates. For T small, $\theta^2 < 1$, so that the between variation is allowed to play a greater role. When the intraclass correlation, ρ, is close to one, the unobserved, residual cross-section variation is large relative to the unobserved individual variation.

$$\theta^2 = \frac{1}{1 + T\dfrac{\rho}{1-\rho}} = \frac{1}{1 + T\dfrac{\sigma^2_\mu}{\sigma^2_\varepsilon}}$$ is smaller for fixed T than when ρ is small.

Between information gets a lower relative weight when ρ is large than when ρ is small, which corresponds to the usual weighting of data from sources with varying degrees of error.

To obtain an estimate of ρ for use in a feasible GLS, I prefer to obtain both an estimate of σ^2 from the pooled regression, as indicated above. Although this estimate is not consistent, it is never negative and empirically it gives, at least the appearance of, a tighter upper bound to the true value of γ than the pooled regression does and a closer approximation to the ML estimate.

3.4 *Bounds for the coefficient of the lagged dependent variable*

As Maddala (1971) has pointed out, the GLS estimates with $\lambda = 1/\theta^2$ can be considered members of a more general class of estimators obtained through different choices of λ. Let $\hat{\gamma}(\lambda)$ be the estimator of γ obtained by solving the GLS normal equations for an arbitrary value of λ. Sevestre and Trognon (1996, pp. 130–133) show that for the case in which $\beta = 0$, the purely autoregressive case, the following inequality holds:

$$\underset{\text{fixed-effects}}{\text{plim}\,\hat{\gamma}(0)} < \gamma < \underset{\text{GLS}}{\text{plim}\,\hat{\gamma}(\lambda)} < \underset{\text{OLS pooled}}{\text{plim}\,\hat{\gamma}(1)} < \underset{\text{means}}{\text{plim}\,\hat{\gamma}(\infty)} \tag{9}$$

Remarkably, the GLS estimate is inconsistent even when a consistent estimate of ρ is used to compute FGLS estimates. The problem is that the lagged dependent variable is correlated even with the transformed disturbance.

Since plim $\hat{\gamma}(\lambda)$ is a continuous function of λ, there exists a value λ^* in the interval $[0, 1/\theta^2]$ for which plim $\hat{\gamma}(\lambda) = \gamma$. Sevestre and Trognon (1983) show that this value is

$$\lambda^* = K(1-\rho)/\left\{\frac{(1-\gamma^T)E(y_{i0}\mu_i)}{(1-\gamma)\sigma^2} + K\xi\right\} \tag{10}$$

where $K = \dfrac{T-1-T\gamma+\gamma^T}{T(1-\gamma)^2}$, and ρ, ξ, and σ^2 are as before.

They also show that when $\beta \neq 0$, the estimate $\hat{\gamma}(\lambda)$ behaves almost the same as in the purely autoregressive case. Since the λ^* estimate is consistent when there are no exogenous variables, it remains so when there are. The trick is to obtain a consistent estimate of λ^* which can be accomplished by finding an appropriate instrumental variable for y_{-1}. Even in this case the results depend heavily on the distribution of the estimate of λ^*.

In the dynamic error-components model, not only are the OLS pooled regression estimates, the fixed-effect or within estimates, and the between estimates inconsistent, but so are the GLS estimates using the true value of ρ. However, the method of instrumental variables may be used to obtain a feasible member of the λ-class of estimates which is consistent (see Sevestre and Trognon, 1996). Unfortunately, this estimate may have a very large variance, as demonstrated in Nerlove (1971).

Nonetheless, the fixed-effects and the pooled regression may be used to bound the true value of γ even when exogenous regressors are also included. Empirically, I have found that FGLS appears to provide an even tighter bound, although since FGLS is also based on an inconsistent estimate of ρ, there is no guarantee that this is in fact an upper bound.

3.5 Maximum likelihood conditional on the initial value of the lagged dependent variable

When the likelihood function for the model (2) with $u_{it} = \mu_i + \varepsilon_{it} \sim N(0, \sigma^2\Omega)$ is derived in the usual way from the product of the densities of y_{it} conditional on x_{it} and y_{it-1}, the joint density is conditional on y_{io}. This likelihood function can be written in terms of the earlier notation introduced as,

$$\log L(\alpha,\beta,\gamma,\sigma_\mu^2,\sigma_\varepsilon^2 | y_{11},\ldots,y_{NT}; x_{11},\ldots,x_{NT}; y_{10},\ldots,y_{N0})$$
$$= -\frac{NT}{2}\log 2\pi - \frac{NT}{2}\log\sigma^2 - \frac{N}{2}\log\xi - \frac{N(T-1)}{2}\log\eta$$
$$-\frac{1}{2\sigma^2}\sum_{i=1}^{N}\sum_{t=1}^{T}(y_{it}^* - \alpha\xi^{-1/2} - \beta x_{it}^* - \gamma y_{it-1}^*)^2 \tag{11}$$

where y^*, x^*, y_{-1}^* are the transformed variables. Since

$\xi = \dfrac{\lambda}{1-(\lambda-1)/T}$ and $\eta = \dfrac{1}{1-(\lambda-1)/T}$, $\log L$ can be expressed as a function solely of λ, σ^2, α, β, and γ. Trognon (1978) shows that, when the exogenous variable x is generated by a first-order autoregression with white-noise input, $w \sim wn(0, \sigma_w^2 I)$. Also assumed in the Monte Carlo experiments reported in Nerlove (1971)

$$x = \delta x_{-1} + w \tag{12}$$

maximization of the conditional likelihood function (12) yields boundary solutions $\hat{\rho} = 0$, which, unlike interior maximum likelihood solutions, are inconsistent, for a considerable, and indeed likely, range of parameter values. In particular, there is a value of γ in (2)

$$\gamma^* = \frac{(T-3)^2 - 8}{(T+1)^2}$$

such that when $\gamma < \gamma^*$ there exists an interior maximum of (11) which yields consistent ML estimates, but that when $\gamma \geq \gamma^*$ there are values of ρ for which the conditional likelihood function (2) is maximized at the boundary $\rho = 0$, i.e., for the OLS estimates of the pooled regression, which we know to be inconsistent. The problem is that when T is small the permissible range of γ, the coefficient of the lagged dependent variable, is implausible (e.g. negative or very small). For example, for $T = 5$, $\gamma^* = -0.11$, while for $T = 10$, $\gamma^* = 0.34$. When $\gamma \geq \gamma^*$, whether or not an interior maximum with consistent ML estimates occurs depends on the value of ρ. For $\rho < \rho^*$ boundary maxima occur where

$$\rho^* = \left(\frac{T-1}{T+1}\right)^2 \frac{\beta^2 \sigma^2_w}{\sigma^2} \frac{1-\gamma}{(\gamma-\gamma^*)(1-\gamma\delta)^2}.$$

For example, when $T=5$, $\beta=1.0$, $\gamma=0.75$, $\delta=0.5$, and $\frac{\sigma_w^2}{\sigma^2}=1.0$, $\gamma^* = -0.11$ and the critical value of ρ is $\rho^* = 0.31$. That means that any true value of the intraclass correlation less than 0.31 is liable to produce a boundary solution to (11) $\rho = 0$ and inconsistent estimates of all the parameters. Using these results, Trognon (1978) is able to replicate the Monte Carlo results reported in Nerlove (1971).

Even though ML may yield inconsistent estimates when the non-negligible probability of a boundary solution is taken into account, it is nonetheless true that the likelihood function summarizes the information contained in the data about the parameters.[16] From a conventional, Neyman–Pearson point of view what matters about the likelihood function is only its maximum and curvature in the neighborhood of the maximum, and all the desirable properties and the assessment of the reliability of the maximum likelihood estimates are only asymptotic. It is perhaps not surprising that only the maximum and the Hessian at the maximum are all that matters from a conventional point of view, in view of the fact that for the mean of a normal distribution, the quadratic approximation is exact and, because of the central limit theorem in its many forms, many estimators, including ML estimators in regular cases, tend to normality in distribution. So the problem of possible inconsistency of the ML estimates should not concern us unduly from the standpoint of likelihood inference. It is the whole shape of the likelihood function, which expresses what the data have to say about the model and its parameters, that matters.[17] For this reason, sections of some of the multidimensional likelihood functions are also presented in the next section. When first differences are taken to eliminate a linear deterministic trend, the individual-specific time-invariant effects become differences in the trend slopes.

[16] Although clearly implied in what Fisher wrote in the 1920s (Fisher (1922, 1925)), the likelihood principle, which essentially holds that the likelihood function is the sole basis for inference, did not come into prominence until the 1950s and 1960s, principally through the work of Barnard, Birnbaum, and Edwards (see the references cited below) written largely in reaction to both the classical Neyman–Pearson (frequentist) and the Bayesian approaches to inference. A good recent discussion is Lindsey (1996).

[17] The principle of likelihood inference and its application to dynamic panel models is elaborated in Nerlove (1997). A maximum at the boundary conveys perfectly valid information about the parameter in question, as does a near-plateau solution at which the asymptotic standard errors derived from the information matrix are huge. More importantly, the existence of two or more local maxima at not very different likelihood values but widely separated values of the parameters, such as I have obtained in the case of regional Indonesian data, is even more revealing.

This makes the interpretation of the model in first-difference form different than that in levels. Moreover, the time- and individual-varying disturbance is now likely to be serially correlated, a fact which needs to be taken into account in the formulation of the unconditional likelihood function. A parallel set of results for the country-specific trends model is presented below.

3.6 *Unconditional likelihood and unconditional maximum likelihood*

While it is not guaranteed that a boundary solution to the likelihood equations is obtained, which would yield ML estimates which are inconsistent, it is apparent, as suggested above, that in panels with a short time dimension the initial values provide important information about the parameters of the model, and to condition on them is to neglect this information.

It is not, in fact difficult to obtain the unconditional likelihood function once the marginal distribution of the initial values is specified. The problem is a correct specification of this distribution. If $|\gamma| \geq 1$ or the processes generating the x_{it} are not stationary, it will not, in general, be possible to specify the marginal distribution of the initial observations. I will assume that, possibly after some differencing, both the y_{it} and the x_{it} are stationary. The derivation of the unconditional likelihood function in the case in which deterministic or stochastic trends are included is contained in Nerlove (1997).[18]

[18] Adding trend, t, to (2)

$$y_{it} = \alpha + \beta x_{it} + \gamma y_{it-1} + \tau_i t + \mu_i + \varepsilon_{it},\ i = 1, \ldots, \mathrm{N},\ t = 1, \ldots \mathrm{T}, \text{ and differencing,} \quad (2')$$

$$\Delta y_{it} = \beta \Delta x_{it} + \gamma \Delta y_{it-1} + \tau_i + \Delta\varepsilon_{it},\ i = 1, \ldots, \mathrm{N},\ t = 1, \ldots, \mathrm{T}, \quad (2'')$$

where Δ denotes the first-difference operator and τ_i is the individual-specific trend coefficient, assumed to have mean zero (enforced by eliminating any overall constant in the differences by deducting the sample mean). Thus, not only is the meaning of ρ altered, but if ε_{it} did not contain a unit root to start with it will now; in particular, if ε_{it} is not serially correlated to start with, it will follow a first-order moving average process with unit root. The variance–covariance matrix of the new disturbances $\tau_i + \Delta\varepsilon_{it}$ is now block diagonal with blocks

$$A = \sigma^2 \begin{bmatrix} 1 & a & b & \ldots b \\ a & 1 & a & b.. \\ b & a & 1 & a\ldots \\ \vdots & \vdots & \vdots & \ldots 1 \end{bmatrix} \text{ where } \sigma^2 = \sigma_\tau^2 + \sigma_\varepsilon^2,\ a = \frac{\sigma_\tau^2 - \sigma_\varepsilon^2}{\sigma^2}, \text{ and } b = \frac{\sigma_\tau^2}{\sigma^2}.$$

The characteristic roots of A give the necessary transform and Jacobian. This is taken into account in the formulation of both the conditional and the unconditional likelihood functions. As indicated, however, differencing is unnecessary when the initial values are conditioning.

Under this assumption, the dynamic relationship to be estimated is stationary and $|\gamma|<1$. Consider equation (3)[19] with the intercept eliminated, for y_{i0} and the infinite past

$$y_{i0}=\sum_{j=1}^{\infty}\gamma^j\beta x_{i,-j}+\frac{1}{1-\gamma}\mu_t+v_{i0},\ \text{where } v_{it-1}=\gamma v_{it}+\varepsilon_{it}.^{20} \tag{13}$$

If $\beta=0$, so that the relationship to be estimated is a pure autoregression for each y_{it}, the vector of initial values $y_0=(y_{10},\ldots,y_{N0})$, has a joint normal distribution with means 0 and variance–covariance matrix $\left[\frac{\sigma_\mu^2}{(1-\gamma)^2}+\sigma_v^2\right]I_N=\left(\frac{\sigma_\mu^2}{(1-\gamma)^2}+\frac{\sigma_\varepsilon^2}{1-\gamma^2}\right)I_N$. The unconditional likelihood is therefore

$$\log L(\gamma,\rho,\sigma_\mu^2,\sigma_\varepsilon^2|y_{11},\ldots,y_{NT};\ldots;y_{10},\ldots,y_{N0})$$

$$=-\frac{NT}{2}\log 2\pi-\frac{NT}{2}\log\sigma^2-\frac{N}{2}\log\xi-\frac{N(T-1)}{2}\log\eta$$

$$-\frac{1}{2\sigma^2}\sum_{i=1}^{N}\sum_{t=1}^{T}(y_{it}^*-\gamma y_{it-1}^*)^2$$

$$-\frac{N}{2}\log\left(\frac{\sigma_\mu^2}{(1-\gamma)^2}+\frac{\sigma_\varepsilon^2}{1-\gamma^2}\right)-\left[\frac{1}{2\left(\frac{\sigma_\mu^2}{(1-\gamma)^2}+\frac{\sigma_\varepsilon^2}{1-\gamma^2}\right)}\right]\sum_{i=1}^{N}y_{i0}^2. \tag{14}$$

This likelihood function can easily be concentrated: To maximize, express $\sigma_\mu^2,\sigma_\varepsilon^2,\xi$, and η in terms of ρ and γ. For given ρ and γ in the interval [0,1), concentrate the likelihood function with respect to σ^2. It follows that

$$\hat{\sigma}^2(\gamma,\rho)=\frac{RSS^*(\gamma,\rho)}{N(T+1)}$$

where

$$RSS^*(\gamma,\rho)=\sum_{i=1}^{N}\sum_{t=1}^{T}(y_{it}^*-\gamma y_{it-1}^*)^2+\left(\sum_{i=1}^{N}y_{i0}^2\Big/\left[\frac{\rho}{(1-\gamma)^2}+\frac{1-\rho}{1-\gamma^2}\right]\right).$$

[19] For a particular time period T and the infinite past $y_{iT}=\gamma^\infty y_{i-\infty}+\sum_{j=0}^{\infty}\gamma^j\beta x_{i-j}+\frac{1-\gamma^\infty}{1-\gamma}\mu_i+v_{iT}$, where $v_{iT}=\sum_{j=0}^{\infty}\gamma^j\varepsilon_{iT-j}$. Since $1\geq|\gamma|$ and $v_{iT}=\sum_{j=0}^{\infty}\gamma^j\varepsilon_{iT-j}$ is the MA form of a first-order autoregression with white-noise input, equation (13) follows.

[20] If all variables are expressed as deviations from their overall means, there is no need to include an intercept; if not, μ_i should be replaced by $\alpha+\mu_i$.

Thus, the concentrated LF is

$$\log L^*(\gamma,\rho) = -\frac{N(T+1)}{2}\log 2\pi - \frac{N}{2}\log\xi - \frac{N(T-1)}{2}\log\eta$$

$$-\frac{N(T-1)}{2}\log\left\{\frac{RSS^*(\gamma,\rho)}{N(T-1)}\right\} - \frac{N}{2}\left\{\frac{\rho}{(1-\gamma)^2} + \frac{1-\rho}{1-\gamma^2}\right\}$$

$$-\left({}^{1}/_{2RSS^*/N(T+1)}\right)\sum_{i=1}^{N}\sum_{t=1}^{T}(y_{it}^* - \gamma y_{it-1}^*)^2$$

$$-\sum_{i=1}^{N} y_{i0}^2 / \left\{(2/N(T+1))\left[\frac{\rho}{(1-\gamma)^2} + \frac{1-\rho}{1-\gamma^2}\right] RSS^*\right\}$$

Maximizing L^* is quite a bit more complicated than the usual minimization of the sum of squares in the penultimate term because RSS*, in that term, depends on $\sum_{i=1}^{N} y_{i0}^2$, as well as on ρ and γ, which enter the final terms as well. When $\beta \neq 0$, things are more complicated still. But more important than finding the maximum of L^* is its shape above the γ–ρ plane. It is apparent from the results presented below that there may be significant trade-offs between γ and ρ without large effects on the value of the likelihood.

Various alternative specifications of the likelihood function considered in the literature are reported and analyzed in Sevestre and Trognon (1996, pp. 136–138).[21] Considerable simplification, however, can be obtained if, following Nerlove (1971), we are willing to assume that x_{it} follows a well-specified common stationary time series model for all individuals i. The first term in (13) is $\varphi_{i0} = \beta\sum_{j=0}^{\infty}\gamma^j x_{i,-j}$. Hence, for any stationary processes x_{it}, which may be serially correlated

$$\frac{\varphi_{it}}{\beta} = \gamma\frac{\varphi_{it-1}}{\beta} + x_{it}$$

with variances

$$\sigma_{\varphi_i}^2 = \frac{\beta^2\sigma_{x_i}^2}{1-\gamma^2} \tag{15}$$

[21] One interesting possibility discussed by Sevestre and Trognon (1996, pp. 136–138) is to choose y_{i0} a linear function of some *observed* individual-specific time-invariant exogenous variables and a disturbance which is decomposed as the sum of the individual-specific disturbances u_i and a remainder. The first-order equations for maximizing the likelihood then take on a simple recursive form when $\beta = 0$, and permit other simplifications when $\beta \neq 0$. But if we knew that some individual-specific time-invariant observed variables influenced behavior why not incorporate them directly in (2), the equation to be estimated?

If we suppose that the variance of the x_{it} is the same for all i, then the random variable

$$\phi_{it} = \sum_{j=0}^{\infty} \gamma^j \beta x_{it-j}$$

has a well-defined variance which is the same for all i and a function of β, γ, and σ_x^2. This then enters the final term in the unconditional likelihood (14), which now becomes

$$\begin{aligned}
&\log L(\beta,\gamma,\sigma_\mu^2,\sigma_\varepsilon^2 | y_{11},\ldots,y_{NT};x_{11},\ldots x_{NT};y_{10},\ldots,y_{N0}) \\
&= -\frac{N(T+1)}{2}\log 2\pi - \frac{NT}{2}\log\sigma^2 - \frac{N}{2}\log\xi - \frac{N(T-1)}{2}\log\eta \\
&\quad - \frac{1}{2\sigma^2}\sum_{i=1}^{N}\sum_{t=1}^{T}(y_{it}^* - \beta x_{it}^* - \gamma y_{it-1}^*)^2 \\
&\quad - \frac{N}{2}\log\left(\frac{\beta^2\sigma_x^2}{1-\gamma^2} + \frac{\sigma_\mu^2}{(1-\gamma)^2} + \frac{\sigma_\varepsilon^2}{1-\gamma^2}\right) \\
&\quad - \left[\frac{1}{2\left(\frac{\beta^2\sigma_x^2}{1-\gamma^2} + \frac{\sigma_\mu^2}{(1-\gamma)^2} + \frac{\sigma_\varepsilon^2}{1-\gamma^2}\right)}\right]\sum_{i=1}^{N} y_{i0}^2 .
\end{aligned} \tag{16}$$

Concentrating the likelihood function to permit a one- or two-dimensional grid search is no longer possible. Nor is it possible to graph the likelihood surface with respect to variations in all of the parameters; although "slicing" the likelihood function along any hyperplane in the parameter space can reveal the trade offs between any pair of parameters. If gradient or search procedures yield an interior maximum, the ML estimates obtained are consistent as long as the random variables $\phi_{it} = \sum_{j=0}^{\infty} \gamma^j \beta x_{i,t-j}$ have well-defined variances and covariances, which they will if the x_{it} are generated by a stationary process. It does not really matter what this process is as long as it is stationary. Besides, since the x_{it} are assumed to be exogenous, we really have no basis on which to model their determination and are likely to misspecify this part of the model. In this case we ought to prefer this kind of "almost full-information" maximum likelihood. Still we have to assume something about the variance of the x process in order to proceed. I suggest estimating σ_x^2 from the sample data.

To generalize these results to the case in which there are several explanatory variables in addition to the lagged value of the dependent variable, assume that X_{it} follows a stationary VAR process and replace βx_{it}^* by $X_{it}^*\beta$ and $\beta^2\sigma_x^2$ by $\beta'\Sigma_{xx}\beta$ in the above formula.

4 Empirical evidence on the comparative performance of different panel data methods

In order to examine the effects of the econometric methods employed on the finding of growth rate convergence or the lack of it, I initially used data on 94 countries for the period 1960–1985, and a sub-sample of 22 OECD countries, from the Penn World Tables 5.6, publicly available from the NBER web site at ftp://nber.harvard.edu/pub/. This is the same data set which has been used in dozens of previous studies. Following Islam (1995), s and n were computed as quinquennial means over the preceding five-year span for the years 1965, 1970, 1975, 1980, 1985; y was taken as the value reported in that year and in 1960 for the lagged value applicable to 1965. The results of the six methods applied to these data are reported in table 6.1 for the usual undifferenced model. Table 6.2 reports the results for the country-specific trends model which requires differencing to reduce the process to stationarity. In this case, the conditional and unconditional likelihood functions are defined for the first difference of the original data.

I have listed the regression methods in the order in which the corresponding estimates of γ appear in the inequality of Sevestre and Trognon (1996) (equation 9 above). These estimates are followed by the maximum likelihood estimates conditional on the initial values y_{i0} or Δy_{il} and the ML estimates unconditional on the initial values, assuming stationarity of both the processes generating the exogenous variable and real GDP per capita. In a substantive study of growth rate convergence, it would clearly be important to include additional explanatory variables such as, for example, the stock of human capital, also available at the NBER internet site, infrastructure investment, and so forth. However, my focus here is on properties of alternative estimators and for this purpose, omission of relevant variables simply increases the unexplained disturbance variance and thus heightens the contrast among alternative estimators.

Turning now to the regression estimates presented in Table 6.1, consider the first four methods. The estimates of γ for the 94-country sample range from a low of 0.72 (fixed-effects regression) to a high of 0.98 (country means regression) with pooled OLS and FGLS falling in

Table 6.1. *Parameter estimates for the model in levels, alternative econometric analyses*

Method of analysis	94-country sample	22-country sample
1 Fixed effects OLS		
γ	0.7204 (0.0211)	0.7645 (0.0166)
β	0.1656 (0.0172)	0.1634 (0.0510)
Implied α	0.3719 (0.0278)	0.4096 (0.0783)
Residual variance	0.0113	0.0020
2 Feasible GLS		
estimate of ρ used*	0.2675	0.4027
γ	0.9130 (0.0119)	0.8282 (0.0156)
β	0.1520 (0.0135)	0.1913 (0.0422)
Implied α	0.6362 (0.0247)	0.5269 (0.0579)
Residual variance	0.0213	0.0047
3 Pooled OLS		
γ	0.9487 (0.0090)	0.8857 (0.0125)
β	0.1244 (0.0108)	0.1764 (0.0308)
Implied α	0.7080 (0.0271)	0.6067 (0.0452)
Residual variance	0.0193	0.0041
4 Country means OLS		
γ	0.9817 (0.0112)	0.9320 (0.0148)
β	0.0919 (0.0138)	0.1493 (0.0343)
Implied α	0.8339 (0.0704)	0.6870 (0.0593)
Residual variance	0.0047	0.0580
5 Conditional ML		
ρ	0.1133 (0.0497)	0.4796 (0.1584)
γ	0.9339 (0.0122)	0.8189 (0.0245)
β	0.1370 (0.0131)	0.1908 (0.0438)
Implied α	0.6744 (0.0289)	0.5131 (0.0664)
Residual variance	0.0194 (0.0013)	0.0052 (0.0012)
6 Unconditional ML		
estimates of σ_x^2 used	0.0826	0.0069
ρ	0.1288 (0.0456)	0.7700 (0.0731)
γ	0.9385 (0.0105)	0.8085 (0.0228)
β	0.1334 (0.0124)	0.1815 (0.0521)
Implied α	0.6846 (0.0277)	0.4865 (0.0791)
Residual variance	0.0197 (0.0013)	0.0113 (0.0028)

Notes:
Figures in parentheses are standard errors.
* Estimated by the method suggested in Balestra and Nerlove (1966).

Table 6.2. *Parameter estimates for the model in first differences, alternative econometric analyses*

Method of analysis	94-country sample	22-country sample
1 Fixed-effects OLS		
γ	0.4007 (0.0375)	0.4544 (0.0611)
β	0.1199 (0.0187)	−0.0126 (0.0637)
Implied α	0.1667 (0.0246)	−0.0237 (0.1209)
Residual variance	0.0077	0.0014
2 Feasible GLS		
estimate of ρ used*	0.4866	0.3628
γ	0.4227 (0.0406)	0.5833 (0.0531)
β	0.1520 (0.0135)	0.1913 (0.0422)
Implied α	0.1864 (0.0259)	0.1322 (0.1218)
Residual variance	0.0213	0.0047
3 Pooled OLS		
γ	0.7031 (0.0328)	0.6237 (0.0453)
β	0.1632 (0.0195)	0.0845 (0.0586)
Implied α	0.3548 (0.0373)	0.1834 (0.1121)
Residual variance	0.0141	0.0022
4 Country means OLS		
γ	0.9178 (0.0471)	0.7215 (0.0572)
β	0.1719 (0.0339)	0.1174 (0.0978)
Implied α	0.6763 (0.1263)	0.2965 (0.1873)
Residual variance	0.0041	0.0005
5 Conditional ML		
ρ	0.2267 (0.0664)	0.0126 (0.0405)
γ	0.4540 (0.0651)	0.6187 (0.0490)
β	0.1368 (0.0208)	0.0815 (0.0601)
Implied α	0.2004 (0.0358)	0.1762 (0.1159)
Residual variance	0.0122 (0.0009)	0.0021 (0.0003)
6 Unconditional ML		
estimates of σ_x^2 used	0.0597	0.0058
ρ	0.2335 (0.0632)	0.0936 (0.0696)
γ	0.4364 (0.0578)	0.7254 (0.0512)
β	0.1340 (0.0201)	0.1478 (0.0727)
Implied α	0.1921 (0.0317)	0.3500 (0.1326)
Residual variance	0.0120 (0.0008)	0.0027 (0.0004)

Notes:
Figures in parentheses are standard errors.
* Estimated by the method suggested in Balestra and Nerlove (1966).

between.[22] For the OECD countries the range is 0.76 to 0.93. The implied speed of convergence thus ranges from 90 percent in 35 years to 90 percent in 570 years. None could be characterized as evidence of reasonably rapid convergence. All of the estimates γ satisfy the Sevestre–Trognon inequality, although the regressions contain an exogenous explanatory variable in contrast to the case considered by Sevestre and Trognon. Pooled OLS and FGLS also stand in the order predicted by the Sevestre–Trognon results. While it is tempting to infer that FGLS provides a tighter upper bound to the true value of γ than the pooled OLS regression estimate, the temptation should be resisted. The FGLS estimates are doubly inconsistent: they are based on an inconsistent estimate of ρ reflecting the inconsistency of the estimates of the residual variance and the fixed effects depending on which regressions they are derived from. Not only is the estimated value of β sensitive to the method of estimation but the estimate of α, the elasticity of output with respect to capital stock in the production function, is extremely so, reflecting the dependence of the estimated value on the coefficient of the lagged dependent variable, γ. This parameter should estimate approximately (1 – the share of labor in the real GDP). It is clear that all of the estimates of α are wide of the mark. If therefore one were to infer policy implications from this parameter, it could be seriously misleading.

The most interesting estimates are those for conditional and unconditional maximum likelihood presented as methods 5 and 6 in tables 6.1 and 6.2 for the level model and the first-difference model, respectively. For the

[22] In the following table, I present the three estimates of ρ discussed above as possible candidates for the transformation involved in FGLS for the 94-country sample and the model in levels. It is argued above that the Greene–Judge estimate is sharply biased downwards and prone to be negative; similarly, the argument Nickell gives with reference to the downward bias in the coefficient of the lagged dependent variable in a fixed-effects regression suggests that the other coefficients will be biased upwards, including the variance of the estimated fixed effects. Coupled with a downward bias in the estimate of the residual variance in the fixed-effects regression, this provides an explanation of the extremely high estimates obtained by the Nerlove (1971) method. It is interesting to note that the Balestra–Nerlove estimate, while substantially higher than the GJ estimate (it can never be negative) is, nonetheless, not too far out of line with the estimate of ρ obtained from the conditional likelihood function for the OECD countries and for both the conditional and unconditional likelihood for the 94-country sample.

Method	94-countries	22-countries
Balestra-Nerlove (1966)	0.2678	0.4027
Nerlove (1971)	0.7790	0.7038
G-J (1983/88)	0.0983	0.0804
Conditional ML	0.1133	0.4796
Unconditional ML	0.1288	0.7700

model in levels and the 22-country OECD sample, these estimates differ quite a bit from one another, although unconditional ML is not far from the fixed-effects OLS regression, while conditional ML yields results close to FGLS using the Balestra–Nerlove (1966) first-round estimate of ρ. For the 94-country sample, the conditional and the unconditional ML estimates differ little from one another. They are close to the pooled OLS regression estimates (a consequence of the fact that the estimated value of ρ is small although significantly different from zero), but are both quite different than any of the inconsistent regression estimates. The estimates of β are quite insensitive to the method used, presumably because the estimates of γ are not very different; consequently the implied estimates of α are similar, albeit different for the two samples. While the results for the first-difference model are quite different from those for the levels model, the same pattern of relation between conditional and unconditional estimates emerges.

To understand better the relation between the conditional and the unconditional ML estimates, consider the log of the ratio of the unconditional to the conditional likelihood, i.e., the marginal density of y_{i0}:

$$\log\{\text{unconditional/conditional likelihood}\} =$$

$$-\frac{N}{2}\log 2\pi - \frac{N}{2}\log\left(\frac{\beta^2\sigma_x^2}{1-\gamma^2} + \frac{\rho\sigma^2}{(1-\gamma)^2} + \frac{(1-\rho)\sigma^2}{1-\gamma^2}\right)$$
$$-\left[\frac{1}{2\left(\frac{\beta^2\sigma_x^2}{1-\gamma^2} + \frac{\rho\sigma^2}{(1-\gamma)^2} + \frac{(1-\rho)\sigma^2}{1-\gamma^2}\right)}\right]\sum_{i=1}^{N} y_{i0}^2.$$

Let the sample variance of y_{i0} be var y_0 and let

$$\varphi^2 = \left(\frac{\beta^2\sigma_x^2}{1-\gamma^2} + \frac{\rho\sigma^2}{(1-\gamma)^2} + \frac{(1-\rho)\sigma^2}{1-\gamma^2}\right).$$

Then

$$\log\{\text{unconditional/conditional likelihood}\} = f(\varphi^2) =$$

$$-\frac{N}{2}\log 2\pi - \frac{N}{2}\log(\varphi^2) - \left[\frac{N \operatorname{var} y_0}{2\varphi^2}\right].$$

The maxima of the two likelihood functions will occur at about the same values of the parameters on which φ depends when $df(\varphi^2)$ is close to zero, which occurs at $\varphi^2 = \operatorname{var} y_0$. At the unconditional ML estimates for the levels model, for example, for the 94-country sample, at $\varphi^2 = 0.91$

and var $y_0 = 0.80$, while, for the 22-country sample $\varphi^2 = 0.25$ and var $y_0 = 0.26$.

Table 6.2 presents parallel results for the first-difference model. Once again the first four estimates of γ fall in the order to be expected from the Trognon–Sevestre inequality, although they are all lower than for the levels model, in the first three cases much lower, implying much more rapid convergence to equilibrium. The estimates of all the parameters are much different for the 22-country sample and quite variable. Perhaps the most interesting findings, however, are for the conditional and unconditional ML estimates. The estimates of ρ for the 94-country sample are quite close to one another and those for the 22-country sample far apart, but now there is a remarkable reversal of the magnitudes of ρ and γ as between the 94-country sample and the 22-country sample: for the former ρ is about one-half of the estimated value for γ, but in the last case of the 22-country sample ρ is only a small fraction of the estimated value of γ.

Further insight into the conditional and unconditional likelihood functions for the two samples can be obtained graphically. Having eliminated the constant term by taking deviations from the overall means of all variables, we are left with four parameters: ρ, γ, β, and σ^2. Figure 6.1 plots the unconditional likelihood function for the 94-country sample, levels model. Figure 6.2 plots the likelihood function for the 22-country sample, levels model. Likelihood functions are plotted in figures 6.3 and 6.4 for the first-difference model, respectively for the 94- and 22-country samples. I have plotted both three-dimensional likelihood surfaces for pairs of variables and two-dimensional contours. "Slices" are taken at the likelihood maximizing values for the parameters not plotted. These plots clearly reveal the implications of the data for the "interactions" between pairs of parameters. Although there are $\binom{5}{2} = 10$ possible pairs to consider, I focus on the crucial pairs: ρ versus γ and β versus σ^2.

Although the likelihood reaches a unique maximum in every case, which is quite well defined, it is clear that there are significant trade offs between each pair of parameters. In the case of the 22 OECD countries, the unconditional ML estimates are precisely determined. As suggested above, this is because for small N, the weight of the initial observations and the parameters determining them is more substantial than for large cross-sectional samples. As indicated above, the likelihood function is sufficient for the parameters of the model and provides useful insight into what the data tell us about these parameters quite apart from the values that maximize it.

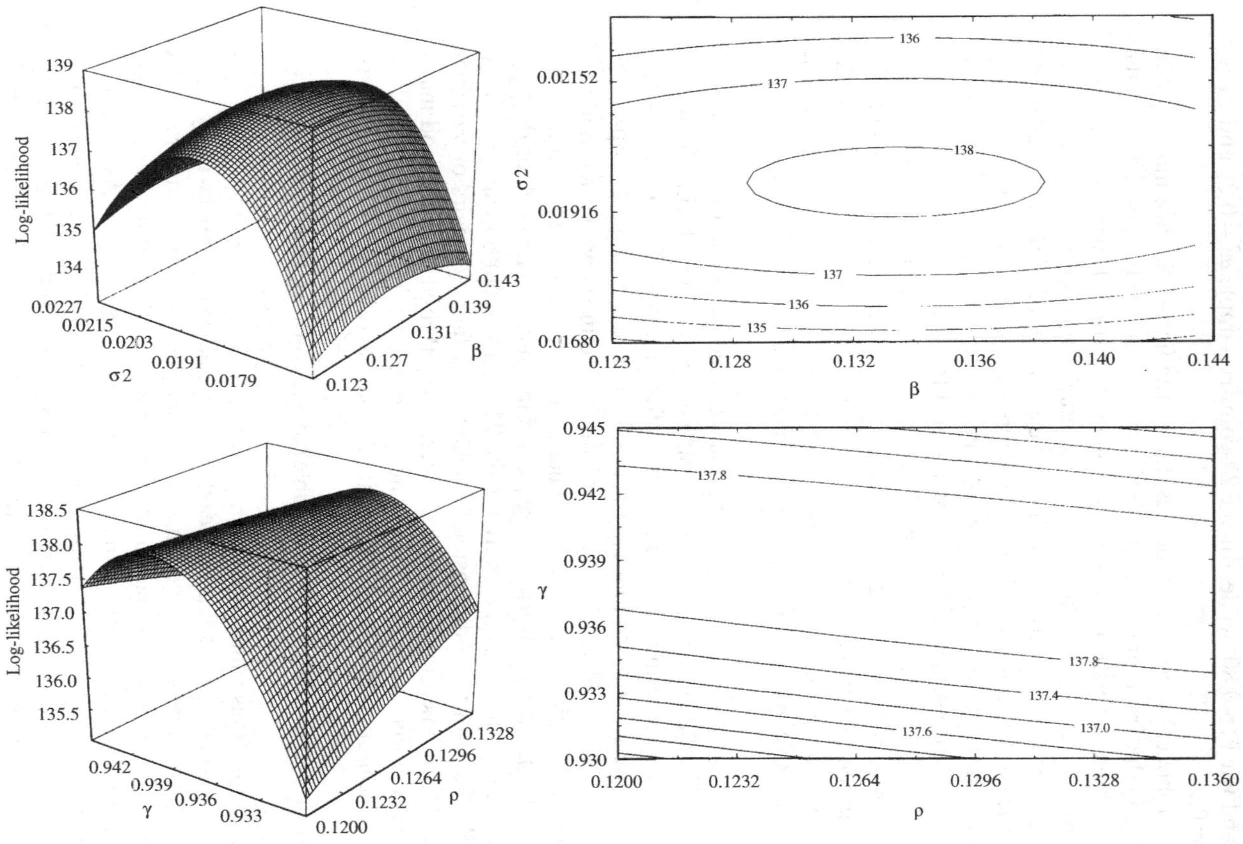

Figure 6.1 Unconditional likelihood, 94-country sample, levels model

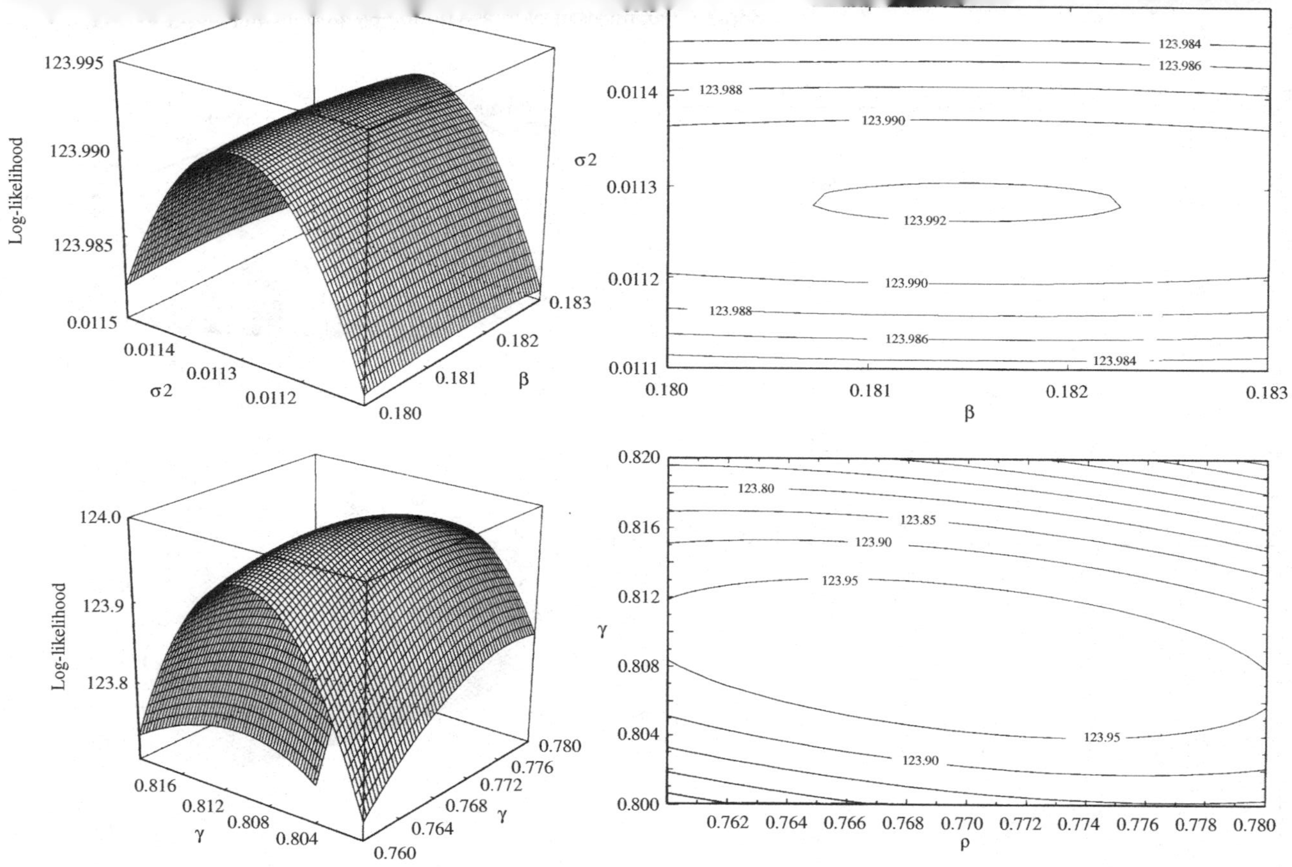

Figure 6.2 Unconditional likelihood, 22-country sample, levels model
Estimated values: $\rho = 0.770$ (0.0740); $\gamma = 0.808$ (0.0230); $\beta = 0.1815$ (0.0520); $\sigma^2 = 0.0113$ (0.0029)

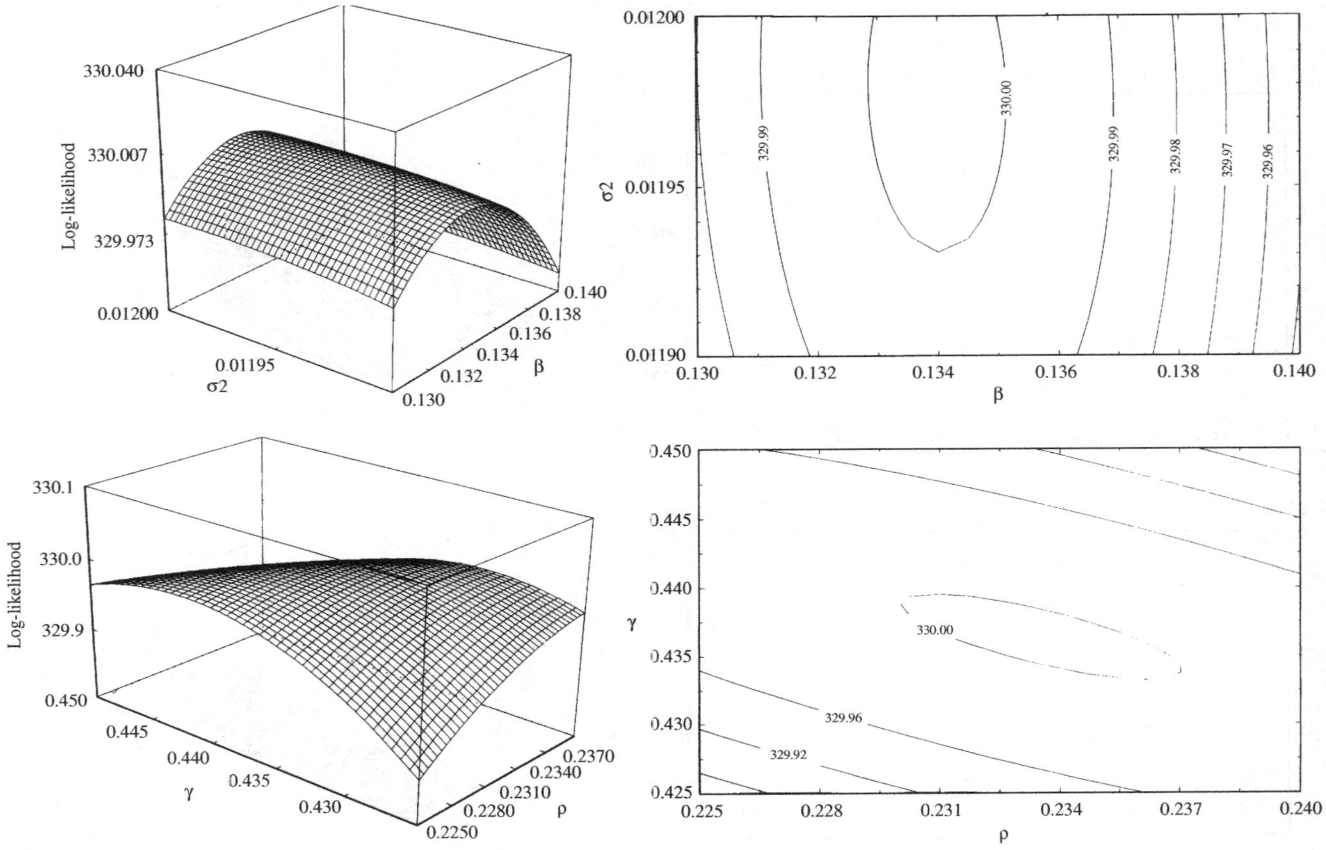

Figure 6.3 Unconditional likelihood, 94-country sample, first-difference model

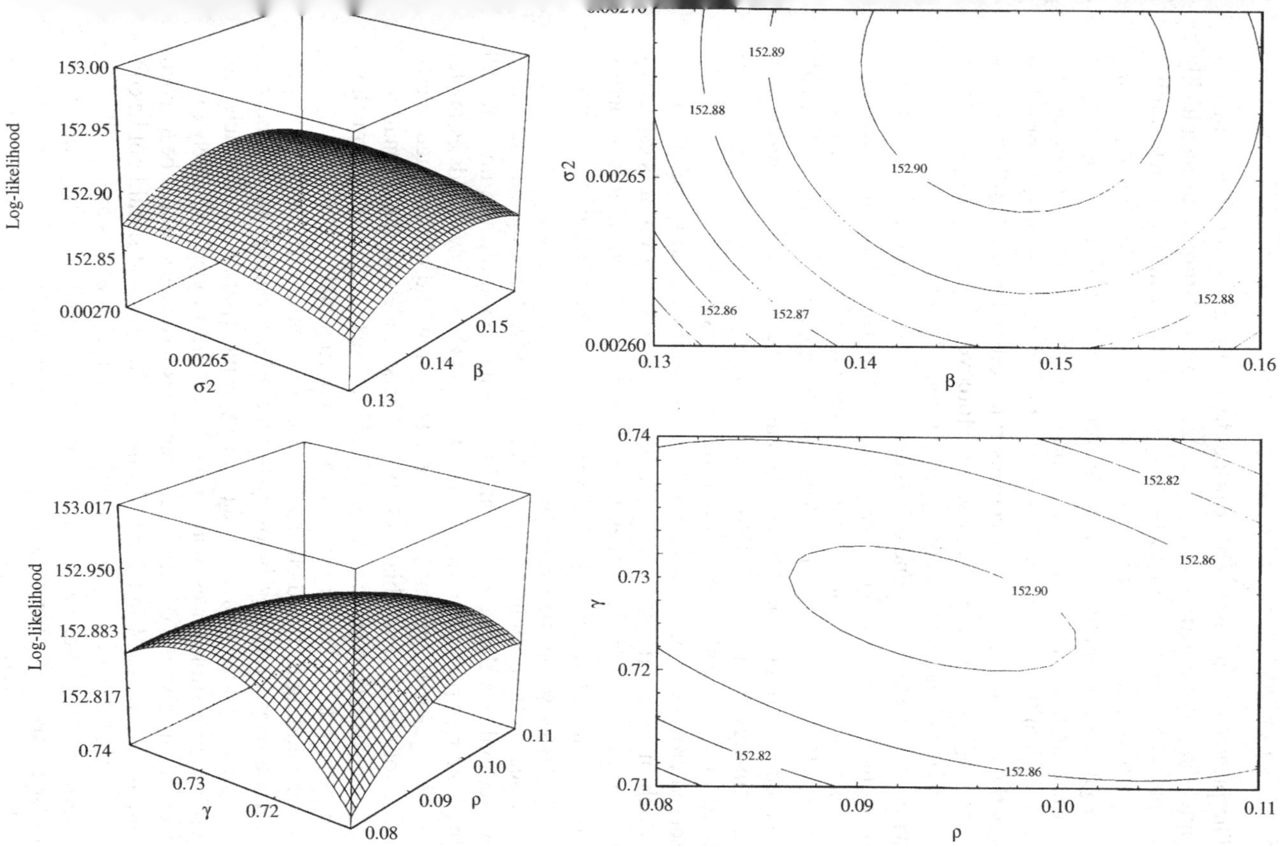

Figure 6.4 Unconditional likelihood, 22-country sample, first-difference model
Estimated values: $\rho = 0.094$ (0.0696); $\gamma = 0.725$ (0.0512); $\beta = 0.148$ (0.0727); $\sigma^2 = 0.0027$ (0.0004)

5 Conclusions

The principal conclusion that can be drawn from this analysis is that, in panel data econometrics, method matters – a lot. Although using a highly simplified Solow (1956) and Swan (1956) model without human capital stocks or infrastructure, I have found estimates of the adjustment parameter significantly different than one in every case, indicating convergence. All of the estimates for the model in levels, however, are so close to one, always greater than 0.7, that convergence to within 90 per cent of equilibrium in less than one generation is effectively ruled out. This can hardly be called "convergence" in any relevant sense. Moreover, the estimates range from 0.72 to 0.98, suggesting a convergence range of from 33 to over 500 years, with most clustering around 0.8, underscoring the importance of choice of econometric method. When the model is estimated in first-difference form, the estimates of γ are much lower, indicating rapid convergence in the case of the 94-country sample. The method of choice, unconditional ML, yields well-defined and reasonable estimates in every case. Much of the variation in estimates of the speed of convergence appears to be due to trade offs between the crucial parameter ρ, which measures the importance of unobserved cross-sectional variation relative to total residual variation, and γ, which measures the speed of adjustment. For this reason, it is especially important to introduce other relevant variables, such as infrastructure investment and human capital stock, in order to reduce the importance of *unobserved* cross-sectional variation.

A second important finding is that the Sevestre–Trognon inequality, proved only for the case $\beta = 0$, and then only asymptotically, holds for all the examples presented. Indeed, fixed-effects OLS always yields estimates of the adjustment parameter at the extreme low end of the range of estimates obtained. The "bias" of fixed-effects models in the estimation of dynamic panel models is apparent. In this context, the use of such methods biases a test for convergence, or more appropriately rapid convergence, toward finding it. Fixed-effects models, however, are widely used, in part because they are the basis for two-round FGLS estimators, and because computer packages for panel data analysis incorporate an extremely misguided suggestion for estimating ρ, guaranteed to yield extremely low or even negative values of this parameter. These packages should be avoided, and, if they are used and do yield a negative estimate, it should not be concluded that the model is misspecified or that fixed effects are a preferable alternative. Fixed-effects OLS remains badly biased in a dynamic context irrespective of whether the packaged routines fail.

I do find, however, that FGLS, using the Balestra-Nerlove (1966) estimates of ρ, which can never be negative, always lie between the fixed-effects

OLS estimates and the pooled OLS estimates, which are known to yield upwardly biased estimates of γ. It is not appropriate to conclude that these FGLS estimates, however, represent a tighter upper bound to the true value of γ, since they are doubly inconsistent estimates and may lie below the true value. This is underscored by the finding that both conditional and unconditional ML yield different estimates of ρ and γ, sometimes higher and sometimes lower than FGLS. The interaction between ρ and γ is crucial in this regard.

Finally, maximum likelihood, unconditional on the initial observations, assuming them to be stationary and generated by the same dynamic process we are trying to estimate and assuming the exogenous variables also to be stationary, is feasible and indeed a viable alternative to conventional regression methods or conditional ML. Use of such methods will, however, generally involve removal of the overall means of all variables prior to analysis and omission of a constant term and may also involve differencing to remove deterministic or stochastic trends. Formulation of the unconditional likelihood function is somewhat more complicated in the case of differenced variables but, as demonstrated, quite feasible nonetheless. The unconditional and simpler conditional ML method may yield similar results under certain circumstances, but cannot generally be expected to do so.

References

Arellano, M. and S. Bond (1991), "Some Tests of Specification for Panel Data: Monte Carlo Evidence and an Application to Employment Equations," *Review of Economic Studies*, 58: 277–297.

Balestra, P. and M. Nerlove (1966), "Pooling Cross-Section and Time-Series Data in the Estimation of a Dynamic Economic Model: The Demand for Natural Gas," *Econometrica*, 34: 585–612.

Barnard, G.A. (1949), "Statistical Inference," *Journal of the Royal Statistical Society, Series B*, 11: 115–149.

(1951), "The Theory of Information," *Journal of the Royal Statistical Society, Series B*, 13: 46–64.

(1966), "The Use of the Likelihood Function in Statistical Practice," *Proceedings of the Fifth Berkeley Symposium on Mathematical Statistics and Probability*, 1: 27–40.

(1967), "The Bayesian Controversy in Statistical Inference," *Journal of the Institute of Actuaries*, 93, 229–69.

Barnard, G.A., G.M. Jenkins, and C.B. Winsten (1962), "Likelihood Inference and Time Series" (with discussion), *Journal of the Royal Statistical Society, Series A*, 125: 321–375.

Bernard, A.B. and S.N. Durlauf (1995), "Convergence in International Output," *Journal of Applied Econometrics*, 10: 97–108.

(1996), "Interpreting Tests of the Convergence Hypothesis," *Journal of Econometrics*, 71: 161–173.

Barro, R.J. (1991), "Economic Growth in a Cross-Section of Countries," *Quarterly Journal of Economics*, 106: 407–443.

Barro, R.J. and Jong-Wha Lee (1993), "International Comparisons of Educational Attainment," NBER Working Paper No. 4349.

Barro, R.J. and X. Sala-i-Martin (1995), *Economic Growth*, New York: McGraw-Hill.

Baumol,W. (1986), "Productivity Growth, Convergence, and Welfare: What the Long-Run Data Show," *American Economic Review*, 76: 1072–1085.

Binder, M. and M.H. Pesaran (1996), "Stochastic Growth," Working Paper No. 19–18, Department of Economics, University of Maryland.

Birnbaum, A. (1962), "On the Foundations of Statistical Inference" (with discussion) *Journal of the American Statistical Association*, 57: 269–306.

Caselli, F., G. Esquivel, and F. Lefort (1996), "Reopening the Convergence Debate: A New Look at Cross-Country Growth Empirics," *Journal of Economic Growth*, 1: 363–389.

Crépon, B. and J. Mairesse (1996), "The Chamberlain Approach," in L. Mátyás and P. Sevestre, *The Econometrics of Panel Data: Handbook of Theory and Applications*, 2nd edn, Boston: Kluwer, 323–391.

Chamberlain, G. (1984), "Panel Data," in Z. Griliches and M. Intriligator (eds.), *Handbook of Econometrics, II*, Amsterdam: Elsevier, 1247–1313.

Diebold, F.X. and M. Nerlove (1990), "Unit Roots in Economic Time Series: A Selective Survey," in T.B. Fomby and G.F. Rhodes (eds.), *Advances in Econometrics, Vol. VIII: Co-integration, Spurious Regressions, and Unit Roots*, Greenwich, CT: JAI Press.

de la Fuente, A. (1997), "The Empirics of Growth and Convergence: A Selective Review," *Journal of Economic Dynamics and Control*, 21: 23–73.

Edwards, A.W.F. (1972), *Likelihood*, Cambridge University Press.

Fisher, R.A. (1922), "On the Mathematical Foundations of Theoretical Statistics," *Philosophical Transactions of the Royal Society of London, Series A*, 222: 309–368.

(1925), "Theory of Statistical Estimation," *Proceedings of the Cambridge Philosophical Society*: 700–725.

Greene, W. (1993), *Econometric Analysis*, 2nd edn, New York: Macmillan.

Holtz-Eakin, D., W. Newey, and H. Rosen (1988), "Estimating Vector Autoregressions with Panel Data," *Econometrica*, 56: 1371–1395.

Islam, N. (1995a), "Growth Empires: A Panel Data Approach," *Quarterly Journal of Economics*, 110: 1127–1170.

(1995b), "Convergence: Variations in Concept and Results," Unpublished. International Institute for Advanced Studies, Cambridge, MA.

Judge, G., R.C. Hill, W. Griffiths, H. Lütkepohl, and T-C. Lee (1988), *Introduction to the Theory and Practice of Econometrics*, 2nd edn, New York: John Wiley & Sons.

Kiviet, Jan F. (1995), "On the Bias, Inconsistency and Efficiency of Various Estimators in Dynamic Panel Models," *Journal of Econometrics*, 68: 53–78.

Knight, M., N. Loazya and D. Villaneuva (1993), "Testing the Neoclassical Growth Model," *IMF Staff papers*, 40: 512–541.

Lee, K., M.H. Pesaran, and R. Smith (1997), "Growth and Convergence in a Multi-Country Empirical Stochastic Solow Model," *Journal of Applied Econometrics*, 12: 357–392.

Lindsey, J.K. (1996), *Parametric Statistical Inference*, Oxford: Clarendon Press.

Loayza, N. (1994), "A Test of the International Convergence Hypothesis Using Panel Data," Policy Research Working Paper No. 1333, The World Bank.

Maddala, G.S. (1971), "The Use of Variance Component Models in Pooling Cross-Section and Time Series Data," *Econometrica*, 39: 341–358.

Mankiw, N.G., D. Romer, and D.N. Weil (1992), "A Contribution to the Empirics of Economic Growth." *Quarterly Journal of Economics*, 108: 407–437.

Mátyás. L. and P. Sevestre (1996), *The Econometrics of Panel Data: Handbook of Theory and Applications*, 2nd edn., Boston: Kluwer Academic Publishers.

Mundlak, Y. (1978), "On the Pooling of Cross-Section and Time-Series Data," *Econometrica*, 46: 69–86.

Nerlove, M. (1971), "Further Evidence on the Estimation of Dynamic Economic Relations from a Time Series of Cross-Sections," *Econometrica*, 39: 359–382.

(1996), "Growth Rate Convergence, Fact or Artifact? An Essay in Panel Data Econometrics," Paper presented to the Sixth Conference on Panel Data Econometrics, Amsterdam, June 28–29, 1996.

(1997), "Likelihood Inference for Dynamic Panel Models." *L'Annales d'Économie et de Statistique de l'INSEE* (forthcoming).

Nerlove, M. and P. Balestra (1996), "Formulation and Estimation of Econometric Models for Panel Data," in L. Mátyás and P. Sevestre (1996).

Nerlove, M. and L.K. Raut (1997), "Growth Models with Endogenous Population: A General Framework," in M.R. Rosenzweig and O. Stark (eds.), *The Handbook of Family and Population Economics*, New York: Elsevier Scientific Publishers, pp. 1117–1174.

Nickell, S. (1981), "Biases in Dynamic Models with Fixed Effects," *Econometrica*, 49: 1417–1426.

Quah, D. (1996), "Empirics for Economic Growth and Convergence," *European Economic Review* (forthcoming).

Sevestre, Patrick and Alain Trognon (1983), "Propiétés de grands échantillons d'une classe d'estimateurs des modéles autoregréssives à erreurs compossées," *Annales de l'INSEE*, 50: 25–49.

(1996), "Linear Dynamic Models," in Mátyás and Sevestre (1996), pp. 126–144.

Solow, R.M. (1956), "A Contribution to the Theory of Economic Growth," *Quarterly Journal of Economics*, 70: 65–94.

Swan, T.W. (1956), Economic Growth and Capital Accumulation," *Economic Record*, 32: 324–361.

Trognon, Alain (1978), "Miscellaneous Asymptotic Properties of Ordinary Least Squares and Maximum Likelihood Methods in Dynamic Error Components Models," *Annales de l'INSEE*, 30–31: 631–657.

7 Modified generalized instrumental variables estimation of panel data models with strictly exogenous instrumental variables

SEUNG CHAN AHN AND PETER SCHMIDT

1 Introduction

Use of the generalized method of moments (GMM) has been increasingly popular in the panel data literature. Exogeneity assumptions usually imply a large number of moment conditions in panel data models. Imposing a subset of such moment conditions in GMM, researchers can easily obtain a consistent estimator. GMM also provides simple guidance for efficient estimation: since imposing more moment conditions never decreases asymptotic efficiency, an efficient estimator can be obtained by utilizing all of the moment conditions implied by a model. Based on this idea, Ahn and Schmidt (1995, 1997) and Crépon, Karamarz, and Trognon (1995) examine the moment conditions implied by dynamic panel data models, and show how these moment conditions can be efficiently implemented in GMM.

In terms of asymptotic efficiency, it would always be desirable to use as many moment conditions as possible. However, GMM using a large number of moment conditions may be infeasible or impractical in many cases. In panel data models with strictly exogenous time-varying regressors, the number of moment conditions rapidly increases with the number of time series observations. For example, a model with five strictly exogenous regressors and ten time periods generates 500 moment conditions. It is practically impossible to impose all of these conditions in GMM. There are also statistical reasons why it may not be desirable to use too many moment conditions. As recent studies (e.g., Tauchen (1986), Andersen and Sørensen (1996)) have shown, finite-sample biases in GMM estimates tend to

The first author gratefully acknowledges the financial support of the College of Business and Dean's Council of 100 at Arizona State University, the Economic Club of Phoenix, and the alumni of the College of Business. The second author gratefully acknowledges the financial support of the National Science Foundation.

increase with the number of moment conditions used.[1] These practical and statistical problems in efficient GMM estimation of panel data models naturally raise an interesting question: Under what conditions can we use a smaller set of moment conditions without incurring any loss of asymptotic efficiency? In other words, under what conditions are some moment conditions redundant in the sense that utilizing them does not improve efficiency? The main motivation of this chapter is to provide a partial answer to this question.

There have been some previous efforts to identify redundant moment conditions for panel data models. Im, Ahn, Schmidt, and Wooldridge (1996), hereafter IASW, consider conventional models, such as fixed effects (FE), random effects (RE), and Hausman and Taylor-type models (see Hausman and Taylor (1981), hereafter HT; Amemiya and MaCurdy (1986), hereafter AM; and Breusch, Mizon and Schmidt (1989), hereafter BMS). These models assume that all regressors are strictly exogenous. This strict exogeneity assumption generates a large set of moment conditions. GMM utilizing all of these moment conditions leads to an efficient estimator. IASW show that when the errors are conditionally homoskedastic, a large number of moment conditions generated by the strict exogeneity assumption are redundant even in cases in which the errors are serially correlated.

In this chapter, we re-examine and generalize the redundancy results of IASW. We consider a general error-components model which subsumes conventional models with time-invariant effects, as well as the model with time-varying effects considered by Cornwell, Schmidt and Sickles (1990). For this general model, we can define a generalized instrumental variables (GIV) estimator which uses the same instruments as HT, AM, or BMS. An advantage of using this GIV estimator is that it utilizes only a small subset of the moment conditions implied by HT, AM, or BMS assumptions regarding the regressors. Unfortunately, however, the GIV estimator is inconsistent in some cases. In response to this problem, we propose a modified GIV (MGIV) estimator which uses the same instruments as the GIV estimator does. When the errors in the model are conditionally homoskedastic, the MGIV estimator is shown to be as asymptotically efficient as GMM using a much larger set of moment conditions. This result is obtained by showing that the MGIV estimator is numerically identical to a three-stage least squares (3SLS) estimator using all of the instrumental variables implied by the HT, AM, or BMS assumptions.

Although some of our results overlap with those of IASW, this chapter

[1] Andersen and Sørensen (1996) argue that GMM estimators using too few moment conditions are as bad as estimators using too many conditions. They show that there is a trade-off between informational gain and finite-sample bias caused by using more instruments.

takes a more systematic approach which is able to handle more complicated models. IASW focus on identifying redundant moment conditions in 3SLS and/or GIV for the FE, RE, and Hausman–Taylor models. It is not obvious how their redundancy results could be generalized to other models. In contrast, our MGIV approach permits a unified treatment of a wider variety of models in which a GIV estimator is inconsistent.

This chapter is organized as follows. Section 2 introduces the model and defines the MGIV estimator. We also examine general conditions under which moment conditions become redundant in instrumental variables (IV) estimation. Section 3 examines properties of the MGIV estimator. We also derive sufficient conditions under which the 3SLS estimator using a large set of instruments becomes equivalent to the MGIV or GIV estimators exploiting a much smaller set of instruments. Section 4 applies MGIV to conventional panel data models with time-invariant effects, while section 5 considers MGIV estimation of the model with time-varying effects. Section 6 conducts some limited Monte Carlo experiments in order to investigate the finite-sample properties of the MGIV estimator. Some concluding remarks follow in section 7.

2 Setup

2.1 *The model and instrumental variables estimation*

The model of our interest in this paper is given by

$$y_i = H_i\delta + u_i;\ u_i = A\alpha_i + \varepsilon_i. \tag{1}$$

Here $i = 1,\dots,N$ indexes the cross-sectional unit, $i = 1,\dots,T$ indexes time, $y_i = [y_{i1},\dots,y_{iT}]'$ is a $T\times 1$ vector, $H_i = [h_{i1}',\dots,h_{iT}']'$ is a $T\times r$ matrix of regressors, δ is an $r\times 1$ vector of unknown parameters, and $u_i = [u_{i1},\dots,u_{iT}']'$ is a $T\times 1$ vector of errors with $E(u_i) = 0$. We allow the error u_i to contain multiple individual effects which are denoted by a $p\times 1$ $(p<T)$ vector $\alpha_i = [\alpha_{i1},\dots,\alpha_{ip}]'$. The $T\times 1$ vector $\varepsilon_i = [\varepsilon_{i1},\dots,\varepsilon_{iT}]'$ contains random noises. The $T\times p$ matrix $A = [a_{tj}]$ is assumed to be known; it does not depend on i. The dimension T is held fixed, so that asymptotics apply as N gets large. We also assume that $\{(y_i',\text{vec}(H_i)')' \mid i = 1,\dots,N\}$ is independently and identically distributed over different i.

To express the model for all observations, we need some additional notation. For any $T\times p$ matrix M_i or $T\times 1$ vector m_i, we denote $M \equiv (M_1',\dots,M_T')'$ and $m = (m_1',\dots,m_N')'$. Accordingly, X, Z, and H denote the data matrices of NT rows. With this notation we can rewrite (1) for the entire sample as

$$y = H\delta + u. \tag{2}$$

The model (1) or (2) encompasses a wide range of panel data models. For example, set $A=e_T$, where e_T is the $T\times 1$ vector of ones. Then, the model reduces to a conventional model with time-invariant individual effects. If we set $[a_{ti},a_{i2},a_{i3}]=[1,t,t^2]$ for the tth row of A, we obtain the model with time-varying effects considered by Cornwell, Schmidt, and Sickles (1990). Model (1) would also be useful for the analysis of capital asset pricing models, for which A and α_i can represent a $T\times 1$ vector of market returns and a beta coefficient for asset i, respectively.

We can think of many other possible macroeconomic applications of model (1). For example, consider Keane (1993) which studies the effects on real wages of nominal and real macro variables such as the inflation rate and oil price. While this study assumes that individuals' real wages respond to macroeconomic variables in a uniform way, there are several reasons why the responses might be heterogenous: aggregated macroeconomic variables may have different effects on different industries or occupations, or, simply, individual workers may have different information sets regarding the whole economy. We can incorporate such potential heterogeneity into macroeconomic models, by letting A include aggregated macroeconomic variables and α_i represent individual i's heterogenous responses to the variables.

For this moment, we do not make any specific exogeneity assumption regarding regressors H_i. We here simply assume that there exist instruments which satisfy the following property:

> **Assumption 1** *$E(\varepsilon_i\otimes w_i^0)=0$ and $E(\alpha_i\otimes w_{2i}^0)=0$, where $w_i^0=[w_{1i}^0,w_{2i}^0]$* is $1\times q$, *and w_{1i}^0 and w_{2i}^0* include q_1 and q_2 *variables, respectively*.

This assumption implies that all the variables in w_{1i}^0 and w_{2i}^0 are strictly exogenous with respect to the ε_{it}, in the sense that $E(w_{ji}^{0\prime}\varepsilon_{it})=0$ for all t and j, but only those in w_{2i}^0 are uncorrelated with α_i. Instruments satisfying assumption 1 are readily available in models with strictly exogenous regressors. For these models, w_i^0 contains all leads and lags of the regressors, but w_{2i}^0 contains only the regressors uncorrelated with α_i.

Assumption 1 implies many moment conditions. We can express them as follows. Let A_0 denote a $T\times(T-p)$ matrix of full column rank which is orthogonal to A: $A_0'A=0$. Then, assumption 1 is equivalent to the following set of moment conditions

$$E(W_{A,i}'u_i)=0 \tag{3}$$

where $W_{A,i}=[A_0\otimes w_i^0, A\otimes w_{2i}^0]$ is a $T\times[(T-p)q+pq_2]$ matrix. To see this, note first that $E[(A_0\otimes w_i^0)'u_i]=E[(A_0'A\alpha_i+A_0'\varepsilon_i)\otimes w_i^{0\prime}]$, which equals zero because $A_0'A=0$ and because w_i^0 is strictly exogenous with respect to ε_i.

Similarly $E[(A\otimes w_{2i}^{0})'u_i]=E[(A'A\alpha+A'\varepsilon_i)\otimes w_{2i}^{0}{}']=0$ because w_{2i}^{0} is strictly exogenous with respect to ε_i and uncorrelated with α_i.

We will use the notation "$E_i\subset F_i$", when we wish to say that there exists a matrix G such that $E_i=F_iG$ for all i; that is, $E_i\subset F_i$ means that $[E_1',\ldots,E_N']'$ is in the column space of $[F_1',\ldots,F_N']'$. Using this notation, we will express a subset W_i of the instruments $W_{\mathrm{A},i}$ by $W_i\subset W_{\mathrm{A},i}$.

Under assumption 1, the parameter vector δ can be consistently estimated by 3SLS using a subset of the instruments $W_{\mathrm{A},i}$. We denote the 3SLS estimator using $W_i\subset W_{\mathrm{A},i}$ by

$$\hat{\delta}_{3\mathrm{SLS}}(W_i)\equiv[H'W(W'\Omega W)^{-1}W'H]^{-1}H'W(W'\Omega W)^{-1}W'y \tag{4}$$

where $\Sigma=E(u_iu_i')$ and $\Omega=I_N\otimes\Sigma$. In practice, Σ should be replaced by a consistent estimate. For notational convenience, however, we treat Σ as known throughout this chapter. A consistent estimate of Σ can be obtained by $N^{-1}\Sigma_i\hat{u}_i\hat{u}_i'$, where the $\hat{u}_i$ are 2SLS residuals. The 3SLS estimator is the GMM estimator using the weighting matrix equal to $(W'\Omega W)^{-1}$. Thus, the 3SLS estimator using $W_{A,i}$ as instruments should be the optimal GMM estimator based on assumption 1, if the following additional assumption holds:

Assumption 2 $E(W_{A,i}'u_iu_i'W_{A,i})=E(W_{A,i}'\Sigma W_{A,i})$.

We will refer to assumption 2 as the assumption of no conditional heteroskedasticity. This is a slight misuse of terminology, since assumption 2 is weaker than the assumption that $E(u_iu_i\,|\,w_i^0)=\Sigma$. However, assumption 2 is what is necessary for 3SLS to coincide with the efficient GMM estimator. When assumption 2 is violated, the GMM estimator replacing $W'\Omega W$ in (4) by the weighting matrix $N^{-1}\Sigma_iW_i'\Sigma\hat{u}_i\hat{u}_i'W_i$ is strictly more efficient than the 3SLS estimator using the same instruments.

As an alternative to the 3SLS estimator defined in (4), we may use the generalized instrumental variables (GIV) estimator (White (1984)), which is obtained by premultiplying (1) by $\Sigma^{-1/2}$ to prewhiten the u_i, and then applying the instruments $\Sigma^{-1/2}W_i$

$$\begin{aligned}\hat{\delta}_{\mathrm{GIV}}(W_i)&\equiv[H'\Omega^{-1}W(W'\Omega^{-1}W)^{-1}W'\Omega^{-1}H]^{-1}\\&\quad\times H'\Omega^{-1}W(W'\Omega^{-1}W)^{-1}W'\Omega^{-1}y\\&=\hat{\delta}_{3\mathrm{SLS}}(\Sigma^{-1}W_i)\end{aligned} \tag{5}$$

In some cases, the GIV estimator could be more efficient than the 3SLS estimator using the same instruments. For example, Chamberlain (1987) assumes $E(u_i|W_i)=0$ and $E(u_iu_i')|W_i)=\Sigma$, which are stronger than assumptions 1 and 2. Under these assumptions, Chamberlain shows that the optimal GMM estimator based on $E(u_i\,|\,W_i)=0$ is a GMM estimator using the instruments $\Sigma^{-1}E(H_i|W_i)$. But, it is straightforward to show that this optimal estimator is asymptotically equivalent to the GIV estimator using instruments W_i, if $E(H_i|W_i)$ is linear in W_i.

While this example may provide a good motivation to use GIV, it is important to realize that the GIV estimator defined in (5) is not necessarily consistent under assumptions 1 and 2. In particular, assumption 1 does not guarantee that $E(W_{A,i}'\Sigma^{-1}u_i)=0$. To clarify this point, note that consistency of $\hat{\delta}_{\mathrm{GIV}}(W_{A,i})$ requires

$$E[(A_0\otimes w_i^0)'\Sigma^{-1}u_i]=E[(A_0'\Sigma^{-1}A\alpha_i)\otimes w_i^0]=0. \tag{6}$$

Assumption 1 ensures that w_{2i}^0 is uncorrelated with α_i. However, since no restriction is imposed on the covariances between w_{1i}^0 and α_i, condition (6) may not hold. A sufficient condition for (6) to hold is

$$A_i^{0\prime}\Sigma^{-1}A=0 \tag{7}$$

which in general does not hold. (It does hold for certain special forms of Σ and A.) This result indicates that the GIV estimator using any subset of instruments $A_0\otimes w_{1i}^0$ is in general inconsistent.

To resolve this problem, we need to modify the GIV estimator. Consider the two sets of instruments $W_{1i}\subset A_0\otimes w_i^0$ and $W_{2i}\subset A\otimes w_{2i}^0$. Clearly $E(W_{2i}'\Sigma^{-1}u_i)=0$ under assumption 1. Thus, the instruments w_{2i} are legitimate for GIV. To handle the instruments w_{1i}, we follow IASW and define a $T\times T$ idempotent (though not symmetric) matrix R_Σ:

$$R_\Sigma=I_T-A(A'\Sigma^{-1}A)^{-1}A'\Sigma^{-1}. \tag{8}$$

Then, since $R_\Sigma'\Sigma^{-1}A=0$, we can see that $E(W_{1i}'R_\Sigma'\Sigma^{-1}u_i)=E(W_{1i}'R_\Sigma'\Sigma^{-1}\varepsilon_i)=0$. Thus, the instruments $R_\Sigma W_{1i}$ are also legitimate for GIV. Based on this result, we define the modified GIV (MGIV) estimator by

$$\hat{\delta}_{\mathrm{MGIV}}(W_{1i},W_{2i})\equiv\hat{\delta}_{\mathrm{GIV}}(R_\Sigma W_{1i},W_{2i})=\hat{\delta}_{\mathrm{3SLS}}(Q_\Sigma W_{1i},\Sigma^{-1}W_{2i}) \tag{9}$$

where $W_{1i}\subset A_0\otimes w_i^0$, $W_{2i}\subset A\otimes w_{2i}^0$ and $Q_\Sigma=\Sigma^{-1}R_\Sigma=\Sigma^{-1}-\Sigma^{-1}A(A'\Sigma^{-1}A)^{-1}A'\Sigma^{-1}$. This MGIV estimator plays an important role in the following sections.

2.2 *Redundancy in instrumental variables*

In this subsection, we consider general conditions under which some instruments become redundant in 3SLS. Since the GIV and MGIV estimators can be viewed as 3SLS estimators, the conditions introduced in this section equally apply to them. In what follows, we often use the usual projection notation. For any matrix B of full column rank, we define the projection matrix $P(B)=B(B'B)^{-1}B'$; and we let $Q(B)=I-P(B)$ denote the projection on to the space orthogonal to B.

The following is theorem 2.4 of IASW:

Lemma 1 *Let $W_i=[W_{ci}, W_{di}]$. Assume*

$$W_d'\Omega^{1/2}Q(\Omega^{1/2}W_c)\Omega^{-1/2}H$$
$$= W_d'H - W_d'\Omega W_c(W_c'\Omega W_c)^{-1}W_c'H = 0. \quad (10)$$

Then, $\hat{\delta}_{3SLS}(W_i)=\hat{\delta}_{3SLS}(W_{ci})$. *That is, the instruments W_{di} are redundant.*

Lemma 1 applies to any 3SLS estimator with W and H of unrestricted form. It may also be worth emphasizing that lemma 1 is a numerical, not asymptotic, result. An asymptotic equivalence version of lemma 1 is

$$\text{Proj}(\Omega^{-1/2}H_i|\Omega^{1/2}W_{ci},\Omega^{1/2}W_{di}) = \text{Proj}(\Omega^{-1/2}H_i|\Omega^{1/2}W_{ci}) \quad (11)$$

where $\text{Proj}(E_i|F_i)$ denotes the linear population projection of E_i on F_i. Condition (11) implies that given $\Omega^{1/2}W_{ci}$,$\Omega^{1/2}W_{di}$ has no linear correlation with $\Omega^{1/2}H_i$ asymptotically. Since our concerns are numerical properties of IV estimators, (11) plays no role in this chapter. However, the condition could be important if one's concern is to determine which instruments may be asymptotically redundant in 3SLS. Condition (11) may also provide a plausible empirical strategy for choosing instruments. For example, one may regress $\Omega^{1/2}H_i$ on all available instruments, and then use in 3SLS only the instruments that enter "significantly" (in some sense) into this auxiliary regression. Whether such a strategy can generate 3SLS estimators having better finite sample properties than those using all of the instruments is a question beyond the scope of this chapter. But, future research in this line seems to be worth pursuing.

Another redundancy condition which we use in later sections is as follows:

Lemma 2 *Let $W_i=[W_{ci}, W_{di}]$ and $W_{ci}=[W_{ei}, W_{fi}]$. Assume*

$$W_c'\Omega W_d = 0; \quad (12)$$

$$W_f'\Omega^{1/2}Q(\Omega^{1/2}W_e)\Omega^{-1/2}H = 0. \quad (13)$$

Then, $\hat{\delta}_{3SLS}(W_i)=\hat{\delta}_{3SLS}(W_{ei}, W_{di})$. That is, under (12), the instruments W_{fi} are redundant for $\hat{\delta}_{3SLS}(W_i)$ whenever they are redundant for $\hat{\delta}_{3SLS}(W_{ci})$.

Proof: See the appendix.

Under (12), the 3SLS estimator using the instruments W_i is a convex combination of two 3SLS estimators, $\hat{\delta}_{3SLS}(W_{ci})$and $\hat{\delta}_{3SLS}(W_{di})$, when they exist:

$$\hat{\beta}_{3SLS}(W_i) = [C_c + C_d]^{-1}[C_c\hat{\beta}_{3SLS}(W_{ci}) + C_d\hat{\beta}_{3SLS}(W_{di})] \tag{14}$$

where $C_j = H'W_j(W_j'\Omega W_j)^{-1}W_j'H$ for $j = c, d$. An implication of lemma 2 is that when $\hat{\delta}_{3SLS}(W_i)$ takes the convex combination form (14), any instrument set that is redundant for $\hat{\delta}_{3SLS}(W_{ci})$ or $\hat{\delta}_{3SLS}(W_{di})$ is also redundant for $\hat{\delta}_{3SLS}(W_i)$; that is, we can identify redundant instruments in W_i by applying lemma 1 to W_{ci} and W_{di} separately.

In fact, our MGIV estimator satisfies condition (12), since

$$\hat{\delta}_{MGIV}(W_{1i}, W_{2i}) = [C_1^* + C_2^*]^{-1}[C_1^*\hat{\delta}_{3SLS}(Q_\Sigma W_{1i}) + C_2^*\hat{\delta}_{3SLS}(\Sigma^{-1}W_{2i})] \tag{15}$$

where

$W_1^* = (I_N \otimes Q_\Sigma)W_1$, $W_2^* = \Omega^{-1}W_2$, and $C_j = H'W_j^*(W_j^{*\prime}\Omega W_j^*)^{-1} W_j^* H$ for $j = 1, 2$.[2]

As it turns out in section 3, this result is crucial in showing that a large number of instruments in $A_0 \otimes w_i^0$ are redundant in MGIV when w_i^0 includes all leads and lags of the regressors h_{it}.

3 Properties of MGIV

In this section, we study properties of the MGIV estimator. In section 3.1, we examine the relation between MGIV and GIV. Section 3.2 derives sufficient conditions under which a large number of instruments $W_{A,i}$ become redundant.

3.1 *MGIV and GIV*

In fact, the MGIV estimator (9) is a GIV estimator applied to a linear transformation of the model (1). To show this, we need some preliminary algebraic results:

Lemma 3 *For any choice of* A_0 *and* Σ, $A_0(A_0'\Sigma A_0)^{-1}A_0' = Q_\Sigma$.

Lemma 4 *For any* $W_{2i} \subset A \otimes w_{2i}^0$, $\Sigma^{-1}W_{2i} = P_\Sigma W_{2i}$, *where* $P_\Sigma = \Sigma^{-1}A(A'\Sigma^{-1}A)A'\Sigma^{-1}$.

Proof: See the appendix.

These lemmas imply that the MGIV estimator can be written as

$$\hat{\delta}_{MGIV}(W_{1i}, W_{2i}) = \hat{\delta}_{3SLS}[A_0(A_0'\Sigma A_0')^{-1}A_0' W_{1i}, P_\Sigma W_{2i}]. \tag{16}$$

To motivate this estimator, we can premultiply the model (1) by $[A_0, \Sigma^{-1}A]'$:

[2] This result is obtained because $W_{2i} \subset A \otimes w_{2i}^0$, and thus, $W_{1i}'R_\Sigma'\Sigma^{-1}W_{2i} = 0$.

$$\begin{bmatrix} A_o'y_i \\ A'\Sigma^{-1}y_i \end{bmatrix} = \begin{bmatrix} A_o'H_i \\ A'\Sigma^{-1}H_i \end{bmatrix}\delta + \begin{bmatrix} A_o'u_i \\ A'\Sigma^{-1}u_i \end{bmatrix}. \tag{17}$$

Since $[A_0, \Sigma^{-1}A]$ is non-singular, this model is informatively equivalent to the original model (1). Note that the covariance matrix of errors in (17) equals $\text{diag}(A_0'\Sigma A_0, A'\Sigma^{-1}A)$. Thus, GIV applied to (17) with instruments $\text{diag}(A_0' W_{1i}, A'\Sigma^{-1}W_{2i})$ is equivalent to 3SLS applied to the same model with instruments

$$\text{diag}[(A_0'\Sigma A_0)^{-1}A_0' W_{1i}, (A'\Sigma^{-1}A)^{-1}A'\Sigma^{-1}W_{2i}].$$

Then, it is not difficult to show that this 3SLS estimator is numerically equivalent to the 3SLS estimator given in (16).

In some cases, MGIV using $W_{1i} \subset A_0 \otimes w_i^0$ and $W_{2i} \subset A \otimes w_{2i}^0$ is equivalent to GIV applied to the original model (1) with the same instruments. A sufficient condition for this equivalence is

$$P_\Sigma W_{1i} \subset \Sigma^{-1}W_{2i}. \tag{18}$$

Since $Q_\Sigma = \Sigma^{-1} - P_\Sigma$, (18) implies that 3SLS using instruments $[Q_\Sigma W_{1i}, \Sigma^{-1}W_{2i}]$ is equivalent to 3SLS using instruments $[\Sigma^{-1}W_{1i}, \Sigma^{-1}W_{2i}]$, that is, GIV using $[W_{1i}, W_{2i}]$. Thus, under (18) we must have

$$\hat{\delta}_{\text{MGIV}}(W_{1i}, W_{2i}) = \hat{\delta}_{\text{3SLS}}(Q_\Sigma W_{1i}, \Sigma^{-1}W_{2i}) = \delta_{\text{GIV}}(W_{1i}, W_{2i}). \tag{19}$$

A stronger condition than (18) is (7), $A_0'\Sigma^{-1}A = 0$, under which $Q_\Sigma W_{1i} = \Sigma^{-1}W_{1i}$. Condition (7) trivially holds if Σ is proportional to I_T, which is too restrictive unless $\alpha_i = 0$ in model (1). Alternatively, we may consider cases in which

$$\Sigma = A\Phi A' + \sigma_\varepsilon^2 I_T. \tag{20}$$

This restriction holds if ε_i is independent of α_i, $\Phi = E(\alpha_i\alpha_i')$ and $E(\varepsilon_i\varepsilon_i') = \sigma_\varepsilon^2 I_T$. For this covariance restriction

$$[A\Phi A' + (1/b)I_T]^{-1} = bI_T - b^2A(\Phi^{-1} + bA'A)^{-1}A' \tag{21}$$

where $b = 1/\sigma_\varepsilon^2$. Thus, we can easily show that $A_0'\Sigma^{-1}A = 0$.

Unfortunately, condition (7) is violated if the random noise components ε_{it} are serially correlated. In the next section, we show that condition (18) could hold for unrestricted Σ if the regressors have some special properties.

3.2 *Redundancy results*

In this section, we show that the 3SLS estimator applied to model (1) with instruments $W_{A,i}$ is equivalent to a MGIV estimator using many fewer instruments. To be specific, we make the following assumption:

Assumption 3 $Q(A)H_i \subset I_T \otimes w_i^0$.

Assumption 3 is a sufficient condition for our redundancy result stated below. For a better understanding of this assumption, consider the usual RE model, for which we can set $A = e_T$ and $A_0 = L_T$, where L_T is a $T \times (T-1)$ differencing matrix

$$L_T = \begin{bmatrix} 1 & 0 & 0 & \dots & 0 & 0 \\ -1 & 1 & 0 & \dots & 0 & 0 \\ \vdots & \vdots & \vdots & & \vdots & \vdots \\ 0 & 0 & 0 & \dots & -1 & 1 \\ 0 & 0 & 0 & \dots & 0 & -1 \end{bmatrix}. \tag{22}$$

Suppose that $E[h_{is}'(u_{it} - u_{i,t-1})] = 0$, for any $s \geq 1$ and $t > 1$. Then, we are able to include $v(H_i)'$ in w_i^0, where $v(\bullet)$ denotes vec($\bullet$) with repeated arguments excluded. Thus, assumption 3 holds for this case. If the regressors h_{it} are strictly exogenous with respect to the errors ε_{it}, then we can always include $v(H_i)'$ in w_i^0, and then assumption 3 would hold. However, assumption 3 also holds under weaker conditions. For example, assumption 3 holds if the differenced regressors are strictly exogenous with respect to differenced ε_{it}; that is, if $E[(h_{is} - h_{i,s-1})(u_{it} - u_{i,t-1})] = 0$, for any $s, t > 1$. This condition can be equivalently written as $E[v(Q_T H_i)'(u_{it} - u_{i,t-1})] = 0$, where $Q_T = Q(e_T)$. If w_i^0 includes $v(Q_T H_i)'$, $Q_T H_i \subset I_T \otimes v(Q_T H_i)' \subset I_T \otimes w_i^0$.

The following result plays an important role for our redundancy result:

Lemma 5 $\hat{\delta}_{3SLS}(W_{A,i}) = \hat{\delta}_{3SLS}[A_0 \otimes w_i^0, \Sigma^{-1}(A \otimes w_{2i}^0)]$.

Proof: See the appendix.

This lemma itself might not be of much interest. However, note that since the two sets of instruments $A_0 \otimes w_i^0$ and $\Sigma^{-1}(A \otimes w_{2i}^0)$ satisfy (12), the 3SLS estimator using instruments $A_0 \otimes w_i^0$ and $\Sigma^{-1}(A \otimes w_{2i}^0)$ is of the convex combination form. Thus, any instrument redundant for $\hat{\delta}_{3SLS}(A_0 \otimes w_i^0)$ can be shown to be also redundant for $\hat{\delta}_{3SLS}[A_0 \otimes w_i^0, \Sigma^{-1}(A \otimes w_{2i}^0)]$ by lemma 2. Based on this observation, we can obtain our major redundancy result:

Theorem 1 *Under assumptions 1 and 3*

$$\hat{\delta}_{3SLS}(W_{A,i}) = \hat{\delta}_{MGIV}[Q(A)H_i, A \otimes w_{2i}^0]. \tag{23}$$

Proof: See the appendix.

Theorem 1 means that among the instruments $A_0 \otimes w_{1i}^0$, only the subset of instruments $Q(A)H_i$ is relevant for MGIV. This result also implies that whenever the instruments $W_{A,i}$ satisfy assumptions 1–3, the MGIV estimator using instruments $[Q(A)H_i, A\otimes \mathrm{w}_{2i}^0]$ is the efficient GMM estimator.

When some restrictions are imposed on the regressors, the MGIV estimator becomes equivalent to the GIV estimator using the same instruments. As we discussed in the previous subsection, condition (18) is sufficient for this equality. We can in turn show that (18) is guaranteed if the regressors H_i have the following property:

Assumption 4 $v[Q(A)H_i]' \subset w_{2i}^0$.

This assumption is a generalization of the stationarity condition of Breusch, Mizon, and Schmidt (1989). To see why, consider panel data models with time-invariant effects; i.e., $A = e_T$ and $v[Q(A)H_i]' = v(Q_T, H_i)'$. For this case, assumption 4 means that for any t, the demeaned regressors $h_{it} - \bar{h}_i$ are uncorrelated with α_i. This will be so if $E(h_{it}'\alpha_i)$ does not depend on t, which is the Breusch, Mizon, and Schmidt condition.

Theorem 2 *Under assumptions* 1, 3, *and* 4

$$\hat{\delta}_{3SLS}(\mathrm{W}_{A,i}) = \hat{\delta}_{GIV}[\mathrm{Q(A)H_i, A}\otimes \mathrm{w}_{2i}^0]. \tag{24}$$

Proof: See the appendix.

4 Application to models with time-invariant effects

In this section, we consider a model with time-invariant individual effects

$$y_i = X_i\beta + (e_T\otimes z_i)\gamma + u_i = H_i\delta + u_i;\ u_i = (e_T\otimes \alpha_i) + \varepsilon_i \tag{25}$$

where $X_i = [x_{i1}', \ldots, x_{iT}']'$ is a $T\times k$ matrix of time-varying regressors, $e_T\otimes z_i = [z_i', \ldots, z_i']'$ is a $T\times g$ matrix of time-invariant regressors, and β and γ are $k\times 1$ and $g\times 1$ vectors of unknown parameters, respectively. We assume that α_i and ε_i are uncorrelated. The following assumption is also maintained throughout this section.

FE assumption *The regressors,* x_{it} *and* z_i, *are strongly exogenous with respect to the* ε_{it}*; i.e.,* $E(x_{it}'\varepsilon_{is}) = 0$ *and* $E(z_i'\varepsilon_{is}) = 0$ *for any* t *and* s.

The appropriate choice of estimation methods for the model (25) crucially depends on the assumptions about correlations between regressors and the effects α_i. Section 4.1 deals with IV estimation of FE models in which all of the regressors are allowed to be correlated with the individual effect, and section 4.2 considers RE models in which all of the regressors are assumed to be uncorrelated with the individual effect. Section 4.3 considers Hausman and Taylor-type models in which some, but not necessarily all, regressors are uncorrelated with the individual effect.

4.1 *Fixed-effects models*

In this subsection, we study the 3SLS estimator using the orthogonality conditions implied by the FE assumption. Since the regressors are allowed to be correlated with the effect α_i, the available orthogonality conditions are

$$\mathrm{E}(\varepsilon_i \otimes s_i) = 0 \tag{26}$$

where $s_i = [v(Xi)', z_i]$. (Thus s_i corresponds to w_i^0 in the general setup of section 2 and 3.) This is a strict exogeneity assumption after removing α_i from the error u_i. GMM based on (26) can identify β only, not γ; thus, for this subsection, our discussion will be restricted to the estimation of β.

The legitimate instruments under the FE assumption are given by

$$W_{FE,i} = L_T \otimes s_i. \tag{27}$$

The total number of instruments included in (27) equals $(T-1)(Tk+g)$. Observe that $E(W_{FE,i}' u_i u_i' W_{FE,i}) = E(W_{FE,i}' \varepsilon_i \varepsilon_i' W_{FE,i})$. This implies that the relevant covariance matrix for 3SLS using the instruments (27) can be taken to be just $E(\varepsilon_i \varepsilon_i')$, not $E(u_i u_i')$. For this reason, this subsection uses Λ to denote $E(\varepsilon_i \varepsilon_i')$ in order to distinguish it from $\Sigma = E(u_i u_i')$. That is, $\Sigma = \sigma_\alpha^2 e_T e_T' + \Lambda$. Of course, $W_{FE,i}' \Sigma W_{FE,i} = W_{FE,i}' \Lambda W_{FE,i}$ in light of $W_{FE,i}' e_T = 0$.

In fact, we can show that many instruments in (27) are redundant. Note that $W_{FE,i}$ is of the form $A_0 \otimes w_i^0$ with $A_0 = L_T$, $w_i^0 = s_i$ and $A = e_T$. Thus, theorem 1 immediately follows

$$\hat{\beta}_{\mathrm{3SLS}}(W_{\mathrm{FE},i}) = \hat{\beta}_{\mathrm{MGIV}}(Q_T X_i). \tag{28}$$

This MGIV estimator utilizes only $(T-1)k$ instruments. That is, $((T-1)^2 k + g)$ instruments in $W_{\mathrm{FE},i}$ are redundant.

Kiefer (1980) considers a GLS estimator for the FE model with known Λ, which is defined by

$$\hat{\beta}_{\mathrm{KGLS}} = [X'(I_N \otimes Q_\Lambda)X]^{-1} X'(I_N \otimes Q_\Lambda)y \tag{29}$$

where $Q_\Lambda = \Lambda^{-1} - \Lambda^{-1} e_T (e_T' \Lambda^{-1} e_T)^{-1} e_T' \Lambda^{-1}$. Note that $\hat{\beta}_{\mathrm{KGLS}}$ equals the usual within estimator when Λ is a scalar matrix. In fact $\hat{\beta}_{\mathrm{KGLS}}$ coincides with $\hat{\beta}_{\mathrm{MGIV}}(Q_T X_i)$. Stated formally:

Theorem 3 $\hat{\beta}_{\mathrm{KGLS}} = \hat{\beta}_{\mathrm{MGIV}}(Q_T X_i)$.

Proof: See the appendix.

This result might not be too surprising, but it does imply an efficiency result. If the instruments $W_{FE,i}$ satisfy assumption 2, that is, if $E(W_{FE,i}'u_i u_i' W_{FE,i}) = E(W_{FE,i}'\Sigma W_{FE,i})$, the KGLS estimator is efficient because the 3SLS estimator using $W_{FE,i}$ is the efficient GMM estimator.

A troublesome aspect of the MGIV (and KGLS) estimator is that in practice it requires estimation of $\Lambda = E(\varepsilon_i \varepsilon_i')$, which is not identified if the model (25) includes time-invariant regressors or individual effects. In response to this problem, Kiefer (1980) proposed an alternative GLS estimator based on the demeaned data, using $(Q_T \Sigma Q_T)^-$, a g-inverse of the error covariance matrix on the demeaned data. This estimator, which we name feasible KGLS (FKGLS), is of the form

$$\hat{\beta}_{\mathrm{FKGLS}} = [X'(I_N \otimes Q_T(Q_T\Sigma Q_T)^- Q_T)X]^{-1} X'(I_N \otimes Q_T(Q_T\Sigma Q_T)^- Q_T)y. \tag{30}$$

This estimator is feasible because $Q_T \Sigma Q_T$ can be consistently estimated, for example, by

$$Q_T[N^{-1}\Sigma_i(y_i - X_i\hat{\beta})(y_i - X_i\hat{\beta})']Q_T$$

where $\hat{\beta}$ is any consistent estimator of β.

There are many equivalent representations of FKGLS estimator. Observe that $Q_T(Q_T\Sigma Q_T)^- Q_T$ is invariant for any choice of g-inverse, since Rank $(Q_T \Sigma Q_T) =$ Rank (Q_T) (see Rao and Mitra (1971, lemma 2.2.6(g)). But, since $L_T(L_T'\Sigma L_T)^{-1}L_T'$ is a g-inverse of $Q_T\Sigma Q_T$, we have

$$Q_T(Q_T\Sigma Q_T)^- Q_T = Q_T L_T (L_T'\Sigma L_T)^{-1} L_T' Q_T = L_T(L_T'\Sigma L_T)^{-1} L_T'.$$

If we replace $Q_T(Q_T\Sigma Q_T)^- Q_T$ in (30) by $L_T(L_T'\Sigma L_T)^{-1}L_T'$, we can see that the FGKLS estimator is equivalent to the GLS estimator ($\hat{\beta}_{\mathrm{DF}}$) in the differenced set of equations. Furthermore, lemma 3 implies that L_T can be replaced by any $T \times (T-1)$ full-column rank matrix orthogonal to e_T. For example, if we choose Q_T^* which equals Q_T with one column deleted, the resulting estimator is equivalent to the GLS estimator ($\hat{\beta}_{\mathrm{DM}}$) in the demeaned equation after deleting any one time period.

Lemma 3 also implies that all of these alternative GLS estimators are equivalent to the KGLS estimator. Therefore, we have

$$\hat{\beta}_{\mathrm{3SLS}}(W_{\mathrm{FE},i}) = \hat{\beta}_{\mathrm{KGLS}} = \hat{\beta}_{\mathrm{FKGLS}} = \hat{\beta}_{\mathrm{DM}} = \hat{\beta}_{\mathrm{DF}}. \tag{31}$$

The equivalence among these estimators, except $\hat{\beta}_{\mathrm{KGLS}}$, has been shown by IASW (theorem 4.3). It follows immediately from this result that, whenever the 3SLS estimator using instruments $W_{\mathrm{FE},i}$ is the efficient GMM estimator (i.e., if assumptions 1 and 2 hold for $W_{\mathrm{FE},i}$), so are any of the GLS estimators.

The result (31) also implies that under the FE assumption, the feasible GLS estimates applied to the demeaned or differenced data are asymptotically equivalent to the GLS estimator obtained with Λ ($\hat{\beta}_{\mathrm{KGLS}}$). This essentially means that demeaning the data does not cause any information (efficiency) loss in GLS, whether $\Lambda = E(\varepsilon_i\varepsilon_i')$ is known or not.

Before we leave this subsection, it might be worth noting that (28) and (31) hold under assumptions weaker than the FE assumption. Suppose that the differenced regressors $x_{it} - x_{i,t-1}$ are strictly exogenous to the differenced errors $u_{it} - u_{i,t-1}$; this is a weaker assumption than strict exogeneity in levels. For this case, the valid instruments are $W^*_{\mathrm{FE},i} = L_T \otimes v(Q_T X_i)'$. Replacing $W_{\mathrm{FE},i}$ by $W^*_{\mathrm{FE},i}$, we can obtain the same results as in (28) and (31). This implies that when the instruments $W^*_{\mathrm{FE},i}$ satisfy assumption 2, all of the GLS estimators in (31) preserve their efficiency among GMM estimators based on the condition $E(W^{*\prime}_{\mathrm{FE},i} u_i) = 0$.

4.2 *Random-effects models*

This subsection studies 3SLS estimation of the model (25) under the usual RE assumption:

> **RE Assumption:** *In addition to the FE assumption, the regressors x_{it} and z_i are uncorrelated with the individual effect α_i; that is $E(x_{it}'\alpha_i) = 0$ and $E(z_i'\alpha_i) = 0$ for any t.*

Under this assumption, we have the orthogonality conditions

$$E(u_i \otimes s_i) = 0. \tag{32}$$

Since these orthogonality conditions are based on the errors in levels, we can identify both β and γ. As before, we let $\delta = (\beta', \gamma')'$ and let $\hat{\delta}_{\mathrm{3SLS}}(W_i)$ be the 3SLS estimator with instruments W_i.

The valid instruments under (32) are $I_T \otimes s_i$, or equivalently

$$W_{\mathrm{RE},i} \equiv [L_T \otimes s_i, e_T \otimes s_i] = [W_{\mathrm{FE},i}, e_T \otimes s_i]. \tag{33}$$

These instruments satisfy assumptions 1, 3, and 4. Therefore, a redundancy result immediately follows:

$$\hat{\delta}_{\mathrm{3SLS}}(W_{\mathrm{RE},i}) = \hat{\delta}_{\mathrm{MGIV}}[Q_T X_i, e_T \otimes s_i] = \hat{\delta}_{\mathrm{GIV}}(Q_T X_i, e_T \otimes s_i) \tag{34}$$

where the first equality results from theorem 1 and the second from theorem 2. Further, since $H_i = [X_i, e_T \otimes z_i] \subset [Q_T X_i, e_T \otimes s_i]$, we can easily show that

$\hat{\delta}_{\text{GIV}}(Q_T X_i, e_T \otimes s_i)$ equals the GLS estimator $\hat{\delta}_{\text{GIV}}(H_i)$. This means that when the set of instruments $W_{\text{RE},i}$ satisfies assumption 2, $\hat{\delta}_{\text{GLS}}$ is efficient among the GMM estimators based on $E(W_{RE,i}{}'u_i) = 0$.

Some redundancy results similar to (34) can be obtained under assumptions weaker than the RE assumption. For example, suppose that only the mean of x_{it} ($\bar{x}_i$), not each of the x_{it} individually, is uncorrelated with the effect (as in Hausman and Taylor (1981)). For this case, the valid set of instruments is $W_{A,i} = [W_{\text{FE},i}, e_T \otimes \bar{s}_i]$, where $\bar{s}_i = [\bar{x}_i, z_i]$. Similarly to (34), we still can show that $\hat{\delta}_{\text{3SLS}}(W_{A,i}) = \hat{\delta}_{\text{MGIV}}(Q_T X_i, e_T \otimes \bar{s}_i)$. However, the equivalence of this MGIV estimator and the GLS estimator $\hat{\delta}_{\text{GIV}}(H_i)$ crucially depends on the structure of Σ. Note that assumption 4 does not hold for $W_{A,i}$, so theorem 2 does not apply here; that is, MGIV using the instruments $[Q_T X_i, e_T \otimes \bar{s}_i]$ may not be the same as GIV using the same instruments. Accordingly, the GLS estimator $\hat{\delta}_{\text{GIV}}(H_i)$ could be different from the MGIV estimator. Nonetheless, these two estimators are equivalent if Σ is of the usual RE form, $\Sigma = \sigma_\alpha^2 e_T e_T' + \sigma_\varepsilon^2 I_T$. This is because this form for Σ guarantees (7). This example demonstrates that the efficiency or consistency of the GLS estimator may depend not only on the assumptions about correlations between regressors and the effect, but also on the structure of the covariance matrix of u_i.

4.3 *Hausman and Taylor-type models*

Hausman and Taylor (1981, HT) studied an unobservable effects model where certain explanatory variables are uncorrelated with the effect. Extending their study, Amemiya and MaCurdy (1986, AM), and Breusch, Mizon, and Schmidt (1989, BMS) considered the same model under stronger assumptions and derived alternative IV estimators that are more efficient than the HT estimator. While these studies assumed the RE error covariance structure, $\Sigma = \sigma_\alpha^2 e_T e_T' + \sigma_\varepsilon^2 I_T$, we relax the assumption by allowing the ε_{it} to be intertemporally correlated.

Following HT, we decompose x_{it} and z_i into

$$x_{it} = [x_{1it}, x_{2it}];\; z_i = [z_{1i}, z_{2i}] \tag{35}$$

where x_{1it} and x_{2it} are $1 \times k_1$ and $1 \times k_2$, respectively, and z_{1i} and z_{2i} are $1 \times g_1$ and $1 \times g_2$. With this notation, define

$$s_{\text{HT},i} = [\bar{x}_{1i}, z_{1i}];\; s_{\text{AM},i} = [v(X_{1i})', z_{1i}];\; s_{\text{BMS},i} = [\bar{x}_{1i}, v(Q_T X_i)', z_{1i}]. \tag{36}$$

HT, AM, and BMS impose the following assumptions, respectively, on the model (25):

HT assumption: In addition to the FE assumption, the effect α_1 is uncorrelated with $s_{\text{HT},i}$.

AM assumption: In addition to the FE assumption, the effect α_1 is uncorrelated with $s_{\text{AM},i}$.

BMS assumption: In addition to the FE assumption, the effect α_1 is uncorrelated with $s_{\text{BMS},i}$.

These assumptions are sequentially stronger. The HT assumption is weaker than the AM assumption, since it only requires the individual means of x_{1it} to be uncorrelated with the effect, rather than requiring x_{1it} to be uncorrelated with α_1 for each t. The BMS assumption is based on the stationarity condition that $E(x'_{2it}\alpha_i)$ is the same for any t, which means that, even though the unobserved effect might be correlated with x_{2it}, this covariance does not change over time.

HT, AM, and BMS consider GIV estimation of the model (25) under the RE error assumption, while AM also consider the case with unrestricted Σ, as we discuss below. The instruments used by HT, AM, and BMS are of the common form $[Q_T X_i, G_i]$, where the form of G_i varies across authors

$$G_{\text{HT},i} = e_T \otimes s_{\text{HT},i};\ G_{\text{AM},i} = e_T \otimes s_{\text{AM},i};\ G_{\text{BMS},i} = e_T \otimes s_{\text{BMS},i}. \tag{37}$$

Under the RE covariance restriction, the HT, AM, and BMS estimators are essentially GIV estimators using instruments $[Q_T X_i, G_{h,i}]$, where h denotes "HT," "AM," or "BMS."

An alternative estimator is the 3SLS estimator exploiting all of the orthogonality conditions implied by the HT, AM, or BMS assumptions. Under each assumption, the valid set of instruments is given by

$$[W_{\text{FE},i}, G_i] \tag{38}$$

where G_i equals $G_{\text{HT},i}$, $G_{\text{AM},i}$, or $G_{\text{BMS},i}$. The 3SLS estimator using the instruments (38) has been considered by Arellano and Bover (1995). In particular, they provide a redundancy result: when $\Sigma = \sigma_\alpha^2 e_T e_T' + \sigma_\varepsilon^2 I_T$, the 3SLS estimator is equivalent to a GIV estimator using instruments $[Q_T X_i, G_{h,i}]$. Extending this result to cases with unrestricted Σ, IASW (theorem 4.8) show that the 3SLS estimator is numerically identical to the GIV estimator using instruments $[R_\Sigma Q_T X_i, G_{h,i}]$, which is our MGIV estimator. While they obtain this result by brute-force algebra, we can provide a more concise proof: observe that the instruments (38) satisfy assumptions 1 and 3. Thus, theorem 1 implies that the 3SLS estimator using the instruments (38) must be equal to the MGIV estimator using the instruments $[Q_T X_i, G_{h,i}]$.

IASW (theorem 4.7) also show that 3SLS using instruments $[W_{\text{FE},i}, G_{\text{BMS},i}]$ is equivalent to GIV using instruments $[Q_T X_i, G_{\text{BMS},i}]$. Our results from section 3 are sufficient to prove the same result: theorem 2 applies to the instruments $[W_{\text{FE},i}, G_{\text{BMS},i}]$, since they satisfy assumptions 1, 3, and 4.

As IASW have discussed, GIV estimators using instruments $[Q_T X_i, G_{\text{HT},i}]$ or $[Q_T X_i, G_{\text{AM},i}]$ are inconsistent unless Σ is of RE form, while the MGIV estimator using the same instruments is consistent. IASW also show that the MGIV estimator using $[Q_T X_i, G_{AM,i}]$ is another representation of an efficient GIV estimator proposed by AM for cases in which the AM assumption holds and Σ is unrestricted. Thus, our MGIV estimator could be viewed as a generalization of AM.

5 Application to models with time-varying effects

In this section, we consider a model with time-varying individual effects

$$y_i = X_i\beta + F_i\gamma + u_i = H_i\delta + u_i;\ u_i = A\alpha_i + \varepsilon_i \tag{39}$$

where $F_i = [f'_{i1}, \ldots, f'_{iT}]'$ is a $T \times g$ matrix of regressors in the space of A (e.g., $P(A)F_i = F_i$). Here, A is $T \times p$ and α_i is $p \times 1$. Matrix A can be included in F_i. Also, if A contains e_T, F_i will include all time-invariant regressors. Cornwell, Schmidt, and Sickles (1990, CSS hereafter) used the same model to estimate firms' time-varying technical inefficiencies. Their study allows the matrix A to vary over i, but here we assume that it is the same for all i. This restriction is purely for notational convenience. All the results obtained below can be generalized to cases with different A for different i at the cost of using more notation.

Consistent with CSS, we make the following assumptions:

> **CSS assumption** $E[\varepsilon_i \otimes v(H_i)] = 0$ *and* $E[\alpha_i \otimes s_{CSS,i}] = 0$, where $s_{CSS,i} = [v(X_{1i})', v(F_{1i})']$ *and* X_{1i} *and* F_{1i} are some *submatrices of* X_i *and* F_i, *respectively.*

Under this assumption, the instruments legitimate for 3SLS are

$$W_{CSS,i} = [A_0 \otimes v(H_i)', A \otimes s_{CSS,i}] \tag{40}$$

where A_0 is a $T \times (T-p)$ matrix orthogonal to A. Since the instruments $W_{CSS,i}$ satisfy assumptions 1 and 3, our redundancy result (theorem 1) immediately follows; that is

$$\hat{\delta}_{3SLS}(W_{CSS,i}) = \hat{\delta}_{MGIV}[Q(A)X_i, A \otimes s_{CSS,i}]. \tag{41}$$

Thus, whenever $\hat{\delta}_{3SLS}(W_{CSS,i})$ is efficient (i.e., assumption 2 holds for $W_{CSS,i}$), so is the MGIV estimator using the smaller set of instruments $[Q(A)X_i, A \otimes s_{CSS,i}]$.

CSS consider a GIV estimator which is different from the MGIV estimator given in (41). Their GIV estimator can be written in our notation as

$$\hat{\delta}_{CSS} = [H'\Omega^{-1}G(G'\Omega^{-1}G)^{-}G'\Omega^{-1}H]^{-1}H'\Omega^{-1}G(G'\Omega^{-1}G)^{-}G'\Omega^{-1}y \tag{42}$$

where $G = [I_N \otimes Q(A), X_1, F_1]$. We need to use a g-inverse of $(G'\Omega^{-1}G)$ for $\hat{\delta}_{CSS}$, since G is not of full column rank. CSS assume condition (7), $\Sigma = A\Phi A' + \sigma_\varepsilon^2 I_T$. This condition can be used to justify the consistency of $\hat{\delta}_{CSS}$. In addition, under (7) many instruments in G become redundant for $\hat{\delta}_{CSS}$. Stated formally:

Theorem 4 *Suppose condition* (7) *holds. Then,* $\hat{\delta}_{CSS} = \hat{\delta}_{GIV}[Q(A)X_i, P(A)X_{1i}, F_{1i}]$.

Proof: See the appendix.

This theorem naturally suggests a MGIV version of the CSS estimator which is consistent even if Σ is unrestricted; that is, $\hat{\delta}_{MGIV}[Q(A)X_i, P(A)X_{1i}, F_{1i}]$. As discussed in section 3.1, under condition (7), this MGIV estimator is equivalent to the GIV estimator using the same instruments. Furthermore, it is clear that the CSS estimator is inefficient when the instruments $W_{CSS,i}$ are legitimate and satisfy assumption 2. This is so because the CSS estimator is the MGIV estimator using only a subset of the non-redundant instruments $[Q(A)X_i, A \otimes s_{CSS,i}]$. This result is not surprising. The relationship of the efficient MGIV estimator to the CSS estimator is the same as the relationship of the AM estimator to the HT estimator in the time-invariant individual effects model. While the efficient MGIV estimator exploits all of the non-redundant moment conditions implied by $E[(A \otimes v(X_{1i})')'u_i] = 0$, the CSS estimator uses the smaller set of conditions $E[X_{1i}'P(A)u_i] = 0$.

We may consider an MGIV estimator which is comparable to the BMS estimator. Suppose that in addition to the CSS assumption, the following condition holds

$$E[A\alpha_i \otimes v(Q(A)X_{2i})] = 0 \tag{43}$$

where $X_i = [X_{1i}, X_{2i}]$. This condition would be reasonable when A is a matrix of polynomial trend variables. For example, similarly to the empirical study of CSS, suppose that the individual effects are deterministic time trends: specifically, assume $a_t\alpha_i = \alpha_{1i} + t\alpha_{2i} + t^2\alpha_{3i}$, where a_t is the tth column of A. For this case, it may be reasonable to assume that the effects in α_i are correlated with the deterministic trend components of the regressors only. If this is the case, the effects may not be correlated with the detrended regressors $Q(A)X_{2i}$.

Under the CSS assumption and (43), we have the instruments $W_{A,i} = [W_{CSS,i}, A \otimes s^*_{CSS,i}]$, where $s^*_{CSS,i} = v(Q(A)X_{2i})$. Clearly, the instruments $W_{A,i}$ satisfy assumptions 1, 3, and 4. Thus, the 3SLS estimator using the instruments $W_{A,i}$ must be equivalent to the GIV estimator using the instruments

$[Q(A)X_i, A \otimes (s_{\text{CSS},i}, s^*_{\text{CSS},1})]$. In addition, when the instruments $W_{A,i}$ also satisfy assumption 2, this GIV estimator is efficient.

6 Monte Carlo experiments

In this section we report the results of some limited Monte Carlo experiments in which we compare the finite sample properties of our MGIV estimator and the GMM estimator using a much larger number of moment conditions and an unrestricted optimal weighting matrix. The foundation for our Monte Carlo experiments is equation (25) with two time-varying regressors, x_{1it} and x_{2it}, and two time-invariant regressors, z_{1i} and z_{2i}. For $T = 5$, we set $\beta_1 = \beta_2 = \gamma_1 = \gamma_2 = 1$. We choose $N = 100$ and 300, and specify i.i.d. effects over i: $\alpha_i \sim N(0,1)$. In order to allow autocorrelation and/or heteroskedasticity in ε_i, we specify

$$\varepsilon_{it} = \rho\varepsilon_{i,t-1} + v_{it}[(1-b) + bx_{1it}/\text{se}(x_{1it})] \tag{44}$$

where $b = 0$ or 1, the v_{it} are i.i.d. random draws from $N(0,2)$, $\varepsilon_{i1} = v_{1t}/(1-\rho)^{1/2}$, and $\text{se}(x_{1it})$ is the sample standard error of the x_{1it}. Two regressors, x_{1it} and z_{1i}, are uncorrelated with α_i. We specify $z_{1i} = 1$ for all t and $x_{1it} = 0.7x_{1i,t-1} + f_i + \eta_{1it}$, where $x_{1i,1}, f_i$ and η_{1it} are each uniformly distributed on the interval $[-2,2]$. The other two regressors, x_{2it} and z_{2i}, are correlated with α_i. We specify $x_{2it} = 0.7x_{2i,t-1} + \alpha_i + \eta_{2it}$ and $z_{2i} = f_i + \alpha_i + \xi_i$. Again, $x_{2i,1}$, η_{2it} and ξ_i are uniformly distributed $[-2,2]$. For each value of ρ, N, and b, the empirical distributions of the estimates are obtained from 1,000 replications.

We consider three estimators; the MGIV estimator using instruments $[Q_T X_i, G_{\text{AM},i}]$ (see (37)); the GMM estimator using all of the moment conditions implied by $E(W'_{\text{FE},i}u_i) = 0$ and $E(G_{\text{AM},i}{}'u_i) = 0$ (see (38)); and the GMM estimator using a subset of the moment conditions, namely $E(X_i' Q_T u_i) = 0$ and $E(G'_{\text{AM},i}u_i) = 0$. We will refer to the GMM estimator using all of the moment conditions as GMM1, and to the GMM estimator using a subset of the moment conditions as GMM2. Note that GMM2 is based on the same set of instruments as the MGIV estimator, but it does not impose the same moment conditions. In cases in which the errors ε_{it} are cross-sectionally homoskedastic ($b = 0$), the MGIV estimator is asymptotically identical to GMM1, and both of these estimators are strictly more efficient than GMM2. In contrast, when the errors are cross-sectionally heteroskedastic ($b = 1$), GMM1 strictly dominates both MGIV and GMM2 in terms of asymptotic efficiency and it is not possible to rank the asymptotic efficiency of MGIV and GMM2. Our motivation for including GMM2 is to examine the effect of using a different number of moment conditions on the finite sample properties of the GMM estimator.

It should be noted that GMM1 and GMM2 use an unrestricted weighting matrix, while MGIV uses a classical (3SLS) weighting matrix that reflects the assumption of no conditional heteroskedasticity. In fact, this difference in weighting matrices is the essential difference between GMM1 and MGIV, because the 3SLS estimator using the full set of moment conditions used by GMM1 is *numerically identical* to MGIV, by our redundancy results above. In other words, under the assumption of no conditional heteroskedasticity, GMM1 uses moment conditions that are redundant, but it is the use of an unrestricted weighting matrix that allows these redundant moment conditions to affect the estimates.

Table 7.1 reports the results from simulations with cross-sectionally homoskedastic errors (i.e., $b=0$). For each estimator, we report the mean and standard error of estimates obtained from 1,000 replications, and the mean over the 1,000 replications of the estimated asymptotic standard errors from each replication.[3] No estimator exhibits large biases. The GMM1 estimator tends to be more biased than the others, but by only a negligible amount. The standard errors reported in table 7.1 indicate that the MGIV estimator has a smaller variance than the two GMM estimators, although the difference between MGIV and GMM2 is in most cases marginal. The variance of the MGIV estimator is considerably smaller than that of GMM1, especially when N is small and/or the errors are highly correlated. These are cases in which the optimal weighting matrix for GMM1 is likely to be poorly estimated. An interesting observation from table 7.1 is that GMM2 has a smaller variance than GMM1 for small N, but this ranking becomes reversed as N gets larger. This finding is similar to that of Andersen and Sørensen (1996), who find that the optimal number of moment conditions to be imposed in GMM increases with sample size.

Table 7.1 also shows that estimated asymptotic standard errors of the MGIV estimator perform well: the means of the asymptotic standard errors are close to the true standard errors. In contrast, the asymptotic standard errors of the GMM1 estimator substantially underestimate the true standard errors. For example, consider the GMM1 estimates of β_1 when $N=100$ and $\rho=0.9$. The mean of the asymptotic standard errors (0.049) is only 41 per cent of the true standard error (0.120). As N increases to 300, the asymptotic standard errors perform better, but even in this case, their mean (0.039)

[3] For MGIV, asymptotic standard errors are estimated using the asymptotic covariance matrix of the form $[H'W(W'\Omega W)^{-1}W'H]^{-1}$, where $W=[(I_N \otimes Q_\Sigma Q_T)X, \Omega^{-1}G_{AM}]$. We estimate Σ using residuals from 2SLS with instruments $[(I_T \otimes Q_T)X, G_{AM}]$. For GMM1, we first compute 2SLS residuals $\hat{u}_i$ using instruments $W=[W_{FE}, G_{AM}]$, and then using the residuals compute asymptotic standard errors from $N^{-1}[H'W\hat{V}^{-1}W'\mathrm{H}]^{-1}$, where $\hat{V}=N^{-1}\Sigma_i W_i'\hat{u}_i\hat{u}_i'W_i$. We do the same thing for the GMM2, but with a smaller instrument set.

Table 7.1. *Results from simulations with homoskedastic errors*

	N = 100			N = 300		
	MGIV	GMM1	GMM2	MGIV	GMM1	GMM2
$\rho = 0.5$						
Coefficient: $\beta_1 = 1$						
mean	0.987	0.979	0.988	0.993	0.990	0.992
s.e.	0.074	0.086	0.081	0.044	0.047	0.049
mean asym. s.e.	0.071	0.048	0.076	0.043	0.038	0.046
Coefficient: $\beta_2 = 1$						
mean	1.020	1.032	1.021	1.006	1.008	1.006
s.e.	0.081	0.091	0.087	0.047	0.050	0.052
mean asym. s.e.	0.077	0.051	0.083	0.046	0.041	0.050
Coefficient: $\gamma_1 = 1$						
mean	0.991	0.983	0.989	0.996	0.995	0.995
s.e.	0.174	0.192	0.183	0.106	0.115	0.108
mean asym. s.e.	0.178	0.125	0.178	0.103	0.094	0.104
Coefficient: $\gamma_2 = 1$						
mean	1.054	1.071	1.051	1.024	1.030	1.026
s.e.	0.240	0.275	0.260	0.145	0.155	0.155
mean asym. s.e.	0.230	0.155	0.237	0.141	0.127	0.148
$\rho = 0.9$						
Coefficient: $\beta_1 = 1$						
mean	0.997	0.985	1.000	0.997	0.994	0.995
s.e.	0.074	0.120	0.097	0.044	0.050	0.058
mean asym. s.e.	0.073	0.049	0.094	0.043	0.039	0.055
Coefficient: $\beta_2 = 1$						
mean	1.006	1.024	1.007	1.001	1.004	1.001
s.e.	0.080	0.113	0.102	0.045	0.049	0.060
mean asym. s.e.	0.076	0.051	0.099	0.044	0.039	0.058
Coefficient: $\gamma_1 = 1$						
mean	0.979	0.958	0.974	0.990	0.990	0.998
s.e.	0.432	0.488	0.452	0.257	0.276	0.265
mean asym. s.e.	0.430	0.302	0.429	0.247	0.226	0.249
Coefficient: $\gamma_2 = 1$						
mean	1.037	1.047	1.028	1.015	1.023	1.020
s.e.	0.442	0.540	0.487	0.259	0.281	0.280
mean asym. s.e.	0.428	0.292	0.446	0.253	0.229	0.268

is only 78 per cent of the true standard error for the estimates of β_1 (0.050). These results indicate that when N is small, t-statistics based on the GMM1 estimates and asymptotic standard errors could result in seriously biased inferences regarding the significance of regressors. The asymptotic standard errors of GMM2 also tend to be downward biased, especially when $N=100$, but their biases are much smaller than those of the GMM1 estimator.

Assumption 2 (no conditional heteroskedasticity) plays a key role in the efficiency of the MGIV estimator. Under this assumption, MGIV is asymptotically efficient as GMM1, but uses a much smaller number of instruments. Thus, it is not too surprising to see that MGIV has better finite sample properties than GMM1. To see how violation of assumption 2 may affect the finite sample properties of MGIV, we conduct additional experiments under which the errors are heteroskedastic ($b=1$). In this case GMM1 strictly dominates MGIV in terms of asymptotic efficiency. These results are reported in table 7.2. All estimators again exhibit only small biases. In terms of finite-sample efficiency (standard error), there is no clear winner, especially when $N=100$. For $N=300$, GMM1 often has smaller variance than MGIV or GMM2, but the efficiency advantage of GMM1 is only marginal. The asymptotic standard errors of GMM1 continue to underestimate the true standard errors, especially when N is small. Not surprisingly, the MGIV estimator has the same problem when the asymptotic standard errors are computed ignoring heteroskedasticity. For $N=100$ and $\rho=0.9$, the asymptotic standard errors for the MGIV estimates of β_1 are seriously downward biased. In response to this problem, table 7.2 also reports heteroskedasticity-robust standard errors for the MGIV estimator.[4] These adjusted asymptotic standard errors approximate the true standard errors fairly well even when N is small.

Table 7.2 also shows that the GMM2 estimator performs quite well when errors are heteroskedastic. The GMM2 estimator tends to have slightly greater variance than the MGIV estimator, but in most cases the difference is not substantial. Similar to the results reported in table 7.1, the biases in the asymptotic standard errors of the GMM2 estimator are much smaller than those of the GMM1 estimator and in general are comparable to those of the MGIV estimator.

The main results from our Monte Carlo experiments can be summarized as follows. First, the MGIV estimator dominates the full GMM estimator

[4] These are computed by the method of White (1982). The asymptotic covariance matrix of the MGIV estimator from which we obtain the standard errors is of the form

$$[H'W(W'\Omega W)^{-1}W'H]^{-1}H'W(W'\Omega W)^{-1}[\Sigma_i W_i'\hat{u}_i\hat{u}_i'W_i] \times (W'\Omega W)^{-1}W'H[H'W(W'\Omega W)^{-1}W'H]^{-1}$$

where $W_i=[Q_\Sigma Q_T X_i, \Sigma^{-1}G_{AM,i}]$, $\Omega=I_N\otimes\Sigma$, and the $\hat{u}_i$ are MGIV residuals.

Table 7.2. *Results from simulations with heteroskedastic errors*

	N = 100			N = 300		
	MGIV	GMM1	GMM2	MGIV	GMM1	GMM2
$\rho=0.5$						
Coefficient: $\beta_1=1$						
mean	0.982	0.974	0.984	0.993	0.991	0.992
s.e.	0.089	0.095	0.095	0.052	0.052	0.054
mean asym. s.e.	0.071	0.046	0.087	0.044	0.043	0.054
	(0.084)*			(0.052)		
Coefficient: $\beta_2=1$						
mean	1.017	1.029	1.019	1.007	1.008	1.009
s.e.	0.081	0.080	0.088.	0.047	0.046	0.051
mean asym. s.e.	0.078	0.042	0.082	0.047	0.039	0.050
	(0.077)			(0.047)		
Coefficient: $\gamma_1=1$						
mean	0.999	0.998	0.996	0.992	0.993	0.993
s.e.	0.183	0.175	0.186	0.103	0.104	0.105
mean asym. s.e.	0.170	0.101	0.167	0.099	0.085	0.099
	(0.172)			(0.100)		
Coefficient: $\gamma_2=1$						
mean	1.060	1.081	1.057	1.027	1.032	1.028
s.e.	0.234	0.228	0.237	0.135	0.136	0.140
mean asym. s.e.	0.222	0.115	0.216	0.139	0.107	0.136
	(0.215)			(0.133)		
$\rho=0.9$						
Coefficient: $\beta_1=1$						
mean	0.990	0.977	0.994	0.997	0.991	0.994
s.e.	0.167	0.190	0.178	0.097	0.096	0.103
mean asym. s.e.	0.098	0.085	0.162	0.058	0.075	0.098
	(0.155)			(0.094)		
Coefficient: $\beta_2=1$						
mean	1.004	1.027	1.007	1.002	1.005	1.005
s.e.	0.104	0.117	0.128	0.062	0.062	0.075
mean asym. s.e.	0.102	0.057	0.122	0.061	0.051	0.074
	(0.101)			(0.060)		
Coefficient: $\gamma_1=1$						
mean	1.007	1.001	0.993	0.992	0.995	0.992
s.e.	0.412	0.379	0.416	0.234	0.227	0.238
mean asym. s.e.	0.389	0.216	0.379	0.226	0.188	0.227
	(0.387)			(0.227)		
Coefficient: $\gamma_2=1$						
mean	1.035	1.075	1.026	1.015	1.032	1.023
s.e.	0.471	0.454	0.472	0.263	0.241	0.262
mean asym. s.e.	0.417	0.210	0.411	0.251	0.196	0.255
	(0.422)			(0.260)		

Note:
* Heteroskedasticity-adjusted asymptotic standard errors.

(GMM1) which exploits all of the moment conditions, if the errors are conditionally homoskedastic. The usual Wald tests based on the full GMM estimator could be substantially biased if N is small. Even when the errors are heteroskedastic and N is relatively large, use of the full GMM estimation instead of MGIV is unlikely to result in any substantial efficiency gain. Second, heteroskedasticity-adjusted standard errors for MGIV appear to be quite reliable, and should probably be used routinely. When the errors are heteroskedastic, the asymptotic standard errors of MGIV computed under the homoskedasticity assumption may result in serious biases. Third, the GMM estimator (GMM2) using the same instruments as the MGIV estimator often performs better than the full GMM estimator in finite samples. The finite-sample performance of this alternative GMM estimator is only slightly dominated by the MGIV estimator.

7 Conclusions

We have shown that, in the context of panel data models with strictly exogenous regressors and intertemporally correlated errors, the 3SLS estimator using a large number of instruments is algebraically identical to a modified GIV estimator using fewer instruments. We also have considered general conditions which are sufficient for this redundancy result. While some of our redundancy results have been given previously by IASW, we provide a more systematic method by which redundant instruments can be found. Further, our results can be generalized to models with time-varying individual effects of aggregated macroeconomic variables.

When the errors are conditionally homoskedastic, our MGIV estimator is asymptotically equivalent to the GMM estimator which exploits all of the moment conditions implied by the strict exogeneity of the regressors. Although the MGIV estimator is less efficient than the full GMM estimator when the errors are conditionally heteroskedastic, our limited Monte Carlo results suggest that, in finite samples, the MGIV estimator with heteroskedasticity-adjusted asymptotic standard errors performs better than the full GMM estimator even when the errors are heteroskedastic. We found that the standard errors of the full GMM estimator could be substantially biased downward when the data contain a small number of cross-sectional units. Our simulation results also indicate that the GMM estimator using the same instrument as the MGIV estimator has good finite-sample properties, and in general performs better than the full GMM estimator.

The strict exogeneity assumption on the regressors plays an important role in our result. A natural extension to this chapter is to consider conditions for models with weakly exogenous regressors. For such models, Keane and Runkle (1992) have proposed a GIV-type estimator. Extending this study, Schmidt, Ahn, and Wykowski (1992) proposed a more efficient 3SLS estimator, which utilizes all of the moment conditions implied by weak exogeneity of the regressors. It would be interesting to see how our MGIV estimator may apply to the case of weak exogeneity.

Appendix

Proof of Lemma 2: By (12), we have $P(\Omega^{1/2}W)=P(\Omega^{1/2}W_c)+P(\Omega^{1/2}W_d)$. Further, condition (13) implies $P(\Omega^{1/2}W_c)\Omega^{-1/2}H=[P(\Omega^{1/2}W_e)+P(Q(\Omega^{1/2}W_e)\Omega^{1/2}W_f)\Omega^{-1/2}H=P(\Omega^{1/2}W_e)\Omega^{-1/2}H$. These results imply $P(\Omega^{1/2}W)\Omega^{-1/2}H=P(\Omega^{1/2}[W_e,W_d])\Omega^{-1/2}H$.

Proof of Lemma 3: By construction of A and A_0, $[\Sigma^{1/2}A_0,\Sigma^{-1/2}A]$ is a non-singular matrix. Note also that $A_0'\Sigma^{1/2}\Sigma^{-1/2}A=A_0'A=0$. Therefore

$$\mathrm{I}=P(\Sigma^{1/2}A_0,\Sigma^{-1/2}A)=P(\Sigma^{1/2}A_0)+P(\Sigma^{-1/2}A).$$

Then we can establish the equality

$$\begin{aligned}\Sigma^{-1}&=\Sigma^{-1/2}[P(\Sigma^{1/2}A_0)+P(\Sigma^{-1/2}A)]\Sigma^{-1/2}\\&=A_0(A_0'\Sigma A_0)^{-1}A_0'+\Sigma^{-1}A(A'\Sigma^{-1}A)^{-1}A'\Sigma^{-1}.\end{aligned}$$

Proof of Lemma 4: Since $W_{2i}\subset A\otimes w_{2i}^0$, there exists a comformable matrix B such that for all i, $W_{2i}=(A\otimes w_{2i}^0)B=A(I_p\otimes w_{2i}^0)B$. Then, we have

$$\begin{aligned}P_\Sigma W_{2i}&=\Sigma^{-1}A(A'\Sigma^{-1}A)^{-1}A'\Sigma^{-1}A(I_p\otimes w_{2i}^0)B\\&=\Sigma^{-1}A(I_p\otimes w_{2i}^0)B=\Sigma^{-1}W_{2i}.\end{aligned}$$

Proof of Lemma 5: Since $w_i^0=[w_{1i}^0,w_{2i}^0]$, $\hat{\delta}_{3SLS}(W_{A,i})=\hat{\delta}_{3SLS}[A_0\otimes w_i^0,A\otimes w_{2i}^0]=\hat{\delta}_{3SLS}[A_0\otimes w_{1i}^0,(A_0,A)\otimes w_{2i}^0]$. Since (A_0,A) is non-singular and $(A_0,A)\otimes w_{1i}^0$ is of Kronecker product form, (A_0,A) can be replaced by any other non-singular matrix without changing the 3SLS estimator. Choose $(A_0,\Sigma^{-1}A)$. Then, we obtain the desired equality

$$\hat{\delta}_{3SLS}[A_0\otimes w_{1i}^0,(A_0,\Sigma^{-1}A)\otimes w_{2i}^0]=\hat{\delta}_{3SLS}(A_0\otimes w_i^0,\Sigma^{-1}(A\otimes w_{2i}^0)).$$

Proof of Theorem 1: Using Lemmas 2 and 5, it is sufficient to show that $\hat{\delta}_{3SLS}(A_0\otimes w_i^0)=[Q_\Sigma Q(A)H_i]$. Since $Q(A)H_i\subset(I_T\otimes w_i^0)$ by Assumption 3, there exists a selection matrix S_H such that

$$(I_N\otimes Q(A))H=(W^0\otimes I_T)S_H. \tag{A1}$$

Since A_0 and Q_Σ span the same space which is orthogonal to the column space of A, and since Rank $(A_0)=\mathrm{Rank}(Q_\Sigma)$, there must exist a $(T-p)\times T$ matrix F such that

$$Q_\Sigma = A_0 F. \tag{A2}$$

Using (A1)–(A2), we can show

$$\begin{aligned}(I_N \otimes Q_\Sigma)(I_N \otimes Q(A))H &= (I_N \otimes A_0 F)(W^0 \otimes I_T)S_H \\ &= (W^0 \otimes A_0)(I_q \otimes F)S_H\end{aligned} \tag{A3}$$

where q equals the number of columns of w_i^0. Thus, without loss of generality we can assume that for some conformable matrix S_0,

$$(W^0 \otimes A_0) = [(I_T \otimes Q_\Sigma Q(A))H, (W^0 \otimes A_0)S_0]. \tag{A4}$$

Observe that $Q_\Sigma \Sigma A_0 = A_0(A_0{'}\Sigma A_0)^{-1}A_0{'}\Sigma A_0 = A_0$ (by lemma 3), $Q(A)A_0 = A_0$ and $Q(A)Q_\Sigma Q(A) = Q_\Sigma Q(A) = Q_\Sigma$. Using the results, we can show

$$\begin{aligned}&S_0{'}(W_0 \otimes A_0)'H - S_0{'}(W_0 \otimes A_0)'\Omega(I_N \otimes Q_\Sigma Q(A))H \\ &\quad \times [H'(I_N \otimes Q(A)Q_\Sigma Q(A))H]^{-1}H'(I_N \otimes Q(A)Q_\Sigma)H = 0.\end{aligned} \tag{A5}$$

Thus, condition (13) holds for $W^0(\otimes A_0)S_0$.

Proof of Theorem 2: We can complete the proof by showing that Assumption 4 implies (18). Note that $P_\Sigma(A)Q(A)X_i = \Sigma^{-1}AMJ_i$, where $M = (A'\Sigma^{-1}A)^{-1}A'\Sigma^{-1}$ and $J_i = Q(A)X_i$. Let m_{jt} be the $(j,t)^{\text{th}}$ element of M and J_{ti} be the tth row of J_i. Then, $MJ_i = [(\Sigma_{t=1}^T m_{1t}J_{ti})', \ldots, (\Sigma_{t=1}^T m_{pt}J_{ti})']'$. Under Assumption 4, $J_{ti} \subset w_{2i}^0$, for all t. Thus, we have

$$MJ_i \subset I_p \otimes w_{2i}^0. \tag{A6}$$

Using (A6) and $\Sigma^{-1}A(I_p \otimes w_{2i}^0) = P_\Sigma(A \otimes w_{2i}^0)$, we can show

$$P_\Sigma(A)Q(A)X_i = \Sigma^{-1}AMJ_i \subset \Sigma^{-1}A(I_p \otimes w_{2i}^0) = P_\Sigma(A \otimes w_{2i}^0).$$

Proof of Theorem 3: For $A = e_T$,

$$Q_\Sigma = L_T(L_T{'}\Sigma L_T)^{-1}L_T{'} = L_T(L_T{'}\Lambda L_T)^{-1}L_T{'} = Q_\Lambda \tag{A7}$$

where the first and third equalities come from Lemma 3; and the second equality from the fact that $L_T{'}\Sigma L_T = L_T{'}(\sigma_\alpha^2 e_T e_T{'} + \Lambda)L_T = L_T{'}\Lambda L_T$. We also have

$$Q_\Sigma X_i = Q_\Sigma(T^{-1}e_T e_T{'} + Q_T)X_i = Q_\Sigma Q_T X_i, \tag{A8}$$

The results (A7) and (A8) imply

$$\begin{aligned}\hat{\beta}_{\text{KGLS}} &= \hat{\beta}_{\text{3SLS}}(Q_\Lambda X_i) = \hat{\beta}_{\text{3SLS}}(Q_\Sigma X_i) = \hat{\beta}_{\text{3SLS}}(Q_\Sigma Q_T X_i) \\ &= \hat{\beta}_{\text{MGIV}}(Q_T X_i).\end{aligned}$$

Proof of Theorem 4: It is sufficient to show that $\hat{\delta}_{CSS}$ is the 3SLS estimator using the instruments $[\Sigma^{-1}Q(A)X_i, \Sigma^{-1}D_i]$, where $D_i = [P(A)X_{1i}, F_{1i}]$. Since G and $[I_N \otimes Q(A), (I_N \otimes P(A))X_1, Z_1]$ span the same space, 3SLS using $\Omega^{-1}G$ is equivalent to 3SLS using $[\Omega^{-1}(I_N \otimes Q(A)), \Omega^{-1}D]$. Thus, we can complete the proof by showing that the two sets of instruments $[\Omega^{-1}(I_N \otimes Q(A)), \Omega^{-1}D]$ and $[\Omega^{-1}(I_N \otimes Q(A))X, \Omega^{-1}D]$ generate the same 3SLS estimator. (7) implies

$$[I_N \otimes Q(A)]'\Omega^{-1}\Omega\Omega^{-1}D = [I_N \otimes Q(A)\Sigma^{-1}P(A)]D = 0.$$

Thus, 3SLS using instruments $[\Omega^{-1}(I_N \otimes Q(A)), \Omega^{-1}D]$ satisfies (12). Clearly, the instruments $(I_N \otimes Q(A))X$ are in the column space of $I_N \otimes Q(A)$. Thus, 3SLS using $\Omega^{-1}(I_N \otimes Q(A))$ is equivalent to 3SLS using $\Omega^{-1}(I_N \otimes Q(A))[X, S_A]$, where S_A is a matrix such that $\text{rank}[X, S_A] = \text{rank}[I_N \otimes Q(A)]$. But

$$\begin{aligned} S_A'(I_N \otimes Q(A))\Omega^{-1}X - S_A'(I_N \otimes Q(A))\Omega^{-1}(I_N \otimes Q(A))X \\ \times [X'(I_N \otimes Q(A))\Omega^{-1}(I_N \otimes Q(A))X]^{-1} \\ X'(I_N \otimes Q(A))\Omega^{-1}X = 0 \end{aligned}$$

using the fact that $Q(A)\Sigma^{-1}Q(A) = Q(A)\Sigma^{-1}$ under condition (7). Thus, Lemma 2 applies.

References

Ahn, S.C. and P. Schmidt (1995), "Efficient Estimation of Models for Dynamic Panel Data," *Journal of Econometrics*, 68: 5–27.

Ahn, S.C. and P. Schmidt (1997), "Efficient Estimation of Dynamic Panel Data Models: Alternative Assumptions and Simplified Assumptions," *Journal of Econometrics*, 76: 309–321.

Amemiya, T. (1985), *Advanced Econometrics*, Cambridge, Mass.: Harvard University Press.

Amemiya, T. and T.E. MaCurdy (1986), "Instrumental-Variables Estimation of an Error-Components Model," *Econometrica* 54: 869–880.

Andersen, T.G. and R.E. Sørensen (1996), "GMM Estimation of a Stochastic Volatility Model: A Monte Carlo study," *Journal of Business and Economic Statistics*, 14: 328–352.

Arellano, M. and O. Bover (1995), "Another Look at the Instrumental Variables Estimation of Error-Component Models," *Journal of Econometrics*, 68: 29–51.

Bowden, R.J. and D.A. Turkington (1984), *Instrumental Variables*, Cambridge University Press.

Breusch, T.S., G.E. Mizon, and P. Schmidt (1989), "Efficient Estimation Using Panel Data," *Econometrica*, 57: 695–700.

Chamberlain, G. (1984), "Panel Data," in Z. Griliches and M.D. Intriligator (eds.), *Handbook of Econometrics*, Vol. II.

Chamberlain, G. (1987), "Asymptotic Efficiency in Estimation with Conditional Moment Restrictions" *Journal of Econometrics*, 34: 305–334.

(1992), "Efficiency Bounds for Semiparametric Regression," *Econometrica*, 60: 567–596.

Cornwell, C., P. Schmidt, and R.C. Sickles (1990), "Production Frontiers with Cross-Sectional and Time-Series Variation in Efficiency Levels," *Journal of Econometrics*, 46: 185–200.

Crépon, B., F. Kramarz, and A. Trognon (1995), "Parameter of Interest, Nuisance Parameter and Orthogonality Conditions," unpublished manuscript, INSEE.

Hansen, L.P. (1982), "Large Sample Properties of Generalized Methods of Moments Estimators," *Econometrica*, 50: 1029–1054.

Hausman, J.A. and W.E. Taylor (1981), "Panel Data and Unobservable Individual Effects," *Econometrica*, 49: 1377–1398.

Im, K.S., S.C. Ahn, P. Schmidt, and J.M. Wooldridge (1996), "Efficient Estimation of Panel Data Models with Strictly Exogenous Explanatory Variables," unpublished manuscript, Michigan State University.

Keane, M.P. (1993), "Nominal-Contracting Theories of Unemployment: Evidence from Panel Data," *The American Economic Review*, 83: 932–952.

Keane, M.P. and D.E. Runkle (1992), "On the Estimation of Panel Data Models with Serial Correlation when Instruments are not Strictly Exogenous," *Journal of Business and Economic Statistics*, 10: 1–10.

Kiefer, N.M. (1980), "Estimation of Fixed Effect Models for Time Series of Cross-Sections with Arbitrary Intertemporal Covariance, *Journal of Econometrics*, 14: 195–202.

Rao, C.R. and S.K. Mitra (1971), *Generalized Inverse of Matrices and Its Applications*, New York: Wiley.

Schmidt, P., S.C. Ahn, and D. Wykowski (1992), "Comment," *Journal of Business and Economic Statistics*, 10: 10–14.

Tauchen, G. (1986), "Statistical Properties of Generalized Method-of-Moments Estimators of Structural Parameters Obtained from Financial Market Data," *Journal of Business and Economic Statistics*, 4: 397–416.

White, H. (1982), "Instrumental Variables Regression with Independent Observations," *Econometrica*, 50: 483–499.

(1984), *Asymptotic Theory for Econometricians*, San Diego: Academic Press.

8 Expectations of expansions for estimators in a dynamic panel data model: some results for weakly exogenous regressors

JAN F. KIVIET*

1 Introduction

In linear dynamic panel data models, the dependent variable (and hence also the lagged dependent regressor variable that makes the model dynamic) is determined by some linear function of present and past values of both the explanatory variables and the various stochastic error components. Since regression coefficient estimators are non-linear in all the regressor variables, the coefficient estimators are also non-linear in the stochastic error components in a linear dynamic panel data model. This non-linearity is the reason why the finite sample properties of inference methods for this type of model are very hard to establish. The actual probability distributions of estimators and test statistics are highly non-standard and usually they also depend on unknown values of nuisance parameters. Some knowledge on their actual shape and behavior can be obtained either experimentally by computer simulation or analytically by asymptotic approximations. For common model specifications the standard first-order asymptotic properties have been assessed for various estimation methods. Some methods are found to be inconsistent, but others are consistent and may even be asymptotically efficient for certain classes of models. However, from simulation studies it has often been found that first-order asymptotic properties do not always offer the right criterion for (dis)qualifying inference procedures as far as their finite sample properties are concerned; see for instance, Nerlove (1971), Arellano and Bond (1991), van den Doel and Kiviet (1995), and Kiviet (1995). For recent overviews on the analysis of dynamic panel data models, see Sevestre and Trognon (1992), Maddala (1993), and Baltagi (1995, chapter 8).

In Kiviet (1995) we found that, due to the linearity of the dependence of

*Tinbergen Institute and Faculty of Economics & Econometrics, University of Amsterdam, Roetersstraat 11, 1018 WB Amsterdam, The Netherlands (JFK@FEE.UvA.NL). The author wants to thank Professor Lung Fei Lee for his constructive comments on an earlier version of this paper and Maurice Bun for repairing some imperfections in the derivations.

the lagged dependent regressor variable on the error components, it is analytically feasible to examine particular higher-order asymptotic properties of relatively simple estimators. Such more refined asymptotic results may approximate the actual finite sample properties more closely than first-order asymptotic techniques; they can also be used to develop more accurate inference methods. More in particular, we found an approximation for the bias of the inconsistent least squares dummy variables (LSDV) estimator in the model with one lagged dependent variable, unobserved individual effects, serially uncorrelated disturbances, and strongly exogenous regressors. When this bias expression, evaluated on the basis of a consistent estimator, is subtracted from the original LSDV estimator, a corrected estimator (LSDVc) results, which, in a rather extensive simulation study, was found to have a mean squared error (MSE) which is not systematically beaten by any of eight other implementations of consistent estimation techniques (all based on instrumental variables). The relative efficiency of LSDVc appeared to be much less dependent on the values of nuisance parameters than for the other techniques, including generalized method of moments (GMM) implementations. The latter were found to be occasionally slightly better than LSDVc, but they also proved to be substantially worse in a considerable number of cases.

In the present study we want to produce further results on higher-order asymptotic approximations of particular finite sample characteristics for various estimation techniques in dynamic panel data models. We shall first reconsider the correction factor derived earlier for the LSDV estimator and we shall improve the order of approximation of the earlier result and investigate to what degree it is determined by the initial conditions of the dynamic panel data relationship under study. We shall also examine the consequences for these results when the exogenous explanatory variable is weakly instead of strongly exogenous. To date, the finite sample effects of weak exogeneity, i.e., dependence of the exogenous regressors on lagged disturbances, are still largely unknown, both analytically and experimentally, since available Monte Carlo results are usually based on strictly exogenous regressors (for an exception see Gierbergen and Kiviet (1996)). This lack of concern stems from the fact that the first-order asymptotic approximations generally imply that weakly exogenous regressors may be treated as strongly exogenous, and therefore it is only when higher-order asymptotic methods are considered that one has to care about this. Finally, we shall also attempt to approximate for particular instrumental variables (IV) estimators the order and magnitude of the finite sample distortions due to weak exogeneity and to any correlation of the regressor variables with the individual effects. As we shall see, all these results can be obtained by deriving the expectation of the initial terms of higher-order expansions of the relevant estimation errors.

The structure of this study is as follows. In section 2 we introduce the model and examine in detail its stochastic characteristics. Then, in section 3, we re-examine LSDV's estimation bias, which is of order $O(T^{-1})$, and obtain for the model with strongly exogenous regressors an approximation to this bias accurate to order $O(n^{-1})$, where $n = NT$ with N the number of cross-section units in the sample and T the number of time series observations per unit. Earlier, we established a result with an approximation error which still included terms of order $O(N^{-1})$. The results obtained now do enable to express the finite sample bias when either of N or T (or both) are finite. Next we examine LSDV under weak exogeneity. In section 4 we apply similar techniques to simple IV estimators. Here we face technical problems because such estimators may not have finite moments. However, we can still obtain the expectation of the initial terms in a higher-order expansion of the estimation error. These do contain information on the major determining factors of the IV estimation error. Section 5 discusses the main findings and concludes. To what degree these theoretical findings are informative and accurate on actual finite sample behavior will be investigated in future research by performing relevant Monte Carlo simulation experiments.

2 The stochastic structure of the model

The most general model that we shall consider in this study is the first-order dynamic panel data model which, apart from a one-period lagged dependent explanatory variable, includes unobserved random individual effects and observed regressors. These may be correlated with the individual effects and could also be correlated with lags of the white-noise disturbances. Hence, instead of strongly, strictly, singly, or doubly exogenous, the regressors may be related to both components of the unobserved random error terms, i.e., the individual effects and the disturbances. To simplify the notation, we restrict ourselves here to the model with just one such weakly exogenous explanatory variable, i.e., the relationship under study is

$$y_{i,t} = \gamma y_{i,t-1} + \beta x_{i,t} + \eta_i + \varepsilon_{i,t} \tag{1}$$

for individuals $i = 1, \ldots, N$ and time periods $t = 1, \ldots, T$. We make the familiar assumptions

$$E\eta_i = 0,\ E\varepsilon_{i,t} = 0,\ E\eta_i\varepsilon_{j,t} = 0,\ \forall i,j,t \tag{2a}$$

$$E\eta_i^2 = \sigma_\eta^2 > 0,\ E\varepsilon_{i,t}^2 = \sigma_\varepsilon^2 > 0,\ \forall i,t \tag{2b}$$

$$E\varepsilon_{i,t}\varepsilon_{j,s} = 0,\ \forall t,s,i \neq j \text{ and } E\varepsilon_{i,t}\varepsilon_{i,s} = 0,\ \forall i,t \neq s \tag{2c}$$

$$|\gamma| < 1,\ Ey_{i,0}\varepsilon_{j,t} = 0,\ \forall i,j,t > 0. \tag{2d}$$

In practice one would like to avoid modeling the exogenous regressor $x_{i,t}$ explicitly. Here, however, where we want to examine the finite sample consequences on inference of particular forms of this variable we shall adopt an explicit model for $x_{i,t}$, viz.

$$x_{i,t} = \bar{x}_{i,t} + \pi\eta_i + \phi\varepsilon_{i,t-1} \tag{3}$$

with $\varepsilon_{i,0}$ distributed as $\varepsilon_{i,t}$ for $t>0$ and

$$E\bar{x}_{i,t}\varepsilon_{j,s} = 0,\ E\bar{x}_{i,t}\eta_j = 0,\ \forall t,s,i,j. \tag{4}$$

Here $\bar{x}_{i,t}$ is the part of $x_{i,t}$ that is stochastically independent of both the random error components of model (1); π parametrizes the presence of any correlation between the observed and the unobserved heterogeneity, and the value of ϕ determines whether or not the regressor $x_{i,t}$ experiences feedback from past disturbances. For $\phi=0$ regressor $x_{i,t}$ is strongly exogenous, and for $\phi\neq 0$ it is weakly exogenous. For a recent discussion of the relevance of weak exogeneity see various contributions in Banerjee and Hendry (1997).

An alternative model for the weakly exogenous regressor, which seems more relevant from an economic point of view, would be the dynamic behavioral equation with feedback mechanism with respect to the target variable $y_{i,t}$ given by

$$x_{i,t} = \rho x_{i,t-1} + \lambda y_{i,t-1} + \pi\eta_i + \nu_{i,t} \tag{5}$$

where the $\nu_{i,t}$ are random error terms independent of all random variables introduced earlier (note that joint dependence of $\nu_{i,t}$ and $\varepsilon_{i,t}$ would render $x_{i,t}$ an endogenous regressor). For such a parametrization, however, it would be very complicated to disentangle the separate effects of correlation between the observed and the unobserved heterogeneity and the correlation between current $x_{i,t}$ and lagged $\varepsilon_{i,t}$. In simulations with specification (5) one would not be able to compare situations of strong versus weak exogeneity, without creating at the same time a difference in impact of the individual effects and of the general dynamic time series properties of the $x_{i,t}$ series. Because of this, we choose the simple formulation (3), where $x_{i,t}$ has been parametrized such that it basically consists of three orthogonal components. We should note, however, that the correlation between the regressor and the disturbance term is of a very special simple nature here and excludes correlation between the current $x_{i,t}$ and any other past disturbance but $\varepsilon_{i,t-1}$.

Upon introducing in the usual way a notation in vectors of T elements, we may rewrite the equations (1) and (3) respectively as

$$y_i = \gamma y_i^{(-1)} + \beta x_i + \eta_i\iota_T + \varepsilon_i \tag{6}$$

and

$$x_i = \bar{x}_i + \pi\eta_i\iota_T + \phi\varepsilon_i^{(-1)} \tag{7}$$

where ι_T indicates a $T\times 1$ vector with all elements unity and $y_i^{(-1)}=By_i=(y_{i,0},\dots,y_{i,T-1})'$, $\varepsilon_i^{(-1)}=B\varepsilon_i$ with B the backward shift operator. All N corresponding vectors of T elements may be stacked in order to arrive at the model in matrix notation, which may be written as

$$y=W\delta+(I_N\otimes\iota_T)\eta+\varepsilon \tag{8}$$

where $y=(y_1',\dots,y_N')'$, $W=[W_1':W_2':\dots:W_N']'$, $W_i=[y_i^{(-1)}:x_i]$, $\delta=(\gamma,\beta)'$, $\eta=(\eta_1,\dots,\eta_N)'$ and $\varepsilon=(\varepsilon_1',\dots,\varepsilon_N')'$.

Substitution of (7) in (6) gives

$$y_i=\gamma y_i^{(-1)}+\beta\bar{x}_i+(\beta\pi+1)\iota_T\eta_i+\varepsilon_i+\phi\beta\varepsilon_i^{(-1)}. \tag{9}$$

From this equation we find that, due to the presence of the lagged dependent regressor variable and under standard stationarity assumptions, the actual contribution of the random individual specific effect to each value of the dependent variable for individual i is time invariant and is given by $[(\beta\pi+1)/(1-\gamma)]\eta_i$. It will prove to be helpful to introduce the latent dependent variables

$$v_{i,t}=y_{i,t}-\alpha\eta_i,\ \forall i,\ t=0,1,\dots,T \tag{10}$$

with

$$\alpha=\frac{\beta\pi+1}{1-\gamma} \tag{11}$$

from which the individual specific effect has been removed completely. From (9) and (10) it follows that for.

$$v_i=y_i-\alpha\eta_i\iota_T \tag{12}$$

we have

$$v_i=\gamma v_i^{(-1)}+\beta\bar{x}_i+\varepsilon_i+\phi\beta\varepsilon_i^{(-1)}. \tag{13}$$

Most estimators of the coefficient δ of model (8) are actually based on the estimation of a transformed model, which includes (or may use as instrumental variables) transformations of the variables W_i, y_i, such as lags, first differences, or deviations from means. In the derivations to follow, we have to be concerned about how such (transformed) variables depend on the stochastic error components. Therefore we shall produce a decomposition of y_i and v_i (as we already have for x_i) in components which may be random (like $\bar{x}_i$) but are unrelated to the error components and any remaining random elements, which are related to the error components η_i and $\varepsilon_{i,t}$ ($i=1,\dots,N$; $t=0,\dots,T$). The latter elements are what we call the *relevant random components* of y_i, v_i, and x_i; they have zero mean and they will be denoted by superimposing a tilde. Below, we condition on all random variables other than the relevant random components. These "non-relevant" random components will be indicated by superimposing a bar. We already have

$$\tilde{x}_i = x_i - \bar{x}_i = \pi \iota_T \eta_i + \phi \varepsilon_i^{(-1)}. \tag{14}$$

Removing all the "non-relevant" components of (6) and (13) we obtain

$$\tilde{y}_i = \gamma \tilde{y}_i^{(-1)} + \beta \tilde{x}_i + \eta_i \iota_T + \varepsilon_i \tag{15}$$

and

$$\tilde{v}_i = \gamma \tilde{v}_i^{(-1)} + \varepsilon_i + \phi \beta \varepsilon_i^{(-1)} \tag{16}$$

respectively.

With respect to the initial condition we specify

$$\tilde{v}_{i,0} = \omega \varepsilon_{i,0}. \tag{17}$$

In the earlier related study Kiviet (1995), where we had $\phi = 0$ (strong exogeneity), we chose $\omega = 0$ and hence $\tilde{v}_{i,0} \neq 0$ (i.e., we conditioned on $v_{i,0}$). Here, where $x_{i,1}$ is related to $\varepsilon_{i,0}$ (when $\phi \neq 0$) and $\varepsilon_{i,0}$ is thus treated as a relevant random component, it seems now more appropriate, since $\tilde{v}_{i,0} = \varepsilon_{i,0} + f(\varepsilon_{i,-1}, \varepsilon_{i,-2}, \dots)$ as follows from (16), to choose $\omega = 1$ instead of $\omega = 0$.

Introducing the $T \times T$ matrix

$$L_T = \begin{bmatrix} 0 & \cdot & \cdot & \cdot & \cdot & 0 \\ 1 & 0 & \cdot & \cdot & \cdot & \cdot \\ 0 & 1 & \cdot & \cdot & \cdot & \cdot \\ \cdot & \cdot & \cdot & \cdot & \cdot & \cdot \\ \cdot & \cdot & \cdot & 1 & 0 & \cdot \\ 0 & \cdot & \cdot & 0 & 1 & 0 \end{bmatrix} \tag{18}$$

and the $q \times 1$ unit vector $e_{q,p}$, which has all elements equal to zero except the pth which is unity ($p = 1, \dots, q$). We may rewrite (16) as

$$[I_T - \gamma L_T]\tilde{v}_i = (\omega\gamma + \phi\beta) e_{T,1} \varepsilon_{i,0} + [I_T + \phi\beta L_T]\varepsilon_i$$

and defining

$$\Gamma_T = [I_T - \gamma L_T]^{-1} \tag{19}$$

this implies

$$\tilde{v}_i = (\omega\gamma + \phi\beta)\Gamma_T e_{T,1} \varepsilon_{i,0} + \Gamma_T [I_T + \phi\beta L_T]\varepsilon_i. \tag{20}$$

From (20) and (10)

$$\tilde{y}_i = (\omega\gamma + \phi\beta)\Gamma_T e_{T,1} \varepsilon_{i,0} + \Gamma_T [I_T + \phi\beta L_T]\varepsilon_i + \alpha \eta_i \iota_T \tag{21}$$

easily follows. Note that all variables are linear in the relevant stochastic elements.

3 The bias of the LSDV estimator

From the above results we can produce an expression for the relatively complex relevant stochastic components of $A_T W_i$, where $A_T = I_T - T^{-1}\iota_T \iota_T'$ is the matrix that takes deviations from individual means. The LSDV estimator uses this transformation to eliminate the unobserved heterogeneity. We have $A_T \tilde{W}_i = [A_T \tilde{y}_i^{(-1)} : A_T \tilde{x}_i]$. It follows from (14) and $A_T \iota_T = 0$ that

$$A_T \tilde{x}_i = \phi A_T \varepsilon_i^{(-1)} = \phi A_T e_{T,1} \varepsilon_{i,0} + \phi A_T L_T \varepsilon_i. \qquad (22)$$

From (12) we find $A_T y_i = A_T v_i$ and hence, using (20), we obtain

$$A_T \tilde{y}_i = A_T \tilde{v}_i = (\omega\gamma + \phi\beta) A_T \Gamma_T e_{T,1} \varepsilon_{i,0} + A_T L_T [I_T + \phi\beta L_T] \varepsilon_i \qquad (23)$$

and using (17) this yields

$$\begin{aligned} A_T \tilde{y}_i^{(-1)} &= A_T \tilde{v}_i^{(-1)} \\ &= A_T [\omega e_{T,1} \varepsilon_{i,0} + L_T \tilde{v}_i] \\ &= A_T [\omega e_{T,1} \varepsilon_{i,0} + (\omega\gamma + \phi\beta) L_T \Gamma_T e_{T,1} \varepsilon_{i,0} L_T + \Gamma_T (I_T + \phi\beta L_T) \varepsilon_i] \\ &= A_T [\omega \Gamma_T + \phi\beta L_T \Gamma_T] e_{T,1} \varepsilon_{i,0} + A_T L_T \Gamma_T [I_T + \phi\beta L_T] \varepsilon_i \end{aligned}$$

where we used $\Gamma_T = I_T + \gamma L_T \Gamma_T$.

The above leads to

$$\begin{aligned} A_T \tilde{W}_i = {} & [\omega A_T \Gamma_T e_{T,1} + \phi\beta A_T L_T \Gamma_T e_{T,1}] \varepsilon_{i,0} e_{2,1}' \\ & + A_T L_T \Gamma_T [I_T + \phi\beta L_T] \varepsilon_i e_{2,1}' \\ & + \phi A_T e_{T,1} \varepsilon_{i,0} e_{2,2}' + \phi A_T L_T \varepsilon_i e_{2,2}'. \end{aligned} \qquad (24)$$

Defining now the $n \times n$ matrices

$$\begin{aligned} A &= I_N \otimes A_T \\ L &= I_N \otimes L_T \\ \Gamma &= I_N \otimes \Gamma_T \end{aligned} \qquad (25)$$

and upon using the notation $\varepsilon_0 = (\varepsilon_{1,0}, \ldots, \varepsilon_{N,0})'$, we have the following expression for the relevant stochastic elements of the matrix AW, viz.

$$\begin{aligned} A\tilde{W} = {} & AL\Gamma\varepsilon e_{2,1}' + \phi\beta AL\Gamma L\varepsilon e_{2,1}' + \phi AL\varepsilon e_{2,2}' \\ & + \omega A\Gamma(I_N \otimes e_{T,1}')\varepsilon_0 e_{2,1}' + \phi\beta AL\Gamma(I_N \otimes e_{T,1}')\varepsilon_0 e_{2,1}' \\ & + \phi A(I_N \otimes e_{T,1}')\varepsilon_0 e_{2,2}'. \end{aligned} \qquad (26)$$

For the case $\phi = 0$ and $\omega = 0$ this simplifies to

$$A\tilde{W} = AL\Gamma\varepsilon e'_{2,1}. \tag{27}$$

The LSDV estimator of δ is $\hat{\delta} = (W'AW)^{-1}W'Ay$, and hence its bias is given by

$$E(\hat{\delta} - \delta) = E[(W'AW)^{-1}W'A\varepsilon]. \tag{28}$$

We shall use now the same type of approach as employed in Kiviet (1995) to approximate this bias, but here we shall aim to obtain results with a slightly higher degree of precision. This means that we have to expand the estimation error

$$\hat{\delta} - \delta = (WAW)^{-1}W'A\varepsilon. \tag{29}$$

First, we examine for each of its two factors $(W'AW)^{-1}$ and $W'A\varepsilon$ the order of magnitude in terms of powers of N and T. When we assume stationarity for the N separate T element time series $\bar{x}_i$, we naturally have $W'AW = O_p(n)$, where $n = NT$, and hence

$$(W'AW)^{-1} = O_p(n^{-1}). \tag{30}$$

In Kiviet (1995) we showed that the stationarity assumption leads to an analysis of the worst case, as far as finite sample problems are concerned. Under non-stationarity, the results will still be valid but they will in fact be more accurate than claimed here. For the second factor of (29) we find

$$W'A\varepsilon = E(W'A\varepsilon) + [W'A\varepsilon - E(W'A\varepsilon)] \tag{31}$$

where

$$E(W'A\varepsilon) = O(N) \tag{32}$$

and

$$[W'A\varepsilon - E(W'A\varepsilon)] = O_p(n^{1/2}) \tag{33}$$

as we shall see. From the above, we directly find the order of the leading terms of the bias (28); these are $O(n^{-1}N)$, i.e., $O(T^{-1})$, and $O(n^{-1/2})$ respectively, showing that LSDV is inconsistent for finite T. Below, we shall evaluate these leading terms, and by expanding (30) we shall also obtain contributions to the bias of smaller order. It will be of interest to examine how these terms are affected by ϕ (the weak exogeneity of $x_{i,t}$) and by ω (the initial conditions); obviously, π (the dependence of the regressor $x_{i,t}$ on the individual effect η_i) has no effect on the bias of the LSDV estimator (28), because the vector η has been eliminated completely from AW.

Defining

$$Q = E(W'AW) \tag{34}$$

we can write

$$\begin{aligned} W'AW &= Q + W'AW - Q \\ &= [I_n + (W'AW - Q)Q^{-1}]Q \end{aligned}$$

so that

$$(W'AW)^{-1} = Q^{-1}[I_n + (W'AW - Q)Q^{-1}]^{-1}.$$

Since $[W'AW - Q] = O_p(n^{1/2})$ and $Q^{-1} = O(n^{-1})$, we can easily expand the first factor of the estimation error (29). Upon using the result that for a general $k \times k$ matrix $C = O_p(n^{-1/2})$ we have $[I_k + C]^{-1} = I_k - C + C^2 + O_p(n^{-1})$, which is a stochastic matrix generalization of a well-known Taylor series expansion, we obtain

$$\begin{aligned} (W'AW)^{-1} = Q^{-1}[I_k &- (W'AW - Q)Q^{-1} \\ &+ (W'AW - Q)Q^{-1}(W'AW - Q)Q^{-1} \\ &+ o_p(n^{-2}) \\ = Q^{-1} &- Q^{-1}(W'AW - Q)Q^{-1} \\ &+ Q^{-1}(W'AW - Q)Q^{-1}(W'AW - Q)Q^{-1} \\ &+ o_p(n^{-2}) \end{aligned} \tag{35}$$

where the three leading terms are of order $O(n^{-1})$, $O_p(n^{-3/2})$ and $O_p(n^{-2})$ respectively. Multiplying these with (31), which contains terms of $O(N)$ and $O_p(n^{1/2})$, we obtain six terms and a remainder term for the estimation error. Omitting the term which is of smaller order than n^{-1} we find

$$\begin{aligned} (W'AW)^{-1}W'A\varepsilon = Q^{-1}&E(W'A\varepsilon) \\ &+ Q^{-1}[W'A\varepsilon - E(W'A\varepsilon)] \\ &- Q^{-1}(W'AW - Q)Q^{-1}E(W'A\varepsilon) \\ &- Q^{-1}(W'AW - Q)Q^{-1}[W'A\varepsilon - E(W'A\varepsilon)] \\ &+ Q^{-1}(W'AW - Q)Q^{-1}(W'AW - Q)Q^{-1}E(W'A\varepsilon) \\ &+ o_p(n^{-1}) \end{aligned} \tag{36}$$

which has five terms whose order of magnitude can be indicated by $O(T^{-1})$, $O_p(n^{-1/2})$, $O_p(N^{-1/2}T^{-3/2})$, $O_p(n^{-1})$, and $O_p(N^{-1}T^{-2})$ respectively. In Kiviet (1995) we did not take into account the fifth of these terms, and therefore the resulting bias approximation error is not $o(n^{-1})$, but includes terms of order $O(N^{-1}T^{-2})$ and $O(N^{-3/2}T^{-3/2})$ and smaller. Hence, it can be indicated by $O(N^{-1}T^{-3/2})$. For that case the bias approximation follows from

$$E[(W'AW)^{-1}W'A\varepsilon] = 2Q^{-1}E(W'A\varepsilon) - Q^{-1}E(W'AWQ^{-1}W'A\varepsilon) + O(N^{-1}T^{-3/2}). \tag{37}$$

Retaining now the fifth term in the approximation (36), we find for the bias of the LSDV estimator for more accurate result

$$E[(W'AW)^{-1}W'A\varepsilon] = Q^{-1}E(W'A\varepsilon) - Q^{-1}E(W'AWQ^{-1}W'A\varepsilon) + Q^{-1}E(W'AWQ^{-1}W'AW)Q^{-1}E(W'A\varepsilon) + o(n^{-1}). \tag{38}$$

The evaluation of this approximation for the general model introduced in section 2 is feasible but intricate. Before we consider that case we therefore return first to the case examined in Kiviet (1995), where the exogenous regressors are strongly exogenous (i.e., $\phi = 0$) and where we condition on $v_{i,0}$ (i.e., $\omega = 0$). We find (see the appendix for proofs) the approximation (which can easily be generalized for the case where one has k instead of just one strongly exogenous regressor)

$$E(\hat{\delta} - \delta) = \sigma_\varepsilon^2[\alpha_1 I_2 + B_1 + \sigma_\varepsilon^2(\alpha_2 I_2 + B_2) + \sigma_\varepsilon^4 \alpha_3 I_2]Q^{-1}e_{2,1} + o(n^{-1}) \tag{39}$$

with

$$a_1 = tr(\Pi) - tr(Q^{-1}\bar{W}'\Pi A\bar{W})$$

$$a_2 = q_{1,1}[-tr(\Pi)tr(\Pi'\Pi) - 2tr(\Pi'\Pi\Pi) + tr(\Pi)tr(Q^{-1}\bar{W}'\Pi\Pi'\bar{W})] + tr(\Pi)[(e_{2,1}'Q^{-1}\bar{W}'\Pi\Pi'\bar{W}Q^{-1}e_{2,1}) + tr(\Pi'\Pi)e_{2,1}'Q^{-1}\bar{W}'A\bar{W}Q^{-1}e_{2,1})]$$

$$a_3 = tr(\Pi)q_{1,1}^2[tr(\Pi'\Pi)tr(\Pi'\Pi) + 2tr(\Pi'\Pi\Pi'\Pi)]$$

$$B_1 = -tr(\Pi)Q^{-1}\bar{W}'A\bar{W} - Q^{-1}\bar{W}'\Pi A\bar{W} + tr(\Pi)Q^{-1}\bar{W}'A\bar{W}Q^{-1}\bar{W}'A\bar{W}$$

$$B_2 = q_{1,1}\,tr(\Pi)[tr(\Pi'\Pi)Q^{-1}\bar{W}'A\bar{W} + 2Q^{-1}\bar{W}'\Pi\Pi'\bar{W}]$$

where

$$\Pi = AL\Gamma, \quad \bar{W} = E(W),$$

$$Q = \bar{W}'A\bar{W} + \sigma_\varepsilon^2 tr(\Pi'\Pi)e_{2,1}e_{2,1}'$$

$$q_{1,1} = e_{2,1}'Q^{-1}e_{2,1}'$$

$I_2 = [e_{2,1} \vdots e_{2,2}]$ is the 2×2 identity matrix.

Instead of $A\tilde{W}$ of (27) we can also employ the more general specification (26) in the derivation of this bias. Doing so leads to many more terms (also in the expression of the Q matrix). Focusing on just the first term of (36) we obtain (see appendix)

$$E(\hat{\delta} - \delta) = \sigma_\varepsilon^2[tr(\Pi)Q^{-1}e_{2,1} + \phi a^*] + O(n^{-1/2}) \tag{40}$$

with

$$a^* = O(T^{-1}).$$

Hence, it is obvious that under weak exogeneity the bias approximation is still given by terms of order $O(T^{-1})$, $O(n^{-1/2})$, etc. However, all these terms are functions now not only of the parameters δ and σ_ε^2, but also of ϕ. We note that the leading term is not affected by ω. The present methods certainly allow to derive an explicit approximation accurate to order $O(n^{-1})$ for the bias of the LSDV estimator in the dynamic panel data model with weakly exogenous regressors, but, in order to exploit such a result in an operational bias corrected estimator would require a consistent estimator of ϕ, and hence it would necessitate a full specification for the data generating process of the exogenous explanatory variables. Usually, that will be considered an impracticable requirement, and therefore we shall not elaborate any further on (40). The above also implies that (39) is inadequate for approximating and correcting bias in a situation where the exogenous explanatory variable is weakly exogenous and T finite. Weak exogeneity has an effect on the LSDV bias of similar magnitude as the presence of a lagged dependent variable. Even if no lagged dependent variable occurs in the model, weak exogeneity will render the LSDV estimator inconsistent for finite T. Since correction is impracticable here, we better focus on alternative estimators.

4 The location of particular IV estimators

Because the LSDV estimator is inconsistent for finite T, the coefficients of the dynamic panel data model are usually estimated by applying instrumental variable (IV) methods. Since the orthogonality conditions in the model transformed by the matrix A are unfavorable, and this not being the case for the model in first differences, this transformation is used here for removing the individual effects. In order to examine the finite sample behavior of such IV estimators, we have to obtain the expression for the relevant random elements in vectors that have been transformed by the $(T-1) \times T$ matrices

$$D_T = \begin{bmatrix} -1 & 1 & 0 & \cdot & \cdot & 0 \\ 0 & -1 & 1 & \cdot & & \cdot \\ \cdot & \cdot & \cdot & \cdot & \cdot & \cdot \\ \cdot & & \cdot & -1 & 1 & 0 \\ 0 & \cdot & \cdot & 0 & -1 & 1 \end{bmatrix}, K_T = \begin{bmatrix} 1 & 0 & \cdot & \cdot & \cdot & 0 \\ 0 & 1 & 0 & \cdot & & \cdot \\ \cdot & \cdot & \cdot & \cdot & \cdot & \cdot \\ \cdot & & \cdot & 1 & 0 & \cdot \\ 0 & \cdot & \cdot & 0 & 1 & 0 \end{bmatrix} \quad (41)$$

for which we also define

$$\begin{aligned} D &= I_N \otimes D_T \\ K &= I_N \otimes K_T \end{aligned} \quad (42)$$

Exploiting $D_T \iota_T = 0$, we transform model (6) into

$$\begin{aligned} D_T y_i &= \gamma D_T y_i^{(-1)} + \beta D_T x_i + \eta_i D_T \iota_T + D_T \varepsilon_i \\ &= V_i \delta + D_T \varepsilon_i \end{aligned} \quad (43)$$

where $V_i = [D_T y_i^{(-1)} \vdots D_T x_i]$. Then the model can be written as

$$Dy = V\delta + D\varepsilon \quad (44)$$

where $V = [V_1' \vdots \ldots \vdots V_N']'$. From $D_T \tilde{y}_i^{(-1)} = D_T \tilde{v}_i^{(-1)}$ (20), (17), and (14) we find

$$\begin{aligned} \tilde{V}_i &= [D_T \tilde{y}_i^{(-1)} \vdots D_T \tilde{x}_i] \\ &= [D_T(\omega e_{T,1} \varepsilon_{i,0} + L_T \tilde{v}_i) \vdots \phi D_T(e_{T,1} \varepsilon_{i,0} + L_T \varepsilon_i)] \\ &= \omega D_T [I_T + \gamma L_T \Gamma_T] e_{T,1} \varepsilon_{i,0} e_{2,1}' + \phi\beta D_T L_T \Gamma_T e_{T,1} \varepsilon_{i,0} e_{2,1}' \\ &\quad + D_T L_T \Gamma_T [I_T + \phi\beta L_T] \varepsilon_i e_{2,1}' - \phi e_{T-1,1} \varepsilon_{i,0} e_{2,2}' + \phi D_T L_T \varepsilon_i e_{2,2}' \end{aligned} \quad (45)$$

which implies

$$\begin{aligned} \tilde{V} &= DL\Gamma\varepsilon e_{2,1}' + \phi\beta DL\Gamma\varepsilon e_{2,1}' + \phi DL\varepsilon e_{2,2}' \\ &\quad + \omega D\Gamma(I_N \otimes e_{T,1})\varepsilon_0 e_{2,1}' + \phi\beta DL\Gamma(I_N \otimes e_{T,1})\varepsilon_0 e_{2,1}' \\ &\quad - \phi(I_N \otimes e_{T-1,1})\varepsilon_0 e_{2,2}'. \end{aligned} \quad (46)$$

For $\phi = 0$ and $\omega = 0$ this simplifies to

$$\tilde{V} = DL\Gamma\varepsilon e_{2,1}'. \quad (47)$$

We shall only consider IV estimators here where the number of instruments is equal to the number of regressors in the model (44). Implementations where more orthogonality conditions are exploited may certainly be of more interest, but finding an expansion for their estimation error, although feasible, is far more complex. Indicating the instrumental variables by $Z = [Z_1' \vdots Z_2' \vdots \ldots \vdots Z_N']'$, the IV estimator is given by

$$\hat{\delta} = (Z'V)^{-1}Z'Dy = \delta + (Z'V)^{-1}Z'D\varepsilon. \quad (48)$$

Because of the equality of the number of instruments and the number of regressors, $\hat{\delta}$ may not have any finite moments. However, as for the LSDV estimator $\hat{\delta}$, the estimation error of $\hat{\delta}$ can be expanded, and the leading terms of this expansion will nevertheless be informative on the finite sample behavior of the estimator. We will examine here the order of magnitude and the expectation of the leading terms in expansions for two particular choices of the set of instrumental variables, viz.

$$H_i = [K_T y_i^{(-1)} : D_T x_i],\ G_i = [K_T y_i^{(-1)} : K_T x_i^{(-1)}] \quad (49)$$

respectively. The implementation using H_i is the (generally preferred) one of the two options suggested by Anderson and Hsiao (1982); G_i follows the recommendations given in Arellano and Bond (1991) for the case where $x_{i,t}$ is a predetermined variable (but their GMM implementations would exploit more linear orthogonality restrictions, leading to the inclusion of more instruments constructed from lagged values of $y_{i,t}$ and $x_{i,t}$).

Using $\tilde{y}_i^{(-1)} = \alpha\iota_T\eta_i + \tilde{v}_i^{(-1)}$, we find

$$\begin{aligned}
\tilde{H}_i &= [K_T\tilde{y}_i^{(-1)} : D_T\tilde{x}_i] \\
&= [\alpha\iota_{T-1}\eta_i + K_T(\omega e_{T,1}\varepsilon_{i,0} + L_T\tilde{v}_i) : \phi D_T(e_{T,1}\varepsilon_{i,0} + L_T\varepsilon_i)] \\
&= \alpha\iota_{T-1}\eta_i e_{2,1}' + K_T[\omega + \omega\gamma L_T\Gamma_T + \phi\beta L_T\Gamma_T]e_{T,1}\varepsilon_{i,0}e_{2,1}' \\
&\quad + K_T L_T\Gamma_T[I_T + \phi\beta L_T]\varepsilon_i e_{2,1}' - \phi e_{T-1,1}\varepsilon_{i,0}e_{2,2}' + \phi D_T L_T\varepsilon_i e_{2,2}' \quad (50)
\end{aligned}$$

which implies

$$\begin{aligned}
\tilde{H} &= \alpha(I_N \otimes \iota_{T-1})\eta e_{2,1}' + KL\Gamma\varepsilon e_{2,1}' + \phi\beta KL\Gamma L\varepsilon e_{2,1}' + \phi DL\varepsilon e_{2,2}' \\
&\quad + \omega K\Gamma(I_N \otimes e_{T,1})\varepsilon_0 e_{2,1}' + \phi\beta KL\Gamma(I_N \otimes e_{T,1})\varepsilon_0 e_{2,2}' \\
&\quad - \phi(I_N \otimes e_{T-1,1})\varepsilon_0 e_{2,2}' \quad (51)
\end{aligned}$$

and, for $\phi = 0$ and $\omega = 0$

$$\tilde{H} = \alpha(I_N \otimes \iota_{T-1})\eta e_{2,1}' + KL\Gamma\varepsilon e_{2,1}'. \quad (52)$$

From $\tilde{x}_i^{(-1)} = \pi\iota_T\eta_i + \phi e_{T,2}\varepsilon_{i,0} + \phi L_T^2\varepsilon_i$, we obtain

$$\begin{aligned}
\tilde{G}_i &= [K_T y_i^{(-1)} : K_T x_i^{(-1)}] \\
&= \alpha\iota_{T-1}\eta_i e_{2,1}' + K_T[\omega + \omega\gamma L_T\Gamma_T + \phi\beta L_T\Gamma_T]e_{T,1}\varepsilon_{i,0}e_{2,1}' \\
&\quad + K_T L_T\Gamma_T[I_T + \phi\beta L_T]\varepsilon_i e_{2,1}' \\
&\quad + \pi\iota_{T-1}\eta_i e_{2,2}' + \phi e_{T-1,2}\varepsilon_{i,0}e_{2,2}' + \phi K_T L_T^2\varepsilon_i e_{2,2}' \quad (53)
\end{aligned}$$

which implies

$$\begin{aligned}\tilde{G} &= \alpha(I_N \otimes \iota_{T-1})\eta e_{2,1}' + \pi(I_N \otimes \iota_{T-1})\eta e_{2,2}' \\ &\quad + KL\Gamma\varepsilon e_{2,1}' + \phi\beta KL\Gamma L\varepsilon e_{2,1}' + \phi KL^2\varepsilon e_{2,2}' \\ &\quad + \omega K\Gamma(I_N \otimes e_{T,1})\varepsilon_0 e_{2,1}' + \phi\beta KL\Gamma(I_N \otimes e_{T,1})\varepsilon_0 e_{2,1}' \\ &\quad + \phi(I_N \otimes e_{T-1,2})\varepsilon_0 e_{2,2}' \end{aligned} \tag{54}$$

and, for $\phi = 0$ and $\omega = 0$

$$\tilde{G} = \alpha(I_N \otimes \iota_{T-1})\eta e_{2,1}' + \pi(I_N \otimes \iota_{T-1})\eta e_{2,2}' + KL\Gamma\varepsilon e_{2,1}'. \tag{55}$$

We find for these Z matrices (see the appendix) that $E(Z'D\varepsilon)$ is either 0 (in this situation the instruments are certainly valid in the usual sense and will yield consistent estimators) or $O(n)$, whereas $[Z'D\varepsilon - E(Z'D\varepsilon)] = O_p(n^{-1/2})$, $Z'V = O_p(n)$ and $[Z'V - E(Z'V)] = O_p(n^{1/2})$. Therefore, we expand as follows. Defining

$$P = E(Z'V) \tag{56}$$

we can write

$$\begin{aligned} Z'V &= P + Z'V - P \\ &= [I_k + (Z'V - P)P^{-1}]P \end{aligned}$$

so that

$$\begin{aligned} (Z'V)^{-1} &= P^{-1}[I_k + (Z'V - P)P^{-1}]^{-1} \\ &= P^{-1} - P^{-1}(Z'V - P)P^{-1} + O_p(n^{-2}). \end{aligned} \tag{57}$$

Thus, the estimation error

$$\check{\delta} - \delta = (Z'V)^{-1}Z'D\varepsilon \tag{58}$$

of the IV estimator can be written as

$$\begin{aligned} (Z'V)^{-1}Z'D\varepsilon &= P^{-1}E(Z'D\varepsilon) + P^{-1}(Z'D\varepsilon - E(Z'D\varepsilon)] \\ &\quad - P^{-1}(Z'V - P)P^{-1}E(Z'D\varepsilon) \\ &\quad - P^{-1}(Z'V - P)P^{-1}[Z'D\varepsilon - E(Z'D\varepsilon)] + O_p(n^{-1}) \end{aligned} \tag{59}$$

where the four terms are either of order $O(1)$, $O_p(n^{-1/2})$, $O_p(n^{-1/2})$ and $O_p(n^{-1})$ respectively, or, if $E(Z'D\varepsilon) = 0$, they are 0, $O_p(n^{-1/2})$, 0, $O_p(n^{-1})$ and then the remainder term is in fact $o_p(n^{-1})$. Note that (59) can also be written as

$$(Z'V)^{-1}Z'D\varepsilon = 2P^{-1}Z'D\varepsilon - P^{-1}Z'VP^{-1}Z'D\varepsilon + O_p(n^{-1}). \tag{60}$$

We now define for $Z = H$ and for $Z = G$

$$E_{n^{-1}}(\check{\delta}_Z - \delta) = 2P^{-1}E(Z'D\varepsilon) - P^{-1}E(Z'VP^{-1}Z'D\varepsilon). \tag{61}$$

This expectation provides information on the location of the IV estimation error $\check{\delta}_Z - \delta$ to order $O(n^{-1/2})$ or $O(n^{-1})$. The above expressions for the relevant stochastic components of V, H, and G enable to derive this approximated "dislocation" of $\check{\delta}$.

We first consider the Anderson–Hsiao estimator and start to focus on the case where $\phi = 0$ and $\omega = 0$. We obtain

$$\begin{aligned}
E_{n^{-1}}(\check{\delta}_H - \delta) &= \sigma_\varepsilon^2[a_1^* I_2 + B^* + p_{1,1}(\sigma_\varepsilon^2 a_2^* + \sigma_\eta^2 a_3^*) I_2]P^{-1}e_{2,1} \\
a_1^* &= tr(P^{-1}\bar{V}'\Omega D'\bar{H}) \\
a_2^* &= tr(\Omega' DL\Gamma D'\Omega) + tr(\Gamma' L' D'\Omega D'\Omega) \\
a_3^* &= -\alpha^2 N\gamma^{T-2} \\
B^* &= P^{-1}\bar{H}' DL\Gamma D'\bar{H} \\
\Omega &= KL\Gamma,\ \bar{V} = E(V),\ \bar{H} = E(H) \\
P &= E(H'V) = \bar{H}'\bar{V} + \sigma_\varepsilon^2 tr(\Gamma' L' D'\Omega)e_{2,1}e_{2,1}' \\
p_{1,1} &= e_{2,1}' P^{-1} e_{2,1}.
\end{aligned} \tag{62}$$

This shows (as would also result from a standard *plim* analysis) that in this case the Anderson–Hsiao estimator of δ is consistent. However, result (62) offers much more. It entails the actual dislocation to the order of $O(n^{-1})$. By substituting consistent estimators ($\check{\delta}$ or other) for all parameters in (62) and subtracting the result from $\check{\delta}$, a corrected estimator is obtained with a dislocation of $o(n^{-1})$. In fact, the estimator for σ_η^2 has to be consistent only for $N \to \infty$, because $p_{1,1}a_3^* = O(T^{-1})$.

For the Anderson–Hsiao estimator under weak exogeneity we find

$$\begin{aligned}
E_{n^{-1}}(\check{\delta}_H - \delta) &= -\phi\sigma_\varepsilon^2 N(T-1)P^{-1}e_{2,2} = O(1) \\
P &= E(H'V) = O(n).
\end{aligned} \tag{63}$$

This shows that this IV estimator is inconsistent now (for $N \to \infty$ or $T \to \infty$ or both). Because the contributions that involve ϕ are of finite magnitude, a correction that could redress the inconsistency would require (as for LSDV) the modeling and consistent estimation of the weak exogeneity, which is not very attractive. Note that for this particular IV estimator the inconsistency problem is worse than for LSDV, because the dislocation is $O(1)$ here, whereas it is $O(T^{-1})$ for LSDV.

Finally, we consider the IV estimator with instruments G. For $\phi = 0$ and $\omega = 0$ we find

$$
\begin{aligned}
E_{n^{-1}}(\breve{\delta}_G-\delta) &= \sigma_\varepsilon^2[a_1^* I_2 + B^* + p_{1,1}(\sigma_\varepsilon^2 a_2^* + \sigma_\eta^2\alpha^2 a_3^*)I_2 \\
&\quad + \sigma_\eta^2\alpha p_{1,2}\pi a_3^* I_2]P^{-1}e_{2,1} + \sigma_\varepsilon^2\sigma_\eta^2 a_3^*(\alpha\pi p_{1,1} \\
&\quad + \pi^2 p_{1,2})P^{-1}e_{2,2} \\
a_1^* &= tr(P^{-1}\bar{V}'\Omega D'\bar{G}) \\
a_2^* &= tr(\Omega' DL\Gamma D'\Omega) + tr(\Gamma' L' D'\Omega D'\Omega) \\
a_3^* &= -N\gamma^{T-2} \\
B^* &= P^{-1}\bar{G}' DL\Gamma D'\bar{G} \\
\Omega &= KL\Gamma,\ \bar{V}=E(V),\ \bar{G}=E(G) \\
P &= E(G'V) = \bar{G}'\bar{V} + \sigma_\varepsilon^2 tr(\Gamma' L' D'\Omega)e_{2,1}e_{2,1}' \\
p_{1,1} &= e_{2,1}' P^{-1} e_{2,1} \\
p_{1,2} &= e_{2,1}' P^{-1} e_{2,2}.
\end{aligned} \tag{64}
$$

The dislocation is $O(n^{-1})$ here. This can be removed by using a correction procedure. It would be of interest to examine whether this leads to a more, or to a less, efficient estimator in finite samples than can be obtained by correcting (and removing bias up to order $O(n^{-1})$ of) the LSDV $\hat{\delta}$ or IV $\breve{\delta}_H$ estimator.

For the general case of the IV estimator with $Z=G$ and $\bar{G}$ as in (54) we obtain

$$
\begin{aligned}
E_{n^{-1}}(\breve{\delta}_G-\delta) &= \sigma_\varepsilon^2[a_1^* I_2 + B_1^* + \sigma_\varepsilon^2 a_3^* I_2]P^{-1}e_{2,1} \\
&\quad + \sigma_\varepsilon^2[a_2^* I_2 + B_2^*]P^{-1}e_{2,2} \\
a_1^* &= tr(P^{-1}\bar{V}'\Omega D'\bar{G}) + \phi\beta tr(P^{-1}\Gamma LD'\bar{G}) \\
a_2^* &= tr(P^{-1}\bar{V}' KL^2 D'\bar{G}) \\
a_3^* &= \text{as defined in the appendix} \\
B_1^* &= P^{-1}\bar{G}' DL\Gamma D'\bar{G} + \phi\beta P^{-1}\bar{G}' DL\Gamma LD'\bar{G} \\
B_2^* &= \phi\bar{G}' DLD'\bar{G} \\
\Omega &= KL\Gamma,\ \bar{V}=E(V),\ \bar{G}=E(G) \\
P &= E(G'V) \\
p_{1,1} &= e_{2,1}' P^{-1} e_{2,1},\ p_{1,2} = e_{2,1}' P^{-1} e_{2,2}.
\end{aligned} \tag{65}
$$

This result can be used to remove contributions to the dislocation of order $O(n^{-1})$, but not those of magnitude $O(N^{-1}T^{-2})$. However, such a correction would again require a consistent estimator of the weak exogeneity parameter ϕ, which makes it impracticable.

5 Conclusions

Economic relationships are often characterized by dynamic adjustment processes and by feedback mechanisms. If the feedback is instantaneous then we have joint dependence, and for efficient structural inference it is required to model and analyse the various endogenous variables as a system. When the feedback is not instantaneous but occurs with at least a one-period lag, then particular limited information techniques may enable consistent estimation of structural parameters, but the finite sample characteristics of such estimators depend on the structural (nuisance) parameters from the feedback mechanism. In order to assess and improve the finite sample properties of inference on the relationship of primary interest, it seems inevitable to analyse and estimate the parameters of the feedback relationship as well.

In this study, some finite sample characteristics are examined of three particular single equation estimation techniques for dynamic models of panel data with time-invariant error components. Estimation of such models requires a transformation that removes this unobserved heterogeneity, but which at the same time complicates the stochastic structure of the resulting transformed model considerably. We consider the situation where next to the lagged dependent regressor there is one other explanatory variable. This regressor is correlated with the unobserved individual specific error component. Furthermore, two situations are compared, viz. the case where this regressor is independent of the random error term (strong exogeneity), and the case where it does depend on the one-period lagged error term (weak exogeneity). In the latter case we encounter the situation just described: accurate finite sample inference requires at least consistent estimation of the feedback mechanism. We find that the dislocation of a consistent IV estimator is determined by terms in the feedback parameter and these are of order $O(n^{-1})$ and $O(n^{-1}T^{-1})$ respectively. Also the bias of the LSDV estimator is a function of the feedback parameters, but its magnitude is more worrying since it is $O(T^{-1})$, which, however, may be better than for the reasonably popular Anderson–Hsiao IV estimator. Under strong exogeneity this is consistent and its dislocation has magnitude $O(n^{-1})$, but under weak exogeneity its dislocation is of finite order, and is given by an $O(1)$ expression involving the nuisance parameter of the feedback mechanism.

We have also examined to what degree the location of the various estimators is determined by initial conditions. We generally find that this aspect seems of secondary importance, because its magnitude never exceeds $O(N^{-1}T^{-2})$.

In a recently published handbook on the econometrics of panel data, the chapter on linear dynamic models could still describe the state of the art as "we do not have analytical results about the small sample properties of the various estimators of these models," see Sevestre and Trognon (1992, p. 95). The analysis of this chapter is meant to start to change this situation. However, in order to find out how substantial the actual relative size of the distinct terms of different orders of magnitude under the various situations considered is, this purely theoretical study has to be supplemented by Monte Carlo simulation experiments. We plan to undertake these in the near future. From those experiments, we should find out at the same time to what degree the analytical results obtained here can be used to produce finite sample improvements to the original estimators, both with respect to mitigating bias and to improving estimator efficiency. Under strong exogeneity the results of this chapter enable to produce estimators which on average deviate from the true parameter value by less than $O(n^{-1})$. It could well be that the least squares based estimator will beat the instrumental variables based estimators. Under weak exogeneity the consistent GMM type estimators seem to have a natural advantage. However, earlier Monte Carlo studies have shown their unstable finite sample behavior under strong exogeneity, which stems from $O(n^{-1})$ terms. Its weak exogeneity nuisance parameters also occur in $O(n^{-1})$ terms, and if these are such that they have to be assessed and removed in order to improve GMM's finite sample behavior, then one could as well assess LSDVs $O(T^{-1})$ and $O(n^{-1})$ bias terms under weak exogeneity, and use them for correcting its bias. After all, it has often been found that least squares estimators tend to have less dispersion than instrumental variables estimators, and hence they may yield more efficient inference in finite samples.

Appendix

In all proofs below we employ the result, see Kiviet and Phillips (1996), that for general $n \times n$ matrices X_1 and X_2 and $n \times 1$ vector $v \sim N(0, I_n)$ we have

$$E(v'X_1v)(v'X_2v) = tr(X_1)tr(X_2) + tr(X_1X_2) + (X_1'X_2)$$

Proof of (39):

In case $\phi = 0$ and $\omega = 0$ we find from (27) that we have

$$A\tilde{W} = \Pi\varepsilon e_{2,1}'$$

with $\Pi = AL\Gamma$ a $n \times n$ matrix. Note that $W = \bar{W} + \tilde{W}$ with $\bar{W}$ such that $E(\bar{W}'A\varepsilon) = 0$. We evaluate the various expectations in the separate terms of (38). We first find

$$E(W'A\varepsilon) = E(\tilde{W}'A\varepsilon) = e_{2,1}E\varepsilon'\Pi\varepsilon = \sigma_\varepsilon^2 tr(\Pi)e_{2,1}.$$

Note that $L_T\Gamma_T$ is the matrix C as used in Kiviet (1995). In Kiviet and Phillips (1996), various properties of the product of a series of (transposed) C matrices have been derived; those results are used below without further reference. We have $tr(\Pi) = -\frac{N}{T}\iota' L_T\Gamma_T\iota = O(N)$.

Next we find

$$E(W'AW) = \bar{W}'A\bar{W} + E(\tilde{W}'A\tilde{W})$$

with

$$E(\tilde{W}'A\tilde{W}) = E(e_{2,1}\varepsilon'\Pi'\Pi\varepsilon e_{2,1}') = \sigma_\varepsilon^2 tr(\Pi)e_{2,1}e_{2,1}'$$

where $tr(\Pi'\Pi) = O(n)$.

We obtain also (upon omitting terms involving odd moments of ε which are zero)

$$\begin{aligned}
E(W'AWQ^{-1}W'A\varepsilon) &= \bar{W}'A\bar{W}Q^{-1}E(\tilde{W}'A\varepsilon) + \bar{W}'E(A\tilde{W}Q^{-1}\bar{W}'A\varepsilon) \\
&\quad + E(\tilde{W}'A\bar{W}Q^{-1}\bar{W}'A\varepsilon) \\
&\quad + E(\tilde{W}'A\tilde{W}Q^{-1}\tilde{W}'A\varepsilon) \\
&= \sigma_\varepsilon^2 tr(\Pi)\bar{W}'A\bar{W}Q^{-1}e_{2,1} \\
&\quad + \bar{W}'E(\Pi\varepsilon e_{2,1}'Q^{-1}\bar{W}'A\varepsilon) \\
&\quad + E(e_{2,1}\varepsilon'\Pi'\bar{W}Q^{-1}\bar{W}'A\varepsilon) \\
&\quad + e_{2,1}E[(\varepsilon'\Pi'\Pi\varepsilon)e_{2,1}'Q^{-1}e_{2,1}(\varepsilon'\Pi'\varepsilon)] \\
&= \sigma_\varepsilon^2 tr(\Pi)\bar{W}'A\bar{W}Q^{-1}e_{2,1} + \sigma_\varepsilon^2\bar{W}'\Pi A\bar{W}Q^{-1}e_{2,1} \\
&\quad + \sigma_\varepsilon^2 tr(Q^{-1}\bar{W}'\Pi A\bar{W})e_{2,1} \\
&\quad + \sigma_\varepsilon^4 tr(\Pi'\Pi)tr(\Pi)(e_{2,1}'Q^{-1}e_{2,1})e_{2,1} \\
&\quad + 2\sigma_\varepsilon^4 tr(\Pi'\Pi\Pi)(e_{2,1}'Q^{-1}e_{2,1})e_{2,1}.
\end{aligned}$$

Finally we evaluate

$$\begin{aligned}
&E(W'AWQ^{-1}W'AW \\
&= \bar{W}'A\bar{W}Q^{-1}\bar{W}'A\bar{W} + \bar{W}'A\bar{W}Q^{-1}E(\tilde{W}'A\tilde{W}) \\
&\quad + \bar{W}'E(A\tilde{W}Q^{-1}\bar{W}'A\tilde{W}) + \bar{W}'E(A\tilde{W}Q^{-1}\tilde{W}'A)\bar{W} \\
&\quad + E(\tilde{W}'A\bar{W}Q^{-1}\bar{W}'A\tilde{W}) + E(\tilde{W}'A\bar{W}Q^{-1}\tilde{W}'A)\bar{W} \\
&\quad + E(\tilde{W}'A\tilde{W}Q^{-1}\bar{W}'A\tilde{W}) + E(\tilde{W}'A\tilde{W}Q^{-1}\tilde{W}'A\tilde{W}) \\
&= \bar{W}'A\bar{W}Q^{-1}\bar{W}'A\bar{W} + \sigma_\varepsilon^2 tr(\Pi'\Pi)\bar{W}'A\bar{W}Q^{-1}e_{2,1}e_{2,1}' \\
&\quad + \bar{W}'E(\Pi\varepsilon e_{2,1}'Q^{-1}\bar{W}'\Pi\varepsilon e_{2,1}') + \bar{W}'E(\Pi\varepsilon e_{2,1}'Q^{-1}e_{2,1}\varepsilon'\Pi')\bar{W} \\
&\quad + E(e_{2,1}\varepsilon'\Pi'\bar{W}Q^{-1}\bar{W}'\Pi\varepsilon e_{2,1}') + E(e_{2,1}\varepsilon'\Pi'\bar{W}Q^{-1}e_{2,1}\varepsilon'\Pi')\bar{W}
\end{aligned}$$

$$
\begin{aligned}
&+\sigma_\varepsilon^2 tr(\Pi'\Pi)e_{2,1}e_{2,1}'Q^{-1}\bar{W}'A\bar{W} \\
&+(e_{2,1}'Q^{-1}e_{2,1})E(e_{2,1}\varepsilon'\Pi'\Pi\varepsilon\varepsilon'\Pi'\Pi\varepsilon e_{2,1}') \\
=\ &\bar{W}'A\bar{W}Q^{-1}\bar{W}'A\bar{W}+\sigma_\varepsilon^2 tr(\Pi'\Pi)\bar{W}'A\bar{W}Q^{-1}e_{2,1}e_{2,1}' \\
&+\bar{W}'E(\Pi\varepsilon\varepsilon'\Pi'WQ^{-1}e_{2,1}e_{2,1}')+(e_{2,1}'Q^{-1}e_{2,1})\bar{W}'E(\Pi\varepsilon\varepsilon'\Pi')\bar{W} \\
&+E(e_{2,1}\varepsilon'\Pi'\bar{W}Q^{-1}\bar{W}'\Pi\varepsilon e_{2,1}')+E(e_{2,1}\varepsilon'\Pi'\bar{W}Q^{-1}e_{2,1}\varepsilon'\Pi')\bar{W} \\
&+\sigma_\varepsilon^2 tr(\Pi'\Pi)e_{2,1}e_{2,1}'Q^{-1}\bar{W}'A\bar{W} \\
&+(e_{2,1}'Q^{-1}e_{2,1})E(e_{2,1}\varepsilon'\Pi'\Pi\varepsilon\varepsilon'\Pi'\Pi\varepsilon e_{2,1}') \\
=\ &\bar{W}'A\bar{W}Q^{-1}\bar{W}'A\bar{W}+\sigma_\varepsilon^2 tr(\Pi'\Pi)\bar{W}'A\bar{W}Q^{-1}e_{2,1}e_{2,1}' \\
&+\sigma_\varepsilon^2\bar{W}'\Pi\Pi'\bar{W}Q^{-1}e_{2,1}e_{2,1}'+\sigma_\varepsilon^2(e_{2,1}'Q^{-1}e_{2,1})\bar{W}'\Pi\Pi'\bar{W} \\
&+\sigma_\varepsilon^2 tr(Q^{-1}\bar{W}'\Pi\Pi'\bar{W})e_{2,1}e_{2,1}'+\sigma_\varepsilon^2 e_{2,1}e_{2,1}'Q^{-1}\bar{W}'\Pi\Pi'\bar{W} \\
&+\sigma_\varepsilon^2 tr(\Pi'\Pi)e_{2,1}e_{2,1}'Q^{-1}\bar{W}'A\bar{W} \\
&+\sigma_\varepsilon^4(e_{2,1}'Q^{-1}e_{2,1})[tr(\Pi'\Pi)tr(\Pi'\Pi)+2tr(\Pi'\Pi\Pi'\Pi)]e_{2,1}e_{2,1}'.
\end{aligned}
$$

Note that occasionally we have taken the transpose of scalar factors in the above terms, in order to obtain equivalent expressions that easily allow to take expectations. For the bias (38) the above yields

$$
\begin{aligned}
E(\hat{\delta}-\delta)=\ &\sigma_\varepsilon^2 tr(\Pi)Q^{-1}e_{2,1}-\sigma_\varepsilon^2 tr(\Pi)Q^{-1}\bar{W}'A\bar{W}Q^{-1}e_{2,1} \\
&-\sigma_\varepsilon^4 tr(\Pi)tr(\Pi'\Pi)(e_{2,1}'Q^{-1}e_{2,1})Q^{-1}e_{2,1} \\
&-\sigma_\varepsilon^2 Q^{-1}\bar{W}'\Pi A\bar{W}Q^{-1}e_{2,1}-\sigma_\varepsilon^2 tr(Q^{-1}\bar{W}'\Pi A\bar{W})Q^{-1}e_{2,1} \\
&-2\sigma_\varepsilon^4 tr(\Pi'\Pi\Pi)(e_{2,1}'Q^{-1}e_{2,1})Q^{-1}e_{2,1} \\
&+\sigma_\varepsilon^2 tr(\Pi)Q^{-1}\bar{W}'A\bar{W}Q^{-1}\bar{W}'A\bar{W}Q^{-1}e_{2,1} \\
&+\sigma_\varepsilon^4 tr(\Pi)tr(\Pi'\Pi)(e_{2,1}'Q^{-1}e_{2,1})Q^{-1}\bar{W}'A\bar{W}Q^{-1}e_{2,1} \\
&+2\sigma_\varepsilon^4 tr(\Pi)(e_{2,1}'Q^{-1}e_{2,1})Q^{-1}\bar{W}'\Pi\Pi'\bar{W}Q^{-1}e_{2,1} \\
&+\sigma_\varepsilon^4 tr(\Pi)(e_{2,1}'Q^{-1}e_{2,1})tr(Q^{-1}\bar{W}'\Pi\Pi'\bar{W})Q^{-1}e_{2,1} \\
&+\sigma_\varepsilon^4 tr(\Pi)(e_{2,1}'Q^{-1}\bar{W}'\Pi\Pi'\bar{W}Q^{-1}e_{2,1})Q^{-1}e_{2,1} \\
&+\sigma_\varepsilon^4 tr(\Pi)tr(\Pi'\Pi)(e_{2,1}'Q^{-1}\bar{W}'A\bar{W}Q^{-1}e_{2,1})Q^{-1}e_{2,1} \\
&+\sigma_\varepsilon^6 tr(\Pi)(e_{2,1}'Q^{-1}e_{2,1})^2[tr(\Pi'\Pi)tr(\Pi'\Pi) \\
&\qquad\qquad\qquad\qquad +2tr(\Pi'\Pi\Pi'\Pi)]Q^{-1}e_{2,1} \\
&+o(n^{-1}).
\end{aligned}
$$

Proof of (40):

Instead of $A\tilde{W}$ of (27), where $\phi=0$ and $\omega=0$, we now employ the more general specification (26) in the derivation of the bias. Focusing on the first term of (36) and using $E(\varepsilon\varepsilon_0')=0$ we obtain now

$$Q^{-1}E(W'A\varepsilon)=Q^{-1}E(\tilde{W}'A\varepsilon)$$
$$=\sigma_\varepsilon^2[tr(\Pi)+\phi\beta tr(\Pi L)]Q^{-1}e_{2,1}+\sigma_\varepsilon^2\phi tr(AL)Q^{-1}e_{2,2}$$

where $tr(\Pi)=O(N)$, $tr(\Pi L)=O(N)$ and $tr(AL)=Ntr(A_T L_T)=-\frac{N}{T}\iota' L_T\iota=-\frac{T-1}{T}N=O(N)$. Hence, we again find $E(W'A\varepsilon)=O(N)$, but now it is linear in ϕ. For $Q=E(W'AW)=\bar{W}'A\bar{W}+E(\tilde{W}'A\tilde{W})$ one again finds $Q=O(n)$. Also $E(\tilde{W}'A\tilde{W})=O(n)$, but one can show that the only contributions that involve ω are $O(N)$, whereas the contributions that involve ϕ are $O(n)$. From this we conclude that the initial term of $E(\hat{\delta}-\delta)$, which is still $O(T^{-1})$ does involve ϕ, but not ω. Only terms of smaller order are affected by the particular assumption that we make on ω, i.e., on the influence of the start-up disturbance $\varepsilon_{i,0}$.

Proof of (62):

For $\phi=0$ and $\omega=0$ the relevant stochastic components of the matrices V and H are given by (47) and (52). Since $E\eta\varepsilon'=O$, we find

$$E(H'D\varepsilon)=E(\tilde{H}'D\varepsilon)$$
$$=E(\varepsilon'KL\Gamma D'\varepsilon)e_{2,1}$$
$$=\sigma_\varepsilon^2 tr(D'KL\Gamma)e_{2,1}=0$$

because $D_T'K_T=L_T-I_T+e_{T,T}e_{T,T}'$ and $L_T\Gamma_T$ is a lower-triangular matrix with zeros on its main diagonal. Next we examine $\mathrm{Cov}(H'D\varepsilon)$. We have

$$E(H'D\varepsilon\varepsilon'D'H)=\sigma_\varepsilon^2\bar{H}'DD'\bar{H}+E(\tilde{H}'D\varepsilon\varepsilon'D'\tilde{H})$$

and substituting $\tilde{H}$, introducing $\Omega=KL\Gamma$, and making use of $D_T'\iota_{T-1}=e_{T,T}-e_{T,1}$, we obtain

$$E(\tilde{H}'D\varepsilon\varepsilon'D'\tilde{H})=E(\varepsilon'\Omega'D\varepsilon\varepsilon'D'\Omega\varepsilon)e_{2,1}e_{2,1}'$$
$$+E\{\eta'[I_N\otimes(e_{T,T}-e_{T,1})']\varepsilon\varepsilon'[I_N\otimes(e_{T,T}-e_{T,1})]\eta\}e_{2,1}e_{2,1}'$$
$$=\sigma_\varepsilon^4[tr(\Omega'DD'\Omega)+tr(D'\Omega D'\Omega)]e_{2,1}e_{2,1}'+2\sigma_\varepsilon^2\sigma_\eta^2Ne_{2,1}e_{2,1}'$$
$$=\sigma_\varepsilon^4 tr(\Omega'DD'\Omega)e_{2,1}e_{2,1}'+2\sigma_\varepsilon^2\sigma_\eta^2Ne_{2,1}e_{2,1}'=O(n)$$

so $H'D\varepsilon = O_p(n^{1/2})$. Next we derive

$$P = E(H'V) = \bar{H}'\bar{V} + E(\tilde{H}'\tilde{V})$$

where

$$E(\tilde{H}'\tilde{V}) = E(\varepsilon'\Omega'DL\Gamma\varepsilon)e_{2,1}e'_{2,1}$$

$$= \sigma_\varepsilon^2 tr(\Gamma'L'D'\Omega)e_{2,1}e'_{2,1} = O(n)$$

and, as expected, we establish $P = O(n)$. Next consider

$$H'V - P = \tilde{H}'\bar{V} + \bar{H}'\tilde{V} + \tilde{H}'\tilde{V} - \sigma_\varepsilon^2 tr(\Gamma'L'D'\Omega)e_{2,1}e'_{2,1}.$$

One can prove that each element of this matrix has a variance which is $O(n^{-1})$. Therefore $(H'V - P) = O_p(n^{1/2})$, so the expansion leading to (60) is valid here, and yields an approximation error which is $o_p(n^{-1})$.

In order to obtain the $O(n^{-1})$ approximation to the location of the Anderson–Hsiao estimator, we have to evaluate expectation (61) for $Z = H$. We have already found $E(H'D\varepsilon) = 0$, so what remains is the derivation of an expression for $P^{-1}E(H'VP^{-1}H'D\varepsilon)$. We have

$$E(H'VP^{-1}H'D\varepsilon) = \bar{H}'\bar{V}P^{-1}E(\tilde{H}'D\varepsilon) + E(\bar{H}'\tilde{V}P^{-1}\tilde{H}'D\varepsilon)$$

$$+ E(\tilde{H}'\bar{V}P^{-1}\tilde{H}'D\varepsilon) + E(\tilde{H}'\tilde{V}P^{-1}\tilde{H}'D\varepsilon).$$

The first term is again zero. Next we obtain

$$E(\bar{H}'\tilde{V}P^{-1}\tilde{H}'D\varepsilon) = \bar{H}'DL\Gamma E(\varepsilon e'_{2,1}P^{-1}\tilde{H}'D\varepsilon) =$$
$$\sigma_\varepsilon^2 \bar{H}'DL\Gamma D'\bar{H}P^{-1}e_{2,1}$$

$$E(\tilde{H}'\bar{V}P^{-1}\tilde{H}'D\varepsilon) = e_{2,1}E(\varepsilon'\Omega'\bar{V}P^{-1}\tilde{H}'D\varepsilon) = \sigma_\varepsilon^2 tr(P^{-1}\bar{V}'\Omega D'\bar{H})e_{2,1}$$

$$E(\tilde{H}'\tilde{V}P^{-1}\tilde{H}'D\varepsilon) = e_{2,1}E(\varepsilon'\Omega'DL\Gamma\varepsilon e'_{2,1}P^{-1}e_{2,1}\varepsilon'\Omega'D\varepsilon)$$

$$+ \alpha^2 e_{2,1}E[\eta'(I_N \otimes \iota_{T-1})'DL\Gamma\varepsilon e'_{2,1}P^{-1}e_{2,1}\eta'(I_N \otimes \iota_{T-1})'D\varepsilon]$$

$$= \sigma_\varepsilon^4(e'_{2,1}P^{-1}e_{2,1})tr(\Omega'DL\Gamma D'\Omega)e_{2,1}$$

$$+ \sigma_\varepsilon^4(e'_{2,1}P^{-1}e_{2,1})tr(\Gamma'L'D'\Omega D'\Omega)e_{2,1}$$

$$+ \sigma_\varepsilon^2\sigma_\eta^2\alpha^2(e'_{2,1}P^{-1}e_{2,1})tr(DL\Gamma D'[I_N \otimes \iota_{T-1}\iota'_{T-1}])e_{2,1}.$$

The final contribution is obtained by using the result that for general $N \times n$ matrices X_1 and X_2 we have $E(\eta'X_1\varepsilon\eta'X_2\varepsilon) = E_\eta E_{\varepsilon|\eta}(\eta'X_1\varepsilon\varepsilon'X'_2\eta) = E_\eta(\sigma_\varepsilon^2\eta'X_1X'_2\eta) = \sigma_\varepsilon^2\sigma_\eta^2 tr(X_1X'_2)$. One can derive that $tr(DL\Gamma D'[I_N \otimes$

$\iota_{T-1}\iota_{T-1}'])=-N\gamma^{T-2}$. Hence, the only term involving σ_η^2 is $O(T^{-1})$, whereas all others are finite, and after pre-multiplication by P^{-1} they are $O(n^{-1})$. Collecting these results yields (62).

Proof of (63): For (51) we obtain

$$E(H'D\varepsilon)=E(\tilde{H}'D\varepsilon)$$

$$=\sigma_\varepsilon^2[tr(D'\Omega)+\phi\beta tr(D'\Omega L)]e_{2,1}+\sigma_\varepsilon^2\phi tr(D'DL)e_{2,2}$$

$$=-\phi\sigma_\varepsilon^2 N(T-1)e_{2,2}=O(n).$$

Proof of (64): Employing (55) we find

$$E(G'D\varepsilon)=E(\tilde{G}'D\varepsilon)=E(\varepsilon'\Omega D'\varepsilon)e_{2,1}=\sigma_\varepsilon^2 tr(D'\Omega)e_{2,1}=0.$$

Next we derive $P^{-1}E(G'VP^{-1}G'D\varepsilon)$. We have

$$E(G'VP^{-1}G'D\varepsilon)=\bar{G}'\bar{V}P^{-1}E(\tilde{G}'D\varepsilon)+E(\bar{G}'\tilde{V}P^{-1}\tilde{G}'D\varepsilon)$$

$$+E(\tilde{G}'\bar{V}P^{-1}\tilde{G}'D\varepsilon)+E(\tilde{G}'\tilde{V}P^{-1}\tilde{G}'D\varepsilon),$$

where the first term is zero. Next we obtain

$$E(\bar{G}'\tilde{V}P^{-1}\tilde{G}'D\varepsilon)=\bar{G}'DL\Gamma E(\varepsilon e_{2,1}'P^{-1}\tilde{G}'D\varepsilon)=$$
$$\sigma_\varepsilon^2\bar{G}'DL\Gamma D'\bar{G}P^{-1}e_{2,1}$$

$$E(\tilde{G}'\bar{V}P^{-1}\tilde{G}'D\varepsilon)=e_{2,1}E(\varepsilon'\Omega'\bar{V}P^{-1}\tilde{G}'D\varepsilon)=\sigma_\varepsilon^2 tr(P^{-1}\bar{V}'\Omega D'\bar{G})e_{2,1}$$

$$E(\tilde{G}'\tilde{V}P^{-1}\tilde{G}'D\varepsilon)$$

$$=e_{2,1}E(\varepsilon'\Omega'DL\Gamma\varepsilon e_{2,1}'P^{-1}e_{2,1}\varepsilon'\Omega'D\varepsilon)$$

$$+\alpha^2 e_{2,1}E[\eta'(I_N\otimes\iota_{T-1})'DL\Gamma\varepsilon e_{2,1}'P^{-1}e_{2,1}\eta'(I_N\otimes\iota_{T-1})'D\varepsilon]$$

$$+\alpha\pi e_{2,1}E[\eta'(I_N\otimes\iota_{T-1})'DL\Gamma\varepsilon e_{2,1}'P^{-1}e_{2,2}\eta'(I_N\otimes\iota_{T-1})'D\varepsilon]$$

$$+\pi\alpha e_{2,2}E[\eta'(I_N\otimes\iota_{T-1})'DL\Gamma\varepsilon e_{2,1}'P^{-1}e_{2,1}\eta'(I_N\otimes\iota_{T-1})'D\varepsilon]$$

$$+\pi^2 e_{2,2}E[\eta'(I_N\otimes\iota_{T-1})'DL\Gamma\varepsilon e_{2,1}'P^{-1}e_{2,2}\eta'(I_N\otimes\iota_{T-1})'D\varepsilon]$$

$$=\sigma_\varepsilon^4(e_{2,1}'P^{-1}e_{2,1})tr(\Omega'DL\Gamma D'\Omega)e_{2,1}$$

$$+\sigma_\varepsilon^4(e_{2,1}'P^{-1}e_{2,1})tr(\Gamma'L'D'\Omega D'\Omega)e_{2,1}$$

$$- \sigma_\varepsilon^2 \sigma_\eta^2 N \gamma^{T-2} [\alpha^2 (e_{2,1}' P^{-1} e_{2,1}) e_{2,1} + \alpha\pi (e_{2,1}' P^{-1} e_{2,2}) e_{2,1}$$

$$+ \alpha\pi (e_{2,1}' P^{-1} e_{2,1}) e_{2,2} + \pi^2 (e_{2,1}' P^{-1} e_{2,2}) e_{2,2}].$$

Hence, again the term involving σ_η^2 is $O(T^{-1})$, and all others are finite, and after premultiplication by P^{-1} they are $O(n^{-1})$. Collecting these results yields (64).

Proof of (65): For the general model we find

$$E(G'D\varepsilon) = E(\tilde{G}'D\varepsilon)$$

$$= \sigma_\varepsilon^2 [tr(D'\Omega) + \phi\beta tr(D'\Omega L)] e_{2,1} + \sigma_\varepsilon^2 \phi tr(D'KL^2) e_{2,2}$$

$$= 0.$$

Analysing $P^{-1}E(G'VP^{-1}G'D\varepsilon)$ we have again

$$E(G'VP^{-1}G'D\varepsilon) = \bar{G}'\bar{V}P^{-1}E(\tilde{G}'D\varepsilon) + E(\bar{G}'\tilde{V}P^{-1}\tilde{G}'D\varepsilon)$$

$$+ E(\tilde{G}'\bar{V}P^{-1}\tilde{G}'D\varepsilon) + E(\tilde{G}'\tilde{V}P^{-1}\tilde{G}'D\varepsilon)$$

with the first term equal to zero. We now obtain

$$E(\bar{G}'\tilde{V}P^{-1}\tilde{G}'D\varepsilon) = \bar{G}'DL\Gamma E(\varepsilon e_{2,1}' P^{-1}\tilde{G}'D\varepsilon)$$

$$+ \phi\beta\bar{G}'DL\Gamma L E(\varepsilon e_{2,1}' P^{-1}\tilde{G}'D\varepsilon)$$

$$+ \phi\bar{G}'DLE(\varepsilon e_{2,2}' P^{-1}\tilde{G}'D\varepsilon)$$

$$= \sigma_\varepsilon^2 [\bar{G}'DL\Gamma D'\bar{G}P^{-1}e_{2,1} + \phi\beta\bar{G}'DL\Gamma LD'\bar{G}P^{-1}e_{2,1}$$

$$+ \phi\bar{G}'DLD'\bar{G}P^{-1}e_{2,2}] = O(1);$$

$$E(\tilde{G}'\bar{V}P^{-1}\tilde{G}'D\varepsilon) = e_{2,1}E(\varepsilon'\Omega'\bar{V}P^{-1}\tilde{G}'D\varepsilon)$$

$$+ \phi\beta e_{2,1}E(\varepsilon'L'\Omega'\bar{V}P^{-1}\tilde{G}'D\varepsilon) + e_{2,2}\phi E(\varepsilon'L'L'K'\bar{V}P^{-1}\tilde{G}'D\varepsilon)$$

$$= \sigma_\varepsilon^2 tr(P^{-1}\bar{V}'\Omega D'\bar{G})e_{2,1} + \phi\beta tr(P^{-1}\bar{V}'\Omega LD'\bar{G})e_{2,1}$$

$$+ tr(P^{-1}\bar{V}'KL^2D'\bar{G})e_{2,2} = O(1).$$

Due to the generality of the matrices G and V one has to evaluate the expectation of 120 separate terms in order to obtain $E(\tilde{G}'\tilde{V}P^{-1}\tilde{G}'D\varepsilon)$. Those involving quadratic forms in η or in ε_0 are all $O(T^{-1})$; for practical reasons we decide to omit these. Therefore, we will not end up with a result with approximation error $o(n^{-1})$, but this error will be $O(N^{-1}T^{-3/2})$. So, we only consider the 27 terms which are all the product of two quadratic forms in ε. These are written below as compactly as possible, and next evaluated

$$E(\tilde{G}'\tilde{V}P^{-1}\tilde{G}'D\varepsilon)$$

$$= e_{2,1}E\{\varepsilon'[\Omega+\phi\beta\Omega L]'[DL\Gamma+\phi\beta DL\Gamma L]\varepsilon e_{2,1}'P^{-1}e_{2,1}\varepsilon'[\Omega+\phi\beta\Omega L]'D\varepsilon\}$$

$$+e_{2,1}E\{\varepsilon'[\Omega+\phi\beta\Omega L]'[DL\Gamma+\phi\beta DL\Gamma L]\varepsilon e_{2,1}'P^{-1}e_{2,1}\varepsilon'[\phi KLL]'D\varepsilon\}$$

$$+e_{2,1}E\{\varepsilon'[\Omega+\phi\beta\Omega L]'[\phi DL]\varepsilon e_{2,2}'P^{-1}e_{2,1}\varepsilon'[\Omega+\phi\beta\Omega L]'D\varepsilon\}$$

$$+e_{2,1}E\{\varepsilon'[\Omega+\phi\beta\Omega L]'[\phi DL]\varepsilon e_{2,2}'P^{-1}e_{2,1}\varepsilon'[\phi KLL]'D\varepsilon\}$$

$$+e_{2,1}E\{\varepsilon'[\phi KLL]'[DL\Gamma+\phi\beta DL\Gamma L]\varepsilon e_{2,1}'P^{-1}e_{2,1}\varepsilon'[\Omega+\phi\beta\Omega L]'D\varepsilon\}$$

$$+e_{2,1}E\{\varepsilon'[\phi KLL]'[DL\Gamma+\phi\beta DL\Gamma L]\varepsilon e_{2,1}'P^{-1}e_{2,1}\varepsilon'[\phi KLL]'D\varepsilon\}$$

$$+e_{2,1}E\{\varepsilon'[\phi KLL]'[\phi DL]\varepsilon e_{2,2}'P^{-1}e_{2,1}\varepsilon'[\Omega+\phi\beta\Omega L]'D\varepsilon\}$$

$$+e_{2,1}E\{\varepsilon'[\phi KLL]'[\phi DL]\varepsilon e_{2,2}'P^{-1}e_{2,1}\varepsilon'[\phi KLL]'D\varepsilon\}+O(T^{-1})$$

$$=\sigma_\varepsilon^4\{p_{1,1}tr([\Omega+\phi\beta\Omega L]'[DL\Gamma+\phi\beta DL\Gamma L][\Omega+\phi\beta\Omega L]'D)$$

$$+p_{1,1}tr([\Omega+\phi\beta\Omega L]'[DL\Gamma+\phi\beta DL\Gamma L][D'\Omega+\phi\beta D'\Omega L])$$

$$+p_{1,1}tr([\Omega+\phi\beta\Omega L]'[DL\Gamma+\phi\beta DL\Gamma L][\phi KLL]'D)$$

$$+p_{1,1}tr([\Omega+\phi\beta\Omega L]'[DL\Gamma+\phi\beta DL\Gamma L][\phi D'KLL])$$

$$+p_{1,2}tr([\Omega+\phi\beta\Omega L]'[\phi DL][\Omega+\phi\beta\Omega L]'D)$$

$$+p_{1,2}tr([\Omega+\phi\beta\Omega L]'[\phi DL][D'\Omega+\phi\beta D'\Omega L])$$

$$+p_{1,2}tr([\Omega+\phi\beta\Omega L]'[\phi DL][\phi KLL]'D)$$

$$+p_{1,2}tr([\Omega+\phi\beta\Omega L]'[\phi DL][\phi D'KLL])$$

$$+p_{1,1}tr([\phi KLL]'[DL\Gamma+\phi\beta DL\Gamma L][\Omega+\phi\beta\Omega L]'D)$$

$$+p_{1,1}tr([\phi KLL]'[DL\Gamma + \phi\beta DL\Gamma L][D'\Omega + \phi\beta D'\Omega L])$$

$$+p_{1,1}tr([\phi KLL]'[DL\Gamma + \phi\beta DL\Gamma L][\phi KLL]'D)$$

$$+p_{1,1}tr([\phi KLL]'[DL\Gamma + \phi\beta DL\Gamma L][\phi D'KLL])$$

$$+p_{1,2}tr([\phi KLL]'[\phi DL][\Omega + \phi\beta\Omega L]'D)$$

$$+p_{1,2}tr([\phi KLL]'[\phi DL][D'\Omega + \phi\beta D'\Omega L])$$

$$+p_{1,2}tr([\phi KLL]'[\phi DL][\phi KLL]'D)$$

$$+p_{1,2}tr([\phi KLL]'[\phi DL][\phi D'KLL])\}e_{2,1} + O(T^{-1})$$

$$= \sigma_\varepsilon^2 a_3^* e_{2,1} + O(T^{-1})$$

where a_3^* is the sum of all the traces given above (some of which are actually zero).

References

Anderson, T.W. and C. Hsiao (1982), "Formulation and Estimation of Dynamic Models Using Panel Data," *Journal of Econometrics*, 18: 47–82.

Arellano, M. and S.R. Bond (1991), "Some Tests of Specification for Panel Data: Monte Carlo Evidence and an Application to Employment Equations," *Review of Economic Studies*, 58: 277–297.

Balestra, P. and M. Nerlove (1966), "Pooling Cross-Section and Time-Series Data in the Estimation of a Dynamic Economic Model: The Demand for Natural Gas," *Econometrica*, 34: 585–612.

Baltagi, B. (1995), *Econometric Analysis of Panel Data*, Chichester: John Wiley & Sons.

Banerjee, A. and D.F. Hendry (eds.) (1997), *The Econometrics of Economic Policy*, Oxford: Blackwell.

Doel, I.T. van den and J.F. Kiviet (1995), "Neglected Dynamics in Panel Data Models: Consequences and Detection in Finite Samples," *Statistica Neerlandica*, 49: 343–361.

Giersbergen, N.P.A. van and J.F. Kiviet (1996), "Bootstrapping a Stable AD Model: Weak versus Strong Exogeneity," *Oxford Bulletin of Economics and Statistics*, 58: 631–656.

Kiviet, J.F. (1995), "On Bias, Inconsistency and Efficiency of Various Estimators in Dynamic Panel Data Models," *Journal of Econometrics*, 68: 53–78.

Kiviet, J.F. and G.D.A. Phillips (1993), "Alternative Bias Approximations in Regressions with a Lagged Dependent Variable," *Econometric Theory*, 9: 62–80.

(1966), "Higher-Order Asymptotic Expansions of the Least-Squares Estimation Bias in First-Order Dynamic Regression Models," Tinbergen Institute discussion paper TI 96–167/7.

Maddala, G.S. (1993), "Introduction," in G.S. Maddala (ed.), *The Econometrics of Panel Data*, vol. I, Aldershot: Edward Elgar.

Nerlove, M. (1971), "Further Evidence on the Estimation of Dynamic Economic Relations from a Time Series of Cross Sections," *Econometrica*, 39: 359–382.

Sevestre, P. and A. Trognon (1992), "Linear Dynamic Models," in L. Mátyás and P. Sevestre (eds.), *The Econometrics of Panel Data*, Dordrecht: Kluwer Academic Publishers.

9 Re-examining the rational expectations hypothesis using panel data on multi-period forecasts

ANTHONY DAVIES AND KAJAL LAHIRI

1 Introduction

In recent years the availability of relatively long panel data on expectations obtained from surveying professional forecasters has made it possible to test the validity of different expectations formations mechanisms in a scientific manner. The use of panel data enables the econometrician to decompose forecast errors into macroeconomic aggregate shocks for which forecasters should not be held responsible, and forecast specific idiosyncratic errors and biases for which they should be held accountable. Muth (1961) suggested that theories of expectation formation should be consistent with the economic model being considered, and defined expectations to be rational if they are equal to mathematical expectations conditional on the set of all information relevant for forecasting. Since the rational expectations hypothesis (REH) has wide-ranging implications for economic theory and policy, it is not surprising that several economists have used survey data on expectations in order to test REH directly.[1] Using the American Statistical Association – National Bureau of Economic Research (ASA-NBER) survey of professional forecasters, Zarnowitz (1985) has performed tests of rationality of

Earlier versions of this chapter were presented at the 5th. Biennial International Conference on Panel Data (Paris 1994), the 7th World Congress of the Econometric Society (Tokyo 1995), and at the 17th International Forecasting Symposium (Istanbul 1996). We thank G.S. Maddala, Carl Bonham, Michael Keane, Steven McNees, Hashem Pesaran, Christopher Sims, and Victor Zarnowitz for many comments and suggestions. We alone are responsible for any errors and shortcomings.

[1] Notable examples of studies which have used individual data in the US are Hirsch and Lovell (1969) using Manufacturer's Inventory and Sales Expectations surveys, Figlewski and Wachtel (1981) using Livingston's surveys, DeLeeuw and McKelvey (1984) using the Survey of Business Expenditures on Plant and Equipment data, Muth (1985) using data on some Pittsburgh plants, and Batchelor and Dua (1991) using the Blue Chip surveys. See Lahiri (1981), Visco (1984), Lovell (1986), Pesaran (1988), and Davies and Lahiri (1995) and Maddala (1990) for reviews of many of the early studies.

forecasts of inflation and other macroeconomic variables.[2] He found that the inflation forecasts did not satisfy rationality; even though many of the other forecasts were rational.[3] Keane and Runkle (1990) have argued that the inability of most researchers to accept REH is due to the use of incorrect methodology. While evaluating the ASA-NBER price forecasts, they suggest that: (1) aggregate shocks should be properly taken into account when constructing the covariance matrix of forecast errors, (2) 60-day preliminary announcements rather than yearly July revised figures should be used as the target variable, and (3) due to July revisions, only one quarter ahead forecasts should be evaluated. They found the price level forecasts to be rational, even though in a recent paper Bonham and Cohen (1995) have shown that Keane and Runkle (1990) have reached the wrong conclusion due to incorrect integration accounting.

In this chapter we develop an econometric framework to model the generating process of the forecast errors in the ASA-NBER surveys. The most important implication of the points raised by Keane and Runkle is that without an appropriate Generalized Method of Moments (GMM) estimator which takes care of the substantial covariance between individual errors due to aggregate shocks, the standard errors of the estimates of the biases in the forecast errors will be severely underestimated. We generalize their model by allowing for a more complex correlation among forecast errors made by different individuals, for different targets, and at different horizons to be expressed as a function of a few fundamental parameters. This allows for more comprehensive tests of the REH with a very general covariance structure of errors. Using our econometric framework to characterize the forecast errors, we examine the implications of the July revisions on multi-period rationality tests. More importantly, we also provide measures of aggregate shocks and their volatility, both of which are estimated prior to the series being realized.

The plan of the chapter is as follows: in section 2, we develop the econometric framework to characterize the ASA-NBER data; the structure of the covariance matrix of forecast errors is derived in section 3. In section 4, we introduce the data and present the estimates of the error components and their variances. In section 5, we examine whether the July data revisions can jeopardize the tests for multi-period rationality. Sections 6 and 7 contain tests for forecast bias and efficiency. Finally, conclusions are summarized in section 8.

[2] For a recent introduction of the ASA-NBER Survey of the Professional Forecasters, which is currently conducted and maintained by the Federal Reserve Bank of Philadelphia, see Croushore (1993). Zarnowitz and Braun (1993) contains the latest and most comprehensive analysis of the data.

[3] See also Lahiri and Teigland (1982).

2 The econometric framework

Let A_t be the actual growth rate in the target variable from the beginning of period t to the beginning of period $t+1$. For N individuals, T target years, and H forecast horizons, let F_{ith} be the forecast of A_t formed by individual i, h periods prior to the end of period t. Let the expectations data be sorted first by individual, then by target period, and lastly by horizon.[4] The forecaster who forecasts at horizon h the growth rate of the actual for period t knows A_{t-h} and a no-change forecast for A_t would be $F_{ith} = A_{t-h}$.[5] If the forecaster correctly interprets all of the information available at the end of period $t-h$, he will anticipate that the actual will change from the end of period $t-h$ to the end of period t by an amount γ_{th}. Further, his anticipated change (γ_{th}) will be, by definition, the same as that of all other forecasters who also correctly interpreted all of the available information. Thus γ_{th} is the "full information" anticipated forecast at period $t-h$ for the change in the actual from the end of period $t-h$ to the end of period t. Because we can expect errors in information collection, judgment, calculation, transcription, etc., as well as private information, we would expect that, even in the absence of individual biases, not all forecasts will be identical. Let us call these differences "idiosyncratic" errors and let ε_{ith} be individual i's idiosyncratic error associated with his forecast for target t made at horizon h.[6] Finally, let ϕ_i be individual i's overall average bias. The individual's forecast can then be expressed as

$$F_{ith} = A_{t-h} + \gamma_{th} - \phi_i - \varepsilon_{ith} \tag{1}$$

where A_{t-h}, γ_{th}, ϕ_i, and ε_{ith} are mutually independent.

Assuming rationality, and in the absence of aggregate shocks, the actual at the end of period t will be the actual at the end of period $t-h$ (A_{t-h}) plus the full information anticipated change in the actual from the end of period $t-h$ to the end of period t (γ_{th}). Let the cumulative aggregate shocks occur-

[4] This notation implies that the forecast $F_{i,t,h+k}$ is made k periods *before* the forecast F_{ith}, while the actual A_{t+k} occurs k periods *after* A_t. Note that while horizons are counted down (i.e., from H to 1) as one moves forward in time, the targets are counted up (i.e., from 1 to T). This notation preserves the concept of "horizon" as the distance between the now and the future.

[5] For example, an individual forecasting the growth rate from the beginning of period 4 to the end of period 4 at a horizon of 2 is standing at the beginning of period 3 and produces the forecast $F_{i,4,2}$. He knows the actual growth rate from the beginning of period 2 to the beginning of period 3. That is, the forecaster knows A_{4-2}. The complications resulting from delays in the processing and transmittal of official data will be dicussed later.

[6] Note that a straightforward extension of this model is to allow for horizon specific biases for each forecaster. Such an extension would require the estimation of NH–N additional parameters.

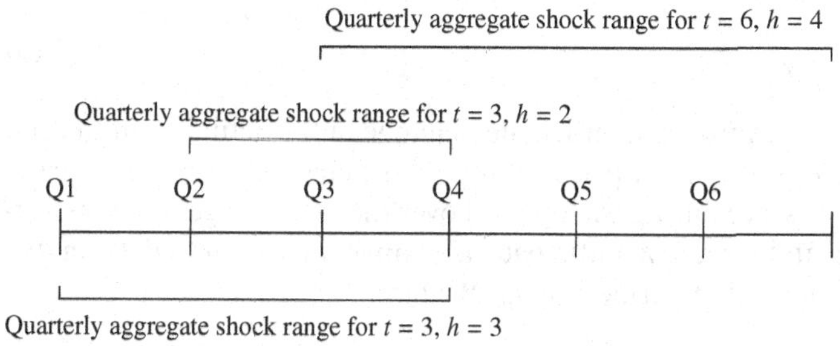

Figure 9.1 A schematic representation of the aggregate shocks

ring from the end of period $t-h$ to the end of period t be represented by λ_{th}. By definition, λ_{th} is the component of the actual which is not anticipated by any forecaster. The actual at the end of period t (A_t) is the actual h periods prior to the end of period t (A_{t-h}) plus the full information anticipated change at the end of period $t-h$ (γ_{th}) plus the aggregate shocks which occurred from the end of period $t-h$ to the end of period t (λ_{th}). We have

$$A_t = A_{t-h} + \lambda_{th} + \gamma_{th} \tag{2}$$

where A_{t-h} is predetermined with respect to λ_{th} and γ_{th}. Note that the aggregate shocks from the end of period $t-h$ to the end of period $t(\lambda_{th})$ are comprised of two components: changes in the actual that occurred but were not anticipated, and changes in the actual that were anticipated but that did not occur.

Figure 9.1 illustrates the construct of the forecasts and aggregate shocks where the horizontal line represents six quarters. Each vertical bar marks the first day of the quarter. The two upper horizontal brackets show the range over which aggregate shocks can occur that will affect the error of forecasts made for quarter 3 at a horizon of two quarters and the error of forecasts made for quarter 6 at a horizon of four quarters, respectively ($F_{i,3,2}$ and $F_{i,6,4}$). The subrange common to both ranges contains the aggregate shocks which will affect both forecasts equally ($\lambda_{3,1}$ and $\lambda_{3,2}$). The lower horizontal bracket shows the range over which shocks can occur that will affect a forecast made for quarter 3 at a horizon of three quarters ($F_{i,3,3}$). The range common to this and to the two quarter horizon forecast for target period 3 ($F_{i,3,2}$) contains aggregate shocks affecting both forecasts equally.

The cumulative aggregate shocks represented by λ_{th} can be expressed as the aggregate shocks that occurred in each period from the end of period $t-h$ to the end of period t. Let u_t be the quarterly aggregate shocks which occur from the beginning to the end of period t. We have

$$\lambda_{th} = \sum_{j=t-h+1}^{t} u_j. \tag{3}$$

We can similarly express the anticipated change in the actual from the end of period $t-h$ to the end of period t (γ_{th}) as the changes that the forecasters expect to observe during each period over the same range. Let forecasters standing at horizon h anticipate a change in the actual from the beginning to the end of period t of a_{th}. We have

$$\gamma_{th} = \sum_{j=0}^{h-1} a_{t-j,h-j}. \tag{4}$$

For example, suppose a forecaster at the beginning of period 6 expects the total change in the actual from the beginning of period 6 to the end of period 7 to be $\gamma_{7,2}$. Further, he expects some of this total change to occur in period 6 and some to occur in period 7. Thus we have

$$\gamma_{7,2} = a_{6,1} + a_{7,2} \tag{5}$$

where $a_{6,1}$ is the change the forecaster expects to occur from the beginning of period 6 to the end of period 6 and $a_{7,2}$ is the change he expects to occur from the beginning of period 7 to the end of period 7. The sum of these anticipated changes is the change in the actual that he expects to occur from the beginning of period 6 to the end of period 7.

3 Forecast errors and their covariances

Subtracting (1) from (2) yields an expression for forecast error where forecasts differ from actuals due to individual biases, cumulative aggregate shocks, and idiosyncratic errors

$$A_t - F_{ith} = \phi_i + \lambda_{th} + \varepsilon_{ith}. \tag{6}$$

A positive ϕ_i would indicate that the ith individual is persistently underestimating inflation on average over the sample period. Notice that the forecast error does not include the average anticipated change (γ_{th}). Anticipated changes which are realized appear in both the forecast and the actual and are canceled by the subtraction in (6). Anticipated changes which are not realized are so because of aggregate shocks, making them part of λ_{th}, which appear on the right-hand side of (6). A somewhat obvious formulation for testing rationality will be to expand (6) to a regression equation

$$A_t - F_{ith} = \phi_i D_i + \delta X_{ith} + e_{ith} \tag{7}$$

where D_i is the dummy for the ith individual, X_{ith} represent variables known to the forecaster at the time the forecast was made, and $e_{ith} = \varepsilon_{ith} + \lambda_{th}$. Thus the test for rationality appears to be a joint test of $\phi_i = \delta = 0$ $(i = 1, \ldots, N)$ in equation (7). Let us further assume that $E(\varepsilon^2_{ith}) = \sigma^2_{\varepsilon i}$ and $E(u^2_{th}) = \sigma^2_{u_{th}}$.[7]

It so turns out that Lovell (1986), Muth (1985), and Palm and Zellner (1992) have suggested similar frameworks to analyze survey forecasts, where a convenient formulation is to analyze the forecast error $A_t - F_{ith}$ directly as in (7). This formulation will also avoid certain complications in statistical inference in models with integrated dependent variables, see Bonham and Cohen (1995). Apart from the "actual-specific" error (λ_{th}), the composite error term (e_{ith}) also includes explicitly a "forecast-specific" measurement error term (ε_{ith}) which will be correlated with F_{ith}.[8] Note that, in the presence of ε_{ith}, the conventional rationality tests, like those in Keane and Runkle (1990), will be biased and inconsistent. The so-called implicit expectations and rational expectations hypotheses are special cases of this model when $\lambda_{th} = 0\ \forall t,h$ and $\varepsilon_{ith} = 0\ \forall\ i,t,h$, respectively.

The covariance between two typical forecast errors under REH (i.e., in (6), $\phi_i = 0\ \forall i$) can be written as

$$\mathrm{cov}(A_{t_1} - F_{i_1 t_1 h_1}, A_{t_2} - F_{i_2 t_2 h_2}) = \mathrm{cov}(\lambda_{t_1 h_1} + \varepsilon_{i_1 t_1 h_1}, \lambda_{t_2 h_2} + \varepsilon_{i_2 t_2 h_2})$$

$$= \mathrm{cov}\left(\sum_{j_1 = t_1 - h_1 + 1}^{t_1} u_{j_1} + \varepsilon_{i_1 t_1 h_1}, \sum_{j_2 = t_2 - h_2 + 1}^{t_2} u_{j_2} + \varepsilon_{i_2 t_2 h_2} \right)$$

$$= \sigma^2_{\varepsilon_1} + \sum_{j = t_{\max} - h_{\min} + 1}^{t_{\min}} \sigma^2_{u_j}\ \forall i_1 = i_2 = i,\ t_{\max} - h_{\min} + 1 < t_{\min} \tag{8}$$

$$= \sum_{j = t_{\max} - h_{\min} + 1}^{t_{\min}} \sigma^2_{u_j}\quad \forall i_1 \neq i_2,\ t_{\max} - h_{\min} + 1 < t_{\min}$$

$$= 0 \qquad \text{otherwise}$$

where $t_{\max} = \max(t_1, t_2)$, $h_{\min} = \min(h_1, h_2)$, $t_{\min} = \min(t_1, t_2)$

From (8) the $NTH \times NTH$ forecast error covariance matrix (Σ) can be written as

$$\Sigma = \begin{bmatrix} A_1 & B & B & \ldots & B & B \\ B & A_2 & B & \ldots & B & B \\ \vdots & & & & & \\ B & B & B & \ldots & B & A_N \end{bmatrix}_{NTH \times NTH} \quad \text{where } A_i = \sigma^2_{\varepsilon_i} I_{TH} + B_{TH}$$

[7] It may be interesting to explore the possibility that the idiosyncratic error variances, $E(\varepsilon^2_{ith}) = \sigma^2_{\varepsilon_i}$, are functions of forecast horizons also.

[8] Jeong and Maddala (1991, 1996) have analyzed such measurement errors in expectational survey data.

$$B=\begin{bmatrix} b_4 & c_5 & d_6 & e_7 & 0 & 0 & 0 & 0 & 0 & \dots & 0 \\ c_5' & b_5 & c_6 & d_7 & e_8 & 0 & 0 & 0 & 0 & \dots & 0 \\ d_6' & c_6' & b_6 & c_7 & d_8 & e_9 & 0 & 0 & 0 & \dots & 0 \\ e_7' & d_7' & c_7' & b_7 & c_8 & d_9 & e_{10} & 0 & 0 & \dots & 0 \\ 0 & e_8' & d_8' & c_8' & b_8 & c_9 & d_{10} & e_{11} & 0 & \dots & 0 \\ \vdots & & & & & & & & & & \\ 0 & 0 & 0 & 0 & 0 & \dots & 0 & e_{T-3}' & d_{T-3}' & c_{T-3}' & b_{T-3} \end{bmatrix}_{TH \times TH} \tag{9}$$

The matrix **B** in the (i, j) block of Σ contains the covariances of forecast errors across individuals i and j for various targets and horizons. The component matrices **b**, **c**, **d**, and **e** are all $H \times H$ matrices. The matrix $\mathbf{b}_t$ contains the covariances of forecast errors across individuals i and j for target t and various horizons. The matrix $\mathbf{c}_t$ contains the covariances of forecast errors across individuals for targets t and $t-1$ and for various horizons. Similarly, $\mathbf{d}_t$ and $\mathbf{e}_t$ contain covariances of forecast errors across individuals i and j for targets t and $t-2$ and for targets t and $t-3$, respectively.[9]

Allowing the variance of the shocks to change over time introduces possible conditional heteroskedasticity in forecast errors. The covariance between two forecast errors is the sum of the variances of the innovations common to both forecast errors.[10] For example, the aggregate shocks affecting a forecast for target 8 at a horizon of 4 are $\lambda_{8,4}$ where

$$\lambda_{8,4} = \sum_{j=8-4+1}^{8} u_j = u_5 + u_6 + u_7 + u_8. \tag{10}$$

The aggregate shocks affecting a forecast for target 9 at a horizon of 3 are $\lambda_{9,3}$ where

$$\lambda_{9,3} = \sum_{j=9-3+1}^{9} u_j = u_7 + u_8 + u_9. \tag{11}$$

The aggregate shocks common to both of these forecast errors are the source of the covariance between the forecast errors. Under the assumption of rationality, the aggregate shocks must have zero covariance, therefore the covariance of these forecast errors is

9 Because the longest forecast horizon in the ASA–NBER data set is four periods, there are no aggregate shocks common to any two forecasts made more than four periods apart. Hence, all the matrices beyond **e** are zero matrices.

10 Under the assumption of rationality, the covariance between aggregate shocks must be zero. Any persistent non-zero correlation in innovations represents information which can be exploited by forecasters. Once the forecasters incorporate the correlation in aggregate shocks into their forecasts, the correlation disappears.

$$\operatorname{cov}(\lambda_{8,4},\lambda_{9,3}) = \operatorname{cov}(u_5 + u_6 + u_7 + u_8,\ u_7 + u_8 + u_9) = \sum_{j=7}^{8} \sigma_{u_j}^2 \tag{12}$$

We have T **b** matrices down the diagonal of **B**; each shows the covariance of forecast errors for various horizons and a particular target. We can now show that the matrix $\mathbf{b}_t$ is a function of the conditionally heteroskedastic variances. Let t be the target to which the $\mathbf{b}_t$ matrix refers. We have

$$\mathbf{b}_t = \begin{bmatrix} \sum_{j=1}^{4}\sigma^2_{u_{t-4+j}} & \sum_{j=2}^{4}\sigma^2_{u_{t-4+j}} & \sum_{j=3}^{4}\sigma^2_{u_{t-4+j}} & \sum_{j=4}^{4}\sigma^2_{u_{t-4+j}} \\ \sum_{j=2}^{4}\sigma^2_{u_{t-4+j}} & \sum_{j=2}^{4}\sigma^2_{u_{t-4+j}} & \sum_{j=3}^{4}\sigma^2_{u_{t-4+j}} & \sum_{j=4}^{4}\sigma^2_{u_{t-4+j}} \\ \sum_{j=3}^{4}\sigma^2_{u_{t-4+j}} & \sum_{j=3}^{4}\sigma^2_{u_{t-4+j}} & \sum_{j=3}^{4}\sigma^2_{u_{t-4+j}} & \sum_{j=4}^{4}\sigma^2_{u_{t-4+j}} \\ \sum_{j=4}^{4}\sigma^2_{u_{t-4+j}} & \sum_{j=4}^{4}\sigma^2_{u_{t-4+j}} & \sum_{j=4}^{4}\sigma^2_{u_{t-4+j}} & \sum_{j=4}^{4}\sigma^2_{u_{t-4+j}} \end{bmatrix}_{HxH} \tag{13}$$

The matrix $\mathbf{b}_t$ takes the form shown because given two forecasts for the same target made at different horizons, both are affected by a common set of shocks. The number of innovations common to the two forecast errors is equal to the magnitude of the lesser forecast horizon. For example, a forecast made for target period 12 at a horizon of three periods is subject to news that will occur over the span from period 10 through period 12. A forecast made for the same target at a horizon of four periods is subject to the same news affecting the three period horizon forecast *plus* the news occurring in period 9. The innovations common to the two horizons are those occurring in periods 10 through 12.

The matrix $\mathbf{c}_t$ in row i column j of **B** shows the covariance of forecast errors across targets i and j for various horizons. For example, a forecast made for target period 12 at a horizon of four periods is subject to news that will occur over the span from period 9 through period 12. A forecast made for target period 13 at a horizon of two periods is subject to the innovations that occur over periods 12 and 13. The innovations common to the two forecast errors are those occurring in period 12. If we let $\mathbf{c}_t$ be the covariance matrix for targets t and $t-1$, we have

$$\mathbf{c}_t = \begin{bmatrix} \sum_{j=2}^{4}\sigma^2_{u_{t-4+j}} & \sum_{j=3}^{4}\sigma^2_{u_{t-4+j}} & \sum_{j=4}^{4}\sigma^2_{u_{t-4+j}} & 0 \\ \sum_{j=2}^{4}\sigma^2_{u_{t-4+j}} & \sum_{j=3}^{4}\sigma^2_{u_{t-4+j}} & \sum_{j=4}^{4}\sigma^2_{u_{t-4+j}} & 0 \\ \sum_{j=3}^{4}\sigma^2_{u_{t-4+j}} & \sum_{j=3}^{4}\sigma^2_{u_{t-4+j}} & \sum_{j=4}^{4}\sigma^2_{u_{t-4+j}} & 0 \\ \sum_{j=4}^{4}\sigma^2_{u_{t-4+j}} & \sum_{j=4}^{4}\sigma^2_{u_{t-4+j}} & \sum_{j=4}^{4}\sigma^2_{u_{t-4+j}} & 0 \end{bmatrix}_{HxH} \tag{14}$$

Similarly, the $\mathbf{d}_t$ and $\mathbf{e}_t$ matrices show the covariance between forecast errors for targets which are two and three periods apart, respectively. These matrices take the form

$$\mathbf{d}_t = \begin{bmatrix} \sum_{j=3}^{4}\sigma^2_{u_{t-4+j}} & \sum_{j=4}^{4}\sigma^2_{u_{t-4+j}} & 0 & 0 \\ \sum_{j=3}^{4}\sigma^2_{u_{t-4+j}} & \sum_{j=4}^{4}\sigma^2_{u_{t-4+j}} & 0 & 0 \\ \sum_{j=3}^{4}\sigma^2_{u_{t-4+j}} & \sum_{j=4}^{4}\sigma^2_{u_{t-4+j}} & 0 & 0 \\ \sum_{j=4}^{4}\sigma^2_{u_{t-4+j}} & \sum_{j=4}^{4}\sigma^2_{u_{t-4+j}} & 0 & 0 \end{bmatrix}_{HxH} \tag{15}$$

$$\mathbf{e}_t = \begin{bmatrix} \sum_{j=4}^{4} \sigma^2_{u_{t-4+j}} & 0 & 0 & 0 \\ \sum_{j=4}^{4} \sigma^2_{u_{t-4+j}} & 0 & 0 & 0 \\ \sum_{j=4}^{4} \sigma^2_{u_{t-4+j}} & 0 & 0 & 0 \\ \sum_{j=4}^{4} \sigma^2_{u_{t-4+j}} & 0 & 0 & 0 \end{bmatrix}_{HxH} \tag{16}$$

Because our model shows the sources of forecast error, we can express the entire forecast error covariance matrix as a function of the individual specific idiosyncratic variances and the time dependent variances of the quarterly aggregate shocks.

Keane and Runkle (1990) use forecasts of IPD levels from the ASA-NBER data set and estimate (17) by GMM

$$A_t = \alpha_0 + \alpha_1 F_{ith} + \alpha_2 X_{ith} + e_{ith} \tag{17}$$

where X_{ith} is information available to the ith forecaster h months prior to the end of period t. Keane and Runkle's model is a special case of our framework in which the following restrictions are imposed: homoskedasticity of forecast errors across individuals, homoskedasticity of aggregate shocks over time, homogeneity of individual biases, and only one period ahead forecast horizons. Although they describe the error covariance matrix that applies to forecast errors across multiple individuals, multiple targets, and multiple horizons, they claimed that the presence of July data revisions precludes them from using forecasts with a horizon greater than one quarter. Applying our model to their data set of only one period horizons eliminates submatrices **d** and **e** (see equations (15) and (16)) as there are no error covariances across targets when the targets are not adjacent.[11]

Confining the analysis to one quarter ahead horizons also reduces

[11] Because the ASA-NBER forecasters report their forecasts for target t by the end of the second month of quarter t-1, there is at least one month of aggregate shocks which affect both the forecasts for target t and the forecasts for target t-1. Thus the forecast errors will be correlated across adjacent targets.

sub-matrices **b** and **c** (see equations (13) and (14)) to scalars. While Keane and Runkle do not make the distinction between aggregate shocks and idiosyncratic errors, they do imply that the forecast error variances within individuals should be treated differently than the forecast error covariances across individuals. Their forecast error covariances take the form

$$\operatorname{cov}(e_{i_1 t_1 h}, e_{i_2 t_2 h}) = \begin{Bmatrix} \sigma^2_{|t_1 - t_2|} \ \forall i_1 = i_2, |t_1 - t_2| \le h \\ \delta_{|t_1 - t_2|} \ \forall i_1 \ne i_2, |t_1 - t_2| \le h \\ 0 \text{ otherwise} \end{Bmatrix} \tag{18}$$

where (18) implies that idiosyncratic error variances do exist (i.e., $\sigma_0 = \delta_0 +$ average idiosyncratic variance), that the idiosyncratic error variances are constant across individuals (i.e., $\sigma_i = \sigma \ \forall i$), and that the variance of the aggregate shocks is constant over time (i.e., $\sigma_t = \sigma \forall t$) and $\delta_t = \delta \ \forall t$). Using our notation, Keane and Runkle's assumptions restrict $\mathbf{A}_i = \mathbf{A} \ \forall i$, and $\mathbf{b}_t =$ $\mathbf{b}$ and $\mathbf{c}_t = \mathbf{c} \ \forall t$. Thus our forecast error covariance matrix (Σ) under Keane and Runkle's data restriction and assumptions becomes

$$\Sigma = \begin{bmatrix} A & B & 0 & 0 & \dots & 0 \\ B & A & B & 0 & \dots & 0 \\ \vdots \\ 0 & \dots & 0 & B & A & B \\ 0 & \dots & 0 & 0 & B & A \end{bmatrix}_{NT \times NT}$$

$$A = \begin{bmatrix} \sigma_0 & \sigma_1 & 0 & 0 & \dots & 0 \\ \sigma_1 & \sigma_0 & \sigma_1 & 0 & \dots & 0 \\ \vdots \\ 0 & \dots & 0 & \sigma_1 & \sigma_0 & \sigma_1 \\ 0 & \dots & 0 & 0 & \sigma_1 & \sigma_0 \end{bmatrix}_{T \times T} \quad B = \begin{bmatrix} \delta_0 & \delta_1 & 0 & 0 & \dots & 0 \\ \delta_1 & \delta_0 & \delta_1 & 0 & \dots & 0 \\ \vdots \\ 0 & \dots & 0 & \delta_1 & \delta_0 & \delta_1 \\ 0 & \dots & 0 & 0 & \delta_1 & \delta_0 \end{bmatrix}_{T \times T} \tag{19}$$

where σ_0 is the variance of the forecast errors for the same individual and target, σ_1 is the covariance of the forecast errors for the same individual across adjacent targets; δ_0 is the covariance of the forecast errors for the same target across different individuals; and δ_1 is the covariance of the forecast errors across different individuals and adjacent targets.

From our model formulation, we know that σ_1 represents only aggregate shock variances (idiosyncratic error variances only show up for the same individual, target, and horizon). Because they do not have an underlying model generating the forecast errors Keane and Runkle (1990) did not realize that σ_1 and δ_1 are identical and so fail to make this restriction in their error covariance matrix. Further, because they do not allow the aggregate shock variances to change over time, their elements σ and δ are *averages* of the aggregate shocks over t. If we average the aggregate shocks over t, we lose the distinction between δ_0, δ_1, and σ_1 except for the fact that δ_1 and σ_1 will be one third the size of δ_0 because the covariance across adjacent targets covers a one month span instead of an entire quarter. In short, we can interpret their equation (18) in the following way

$$\delta_0 = 3\delta_1 = 3\sigma_1 = \frac{1}{T}\sum_{t=1}^{T}\sigma_{u_t}^2$$
$$\sigma_0 = \delta_0 + \frac{1}{N}\sum_{i=1}^{N}\sigma_{\varepsilon_1}^2 = \frac{1}{T}\sum_{t=1}^{T}\sigma_{u_t}^2 + \frac{1}{N}\sum_{i=1}^{N}\sigma_{\varepsilon_i}^2 \tag{20}$$

Their data restrictions and assumptions reduce the number of error covariance matrix terms to be estimated to 4. Using our underlying model, however, we can relax the restrictions and assumptions that they impose and still need only estimate $N+T$ terms. Keane and Runkle (1990) find the ASA-NBER forecasters to be rational, but make two assumptions which might have biased their results in favor of rationality: (1) since they restrict all forecasters to have the same bias, positive biases will cancel negative biases so that even if all the individuals are biased, the average bias could be zero; (2) they restrict their data set to the forecasts which one would expect to show the least bias (one quarter ahead forecasts).

4 Data and estimates of the error components

The ASA-NBER panel forecasts a number of macroeconomic variables including the implicit price deflator (level, not growth rate), the quarterly change in business inventories, net investment, industrial production, the short-term interest rate, and nominal GDP. Each quarter the panel forecasts for the previous quarter (which has not been announced), the current quarter, and the next four consecutive quarters. In this analysis we include 89 target periods (1969:IV through 1991:IV), four forecast horizons (from four periods to one period prior to the end of each target), and 171 respondents who responded most frequently over the sample period. The number of respondents in any given period ranges from a high of 83 to a low of 9. On average, 39 individuals respond each period. To average the forecast errors, only non-missing data are considered. Because we compute the respondents' implied forecasts for period over period growth rates, we lose several additional observations.

Because ε_{ith} is white noise across all dimensions, the aggregate shocks can be extracted by first differencing (1) over h.

$$F_{i,t,h} - F_{i,t,h+1} = A_{t-h} + \gamma_{th} + \phi_i + \varepsilon_{ith} - A_{t-(h+1)} - \gamma_{t,h+1} - \phi_i - \varepsilon_{i,t,h+1}$$

and substituting (2) for A_{t-h} and $A_{t-(h+1)}$ where

$$A_{t-h} = A_t - \lambda_{th} - \gamma_{th} \text{ and } A_{t-(h+1)} = A_t - \lambda_{t,h+1} - \gamma_{t,h+1}$$

Thus, we have

$$F_{ith} - F_{i,t,h+1} = u_{th} - \varepsilon_{ith} + \varepsilon_{i,t,h+1} \tag{21}$$

Averaging $F_{ith} - F_{i,t,h+1}$ over i yields

$$\hat{u}_{th} = \frac{1}{N}\sum_{i=1}^{N}(F_{ith} - F_{i,t,h+1}) \tag{22}$$

which gives us a *TH* vector of quarterly aggregate shocks. Note that, because we calculate the aggregate shocks from the forecast revisions over horizons, the shocks are measured prior to the actual being realized, and hence are robust to data revisions. For simplicity we refer to the u_t as "quarterly aggregate shocks" although, technically, they are the consensus' *perception of the impact* of the quarterly aggregate shocks on the actual.

Because we are using forecasts for four horizons, we can obtain three observations per individual (ignoring the beginning and ending points of the data set) for every quarterly aggregate shock. For example, one can obtain a measure of the aggregate shock occurring in quarter 9 by averaging over i any of the following three differences: $F_{i,12,3} - F_{i,12,4}$, $F_{i,11,2} - F_{i,11,3}$, or $F_{i,10,1} - F_{i,10,2}$. These are then the consensus' perceptions on how the 9th quarter shock is going to affect inflation during quarters 12, 11, and 10 respectively. Although it may be interesting to examine the differences in these series in general to study the impact of news at various horizons, we found no systematic differences in the series and so treated them as three sets of observations of the same aggregate shocks.

In normal times all positive aggregate shocks can be regarded as "bad" news (i.e., an increase in inflation) and all negative aggregate shocks can be regarded as "good" news. Figure 9.2 shows a series of inflationary shocks from mid-1973 to late 1974 (the Arab oil embargo). (Note that the dates shown on the horizontal axis indicate the quarter in which the aggregate shock hit the economy.) Notice also a turbulent period of inflationary shocks in the early 1980s (when considered in light of the low economic growth of the period, this is an expectation of stagnation). No significant shock appears in the fourth quarter of 1987 (the Stock Market Crash of October 1987) presumably because the crash reversed itself before the forecasters could give their next forecast. Interestingly, in Davies and Lahiri (1995), this shock was clearly discernible because the Blue Chip surveys, which were analyzed in the study, are conducted on a monthly basis. That is, while the crash was a large negative shock, its reversal was a positive shock of similar magnitude. Because the two shocks occurred within a one quarter span of each other, they canceled each other out due to time aggregation and so neither appears on the graph.

We found the shocks to exhibit a significant first-order autocorrelation.

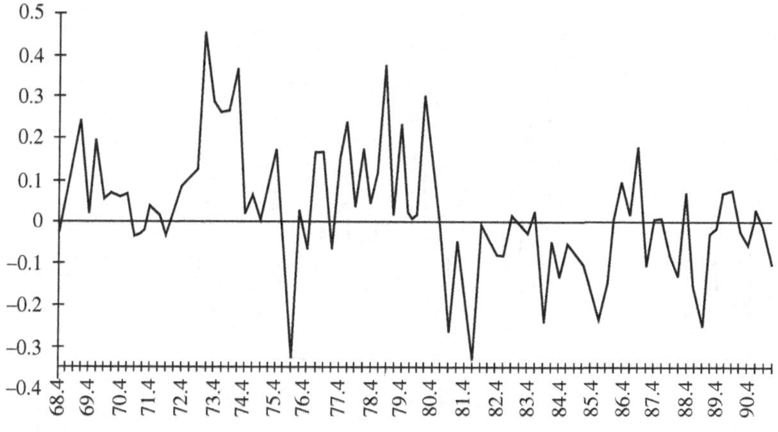

Figure 9.2 Aggregate shocks to IPD inflation

Because the individuals do not forecast at the exact same point in time (there is a range of one month over which the forecasts are made), those who forecast early will be subject to more shocks than those who forecast later. For example, an individual who forecasts at the beginning of the second month of the quarter is subject to 30 more days' worth of shocks than someone who forecasts at the beginning of the third month of the quarter. When we subtract the forecasts made at horizon $h-1$ from the forecasts made at horizon h, some of the shocks in this one month period will show up as shocks occurring at horizon h while others will show up as shocks occurring at horizon $h+1$. Because the shocks are computed by averaging this forecast revision over all individuals, the estimated shocks will exhibit serial correlation of order one even when forecasts are rational.

Estimating Σ requires estimating $N+TH$ parameters ($TH\sigma^2_{u_{th}}$'s, $t=[1,T]$, $h=[1,H]$ and $N\,\sigma^2_{\varepsilon_i}$'s, $i=[1,N]$). Averaging (6) over combinations of i, t, and h gives the following estimates

$$\frac{1}{TH}\sum_{t=1}^{T}\sum_{h=1}^{H}(A_t-F_{ith})=\hat{\phi}_i \tag{23}$$

$$\frac{1}{N}\sum_{i=1}^{N}(A_t-F_{ith}-\hat{\phi}_i)=\hat{\lambda}_{th} \tag{24}$$

$$A_t-F_{ith}-\hat{\phi}_i-\hat{\lambda}_{ith}=\hat{\varepsilon}_{ith} \tag{25}$$

Since $E(\varepsilon^2_{ith})=\sigma^2_{\varepsilon_i}$, consistent estimates of these individual specific forecast error variances can be obtained by regressing $\hat{\varepsilon}^2_{ith}$ on N individual specific dummy variables. The test for individual heterogeneity is achieved by regressing $\hat{\varepsilon}^2_{ith}$ on a constant and $N-1$ individual dummies. The resulting

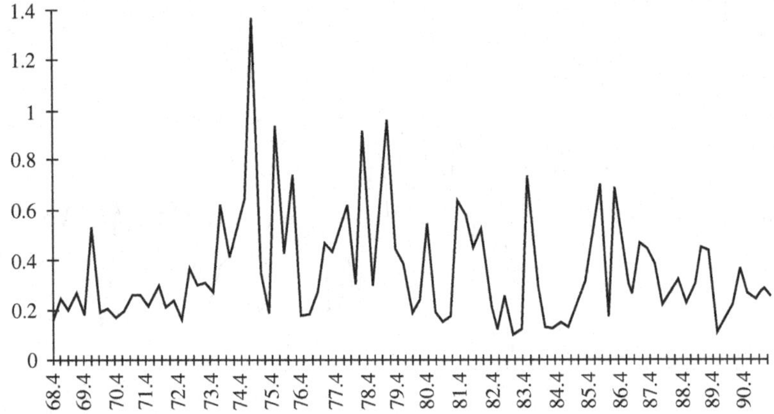

Figure 9.3 Variance of aggregate shocks to inflation

R^2 multiplied by NTH is distributed χ^2_{N-1} under the null hypothesis of $\sigma^2_{\varepsilon_i} = \sigma^2_\varepsilon\ \forall i$. The calculated statistic of 398.98 for our data set far exceeded the critical value of 7.96 at the 95 percent confidence level thus overwhelmingly rejecting the individual homogeneity hypothesis.[12] Estimates for the individual forecast error variances for IPD inflation are given in table 9.1 and show considerable variability.

Since the quarterly aggregate shocks ($\sigma^2_{u_{th}}$) are computed as the mean of $3N$ observations, we can also estimate the volatility of the quarterly aggregate shocks by calculating the variance of the forecast revision across individuals from equation (21)

$$\mathrm{var}_{th}(F_{ith} - F_{i,t,h+1}) = \sigma^2_{u_{th}} + 2\bar{\sigma}^2_\varepsilon \tag{26}$$

where $\bar{\sigma}^2_\varepsilon$ is the mean of the variances of the $\sigma^2_{\varepsilon_i}$ computed as the variance of the ε_{ith} over all i, t, and h. By computing the variance in (26) and subtracting twice the mean idiosyncratic variance ($\bar{\sigma}^2_\varepsilon$), we obtain consistent estimates of the $\sigma^2_{u_{th}}$ which are based on $3TH$ independent observations. The greater the variance of a single u_t, the greater is the volatility of the aggregate shocks hitting the economy in quarter t.[13] These are actually measures of disagreement among the respondents which tend to be highly correlated with alternative measures of volatility. Figure 9.3 shows the volatility of the aggregate shocks. Notice that the volatility was high during the mid seventies due to the Arab oil embargo and during the early eighties due to uncertainty as to the effectiveness of supply-side economics combined with the double-dip recessions starting in 1982. The important point to note is that it shows considerable variability over time.

Because the respondents in the ASA-NBER surveys forecast for one, two,

[12] Bonham and Cohen (1996) also found similar individual heterogeneity.
[13] cf. Lahiri *et al.* (1988), Rich *et al.* (1992), and Zarnowitz (1992).

Table 9.1. *Test for forecast bias (one quarter horizon forecasts versus all horizons and preliminary versus revised actuals)*

	Horizon 1 forecasts		All forecasts		
	Preliminary	July revised	Preliminary	July revised	$\sigma^2_{\varepsilon i}$
ϕ_1	0.07 (0.09)	0.06 (0.09)	0.10 (0.14)	0.08 (0.14)	0.13
ϕ_2	0.16 (0.11)	0.13 (0.11)	0.20 (0.16)	0.17 (0.16)	0.15
ϕ_3	0.09 (0.10)	0.08 (0.10)	0.05 (0.14)	0.07 (0.14)	0.14
ϕ_4	0.03 (0.10)	0.05 (0.10)	0.04 (0.14)	0.02 (0.14)	0.22
ϕ_5	0.00 (0.10)	0.04 (0.10)	−0.07 (0.15)	−0.08 (0.15)	0.14
ϕ_6	−0.06 (0.09)	−0.05 (0.09)	−0.10 (0.14)	−0.10 (0.14)	0.18
ϕ_7	0.32 (0.12)**	0.31 (0.12)*	0.37 (0.17)*	0.37 (0.17)*	0.26
ϕ_8	0.10 (0.09)	0.08 (0.09)	0.15 (0.13)	0.13 (0.13)	0.08
ϕ_9	0.30 (0.12)*	0.29 (0.11)*	0.27 (0.16)	0.26 (0.16)	0.28
ϕ_{10}	0.15 (0.11)	0.17 (0.11)	0.22 (0.17)	0.24 (0.17)	0.14
ϕ_{11}	0.01 (0.11)	−0.03 (0.10)	0.02 (0.18)	−0.01 (0.18)	0.29
ϕ_{12}	0.24 (0.11)*	0.31 (0.10)**	0.36 (0.18)*	0.35 (0.18)*	0.13
ϕ_{13}	0.09 (0.11)	0.13 (0.11)	0.05 (0.14)	0.07 (0.14)	0.09
ϕ_{14}	0.01 (0.12)	−0.03 (0.11)	−0.04 (0.19)	−0.07 (0.19)	0.27
ϕ_{15}	0.30 (0.11)**	0.23 (0.12)*	0.37 (0.17)*	0.36 (0.17)*	0.16
ϕ_{16}	0.11 (0.11)	0.10 (0.11)	0.13 (0.15)	0.13 (0.15)	0.12
ϕ_{17}	0.03 (0.11)	0.01 (0.11)	−0.03 (0.16)	−0.06 (0.16)	0.20
ϕ_{18}	−0.21 (0.13)	−0.18 (0.15)	0.20 (0.21)	0.23 (0.21)	1.11
ϕ_{19}	−0.04 (0.12)	−0.08 (0.11)	−0.22 (0.20)	−0.24 (0.20)	0.26
ϕ_{20}	0.14 (0.12)	0.18 (0.12)	0.23 (0.18)	0.23 (0.18)	0.19
ϕ_{21}	0.31 (0.12)**	0.32 (0.11)**	0.42 (0.19)*	0.43 (0.19)*	0.18
ϕ_{22}	0.09 (0.12)	0.03 (0.11)	0.10 (0.16)	0.07 (0.16)	0.14
ϕ_{23}	0.04 (0.12)	0.14 (0.11)	0.16 (0.16)	0.15 (0.16)	0.12
ϕ_{24}	0.31 (0.13)*	0.38 (0.12)**	0.41 (0.17)*	0.38 (0.17)*	0.11
ϕ_{25}	0.17 (0.12)	0.21 (0.11)	0.28 (0.17)	0.30 (0.17)	0.20
ϕ_{26}	0.03 (0.13)	0.08 (0.11)	0.12 (0.18)	0.13 (0.18)	0.12
ϕ_{27}	0.17 (0.12)	0.13 (0.12)	0.18 (0.18)	0.15 (0.18)	0.17
ϕ_{28}	0.38 (0.12)**	0.32 (0.12)*	0.40 (0.18)*	0.38 (0.18)*	0.16
ϕ_{29}	0.33 (0.14)*	0.30 (0.15)*	0.41 (0.20)*	0.39 (0.20)*	0.30
ϕ_{30}	0.30 (0.13)*	0.27 (0.14)	0.27 (0.19)	0.25 (0.19)	0.16
ϕ_{31}	0.29 (0.15)	0.32 (0.15)*	0.41 (0.21)*	0.45 (0.21)*	0.18
ϕ_{32}	0.32 (0.14)*	0.28 (0.14)*	0.40 (0.19)*	0.40 (0.19)*	0.40
ϕ_{33}	−0.05 (0.14)	−0.09 (0.15)	0.02 (0.17)	0.00 (0.17)	0.19
ϕ_{34}	0.01 (0.12)	0.02 (0.12)	0.17 (0.19)	0.21 (0.19)	0.13
ϕ_{35}	0.23 (0.13)	0.22 (0.13)	0.40 (0.20)*	0.42 (0.20)*	0.51
ϕ_{36}	0.23 (0.15)	0.20 (0.14)	0.22 (0.17)	0.18 (0.17)	0.23
ϕ_{37}	0.23 (0.16)	0.25 (0.16)	0.16 (0.19)	0.17 (0.19)	0.27
ϕ_{38}	0.10 (0.12)	0.15 (0.12)	0.22 (0.18)	0.25 (0.18)	0.12
ϕ_{39}	0.43 (0.13)**	0.41 (0.13)**	0.55 (0.19)**	0.54 (0.19)**	0.19
ϕ_{40}	−0.09 (0.16)	−0.04 (0.16)	−0.00 (0.18)	0.00 (0.18)	0.21
ϕ_{41}	0.14 (0.13)	0.12 (0.13)	0.19 (0.18)	0.18 (0.18)	0.16
ϕ_{42}	0.40 (0.13)**	0.34 (0.15)*	0.43 (0.18)*	0.43 (0.18)*	0.20
ϕ_{43}	0.09 (0.17)	0.17 (0.16)	0.16 (0.21)	0.22 (0.21)	0.14
ϕ_{44}	−0.16 (0.13)	−0.16 (0.13)	−0.18 (0.21)	−0.17 (0.21)	0.60
ϕ_{45}	0.03 (0.16)	−0.04 (0.17)	−0.02 (0.21)	−0.04 (0.21)	0.37

Notes:
Numbers in parentheses are standard errors.
* Significant at 5% level. ** Significant at 1% level.

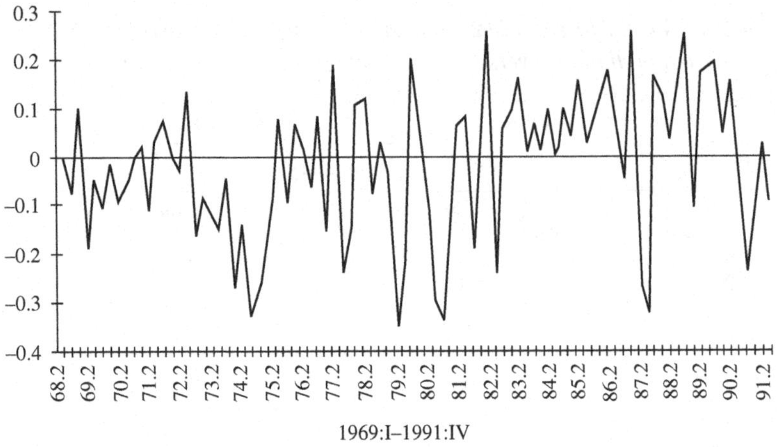

Figure 9.4 Anticipated change in IPD inflation

three, and four quarters ahead *every quarter*, we can deduce from their forecasts implied changes in the actual that they expected to see over those specific future quarters. We call these "anticipated changes," and they include such things as expected trends and cyclical movements. We can estimate the anticipated changes by taking the following first difference of (1) over t and h

$$\begin{aligned} F_{ith} - F_{i,t-1,h+1} &= \gamma_{th} - \gamma_{t-1,h+1} - \varepsilon_{ith} + \varepsilon_{i,t-1,h+1} \\ &= a_{th} - \varepsilon_{ith} + \varepsilon_{i,t-1,h+1} \end{aligned} \tag{27}$$

By averaging (27) over i, we can obtain estimates of the changes anticipated for quarter t at horizon h, $\hat{a}_{th}$. Figure 9.4 shows the anticipated quarterly changes in IPD inflation at two quarters in the future, i.e., it shows the anticipation at the beginning of quarter t of the change in actual from the beginning to the end of quarter $t+2$. The graphs of anticipated changes for longer horizons looked similar but increasingly muted. This is because at longer horizons the forecasters are apt to be less sure of the changes. This was evidenced by the fact that the variance of a_{th} over individuals became significantly more volatile as the horizon increased from 2 to 4.

5 Preliminary versus revised data

There has been much discussion concerning the degree of data revision in actuals. Keane and Runkle (1990) argue that the July data revisions for IPD have been systematic and were consistently positive. They claim that when this revision occurs between the time a forecast is made and the time the actual is realized, the forecast will falsely test negative for rationality. Because the IPD level in any period is dependent on the IPD level in the previous period, when the previous period's IPD level is revised *after* a forecast is made, it will appear that the forecaster based his forecast on a different information set than he actually used. For example, if the forecaster thinks that IPD at time t is 100 and he believes inflation will be 5 percent between time t and time $t+2$, he will report a forecast for period $t+2$ IPD of 105. Suppose that at time $t+1$ data revisions are made which show that the true IPD at time t was 101, not 100. Suppose further that the forecaster was correct in that inflation was 5 percent from time t to time $t+2$. Given the data revision, the IPD reported at time $t+2$ will be 106.05, not 105. That is, the forecaster was correct in believing inflation would be 5 percent, but his *level* forecast was incorrect due to the revision of the time t IPD.

This data revision problem would not cause rationality tests to yield biased results if the data revisions were white noise. They claim, however, that the July data revisions have been systematic.[14] We argue that if there is any systematic component to the data revisions, the rational forecaster will incorporate the component into his forecast. The non-systematic component, by definition, will resemble white noise and will not affect the rationality test. The July data revisions are then nothing more than aggregate shocks which occur every July. To the extent that the revisions would be systematic, that systematic component represents information which could be exploited by the forecasters and for which the forecasters should be held responsible. To the extent that the revisions would not be systematic, that non-systematic component represents an aggregate shock to the actual for which our model accounts along with all other aggregate shocks occurring in that period.[15]

To avoid the supposed data revision problem, Keane and Runkle (1990) compare IPD forecasts extending no more than one quarter into the future (i.e., horizon one forecasts) to the preliminary data released 45 days after the end of the quarter. In this way, they claim that their forecasts and their actuals do not fall on opposite sides of the July revisions. Needless to say, this restriction dramatically limits their data set.

We use anticipated changes (a_{th}) and aggregate shocks (u_j) to test if the forecasters do anticipate systematic data revisions and incorporate these anticipations into their forecasts. To compare our results with Keane and Runkle's, we use both level data and growth rates. Figure 9.5 shows the effect of the July revision on changes anticipated at one, two, and three quarter horizons, i.e. ($a_{t,1}, a_{t,2}, a_{t,3}\ \forall\ t$). It shows two years marked off in quarters and

[14] In support of this claim, Keane and Runkle (1990, p. 723) plot benchmark revised data against preliminary IPD data and find a significant and systematic difference. The appropriate comparison of July revised versus preliminary IPD series exhibits no such systematic difference.

[15] Mankiw and Shapiro (1986) examine the size and nature of data revisions in the growth rate of GDP (real and nominal). They find that the data revisions are better characterized as news than as forecasters' measurement errors. We find that the aggregate shocks that occur in July are not significantly different from the aggregate shocks that occur in any other month (see figure 9.2). That is, whatever the portion of the shock that is represented by the data revision, it is drowned out by other shocks that have nothing to do with the data revision.

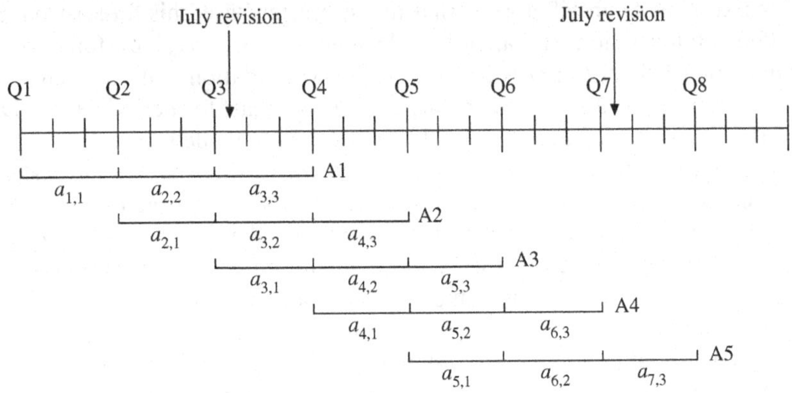

Figure 9.5 A schematic representation of the effect of data revision

months and the times at which July revisions are made. The set of brackets marked A1 show the ranges over which changes are anticipated at quarter 1 to occur for quarters 1, 2, and 3. The set of brackets marked A2 show the ranges over which changes are anticipated at quarter 2.

According to Keane and Runkle, data revisions introduce bias when the revision occurs after a forecast is made but before the target is realized. Of all the anticipated changes, only changes anticipated for the third quarter of a year are affected by July revisions. To see this, let us suppose that a forecaster is forecasting at the end of quarter 1. The difference between the forecaster's forecast for IPD for the end of quarter 1 and IPD for the end of quarter 2 is the forecaster's anticipated change in IPD for quarter 2. Because a July revision does not occur in this interval, July revisions do not affect changes anticipated for second quarters. The difference between the forecaster's forecast for IPD for the end of quarter 3 and IPD for the end of quarter 4 is the forecaster's anticipated change in IPD for quarter 4. Because a July revision occurs between the time the forecaster made his forecast (the end of quarter 1) and the time the actual was realized (the end of quarter 4), the July revision does affect the forecasts for quarters 3 and 4. The July revision does not, however, affect the anticipated change from quarter 3 to 4 because the subtraction of the forecasts to obtain the anticipated change eliminates the effect of the revision. The difference between a forecaster's forecast for IPD for the end of quarter 2 and IPD for the end of quarter 3 is the forecaster's anticipated change in IPD for quarter 3. Because a July revision occurs between the time the forecaster made his forecast for quarter 3 (the end of quarter 1) and the time the actual was realized (the end of quarter 3), the July revision does affect the forecast for quarter 3. However, the July revision does not occur between the time the forecaster made his forecast for quarter 2 and the time the actual was realized. Because of this, the subtraction which yields the anticipated change in IPD for quarter 3 will be affected by the July revision. Thus, the only anticipated change the July revision affects is the change anticipated for quarter 3.

If the forecasters do anticipate the July data revisions and incorporate these revisions into their forecasts, then the anticipated changes for the third quarters should be different than the anticipated changes for the other quarters. To test for the forecasters' anticipation of the data revisions, we regress the anticipated changes on a constant and a dummy which is one if the anticipated change was for the third quarter of the year, zero otherwise. We run this regression for all the anticipated changes ($a_{t,2}$, $a_{t,3}$, and $a_{t,4}$) pooled together (see table 9.3). Results are shown using anticipated changes derived from forecasted levels and anticipated changes derived from forecasted growth rates. We also regress the aggregate shocks on a dummy which is one if the aggregate shock occurred in the third quarter to test if the July revisions show up as a component of the third quarter aggregate shocks (see table 9.3). Results are shown using aggregate shocks derived from forecasted levels and aggregate shocks derived from forecasted growth rates.

These tests show that the only thing affected by the July revisions is the third quarter aggregate shocks derived from the forecasted levels. Under rationality, we would expect that systematic July revisions would be expected and would show up as a component of the third quarter anticipated changes; however, no anticipated changes (neither those based on levels nor those based on growth rates) are significantly affected by the July revisions. Rather, the aggregate shocks derived from the forecasted levels do show a significant effect from the July revisions indicating that the forecasters failed to incorporate into their forecasts a systematic data revision that, under rationality, they should have anticipated. The aggregate shocks derived from the forecasted growth rates, however, are not significantly affected by the July data revisions indicating that whatever systematic revision occurred was incorporated into the forecasted growth rates. Under rationality, we must conclude that the forecasters do not forecast in terms of levels but in terms of growth rates and convert these growth rate forecasts to levels for the purpose of reporting to the ASA-NBER surveys. As the July revisions do not significantly affect the third quarter aggregate shocks derived from the forecasted inflation rates, we can also conclude that the July data revisions do not introduce any systematic bias in multi-period rationality tests when one works with inflation (rather than price level) forecasts.

6 GMM tests for bias

For the purpose of GMM estimation we use the 45 forecasters who report more than 50 percent of the time. The total number of observations present is 7,449 out of a possible 16,020. Because we compute the forecasters' implied forecast for period over period growth rates, we lose several more observations.

Thus we have an incomplete panel with over 50 percent of the entries missing. In order to estimate a relationship with OLS or GMM the data and covariance matrices have to be appropriately *compressed.* To compress the data matrix, we delete every row of the matrix containing a missing observation. To compress the covariance matrix, we delete every row and column corresponding to a missing observation in the data matrix. The compressed matrices can then be directly used in OLS or GMM estimations.[16] All our variance estimations also account for the fact that N varies over the sample.[17]

The error covariance structure shown in (8) is constructed on the assumption that forecasts are made on the first day of the period. In actuality, the ASA-NBER forecasters make their forecasts anywhere from one month to two months prior to the beginning of the period. We adjust the error covariance matrices based on the simplifying assumption that the individuals make their forecasts one month prior to the beginning of the period.

This means that forecast errors associated with horizon h are also subject to the last month's worth of unanticipated shocks from horizon $h+1$. For simplicity, let us measure the aggregate shocks as if they occurred monthly instead of quarterly where each monthly shock occurring in a period is estimated as one-third of the shocks occurring over the whole period.[18] Accounting for the exact time that the forecasts are made changes the submatrices in (13)–(16) to

$$b_t = \begin{bmatrix} \sum_{j=0}^{12}\sigma^2_{u_{3(t-1)+j}} & \sum_{j=3}^{12}\sigma^2_{u_{3(t-1)+j}} & \sum_{j=6}^{12}\sigma^2_{u_{3(t-1)+j}} & \sum_{j=9}^{12}\sigma^2_{u_{3(t-1)+j}} \\ \sum_{j=3}^{12}\sigma^2_{u_{3(t-1)+j}} & \sum_{j=3}^{12}\sigma^2_{u_{3(t-1)+j}} & \sum_{j=6}^{12}\sigma^2_{u_{3(t-1)+j}} & \sum_{j=9}^{12}\sigma^2_{u_{3(t-1)+j}} \\ \sum_{j=6}^{12}\sigma^2_{u_{3(t-1)+j}} & \sum_{j=6}^{12}\sigma^2_{u_{3(t-1)+j}} & \sum_{j=6}^{12}\sigma^2_{u_{3(t-1)+j}} & \sum_{j=9}^{12}\sigma^2_{u_{3(t-1)+j}} \\ \sum_{j=9}^{12}\sigma^2_{u_{3(t-1)+j}} & \sum_{j=9}^{12}\sigma^2_{u_{3(t-1)+j}} & \sum_{j=9}^{12}\sigma^2_{u_{3(t-1)+j}} & \sum_{j=9}^{12}\sigma^2_{u_{3(t-1)+j}} \end{bmatrix}_{HxH} \tag{28}$$

16 cf. Blundell *et al.* (1992).

17 All calculations reported were done using two sets of actuals: preliminary data (released one month after the end of the target period), and revised data (released in the first July following the end of the period) – the differences in the results were negligible. Zarnowitz (1992) has also obtained similar results.

18 Instead of being indexed from 1 to T, the u_t will now be indexed from 1 to 3T. One extra observation, u_0, will also be needed.

$$c_t = \begin{bmatrix} \sum_{j=3}^{12}\sigma^2_{u3(t-1)+j} & \sum_{j=6}^{12}\sigma^2_{u3(t-1)+j} & \sum_{j=9}^{12}\sigma^2_{u3(t-1)+j} & 0 \\ \sum_{j=3}^{12}\sigma^2_{u3(t-1)+j} & \sum_{j=6}^{12}\sigma^2_{u3(t-1)+j} & \sum_{j=9}^{12}\sigma^2_{u3(t-1)+j} & 0 \\ \sum_{j=6}^{12}\sigma^2_{u3(t-1)+j} & \sum_{j=6}^{12}\sigma^2_{u3(t-1)+j} & \sum_{j=9}^{12}\sigma^2_{u3(t-1)+j} & 0 \\ \sum_{j=9}^{12}\sigma^2_{u3(t-1)+j} & \sum_{j=9}^{12}\sigma^2_{u3(t-1)+j} & \sum_{j=9}^{12}\sigma^2_{u3(t-1)+j} & 0 \end{bmatrix}_{HxH} \quad (29)$$

$$d_t = \begin{bmatrix} \sum_{j=6}^{12}\sigma^2_{u3(t-1)+j} & \sum_{j=9}^{12}\sigma^2_{u3(t-1)+j} & 0 & 0 \\ \sum_{j=6}^{12}\sigma^2_{u3(t-1)+j} & \sum_{j=9}^{12}\sigma^2_{u3(t-1)+j} & 0 & 0 \\ \sum_{j=6}^{12}\sigma^2_{u3(t-1)+j} & \sum_{j=9}^{12}\sigma^2_{u3(t-1)+j} & 0 & 0 \\ \sum_{j=9}^{12}\sigma^2_{u3(t-1)+j} & \sum_{j=9}^{12}\sigma^2_{u3(t-1)+j} & 0 & 0 \end{bmatrix}_{HxH} \quad (30)$$

$$e_t = \begin{bmatrix} \sum_{j=9}^{12} \sigma^2_{u_{3(t-1)+j}} & 0 & 0 & 0 \\ \sum_{j=9}^{12} \sigma^2_{u_{3(t-1)+j}} & 0 & 0 & 0 \\ \sum_{j=9}^{12} \sigma^2_{u_{3(t-1)+j}} & 0 & 0 & 0 \\ \sum_{j=9}^{12} \sigma^2_{u_{3(t-1)+j}} & 0 & 0 & 0 \end{bmatrix}_{HxH} \qquad (31)$$

With estimates of $\sigma^2_{u_{th}}$ and $\sigma^2_{\varepsilon_i}$ we construct the error covariance matrix (Σ) and perform GMM (cf. Hansen (1982)) on equation (7) using dummy variables to estimate the ϕ_i's. The estimates we get for the ϕ_i are identical to those obtained through the simple averaging in equation (23); it is the GMM standard errors that we seek.

To obtain a better comparison with Keane and Runkle's (1990) results in which they restrict the ASA-NBER forecasts to one quarter ahead horizons and use preliminary actuals, we show the results of applying GMM rationality tests to our model for all forecast horizons pooled together and for horizon one forecasts only under both preliminary and July revised actuals. The first four columns of table 9.1 show the bias for each forecaster under preliminary and July revised actuals when the data set is restricted to horizon one forecasts only. The last four columns show the bias for each forecaster under preliminary and July revised actuals when all four horizons are pooled together. Of 45 forecasters, all four tests show the same 12 forecasters to have a significant bias at the 5 percent level. In addition, the results show that (1) there is strong heterogeneity across individuals, (2) the vast majority of the forecasters exhibit a greater bias for all horizons pooled together than for horizon one forecasts alone (under both preliminary and July revised actuals), (3) the standard errors of the estimated biases are similar under preliminary and revised data and are greater under pooled horizons than under horizon one alone. In addition, table 9.1 shows significant differences in the idiosyncratic error variances across individuals. Note that a large proportion of respondents are making systematic and fairly sizeable errors whereas others are not. In terms of the root mean square error of forecasts (RMSE), the performance of the forecasters varied quite widely. Over this period, the worst forecaster in

Table 9.2. *Martingale efficiency tests (pooled forecast revisions regressed on various past information)*

$$F_{ith} - F_{i,t,h+1} = \alpha + \beta\,(A_{t,h+2} - A_{t,h+3})$$

α	0.0348	(0.0062)**
β	0.0407	(0.0111)**
$\bar{R}^2$	0.0029	

The regressor is the two-period lagged change in quarterly IPD growth.

$$F_{ith} - F_{i,t,h+1} = \alpha + \beta\,(F_{i,t,h+2} - F_{i,t,h+3})$$

α	0.0273	(0.0061)**
β	0.2045	(0.0151)**
$\bar{R}^2$	0.0416	

The regressor is the two-period lagged forecast revision.

$$F_{ith} - F_{i,t,h+1} = \alpha + \beta\,(\bar{F}_{t,h+2} - F_{i,t,h+2})$$

α	0.0243	(0.0062)**
β	0.6735	(0.0199)**
$\bar{R}^2$	0.2836	

The regressor is the two-period lagged deviation from the consensus.

Notes:
Numbers in parentheses are standard errors.
* Significant at 5% level.
** Significant at 1% level.

the panel had a RMSE of 1.73 compared to the best forecaster whose RMSE was only 0.53. Thus, as Batchelor and Dua (1991) have pointed out, the inefficiencies of these forecasters cannot be attributed to such factors as peso problems, learning due to regime shifts, lack of market incentives, etc.

7 Martingale test for efficiency

The standard tests of the REH check for zero correlation between the forecast errors and the variables in the information set that were known to the forecaster at the time the forecast was made. That is, in the regression

$$A_t - F_{ith} = \delta X_{t,h+1} + \phi_i + \lambda_{th} + \varepsilon_{ith} \qquad (32)$$

where $X_{t,h+1}$ is information known to the forecaster at the time the forecast was made, the result $\hat{\delta} \neq 0$ rejects the hypothesis of efficiency.[19] This is the so-called efficiency test.

[19] Note that because the horizon index *declines* as one moves forward in time, a variable indexed $h+1$ is realized one period *before* a variable indexed h.

However, since $X_{t,h+1}$ is predetermined but not strictly exogenous, the use of individual dummies will make OLS estimation inconsistent, see Lahiri (1993). Since past innovations can affect future X_{th}'s, the error and the regressor in the demeaned regression will be cotemporaneously correlated.[20] Looking for a legitimate instrument in this case is a hopeless endeavor since one has to go beyond the sample period to find one.

The optimal solution is to apply GMM to the first-difference transformation of (32)[21]

$$F_{ith} - F_{i,t,h+1} = \delta(X_{t,h+1} - X_{t,h+2}) + u_{t,h+1} - \varepsilon_{ith} + \varepsilon_{i,t,h+1} \tag{33}$$

With the ASA-NBER data set, since A_t is the same over h, the first-difference transformation gives us the martingale condition put forth by Batchelor and Dua (1991). This condition requires that revisions to the forecasts be uncorrelated with variables known at the time of the earlier forecast. We perform three sets of martingale tests using the following proxies for $X_{t,h+1} - X_{t,h+2}$. (1) the change in the growth rate of IPD lagged two periods, (2) the change in each individual's forecast lagged two periods, and (3) the deviation of each individual's forecast from the consensus (mean forecast) lagged two periods. We use each of the three sets of information in both pooled and individual regressions.

The ASA-NBER forecasters receive their questionnaires near the end of the first month of each quarter and respond by the end of the second month of that quarter. We use the first available actuals in the martingale tests which are released one month after the end of each quarter. Thus the one quarter lagged change in the actual is known to the forecasters at the time they make their forecasts. For example, consider the forecasts for target four made at horizons one and two. The forecast revision $(F_{i4,1} - F_{i4,2})$ is realized no earlier than August 1. The earlier of the two forecasts is made no earlier than May 1. The actual $A_{4,4}$ is the actual for the quarter that begins four quarters before the end of quarter four (i.e., $A_{4,4}$ is the actual for quarter one). This actual is known by May 1 (one month after the end of quarter one). The actual $A_{4,5}$ is the actual for the quarter that begins five quarters before the end of quarter four (i.e., $A_{4,5}$ is the actual for quarter four of the previous year). This actual is known by February 1. The difference in the actuals $(A_{4,4,} - A_{4,5})$ is known at the time that the forecast $F_{i4,2}$ is made. Thus regressing $F_{i,t,h} - F_{i,t,h+1}$ on $F_{t,h+2} - F_{t,h+3}$ is a legitimate martingale test for forecast efficiency. Table 9.2 shows that for IPD, the change in the quarterly growth rate of IPD lagged two quarters significantly explains the forecast revision for the 45 forecasters pooled together at a 5 percent level of significance.

20 Note that irrespective of the individual dummies, for the same basic reason, the inconsistency will arise even with a constant term, cf. Goodfriend (1992). Thus, the conventional efficiency tests as reported by Keane and Runkle (1990) are not strictly valid.

21 cf. Schmidt *et al.* (1992) and Lahiri (1993).

Table 9.3. *Effect of July data revisions on aggregate shocks and anticipated changes (levels and growth rates)*

	$a_{t,h} = \alpha + \beta D1_t$	$u_t = \alpha + \beta D2_t$
Price level forecasts		
α	2.0041 (0.0303)**	−2.5540 (0.3107)**
β	0.0572 (0.0622)	3.0260 (0.6221)**
Inflation rate forecasts		
α	−0.0319 (0.0270)	0.0235 (0.0112)*
β	0.0210 (0.0556)	−0.0076 (0.0225)

where $D1_t = 1$ if forecast was made in the third quarter $D1_t = 0$ otherwise; $D2_t = 1$ if the aggregate shock occurred in the third quarter $D2_t = 0$ otherwise.

Notes:
Numbers in parentheses are standard errors.
* Significant at 5% level.
** Significant at 1% level.

Table 9.2 also shows the results of the martingale test using the two period lagged forecast revision $(F_{i,t,h+2} - F_{i,t,h+3})$ as the exogenous regressor for all the forecasters pooled together. This test indicates that the two period lagged forecast revision significantly explains the current forecast revision and thus this test rejects rationality for the forecasters as a whole. Further, the results indicate that the nature of the irrationality is a failure to fully adjust forecasts to news as the coefficients of the two period lagged forecast revisions are positive. The results of the martingale test using the forecasters' two period lagged deviation from the consensus $(\bar{F}_{t,h+2} - F_{i,t,h+2})$ as the exogenous regressor is given in the lowest panel of table 9.2. We calculate $\bar{F}_{th}$ as the mean of the reported forecasts for target t, horizon h. The difference $\bar{F}_{th} - F_{ith}$ is forecaster i's deviation from the consensus forecast for target t, horizon h. We find that the deviation from the consensus forecast lagged two periods significantly explains the forecast revision and thus this test rejects efficiency for the forecasters as a whole. Further, the results indicate that the nature of the irrationality is a failure to fully adjust forecasts based on information contained in the consensus. These results are consistent with those of Bonham and Cohen (1995) who have shown that Keane and Runkle's failure to reject the efficiency tests using either oil prices or M1 as information-set variables are flawed because of incorrect integration accounting.

We have also conducted these efficiency tests for each forecaster individually, and found that many of them failed the efficiency test. Not all of the forecasters who showed bias failed the tests of efficiency; similarly not all of those who failed the test of efficiency showed a significant bias. Because rationality requires both unbiasedness and efficiency, a forecaster who fails either is considered irrational. The total number of forecasters who failed one or more of the bias and efficiency tests is thirty. Thus, based on the bias and martingale tests, we overwhelmingly reject the hypothesis that the ASA-NBER panel as a whole has been rational in predicting IPD over 1968:IV–1991:IV. Individually, more than 70 percent of the forecasters fail to meet the rationality criteria in the sense of Muth (1961).

8 Conclusion

While summarizing over 20 years of empirical work on various expectational survey data sets, Maddala (1990) asked, "What have we learned?", and concluded that "possibly too much attention has been devoted to tests of rationality and not too much to the question of how survey data can be used effectively in econometric modeling." Pursuing this line of thought we argue that the full potential of panel data of survey forecasts can not be harnessed unless we develop the econometric model that is presumably generating the forecast errors. In Davies and Lahiri (1995), we developed such a framework and applied it to the study of the Blue Chip forecasts. In this chapter we have extended the econometric model to study the ASA-NBER professional forecasts. The advantage of this data set over the Blue Chip data is that in the ASA-NBER survey, individuals forecast for multiple targets at *each* horizon, (i.e., at any given point in time, the individuals are making four forecasts as opposed to one forecast for the Blue Chip data set). Forecasts for multiple targets at each point in time provide additional information with which we can calculate anticipated changes. In addition, these data enable us to estimate aggregate shocks and their volatility independent of data revisions and, more importantly, prior to the availability of the actual data series. With these measures, we empirically examined whether the July data revisions render multi-period survey forecasts unusable for testing rationality. In terms of level forecasts, the regression results support the Keane–Runkle point that the systematic July revisions are not anticipated, and appear as part of the aggregate shocks. In terms of inflation forecasts, however, we find that the July revisions are neither anticipated nor significant in explaining aggregate shocks. Thus, the July revisions are not an issue in evaluating multi-period forecast efficiency provided the inflation (rather than price level) forecasts are analyzed.

We show that the seemingly complex covariance structure of forecast errors made by different individuals, for different targets, and at different horizons can be represented in terms of a few fundamental parameters (*viz.* the variances of the aggregate shocks) which allows for a more comprehensive test for the rational expectations hypothesis. This covariance matrix is used in a GMM framework to test for forecast bias under individual heterogeneity. The efficiency criterion was studied by directly testing the martingale property of forecast revisions. Employing a wide battery of tests, we find that a substantial number of ASA-NBER forecasters do not fulfill the twin criteria of unbiasedness and efficiency of the rational expectations hypothesis in predicting inflation.

References

Batchelor, R. and P. Dua (1991), "Blue Chip Rationality Tests," *Journal of Money, Credit, and Banking*, 23: 692–705.

Blundell, R., S. Bond, M. Devereux, and F. Schiantarelli (1992), "Investment and Tobin's Q: Evidence from Company Panel Data," *Journal of Econometrics*, 51: 233–257.

Bonham, C.S. and R. Cohen (1995), "Testing the Rationality of Price Forecasts: Comment," *American Economic Review*, 85: 284–289.

Bonham, C.S. and R. Cohen (1996), "Heterogeneous Expectations: Aggregation Bias and the Poolability of Survey Forecasts in Tests of the Rational Expectations Hypothesis," paper presented at Conference on Expectations in Economics: In Honor of the 50th Anniversary of the Livingston Survey, Federal Reserve Bank of Philadelphia, October.

Croushore, D. (1993), "Introducing: The Survey of Professional Forecasters," *Business Review*, Federal Reserve Bank of Philadelphia, Nov/ Dec, 3–15.

Davies, A. and K. Lahiri (1995), "A New Framework for Analyzing Survey Forecasts Using Three-Dimensional Panel Data," *Journal of Econometrics*, 68: 205–227.

DeLeeuw, F. and M.J. McKelvey (1984), "Price Expectations of Business Firms," *American Economic Review*, 74: 99–110.

Figlewski, S.F. and P. Wachtel (1981), "The Formation of Inflationary Expectations," *Review of Economics and Statistics*, 63: 1–10.

Goodfriend, M. (1992), "Information Aggregation Bias," *American Economic Review*, 82: 508–519.

Hansen, L. P. (1982), "Large Sample Properties of Generalized Method of Moments Estimators," *Econometrica*, 50: 1019–1054.

Hirsch, A.A. and M.C. Lovell (1969), *Sales Anticipations and Inventory Behavior*, New York: Wiley and Sons.

Jeong, J. and G.S. Maddala (1991), "Measurement Errors and Tests for Rationality," *Journal of Business and Economic Statistics*, 9: 431–439.

(1996), "Testing the Rationality of Survey Data Using the Weighted Double-Bootstrapped Method of Moments," *Review of Economics and Statistics*, 78: 296–302

Keane, M.P. and D.E. Runkle (1990), "Testing the Rationality of Price Forecasts: New Evidence From Panel Data," *American Economic Review*, 80: 714–735.

Lahiri, K. (1981), *The Econometrics of Inflationary Expectations*, Amsterdam: North-Holland.

(1993), "Panel Data Models with Rational Expectations," *Handbook of Statistics, vol.11: Econometrics*, in G.S. Maddala, C.R. Rao, and H.D. Vinod (eds.), Amsterdam: North-Holland.

Lahiri, K. and C. Teigland (1982), "On the Rationality of ASA-NBER Survey Data on Expectations," *Proceedings of the 1982 Annual Meeting of the American Statistical Association*, Business and Economic Statistics Section, ASA, Washington DC, pp. 448–453.

Lahiri, K., C. Teigland, and M. Zaprowski (1988), "Interest Rates and the Subjective Probability Distribution of Forecasts," *Journal of Money, Credit, and Banking*, 20: 233–248.

Lovell, M.C. (1986), "Tests of the Rational Expectations Hypothesis," *American Economic Review*, 79: 110–124.

Maddala, G.S. (1990), "Survey Data on Expectations: What Have We Learnt?" in M. Nerlove (ed.), *Issues in Contemporary Economics, vol. II, Macroeconomics and Econometrics*, London: Macmillan, pp. 319–344.

Mankiw, N.G. and M.D. Shapiro (1986), "News or Noise: An Analysis of GNP Revisions," *Survey of Current Business*, 66: 20–25.

Muth, J.F. (1961), "Rational Expectations and the Theory of Price Movements," *Econometrica*, 29: 315–355.

(1985), "Properties of Some Short-Run Business Forecasts," *Eastern Economic Journal*, 11: 200–210.

Palm, F.C. and A. Zellner (1992), "To Combine or Not to Combine? Issues of Combining Forecasts," *Journal of Forecasting*, 11: 687–701.

Pesaran, M.H. (1988), *Limits to Rational Expectations*. Oxford: Basil Blackwell.

Rich, R.W., J.E. Raymond, and J.S. Butler (1992), "The Relationship Between Forecast Dispersion and Forecast Uncertainty: Evidence From a Survey Data – ARCH Model," *Journal of Applied Econometrics*, 7: 131–148.

Schmidt, P., S.C. Ahn, and D. Wyhowski (1992), "Comment," *Journal of Business and Economic Statistics*, 10: 15–21.

Visco, I. (1984), *Price Expectations in Rising Inflation*, Amsterdam: North-Holland.

Zarnowitz, V. (1985), "Rational Expectations and Macroeconomic Forecasts," *Journal of Business and Economic Statistics*, 3: 293–311.

(1992), "Business Cycles: Theory, History, Indicators, and Forecasting," *Studies in Business Cycles, vol. XXVII*, National Bureau of Economic Research, The University of Chicago Press.

Zarnowitz, V. and P. Braun (1993), "Twenty-two Years of the NBER-ASA Quarterly Economic Outlook Surveys: Aspects and Comparisons of Forecasting Performance," in J.H. Stock and M.W. Watson (eds.), *Business Cycles, Indicators, and Forecasting*, The University of Chicago Press.

10 Prediction from the regression model with one-way error components

RICHARD T. BAILLIE AND BADI H. BALTAGI

Econometrics had its origin in the recognition of empirical regularities and the systematic attempt to generalize these regularities into "laws" of economics. In a broad sense, the use of such "laws" is to make predictions – about what might have been or what will come to pass. Econometrics should give a base for economic prediction beyond experience if it is to be useful. In this broad sense it may be called the science of economic prediction. Lawrence R. Klein (1971)

1 Introduction

Following the work of Balestra and Nerlove (1966) the regression model with error components, or variance components, has become a popular method for dealing with panel data. A summary of the main features of the model, together with a discussion of some applications, is available in Hsiao (1986), Mátyás and Sevestre (1992), Maddala (1993), and Baltagi (1995). However, relatively little is known about prediction from the model. Assuming that all the regression parameters and the error process parameters are known, the form of the optimal (in the sense of minimum MSE predictor) has been obtained by Wansbeek and Kapteyn (1978) and Taub (1979). This was extended to the case of serially correlated error components by Baltagi and Li (1992).

This chapter investigates some potentially important practical problems associated with prediction from the error components regression model. In particular, we derive the asymptotic mean squared error (AMSE) of multi-step prediction from the model, which takes into account the additional inherent uncertainty associated with estimating both the regression parameters and the error components parameters. The adequacy of the prediction AMSE formula is also investigated by the use of Monte Carlo methods. The effect of parameter estimation is found to be quite substantial

* We are very grateful to Kajal Lahiri, Lung-Fei Lee and Peter Schmidt for helpful comments on an earlier version of this chapter and to Michel Vanderhart for his research assistance.

and is clearly important to take into account when forming prediction confidence intervals, or undertaking *ex ante* model stability testing.

We also provide both theoretical and simulation evidence as to the relative efficiency of four alternative predictors; (i) an ordinary predictor, based on the form of the optimal predictor, but with MLEs replacing population parameters, (ii) a truncated predictor that ignores the error component correction but uses MLEs for its regression parameters, (iii) a misspecified predictor which uses OLS estimates of the regression parameters, and (iv) a fixed effects predictor which assumes that the individual effects are fixed parameters that can be estimated. We compare the asymptotic efficiencies of these alternative predictors. Numerical examples and simulation results indicate the importance of taking into account the individual effects. We recommend using the fixed effects and the ordinary predictor in applied work. Both predictors specifically allow for the individual effects. Our results also show that the asymptotic formula for MSE prediction performs adequately in realistic sample sizes.

The regression model with T pooled time series and N pooled cross sections is defined as

$$y_{it} = x_{it}'\beta + u_{it} \qquad i=1,\dots,N; t=1,\dots,T \tag{1}$$

where x_{it} is a k dimensional vector of explanatory variables associated with the tth time period for the ith cross section of individuals, firms, or countries. The disturbances u_{it} follow the one-way error component model

$$u_{it} = \mu_i + v_{it}, \tag{2}$$

where μ_i denotes the firm-specific effect which is assumed to be NID$(0,\sigma_\mu^2)$ and v_{it} is the remaining disturbance, which is also assumed to be NID$(0,\sigma_v^2)$. The μ_is and the v_{it}s are independent of each other.

With known parameters $(\beta,\sigma_\mu^2,\sigma_v^2)$ and known future exogenous variables $x_{i,T+s}$, the optimal, i.e., minimum mean squared error (MSE) predictor of $y_{i,T+s}$ is denoted by $y_{i,T,s}$ and is the optimal prediction of the ith component at time T with an s step ahead forecast horizon. From Goldberger (1962) the form of this optimal predictor is given by

$$y_{i,T,s} = x_{i,T+s}'\beta + \theta\bar{u}_i \qquad s \geq 1 \tag{3}$$

where for a fixed number of T time periods

$$\theta = T\sigma_\mu^2/(T\sigma_\mu^2 + \sigma_v^2) \tag{4}$$

and $\bar{u}_i = \sum_{t=1}^{T} u_{it}/T$. The feasible optimal predictor $\hat{y}_{i,T,s}$, is obtained by substituting MLE for corresponding unknown population parameters into (3).

For the case where the true variance components are known, Wansbeek and Kapteyn (1978) and Taub (1979) have applied Goldberger's (1962) result to show that the best linear unbiased predictor (BLUP) for the ith individual s periods ahead, is given by

$$\hat{y}_{i,T,s} = x'_{i,T+s}\hat{\beta}_{\text{GLS}} + \theta\bar{\hat{u}}_i \qquad s \geq 1 \tag{5}$$

where θ is defined in (4) and $\bar{\hat{u}}_i$ is the average of the GLS residuals over time, for the ith individual. Hence $\hat{u}_{it} = y_{it} - x'_{it}\hat{\beta}_{\text{GLS}}$ and $\bar{\hat{u}}_i = \sum_{t=1}^{T} \hat{u}_{it}/T$, where $\hat{\beta}_{\text{GLS}}$ is the GLS estimator of β based on the true variance components

$$\hat{\beta}_{\text{GLS}} = (X'\Omega^{-1}X)^{-1}X'\Omega^{-1}y,$$

Also, $y' = (y_{11}, \ldots, y_{IT}, \ldots, y_{N1}, \ldots, y_{NT})$, and X is the $NT \times k$ dimensional matrix with the itth row being x'_{it} stacked in the same way as defined for y. In this case

$$\Omega = E(uu') = \sigma^2_\mu(I_N \otimes \iota_T\iota'_T) + \sigma^2_\nu I_{NT}, \tag{6}$$

where, $u' = (u_{11}, \ldots, u_{1T}, \ldots, u_{N1}, \ldots, u_{NT})$, I_N is an identity matrix of dimension N and ι_T is a vector of ones of dimension T. It is well known that Ω^{-1} is given by

$$\Omega^{-1} = (1/\sigma^2_\nu)Q + \{1/(T\sigma^2_\mu + \sigma^2_\nu)\}P \tag{7}$$

where $P = (I_N \otimes \iota_T\iota'_T)/T$ and $Q = I_{NT}\text{-}P$.

To obtain the fully feasible optimal predictor it is necessary to replace the unknown variance components with consistent estimates; Wallace and Hussain (1969) and Amemiya (1971) describe two such estimators. More recently, Breusch (1987) showed that the MLE of β and θ can be obtained by using a simple iterative procedure which guards against local maxima. When the parameters in this predictor are replaced with their corresponding MLEs, the feasible predictor, or "ordinary predictor," becomes

$$\hat{y}_{i,T,s} = x'_{i,T+s}\hat{\beta} + \hat{\theta}\bar{\hat{u}}_i \qquad s \geq 1 \tag{8}$$

where $\hat{u}_{it} = y_{it} - x'_{it}\hat{\beta}$ and $\hat{\beta}$ and $\hat{\theta}$ are the MLEs of β and θ respectively. In this chapter, we derive the asymptotic mean square error of $\hat{y}_{i,T,s}$, and compare the efficiency of this predictor with three alternative predictors. The first is the truncated predictor

$$\hat{\hat{y}}_{i,T,s} = x'_{i,T+s}\hat{\beta} \tag{9}$$

which is based on efficient estimates of the regression parameters, but is sub-optimal in the sense that it ignores the contribution of autocorrelation to the predictor. This truncated predictor corresponds to the expected value predictor in the terminology of Goldberger (1962) and Baillie (1980).

Another predictor of considerable practical relevance is the predictor based on inefficient OLS estimates of the regression parameters

$$y^{*}_{i,T,s} = x'_{i,T+s}\hat{\beta}_{\text{OLS}} \tag{10}$$

where $\hat{\beta}_{\text{OLS}}$ is the least squares estimator and clearly ignores the autocorrelated error components phenomenon in both estimation and formation of the predictor. It should be noted that the truncated predictor in (10) has been previously analyzed by Baillie (1980) in the context of the regression model with ARMA disturbances and by Yamamoto (1979) for the AR(1) process. This predictor ignores the extra term in (3), which arises from Ω being non-spherical. Hence (10) corresponds to the situation where the investigator is oblivious to the presence of the error components and merely uses standard regression software to calculate predictions and their associated MSE.

Finally, we consider the fixed effects predictor which is based on the within estimates of the regression parameters. This assumes that the μ_is are fixed parameters to be estimated

$$\tilde{y}_{i,T,s} = x'_{i,T+s}\tilde{\beta} + \tilde{\mu}_i \tag{11}$$

with

$$\tilde{\beta} = (X'QX)^{-1}X'Qy$$

and

$$\tilde{\mu}_i = \bar{y}_i - \bar{x}'_i\tilde{\beta}$$

where $\bar{y}_i = \sum_{t=1}^{T} y_{it}/T$ and $\bar{x}_i = \sum_{t=1}^{T} x_{it}/T$; see Baltagi (1995). The predictor in (11) is the BLUP given that the μ_is are constants.

2 Asymptotic mean squared error (AMSE) of prediction

In order to compare the relative efficiencies of predictors it is necessary to examine their asymptotic MSE or AMSE. There is a substantial previous literature on the effect of parameter estimation and the prediction of exogenous variables in the context of dynamic econometric models, e.g., Schmidt (1974, 1977), Lahiri (1975), Baillie (1979, 1980), Yamamoto (1979), and Lütkepohl (1988). The method of analysis in this chapter is similar to the above literature, except the crucial parameters of interest in the predictor arise from error components effects rather than a dynamic model. For example, Baillie (1980) compared the asymptotic efficiencies of the predictors given by (8), (9) and (10) for the time series regression model with ARMA(p,q) disturbances and Yamamoto (1979) provided a related treatment for the pure AR(1) process. This chapter examines the panel data regression and compares the relative efficiency of predictors given in (8) through (11) using analytical as well as sampling results.

The optimal predictor with known parameters $y_{i,T,s}$, defined in (3) has prediction MSE of

$$\sigma^2_{T+s} = E(y_{i,T+s} - y_{i,T,s})^2 = E(u_{i,T+s} - \theta\bar{u}_i)^2 \tag{12}$$

where the population expected value of the ith cross-section departure over the T time periods is replaced with the sample average. On using the fact that

$$u_{i,T+s} - \theta\bar{u}_i = (1-\theta)\mu_i + (\nu_{i,T+s} - \theta\bar{\nu}_i)$$

it follows that

$$\sigma^2_{T+s} \equiv E(y_{i,T+s} - y_{i,T,s})^2 = (1-\theta)^2\sigma^2_\mu + \sigma^2_\nu + (\theta^2\sigma^2_\nu)/T. \tag{13}$$

Since this predictor is entirely dependent on known parameter values its prediction AMSE is equivalent to its MSE, which is denoted by σ^2_{T+s}.

2.1 *The ordinary predictor with estimated parameters*

The practically feasible version of the ordinary predictor in (8) with MLEs of its parameters $(\hat{\beta},\hat{\theta})$, replacing population parameters, has a prediction error given by

$$y_{i,T+s} - \hat{y}_{i,T,s} = (y_{i,T+s} - y_{i,T,s}) - (\hat{y}_{i,T,s} - y_{i,T,s}) \tag{14}$$

where

$$\begin{aligned}\hat{y}_{i,T,s} - y_{i,T,s} &= x'_{i,T+s}(\hat{\beta}-\beta) + \hat{\theta}\bar{\hat{u}}_i - \theta\bar{u}_i \\ &= x'_{i,T+s}(\hat{\beta}-\beta) - \theta\bar{u}_i + \{\theta + (\hat{\theta}-\theta)\}\{\bar{u}_i + (\bar{\hat{u}}_i - \bar{u}_i)\} \\ &= x'_{i,T+s}(\hat{\beta}-\beta) + \theta(\bar{\hat{u}}_i - \bar{u}_i) + (\hat{\theta}-\theta)\bar{u}_i + (\hat{\theta}-\theta)(\bar{\hat{u}}_i - \bar{u}_i).\end{aligned}$$

On using the fact that $\bar{\hat{u}}_i - \bar{u}_i = -\bar{x}'_i(\hat{\beta}-\beta)$, it follows that

$$\hat{y}_{i,T,s} - y_{i,T,s} = (x_{i,T+s} - \theta\bar{x}_i)'(\hat{\beta}-\beta) + (\hat{\theta}-\theta)\bar{u}_i - (\hat{\theta}-\theta)\bar{x}'_i(\hat{\beta}-\beta). \tag{15}$$

For the derivation of the AMSE prediction of $\hat{y}_{i,T,s}$, it is necessary to consider the asymptotic covariance matrix of the MLE of (β,θ). It can be shown that the MLE $\hat{\gamma}$, where

$$\gamma' = (\beta',\rho') \text{ and } \rho' = (\sigma^2_\mu,\sigma^2_\nu) \tag{16}$$

has the asymptotic distribution

$$n^{1/2}(\hat{\gamma}-\gamma) \rightarrow N\{0, J^{-1}(\gamma)\} \tag{17}$$

where $n=NT$ and the asymptotics are in terms of T being fixed and $N\rightarrow\infty$ and hence $n\rightarrow\infty$. The information matrix $J(\gamma)$ is block diagonal and is defined as

$$J^{-1}(\gamma)=\begin{bmatrix} V_\beta & 0 \\ 0 & V_\rho \end{bmatrix}$$

where

$$V_\beta=(X'\Omega^{-1}X)^{-1} \tag{18}$$

$$V_\rho=2\sigma_\nu^4/NT(T-1)\begin{bmatrix} \left(\dfrac{T-1}{T}\right)[(T\sigma_\mu^2+\sigma_\nu^2)/\sigma_\nu^2]^2+(1/T) & -1 \\ -1 & T \end{bmatrix} \tag{19}$$

However, the main parameter of interest, θ, is defined in (4) and is a non-linear function $f(\sigma_\mu^2,\sigma_\nu^2)$, of the elements of V_ρ. By means of first-order Taylor series approximation around the true parameter θ

$$\hat{\theta}=\theta+g(\hat{\rho}-\rho)$$

where

$$g=[\partial f(.)/\partial\rho]=[T\sigma_\nu^2/(T\sigma_\mu^2+\sigma_\nu^2)^2, -T\sigma_\mu^2/(T\sigma_\mu^2+\sigma_\nu^2)^2].$$

Then

$$\begin{aligned}\text{var}(\hat{\theta})&=g\{\text{var}(\hat{\rho})\}g' \\ &=T^2/(T\sigma_\mu^2+\sigma_\nu^2)^4\{\sigma_\nu^4\text{var}(\hat{\sigma}_\mu^2)-2\sigma_\mu^2\sigma_\nu^2\text{cov}(\hat{\sigma}_\mu^2,\hat{\sigma}_\nu^2)+\sigma_\mu^4\text{var}(\hat{\sigma}_\nu^2)\}.\end{aligned} \tag{20}$$

Substituting $\text{var}(\hat{\rho})=V_\rho$ from (19), and after some algebra

$$\text{var}(\hat{\theta})=2T\sigma_\nu^4/N(T-1)(T\sigma_\mu^2+\sigma_\nu^2)^2. \tag{21}$$

The prediction AMSE can then be obtained from (14) and (15) and by using the fact that $E(\hat{\beta}-\beta)(\hat{\theta}-\theta)\approx o_p(n^{-1/2})$ and $E(\hat{\beta}-\beta)(\hat{\theta}-\theta)^2\approx o_p(n^{-3/2})$. Then

$$\begin{aligned}\text{AMSE}(\hat{y}_{i,T,s})&=\sigma_{T+s}^2+(x_{i,T+s}-\theta\bar{x}_i)'V_\beta(x_{i,T+s}-\theta\bar{x}_i)+E\{(\hat{\theta}-\theta)\bar{u}_i\}^2 \\ &=\sigma_{T+s}^2+(x_{i,T+s}-\theta\bar{x}_i)'V_\beta(x_{i,T+s}-\theta\bar{x}_i)+\text{var}(\hat{\theta})\{\bar{x}_i'\beta\}^2\end{aligned} \tag{22}$$

where σ^2_{T+s} is given in (13), V_β in (18) and var($\hat{\theta}$) in (21). The last two terms of (22) represent the increase in the AMSE($\hat{y}_{i,T,s}$) over the MSE($y_{i,T,s}$) which is caused by the estimation of the regression parameters β and the error components parameters ρ, respectively.

2.2 *The truncated predictor*

A possible alternative predictor is given by (9) and is referred to as the truncated predictor, since it utilizes efficient MLEs of the regression parameters but ignores the last term in the optimal predictor (3), which is due to the predictable systematic behavior of the error components. The prediction error associated with (9) is given by

$$y_{i,T+s} - \hat{\hat{y}}_{i,T,s} = x'_{i,T+s}(\beta - \hat{\beta}) + u_{i,T+s}. \tag{23}$$

On using the fact that $E(\beta - \hat{\beta})u_{i,T+s} = -(T\sigma^2_\mu / T\sigma^2_\mu + \sigma^2_\nu)\,(X'\Omega^{-1}X)^{-1}\bar{x}_i$, it follows that the AMSE of the truncated predictor is given by

$$\begin{aligned} \text{AMSE}(\hat{\hat{y}}_{i,T,s}) = {} & x'_{i,T+s}(X'\Omega^{-1}X)^{-1}x_{i,T+s} + (\sigma^2_\mu + \sigma^2_\nu) \\ & - 2T\sigma^2_\mu x'_{i,T+s}(X'\Omega^{-1}X)^{-1}\bar{x}_i/(T\sigma^2_\mu + \sigma^2_\nu). \end{aligned} \tag{24}$$

In the case of the regression model with ARMA(p,q) errors, Baillie (1980) found there were some situations where the truncated predictor had smaller prediction AMSE than the ordinary predictor. This possibility arose when the variability of estimating the error process parameters exceeded the efficiency gain from using the optimal predictor rather than just ignoring the effect of autocorrelated errors when forming predictions. Section 3 of this chapter analyzes a similar situation in the context of the error components model; analogous results are not found for the error components model, indicating the desirability of using the ordinary predictor (8), rather than (9).

2.3 *The misspecified OLS predictor*

The misspecified predictor for $y_{i,T+s}$, given by $y^*_{i,T,s} = x'_{i,T+s}\hat{\beta}_{\text{OLS}}$ in (10), is obtained from using OLS and ignoring the presence of error components both in estimation and in terms of forming the predictor. In this case, the prediction error is given by

$$y_{i,T+s} - y^*_{i,T,s} = x'_{i,T+s}(\beta - \hat{\beta}_{\text{OLS}}) + u_{i,T+s}. \tag{25}$$

On defining

$$\text{var}(\hat{\beta}_{\text{OLS}}) = (X'X)^{-1}(X'\Omega X)(X'X)^{-1}$$

and noting that

$$E[(\beta-\hat{\beta}_{OLS})u_{i,T+s}]=-T\sigma_{\mu}^{2}(X'X)^{-1}\bar{x}_{i} \tag{26}$$

it follows that

$$\begin{aligned}\mathrm{AMSE}(y_{i,T,s}^{*})=&x_{i,T+s}'(X'X)^{-1}(X'\Omega X)(X'X)^{-1}x_{i,T+s}+(\sigma_{\mu}^{2}+\sigma_{\nu}^{2})\\&-2T\sigma_{\mu}^{2}x_{i,T+s}'(X'X)^{-1}x_{i}\end{aligned} \tag{27}$$

Since the last terms of (27) and (24) are of $o_p(1/n)$, then the AMSE$(y_{i,T,s}^{*})$ $-$ AMSE$(\hat{y}_{i,T+s})\geq 0$ for every γ, N, T and s. This means that the truncated predictor is more efficient than the misspecified predictor.

2.4 *The fixed effects predictor*

The fixed effects predictor for $y_{i,T+s}$ given by $\tilde{y}_{i,T,s}=x_{i,T+s}'\tilde{\beta}+\tilde{\mu}_i$ in (11), is obtained by estimating the μ_i for the ith individual as a fixed parameter. In this case, the prediction error is given by

$$\begin{aligned}y_{i,T+s}-\tilde{y}_{i,T,s}&=x_{i,T+s}'(\beta-\tilde{\beta})+u_{i,T+s}-\tilde{\mu}_i\\&=(x_{i,T+s}'-\bar{x}_i')(\beta-\tilde{\beta})+u_{i,T+s}-(\bar{y}_i-\bar{x}_i'\beta)\\&=(x_{i,T+s}'-\bar{x}_i')(\beta-\tilde{\beta})+u_{i,T+s}-\bar{u}_{i}.\end{aligned} \tag{28}$$

Using the fact that

$$\mathrm{var}(\tilde{\beta})=\sigma_{\nu}^{2}(X'QX)^{-1} \tag{29}$$

and noting that

$$E(\beta-\tilde{\beta})\bar{u}_i=-(X'QX)^{-1}X'QE(\bar{u}_iu)=0$$

$$E(\beta-\tilde{\beta})u_{i,T+s}=-(X'QX)^{-1}X'QE(u_{i,T+s}u)=0$$

and $E(u_{i,T+s}\bar{u}_i)=\sigma_{\mu}^{2}$, it follows that

$$\begin{aligned}\mathrm{AMSE}(\tilde{y}_{i,T,s})=&\sigma_{\nu}^{2}(x_{i,T+s}-\bar{x}_i)'(X'QX)^{-1}(x_{i,T+s}-\bar{x}_i)+\sigma_{\nu}^{2}\\&+(\sigma_{\nu}^{2}/T).\end{aligned} \tag{30}$$

3 Monte Carlo results

Some Monte Carlo experiments were performed to determine the accuracy of the asymptotic approximation of the MSE of the predictors in the type of sample sizes commonly encountered with panel data. The data are generated from the simple regression

$$y_{it}=\alpha+\beta x_{it}+u_{it}\qquad i=1,2,\dots,N;\ t=1,2,\dots,T+s$$

with one-way error components, $u_{it} = \mu_i + \nu_{it}$. Throughout the experiment the parameters were set at $\alpha = 5$, $\beta = 0.5$, with the total variance $\sigma^2 = \sigma_\mu^2 + \sigma_\nu^2$ fixed at 20. The variable x_{it} was generated as in Nerlove (1971) with

$$x_{it} = 0.1t + 0.5x_{i,t-1} + \omega_{it}$$

where ω_{it} is a random variable uniformly distributed on the interval $[-0.5,0.5]$ and $x_{i0} = 5 + 10\omega_{i0}$. The first 20 period observations were discarded to minimize the effect of initial values. Predictions were made for only ($s = 1$) one period ahead. It is important to note that the predictor for this panel data model changes with s only through $x_{i,T+s}$. In fact, it is the presence of the same individual in the panel that creates the correlation over time, and this is constant correlation that does not die out no matter how far ahead we are predicting. In order to depict the typical labor or consumer panel where N is large and T is small, the sample sizes in the different experiments were chosen as $N = 50$ or 500 and $T = 10$ or 20; with 1,000 replications performed for each experiment. For each replication, $(N + N(T + s))$ NID(0,1) random numbers are generated. The first N random numbers were used to generate the μ_is from NID$(0,\sigma_\mu^2)$ and the remaining $N(T + s)$ random numbers are used to generate the ν_{it}s from NID$(0,\sigma_\nu^2)$. With this design the implied values of $\rho = \sigma_\mu^2/\sigma^2$ are 0, 0.3, 0.6, and 0.9. For each of the predictors considered in this chapter, the AMSE for a one-step ahead prediction were computed from the formulas derived in the chapter, and the sampling MSE were computed as

$$\text{MSE} = \sum_{r=1}^{R} \sum_{i=1}^{N} (y_{i,T+s} - \hat{y}_{i,T,s})^2/NR.$$

Following Spitzer and Baillie (1983), the quantity

$$\text{AMSE BIAS VARIANCE} = \sum_{r=1}^{R} \sum_{i=1}^{N} \{(y_{i,T+s} - \hat{y}_{i,T,s})^2 - \text{AMSE}(\hat{y}_{i,T,s})\}^2/NR$$

where the summation extends over all $R = 1{,}000$ replications and N individuals for each (T,ρ,s). On defining $q = (\text{MSE-AMSE})$, it is possible to test H_0: $q = 0$ versus H_1: $q \neq 0$, by using the statistic

$$Z = \sqrt{R}\, q/(\text{AMSE BIAS VARIANCE})^{1/2}.$$

Since N is fixed for each particular experiment, then for large R, it can be seen that Z will be approximately distributed as $N(0,1)$, since AMSE BIAS VARIANCE is an estimate of the population variance of q and both MSE and AMSE are χ_1^2 variables.

Table 10.1 gives the results of MSE and AMSE for the ordinary, truncated, misspecified, and fixed effects predictors, averaged over all individuals and replications. The results can be summarized as follows:

(1) The sampling results are very close to the analytical ones as evident by the closeness of MSE to AMSE for all experiments and predictors considered. The only exception is for $N=50$ and $\rho=0$, and then only for the ordinary predictor. The MSE of the ordinary predictor tends to understate its AMSE, but this difference is not statistically significant. In fact, the difference between MSE and AMSE is insignificant for all experiments and predictors considered.

(2) Both the analytical and sampling results in table 10.1 show that there are substantial gains in mean square error prediction by using the ordinary predictor instead of the misspecified or the truncated predictors, especially with increasing ρ values. The reduction in MSE is about ten fold for $\rho=0.9$ and a little more than two fold for $\rho=0.6$ for various values of N and T. Unlike the results for the regression model with AR(2) errors in Baillie (1980) and the AR(1) model in Yamamoto (1979), the ordinary predictor for the error component model comprehensively outperforms the truncated and misspecified predictors and is recommended when predicting with panel data.

(3) The fixed effects predictor performs remarkably well being a close second to the ordinary predictor for all experiments. The MSE and AMSE of the fixed effects and the ordinary predictors decrease by ten fold as ρ increases from 0 to 0.9. This is true for all values of N and T considered.

(4) Both the truncated and misspecified predictors perform badly (except when $\rho=0$) when compared to the ordinary and fixed effects predictors. OLS ignores the individual effects in estimation and prediction, while the truncated estimator ignores the individual effects only in prediction.

4 Conclusion

This chapter has derived the asymptotic MSE of the ordinary and fixed effects predictors of the regression model with error components. Simulation evidence has confirmed the adequacy of the asymptotic approximation in realistic sample sizes and indicates the importance of allowing for parameter uncertainty when forming prediction confidence intervals or when undertaking *ex ante* prediction stability testing. Interestingly enough, the gain in efficiency from allowing for the autocorrelated error components is considerable compared to the sub-optimal truncated predictor, or from using OLS. This is in contrast to previously derived results for the regression model with dynamic disturbances, such as

Table 10.1. *Experimental and analytical mean square prediction errors one period ahead*

Prediction	Ordinary			Truncated			Misspecified			Fixed effect		
period	MSE	AMSE	Z	MSE	AMSE	Z	MSE	AMSE	Z	MSE	AMSE	Z
$N=50$, $T=10$												
$\rho=0.0$	20.291	21.395	−1.227	20.200	20.099	0.113	20.200	20.099	0.113	22.213	22.092	0.123
$\rho=0.3$	15.281	15.242	0.058	20.079	19.952	0.141	20.095	19.961	0.149	15.549	15.464	0.123
$\rho=0.6$	8.833	8.791	0.108	20.011	19.802	0.233	20.039	19.823	0.241	8.885	8.837	0.123
$\rho=0.9$	2.219	2.207	0.120	19.967	19.651	0.354	20.008	19.685	0.361	2.221	2.209	0.123
$N=500$, $T=10$												
$\rho=0.0$	20.031	20.138	−0.120	20.021	20.009	0.014	20.021	20.009	0.014	22.010	22.007	0.003
$\rho=0.3$	15.138	15.145	−0.009	19.980	19.994	−0.016	19.978	19.994	−0.018	15.407	15.405	0.003
$\rho=0.6$	8.752	8.753	−0.002	19.967	19.979	−0.014	19.965	19.979	−0.016	8.804	8.803	0.003
$\rho=0.9$	2.199	2.199	0.001	19.970	19.965	0.005	19.968	19.964	0.004	2.201	2.201	0.003
$N=50$, $T=20$												
$\rho=0.0$	20.056	21.313	−1.398	20.010	20.040	−0.034	20.010	20.040	−0.034	21.005	21.029	−0.026
$\rho=0.3$	14.637	14.662	−0.038	19.942	19.911	0.035	19.963	19.928	0.039	14.704	14.721	−0.026
$\rho=0.6$	8.391	8.400	−0.025	19.805	19.778	0.031	19.850	19.816	0.038	8.402	8.412	−0.026
$\rho=0.9$	2.100	2.102	−0.025	19.633	19.644	−0.013	19.702	19.703	−0.001	2.101	2.103	−0.026
$N=500$, $T=20$												
$\rho=0.0$	19.999	20.131	−0.148	19.995	20.005	−0.011	19.995	20.005	−0.011	21.005	21.004	0.002
$\rho=0.3$	14.630	14.631	−0.001	19.984	19.992	−0.009	19.984	19.993	−0.010	14.704	14.703	0.002
$\rho=0.6$	8.389	8.389	0.001	19.970	19.978	−0.010	19.971	19.981	−0.011	8.402	8.401	0.002
$\rho=0.9$	2.100	2.100	0.002	19.954	19.965	−0.012	19.957	19.968	−0.013	2.101	2.100	0.002

ARMA. The fixed effects predictor performs well and is a close second to the ordinary predictor. Both predictors account for the individual effects in estimation and prediction. Given the robustness of the fixed effects predictor with respect to the correlation with regressors and possible infinite variance of the μ_is (when they are actually random), it seems fair to conclude that the fixed predictor comes out with a clear bill of health and is recommended.

References

Amemiya, T. (1971), "The Estimation of Variances in a Variance Components Model," *International Economic Review*, 12: 1–13.

Baillie, R.T (1979), "The Asymptotic Mean Squared Error of Multistep Prediction from the Regression Model with Autoregressive Errors," *Journal of the American Statistical Association*, 74: 175–184.

(1980), 'Prediction from ARMAX Models," *Journal of Econometrics*, 12: 365–374.

Balestra, P. and M. Nerlove (1966), "Pooling Cross-Section and Time-Series Data in the Estimation of a Dynamic Model: The Demand for Natural Gas," *Econometrica*, 14: 381–394.

Baltagi, B.H. (1995), *Econometric Analysis of Panel Data*, Chichester: John Wiley and Sons.

Baltagi, B.H. and Q. Li (1992), "Prediction in the One-Way Error Component Model with Serial Correlation," *Journal of Forecasting*, 11: 561–567.

Breusch, T.S. (1987), "Maximum Likelihood Estimation of Random Effects Models," *Journal of Econometrics*, 36: 383–389.

Goldberger, A.S. (1962), "Best Linear Unbiased Prediction in the Generalized Linear Regression Model," *Journal of The American Statistical Association*, 57: 369–375.

Hsiao, C. (1986), *Analysis of panel data*, Cambridge: Cambridge University Press.

Judge, G.G., W.E. Griffiths, R.C. Hill, H. Lutkepohl, and T.C. Lee (1985), *The Theory and Practice of Econometrics*, New York: Wiley.

Klein, L.R. (1971), "Whither Econometrics?," *Journal of the American Statistical Association*, 66: 415–421.

Lahiri, K. (1975), "Multiperiod Predictions in Dynamic Models," *International Economic Review*, 16: 699–711.

Lutkepohl, H. (1988), "Prediction Tests for Structural Stability," *Journal of Econometrics*, 39: 267–296.

Maddala, G.S. (ed.) (1993), *The Econometrics of Panel Data*. Vols. I and II, Cheltenham: Edward Elgar Publishing.

Mátyás, L. and P. Sevestre (eds.) (1992), *The Econometrics of Panel Data: Handbook of Theory and Applications*, Dordrecht: Kluwer Academic Publishers.

Nerlove, M. (1971), "Further Evidence on the Estimation of Dynamic Economic Relations from a Time-Series of Cross-Sections," *Econometrica*, 39: 359–383.

Schmidt, P. (1974), "The Asymptotic Distribution of Forecasts in the Dynamic Simulation of an Econometric Model," *Econometrica*, 42: 303–309.

(1977), "Some Small Sample Evidence on the Distribution of Dynamic Simulation Forecasts," *Econometrica*, 45: 997–1005.

Spitzer, J.J. and R.T. Baillie (1983), "Small-Sample Properties of Predictions from the Regression Model with Autoregressive Errors," *Journal of the American Statistical Association*, 78: 258–263.

Taub, A.J. (1979), "Prediction in the Context of the Variance-Components Model," *Journal of Econometrics*, 10: 103–107.

Wallace, T.E. and A. Hussain (1969), "The Use of Error Component Models in Combining Cross Section and Time Series Data," *Econometrica*, 37: 55–72.

Wansbeek, T. and A. Kapteyn (1978), "The Separation of Individual Variation and Systematic Change in the Analysis of Panel Data," *Annales de l'INSEE*, 30–31: 659–680.

Yamamoto, T. (1979), "On the Prediction Efficiency of the Generalized Least Squares Model with an Estimated Variance Covariance Matrix," *International Economic Review*, 20: 693–705.

11 Bayes estimation of short-run coefficients in dynamic panel data models

CHENG HSIAO, M. HASHEM PESARAN, AND A. KAMIL TAHMISCIOGLU

1 Introduction

This chapter considers the estimation of the mean coefficients of dynamic panel data models in the presence of coefficient heterogeneity across cross-sectional units. It is well known that when the regressors are exogenous, the estimators based on the sampling approach such as fixed and random effects yield consistent estimates of the mean coefficients when the number of cross-sectional units approaches infinity (see, for example, Zellner (1969)). However, Pesaran and Smith (1995) have demonstrated that the same results do not carry over to dynamic models. The neglect of coefficient heterogeneity in dynamic models creates correlation between the regressors and the error term as well as causing serially correlated disturbances, thus rendering the within estimators biased. Moreover, the bias of the within estimators does not disappear even asymptotically. Neither do the usual remedies such as instrumental variables estimation technique or differencing the variables work in this case. The asymptotic bias of the usual within estimator is a function of the degree of coefficient heterogeneity and the extent of serial correlation in the regressors.

While the inconsistency of traditional pooled panel estimators have been well established for dynamic random coefficient models, it is hard to say that there is similar clarity in the literature about the appropriate estimation technique that needs to be used (see Maddala *et al.* (1997) for a review). Not only does recent research neglect some important estimators that are relevant for this case, but it also conveys the impression that there is not much one can do if the time dimension of panel is short. This latter

An earlier version of this chapter was presented at the Seventh International Conference on Panel Data, Paris, June 1997. We are grateful to Ron Smith and Kajal Lahiri for helpful comments.

Cheng Hsiao would like to acknowledge the research support of NSF grant number 96-19330. Hashem Pesaran also gratefully acknowledges partial financial by the ESRC grant H519255003 and the Isaac Newton Trust of the Trinity College, Cambridge.

conclusion is very troubling in view of the fact that panels with large T are typically the exception in economics. In this chapter we suggest a Bayesian approach to the estimation of dynamic panel data models that seem to perform reasonably well. We establish the asymptotic equivalence of the Bayes estimator and the mean group estimator proposed by Pesaran and Smith (1995), and show that the mean group estimator is asymptotically normal for large N (the number of units) and large T (the number of time periods) so long as $\sqrt{N}/T \to 0$ as both N and $T \to \infty$. This is a new result with important practical implications where N is often much larger than T, in practice.

After discussing different ways of estimating the mean coefficients, we present the results of a limited Monte Carlo study that was conducted to investigate the small sample performance of the estimators of the means of short-run coefficients in the dynamic heterogeneous panel data models. We also provide an illustration with real data. When different estimators are compared on the basis of their sampling properties, the Bayes estimator turns out to have very good properties in both small and moderate T samples. Although the knowledge of variance components that is essential for the computation of the Bayes estimator may not be available, this does not appear to pose any great difficulties in practice. The problem of unknown variances is easily handled by taking a hierarchical Bayes approach and by putting a prior distribution on the hyperparameters. The desired marginal posterior densities of the parameters can be obtained by iterative Markov Chain Monte Carlo methods, even though they cannot be evaluated analytically. When the time dimension of the panel is sufficiently large (e.g. $T=20$), even empirical Bayes methods which substitute consistent estimates of the variance components into the Bayes formula seem to yield good results. Our results also caution against the use of the mean group estimator (MGE) unless T is sufficiently large relative to N (namely when $\sqrt{N}/T$ is sufficiently small). The bias in the mean coefficient of the lagged dependent variable appears to be serious when T is very small (e.g., $T=5$) and the true value of this coefficient is large (in excess of 0.6).

The plan of the chapter is as follows: section 2 presents the dynamic panel data model we consider in this study. Alternative ways of estimating this model (Classical and Bayesian) are discussed in sections 3 and 4. Section 5 deals with the asymptotics and establishes the required relative rates of convergence of N and T for the asymptotic theory to hold. Section 6 discusses the design of the Monte Carlo study and section 7 presents the results. In section 8, we re-examine the empirical evidence for the q investment model using a panel of 273 US firms over the period 1973–1992. Concluding remarks are given in section 9.

2 Model

We consider the following dynamic model

$$y_i = \gamma_i y_{i,-1} + X_i \beta_i + u_i, \qquad |\gamma_i| < 1, \qquad i = 1,2,\ldots, N \tag{1}$$

where $y_i = (y_{i1}, y_{i2,\ldots,} y_{iT})'$ is a $T \times 1$ vector of observations for the dependent variable and $y_{i,-1} = (y_{i0}, y_{i1,\ldots,} y_{iT-1})'$ and $X_i = (x_{i1}, x_{i2}, \ldots, x_{iT})'$ are matrices of explanatory variables with dimensions $T \times 1$ and $T \times (k-1)$ for the ith individual (group). This can be written more compactly as

$$y_i = Z_i \theta_i + u_i \tag{2}$$

where

$$Z_i = (y_{i-1}, X_i), \qquad \theta_i = \begin{pmatrix} \gamma_i \\ \beta_i \end{pmatrix}.$$

We shall make the following assumptions on this model:

Assumption 1 $\theta_i = \bar{\theta} + \varepsilon_i$, *where* $\bar{\theta} = (\bar{\gamma}, \bar{\beta}')'$ *and* $\varepsilon_i = (\varepsilon_{1i}, \varepsilon'_{2i})'$ *are independently normally distributed with mean* 0 *and covariance* Δ, *i.e.* $\theta_i \sim N(\bar{\theta}, \Delta)$ *and* $\mathrm{Cov}(\theta_i, \theta_j) = 0$ *if* $i \neq j$.

Assumption 2 x_{it} *and* u_{is} *are independent for all t and s, i.e.,* $x'_{it}s$ *are strictly exogenous.*

Assumption 3 *The product-moment matrices* $T^{-1}(X_i'X_i)$ *have full ranks and tend to finite non-singular matrices as* $T \rightarrow \infty$.

Assumption 4 *The disturbances are heteroscedastic and are uncorrelated across different units, i.e.* $u_{it} \sim iid(0, \sigma_i^2)$ *and* $Eu_iu_j' = 0$ *if* $i \neq j$.

The main emphasis of this study will be the estimation of the mean coefficient vector $\bar{\theta}$. Although the focus will be on the estimates of the short-run coefficients throughout the study, we will also discuss the implications of them for long-run coefficient estimates. The estimates of the covariance matrix Δ will receive attention to find out if the degree of coefficient heterogeneity can be correctly detected from them.

3 Classical approach

Substituting $\theta_i = \bar{\theta} + \varepsilon_i$ into (2) yields

$$y_i = Z_i \bar{\theta} + v_i, \qquad i = 1,2,\ldots, N, \tag{3}$$

where

$$v_i = Z_i\varepsilon_i + u_i \tag{4}$$

Since

$$y_{i,t-1} = \sum_{j=0}^{\infty}(\bar{\gamma} + \varepsilon_{1i})^j x'_{i,t-j-1}(\bar{\beta} + \varepsilon_{2i}) + \sum_{j=0}^{\infty}(\bar{\gamma} + \varepsilon_{1i})^j u_{i,t-j-1} \tag{5}$$

it follows that $E(v_i|Z_i) \neq 0$. Therefore, the least squares estimator of $\bar{\theta}$ is inconsistent.

Equations (4) and (5) also demonstrate that the covariance matrix of v_i is not easily derivable. In other words, the generalized least squares method that transforms (3) into a model with serially uncorrelated error is not implementable. Neither is the instrumental variable method feasible because the instruments that are uncorrelated with v_i are most likely uncorrelated with Z_i as well.

Pesaran and Smith (1995, Appendix) have derived the asymptotic bias of the conventional fixed effects (within) estimator for model (3). In the special case where there is a single exogenous regressor which is generated according to a first-order autoregressive process

$$x_{it} = \mu_i(1-\rho) + \rho x_{i,t-1} + \nu_{it}$$

and there is no heterogeneity in the coefficient of the lagged dependent variable, i.e., $\gamma_i = \bar{\gamma}$, they show that[1]

$$\operatorname*{plim}_{N,T\to\infty} \hat{\gamma} = \bar{\gamma} + \frac{\rho(1-\bar{\gamma}\rho)(1-\bar{\gamma}^2)\delta_2}{\Psi_1}$$

$$\operatorname*{plim}_{N,T\to\infty} \hat{\beta} = \bar{\beta} - \frac{\bar{\beta}\rho^2(1-\bar{\gamma}^2)\delta_2}{\Psi_1}$$

where

$$\Psi_1 = (\sigma^2/\tau^2)(1-\rho^2)(1-\bar{\gamma}\rho)^2 + (1-\bar{\gamma}^2\rho^2)\delta_2 + (1-\rho^2)\bar{\beta}^2.$$

The size of the asymptotic bias depends on the mean coefficients $\bar{\beta}$ and $\bar{\gamma}$, ρ, the variance of β_i, denoted by δ_2, and the means of σ_i^2 and τ_i^2, denoted by σ^2 and τ^2, where τ_i^2, is the variance of ν_{it}. It is easy to check that $\hat{\beta}$ always underestimates $\bar{\beta}$, whereas $\hat{\gamma}$ over- or underestimates $\bar{\gamma}$ depending on whether ρ is positive or negative, respectively.

Thus, there are serious difficulties with the sampling approach to deriving consistent estimators of the mean coefficients. Pesaran and Smith (1995) advocate an estimator which they call the mean group estimator.[2]

[1] These results do not depend on the order by which N or T is allowed to tend to infinity.
[2] They also consider the Swamy estimator, referred to as the empirical Bayes estimator in this chapter.

This estimator is obtained by estimating the coefficients of each cross-sectional unit separately by OLS and then by taking an arithmetic average of them

$$\hat{\bar{\theta}} = \frac{1}{N}\sum_{i=1}^{N}\hat{\theta}_i \tag{6}$$

where $\hat{\theta}_i$ are OLS estimates from individual regressions. When $T \to \infty$, $\hat{\theta}_i \to \theta_i$ and (6) will be consistent when N also goes to infinity. This estimator has obviously only asymptotic justification. A discussion of the asymptotic properties of the mean group estimator is provided below in section 6. However, it would be interesting to have some idea about its performance in finite samples, particularly as compared to Bayesian type estimators and estimators that attempt to correct for the finite T bias of the individual estimates, $\hat{\theta}_i$. We shall now turn our attention to these estimators.

4 Bayesian approach

In this section, we consider various Bayes methods of estimating the mean coefficients for a dynamic panel data model. For finite T, we need to be more specific about the initial values of the dependent variable y_{i0} (e.g., Anderson and Hsiao (1981, 1982)). We could either assume that y_{i0} are fixed and known or alternatively specify the distribution of y_{i0} assuming stationarity. The latter case is obviously of great interest but it would complicate the analysis significantly. Therefore, in this study, we shall consider the Bayes estimator conditional on the initial values y_{i0} and report on the unconditional Bayes estimator in our future work.

When there is reliable prior information about Δ and σ_i^2, the posterior distribution of $\bar{\theta}$ can be derived by expressing the likelihood function conditional on the initial values y_{i0} and combining it with the prior distribution of $\bar{\theta}$, i.e.

$$p(\bar{\theta} \mid y, y_0) \propto p(y \mid \bar{\theta}) p(\bar{\theta}).$$

Lindley and Smith (1972) and Smith (1973) discuss the derivation of the Bayes estimator of $\bar{\theta}$ and for completeness we sketch it here. In their approach, there is a three-stage hierarchy. The joint density function for data $y = (y_1', y_2', \ldots, y_N')'$

$$y \sim N(\tilde{Z}\theta, \Omega)$$

is indexed by a parameter vector θ which is in turn also assumed to be normally distributed

$$\theta \sim N(A\bar{\theta}, \Gamma)$$

where $\tilde{Z} = \text{diag}(Z_1, Z_2, \ldots, Z_N)$, $\theta = (\theta'_1, \theta'_2, \ldots, \theta'_N)'$, $A = e_N \otimes I_k$, e_N is a column vector of ones, $\Gamma = I_N \otimes \Delta$ and Ω is a block diagonal matrix with the ith diagonal block given by $\Omega_i = \sigma_i^2 I_T$. The dimensions of y, $\tilde{Z}$, θ are $NT \times 1$, $NT \times Nk$, and $Nk \times 1$, respectively. The third stage of the hierarchy corresponds to the prior distribution of $\bar{\theta}$

$$\bar{\theta} \sim N(\mu, \Psi).$$

Note that the marginal distribution of y is given by

$$y \sim N(Z\bar{\theta}, \Phi)$$

where $Z = (Z'_1, Z'_2, \ldots, Z'_N)'$ and $\Phi = \Omega + \tilde{Z}\Gamma\tilde{Z}'$. Combining this with the prior distribution of $\bar{\theta}$ yields the posterior density of $\bar{\theta}$. The posterior density is proportional to $exp\,(-\frac{1}{2}S)$ where

$$\begin{aligned} S &= (y - Z\bar{\theta})'\Phi^{-1}(y - Z\bar{\theta}) + (\bar{\theta} - \mu)'\Psi^{-1}(\bar{\theta} - \mu), \\ &= \bar{\theta}' B^{-1}\bar{\theta} - 2b'\bar{\theta} + \text{constant}, \\ &= (\bar{\theta} - Bb)' B^{-1}(\bar{\theta} - Bb) + \text{constant}, \end{aligned}$$

$B = (Z'\Phi^{-1}Z + \Psi^{-1})^{-1}$ and $b = Z'\Phi^{-1}y + \Psi^{-1}\mu$. Thus, it is clear that

$$\bar{\theta} \sim N(\theta^*, V^*)$$

where $\theta^* = Bb$ and $V^* = B$. Assuming prior ignorance at the third stage of the hierarchy, i.e., $\Psi^{-1} = 0$, yields the following alternative form of the posterior distribution of $\bar{\theta}$

$$\bar{\theta} \sim N((Z'\Phi^{-1}Z)^{-1}Z'\Phi^{-1}y, (Z'\Phi^{-1}Z)^{-1}).$$

Moreover, after some algebra it can be shown that

$$\theta^* = \sum_{i=1}^{N} W_i \hat{\theta}_i \tag{7}$$

where

$$W_i = \left[\sum_{j=1}^{N} (\sigma_j^2 (Z_j' Z_j)^{-1} + \Delta)^{-1}\right]^{-1} [\sigma_i^2 (Z_i' Z_i)^{-1} + \Delta]^{-1}.$$

Thus, the posterior mean has the form of a weighted average of the least squares estimates of individual units with the weights being inversely proportional to individual variances. The posterior mean can be used as a point estimate of $\bar{\theta}$.

In practice, the variance components in (7) will be rarely known in economics and the Bayes estimator derived above is not a feasible estimator. Therefore, we shall call (7) the "infeasible Bayes" estimator. This estimator will be of interest only for the purpose of comparing the performance of other estimators with it. When variance components are unknown, an alternative approach can be taken following Lindley and Smith (1972). The prior distribution of the hyperparameters can be incorporated into the model and then the marginal posterior densities of the parameters of interest can be obtained by integrating out the hyperparameters from the joint posterior density. However, the required integrations pose an insurmountable challenge in our case and closed-form analytic solutions cannot be obtained. Nevertheless, a full Bayesian implementation of this model is now feasible as a result of recent advances in sampling-based approaches to calculating marginal densities. A particular algorithm known as Gibbs sampling has been used successfully in recent research in multi-dimensional problems similar to the one considered here. It is discussed in detail in Gelfand and Smith (1990) and illustrations of it using various well-known models in statistics are provided in Gelfand *et al.* (1990).

The Gibbs sampler is an iterative Markov Chain Monte Carlo method which is most easy to implement among various sampling-based approaches and which only requires the knowledge of the full conditional densities of the parameter vector. Starting from some arbitrary initial values, say $(\theta_1^{(0)}, \theta_2^{(0)}, \ldots, \theta_k^{(0)})$ for a parameter vector $\theta = (\theta_1, \theta_2, \ldots, \theta_k)$, it samples alternately from the conditional density of each component of the parameter vector conditional on the values of other components sampled in the latest iteration. That is:

$$\text{(1) Sample } \theta_1^{(i+1)} \text{ from } p(\theta_1 \mid \theta_2^{(i)}, \ldots, \theta_k^{(i)}, y)$$

$$\text{(2) Sample } \theta_2^{(i+1)} \text{ from } p(\theta_2 \mid \theta_1^{(i+1)}, \ldots, \theta_k^{(i)}, y)$$

$$\vdots \qquad \vdots$$

$$\text{(3) Sample } \theta_k^{(i+1)} \text{ from } p(\theta_k \mid \theta_1^{(i+1)}, \ldots, \theta_{k-1}^{(i+1)}, y).$$

The vectors $\theta^{(0)}, \theta^{(1)}, \ldots, \theta^{(m)}, \ldots$ will form a Markov Chain with transition probability from stage θ' to the next one θ being

$$K(\theta', \theta) = p(\theta_1 \mid \theta_2', \ldots, \theta_k', y) p(\theta_2 \mid \theta_1, \theta_3', \ldots, \theta_k', y) \ldots p(\theta_k \mid \theta_1, \ldots, \theta_{k-1}, y).$$

As the number of iterations m approaches infinity, the sampled values in effect can be regarded as drawing from true joint and marginal posterior densities. Moreover, the ergodic averages of functions of the sampled values will be consistent estimators of the expected values.

In order to implement Gibbs sampling, we need to specify the prior distribution of the hyperparameters. The hyperparameters in our study are assumed to be independent and distributed as

$$p(\Delta^{-1},\Omega) = W(\Delta^{-1}|(\rho R)^{-1},\rho)^{-1},\rho)\prod_{i=1}^{N}\sigma_i^{-2}$$

where W represents the Wishart distribution with scale matrix (ρR) and degrees of freedom ρ. Although it may be interesting to incorporate an informative prior distribution for σ_i^2 by making them exchangeable in a fashion similar to θ_i, we do not explore this possibility in this chapter and find it satisfactory to proceed with a non-informative prior distribution for σ_i^2.

With this structure the joint density of all the parameters can be written as

$$p(\theta_i,\bar{\theta},\Delta,\sigma_i^2|y,y_{i0}) \alpha \prod_{i=1}^{N}\sigma_i^{-T} exp\left[-\frac{1}{2}\sum_{i=1}^{N}\sigma_i^{-2}(y_i - Z_i\theta_i)'\,(y_i - Z_i\theta_i)\right]$$

$$\times|\Delta|^{-\frac{N}{2}} exp\left[-\frac{1}{2}\sum_{i=1}^{N}(\theta_i - \bar{\theta})'\Delta^{-1}(\theta_i - \bar{\theta})\right]$$

$$\times|\Psi|^{-\frac{1}{2}} exp\left[-\frac{1}{2}(\bar{\theta} - \mu)'\Psi^{-1}(\bar{\theta} - \mu)\right]$$

$$\times|\Delta|^{-\frac{1}{2}(\rho-k-1)} exp\left[-\frac{1}{2}tr(\rho R)\Delta^{-1}\right]$$

$$\times\prod_{i=1}^{N}\sigma_i^{-2}.$$

The first line of the above formula corresponds to the standard likelihood function and the others represent the prior information.

The relevant conditional distributions that are needed to implement the Gibbs sampler in our case are easily obtained from the joint posterior density

$$p(\theta_i|y,\bar{\theta},\Delta^{-1},\sigma_1^2,\ldots,\sigma_N^2) = N[A_i(\sigma_i^{-2}Z_i'y_i + \Delta^{-1}\bar{\theta}),A_i]\; i=1,2,\ldots,N,$$

$$p(\bar{\theta}|y,\theta_1,\ldots,\theta_N,\Delta^{-1},\sigma_1^2,\ldots,\sigma_N^2) = N[B(N\Delta^{-1}\tilde{\theta} + \Psi^{-1}\mu),B]$$

$$p(\Delta^{-1}|y,\theta_1,\ldots,\theta_N,\bar{\theta},\sigma_1^2,\ldots,\sigma_N^2) = W\Big[\big(\textstyle\sum_{i=1}^{N}(\theta_i - \bar{\theta})(\theta_i - \bar{\theta})' + \rho R\big)^{-1},\rho + N\Big]$$

$$p(\sigma_i^2|y,\theta_1,\ldots,\theta_N,\bar{\theta},\Delta^{-1}) = IG[T/2,((y_i - Z_i\theta_i)'(y_i - Z_i\theta_i)/2]\quad i=1,2,\ldots,N$$

where $A_i = (\sigma_i^{-2}Z_i'Z_i + \Delta^{-1})^{-1}, B = (N\Delta^{-1} + \Psi^{-1})^{-1}, \tilde{\theta} = \frac{1}{N}\sum_{i=1}^{N}\theta_i$, and IG denotes the inverse gamma distribution. The values sampled after some initial number of iterations can be used to construct estimates of the parameters of interest. We shall call the estimator of $\bar{\theta}$ obtained using Gibbs sampling the "hierarchical Bayes" estimator.

Although we choose to model the data and the parameters by normal distributions in the above discussion, the Bayesian framework is quite flexible and can easily accommodate other distributional forms. It is well known that the normal distribution may be quite misleading as the outliers in the data and in the parameters may have undue influence on overall inferences. In some instances, it may be a better idea to use a longer-tailed distribution such as the t-distribution instead of the normal distribution to lessen the influence of the extreme values. Markov Chain Monte Carlo methods can be easily used to check the sensitivity of inferences to the specific assumptions made regarding distributions of the data and parameters.

A somewhat different approach to the estimation of mean coefficients is the so-called empirical Bayes approach which can be viewed as an attempt to operationalize the infeasible Bayes estimator presented earlier. In this approach, the estimates of hyperparameters are directly substituted into the Bayes formula after they are obtained by some familiar method such as method of moments, maximum likelihood, etc. Since the uncertainty in the estimation of hyperparameters is not taken into account, the empirical Bayes approach is expected to give better results when T and N are large. In more sophisticated versions of the empirical Bayes approach (e.g., Morris (1983)), this uncertainty is also incorporated into the model. However, in our case, this potentially useful extension does not seem to be easy and straightforward. In this chapter we implement the empirical Bayes approach by estimating the variance components by the method originally proposed by Swamy (1971), i.e.

$$\hat{\Delta}=\frac{1}{N}\sum_{i=1}^{N}\left(\hat{\theta}_i-\frac{1}{N}\sum_{i=1}^{N}\hat{\theta}_i\right)\left(\hat{\theta}_i-\frac{1}{N}\sum_{i=1}^{N}\hat{\theta}_i\right)'-\frac{1}{N}\sum_{i=1}^{N}\hat{\sigma}_i^2(Z_i'Z_i)^{-1}, \qquad (8)$$

$$\hat{\sigma}_i^2=\frac{\hat{u}_i'\hat{u}_i}{T-k}$$

where $\hat{\theta}_i$ and $\hat{u}_i$ are obtained from OLS estimation for each cross-sectional unit. It is possible that $\hat{\Delta}$ may not be non-negative definite. An easy way to fix this problem is to drop the second term on the right-hand side.[3] While the variance components can be estimated in alternative ways and it may be interesting to compare the performance of the empirical Bayes estimator using different estimates of hyperparameters, we do not pursue this extension

[3] Notice that under assumption 3 the second term in (8) is $O_p(T^{-1})$.

and instead focus our attention on the performance of a particular version of the empirical Bayes estimator against other alternative estimators.

5 Asymptotics

For *all* values of $0<\sigma_i^2<\infty$, and for *all* non-singular matrices Δ, the Bayes estimator defined by (7) is asymptotically equivalent to the mean group estimator, (6), as $T\rightarrow\infty$, $N\rightarrow\infty$ and $\sqrt{N}/T^{3/2}\rightarrow 0$. To see this consider the difference between the two estimators and note that this difference can be written as

$$\sqrt{N}(\theta^* - \hat{\bar{\theta}}) = N^{-\frac{1}{2}}\sum_{i=1}^{N}(\psi_{NT}^{-1}\psi_{iT} - \mathrm{I}_k)\hat{\theta}_i \tag{9}$$

where I_k is an identity matrix of order k

$$\psi_{iT} = \left(\frac{\sigma_i^2}{T}\left(\frac{Z_i'Z_i}{T}\right)^{-1} + \Delta\right)^{-1}$$

and

$$\psi_{NT} = N^{-1}\sum_{j=1}^{N}\psi_{jT}.$$

Under assumption 3 and for $|\gamma_i|<1$ we have (for each i)

$$\operatorname*{plim}_{T\rightarrow\infty}\left(\frac{Z_i'Z_i}{T}\right) = Q_i \qquad \text{(a positive definite matrix).}$$

$$\hat{\theta}_i = \theta_i + (Z_i'Z_i)^{-1}Z_i'u_i = \theta_i + O_p(T^{-\frac{1}{2}}).$$

Hence

$$\psi_{iT}^{-1} = \Delta + T^{-1}(\sigma_i^2 Q_i^{-1}) + O_p(T^{-\frac{3}{2}}).$$

and

$$\psi_{iT} = \Delta^{-1} - T^{-1}\sigma_i^2(\Delta Q_i \Delta)^{-1} + O_p(T^{-\frac{3}{2}}). \tag{10}$$

Similarly

$$\psi_{NT}^{-1} = \Delta + T^{-1}\Delta\left[N^{-1}\sum_{i=1}^{N}\sigma_i^2(\Delta Q_i\Delta)^{-1}\right]\Delta + O_p(T^{-\frac{3}{2}}). \tag{11}$$

Also under assumptions 2–4

$$\hat{\theta}_i = \theta_i + (Z_i'Z_i)^{-1}Z_i'u_i = \theta_i + O_p(T^{-\frac{1}{2}}).$$

Using these results in (9), and after some algebra we have

$$\sqrt{N}(\theta^* - \hat{\bar{\theta}}) = \frac{\sqrt{N}}{T}\Delta\left\{\begin{array}{l}[N^{-1}\sum_{i=1}^{N}\sigma_i^2(\Delta Q_i\Delta)^{-1}]\bar{\theta} \\ - N^{-1}\sum_{i=1}^{N}\sigma_i^2(\Delta Q_i\Delta)^{-1}\theta_i\end{array}\right\} + O_p\left(\frac{\sqrt{N}}{T^{3/2}}\right). \tag{12}$$

The terms in the curly brackets are bounded in N for finite values of σ_i^2 and θ_i, and for all positive definite matrices Δ and Q. Therefore, $\sqrt{N}(\theta^* - \hat{\bar{\theta}})$ is of order $\sqrt{N}/T$ in probability and for *all* feasible parameter values the Bayes and the mean group estimators are therefore asymptotically equivalent as $T \to \infty$, $N \to \infty$ and $\sqrt{N}/T \to 0$. Under assumption 1 where $\theta_i = \bar{\theta} + \varepsilon_i$, the terms in the curly brackets in (12) tend to zero as $N \to \infty$, and

$$\sqrt{N}(\theta^* - \bar{\theta}) - \sqrt{N}(\hat{\bar{\theta}} - \bar{\theta}) = O_p\left(\frac{\sqrt{N}}{T^{3/2}}\right).$$

This result also clearly shows that the choices of σ_i^2 and Δ in the construction of the Bayes estimator is important only when T is small.

Given the asymptotic equivalence of the two estimators, in what follows we focus our analysis on the asymptotic distribution of the mean group estimator, $\hat{\bar{\theta}}$. Using (6) and recalling that

$$\hat{\theta}_i = \theta_i + (Z_i'Z_i)^{-1}Z_i'u_i, \qquad \theta_i = \bar{\theta} + \varepsilon_i$$

we have

$$\sqrt{N}(\hat{\bar{\theta}} - \bar{\theta}) = N^{-\frac{1}{2}}\sum_{i=1}^{N}\varepsilon_i + N^{-\frac{1}{2}}\sum_{i=1}^{N}\xi_{iT} \tag{13}$$

where

$$\xi_{iT} = (Z_i'Z_i)^{-1}Z_i'u_i, \qquad i = 1,2,\ldots,N. \tag{14}$$

It is clear that for a fixed T, and assuming $\varepsilon_i \sim iid(0,\Delta)$, the first term on the right-hand side of (13) converges to $N(0,\Delta)$ as $N \to \infty$.[4] The contribution of the second term in (13) to the asymptotic distribution of $\sqrt{N}(\hat{\bar{\theta}} - \bar{\theta})$ critically depends on whether the underlying group regressions, (6), contain lagged values of the dependent variable or not. Under the latter case $E(\xi_{iT}) = 0$ (exactly), and assuming that (Z_i, u_i) are independently distributed across i, as $N \to \infty$ the second term in (13) will tend to a normal distribution with mean zero and the covariance matrix

$$\Phi_T = \frac{1}{T}\lim_{N\to\infty}\left\{N^{-1}\sum_{i=1}^{N}\sigma_i^2\left(\frac{Z_i'Z_i}{T}\right)^{-1}\right\}$$

for a finite T. In the case where T is also allowed to tend to infinity, the contribution of the second term in (13) becomes negligible and $\sqrt{N}(\hat{\bar{\theta}} - \bar{\theta}) \overset{a}{\sim} N(0,\Delta)$ for sufficiently large N and T; and it does not matter whether N and/or T is allowed to tend to infinity first.

[4] Note that the assumption that θ_i (and hence ε_i) are normal, made earlier in the chapter to implement the Bayes procedure, is not needed.

When Z_i contains lagged values of the dependent variable, $\hat{\theta}_i$ is no longer an unbiased estimator of θ_i and the above reasoning will not be applicable. For this case using familiar results (for example, Kiviet and Phillips (1993)) we have (for each i)

$$E(\xi_{iT}) = E(\hat{\theta}_i - \theta_i) = \delta_{iT} = \frac{K_{it}}{T} + O(T^{-\frac{3}{2}}) \tag{15}$$

where K_{iT} is a non-stochastic variable bounded in T, such that

$$\lim_{N\to\infty} \left(N^{-1} \sum_{i=1}^{N} K_{iT} \right) = \bar{K}_T < \infty, \qquad \text{for all } T.$$

Now write (13) as

$$\sqrt{N}(\hat{\bar{\theta}} - \bar{\theta}) = N^{-\frac{1}{2}} \sum_{i=1}^{N} \varepsilon_i + N^{-\frac{1}{2}} \sum_{i=1}^{N} (\xi_{iT} - \delta_{iT}) + N^{-\frac{1}{2}} \sum_{i=1}^{N} \delta_{iT} \tag{16}$$

and using (15), we have

$$\sqrt{N}(\hat{\bar{\theta}} - \bar{\theta}) = N^{-\frac{1}{2}} \sum_{i=1}^{N} \varepsilon_i + N^{-\frac{1}{2}} \sum_{i=1}^{N} (\xi_{iT} - \delta_{iT})$$
$$+ \frac{\sqrt{N}}{T} \left(N^{-1} \sum_{i=1}^{N} K_{iT} \right) + O_p\left(\frac{\sqrt{N}}{T^{\frac{3}{2}}} \right).$$

In this case it is clear that the finite T distribution of $\sqrt{N}(\hat{\bar{\theta}} - \bar{\theta})$ will depend on the nuisance parameters in K_{iT} and the higher-order terms of the bias term $E(\xi_{iT})$. To obtain the asymptotic distribution of the mean group estimator (and hence the asymptotic distribution of the Bayes estimator) we need to assume that N is a monotonic function of T (say $N(T)$), such that $\sqrt{N(T)}/T \to 0$, as $T \to \infty$. The first condition is needed so that the central limit theorem for triangular arrays can be applied to the sum $N(T)^{-\frac{1}{2}} \sum_{i=1}^{N(T)} (\xi_{iT} - \delta_{iT})$ (see Billingsley (1979, theorem 27.2)).[5] The second condition $\sqrt{N(T)}/T \to 0$ is needed so that the terms involving the nuisance parameters are eliminated, asymptotically. We summarize the above results in the following proposition:

> ***Proposition 1*** *Under Assumptions 1–4, and assuming that N is a monotonic function of T, say $N = N(T)$, such that as $T \to \infty$, then $N(T) \to \infty$ and $\sqrt{N(T)}/T \to 0$, we have*[6]
>
> $$\sqrt{N(T)}(\theta^* - \bar{\theta}) \overset{a}{\sim} \sqrt{N(T)}(\hat{\bar{\theta}} - \bar{\theta}) \overset{a}{\sim} N(0, \Delta).$$

[5] For more details and relevant references to the literature, see the appendix to Im *et al.* (1997).

[6] The part of assumption 1 which requires θ_i to be normally distributed is not needed for the validity of this proposition.

Notice that the condition $\sqrt{N}/T \to 0$ is weaker than the condition requiring that N and T tend to infinity at the same rate, and permits N to grow at a faster rate than T. This allows the application of the theorem to panels where N could be much larger than T, which is an important consideration in practice. To highlight this point condition $\sqrt{N}/T \to 0$ in the above proposition can also be written as $T = O(N^{\frac{1}{2}+d})$, or $N = O(T^{2-d})$, for $2 > d > 0$.

Using the above results it also readily follows that

$$(\hat{\bar{\theta}} - \bar{\theta}) = N^{-1}\sum_{i=1}^{N}\varepsilon_i + N^{-1}\sum_{i=1}^{N}(\xi_{iT} - \delta_{iT}) + \frac{1}{T}\left(N^{-1}\sum_{i=1}^{N}K_{iT}\right) + O_p(T^{-\frac{3}{2}})$$

and $\hat{\bar{\theta}}$ will be an asymptotically unbiased estimator of $\bar{\theta}$ so long as $T \to \infty$. Notice that

$$E(\hat{\bar{\theta}} - \bar{\theta}) = \frac{1}{T}\left(N^{-1}\sum_{i=1}^{N}K_{iT}\right) + O_p(T^{-\frac{3}{2}})$$

and hence

$$E(\hat{\bar{\theta}}) \to \bar{\theta}, \qquad \text{as} \qquad T \to \infty$$

for all values of N. For reducing the bias we need sufficiently large T; not surprisingly increasing N does not help the small sample bias of the dynamic coefficients.

Because the finite T properties of $\hat{\bar{\theta}}$ hinge on how good $\hat{\theta}_i$ is as an estimator of θ_i, one way to improve upon $\hat{\bar{\theta}}$ is to improve the initial estimator of θ_i. It is well known that the asymptotic bias of $\hat{\theta}_i$ is $O(T^{-1})$ (Hurwicz (1950)). Kiviet and Phillips (1993) have proposed a bias corrected estimator that is unbiased to $O(T^{-1})$. They claim that the bias-corrected estimator achieves significant decreases in bias without accompanying deterioration in mean squared error. It may be interesting to construct an estimator analogous to the mean group estimator following their method. We call it the bias-corrected mean group estimator and define it as

$$\breve{\theta} = \frac{1}{N}\sum_{i=1}^{N}\breve{\theta}_i \tag{17}$$

where $\breve{\theta}_i$ is the bias-corrected estimator for the ith cross-sectional unit.[7]

[7] Using Monte Carlo simulation techniques, the small sample properties of the mean group estimators of the long-run coefficients, are investigated by Pesaran *et al.* (1996). In chapter 12 of this volume, Pesaran and Zhao investigate alternative bias corrected mean group estimators of the long-run coefficients.

6 The design of the Monte Carlo study

The data are generated from the model

$$y_{it} = \gamma_i y_{i,t-1} + \beta_i x_{it} + u_{it}$$

where

$$x_{it} = \mu_i(1-\phi) + \phi x_{i,t-1} + \varepsilon_{it}, \quad i=1,\dots,N, \quad t=1,\dots,T.$$

The disturbances are generated from

$$u_{it} \sim N(0,\sigma_i^2), \quad \varepsilon_{it} \sim N(0,\tau_i^2), \quad \sigma_i \sim N(\sigma,\eta^2), \quad \tau_i \sim N(\tau,\xi^2).$$

When negative σ_i and τ_i are drawn, their absolute values are taken. In all simulations the x series is generated in the same way by setting $\tau=0.3$, $\xi=0.1$, $\phi=0.7$ and $\mu \sim N(1,0.09)$. Random coefficients γ_i and β_i are obtained from independent normal distributions

$$\gamma_i \sim N(\bar{\gamma},\sigma_\gamma^2), \quad \beta_i \sim N(\bar{\beta},\sigma_\beta^2).$$

Since the bias of the estimators depend on the degree of coefficient heterogeneity, data with both low and high degrees of heterogeneity are generated. Specifically, σ_γ and σ_β are chosen to be equal to 50 percent and 100 percent of their mean coefficients, i.e., $\sigma_\gamma \varepsilon \{\bar{\gamma}/2,\bar{\gamma}\}$ and $\sigma_\beta \varepsilon \{\bar{\beta}/2,\bar{\beta}\}$. The mean coefficients take the values $\bar{\gamma}=0.3$, 0.6 and $\bar{\beta}=0.1$, 1. The bias of the estimators also depend on the signal to noise ratio and we pay particular attention to the average values of R^2.

To avoid explosive (or unstable) simulated y series we generated γ_i from the truncated normal distribution for $\bar{\gamma}=0.6$ and $T=20$ by truncating the distribution to the unit interval. The mean and variance of the γ_i generated in this manner can be obtained from the standard formulas

$$E(\gamma_i \mid -1<\gamma_i<1) = \bar{\gamma} + \sigma_\gamma M, \tag{18}$$

$$\text{var}(\gamma_i \mid -1<\gamma_i<1) = \sigma^2_\gamma(1-M^2+P)$$

where $\alpha_1=(-1-\bar{\gamma})/\sigma_\gamma, \alpha_2=(1-\bar{\gamma})/\sigma_\gamma, M=\phi(\alpha_1)-\phi(\alpha_2)/\Phi(\alpha_2)-\Phi(\alpha_1)$ and $P=\alpha_1\phi(\alpha_1)-\alpha_2\phi(\alpha_2)/\Phi(\alpha_2)-\Phi(\alpha_1)$. Note that when the coefficients are generated from the truncated normal distribution, the prior distribution of γ_i would be different and the derivation of the Bayes estimator should take this into account. Although we could have attempted to do this, it would also be interesting to see the performance of the Bayes estimator without making this adjustment.

The number of cross-sectional units is $N=50$ in all simulations and $T=5, 20$. For each cross-sectional unit $T+10$ observations are generated starting from $y_{i0}=0$ and $x_{i0}=0$. The first ten observations are then dropped in order to reduce the dependency on initial values. The number

Table 11.1. *Monte Carlo design**

	T	$\bar{\gamma}$	σ_γ	$\bar{\beta}$	σ_β	σ	η	$\bar{R}^2$
1	5	0.3	0.3	0.1	0.1	0.2	0.1	0.57
2	5	0.3	0.3	1	1	2	0.5	0.58
3	5	0.6	0.6	0.1	0.1	0.2	0.1	0.64
4	5	0.6	0.6	1	1	2	0.5	0.71
5	5	0.3	0.15	0.1	0.05	0.2	0.1	0.51
6	5	0.3	0.15	1	0.5	2	0.5	0.54
7	5	0.6	0.3	0.1	0.05	0.2	0.1	0.66
8	5	0.6	0.3	1	0.5	2	0.5	0.68
9	20	0.3	0.3	0.1	0.1	0.2	0.1	0.43
10	20	0.3	0.3	1	1	2	0.5	0.46
11	20	0.6	0.6	0.1	0.1	0.2	0.1	0.51
12	20	0.6	0.6	1	1	2	0.5	0.54
13	20	0.3	0.15	0.1	0.05	0.2	0.1	0.36
14	20	0.3	0.15	1	0.5	2	0.5	0.40
15	20	0.6	0.3	0.1	0.05	0.2	0.1	0.55
16	20	0.6	0.3	1	0.5	2	0.5	0.58

Note:
* The underlying data generation process is described in section 6.

of replications is chosen as 500. To implement the hierarchical Bayes analysis, we specify vague priors for Ψ^{-1} and ρ by setting $\Psi^{-1}=0$ and $\rho=2$. We originally considered a diffuse prior for Δ. However, the Gibbs algorithm breaks down completely in some experiments when a diffuse prior is specified. This may be the result of having an improper posterior density when the prior is diffuse (see Hobert and Casella (1996)). For this reason, we proceed with an informative prior distribution for Δ and choose the prior scale matrix R equal to the Swamy estimate of Δ. The parameters of different Monte Carlo designs are summarized in Table 11.1.

An important issue in the implementation of the Gibbs sampler is the detection of convergence. Although a large number of diagnostic tools for checking convergence has been proposed in recent literature, none of them appears to be foolproof as demonstrated in a recent review article by Cowles and Carlin (1996). In fact, they recommend that "automated convergence monitoring (as by a machine) is unsafe and should be avoided." In this study we try to get some idea about convergence by experimenting with different numbers of iterations and by examining the output of the

Table 11.2. *Bias of the short-run coefficient, $\bar{\beta}$*

	$\bar{\beta}$	Pooled OLS	Mean group	Bias-corrected mean group	Infeasible Bayes	Empirical Bayes	Hierarchical Bayes
$T=5$							
1	0.1	−0.03647	0.02838	0.01419	−0.00594	0.02091	0.00779
2	1	−0.44095	0.29004	0.14631	−0.06237	0.17418	0.03993
3	0.1	−2.46840	0.03168	0.01956	−0.00590	0.01425	0.00325
4	1	−12.6822	0.27987	0.12711	−0.12751	0.06032	−0.09211
5	0.1	−0.00445	0.03564	0.02241	−0.00144	0.02614	0.01486
6	1	−0.06367	0.35721	0.22241	0.00286	0.26849	0.14975
7	0.1	−0.11340	0.05409	0.02780	−0.00862	0.03323	0.01284
8	1	−1.23366	0.51018	0.25752	−0.12327	0.26294	0.05563
$T=20$							
9	0.1	−0.05136	0.00960	0.00114	−0.0011	0.00039	−0.00140
10	1	−0.55847	0.11376	0.03153	0.00830	0.02240	0.00772
11	0.1	−0.00219	0.01247	0.00140	−0.00012	0.00243	−0.00002
12	1	0.05894	0.10257	−0.00059	−0.00903	0.00933	−0.01103
13	0.1	−0.00548	0.01065	0.00232	0.00033	0.00289	0.00133
14	1	−0.08267	0.09708	0.01564	−0.00122	0.02212	0.00650
15	0.1	−0.03620	0.02107	0.00456	0.00023	0.00568	0.00196
16	1	−0.43800	0.19625	0.03863	0.00047	0.04407	0.01136

Notes:
The true parameter values and sample sizes for all the 16 experiments are set out in table 11.1. "Pooled OLS" refers to the OLS estimator of the pooled model. "Mean group" is the mean group estimator defined by (6). "Biased-corrected mean group" is defined by (17). "Infeasible Bayes" is the Bayes estimator defined by (7) based on the true values of σ_i^2 and Δ. "Empirical Bayes" is the Bayes estimator which uses the Swamy estimators of σ_i^2 and Δ given by (8). "Hierarchical Bayes" is the Bayes estimator with σ_i^2 and Δ integrated out using Gibbs sampling.

Gibbs sampler carefully. It appears that convergence is usually achieved fairly quickly. For $T=5$, the number of iterations is set to 2,500 and the values from the first 500 iterations are discarded. For $T=20$, the corresponding values are chosen as 1,000 and 200.

7 Monte Carlo results

Tables 11.2–11.8 present the simulation results. The bias and the root mean squared error of the alternative estimators are reported. Table 11.2 shows the bias of $\bar{\beta}$. The infeasible Bayes estimator appears to have very small

Table 11.3. *Bias of the short-run coefficient, $\bar{\gamma}$*

	$\bar{\gamma}$	Pooled OLS	Mean group	Bias-corrected mean group	Infeasible Bayes	Empirical Bayes	Hierarchical Bayes
$T=5$							
1	0.3	0.36859	−0.23613	−0.14068	0.05120	−0.12054	−0.02500
2	0.3	0.41116	−0.23564	−0.14007	0.04740	−0.11151	−0.01500
3	0.6	1.28029	−0.17924	−0.10969	0.05751	−0.02874	0.02884
4	0.6	1.29490	−0.18339	−0.10830	0.06879	−0.00704	0.06465
5	0.3	0.06347	−0.26087	−0.15550	0.01016	−0.18724	−0.10068
6	0.3	0.08352	−0.26039	−0.15486	0.01141	−0.18073	−0.09544
7	0.6	0.54756	−0.28781	−0.17283	0.05441	−0.12731	−0.02997
8	0.6	0.57606	−0.28198	−0.16935	0.06258	−0.10366	−0.01012
$T=20$							
9	0.3	0.44268	−0.07174	−0.01365	0.00340	−0.00238	0.00621
10	0.3	0.49006	−0.06910	−0.01230	0.00498	−0.00106	0.00694
11	0.35	0.25755	−0.06847	−0.01209	−0.00172	−0.01004	−0.00011
12	0.35	0.25869	−0.06644	−0.01189	−0.00229	−0.00842	0.00116
13	0.3	0.07199	−0.07966	−0.01508	−0.00054	−0.01637	−0.00494
14	0.3	0.09342	−0.07659	−0.01282	0.00244	−0.01262	−0.00107
15	0.55	0.26997	−0.09700	−0.02224	−0.00062	−0.01630	0.00011
16	0.55	0.29863	−0.09448	−0.02174	−0.00053	−0.01352	0.00198

Note:
See the notes to table 11.2.

bias even for $T=5$. For $T=5$, its bias falls within the range of 1 to 13 percent. For $T=20$, the bias is at most about 1 percent. The hierarchical Bayes performs estimator also very well, particularly when the degree of coefficient heterogeneity is relatively high. For $T=5$, its bias does not exceed 10 percent and in some cases also turns out to be slightly less than the bias of the infeasible Bayes estimator! However, when the degree of coefficient heterogeneity is reduced, the bias increases somewhat, e.g., designs 5,6, and 7, although it still remains less than 15 percent in all cases. This sensitivity seems to be related to the specification of the prior scale matrix R. Recall that it is specified in terms of the Swamy estimate of Δ. When the degree of coefficient heterogeneity decreases, the Swamy estimate of Δ deteriorates and this affects the hierarchical Bayes estimates of $\bar{\beta}$ and $\bar{\gamma}$ adversely. Although the idea of using a diffuse prior for Δ to improve the estimates is attractive, it does not work in this case as we explained earlier. For $T=20$, the bias of the hierarchical Bayes estimator is always less than 2 percent.

Table 11.4. *Bias of the long-run coefficient,* $\bar{\lambda} = \bar{\beta}/(1 - \bar{\gamma})$

	Pooled OLS	Mean group	Corrected mean group	Infeasible Bayes	Empirical Bayes	Hierarchical Bayes
$T=5$						
1	0.0488	−0.00572	−0.00703	0.00212	0.00450	0.00582
2	0.5069	−0.04979	−0.06403	0.00819	0.01834	0.02588
3	2.4405	−0.02267	−0.01543	0.02475	0.01648	0.02818
4	10.5542	−0.30615	−0.28259	0.13425	0.10495	0.20729
5	0.0073	−0.00169	0.00023	0.00002	−0.00069	0.00060
6	0.0903	−0.01539	0.00138	0.02782	0.01170	0.01686
7	−0.1592	−0.02597	−0.02690	0.01442	0.00266	0.01244
8	−1.1728	−0.28559	−0.29131	0.09833	0.00752	0.07395
$T=20$						
9	0.04617	−0.00084	−0.00113	−0.00088	0.00007	−0.00073
10	0.67455	0.01956	0.01959	0.02217	0.02979	0.02544
11	0.09578	0.00267	−0.00070	−0.00059	0.00134	−0.00005
12	1.17224	0.00027	−0.02861	−0.01928	0.00554	−0.01426
13	0.00765	−0.00093	0.00023	0.00036	0.00077	0.00088
14	0.08373	−0.01588	−0.00375	0.00324	0.00574	0.00709
15	0.12642	−0.00053	−0.00071	0.00020	0.00444	0.00437
16	1.41453	−0.02161	−0.01945	−0.00153	0.03056	0.03478

Note:
See the notes to table 11.2.

The pooled OLS estimator is very badly biased in most cases and the bias persists as T increases.[8] When coefficient heterogeneity is lowered, the bias of the pooled OLS estimator decreases dramatically in certain cases, e.g., compare designs 5 and 6 to 1 and 2. These results suggest that the pooled OLS estimator may yield reasonable estimates even in the presence of coefficient heterogeneity provided that the coefficient heterogeneity is not too excessive. The mean group estimate of $\bar{\beta}$ improves as T increases but nevertheless the bias still seems to be relatively high even for $T=20$. The bias ranges from a low of 10 percent to a high of approximately 20 percent in some designs. The bias-corrected mean group estimator appears to be a much better alternative to the mean group estimator and especially appears to have a very respectable performance as T rises. For $T=20$, the bias is only about 1–5 percent. The empirical Bayes estimator is very much like the

[8] Notice that since intercepts are not included in the Monte Carlo experiments the fixed effect estimator is the same as the pooled OLS estimator.

Table 11.5. *RMSE ratios for* $\bar{\beta}$

	Pooled OLS	Mean group	Corrected mean group	Infeasible Bayes	Empirical Bayes	Hierarchical Bayes
$T=5$						
1	1.932	2.188	1.903	1.000	1.590	1.185
2	2.188	1.975	1.677	1.000	1.470	1.114
3	440.8	2.327	2.244	1.000	1.457	1.204
4	151.6	1.946	1.724	1.000	1.187	1.088
5	1.030	2.831	2.364	1.000	2.063	1.510
6	1.069	2.848	2.346	1.000	2.082	1.473
7	6.207	3.453	2.603	1.000	2.288	1.380
8	6.162	2.883	2.069	1.000	1.859	1.135
$T=20$						
9	3.735	1.255	1.080	1.000	1.025	1.017
10	3.901	1.319	1.090	1.000	1.042	1.015
11	6.720	1.275	1.016	1.000	1.018	1.010
12	9.677	1.281	1.050	1.000	1.044	1.027
13	1.136	1.542	1.189	1.000	1.118	1.044
14	1.227	1.416	1.104	1.000	1.075	1.039
15	3.008	2.082	1.274	1.000	1.194	1.077
16	3.656	1.980	1.188	1.000	1.183	1.078

Note:
See the notes to table 11.2.

bias-corrected mean group estimator in terms of the bias of $\bar{\beta}$. It gives more reasonable results as T increases and its performance shows some sensitivity to the accuracy of the Swamy estimates of Δ.

The bias of $\bar{\gamma}$ seems to be a slightly more serious issue. Table 11.3 summarizes these results. The bias of the infeasible Bayes estimator ranges from 3 percent to 17 percent for $T=5$. For $T=20$, it is always less than 2 percent. For $T=5$, the hierarchical Bayes estimator has very small bias as long as the degree of coefficient heterogeneity is relatively high and the scale matrix R is not specified very badly as we discussed above. With the exceptions of designs 5 and 6, its bias is even smaller than the bias of the infeasible Bayes estimator which assumes knowledge of true variances. For $T=20$, its bias is always less than 3 percent. The pooled OLS estimator overestimates $\bar{\gamma}$ substantially both for $T=5$ and $T=20$. The mean group estimator is downward biased and the bias for $T=20$ varies from 17 percent to 28 percent. The bias-corrected mean group estimator again gives reasonably good results for $T=20$ even though for smaller T it is substantially biased.

Table 11.6. *RMSE ratios for* $\bar{\gamma}$

	Pooled OLS	Mean group	Corrected mean group	Infeasible Bayes	Empirical Bayes	Hierarchical Bayes
$T=5$						
1	4.345	2.612	1.788	1.000	1.642	1.008
2	4.974	2.720	1.835	1.000	1.658	1.048
3	11.219	1.776	1.335	1.000	0.980	0.992
4	11.108	1.771	1.325	1.000	0.931	1.076
5	1.534	4.326	2.826	1.000	3.207	1.945
6	1.643	3.833	2.559	1.000	2.775	1.714
7	7.011	3.543	2.284	1.000	1.906	0.990
8	6.573	3.200	2.109	1.000	1.736	1.008
$T=20$						
9	9.192	1.598	1.028	1.000	1.016	1.033
10	10.397	1.619	1.027	1.000	1.013	1.035
11	10.097	1.467	1.054	1.000	1.052	1.058
12	10.857	1.421	1.026	1.000	1.051	1.060
13	2.423	2.393	1.159	1.000	1.218	1.085
14	2.996	2.400	1.137	1.000	1.169	1.088
15	6.415	2.446	1.209	1.000	1.176	1.140
16	7.067	2.410	1.210	1.000	1.154	1.146

Note:
See the notes to table 11.2.

It has a bias of 3–6 percent for $T=20$. The empirical Bayes estimator gives very good results even for $T=5$ in some cases but the bias also appears to be quite high in certain other cases. As T gets larger its bias decreases considerably.

It would also be interesting in dynamic models to have some idea about the bias of the long-run coefficients. Table 11.4 presents the bias of the long-run coefficient $\bar{\lambda}=E(\beta_i/(1-\gamma_i))$, estimated as $\hat{\bar{\beta}}/(1-\hat{\bar{\gamma}})$. It is clear from this table that if one is interested in the bias of the long-run coefficients then giving consideration *only* to the bias of the short-run estimates may be quite misleading. Since the biases in $\bar{\beta}$ and $\bar{\gamma}$ are in opposite directions for most estimators, it is possible to get a small bias for the long-run coefficient even if the biases of short-run coefficients are quite large. For example, the mean group estimator appears to have smaller bias than the infeasible Bayes estimator 1 in experiments 3, 6, 9, 10, and 12 even though the bias of the short-run coefficients for the mean group estimator is much larger than that of the Bayes estimator. The opposite is also true; namely that if one is

Table 11.7. *Estimates of* σ_γ and σ_β

	σ_γ			σ_β		
	True value	Swamy estimate	Hierarchical Bayes	True value	Swamy estimate	Hierarchical Bayes
$T=5$						
1	0.300	0.481	0.372	0.100	0.299	0.163
2	0.300	0.473	0.372	1.000	2.440	1.414
3	0.600	0.675	0.659	0.100	0.446	0.254
4	0.600	0.645	0.635	1.000	2.266	1.367
5	0.150	0.476	0.313	0.050	0.269	0.135
6	0.150	0.490	0.312	0.500	2.326	1.200
7	0.300	0.488	0.383	0.050	0.296	0.149
8	0.300	0.476	0.380	0.500	2.482	1.306
$T=20$						
9	0.300	0.270	0.306	0.100	0.112	0.103
10	0.300	0.270	0.306	1.000	1.113	1.041
11	0.425	0.394	0.430	0.100	0.117	0.106
12	0.425	0.396	0.429	1.000	1.121	1.042
13	0.150	0.167	0.160	0.050	0.072	0.058
14	0.150	0.163	0.158	0.500	0.678	0.562
15	0.256	0.247	0.245	0.050	0.077	0.061
16	0.256	0.247	0.246	0.500	0.685	0.575

Note:
See the notes to table 11.2.

interested in small sample bias of long-run estimates, the use of unbiased (or reduced bias) estimates of the short-run coefficients does not necessarily yield a reduced-biased estimate of the long-run coefficients. This is largely due to the non-linearity of the relationship between the short-run and the long-run coefficients. Notice that in general

$$\bar{\lambda} = E(\lambda_i) = E\left(\frac{\beta_i}{1-\gamma_i}\right) \neq \frac{E(\beta_i)}{1-E(\gamma_i)} = \frac{\bar{\beta}}{1-\bar{\gamma}}$$

Therefore, a procedure which is successful in reducing the bias of the short-run coefficients ($\bar{\beta}$ and $\bar{\gamma}$) may perform very poorly when it comes to estimating the long-run coefficients, $\bar{\lambda}$, in a small sample. For more details and an alternative bias-correction procedure applied to the long-run coefficients see chapter 12 in this volume, Pesaran and Zhao (1999).

Table 11.8. *Posterior quantiles*

	$\bar{\gamma}$				$\bar{\beta}$			
	25	75	2.5	97.5	25	75	2.5	97.5
$T=5$								
1	0.209	0.331	0.114	0.435	0.089	0.126	0.048	0.168
2	0.231	0.344	0.079	0.463	0.866	1.227	0.529	1.587
3	0.555	0.718	0.403	0.823	0.074	0.132	0.009	0.209
4	0.599	0.740	0.426	0.887	0.713	1.098	0.322	1.479
5	0.153	0.245	0.072	0.334	0.098	0.131	0.067	0.160
6	0.153	0.257	0.059	0.353	0.993	1.282	0.791	1.586
7	0.520	0.622	0.413	0.716	0.094	0.131	0.066	0.160
8	0.523	0.660	0.395	0.771	0.886	1.217	0.595	1.550
$T=20$								
9	0.270	0.343	0.191	0.419	0.084	0.110	0.065	0.135
10	0.273	0.344	0.196	0.409	0.889	1.124	0.666	1.357
11	0.303	0.394	0.227	0.475	0.087	0.112	0.068	0.135
12	0.309	0.391	0.226	0.494	0.875	1.109	0.626	1.293
13	0.271	0.321	0.211	0.364	0.093	0.109	0.078	0.126
14	0.275	0.324	0.220	0.371	0.928	1.083	0.759	1.246
15	0.514	0.579	0.443	0.642	0.092	0.111	0.073	0.131
16	0.516	0.576	0.453	0.649	0.916	1.101	0.775	1.293

Tables 11.5 and 11.6 present the root mean squared errors (rmse) of alternative estimators relative to the root mean squared error of the infeasible Bayes estimator. Table 11.5 reports the rmse ratios for $\bar{\beta}$. It is clear that the infeasible Bayes estimator which utilizes the true variances has the smallest rmse among all estimators both for $T=5$ and $T=20$. The hierarchical Bayes estimator also compares favorably with the infeasible Bayes estimator with the exceptions of designs 5 and 6. The designs 5 and 6 are also those in which the pooled OLS estimator yields good results. For $T=20$, the rmse of the hierarchical Bayes estimator is never more than 8 percent larger than the rmse of the infeasible Bayes estimator. In general, the bias-corrected mean group and empirical Bayes estimators have good rmse properties for $T=20$, but their performance in small T panels is far from satisfactory. Their rmse is 40–80 percent larger than the rmse of the hierarchical Bayes estimator in several cases for $T=5$. The rmse of the empirical Bayes estimator is slightly smaller than that of the bias-corrected mean group estimator in all cases.

Table 11.6 shows the rmse ratios for $\bar{\gamma}$. The hierarchical Bayes estimator again yields very good results with the exceptions of the same designs.[9] The pooled OLS estimator again performs very poorly. It is interesting to note that even though the rmse of the pooled OLS estimator for $\bar{\beta}$ is quite reasonable for designs 5, 6, 13, and 14, the rmse for $\bar{\gamma}$ is much higher for the same designs. The mean group estimator also has unsatisfactory performance even for $T=20$.

It is quite important to be able to assess the degree of heterogeneity in the coefficients accurately from the existing data. Good estimates of Δ can aid in the choice of an appropriate estimator. If Δ is small, then there is no harm in using the pooled OLS estimators. On the other hand, if the components of Δ are large, imposing coefficient homogeneity will be very misleading.[10] In table 11.7 we report two different estimates of σ_γ and σ_β. The construction of the Swamy estimate of Δ is already discussed. In addition, it is also possible to obtain an estimate of Δ from the Gibbs sampler. The Δ sampled in successive iterations of the Gibbs algorithm from its conditional distribution can be used for this purpose. A comparison of the Swamy estimates with the ones used to generate the data indicate that Swamy estimates are significantly larger than the true values. The accuracy of Swamy estimates depends both on T and the degree of heterogeneity in the coefficients. For larger T, the Swamy estimates appear to be much more reasonable. Also, as heterogeneity decreases, they become less reliable. The bias of σ_γ is smaller relative to the bias of σ_β but it is difficult to make generalizations from this. This result may be due to the larger variability in the y series we have generated. The results for $T=5$ caution against drawing any firm conclusions from Swamy estimates in small samples. They may substantially overestimate the true variances in small samples. On the other hand, Bayes estimates of Δ in general are much better than the Swamy estimates even though not perfect at least for small T.

So far we have focused on the sampling properties of alternative estimators such as bias and root mean squared error. However, our approach to the comparison of alternative estimators may not be palatable to Bayesians. It is considered inappropriate by Bayesians to summarize inference only by a single value. Point estimates make sense to Bayesians only in large

[9] In the case of experiments 3 and 7 the hierarchical Bayes estimator of $\bar{\gamma}$ performs even slightly better than the infeasible estimator when $T=5$, which in the first instance may seem rather surprising (see table 11.6). However, this could be due to a number of factors: When T is small initial observations play an important role and none of the Bayes estimators, including the classical infeasible one, account for them, and the infeasible Bayes estimator need not be better than the other estimators in all experiments. Also in the case of these experiments (3 and 7) where $\bar{\gamma}=0.6$, some of the simulated values of γ could be in the unstable region with unexpected consequences for the different estimators. Notice that simulated values of γ were trimmed only for the case of $T=20$ and not when $T=5$ which is applicable to the experiments under consideration.

[10] Formal tests of coefficient homogeneity are discussed in Pesaran *et al.* (1996).

samples when the posterior mode is the center of the posterior distribution and the uncertainty as expressed in the standard errors are small enough to be neglected. Bayesians would point to the richness of inferences that can be drawn from the entire posterior distribution. We report in table 11.8 the 2.5, 25, 75, and 97.5 percentiles of the posterior distribution of $\bar{\gamma}$ and $\bar{\beta}$ obtained from Gibbs sampling. It is worth noting that in all cases 95 percent posterior intervals include the true mean coefficients. Moreover, the entries to the table can be used to infer useful information about the other features of the posterior distribution.

In summary, the limited Monte Carlo experience appears to indicate that when T is large, then various consistent estimators perform fairly well. When T is small, then the hierarchical Bayes estimator of the short-run coefficients (computed via Gibbs sampling) performs the best. The uncorrected mean group estimator does not have good properties, neither does the least squares estimator. The good performance of the hierarchical Bayes estimator for very small T is quite surprising in view of the fact that they are derived conditional on initial y_{i0}, which as demonstrated by Anderson and Hsiao (1981, 1982), and cannot be viewed as the proper likelihood function for $(y_{i0},\ldots,y_{iT})$. It has been confirmed by many Monte Carlo studies (e.g. Blundell and Bond (1998)) that the bias of ignoring the initial observation is quite significant in a sampling approach. One possible explanation of the better performance of the Bayes estimators in the present application may be due to the fact that by weighing the OLS estimates of the individual coefficients, the Bayes estimators in effect appropriately trim the individual estimates that could be extremely unreliable in small samples. It is worth noting that for $T=5$, the OLS estimates of the individual coefficients that underlie the Bayes or the mean group estimators may not even have moments, and thus could result in extreme value estimates. Trimming such estimates before using them in the mean group estimation procedure may be a sensible strategy when T is small.

8 An empirical application: the *q* investment model re-examined

The q investment model has been used to study a large number of theoretical and empirical issues relating to investment in recent years (for references, see, e.g., Chirinko (1993)). The origins of the q model go back to Brainard and Tobin (1968) and Tobin (1969) and a formal derivation of the model from the firm's value maximization problem was given by Hayashi (1982). The q theory relates investment to marginal q which is the ratio of the market value of new investment goods to their replacement cost. The intuition behind the theory is easy to understand. Suppose a firm increases its capital stock by one more dollar. If the firm has unexploited profit opportunities, its market value, which is the present discounted value of its future profits, will increase by more than one dollar in response to the addition of the last unit of capital. In this case, firm managers should acquire the new capital goods if they pursue the objective of maximizing shareholder value. Investment will continue to increase until the marginal increase in firm value equals the marginal cost of additional capital, i.e., until marginal q equals one. On the other hand, if a firm already has more than adequate capital, its market value will increase by less than one dollar when new capital is added. In this case, shareholder value maximization dictates that managers should abandon the marginal project. Thus, investment will be an increasing function of marginal q. The steady-state value of marginal q will be equal to one, not allowing for tax considerations, etc. The attractive feature of the model is that it introduces forward-looking expectations into the study of investment behavior through the asset prices which are supposed to capture those expectations.

One of the most troubling findings regarding the q investment model has been the extremely large estimates often obtained for the adjustment cost parameters and the implied slow speeds of adjustment of the capital stock to its equilibrium value. We suspect that this finding may be due, at least partly, to the use of inappropriate estimation techniques when there is significant heterogeneity in firm investment responses to the q variable. To evaluate the importance of this heterogeneity we estimate the following simple dynamic version of the q model for a panel of a large number of US companies

$$\left(\frac{I}{K}\right)_{it} = a_i + b_i\left(\frac{I}{K}\right)_{i,t-1} + c_i q_{it} + u_{it}$$

where I_{it} is investment expenditures by firm i during the period t, K_{it} is the replacement value of the capital stock, and q_{it} is Tobin's q of the firm. Our data set is the one which has been used by Hsiao and Tahmiscioglu (1997). It is a subset of the original data set and contains 273 firms with complete observations over the 20 years: 1973–1992. Readers interested in the construction of the variables should consult Hsiao and Tahmiscioglu (1997).

The estimation results are presented in table 11.9. The fixed-effect (within) estimate of the coefficient of the q variable is within the range (i.e., 0.005 to 0.010) reported in previous panel studies. A comparison of the pooled OLS and the hierarchical Bayes estimates indicates that there is significant underestimation of the coefficients of the q and the lagged investment variable. We also think that the substantial serial correlation reported by researchers in previous studies is most likely the consequence of the incorrect imposition of slope homogeneity and not paying enough attention to the dynamic nature of investment models. Although our purpose here is not to salvage the q investment model, it is clear that some of the

Table 11.9. *Estimates of Tobin's* q *model* $\left(\text{dependent variable is } \left(\frac{I}{K}\right)_{it}\right)$

Variables	Fixed effects	Mean group	Corrected mean group	Empirical Bayes	Hierarchical Bayes
Intercept		0.1127	0.0921	0.0972	0.0984
		(0.0043)	(0.0043)	(0.0030)	(0.0034)
$\left(\frac{I}{K}\right)_{i,t-1}$	0.2947	0.3233	0.4245	0.4052	0.4305
	(0.0137)	(0.0150)	(0.0167)	(0.0138)	(0.0154)
q_{it}	0.0086	0.0369	0.0351	0.0245	0.0174
	(0.0006)	(0.0032)	(0.0031)	(0.0024)	(0.0014)

problems attributed to it are the artifact of an inappropriate choice of estimation techiques and the neglect of slope heterogeneity.

The Bayes estimate of the q coefficient is 0.017, whereas the coefficient estimates for the mean group and the bias-corrected mean group estimators are 0.037 and 0.035, respectively. All these estimates are substantially larger than the ones reported in the literature. The discrepancy in these estimates of the coefficient of the q variable (between the hierarchical Bayes estimator and the mean group and the bias-corrected mean group estimators) is intriguing. We would expect the estimates to be much closer to each other, particularly considering that in the present application $T=20$, which is relatively large. Since it is difficult to know which estimation technique gives better results, we resort to prediction comparison. We estimate the model using the observations from 1973 to 1987 and reserve the last five years for obtaining forecasts. As prediction criteria, root mean squared error and mean absolute forecast error are chosen. The results are reported in table 11.10. It is clear that the hierarchical Bayes estimator gives the best predictions. It is interesting to note that the predictive performance of the mean group and the bias-corrected mean group estimators is even worse than the within estimator. Thus, there is much reason to be suspicious about the mean and bias-corrected mean group estimates. We suspect that the cause of the discrepancy in the estimates of the hierarchical Bayes and the mean group estimators may be the collinearity between the q variable and other variables, particularly the constant term. The q variable changes very slowly for many firms and this creates a linear dependency with the constant term.

9 Conclusion

This chapter shows that in the case of dynamic panel data model with coefficient heterogeneity where there does not exist a consistent estimator

Table 11.10. *Prediction comparison of the* q *model*

Year	Fixed effects	Mean group	Corrected mean group	Empirical Bayes	Hierarchical Bayes
Root mean squared error					
1988	0.093	0.096	0.093	0.088	0.085
1989	0.095	0.116	0.114	0.100	0.091
1990	0.096	0.134	0.129	0.094	0.086
1991	0.114	0.145	0.142	0.110	0.104
1992	0.216	0.227	0.224	0.202	0.199
Mean absolute forecast error					
1988	0.070	0.071	0.069	0.065	0.061
1989	0.071	0.083	0.080	0.072	0.065
1990	0.072	0.089	0.085	0.069	0.064
1991	0.083	0.097	0.094	0.079	0.075
1992	0.100	0.119	0.114	0.099	0.091

of the mean parameters unless N and T both tend to infinity, the Bayesian approach performs fairly well even when T is small. Contrary to the sampling approach where the correct modeling of initial observations is quite important (e.g. Anderson and Hsiao (1981, 1982)), Bayesian methods can be a viable alternative in the estimation of the mean coefficients in dynamic panel data models even if initial observations are treated as fixed constants. This study also cautions against the practice of generalizing from the asymptotic properties of the estimators about their finite sample performance. The Monte Carlo results indicate that some consistent estimators may have disastrous implications in panels with very small T. Our results using both simulated and real data suggest that the hierarchical Bayes estimator is preferable to the other consistent estimators unless the time dimension of the panel is sufficiently large relative to the cross-sectional dimension.

The difficulties of implementing the Bayesian approach have been substantially eliminated by the recent advances in sampling-based approaches to calculating posterior densities. Thus, there is no excuse any longer for not considering Bayesian methods because of practical difficulties. Since the comparison of alternative estimators in this study is undertaken to a large extent using the sampling properties of estimators, econometricians who adopt the sampling theory framework should find the Bayesian approach more attractive in the light of our findings.

References

Anderson, T.W. and C. Hsiao (1981), "Estimation of Dynamic Models with Error Components," *Journal of the American Statistical Association*, 76: 598–606.

(1982), "Formulation and Estimation of Dynamic Models Using Panel Data," *Journal of Econometrics*, 18: 47–82.

Billingsley, P. (1979), *Probability and Measure*, New York: John Wiley & Sons.

Blundell, R. and S. Bond (1998), "Initial Conditions and Moment Restrictions in Dynamic Panel Data Models," *Journal of Econometrics*, forthcoming.

Brainard, W.C. and J. Tobin (1968), "Pitfalls in Financial Model Building," *American Economic Review*, 58: 99–122.

Chirinko, R. (1993), "Business Fixed Investment Spending: Modeling Strategies, Empirical Results, and Policy Implications," *Journal of Economic Literature*, 31: 1875–1911.

Cowles, M.K. and B.P. Carlin (1996), "Markov Chain Monte Carlo Convergence Diagnostics: A Comparative Review," *Journal of the American Statistical Association*, 91: 883–904.

Gelfand, A.E., S.E. Hills, A. Racine-Poon, and A.F.M. Smith (1990), "Illustration of Bayesian Inference in Normal Data Models Using Gibbs Sampling," *Journal of the American Statistical Association*, 85: 972–985.

Gelfand, A.E. and A.F.M. Smith (1990), "Sampling-Based Approaches to Calculating Marginal Densities," *Journal of the American Statistical Association*, 85: 398–409.

Hayashi, F. (1982), "Tobin's Marginal q and Average q: A Neoclassical Interpretation," *Econometrica*, 50: 213–224.

Hobert, J.P. and G. Casella (1996), "The Effect of Improper Priors on Gibbs Sampling in Hierarchical Linear Mixed Models," *Journal of the American Statistical Association*, 91: 1461–1473.

Hsiao, C. and A.K. Tahmiscioglu (1997), "A Panel Analysis of Liquidity Constraints and Firm Investment," *Journal of the American Statistical Association*, 92: 455–465.

Hurwicz, L. (1950), "Least Squares Bias in Time Series," in T.C. Koopmans (ed.), *Statistical Inference in Dynamic Economic Models*, Cowles Commission Monograph 10, New York: John Wiley & Sons.

Im, K-S., M.H. Pesaran, and Y. Shin (1997), "Testing for Unit Roots in Heterogeneous Panels", unpublished manuscript, University of Cambridge. (http://www.econ.cam.ac.uk/faculty/pesaran/).

Kiviet, J. and G. Phillips (1993), "Alternative Bias Approximations in Regressions with a Lagged-Dependent Variable," *Econometric Theory*, 9:62–80.

Lindley, D.V. and A.F.M. Smith (1972), "Bayes Estimates for the Linear Model," *Journal of the Royal Statistical Society*, 34: 1–41.

Maddala, G.S., R.P. Trost, H. Li, and F. Joutz (1997), "Estimation of Short-Run and Long-Run Elasticities of Energy Demand from Panel Data Using Shrinkage Estimators," *Journal of Business and Economic Statistics*, 15: 90–100.

Morris, C. (1983), "Parametric Empirical Bayes Inference: Theory and Applications," *Journal of the American Statistical Association*, 78: 47–59.

Pesaran, M.H. and R. Smith (1995), "Estimating Long-Run Relationships from Dynamic Heterogeneous Panels," *Journal of Econometrics*, 68: 79–113.

Pesaran, M.H., R. Smith, and K-S. Im, (1996), "Dynamic Linear Models for Heterogeneous Panels", in L. Matyas and P. Sevestre (eds.), *The Econometrics of Panel Data* (second edn), Dordrecht: Kluwer Academic Publishers.

Pesaran, M.H. and Z. Zhao (1999), "Bias Reduction in Estimating Long-run Relationships from Dynamic Heterogenous Panels," in Hsiao, C., K. Lahiri, L-F. Lee, and M.H. Pesaran (eds.), *Analysis of Panels and Limited Dependent Variables: A Volume in Honour of G.S. Maddala*, Cambridge University Press, this volume.

Smith, A.F.M. (1973), "A General Bayesian Linear Model," *Journal of the Royal Statistical Society*, series B, 35: 67–75.

Swamy, P.A.V.B. (1971), *Statistical Inference in Random Coefficient Regression Models*, Berlin: Springer-Verlag.

Tobin, J. (1969), "A General Equilibrium Approach to Monetary Theory," *Journal of Money, Credit and Banking*, 1: 15–29.

Zellner, A. (1969), "On the Aggregation Problem: A New Approach to a Troublesome Problem," in K.A. Fox *et al.*(eds.), *Economic Models, Estimation and Risk Programming: Essays in Honor of Gerhard Tintner*, Berlin: Springer-Verlag, pp. 365–378.

12 Bias reduction in estimating long-run relationships from dynamic heterogeneous panels

M. HASHEM PESARAN AND ZHONGYUN ZHAO

1 Introduction

In panel data models it is often of interest to estimate the average long-run effects of some exogenous variables (x) on a dependent variable of interest (y). In situations where T (the number of time periods) is sufficiently large there are four procedures that can be used to estimate this average effect (Pesaran and Smith (1995)). The first involves estimating separate regressions for each group and averaging the long-run coefficients over groups, which Pesaran and Smith refer to as the mean group estimator (MGE). The second procedure is to pool the separate regressions by imposing common slopes (but allowing for fixed or random intercepts), with the long-run effects estimated using standard fixed or random effects pooled regressions. The third is to average the data over groups and estimate aggregate time series regressions based on group averages. The last is to average the data over time and estimate cross-section regression based on long-time averages. In the static case, where the regressors are strictly exogenous and the coefficients differ randomly and are distributed independently of the regressors across groups, all four procedures provide consistent (and unbiased) estimates of the average (long-run) effects (Zellner (1969)). For some time it was wrongly believed that a similar result held for dynamic panel data models, namely that all the above four procedures yield consistent estimators. However, recently Pesaran and Smith (1995) have shown that the pooled and aggregate time series estimators are not consistent in dynamic models, even for large N (the number of groups) and T, and the traditional panel procedures (such as the fixed and random effects estimators) which pool the data by imposing slope homogeneity can be subject to substantial estimation bias when applied to heterogeneous dynamic panel data models. They also show that under certain conditions the mean group and the

We are grateful to Jan Kiviet for helpful comments on a previous version of the chapter. The first author wishes to acknowledge partial financial support from the ESRC and the Isaac Newton Trust of Trinity College, Cambridge.

cross-section estimates based on long time averages yield consistent estimates of the average long-run effects.

Pesaran, Smith, and Im (1996), using Monte Carlo simulations, investigate the small sample properties of the various estimators of the long-run coefficients, and discuss a number of procedures for testing the slope homogeneity hypothesis. Their findings indicate that the mean group estimator performs reasonably well for large T. However, when T is small, the mean group estimator could be seriously biased, particularly when N is large relative to T.

This chapter considers further the small sample properties of the mean group estimator in dynamic heterogeneous panels, and examines the effectiveness of alternative bias-correction procedures in reducing the small sample bias of these estimators. In particular, three procedures will be considered. An indirect procedure which attempts to bias-correct the estimator of the long-run coefficients by using the bias-corrected estimators of the short-run coefficients proposed by Kiviet and Phillips (1993). Due to the non-linear dependence of the long-run coefficients on the short-run coefficients it is easily seen that such an indirect approach does not lead to an estimator which is unbiased to order $O(T^{-1})$; and it is included to demonstrate the problem that surrounds a careless use of the result in Kiviet and Phillips (1993). We refer to this as the "naive" bias-corrected (NBC) estimator. More appropriately, we derive large sample approximation formulae directly for the bias of the least squares estimators of the long-run coefficients. In particular, we consider two variations of this direct approach and obtain estimators of the long-run coefficients which we call the "direct" bias-corrected estimators, DBC_1 and DBC_2. The bias in both of these estimators are of $O(T^{-1})$ order, but the DBC_1 estimator contains some higher-order bias corrections. The third procedure we shall consider employs the bootstrap method to compute the bias of the estimates of the long-run coefficients, which is subsequently used to construct a new bias-corrected estimator. This will be referred to as the bootstrap bias-corrected (BSBC) estimator.

The effectiveness of these procedures in small samples is examined by Monte Carlo experiments, both in the case of a single regression (namely when $N=1$), and for panel data models with $N=20$. We also compare the relative small sample performances of the Kiviet and Phillips bias-corrected (KPBC) and BSBC estimators of the short-run coefficients. Our experimental results indicate that both the KP and bootstrap estimators perform quite well in estimating the short-run coefficients, but the situation is different when the parameter of interest is the long-run coefficient. Not surprisingly the NBC procedure fails in all cases, and the bootstrap method performs poorly in cases where the true coefficient of the lagged dependent variable is relatively large. Both of the direct bias-corrected estimators perform reasonably well, although only the DBC_1 estimator which allows for some higher-order bias-correction terms out performs the bootstrap method. None of the estimators seem to be effective when the coefficient of the lagged dependent variable is around 0.8. For large values of the lagged dependent variable coefficient it may be worthwhile to derive higher-order bias-corrected estimators along the lines advanced recently by Kiviet and Phillips (1996).

Section 2 sets out the dynamic heterogeneous panel data model and provides a brief review of the literature on small sample bias of the least squares estimation of the slope coefficients in dynamic models. Section 3 discusses the alternative procedures for correcting the small sample bias of the MG estimator of the long-run coefficients. Section 4 examines their finite sample performances by means of Monte Carlo experiments. A brief summary of the chapter's main findings is given in section 5.

2 Dynamic models of heterogeneous panels

We assume that the data are generated by a set of relationships with coefficients that are constant over time but differ randomly across groups, and that the distribution of the coefficients is independent of the regressors. The parameters of interest are the averages, over groups, of the long-run coefficients. Consider the following heterogeneous dynamic model, also examined by Pesaran and Smith (1995).

$$y_{it} = \alpha_i + \lambda_i y_{i,t-1} + \beta_i' x_{it} + \varepsilon_{it}, \qquad i = 1,2,\ldots,N,\ t = 1,2,\ldots,T, \tag{1}$$

where i denotes cross-sectional units (groups) and t is the time index, ε_{it} is assumed to be independently and identically distributed with mean zero and variance σ_i^2, and ε_{it} is independent of α_i, λ_i, β_i, and x_{it}. It will be assumed that the process is stable $(-1<\lambda_i<1)$ and has started a long time ago, the between-group disturbance covariances are zero, i.e., $E(\varepsilon_{it}\varepsilon_{js})=0$, for all t and s, $i \neq j$, and the parameters λ_i and β_i are random and can be characterized by

$$\lambda_i = \lambda + \eta_{1i}, \quad \beta_i = \beta + \eta_{2i} \tag{2}$$

where η_{1i} and η_{2i} are assumed to have zero means and have a constant variance covariance matrix

$$\Omega = \begin{pmatrix} \omega_{11} & \omega_{12} \\ \omega_{21} & \omega_{22} \end{pmatrix}$$

We also assume that the higher-order moments of η_{1i} and η_{2i}, and their cross-moments exist and are finite, such that $\beta = E(\beta_i)$, $\lambda = E(\lambda_i)$ and the following (average) long-run parameter of interest exists:

$$\theta = E(\theta_i) = E(\beta_i/(1-\lambda_i)) \tag{3}$$

We also assume that x_{it} is generated by a stationary first-order vector autoregressive process:

$$x_{it} = (I_k - \Phi)\mu_i + \Phi x_{i,t-1} + u_{it} \tag{4}$$

where all the eigenvalues of Φ lie within the unit circle, and for each i, u_{it} is independently and identically distributed with zero mean and variance δ_i^2, and $E(u_{it}u'_{js}) = 0$, $t \neq s$, $i \neq j$. The assumption is made for convenience, and, except for the stationarity condition, can be readily relaxed.

In the case of a single group, namely for $N = 1$, there is a sizeable literature on the small sample bias of the least squares estimators of the slope coefficients λ_i and β_i. In the relatively simple case where $\beta_i = 0$, the order of the bias of the OLS estimator λ_i has been the subject of intensive research since the pioneering work of Hurwicz (1950) and White (1961). See, for example, Orcutt and Winokur (1969), Sawa (1978), Evans and Savin (1981), Tanaka (1983), and Evans and Savin (1984). In this case the bias of the OLS estimator of λ_i, up to order $O(T^{-1})$, is given by $-2\lambda_i/T$, when the model contains no intercepts. Including an intercept, this bias becomes $(1 + 3\lambda_i)/T$. In the more general case where the model contains exogenous regressors, Tse (1982) and Maekawa (1983) derived Edgeworth approximations for the distribution of the OLS estimators of the slope coefficients. Carter and Ullah (1979), Ullah and Maasoumi (1986), Hoque and Peters (1986), Peters (1989), Ullah and Srivastava (1994), on the other hand, derived the exact moments and small error variance approximation for the bias of the OLS estimator of λ_i. However, as shown by Kiviet and Phillips (1993), the small-σ approximation procedure performs rather poorly as compared to the large sample approximation techniques in reducing the bias of the short-run slopes. Grubb and Symons (1987) and Kiviet and Phillips (1993), especially the latter, provide an effective and easy to implement large sample approximation formulae for reducing the bias of the OLS estimators of the short-run coefficients in dynamic regressions. By comparison, little attention has been paid in the literature to the problem of the small sample bias correction of the estimators of the long-run coefficients. This problem is considered in the next section.

3 Bias-reduction techniques for estimation of the long-run coefficients

The focus of our analysis is the estimation of the (average) long-run coefficient, $\theta = E(\beta_i/(1 - \lambda_i))$. The theoretical and Monte Carlo evidence provided by Pesaran and Smith (1995) and Pesaran, Smith, and Im (1996) indicate that the mean group estimator of θ performs well for sufficiently large T. But, when T is small the bias in the estimate of the coefficient of the lagged dependent variable and the inherent non-linearity between the short-run and the long-run coefficients introduce a bias in the mean group estimator of the long-run coefficient which becomes more serious as $N \rightarrow \infty$.

The mean group estimator is based on individual group estimates. For the ith group, write (1) more compactly as

$$y_{it} = \alpha_i + \gamma_i' w_{it} + \varepsilon_{it}, \qquad i = 1,2,\ldots,N, \quad t = 1,2,\ldots,T,$$

where $w_{it} = (y_{i,t-1}, x_{it}')'$, $\gamma_i = (\lambda_i, \beta_i)'$. The OLS estimator of γ_i is given by

$$\hat{\gamma}_i = (W_i' H_T W_i)^{-1} W_i' H_T y_i, \qquad i = 1,2,\ldots,N,$$

where $W_i = (y_{i,-1}, X_i)$, $y_{i,-1} = (y_{i,0}, y_{i,1}, \ldots, y_{i,T-1})'$, $X_i = (x_{i1}, x_{i2}, \ldots, x_{iT})$ and $H_T = I_T - \tau_T(\tau_T'\tau_T)^{-1}\tau_T'$, I_T is the identity matrix of order T, and τ_T is a $T \times 1$ unit vector, and

$$\hat{\gamma}_i = (\hat{\lambda}_i, \hat{\beta}_i')' \tag{5}$$

Then the individual group estimates of the long-run coefficients are given by

$$\hat{\theta}_i = \hat{\beta}_i / (1 - \hat{\lambda}_i), \qquad i = 1,2,\ldots,N. \tag{6}$$

The mean group estimator of $\theta = E(\theta_i) = E(\beta_i/(1 - \lambda_i))$ is given by

$$\hat{\theta}_{MG} = N^{-1} \sum_{i=1}^{N} \hat{\beta}_i / (1 - \hat{\lambda}_i) \tag{7}$$

with its variance consistently estimated by

$$\hat{V}(\hat{\theta}_{MG}) = \frac{1}{N(N-1)} \sum_{i=1}^{N} (\hat{\theta}_i - \hat{\theta}_{MG})(\hat{\theta}_i - \hat{\theta}_{MG})' \tag{8}$$

Theoretically, $\hat{\theta}_{MG}$ converges to the true θ as both T and N go to infinity.[1] However, the estimator in (6) is biased when T is small for two different reasons: one source of the bias is the presence of the lagged dependent variables in the model which biases the OLS estimator of the short-run coefficients $\hat{\lambda}_i$ and $\hat{\beta}_i$. The second source of potential bias is due to the non-linearity of $\hat{\theta}_i$ in terms of $\hat{\lambda}_i$ and $\hat{\beta}_i$. It should be clear that even when exact unbiased estimators of the short-run coefficients are available, the estimator of the long-run coefficient could still be badly biased in finite samples. In case of trended regressors (irrespective of whether such trends are deterministic

[1] The mean group estimator is based on a simple average of the individual group estimates. However, it is also possible to consider weighted averages or individual group estimates with the weights determined either from a Bayesian perspective of a classical viewpoint. A prominent example of such a weighting scheme is Swamy's random coefficient estimator which weighs the individual group estimates by matrices that are inversely proportional to their estimated covariances. See, for example, Swamy (1970) and Hsiao (1986, chapter 6).

or stochastic) it is quite likely for the small sample bias of the estimator of the long-run coefficient to be much less serious than the bias of the estimators of the short-run coefficients (on this see Pesaran and Shin (1997)).

Here we consider three bias reduction models for the estimation of the long-run coefficients.

3.1 *The "naive" bias-corrected estimator (NBC)*

This method employs the bias-corrected estimators of the short-run coefficients proposed by Kiviet–Phillips (1993), and uses these corrected OLS estimators to construct the bias-corrected MG estimators of the long-run coefficients. More specifically, the NBC mean group estimators of θ is given by

$$\hat{\hat{\theta}}_{KP}=\frac{1}{N}\sum_{i=1}^{N}\hat{\hat{\beta}}_i/(1-\hat{\hat{\lambda}}_i)$$

where $\hat{\hat{\lambda}}_i$ and $\hat{\hat{\beta}}_i$ are the Kiviet–Phillips bias-corrected estimates of λ_i and β_i respectively, for $i=1,2,\ldots,N$. As was noted earlier such an indirect method of correcting for the bias of the estimator of the long-run coefficient does not yield a bias-corrected estimator which is of order $O(T^{-1})$, and it is included as a bench mark and to illustrate the pitfalls of an indiscriminate use of bias-corrected estimators of the short-run coefficients.

3.2 *Bias corrections applied directly to the estimator of the long-run coefficients*

Building on the work of Kiviet and Phillips we shall derive an $O(T^{-1})$ approximation formula for the bias of the long-run coefficient. For notational convenience, subscript i will be omitted here. We first note that

$$\begin{aligned}\hat{\theta}-\theta&=[(\hat{\beta}-\beta)+\theta(\hat{\lambda}-\lambda)]/(1-\hat{\lambda})\\&=[(\hat{\beta}-\beta)+\theta(\hat{\lambda}-\lambda)]/[(1-\lambda)-(\hat{\lambda}-\lambda)]\end{aligned}$$

where the letters without hats denote the true values. Let

$$C=(\hat{\beta}-\beta)+\theta(\hat{\lambda}-\lambda),\quad D=(1-\lambda)-(\hat{\lambda}-\lambda),$$

$$B_\theta=E(\hat{\theta}-\theta),\quad B_\beta=E(\hat{\beta}-\beta),\quad B_\lambda=E(\hat{\lambda}-\lambda),$$

where expectations are taken with respect to the joint distribution of the estimators of the short-run coefficients. Then the bias of $\hat{\theta}$ can be expressed as

$$B_\theta=E(\hat{\theta}-\theta)=E\left(\frac{C}{D}\right) \tag{9}$$

The Nagar-type expansion of $E\left(\frac{C}{D}\right)$ can now be used to yield the following bias approximation formula (see Nagar (1959)).

Theorem 1 *The bias B_θ of the OLS estimator of the long-run coefficient for each group can be approximated by $B_\theta = \Psi_\theta + O(T^{-3/2})$, where*

$$\Psi_\theta = \{(1-\lambda-B_\lambda)(B_\beta+\theta B_\lambda)+\text{cov}(\hat{\lambda},\hat{\beta})+\theta\text{var}(\hat{\lambda})\}/(1-\lambda-B_\lambda)^2. \quad (10)$$

Proof: *Let*

$$\bar{C} = E(C)$$
$$= E(\hat{\beta}-\beta)+\theta E(\hat{\lambda}-\lambda)$$
$$= B_\beta + \theta B_\lambda, \quad (11)$$
$$\bar{D} = E(D)$$
$$= (1-\lambda)-E(\hat{\lambda}-\lambda)$$
$$= (1-\lambda)-B_\lambda \quad (12)$$

and note that

$$D^{-1} = \bar{D}^{-1}\bar{D}D^{-1}$$
$$= \bar{D}^{-1}[D-(D-\bar{D})]D^{-1}$$
$$= \bar{D}^{-1}[1-(D-\bar{D})D^{-1}].$$

Substituting in this identity recursively for D^{-1} from its own right-hand side, the following expansion for D^{-1}, in powers of $(D-\bar{D})D^{-1}$, is obtained

$$D^{-1} = \bar{D}^{-1}\{1-(D-\bar{D})\bar{D}^{-1}+(D-\bar{D})^2\bar{D}^{-2}-\ldots\}.$$

Hence

$$B_\theta = E(\hat{\theta}-\theta)$$
$$= E\left(\frac{C}{D}\right)$$
$$= E\{C\bar{D}^{-1}[1-(D-\bar{D})\bar{D}^{-1}]\}+R \quad (13)$$

where R, the remainder term, is composed of a series of terms with elements

$$E\{C\bar{D}^{-1}[-(D-\bar{D})\bar{D}^{-1}]^j\} = \bar{D}^{-(j+1)}E[C(\bar{D}-D)^j],$$
$$\text{for } j=2,3 \quad (14)$$

Under $|\lambda|<1$ and assuming the regressors are covariance stationary we have

$$\hat{\beta}-\beta=O_p(T^{-1/2}), \text{ and } \hat{\lambda}-\lambda=O_p(T^{-1/2}).$$

Now using theorem 8 of Kiviet and Phillips (1993) it also follows that

$$B_\beta=E(\hat{\beta}-\beta)=O(T^{-1}),$$
$$B_\lambda=E(\hat{\lambda}-\lambda)=O(T^{-1}).$$

Similarly

$$C=(\hat{\beta}-\beta)+\theta(\hat{\lambda}-\lambda)=O_p(T^{-1/2}),$$
$$D-\bar{D}=(1-\lambda)-(\hat{\lambda}-\lambda)-[(1-\lambda)-E(\hat{\lambda}-\lambda)]$$
$$=B_\lambda-(\hat{\lambda}-\lambda)=O_p(T^{-1/2}).$$

Therefore

$$(D-\bar{D})^j=O_p(T^{-j/2}).$$

Using these results in (14)

$$E[C(\bar{D}-D)^j]=O(T^{-(j+1)/2}), \qquad \text{for } j=2,3,\ldots$$

Since $\bar{D}=O(1)$, we also have

$$E\{C\bar{D}^{-1}[-(D-\bar{D})\bar{D}^{-1}]^j\}=\bar{D}^{-(j+1)}E[C(\bar{D}-D)^j]$$
$$=O(T^{-(j+1)/2}), \qquad \text{for } j=2,3,\ldots$$

which establishes that the remainder term in (13) is in fact of order $O(T^{-3/2})$.

Now consider the main term of (13). Let

$$\Psi_\theta=E\{C\bar{D}^{-1}[1-(D-\bar{D})\bar{D}^{-1}]\}$$

and note that

$$\Psi_\theta=2E(C\bar{D}^{-1})-E(CD\bar{D}^{-2})$$
$$=2[E(C)]\bar{D}^{-1}-[E(CD)]\bar{D}^{-2}$$
$$=2\bar{C}\bar{D}^{-1}-[E(CD)]\bar{D}^{-2}$$

and

$$E(CD)=E\{[(\hat{\beta}-\beta)+\theta(\hat{\lambda}-\lambda)][(1-\lambda)-(\hat{\lambda}-\lambda)]\}$$
$$=E[(1-\lambda)(\hat{\beta}-\beta)-(\hat{\lambda}-\lambda)(\hat{\beta}-\beta)+\theta(1-\lambda)(\hat{\lambda}-\lambda)-\theta(\hat{\lambda}-\lambda)(\hat{\lambda}-\lambda)]$$
$$=(1-\lambda)B_\beta-E[(\hat{\lambda}-\lambda)(\hat{\beta}-\beta)]+\theta(1-\lambda)B_\lambda-\theta E[(\hat{\lambda}-\lambda)(\hat{\lambda}-\lambda)].$$

Also

$$E[(\hat{\lambda} - \lambda)(\hat{\beta} - \beta)] = \mathrm{cov}(\hat{\lambda}, \hat{\beta}) + B_\beta B_\lambda$$

and

$$E[(\hat{\lambda} - \lambda)(\hat{\lambda} - \lambda)] = \mathrm{var}(\hat{\lambda}) + B_\lambda^2.$$

Therefore

$$E(CD) = (1 - \lambda)B_\beta + \theta(1 - \lambda)B_\lambda - \mathrm{cov}(\hat{\lambda}, \hat{\beta}) - B_\beta B_\lambda - \theta \mathrm{var}(\hat{\lambda}) - \theta B_\lambda^2$$

and, after some simple algebra

$$\Psi_\theta = \{(1 - \lambda - B_\lambda)(B_\beta + \theta B_\lambda) + \mathrm{cov}(\hat{\lambda}, \hat{\beta}) + \theta \mathrm{var}(\hat{\lambda})\}/(1 - \lambda - B_\lambda)^2$$

which completes the proof of the theorem.

Since $B_\beta + \theta B_\lambda = O(T^{-1})$ and $B_\beta B_\lambda = O(T^{-2})$ then Ψ_θ defined by (15) can be further simplified, and the result of theorem 1 is not a parsimonious $O(T^{-1})$ approximation to the bias. Using a more direct approach the following alternative $O(T^{-1})$ approximation for the bias can be obtained.[2]

$$\bar{\Psi}_\theta = \{(1 - \lambda)(B_\beta + \theta B_\lambda) + \mathrm{cov}(\hat{\lambda}, \hat{\beta}) + \theta \mathrm{var}(\hat{\lambda})\}/(1 - \lambda)^2. \quad (15)$$

Based on the result of theorem 1, a bias-corrected estimator for θ can be constructed as follows:

$$\hat{\theta}_{BC} = \hat{\theta}_{MG} - \hat{\Psi}_\theta \quad (16)$$

where $\hat{\Psi}_\theta$ is the expression given by (10) (or alternatively by (15)), with β, λ, $\mathrm{cov}(\hat{\lambda}, \hat{\beta})$ and $\mathrm{var}(\hat{\lambda})$ replaced by their corresponding OLS estimators, whereas B_β and B_λ are replaced by $\hat{B}_\beta$ and $\hat{B}_\lambda$ which are obtained using the approximation formulae provided for the short-run coefficients in Kiviet and Phillips (1993).

3.3 *Bootstrap bias-corrected estimator*

Bootstrap methods (Efron (1979), Bickel and Freedman (1981), Hall (1992), Efron and Tibshirani (1993)) can also be used to make the bias corrections.[3] In the present application the bootstrap bias-corrected (BSBC) estimator of the mean group estimator of the long-run coefficient is computed in the following manner:

[2] We are grateful to Jan Kiviet for pointing this out to us.

[3] It has been pointed out to us by Jan Kiviet that since $(\hat{\theta} - \theta)$ is asymptotically pivotal, then it can be shown that the bootstrap bias correction will also lead to an estimator which is unbiased to order $O(T^{-1})$.

Step 1: Compute the OLS estimators of α_i, λ_i, β_i and the group-specific error variances

$$\hat{\sigma}_i^2 = \frac{1}{T-k-2}(y_i - \hat{\alpha}_i - W_i\hat{\gamma}_i)'(y_i - \hat{\alpha}_i - W_i\hat{\gamma}_i) \tag{17}$$

$$i = 1,2,\ldots,N$$

as well as the least squares estimators of θ_i defined by (6).

Step 2: Generate bootstrap samples $\hat{\varepsilon}_{it}^{(j)}$, $i = 1,2,\ldots,N$; $t = 1,2,\ldots,T$, for the jth replication either using the parametric or non-parametric approaches:

(a) In the case of parametric bootstrap, the errors $\hat{\varepsilon}_{it}^{(j)}$ for the jth replication are drawn from i.i.d. $N(0,\hat{\sigma}_i^2)$

$$i = 1,2,\ldots,N, \qquad \text{and} \qquad t = 1,2,\ldots,T$$

(b) The non-parametric resampling starts from the residuals:

$$\hat{\varepsilon}_{it} = y_{it} - \hat{\alpha}_i - \hat{\lambda}_i y_{i,t-1} - \hat{\beta}_i' x_{it},$$

$$i = 1,2,\ldots,N, \qquad t = 1,2,\ldots,T. \tag{18}$$

For each fixed i, let $A_i = (\hat{\varepsilon}_{i1}, \hat{\varepsilon}_{i2}, \ldots, \hat{\varepsilon}_{iT})$ and attach the weights $1/T$ to each of the values: $\hat{\varepsilon}_{it}$, $t = 1,2,\ldots,T$. A bootstrap sample is then constructed as a random sample of size T drawn from A_i, say

$$A_i^* = (\hat{\varepsilon}_{i1}^{(j)}, \hat{\varepsilon}_{i2}^{(j)}, \ldots, \hat{\varepsilon}_{iT}^{(j)}).$$

Step 3: Generate R bootstrap samples $y_{it}^{(j)}$:

$$y_{it}^{(j)} = \hat{\alpha}_i + \hat{\lambda}_i y_{i,t-1}^{(j)} + \hat{\beta}_i' x_{it} + \hat{\varepsilon}_{it}^{(j)} \tag{19}$$

for $i = 1,2,\ldots,N$, $t = 1,2,\ldots,T$ $j = 1,2,\ldots,R$ where

$$y_{i,0}^{(j)} = y_{i,0}, \qquad i = 1,2,\ldots,N$$

and $\hat{\varepsilon}_{it}^{(j)}$ are from step two above, generated either by parametric or non-parametric techniques.

Step 4: For each replication $j = 1,2,\ldots,R$, use $\{y_{it}^{(j)}: i = 1,2,\ldots,N,\ t = 1,2,\ldots,T\}$ and the original observations $\{x_{it}: i = 1,2,\ldots,N, t = 1,2,\ldots,T\}$ to compute the OLS estimates $\hat{\beta}_i^{(j)}$, $\hat{\lambda}_i^{(j)}$ and $\hat{\theta}_i^{(j)} = \dfrac{\hat{\beta}_i^{(j)}}{(1-\hat{\lambda}_i^{(j)})}$.

Step 5: Repeat steps two through four R times, and compute the bootstrap estimate of the bias

$$\widehat{bias}_R = \hat{\theta}_R - \hat{\theta}_{MG}$$

where

$$\hat{\theta}_R = \frac{1}{NR} \sum_{j=1}^{R} \sum_{i=1}^{N} \hat{\theta}_i^{(j)}.$$

Then the bootstrap bias-corrected (BSBC) estimator is given by

$$\hat{\hat{\theta}}_{MG} = 2\hat{\theta}_{MG} - \hat{\theta}_R. \tag{20}$$

4 Small sample performance of bias-reduction methods

In this section, the three bias-correction procedures discussed above will be illustrated and compared by Monte Carlo methods. Even though our main concern is with the estimation of average long-run effects, our simulations also provide information on the small sample performance of the estimates of the short-run coefficients obtained using the Kiviet–Phillips bias-corrected and the bootstrap methods.

4.1 Monte Carlo results for a single time series regression

We consider first the case where $N = 1$. To allow for the effect of variations in λ on the long-run coefficient, θ and to control the signal-to-noise ratio of the model we use the following parametrization of the Data Generation Process (DGP):

$$y_t = \lambda y_{t-1} + \theta(1-\lambda)x_t + \varepsilon_t \tag{21}$$

and

$$x_t = \rho x_{t-1} + u_t, \tag{22}$$

for $t = 1,2,\ldots,T$, $\varepsilon_t \sim NID(0, \sigma_\varepsilon^2)$ and $u_t \sim NID(0, \sigma_u^2)$ and without loss of generality we set $\theta = 1$ and $\sigma_\varepsilon^2 = 1$ throughout. The signal-to-noise ratio of (21) is given by

$$\frac{\sigma_s^2}{\sigma_\varepsilon^2} = \frac{R^2}{1-R^2} = \frac{\text{var}(y_t) - \sigma_\varepsilon^2}{\sigma_\varepsilon^2} \tag{23}$$

where R^2 is the population value of the squared multiple coefficient of (21). For the variance of y_t we have

$$\text{var}(y_t) = \lambda^2 \text{var}(y_{t-1}) + \theta^2(1-\lambda)^2 \text{var}(x_t) + 2\theta\lambda(1-\lambda)\text{cov}(y_{t-1}, x_t) + \sigma_\varepsilon^2$$

and since y_t is stationary ($|\lambda| < 1$)

$$(1-\lambda^2)\text{var}(y_t) = \theta^2(1-\lambda)^2 \text{var}(x_t) + 2\theta\lambda(1-\lambda)\text{cov}(y_{t-1}, x_t) + \sigma_\varepsilon^2$$

But

$$\text{var}(x_t) = \sigma_x^2 = \sigma_u^2/(1-\rho^2),$$

Table 12.1. *Simulation results for the bias and RMSE of alternative estimates for the single-group dynamic regression model**
($\lambda = 0.2$, $T = 20$, $N = 1$)

			OLS	NBC	DBC_1	DBC_2	BSBC
$\sigma_s^2 = 2$							
$\rho = 0.6$	λ	BIAS	−0.06297	−0.02096	—	—	−0.01885
		RMSE	0.17124	0.16921	—	—	0.17763
	β	BIAS	0.02695	0.00792	—	—	0.00731
		RMSE	0.19646	0.19515	—	—	0.20092
	θ	BIAS	−0.01959	0.02405	−0.00954	−0.01052	−0.00785
		RMSE	0.26034	0.27617	0.26273	0.26261	0.27537
		M	0	0	0	0	0
$\rho = 0.95$	λ	BIAS	−0.10844	−0.03207	—	—	−0.02325
		RMSE	0.23725	0.23258	—	—	0.24304
	β	BIAS	0.07635	0.02107	—	—	0.01627
		RMSE	0.47236	0.45552	—	—	0.45967
	θ	BIAS	−0.01502	0.02191	−0.00378	−0.00482	−0.00353
		RMSE	0.52721	0.56066	0.52842	0.52834	0.57632
		M	0	0	0	0	0
$\sigma_s^2 = 8$							
$\rho = 0.6$	λ	BIAS	−0.02283	−0.00376	—	—	−0.00524
		RMSE	0.10512	0.10516	—	—	0.10589
	β	BIAS	0.00816	−0.00036	—	—	0.00022
		RMSE	0.09943	0.09967	—	—	0.10074
	θ	BIAS	−0.00829	0.00852	−0.00424	−0.00446	−0.00420
		RMSE	0.13576	0.13932	0.13630	0.13628	0.13743
		M	0	0	0	0	0
$\rho = 0.95$	λ	BIAS	−0.07809	−0.01898	—	—	−0.01574
		RMSE	0.19494	0.19214	—	—	0.19699
	β	BIAS	0.05217	0.01061	—	—	0.00865
		RMSE	0.24634	0.24200	—	—	0.24600
	θ	BIAS	−0.01042	0.01371	−0.00423	−0.00492	−0.00424
		RMSE	0.27907	0.30034	0.28220	0.28175	0.28718
		M	0	0	0	0	0

Table 12.1. *(cont.)*

Notes:
* The estimates are based on the regressions $y_t = \lambda y_{t-1} + \beta x_t + \varepsilon_t$, and $x_t = \rho x_{t-1} + u_t$, for $t = 1, 2, \ldots, T$, where T is the number of time periods.
OLS denotes the estimate of θ defined as $\hat{\theta} = \hat{\beta}/(1 - \hat{\lambda})$, where $\hat{\lambda}$ and $\hat{\beta}$ are the OLS estimates of λ and β, respectively. NBC denotes the estimate of θ defined as $\hat{\hat{\theta}} = \hat{\hat{\beta}}/(1 - \hat{\hat{\lambda}})$, where $\hat{\hat{\lambda}}$ and $\hat{\hat{\beta}}$ are the Kiviet–Phillips bias-corrected estimates of λ and β, respectively. DBC_1 and DBC_2 stand for the two variants of the bias-corrected estimator of the long-run coefficient defined by (16), and utilize the correction formula (10) and (15), respectively. BSBC the bootstrap bias-corrected estimator is defined by (20).
σ_s^2 is the signal-to-noise ratio defined by (24). Notice that $\sigma_\varepsilon^2 = 1$. M is the number of cases where the absolute values of the estimates of the coefficients of the lagged dependent variable were greater than 0.99.

and it is easily seen that $\text{cov}(y_{t-1}, x_t) = \rho\theta(1 - \lambda)\sigma_x^2/(1 - \lambda\rho)$. Using these results in (23) we obtain[4]

$$\frac{\sigma_s^2}{\sigma_\varepsilon^2} = \left(\frac{\lambda^2}{1 - \lambda^2}\right) + \theta^2\left(\frac{\sigma_u^2}{\sigma_\varepsilon^2}\right)\left(\frac{1 - \lambda}{1 + \lambda}\right)\left(\frac{1 + \lambda\rho}{1 - \lambda\rho}\right)\left(\frac{1}{1 - \rho^2}\right) \tag{24}$$

We follow Kiviet (1995, table 2) and experiment with two values of the signal-to-noise ratios, $\sigma_s^2/\sigma_\varepsilon^2 = \sigma_s^2 = (2,8)$, and fix σ_u^2 by inverting (24)

$$\sigma_u^2 = \frac{\left(\sigma_s^2 - \dfrac{\lambda^2}{1 - \lambda^2}\right)(1 + \lambda)(1 - \rho^2)(1 - \lambda\rho)}{\theta^2(1 - \lambda)(1 + \lambda\rho)} \tag{25}$$

Finally, we experiment with the following values of λ and ρ: $\lambda = (0.2, 0.6, 0.8)$ and $\rho = (0.60, 0.95)$. Notice that these parameter configurations satisfy the constraint $\sigma_s^2 > \lambda^2/(1 - \lambda^2)$ needed to ensure $\sigma_u^2 > 0$. Throughout we set $T = 20$, and use 2,500 for the number of replications in each experiment, and 500 for the number of bootstrap replications. Only replications yielding a stable estimate for λ (namely those with their absolute values falling below 0.99) are included in the experiments. The number of such cases is denoted by M and reported for each experiment. In general, they form only a very small fraction of the total number of replications, and mainly occur when $\lambda = 0.8$ and ρ is small.

The simulation results for the single-group model (21–22), are reported in tables 12.1 to 12.3. The following general conclusions may be drawn from

[4] See also equation (40) in Kiviet (1995). Despite their apparent differences (24) and (40) are identical. Since $\sigma_s^2/\sigma_\varepsilon^2 = R^2/(1 - R^2)$, it is also interesting to note that we must have $R^2 > \lambda^2$, otherwise we obtain a negative value for σ_u^2 or σ_ε^2.

Table 12.2. *Simulation results for the bias and RMSE of alternative estimates for the single-group dynamic regression model** ($\lambda = 0.6$, $T = 20$, $N = 1$)

			OLS	NBC	DBC_1	DBC_2	BSBC
$\sigma_s^2 = 2$							
$\rho = 0.6$	λ	BIAS	−0.10941	−0.03673	—	—	−0.02067
		RMSE	0.20692	0.18643	—	—	0.19878
	β	BIAS	0.02995	0.01084	—	—	0.00884
		RMSE	0.18596	0.17976	—	—	0.18466
	θ	BIAS	−0.05009	0.16779	−0.03812	−0.18029	−0.03392
		RMSE	0.59893	1.59451	0.56009	4.49575	1.16864
		M	2	2	2	2	2
$\rho = 0.95$	λ	BIAS	−0.17773	−0.07308	—	—	−0.04127
		RMSE	0.27878	0.24006	—	—	0.25240
	β	BIAS	0.09649	0.03873	—	—	0.02646
		RMSE	0.54190	0.50051	—	—	0.50391
	θ	BIAS	−0.04621	0.08964	−0.02814	−0.04838	−0.03078
		RMSE	1.25451	3.93756	1.16511	5.98743	2.82658
		M	1	1	1	1	1
$\sigma_s^2 = 8$							
$\rho = 0.6$	λ	BIAS	−0.04840	−0.01187	—	—	−0.01020
		RMSE	0.12550	0.11801	—	—	0.12049
	β	BIAS	0.01221	0.00305	—	—	0.00339
		RMSE	0.07948	0.07896	—	—	0.08019
	θ	BIAS	−0.02317	0.05865	−0.01202	−0.02047	−0.01202
		RMSE	0.30844	0.41986	0.30384	0.30172	0.33187
		M	0	0	0	0	0
$\rho = 0.95$	λ	BIAS	−0.13413	−0.04669	—	—	−0.02472
		RMSE	0.23014	0.20186	—	—	0.21148
	β	BIAS	0.07031	0.02358	—	—	0.01617
		RMSE	0.24767	0.23196	—	—	0.23578
	θ	BIAS	−0.05699	0.07682	−0.02995	−0.07507	−0.03783
		RMSE	0.56716	1.54967	0.53832	0.88482	1.24221
		M	0	0	0	0	0

Notes:
* See table 12.1.

Table 12.3. *Simulation results for the bias and RMSE of alternative estimates for the single-group dynamic regression model**
($\lambda = 0.8$, $T = 20$, $N = 1$)

			OLS	NBC	DBC_1	DBC_2	BSBC
$\sigma_s^2 = 2$							
$\rho = 0.6$	λ	BIAS	−0.20288	−0.10658	—	—	−0.06609
		RMSE	0.28757	0.23501	—	—	0.23773
	β	BIAS	0.00906	−0.00314	—	—	−0.00493
		RMSE	0.37785	0.36002	—	—	0.35855
	θ	BIAS	−0.13348	−2.28683	−0.14745	−0.18029	0.11388
		RMSE	2.74301	240.514	2.52414	4.49575	20.2499
		M	17	17	17	17	17
$\rho = 0.95$	λ	BIAS	−0.24007	−0.13034	—	—	−0.08341
		RMSE	0.32298	0.25797	—	—	0.26064
	β	BIAS	0.02799	−0.00616	—	—	−0.00815
		RMSE	1.39656	1.27748	—	—	1.26231
	θ	BIAS	−0.32072	−10.2143	−0.09771	12.07933	2.08078
		RMSE	8.85296	444.020	8.14995	476.992	89.7419
		M	13	13	13	13	13
$\sigma_s^2 = 8$							
$\rho = 0.6$	λ	BIAS	−0.08864	−0.03230	—	—	−0.01880
		RMSE	0.15855	0.13437	—	—	0.13933
	β	BIAS	0.00799	0.00103	—	—	0.00064
		RMSE	0.06656	0.06554	—	—	0.06625
	θ	BIAS	−0.07098	0.27077	−0.09588	−1.47219	−0.21754
		RMSE	0.78518	6.45395	0.79922	27.2782	15.7881
		M	14	14	14	14	14
$\rho = 0.95$	λ	BIAS	−0.19516	−0.09776	—	—	−0.05973
		RMSE	0.27634	0.22097	—	—	0.22537
	β	BIAS	0.06963	0.03347	—	—	0.02469
		RMSE	0.26649	0.24208	—	—	0.24197
	θ	BIAS	−0.10507	0.58921	−0.11604	−0.24558	0.95021
		RMSE	1.66245	17.2511	1.12198	69.92237	6.14442
		M	15	15	15	15	15

Notes:
* See table 12.1.

these results: (i) As far as the estimates of the short-run coefficients (λ and β) are concerned, both the bootstrap and Kiviet–Phillips bias-corrected (KPBC) procedures seem to be quite effective. For λ, the bias of the bootstrap method (in absolute value) is less than the bias of the KPBC estimator for all combinations of the parameter values. In terms of root mean square errors (RMSE), the bootstrap method yields a slightly higher value than the KPBC procedure. For the coefficient of the exogenous variable, β, the bias of the bootstrap method, is less than the bias of the KPBC estimator in 8 out of 12 cases. It is also interesting to note that these results continue to hold even for a very small number of bootstrap replications, often as low as 15. The RMSE of the bootstrap estimates of β is, however, slightly larger than that of the KPBC estimators. Overall, both estimators perform very similarly in correcting for the small sample bias of the estimators of the short-run coefficients.

Suppose now the parameter of interest is the long-run coefficient, θ. We experimented with five different ways of estimating it: The standard OLS estimator $\hat{\theta} = \hat{\beta}/(1 - \hat{\lambda})$, where $\hat{\beta}$ and $\hat{\lambda}$ are the OLS estimates of the short-run coefficients. The "naive" bias-corrected (NBC) estimator $\hat{\hat{\theta}} = \hat{\hat{\beta}}/(1 - \hat{\hat{\lambda}})$, where $\hat{\hat{\lambda}}$ and $\hat{\hat{\beta}}$ are the Kiviet–Phillips bias-corrected estimates of λ and β, respectively. The two variants of the bias-corrected estimator of θ, using (15) with the bias-correction factors given by (10) and (13). We shall refer to them as DBC_1 and DBC_2 estimators, respectively. And the bootstrap bias-corrected (BSBC) estimator defined by (20) for $N = 1$. The results are summarised in tables 12.1–12.3. Firstly, the bias of the OLS estimator of the long-run coefficient, although still quite substantial particularly when λ is large (around 0.8), it is nevertheless generally smaller than the bias of the underlying short-run coefficients. Secondly, as expected, the NBC estimator completely fails to correct for the bias of the long-run estimates, and in many cases does even worse than the uncorrected OLS estimator. Thirdly, out of the two variants of the direct approach to bias correction of the long-run estimates the DBC_1 estimator based on (10) does much better particularly in the case of experiments with $\lambda = 0.8$. This seems to be due to the inclusion of terms of order $O(T^{-3/2})$ in (10) not included in (15), the bias correction formulae that underlies the DBC_2 estimator.[5] Finally, both the bootstrap and the DBC_1 procedures perform reasonably well for values of $\lambda = 0.2$ and 0.6, with the DBC_1 method generally yielding a smaller RMSE as compared to the bootstrap procedure. But for $\lambda = 0.8$, none of the procedures seem to work, although the DBC_1 method still outperforms the bootstrap procedure.

[5] An appropriate order $O(T^{-3/2})$ approximation formulae for the bias of the long-run estimator can be obtained along the lines advanced recently by Kiviet and Phillips (1996), which could be a useful topic for future research.

The simulation results also show that the choice of the signal-to-noise ratio, σ_s^2, has a significant impact on the bias and the RMSE of both the short-run and the long-run coefficients. The bias and RMSE of the short-run and long-run estimators decline as σ_s^2 is increased from 2 to 8 in almost all cases for all five estimation methods. However, for a given choice of σ_s^2 the effect of increasing ρ on the various estimators is rather mixed. In the case of the short-run coefficients raising ρ (while keeping σ_s^2 fixed), always increases the bias and the RMSE of the estimators. The situation is more favorable as far as the estimation of the long-run coefficient is concerned.[6] When λ is relatively small increasing ρ seems to have only a very small impact on the bias of the DBC_1 estimator of the long-run coefficient, but its RMSE is always adversely affected when ρ is increased. Finally, another interesting observation concerns the sign of the bias of the various estimators, both for the short-run and long-run coefficients. For λ and β, the biases of the OLS, KPBC, and BSBC estimators are of the same sign, with λ being underestimated and β overestimated, suggesting that the bias corrections have not been large enough to remove the downward (upward) bias of the OLS estimator of λ (β). With a few exceptions the same also applies to the bias of the various estimators of the long-run coefficient, θ. The notable exception is the bias of the NBC of θ which is systematically positive and overcorrects for the negative bias of the OLS estimator of the long-run coefficient.

4.2 *Monte Carlo results for panels*

The DGP underlying the Monte Carlo experiments for the panel data model follows closely the design of the experiments described in the previous section, but allows for parameter heterogeneity across the different groups

$$y_{it} = \alpha_i + \lambda y_{i,t-1} + (1-\lambda)\theta_i x_{it} + \varepsilon_{it}$$

$$i = 1,2,\dots,N,\ t = 1,2,\dots,T \quad (26)$$

where

$$x_{it} = \mu_i(1-\rho) + \rho x_{i,t-1} + u_{it},$$

$$i = 1,2,\dots,N,\ t = 1,2,\dots,T. \quad (27)$$

In each experiment, we generated the disturbances and the parameters according to

$$u_{it} \sim N(0,\tau_i^2),\ \varepsilon_{it} \sim N(0,1), \qquad i = 1,2,\dots,N,\ t = 1,2,\dots,T$$

$$\alpha_i \sim N(1,1),\ \theta_i \sim N(1,1),\ \mu_i \sim N(1,1), \qquad i = 1,2,\dots,N.$$

[6] On this also see Pesaran and Shin (1997).

The values of τ_i^2 across i are generated using the analogue of (25) for panels,

$$\tau_i^2 = \frac{\left(\sigma_s^2 - \dfrac{\lambda^2}{1-\lambda^2}\right)(1-\lambda)(1-\rho^2)(1-\lambda\rho)}{\theta_i^2(1-\lambda)(1+\lambda\rho)}, \tag{28}$$

with two different choices of σ_s^2, namely 2 and 8. The main source of slope heterogeneity in these experiments is through the cross-sectional variations in the long-run parameter, and represents only a mild degree of slope heterogeneity. As in the case of $N=1$, we first generated $T+50$ observations for x and y and then dropped the first 50 observations for each i. Again, the average long-run effect $E(\theta_i)=1$, is the focus of our analysis. As the experiments in Pesaran, Smith, and Im (1996) show, the estimate of θ is sensitive to the degree of regressor serial correlation and the coefficient of the lagged dependent variable, so we shall examine various bias reduction estimators for all combinations of $\lambda=(0.2, 0.6, 0.8)$ and $\rho=(0.6, 0.95)$. The results, summarised in tables 12.4–12.6, are based on 2,500 replications, with the number of bootstrap replications set at 500.

Generally speaking, the simulation results for the dynamic heterogeneous panels are quite similar to the results obtained for the classical dynamic model with $N=1$. The MGE estimator based on the bootstrap and the Kiviet–Phillips bias corrected methods perform quite well in estimating the short-run coefficients λ and β, with the bootstrap estimator having a smaller bias and a slightly larger RMSE than the KPBC method in most cases. This conclusion seems to hold even for relatively large values of λ (see table 12.6).[7] As in the case of the single-group regressions the bias and the RMSE of the different MGE estimates tend to improve as the signal-to-noise ratio, σ_s^2, is raised; and worsens as the degree of regressor serial correlation, ρ, is increased. Once again, as to be expected, the bias-corrected estimators tend to lose their effectiveness as the coefficient of the lagged dependent variable, λ, is increased.

As far as the estimation of the long-run coefficient, θ, is concerned, the mean group estimator based on the NBC procedure fails in all cases. In fact for small and moderate values of λ (≤ 0.6), the bias of the uncorrected MGE of the long-run coefficient is generally less than 5 per cent, often substantially smaller than the bias of the uncorrected mean group estimators of the short-run coefficients. As before, the MGE based on the DBC_1 correction formula

[7] For a Bayesian approach to the problem of bias correction of the short-run coefficients in dynamic panel data models see chapter 11 of this volume, Hsiao *et al.*

Table 12.4. *Simulation results for the bias and RMSE of alternative estimators of heterogeneous dynamic panel models* ($\lambda = 0.2$, $T = 20$, $N = 20$)

			MGE	NBC	DBC_1	DBC_2	BSBC
$\sigma_s^2 = 2$							
$\rho = 0.6$	λ	BIAS	−0.05449	−0.01201	—	—	−0.01033
		STD	0.03559	0.03753	—	—	0.03898
		RMSE	0.06528	0.03973	—	—	0.04080
	β	BIAS	0.02610	0.00690	—	—	0.00686
		STD	0.19174	0.18776	—	—	0.18830
		RMSE	0.19425	0.18868	—	—	0.18933
	θ	BIAS	−0.01263	0.02238	−0.00511	−0.00628	−0.00429
		STD	0.23256	0.24362	0.23376	0.23366	0.23567
		RMSE	0.23288	0.27763	0.23370	0.23365	0.23625
		M	0	0	0	0	0
$\rho = 0.95$	λ	BIAS	−0.10808	−0.03144	—	—	−0.02188
		STD	0.04604	0.05039	—	—	0.05365
		RMSE	0.11798	0.06056	—	—	0.05916
	β	BIAS	0.07558	0.02103	—	—	0.01599
		STD	0.23593	0.22415	—	—	0.22554
		RMSE	0.25637	0.23410	—	—	0.23562
	θ	BIAS	−0.01461	0.01476	−0.00679	−0.00877	−0.00446
		STD	0.26459	0.27684	0.26608	0.26587	0.27141
		RMSE	0.27387	0.29344	0.27571	0.27797	0.28184
		M	0	0	0	0	0
$\sigma_s^2 = 8$							
$\rho = 0.6$	λ	BIAS	−0.02078	−0.00188	—	—	−0.00320
		STD	0.02232	0.02288	—	—	0.02346
		RMSE	0.03056	0.02300	—	—	0.02373
	β	BIAS	0.00658	−0.00190	—	—	−0.00144
		STD	0.18025	0.17844	—	—	0.17867
		RMSE	0.18158	0.17964	—	—	0.18033
	θ	BIAS	−0.00514	0.00836	−0.00185	−0.00216	−0.00184
		STD	0.22276	0.22590	0.22350	0.22346	0.22378
		RMSE	0.22445	0.22757	0.22513	0.22509	0.22548
		M	0	0	0	0	0

Table 12.4. (*cont.*)

			MGE	NBC	DBC_1	DBC_2	BSBC
$\rho = 0.95$	λ	BIAS	−0.07873	−0.01966	—	—	−0.01564
		STD	0.03977	0.04268	—	—	0.04472
		RMSE	0.08832	0.04727	—	—	0.04760
	β	BIAS	0.05782	0.015896	—	—	0.01447
		STD	0.20227	0.19380	—	—	0.19461
		RMSE	0.20827	0.19257	—	—	0.19368
	θ	BIAS	−0.01157	0.01165	−0.00384	−0.00495	−0.00351
		STD	0.23176	0.23795	0.23319	0.23297	0.23476
		RMSE	0.23113	0.23811	0.23246	0.23220	0.23443
		M	0	0	0		0

Notes:
The regressions are based on: $y_{it} = \alpha_i + \lambda_i y_{i,t-1} + \beta_i x_{it} + \varepsilon_{it}$, for $i = 1, 2, \ldots, N$, $t = 1, 2, \ldots, T$, where N is the number of groups, T is the number of time periods. MGE is the Mean Group Estimate of θ, defined as $\hat{\theta} = \frac{1}{N}\sum_{i=1}^{N} \hat{\beta}_i/(1-\hat{\lambda}_i)$, where $\hat{\lambda}_i$ and $\hat{\beta}_i$ are the OLS estimators of λ_i and β_i, for $i = 1, 2, \ldots, N$. NBC is the "naïve" bias-corrected MGE estimator of θ defined as $\hat{\hat{\theta}} = \frac{1}{N}\sum_{i=1}^{N} \hat{\hat{\beta}}_i/(1-\hat{\hat{\lambda}}_i)$, where $\hat{\hat{\lambda}}_i$ and $\hat{\hat{\beta}}_i$ are the Kiviet–Phillips bias-corrected estimates of λ_i and β_i, respectively. DBC_1 and DBC_2 stand for the two variants of the bias-corrected estimator of the long-run coefficient defined by (16), and utilize the correction formula (10) and (15), respectively. BSBC is the bootstrap bias-corrected estimator defined by (20). σ_s^2 is the signal-to-noise ratio defined by (24), Notice that $\sigma_s^2 = 1$. M is the number of cases where the absolute values of the estimates of the coefficients of the lagged dependent variable were greater than 0.99.

does much better than the DBC_2 variant. The bootstrap and DBC_1 methods perform well in terms of their effectiveness in reducing the bias, and the latter method tends to have a smaller RMSE. But as λ is allowed to increase to 0.8 neither of these methods is effective in reducing the bias of the estimator of the long-run coefficient. Even for $\lambda = 0.6$ the bootstrap method yields long-run estimates with unacceptably large RMSE. By comparison, the DBC_1 method continues to perform reasonably well, although it is still not very effective. For $\lambda = 0.8$ there is little to choose between the uncorrected MGE and the DBC_1 methods. Again, for $\lambda = 0.2$ or 0.6, the bias in the estimates of θ decreases (increases) as σ_s^2 (ρ) is increased.

Table 12.5. *Simulation results for the bias and RMSE of alternative estimators of heterogeneous dynamic panel data models*
($\lambda = 0.6$, $T = 20$, $N = 20$)

			MGE	NBC	DBC_1	DBC_2	BSBC
$\sigma_s^2 = 2$							
$\rho = 0.6$	λ	BIAS	−0.10976	−0.03679	—	—	−0.02059
		STD	0.03886	0.04036	—	—	0.04345
		RMSE	0.11677	0.05539	—	—	0.04890
	β	BIAS	0.02739	0.00827	—	—	0.00671
		STD	0.10813	0.10397	—	—	0.10464
		RMSE	0.11331	0.10599	—	—	0.10702
	θ	BIAS	−0.05060	0.10935	−0.04445	0.20754	0.03192
		STD	0.26877	0.52478	0.26883	1.69704	0.36262
		RMSE	0.30739	3.33469	0.30172	46.9459	1.02787
		M	16	16	16	16	16
$\rho = 0.95$	λ	BIAS	−0.18251	−0.07823	—	—	−0.04652
		STD	0.04706	0.04994	—	—	0.05519
		RMSE	0.18904	0.09415	—	—	0.07428
	β	BIAS	0.11038	0.05209	—	—	0.03837
		STD	0.19796	0.18159	—	—	0.18326
		RMSE	0.23569	0.19874	—	—	0.19900
	θ	BIAS	−0.05435	−0.17098	−0.02066	0.61148	−0.03129
		STD	0.42387	1.05218	0.43558	1.79575	0.64939
		RMSE	0.50452	9.23019	0.50753	27.0601	5.36198
		M	20	20	20	20	20
$\sigma_s^2 = 8$							
$\rho = 0.6$	λ	BIAS	−0.04498	−0.00800	—	—	−0.00606
		STD	0.02495	0.02539	—	—	0.02652
		RMSE	0.05167	0.02705	—	—	0.02758
	β	BIAS	0.01138	0.00224	—	—	0.00214
		STD	0.09355	0.09162	—	—	0.09182
		RMSE	0.09364	0.09106	—	—	0.09124
	θ	BIAS	−0.02343	0.05931	−0.00848	−0.05178	−0.00839
		STD	0.23433	0.26617	0.23647	0.26184	0.25937
		RMSE	0.23727	0.30856	0.23903	1.32443	0.57846
		M	2	2	2	2	2

Table 12.5. (*cont.*)

			MGE	NBC	DBC_1	DBC_2	BSBC
$\rho=0.95$	λ	BIAS	−0.13775	−0.05054	—	—	−0.03026
		STD	0.04112	0.04297	—	—	0.04661
		RMSE	0.14431	0.06764	—	—	0.05736
	β	BIAS	0.06837	0.02191	—	—	0.01404
		STD	0.12649	0.11657	—	—	0.11670
		RMSE	0.14549	0.12071	—	—	0.11972
	θ	BIAS	−0.05078	0.48489	−0.03166	−0.07435	−0.02669
		STD	0.26797	0.99023	0.26910	0.51330	0.31712
		RMSE	0.29709	25.7381	0.29823	5.90733	0.57720
		M	14	14	14	14	14

Notes:
* See table 12.4.

5 Concluding remarks

Both theoretical and simulation results from the previous studies (Pesaran and Smith 1995; and Pesaran, Smith, and Im 1996) indicate that the mean group estimates of the long-run coefficient of a heterogeneous dynamic panel can exhibit substantial bias in small samples. This bias becomes particularly troublesome for inference in panels with large N. The small sample bias is caused by the bias in the estimation of the short-run coefficients as well as the non-linearity inherent in estimation of the long-run coefficients from the short-run coefficients. In view of this, four estimation methods are considered in this chapter for correcting the small sample bias of the long-run coefficient in dynamic heterogeneous panels. Intensive Monte Carlo experiments are conducted to evaluate the merits of the alternative estimators. Although, the primary concern in this chapter has been the long-run coefficients, our simulation experiments also shed light on the relative performance of the Kiviet–Phillips bias-corrected (KPBC) and the bootstrap (BSBC) methods as far as the small sample bias of the short-run coefficients are concerned.

All estimation methods are applied to the heterogeneous dynamic panel as well as to the single-group dynamic regression model. For the short-run coefficients, the KPBC and BSBC procedures perform well, although the BSBC method tends to yield a smaller bias with a slightly larger root mean square than the KPBC estimator. For the long-run coefficient, the BSBC method performs reasonably well in cases where λ (the coefficient of the

Table 12.6. *Simulation results for the bias and RMSE of alternative estimators of heterogeneous dynamic panel data models* ($\lambda=0.8$, $T=20$, $N=20$)

			MGE	NBC	DBC_1	DBC_2	BSBC
$\sigma_s^2=2$							
$\rho=0.6$	λ	BIAS	−0.19665	−0.10042	—	—	−0.05909
		STD	0.04439	0.04564	—	—	0.05129
		RMSE	0.20178	0.11071	—	—	0.07905
	β	BIAS	0.01340	0.00074	—	—	−0.00130
		STD	0.12325	0.11730	—	—	0.11939
		RMSE	0.12754	0.12112	—	—	0.12288
	θ	BIAS	−0.20075	2.53054	−0.20943	−3.15370	−0.16566
		STD	0.57557	5.71871	0.55858	6.25829	1.49623
		RMSE	0.79609	73.4231	0.75099	36.0543	10.1978
		M	326	326	326	326	326
$\rho=0.95$	λ	BIAS	−0.23963	−0.12952	—	—	−0.08264
		STD	0.04699	0.04834	—	—	0.05379
		RMSE	0.24429	0.13848	—	—	0.09895
	β	BIAS	0.06942	0.03026	—	—	0.01875
		STD	0.42505	0.38565	—	—	0.37904
		RMSE	0.45284	0.40951	—	—	0.40337
	θ	BIAS	−0.15965	17.2530	−0.15823	2.14009	−0.14362
		STD	1.56680	27.3652	1.56206	16.3541	3.21194
		RMSE	1.96708	826.151	1.97435	146.565	12.6103
		M	294	294	294	294	294
$\sigma_s^2=8$							
$\rho=0.6$	λ	BIAS	−0.08862	−0.03197	—	—	−0.01815
		STD	0.02989	0.02963	—	—	0.03111
		RMSE	0.09349	0.04357	—	—	0.03603
	β	BIAS	0.00918	0.00231	—	—	0.00193
		STD	0.05005	0.04859	—	—	0.04857
		RMSE	0.05138	0.04915	—	—	0.04910
	θ	BIAS	−0.04303	0.18553	−0.09836	−2.90157	0.17850
		STD	0.30830	2.42716	0.30462	3.15425	1.07477
		RMSE	0.38793	36.1323	0.42052	21.6556	17.1475
		M	285	285	285	285	285

Table 12.6. (*cont.*)

			MGE	NBC	DBC_1	DBC_2	BSBC
$\rho=0.95$	λ	BIAS	−0.19388	−0.09643	—	—	−0.05823
		STD	0.04334	0.04375	—	—	0.04800
		RMSE	0.19898	0.10641	—	—	0.07609
	β	BIAS	0.05979	0.02507	—	—	0.01622
		STD	0.09700	0.08797	—	—	0.08677
		RMSE	0.11727	0.09499	—	—	0.09176
	θ	BIAS	−0.12462	−1.52382	−0.12761	−1.23776	−0.12935
		STD	0.39979	3.97741	0.38741	4.18226	1.15955
		RMSE	0.54172	56.1229	0.57693	35.3689	10.5199
		M	314	314	314	314	314

Notes:
* See table 12.4.

lagged dependent variable) is small, around 0.2, but does rather poorly for larger values of λ. In contrast, the DBC_1 estimator which applies the bias corrections directly to the long-run coefficient performs well for small and moderate values of λ. None of the procedures seems to be effective when λ is relatively large. Clearly, further research is required in cases where $\lambda \geq 0.8$.

References

Bickel, P.J. and D.A. Freedman (1981), "Some Asymptotic Theory for the Bootstrap," *The Annals of Statistics*, 9: 1196–1217.

Carter, R.A.L. and A. Ullah (1979), "The Finite Sample Properties of OLS Estimators in Special Rational Distributed Lag Models," *Sankhya*, 41 D: 1–18.

Efron, B. (1979), "Bootstrap Methods: Another Look at the Jackknife," *The Annals of Statistics*, 7: 1–26.

Efron, B. and R.J. Tibshirani (1993), *An Introduction to the Bootstrap*, New York: Chapman and Hall.

Evans, G.B.A. and N.E. Savin (1981), "Testing Unit Roots: 1," *Econometrica*, 49: 753–779.

(1984), "Testing Unit Roots: 2," *Econometrica*, 52: 1241–1270.

Grubb, D. and J. Symons (1987), "Bias in Regressions with Lagged Dependent Variable," *Econometric Theory*, 3: 371–386.

Hall, P. (1992), *The Bootstrap and Edgeworth Expansion*, New York: Springer-Verlag.

Hoque, A. and T.A. Peters (1986), "Finite Sample Analysis of Least Squares in ARMAX Models," *Sankhya, B* 48: 266–283.

Hsiao, C. (1986), *Analysis of Panel Data.* Econometric Society Monograph 11, Cambridge University Press, pp. 128–153.

Hsiao, C., M. Hashem Pesaran, and A. Kamil Tahmiscioglu (1998), "Bayes Estimation of Short-run Coefficients in Dynamic Panel Data Models" in (eds.) C. Hsiao, K. Lahiri, L-F. Lee and M.H. Pesaran, *Analysis of Panels and Limited Dependent Variable Models*, Cambridge University Press, chapter 11, this volume.

Hurwicz, L. (1950), "Least-squares Bias in Time Series," in T.C. Koopmans, *Statistical Inference in Dynamic Economic Models*, Chicago: University of Chicago Press, Monograph number, 10: 365–383.

Kiviet, J.F. (1995), "On Bias Inconsistency and Efficiency in Various Estimators of Dynamic Panel Data Models," *Journal of Econometrics*, 68: 53–78.

Kiviet, J.F. and G.D.A. Phillips (1993), "Alternative Bias Approximations with A Lagged-Dependant Variable," *Econometric Theory*, 9: 62–80.

(1996), "Higher-order Asymptotic Expansions of the Least-Squares Estimation Bias in First-order Dynamic Regression Models," unpublished manuscript, University of Amsterdam.

Maekawa, K. (1983), "An Approximation to the Distribution of the Least Squares Estimator in An Autoregressive Model with Exogeneous Variables," *Econometrica*, 51: 229–238.

Nagar, A.L. (1959), "The Bias and Moment Matrix of the General k-class Estimators of the Parameters in Structural Equations," *Econometrica*, 27: 575–595.

Orcutt, G.H. and J.H.S. Winokur (1969), "First-order Autoregression: Inference, Estimation and Prediction," *Econometrica*, 37: 1–14.

Pesaran, M.H. and Y. Shin (1998), "An Autoregressive Distribute Lag Modelling Approach to Cointegration Analysis," in Centennial Volume of Ragner Frisch, S. Strom, A. Holly, and P. Diamond (eds.), *Econometric Society Monograph*, Cambridge University Press (forthcoming).

Pesaran, M.H. and R. Smith (1995), "Estimating Long-run Relationships from Dynamic Heterogeneous Panels," *Journal of Econometrics*, 68(1): 79–113.

Pesaran, M.H., R. Smith, and K-S. Im (1996), "Dynamic Linear Models for Heterogeneous Panels," in L. Matyas and P. Sevestre (eds.), *The Econometrics of Panel Data (2nd edn)*, Dordrecht: Kluwer Academic Publishers, pp. 145–195.

Peters, T.A. (1989), "The Exact Moments of OLS in Dynamic Regression Models with Non-normal Errors," *Journal of Econometrics*, 40: 279–305.

Sawa, T. (1978), "The Exact Moments of the Least Squares Estimator for the Autoregressive Model," *Journal of Econometrics*, 8: 159–172.

Swamy, P.A.V.B. (1970), "Efficient Inference in a Random Coefficient Regression Model," *Econometrica*, 38: 311–33.

Tanaka, K. (1983), "Asymptotic Expansion Associated with the AR(1) Model with Unknown Mean," *Econometrica*, 51: 1221–1231.

Tse, Y.K. (1982), "Edgeworth Approximations in First-order Stochastic Difference Equations with Exogenous Variables," *Journal of Econometrics*, 20: 175–195.

Ullah, A. and E. Maasoumi (1986), "Moments of OLS Estimators in An Autoregressive Moving Average Model with Explanatory Variables," *Economics Letters*, 21: 265–269.

Ullah, A. and K.V. Srivastava (1994), "Moments of the Ratio of Quadratic Forms in Non-normal Variables with Econometric Examples," *Economics Letters*, 62: 129–141.

White, J.S. (1961), "Asymptotic Expansion for the Mean and Variance of the Serial Correlation Coefficient," *Biometrika*, 48: 85–95.

Zellner, A. (1969), "On the Aggregation Problem: A New Approach to a Troublesome Problem," in K.A. Fox *et al.*, *Economic Models, Estimation and Risk Programming: Essays in honor of Gerhard Tintner*, Berlin: Springer–Verlag, pp. 365–378.

Curriculum vitae of G.S. Maddala

Current position

University Eminent Scholar Professor in Economics, 1992–present, The Ohio State University

Educational background

BA (Mathematics), Andhra University, India, 1955
MA (Statistics), Bombay University, India, 1957
PhD (Economics), University of Chicago, USA, 1963

Previous appointments

Assistant Professor of Economics, Stanford University, 1963–1967
Associate Professor of Economics, University of Rochester, 1967–1970
Visiting Professor of Economics, Cornell University, Spring 1969 and Spring 1972
Professor of Economics, University of Rochester, 1970–1975
Graduate Research Professor in Economics, 1975–1993; Director, Center for Econometrics and Decisions Sciences, 1979–1993. Both at the University of Florida

Other research appointments

Cowles Foundation, Yale University, Fall 1970
Center for Operations Research and Econometrics, Louvain, Belgium, Spring 1971
MIT-NBER Computer Research Center, Summer 1974
Oakridge National Laboratory, Summer 1975
Monash University, Australia, Summer 1983
Columbia University, Center for the Study of Futures Markets, 1984–1985, 1989–1990
Visiting Professor of Economics, California Institute of Technology, Winter 1993
Visiting Professor of Economics, Emory University, Spring 1994, Spring 1995

Scholarly honors and awards

Three gold medals during education in India
Fellow, Econometric Society
Who's Who in Economics (MIT Press, 1982, 1987)
Fairchild Distinguished Scholar, Caltech, 1979–1980, and Winter, 1993
Listed in Who's Who in the World, 1995 Ed., Who's Who in America, 1996, 1997

National Science Foundation research grants

Studies in Monetary Dynamics, 1967–1969
Likelihood Methods in Pooling and Related Problems, 1970–1972
Econometric Methods and Applications, 1972–1974
Statistical Analysis of Economic Disequilibrium, 1975–1977
Econometrics of Cross-Section and Time Series Data, 1978–1980
Econometric Analysis of Expectations Based on Micro Data, 1981–1984
Price Expectations in Regulated Markets, 1985–1987

Offices in professional associations

Associate Editor, *Econometrica*, 1970–1979
Vice-President, Atlantic Economic Society, 1981–1982
Member, Panel on Productivity Statistics, National Academy of Sciences, 1978–1979
Chairman, Program Committee on Business and Economics Statistics, American Statistical Association Annual Meetings, Las Vegas, 1985
Member, Program Committee, Econometric Society Meetings, several years
Reviewer for over 20 journals, for NSF, and the Nobel Prize Committee
Associate Editor, *Journal of Applied Econometrics*, 1993–1996
Associate Editor, *Journal of Statistical Planning and Inference*, 1995–
Advisory Board, *Econometric Theory*, Dec. 1996–Dec. 1999

Publications

Production functions and productivity

1 "Productivity and Technological Change in the Bituminous Coal Industry," *Journal of Political Economy*, Vol. 73, August 1965, pp. 352–365.
2 "Notes on the Estimation of Elasticity of Substitution" (with J.B. Kadane), *Review of Economics and Statistics*, Vol. 48, August 1966, pp. 340–344.
3 "Estimation of Returns to Scale and Elasticity of Substitution" (with J.B. Kadane), *Econometrica*, Vol. 35, July 1967, pp. 419–423.
4 "International Diffusion of Technical Change" (with P.T. Knight), *Economic Journal*, Vol. 77, September 1967, pp. 531–558.
5 "A Note on the Form of the production Function and Productivity" in *Measurement and Interpretation of Productivity* (National Research Council, National Academy of Sciences, Washington, DC 1979), pp. 309–317.

6 "Technical Change, Frontier Production Function and Efficiency Measurement" (with R.P.H. Fishe), *American Statistical Association, Proceedings of the Business and Economic Statistics Section*, December 1979, pp. 470–475.
7 "Discussion of Quality Changes and Productivity Measurement: Hedonics and an Alternative," *Journal of Accounting, Auditing and Finance*, June 1990.

Distributed lag models

8 "Notes on Estimated Aggregate Quarterly Consumption Functions" (with Z. Griliches and others) *Econometrics*, Vol. 30, July 1962, pp. 491–500.
9 "Estimation of Lagged Relationships in Liquid Assets Holdings of Manufacturing Corporations" (with R.C. Vogel), *Review of Economics and Statistics*, Vol. 51, February 1969, pp. 53–61.
10 "Generalized Least Squares with an Estimated Covariance Matrix," *Econometrica*, Vol. 39, January 1971, pp. 23–33.
11 "Maximum Likelihood Estimation of Solow's and Jorgenson's Distributed Lag Models" (with A.S. Rao), *Review of Economics and Statistics*, Vol. 73, February 1971, pp. 80–88.
12 "On the Asymptotic Properties of Two-Step Procedures used in the Estimation of Distributed Lag Models" (with D.M. Grether), *International Economic Review*, Vol. 13, October 1972, pp. 737–744.
13 "Errors in Variables and Serially Correlated Residuals in Distributed Lag Models" (with D.M. Grether), *Econometrica*, Vol. 41, March 1973, pp. 255–262.
14 "Tests for Serial Correlation in Regression Models with Lagged Dependent Variables and Serially Correlated Residuals" (with A.S. Rao), *Econometrica*, Vol. 41, July 1973, pp. 761–774.
15 "Ridge Estimators for Distribution Lag Models" (with A.K. Chanda), *Communications in Statistics, Theory and Methods*, Vol. 13, No. 2, 1984, pp. 217–225.

Panel data

16 "Cross-Section Estimates of Liquid Asset Demand" (with R.C. Vogel), *Journal of Finance*, Vol. 22, December 1967, pp. 557–575.
17 "On the Use of Variance Component Models in Pooling Cross-Section and Time-Series Data," *Econometrica*. Vol. 39, March 1971, pp. 341–358.
18 "The Likelihood Approach to Pooling Cross-Section and Time-Series Data," *Econometrica*, Vol. 39, November 1971, pp. 939–953.
19 "A Comparative Study of Alternative Estimators for Variance Component Models" (with T.D. Mount), *Journal of American Statistical Association*, Vol. 68, June 1973, pp. 324–328.
20 "On the Prediction of Systematic and Specific Risk in Common Stocks: A Discussion of Rosenberg's Model" (July 1979).

21 "Recent Developments in the Econometrics of Panel Data Analysis," *Transportation Research*, A, Vol. 21A (1987), pp. 303–326. (Invited paper for special volume on Longitudinal Data Analysis).
22 "Limited Dependent Variable Models Using Panel Data," *Journal of Human Resources*, Vol. 22, Summer 1987, pp. 307–338.
23 "To Pool or Not to Pool: That is the Question," *Journal of Quantitative Economics*, Vol. 7, No. 2, July 1991, pp. 255–262.
24 "An Unobserved Component Panel Data Model to Study the Effect of Earnings Surprises on Stock Prices. Trading Volumes and Spreads" (with M. Nimalendran), *Journal of Econometrics*, Vol. 68, 1995, 229–242.
25 "The Pooling Problem," in L. Matyas and P. Sevestre (eds.), *Econometrics of Panel Data* (Kluwer, 1996).
26 "Estimation of Short-Run and Long-Run Elasticities of Energy Demand From Panel Data Using Shrinkage Estimators" (with H. Li, R.P. Trost, and F. Joutz) *Journal of Business Economics and Statistics*, 1997, 15, 90–100.
27 "Tobin's Study on the Demand for Food in the US Revisited: An Examination of the issue of Pooling Information from Budget Studies and Time Series," (with S. Wu and Y. Yin), Forthcoming in *An Experiment in Applied Econometrics*, J. Magnus and M. Morgan (eds.), Wiley: New York, 1997.

Simultaneous equations models

28 "Simultaneous Equation Methods for Large and Medium-Size Econometric Models," *Review of Economic Studies*, Vol. 38, October 1971, pp. 435–445.
29 "Some Small Sample Evidence on Tests of Significance in Simultaneous Equation Models," *Econometrica*, Vol. 42, September 1974, pp. 841–851.
30 "Comment" on "Exact Finite Sample Distributions for Econometric Estimators and Test Statistics," in M.D. Intrilligator and D. Kendrick (eds.), *Frontiers in Econometrics*, Vol. II (North-Holland Publishing Company, Amsterdam 1974).
31 "Weak Priors and Sharp Posteriors in Simultaneous Equation Models," *Econometrica*, Vol. 44, March 1976, pp. 345–351.
32 "Constraints Often Overlooked in Analyses of Simultaneous Equation Models: Comment," and "Rejoinder," *Econometrica*, Vol. 44, May 1976, pp. 615–616 and 625.
33 "Statistical Inference in Relation to the Size of the Model," in J. Kemnta (ed.), *Large-Scale Macro-Econometric Models: Theory and Practice* (North Holland Publishing Company, 1981), pp. 191–218.
34 "On the Exact Small Sample Distribution of the Instrumental Variable Estimator" (with J. Jeong), *Econometrica*, Vol. 60, January 1992, pp 181–183.

Qualitative variables models

35 "Specification Errors in Limited Dependent Variable Models" (with F.D. Nelson), July, 1975.

36 "Recursive Models with Qualitative Endogenous Variables" (with L.F. Lee), *Annals of Social and Economic Measurement*, vol. 5, Fall 1976, pp. 525–545.

37 "Recursive Systems Containing Qualitative Endogenous Variables: A Reply" (with L.F. Lee), *Econometrica*, Vol. 48, April 1980, pp. 765–766.

38 "Some Extensions of the Nerlove Press Model" (with R.P. Trost), *American Statistical Association Proceedings of the Business and Economics Section*, 1980, pp. 481–485.

39 "Alternative Formulations of the Nerlove-Press Models" (with R.P. Trost), *Journal of Econometrics*, Vol. 16, 1981, pp. 35–49.

40 "A Time Series Analysis of Popular Expectation Data" (with R.P.H. Fishe and K. Lahiri), in A. Zellner (ed.), *Economic Applications of Time-Series Analysis* (U.S. Census Bureau, December 1983), pp. 278–289.

Limited dependent variable models

41 "Identification and Estimation Problems in Limited Dependent Variable Models," in *Natural Resources, Uncertainty and General Equilibrium Systems*. Essays in Memory of Rafael Lusky, A. Blinder and P. Friedman (eds.) (Academic Press,. 1977), pp. 219–239.

42 "Asymptotic Covariance Matrices of Two-Stage Probit and Two-Stage Tobit Methods for Simultaneous Equations Models with Selectivity" (with L.F. Lee and R.P. Trost), *Econometrica*, Vol. 48, No. 2, March 1980, pp. 491–503.

43 "Multiple Model Testing" for Non-Nested Heteroscedastic Censored Regression Models" (with M. Smith), *Journal of Econometrics*, Vol. 21, 1983, pp. 71–81.

44 "Econometric Issues in the Empirical Analysis of Thrift Institutions" Insolvency and Failure," Invited Research Working Paper #56, Federal Home Loan Bank Board (October 1986), pp. 2–27.

45 "Censored Data Models," *The New Palgrave* (a Dictionary in Economics), Stockton Press, 1987.

46 "A Perspective on the use of Limited Dependent and Qualitative Variable Models in Accounting Research," *The Accounting Review*, Vol. 66, October 1991, pp. 788–807.

47 "Rational Expectations in Limited Dependent Variable Models," *Handbook of Statistics*, Vol. 11 (North-Holland Publishing Company, 1993), pp. 175–194.

48 "Specification Errors in Limited Dependent Variable Models" (Spanish), *Cuadernos Economicos de ICE*, Vol. 55, 1993, 185–223.

49 "Specification Tests in Limited Dependent Variable Models," in *Advances in Econometrics and Quantitative Economics* (Blackwell, 1995), pp. 1–49

50 "Applications of Limited Dependent Variable Models in Finance," in *Handbook of Statistics, Vol. 14: Statistical Methods in Finance* (Elsevier Science, Amsterdam, 1996), pp. 553–566.

51 "Limited Dependent Variable Models," in *Encyclopedia of Statistical Sciences,* Update Vol. I, S. Kotz and C.B. Read (eds.) (Wiley, New York, 1997), pp. 361–366.

52 "Hedonic Price Estimation in a Disequilibrium Setting: The case of Auctioned Apartments in Moscow," with Y. Toda and N. Nozdrina, in "Property Valuation and Investment in Central and Eastern Europe During the Transition to Free Market Economy," 1997.

53 "Tobin's Study on the Demand for Food in the US Revisited: An Examination of the Issue of Pooling Information from Budget Studies and Time Series" (S. Wu and Y. Yin), forthcoming in *An Experiment in Applied Econometrics*, J. Magnus and M. Morgan (eds.) (Wiley, New York, 1997).

Self-selection models

54 "Self-Selectivity Problems in Econometric Models," in *Applications in Statistics*, P.R. Krishniah (ed.) (North-Holland Publishing Company, Amsterdam, 1977), pp. 351–366.

55 "Selectivity Problems in Longitudinal Data," *Annales de l'Insee*, March 1978, pp. 423–450.

56 "Determinants of Rates Requested and Rates Granted in a Formal Regulatory Process" (with R.B. Roberts and G. Enholm), *Bell Journal*, Vol. 9, No. 2, Autumn 1978, pp. 611–621.

57 "Returns to College Education: An Investigation of Self-Selection Bias Based on the Project Talent Data" (with L.W. Kenny, L.F. Lee and R.P. Trost), *International Economic Review*, Vol. 20, No. 3, October 1979, pp. 775–789.

58 "On Measuring Discrimination in Loan Markets" (with R.P. Trost), in *Housing Finance Review*, Vol. 1, No. 1, 1982, pp. 245–268.

59 "The Common Structure of Tests for the Selectivity Bias, Serial Correlation, Heteroscedasticity and Non-Normality in the Tobit Model" (with L.F. Lee), *International Economic Review*, February 1985, pp. 1–20.

60 "A Survey of the Literature on Selectivity Bias as it Pertains to Health Care Markets," in *Advances in Health Economics and Health Related Research* (Greenwich, Connecticut, Jai Press), Vol. 6 (1985), pp. 3–18.

61 "Sequential Selection Rules and Selectivity in Discrete Choice Econometric Models" (with L.F. Lee) (December 1985).

Disequilibrium models

62 "Maximum Likelihood Methods for Models of Markets in Disequilibrium" (with F.D. Nelson), *Econometrica*, Vol. 42, November 1974, pp. 1013–1030.

63 "Switching Regression Models with Exogenous and Endogenous Switching" (with F.D. Nelson), *American Statistical Association Proceedings of the Business and Economic Statistics Section*, December 1975, pp. 423–426.

64 "Testing for Structural Change by D-Methods in Switching Simultaneous Equation Models" (with L.F. Lee and R.P. Trost), *American Statistical Association Proceedings of the Business and Economic Statistics Section*, December 1979, pp. 461–466.

65 "Methods of Estimation for Models of Markets with Bounded Price Variation Under Rational Expectations," *Economics Letters*, 13, 1983, pp. 181–184, Erratum in *Economics Letters*, 15, 1984, pp. 195–196.

66 "Methods of Estimation for Models of Markets with Bounded Price Variation," *International Economic Review*, Vol. 24. No. 2, June 1983, pp. 361–378.

67 "Disequilibrium, Self-Selection and Switching Models" (with Z. Griliches and M.D. Intrilligator), *Handbook for Econometrics*, Vol III (North-Holland Publishing Company, 1985), pp. 1633–1688.

68 "Modelling Expectations of Bounded Prices: An Application to the Market for Corn," (with J.S. Shonkwiler), *Review of Economics and Statistics*, Vol. 67, 1985, pp. 697–702.

69 "Estimation of Dynamic Disequilibrium Models under Rational Expectations: the Case of Commodity Markets," in L. Alan Winters and David Sapsford (eds.), *Primary Commodity Prices: Economic Models and Policy* (Cambridge University Press, 1990), pp. 21–37.

70 "Disequilibrium Modelling, Switching Regressions and Their Relationships to Structural Change," Peter Hackl and Anders H. Weslund (eds.), *Economic Structural Change* (Springer-Verlag, 1991), pp. 159–168.

71 "A Note on the Estimation of Limited Dependent Variable Models under Rational Expectations" (with S.G. Donald), *Economics Letters*, Vol. 38, Jan, 1992, pp. 17–23.

72 "Hedonic Price Estimation in a Disequilibrium Setting: The Case of Auctioned Apartments in Moscow" (with Y. Toda and N. Nozdrina), in "Property Valuation and Investment in Central and Eastern Europe During the Transition to Free Market Economy," 1997.

Time series models

73 "A Time Series Model with Qualitative Variables" (with D.M. Grether), in M. Deistler, E. Fürst and G. Schwödiauer (eds.), Oscar Margenstern Memorial Symposium, *Games, Economic Dynamics and Time-Series Analysis* (Physica Verlag, Wein, 1982), pp. 2391–305.

74 "A Time Series Analysis of Popular Expectation Data" (with R.P.H. Fishe and K. Lahiri), in A. Zellner (ed.), *Economic Applications of Time-Series Analysis* (U.S. Census Bureau, December 1983), pp. 278–289.

75 "Flat Prior vs. Ignorance Priors in the Analysis of the AR(1) Model" (with I.M. Kim), *Journal of Applied Econometrics*, Vol. 6, 1991, pp. 375–380.

76 "Identifying Outliers and Influential Observations in Economic Models" (with S.G. Donald), *Handbook of Statistics*, Vol. 11 (North-Holland Publishing Company, 1993), 663–701.

77 "An Integrated Bayesian Vector Autoregression and Error Correction Model for Forecasting Electricity Consumption and Prices" (with F.L. Joutz and R.P. Trost), *Journal of Forecasting*, Vol. 14, 1995, pp. 287–310.

78 "New Small Sample Estimators for Cointegration Regression: Low Pass Spectral Method" (with Y. Li), *Economics Letters*, Vol. 47, 1995, pp. 123–129.

79 "Bayesian Detection of Structural Breaks" (with I.M. Kim) in D.A. Berry, K.M. Chaloner, and J. Geweke (eds.), *Bayesian Analysis in Statistics and Econometrics*, Essays in Honor of Arnold Zellner (Wiley), 1996.

80 "Structural Change and Unit Roots" (with I.M. Kim), *Journal of Statistical Planning and Inference* (Special Issue on Advances in Econometrics), Vol. 49, 1996, pp. 73–103.

81 "Outliers, Unit Roots and Robust Estimation of Nonstationary Time Series" (with Y. Yin), in *Handbook of Statistics, Vol. 15: Robust Inference* (Elsevier Science, Amsterdam, 1997), pp. 237–266.

82 "The Fisher Test as a Panel Data Unit-Root Test" (1997), paper for the Volume by the Department of Statistics, Bombay University, in honor of the 50th Anniversary.

83 "The Effects of Different Types of Outliers on Unit Root Tests," forthcoming in T. Fomby and R.C. Hill (eds.), *Advances in Econometrics*, Vol. 13 (Jai Press, Greenwich, Conn.).

Bootstrap models

84 "A Perspective on Applications of Bootstrap Methods in Econometrics" (with J. Jeong), *Handbook of Statistics*, Vol. 11 (North-Holland Publishing Company, 1993), pp. 573–610.

85 "Bootstrapping Time Series Models, with discussion" (with H. Li), *Econometric Reviews*, Vol. 15, 1996, pp. 115–195.

86 "Testing for Rationality of Survey Data Using the Weighted Double-Bootstrapped Method of Moments" (with J. Jeong), *Review of Economics and Statistics*, Vol. 78, 1996, pp. 296–302.

87 "Bootstrap Based Tests in Financial Models" (with H. Li) in *Handbook of Statistics Vol. 14:Statistical Methods in Finance* (Elsevier Science, Amsterdam, 1996), pp. 463–488.

88 "Bootstrapping Cointegrating Regressions" (with H. Li), forthcoming in *Journal of Econometrics*.

Errors in variables

89 "Errors in Variables and Serially Correlated Residuals in Distributed Lag Models" (with D.M. Grether), *Econometrica*, Vol. 41, March 1973, pp. 255–262.

90 "Measurement Errors and Test for Rationality" (with J. Jeong), *Journal of Business and Economics Statistics*, Vol. 9, No 4, October 1991, pp. 431–439.

91 "Errors-in-Variables Problems in Financial Models" (with M. Nimaldendran), *Handbook of Statistics, Vol. 14: Statistical Methods in Finance*, (Elsevier Science, Amsterdam, 1996), pp. 507–528.
92 "Econometric Issues Related to Errors in Variables in Financial Models," forthcoming in *Ragnar Frisch Centenary Volume* (Cambridge University Press).

Income distribution

93 "A Stochastic Process of Income Distribution and Tests of Income Distribution Functions" (with S.K. Singh), *American Statistical Association Proceedings of the Business and Economic Statistics Section*, December 1975, pp. 551–553.
94 "A Function for Size Distribution of Incomes" (with S.K. Singh), *Econometrica*, Vol. 44, September 1976, pp. 963–970.
95 "Estimation Problems in Size Distribution of Incomes" (with S.K. Singh), *Economie Appliqueé*, Vol. 30, No. 3, 1977, pp. 461–480.
96 "A Flexible Functional form of Lorenz Curves" (with S.K. Singh), *Economie Appliqueé*, Vol. 30, No. 3, 1977, pp. 481–486.

Pseudo data

97 "Alternative Functional Forms and Errors of Pseudo-Data Estimation" (with R.B. Roberts), *The Review of Economics and Statistics*, Vol. 62, May 1980, pp. 323–327.
98 "Statistical Cost Analysis Revisited: Comment" (with R.B. Roberts), *Quarterly Journal of Economics*, Vol. 96, No. 1, 1981, pp. 177–181.
99 "Pseudo Data: Problems of Design and Statistical Analysis," in V. Kerry Smith (ed.), *Advances in Applied Micro-Economics* (Jai Press, Greenwich, Connecticut), Vol. 2, 1982, pp. 19–29.

Survey data

100 "Survey Data on Expectations: What Have We Learnt?" in Marc Nerlove (ed.), *Issues in Contemporary Economics*, Vol. 2, Macroeconomics and Econometrics (Macmillan I.E.A. 1991), pp. 319–344.
101 "Using Survey Data to Test Market Efficiency in the Foreign Exchange Markets" (with P.C. Liu), *Empirical Economics*, Vol. 17, 1992, pp. 303–314.
102 "Rationality of Survey Data and Tests for Market Efficiency in the Foreign Exchange Markets" (with P.C. Liu), *Journal of International Money and Finance*, Vol. 11, 1992, pp. 366–381.

Others

103 "Demand for Money – A Comment" (with R.C. Vogel), *Quarterly Journal of Economics*, Vol. 79, February 1965, pp. 153–159.
104 "Risk Premia and Price Volatility in Futures Markets" (with J. Yoo), *The Journal of Futures Markets*, Vol. 11, No. 2, April 1991, pp. 165–177.
105 "Estimation and Specification Analysis of Models of Dividend Behavior Based on Censored Panel Data" (with B.S. Kim), *Empirical Economics* Vol. 17 (1992), pp. 111–124.
106 "Option Pricing Using Artificial Neural Networks: The Case of S&P 500 Index Call Options," (1995) (with Min Qi), *Neural Networks in Financial Engineering*. Proceedings of the Third International Conference on Neural Networks in the Capital Markets, London, p. 78–91.
107 "Extracting Economic Information From Data: Methodology in an Empirical Discipline," (with L. Dunn) in *Methodology in Economics* (Edward Elgar, 1996).
108 "Future Directions on Robust Inference" (with C.R. Rao) in *Handbook of Statistics Vol. 15: Robust Inference* (Elsevier Science, Amsterdam, 1997), pp. 661–675.

Books

1 *Econometrics* (New York, McGraw-Hill), 1977. Spanish Edition, 1985.
2 *Econometric Studies in Energy Demand and Supply* (edited) (Praeger Special Studies, Praeger Publishers, New York), March 1978.
3 *Limited Dependent and Qualitative Variables in Econometrics* (Cambridge University Press), 1983.
4 *Introduction to Econometrics* (Macmillan), March 1988. Second Edition, December 1991. Japanese Edition, 1992.
5 *Microeconomics: Theory and Applications* (McGraw-Hill), December 1988. Spanish Edition, 1990.
6 *Econometrics of Panel Data* (edited), Vols. I and II (Edward Elgar), 1992.
7 *Handbook of Statistics, Vol. II: Econometrics* (North-Holland Publishing Company), Co-editor, 1993.
8 *Econometric Methods and Applications*: Selected Papers of G.S. Maddala Vols. I and II (Edward Elgar), 1994.
9 *Statistial Methods of Econometrics and Quantitative Economies* (Blackwell), Co-editor, 1995.
10 *Handbook of Statistics, Vol 14: Statistics Methods and Finance* (Elsevier Science, Amsterdam), with C.R. Rao, December 1996.
11 *Handbook of Statistics, Vol 15: Robust Inference* (Elsevier Science, Amsterdam), with C.R. Rao, April 1997.
12 *Unit Roots and Cointegration* (Cambridge University Press), with In-Moo Kim, 1999.

Edited journal volumes

Model Selection (ed.), *Journal of Econometrics Supplement*, Vol. 16, 1981.

Books forthcoming

Introduction to Econometrics (3rd edn.) (Prentice-Hall), Fall, 1997.

Other

Econometrics (McGraw Hill, 1977) has been written up as a citation classic in *Current Contents*, Vol. 22, Dec. 3, 1990.

Limited Dependent and Qualitative Variables in Econometrics (Cambridge University Press, 1983) has been written up as a citation classic in *Current Contents*, Vol. 30, July 26, 1993.

According to the *Social Science Citation Index* I was one of the top five most cited econometricians during each of the years 1988–1994.

Doctoral dissertations

I supervised 41 doctoral dissertations during the years 1975–1996. I have not kept track of the dissertations supervised during 1963–1974. I have also been a member of numerous other doctoral dissertation committees.

Index